Daystar Television Network has long since been involved in the support of the Nation of Israel, both as the Jewish homeland and historic center of the Judeo-Christian faith, and we are so honored and excited to help Israel celebrate 60 years as a sovereign nation.

Since its inception, the Nation of Israel has played an important role throughout the world and was also instrumental in the foundation of Daystar. It was in the city of Jerusalem where God planted in us the seed that would eventually grow into Daystar, and that is why Israel will forever remain near and dear to our hearts.

It is this love both for the nation and its people which has been the compass that has directed Daystar in support of various projects throughout the country including the building of a medical facility, humanitarian efforts, the planting of olive trees, a variety of economic efforts, prayers for its people and so much more.

So we encourage you to join in the celebration as we commemorate Israel's 60th year as a nation and continue to pray that God would further bless and protect this country as we look ahead to the next 60 years.

Sincerely,

Marcus & Joni

Marcus & Joni Lamb
President /Vice President
Daystar Television Network

DAYST★R.
TELEVISION NETWORK

Marcus & Joni Lamb, Jerusalem 2007

Nissim Mishal

ISRAEL

1948 – 2008

Those Were the Years...

S. Yizhar
Yaron London
Sami Michael
Meir Shalev
Yosef Burg
Amnon Lipkin-Shahak
Ya'acov Sharet
Haim Cohen
Meir Pa'il
Amnon Ahi-No'omi
Shimon Shitrit
Sami Samocha
Isar Harel
Uri Avneri
Haim Beer
Yossi Sarid
Efraim Kishon
Itzhak Shamir
Azmi Bshara
Ariel Sharon
Haim Yavin
Yosi Beilin
David Alexander
Haim Ramon
Ester Shahamorov-Rott
Itzhak Mordechay
Zvulun Hammer
Amir Peretz
Binyamin Netanyahu
Ido Netanyahu
Roni Milo
Shulamit Aloni
Eizer Weizman
Haim Guri
Eytan Ben-Eliahu
A.B. Yehoshua
Avraham Burg
Sever Plotzker
Maski Shibro-Sivan
Dan Abebe
Batya Arad
David Grossman
Ilana Dayan
Shaul Mishal
Aviezer Ravitzky
Dan Meridor
Leah Rabin
Shimon Peres
Yehuda Amital
King Hussein
Ehud Barak
Yosef Lapid
Nahum Barnea
Mickey Haimovich
Eli Amir
Gabi Ashkenazi
Ehud Olmert
Shaul Mofaz
Rona Ramon
Aharon Ciechanover
David Hatuel
Haim Sabato
Shlomo Artzi

Yedioth Books

Nissim Mishal
Israel 60, Those Were the Years

Editor in Chief: **Dov Eichenwald**

Editorial Co-ordinator: **Ruth Ben-Ari**

Design and Graphic Editing: **Studio Joseph Jibri**

Translator: **Baruch Gefen**

Translation Editor (50): **Marion Duman**

Editor (Hebrew 50): **Aliza Ziegler**

Research and Photos: **Eli Shenberg**

Research: **Oriana Almassi, Roni Azulai, Ben Shalev and Tuli Keren**

The publishers wish to thank the following
for providing the photographs for this book:

GPO – Government Press Office
Special thanks to Ya'akov Sa'ar, Moshe Milner, Avi Ohayon
Ilana Dayan and Einat Ankri
The *Yedioth Ahronoth* archives
Special thanks to Dimon Shachar and the archive team
The Central Zionist Archives
The JNF Photo Archive
The IDF Archives
The Israeli Center for the Documentation of Performing Arts
The Theater Department
The Yolanda and David Katz Arts Faculty
Tel Aviv University
The Center for the Heritage of Babylon Jews
The Lavon Institute, the *Davar* newspaper photo collection
Laisha **Archives**
Special thanks to Bathsheba Bibas
The Cameri Theater Archives
The Carmel Ridge Archives

Thanks to Micha Bar-Am, David Rubinger, Ziv Koren,
Ephraim Kishon, Shlomo Nakdimon

Front cover photos by:
Micha Bar-Am, GPO, Michael Kramer, A.P., David Rubinger
Back cover photos by:
Michael Kramer, Ziv Koren, Arad family album, Oren Agmon,
Robert Kappa, GPO

Typesetting: A.N.A.
Scanning: Graphor Inc., Meishav Inc.
Plates and printing: Emanuel Offset Printing Ltd.

Danacode: 362-3728
ISBN 978-965-482-731-7

Printed in Israel 2008

For Idan, Yoav, Or, and Guri
– my beloved.

I wish to thank my brother, Prof.
Shaul Mishal, a creative and loyal
partner in making this book.

Footsteps Ltd.

Exclusive Distributor
In North America

office@footsteps.co.il

Contents

(1948-98

The State Committee approves the state emblem in Tel Aviv, February 1949. Photo: Government Press Office (GPO)

A bird's-eye view of Tel Aviv, 1997. Photo: Albatross Aerial Photography

Making A State

*TV Reporter
and Anchorman
Nissim Mishal*

We were born into the age of togetherness. Now we are in the era of individuality. And in between, 60 years have gone.

With the advent of the 60th anniversary, we are still burdened by questions of identity and meaning, arguing over substance and the boundaries of what is permitted and what is not, wondering where we are headed and how our lives would look if and when there was peace. Will we be more "East" or more "West", and who will rule the future – the right, the left, or perhaps the center? Or perhaps this is all immaterial because these troubles are to be expected in a nation that fought against the world in order to become a part of it, built a state and sang the Song of Peace along with an ancient tune and the Song of Degrees.

The first decade of the State of Israel was dominated by values of "togetherness". Those were the years of collective being, of absorbing immigrants and settling the land, of making the desert flourish and of building the Israel Defense Forces (IDF). We were friends and brothers-in-arms, we settled for less and remained humble. Our parents spoke the tongue of historic longing and national goals and big solutions, around which the masses rallied with vast and sweeping public support. That was a time when individual hardships were suppressed in favor of the overall feeling of being under siege and the constant need for individual sacrifice.

I spent my first decade as a child in the ma'abara [transit camp] of Talpiot in southern Jerusalem. Looking back, my "togetherness" was a close and supportive family of uncles and aunts; a grandmother standing with one hand on the mezuzah, whispering a prayer, pleading with God; a sheltering, encouraging and knowledgeable mother; and a father – a manual laborer – who left for work early in the morning and came back late in the evening, shrouded in silence. Outside, the neighbors were noisy; children and grownups hung around in groups on the street where our hut stood, right next to the synagogue. The grownups would talk loudly, often arguing till they were blue in the face, mainly about family and livelihood, border incidents or politics. And we, the children, built carts out of wooden boxes and four little wheels, and tore down the road to the edge of the dry river bed. In the afternoons, we would play with a ball made of a thick old sock stuffed with rags, or exchange blows and then run to the nearby hills to hide behind a rock, a fig tree, a thick olive tree trunk or a terrace.

Outside that *ma'abara*, Israel was ruled by the social values of the working settlers, dressed in khaki and Russian shirts and Biblical sandals, thick braids blowing in the wind and barefoot. In those years, the group was holier than the family, the team more important than the individual, and bands and duos preferred to the soloist. The symbol of those days was the Sabra – the mythological figure, boyish and romantic, veiled in dreams, feverishly in search of himself, seeking self-fulfillment in the collective. The Sabra had no past. He was born of the sea. His thick hair blew in the wind and his girlfriend, with a raven-black braid or golden locks, wore a full skirt or khaki shorts. They both went to study farming or help in immigrant absorption. They lived in a little room with a Jewish

New immigrants on their arrival in Israel. Photo: Hans Finn, GPO

Introduction

Nissim Mishal

...and the earth filled with tents... Photo: Hans Pin, GPO

Center: Hora dancers on Independence Day. Photo: Fritz Schlezinger

Bottom: Hallelujah by Milk & Honey won the Eurovision song contest in Jerusalem, 1979. Photo: GPO

Agency-sponsored iron bed and a modest bookshelf with books by Alterman, Tolstoy and Pushkin. On the walls hung a reproduction of van Gogh's *Sunflowers* or a photograph of Israel's landscape taken by Peter Merom. Those were the years of austerity, rations and food coupons, reparations from Germany, *ma'abarot* and the draining of the Hula swamps, the construction of the nuclear reactor in Dimona, the establishment of Commando Unit 101 under Arik Sharon's command, the Sinai Campaign and riots in Haifa's slums. Above all we had a regime and a government designed in the spirit of the ruling workers' parties, with David Ben-Gurion as a strong-minded leader and Mapai [Israel's Workers' Party] as the dominant party, and talk of a workers' economy, common destiny and socialism. In those days, literature and poetry, radio and press, movies and theater spoke in one voice: a voice which championed the cause of implementing the values of the "togetherness" culture.

When the 1960s came, "togetherness" changed forever. When the state reached Bar-Mitzvah, the Lavon affair erupted. It centered around the question of who gave the unfortunate order to make Mossad agents out of local Jews to carry out terrorist activities in Egypt. The affair created deep rifts throughout the ruling elite and posed a real threat to the government. The serious disagreements led to Ben-Gurion's resignation and Levi Eshkol's becoming premier, as well as to a split in Mapai and the establishment of Rafi [Israel's Workers' List]. Since then, the individualist culture has been gaining strength – noisy and public or discreet and unthreatening. It discovered the pleasure of ballroom dancing to Paul Anka tunes, thus challenging the traditional *hora* – a circle dance, or "The Little Shepherdess" – a couples dance.

My personal "togetherness" also changed in those years. In the early 1960s, my family and I left the ma'abara, said goodbye to our friends, teachers and relatives, and moved to the working-class suburb of Bnei Brak. For the first time in my life, I was in an Ashkenazi environment with children of my own age from religious-Zionist families – the veteran ruling class. The boys always donned knitted yarmulkes [skullcups] and often wore khaki pants, and the girls mostly wore blue skirts. They were quieter than the ma'abara kids. Their accent was free of glottal consonants. They raised a finger in class to receive permission to speak and addressed the teacher in the third person. Their bags were packed with books, notebooks and sandwiches consisting of a roll and salami. I had two slices of cheap bread with margarine. My new friends encouraged me to join the Bnei Akiva Youth Movement, where I was introduced to values that combined Torah studies with hikes around the country – coast to coast (from Lake Kinneret to the Mediterranean) and from the Galilee to the Negev – as well as the experience of summer camps. It was not long before I replaced my ma'abara beret with a knitted yarmulke.

Ben Gurion with Shimon Peres and Yitzhak Navon, 1958
Photo: David Rubinger

The 1960s brought greater economic, cultural and political openness. Some of the clear signs of the time were free-market economy, ethnic-slapstick movies, free press and the lifting of the military regime which has been imposed on the Israeli Arabs since 1948. In those years, we were torn between loyalty to the founding fathers and walking the path they had created for us, and shaking them off and rebelling; between Mother Earth and a warm, loving, flesh and blood mother; between marching with the crowds and taking side roads; between smooth roads and rough, unknown trails; between the unifying and consolidating and the unique and exclusive. Young Israeli artists, authors, poets and politicians of the generation of Amos Oz, Dalia Rabikovich, Abraham B. Yehoshua, S. Yizhar, Dan Ben-Amotz, David Avidan and Nathan Zach spoke Hebrew that was less flowery, lofty and pompous and more personal. Most of them belonged to the elite of veteran Israel, but the state was no longer an absolute truth for them and the leadership was no longer seen as always wise, honest and just. This was an in-between period in the social, cultural and political sense. Collective decrees, absolute norms and the heroic values of "togetherness" were questioned and challenged.

In the 1960s, Israeli society became more civilian and less cause-oriented. The heroic tone was replaced by a minor-key political style. Informal frameworks and collective concepts gave way to institutionalized thinking, organizations and hierarchic structures. In those years, culture wars and clashes between religious and secular, left and right, center and fringe, rich and poor were nowhere in sight. *Humus* and *masbaha*, *ful* and *kubane*, *shwarma* in a *pita*, Umm Koulthum and Abd al-Wahhab were the culture of the underprivileged neighborhoods and development towns. The Sephardim were still called "communities" and the Arabs and the ultra-Orthodox were "sectors". The veteran Ashkenazi elite regarded both as black masses and monolithic anthropological entities.

The IDF too underwent a transformation in the 1960s, becoming a professional army. The spirit of the paratroopers and Unit 101 with warriors such as Meir Har-Zion, Katcha, Yirmi, Mota, Raful and Davidi gave way to a large-scale army based on battalions and divisions and professional military schools, and not so much on the Palmach fighting spirit and personal initiatives. The army procured new weapon systems and became cognizant with large armored forces, massive air power and co-operation between branches. This paid off in the Six Day War, during which the IDF reached the banks of the Jordan River and the Suez Canal, the beaches of Sharm al-Sheikh and the top of Mount Hermon. The war began with the award-winning song, *Jerusalem of Gold* [*Yerushalaim shel Zahav*] and with longing, and ended with a united Jerusalem and a fragile and tense Jewish-Arab co-existence. The sweeping victory gave Israel a sense of regional supremacy, of being an omnipotent state that enjoyed military control over large territories, and plenty of time to wait for the Arabs to signal that they wished to negotiate agreements with us.

In the meantime, we enjoyed the vast Sinai Desert and became reacquainted with old homeland landscapes that eventually became a bone of contention with our Palestinian neighbors. Israel changed from a political entity with an intimate sense of community into a more abstract entity ruled by the power of contractual relations, institutionalized arrangements, punctilious laws and detailed regulations. Now we speak of immigrant absorption rather than of immigrants, of Judaism rather than of Jews, of poverty rather than of the poor, of landscapes rather than of residents and of territories and terrorists rather than of Palestinians.

Israel is changing. Its landscapes are more diverse, its opinions less unified, its positions more extreme; its music is more pluralistic, its language more sensual and its fashions are more daring. Its foods are becoming richer and its tastes more sophisticated. The younger generation is growing taller and the Hebrew language is becoming more personal, matter-of-fact, sometimes nasal, sometimes dry.

In 1973, we were surprised by the Yom Kippur War. More than 2,000 soldiers perished and many thousands were left scarred. The war made us doubt the reasoning powers of our leaders and military commanders. The Yom Kippur War caused private and public traumas that would surface in the political upheaval of 1977 when, for the first time ever in Israel, the right wing came to power and formed a government under Menachem Begin.

As a young TV correspondent, my encounters with Prime Minister Menachem Begin left me with an impression of a sensitive and humane person who could also be tough and distant. In our interviews, he was careful about every fine detail, crossing every "t" and dotting every "i". At the same time, he was a man of comprehensive vision, able to see the whole picture; a man of pleasant and friendly conversation and careful attentiveness on the one hand, and on the other, a rhetorician who plucked the collective heartstrings of Holocaust and heroism, destruction and resurrection, power and concern for the future of the nation and the state; a man who had a deep awareness of history and a broad Jewish education. Begin, more than any other Israeli prime minister, reminded me of Ben-Gurion. They both foresaw trends and processes and were willing to defy norms and recruit the best people to turn the vision of generations into a living and breathing reality. In their daily lives, they were modest, settling for little. Both of them ended brilliant political careers in despair, remaining, however, in the collective memory as pathbreaking leaders. They knew how to hold on to the hem of history's cloak and force it to change direction; they harnessed the present and set the future on a new road.

My generation changed after the Yom Kippur War. Some chose mysticism and messianic notions, others became nihilists who lost their faith in values, and most wavered between permissiveness and idealism, between cynicism and seriousness, between sin and the fear of God. The war created divisions and drew clear boundaries between secular and religious, Zionism and post-Zionism, Sephardim and Ashkenazim, Arabs and Jews within the Green Line boundaries, Israel and the Palestinians in the territories, rich and poor, veteran Israelis and immigrants.

After the 1973 war and the 1977 change of government, Egyptian President Anwar Sadat arrived in Israel on a visit that initiated peace relations between Egypt and Israel and compelled an Israeli government, under Begin, to recognize the rights of the Palestinian nation. Sixteen years later, this recognition would pave the way for the Israeli-PLO Agreement of Principles that was signed on the White House lawn in September 1993, the establishment of the Palestinian Authority in Jericho and Gaza and the signing of the peace accord with Jordan a year later.

Between one peace agreement and another, we experienced dramatic events: the bombing of the Iraqi nuclear reactor and Operation Moses, in which Ethiopian Jews were brought to Israel. At the same time, Israel gave up the Sinai, Sharm al-Sheikh, Dahab and Nuweiba in April 1982. Two months later, there was lengthy and violent friction with the PLO, which escalated into the Lebanon War in 1982 and the *intifadah* [uprising] in the West Bank and the Gaza Strip at the end of 1987.

The 1990s started with the Gulf War. Israel was hit by more than 40 missiles, refrained from striking back and allowed the US Air Force to do its job. The Palestinian problem, however, did not let up. We have been struggling with it since 1967, using the carrot and stick policy. First we tried saying no: No return to 1967 borders; no negotiations with the PLO; no Palestinian state.

The protracted *intifadah* that erupted in December 1987 could not be eliminated by force. It paved the way to a political dialogue between Israel and leaders from the territories first, and PLO leaders later. That dialogue and the Oslo accords of September 1993 exacerbated political rivalries in Israel even further. The rivalries caused a split in the nation, culminating in the horrendous assassination of Prime Minister Yitzhak Rabin in November 1995.

President Sadat arrived on a historic visit of Israel, 1977

Photo: David Rubinger

Photo: Avi Ohaion, GPO

Photo: Moshe Milner, GPO

Center: Israel-PLO peace treaty - signing ceremony at the White House, 1993

Bottom: Prime Minister Yitzhak Rabin assassinated at a peace rally in Tel Aviv, 1995.

11

Introduction

Nissim Mishal

Top: Prime Minister Ariel Sharon and Foreign Minister Shimon Peres, 2001.

Middle: Terror attack on bus No. 5, Dizengoff St., Tel Aviv, 1995.

Bottom: The intifada in the territories, 1987

Photo: Ziv Koren

Photo: Ziv Koren

Photo: GPO

Right: On the "Mishal Ham" show: Prime Minister Binyamin Netanyahu and Defense Minister Yitzhak Mordechay debate ahead of the 1999 elections. Photo: Tzvika Tischler

The murder has changed Israel. The country has grown more bitter, suspicious and sober. More than ever before, it is worried about its public image and the contents that will shape the lives of its children at the end of the second millennium. This is a period that combines rationalism and mysticism, innovation and nostalgia. Some people have gone to seek their roots in Zen and meditation, others have picked up ancient Jewish texts; still others drift between ashrams, black Hassidic hats, synagogues and knitted *yarmulkes*.

The sixth decade of the State of Israel found us yearning for outstanding leaders who could take us onward to a new reality, great hope, relaxed security, and national consensus. Two young Sayeret Matkal graduates were elected prime ministers subsequently. Binyamin Netanyahu (1996-1999) and Ehud Barak (1999-2001) replaced the old guard, determined and eager to reach their goals: making the pages of history as breakthrough leaders who introduced substantive changes to the region, and leading us all to a "dawn of a new day." Reality, however, slapped them on the face and the great euphoria of their election ended in disappointment. The two performed as impatient and intolerant soloists, acknowledging nothing but their own skills and ability to attain rapid achievements in every field.

Both seemed to ignore the rules of the Middle Eastern game and believed they would be able to make other regional leaders follow their will and plans. Barak even went as far as setting terms and schedules for ending the conflict with the Palestinians and signing a peace accord with the Syrians, acting as if there was no one on the other side who would haggle, as if it were all exclusively up to him. Later, experts who accompanied the negotiations with the Syrians said that Barak had a historic opportunity to reach an agreement with Hafez Asad, but lacked the courage to make a Ben Gurion-like decision that could reshape the history of the Middle East. Thus, in less than 2 years, Barak reached the end of his term without his coalition, no support from his own party, and no diplomatic achievements. Subsequently, he crashed in the 2001 elections, losing to Sharon, who received 61% of the votes.

In 2001, the new Israeli prime minister appeared as kind-hearted grandfather. Ariel Sharon - for many years one of the most publicly disputed politicians - promised peace, security, and national unity. The people loved his new image and his popularity rates soared, regardless of police investigations into his affairs.

Sharon's term in office was marked by the Al-Aksa intifadah, which broke out on the day he toured Temple Mount, 28 September 2000. The violent outbreak shattered the dream of coexistence with the Palestinians, leaving not only 1,099 Israelis dead, but also ripping apart the disappointed Israeli peace camp that lost hope of attaining an arrangement with them. At the same time, Israel won international scientific recognition. Four of its top researchers won the prestigious Nobel Prize, shining precious light on Israel. Professors Avraham Hershko, Israel Auman, Daniel Kahneman, and Aharon Ciechanover presented groundbreaking discoveries in their scientific fields, won global appreciation, and showed the Jewish brain at its best.

In this decade, I made a professional transition. Leaving national TV Channel 1, I joined the commercial Channel 2 and found a new home with Reshet. I started narrating the current-affairs talk show *"Mishal Ham"* [Hot Mishal], and together with editor Israel Segal, my dear friend who passed away in September 2007, we brought stormy public political and social debates that characterized the period to the screen. Political interviews and social disclosures made the show. While I enjoyed a professional bloom, we could watch a new TV-oriented elite of politicians who started believing that they should communicate with the public through the screen, and not in party gatherings or outdoor rallies. Happily for us, the *"Mishal Ham"* studio turned into a ring of political drama, such as the debate between Prime Minister Binyamin Netanyahu and Defense Minister Yitzhak Mordechay who vied for the premiership in 1999. Additional political figures such as Sharon, Barak, Netanyahu, Deri, Peres, Olmert, Lapid and others seized the medium and appeared on TV trying to sell their political goods, following the new rules it dictated.

In 2005, Prime Minister Sharon ruled in favor of the disengagement plan, making a disputed decision that would rip the nation apart and sharpen the left-right split in the Israeli society. The right came up with a slogan, "Withdrawals Go as Deep as Police Investigations," in an attempt to undermine Sharon's moral standing. Sharon was not deterred, did not hesitate, and went on to execute his plan, to the chagrin of the settlers, previously his ardent followers. Clearly, this was one of the most difficult, dramatic, and traumatic events Israel has ever experienced. The disengagement wounds are still sore, as the security and political benefits of the withdrawal from the Gaza Strip are widely questioned.

Yet, despite grave terror attacks (the intifadah), stormy clashes (the disengagement), and endless debates on the path and nature of the State of Israel, our economy reached previously unseen records. Quality of life levels soared, exports expanded, gross national product grew, the number of unemployed dropped, and foreign investors infused the Israeli market with billions of dollars, showing their appreciation for its performance. Big economic reforms that Prime Minister Sharon and Finance Minister Netanyahu introduced promoted the huge economic shift that was internationally praised and acknowledged by global economic leaders. Only poverty remained etched on our national and societal foreheads like Cain's stigma.

The curse of Lebanon haunted us in this decade as well. In 2000, we pulled out of there with loud fanfare ("Mom, we're out!"), locked the gates behind us, and prayed to the Almighty that it would be the last time. Deceitful fate sent us right back into the Lebanese mud as if nothing ever happened. Six years later, in July 2006, with Ehud Olmert as prime minister after he replaced comatose Sharon, we found ourselves right back there, conducting a war that was botched by inexperienced leaders (Olmert, Peretz, and Halutz) who turned a retaliation operation into Israel's longest war since the War of Independence.

This was the decade that saw my grandchildren born: Idan and Yoav and Or and Gur-Arye-Yehuda - each with his smile and charm. Together they formed the world of grandchildren for me, a world of innocence, love, and longing. A world that engulfs me with soft shades, filled with a joy of life. When I look at their innocent eyes, charming smiles, and tiny hands reaching out to me, I am filled with great joy, pleasure, and peace. I give myself to them easily, happily listening to them pronounce their first syllables and broken words, diving right back into the magical world of fairytales and children's books. The world of grandchildren is for me a land unto itself, including its inhabitants.

My grandchildren are growing right into the world of Internet, where everyone is gazing at a computer screen, Playstation screen, or the screen of their small digital helper. For the first time in the history of mankind it seems that what appears on screen is more important than reality. The Internet and cellular phone revolution changed language, which turned shorter, sharper, keeping only consonants and losing its vowels. At the same time, the Internet industry placed Israel on the shortlist of the world's most promising countries, following the USA and Britain. Silicone Wadi is the busiest place after Silicone Valley.

And a glimpse of the future: Despite the ups and downs we expect in the coming years, we will probably keep living here in the space between two extremes, walking between the raindrops. Our ship will remain one and we will all sit in it, bent over the oars - some joyful, others sad; some fearful, others enthusiastic; some willingly, others for lack of a better choice. We will probably fight over the direction we should take and argue about whether we belong on deck, below it, or right at the helm. We will wonder if we are right and whether things could be done differently. Our voyage will continue, through relatively calm or rough waters, until the next eruption.

Those Were the Years offers a comprehensive review Israel's first 60 years, thoroughly analyzing and describing events and persons; victories and defeats; moments of glory and despair; times of exhilaration and agony; grand achievements in the battlefields and miserable failures we would rather forget. This is all accompanied by many photos and comments by famous individuals, some of whom took part in shaping our reality and creating our history.

Top: President Clinton, Prime Minister Barak, Syrian Foreign Minister Al-Shara at the Israeli-Syrian peace talks, 2000.

Middle: Soldiers evicting a Nisanit resident from the Katif Bloc as part of the disengagement plan, 2005.

Bottom: IAF raids Lebanon, 2006

(1948

David Ben-Gurion in his study at Sde Boker during an interview on his 80th birthday, December 1966.
Photo: Micha Bar-Am

Jubilant citizens celebrating the United Nations decision on partition of Palestine in front of the Mugrabi cinema in Tel Aviv. 29 November, 1949.
Photo: Hans Pin, GPO

The Moment Before the State Erupted

Writer S. Yizhar

Only on very rare occasions does it happen that an entire population comes together at a single spot – a spot that includes everything, from which everything changes for the best, where all that is unresolved is resolved and where all that is unopened suddenly opens, revealing the long-awaited beginning.

It is, perhaps, like a giant triangle: At its base, piled up and pressed together, lurk the darkness, the evils, the worries, the fears, the despair, the cul-de-sacs and the recurring uncertainties; at the apex, a light is turned on from which the change will surely start, from which we will break out into the open, and from which security, solutions and salvation will flow.

This is how the Jewish population in Eretz Yisrael looked on the eve of the foundation of the State. Everything was terribly difficult, but all eyes were turned to that light above, at the apex: Look, a state will be founded here and everything will be resolved – for the individual, for the population as a whole and for history – and a life of freedom will begin. Everything will change at once and everything will be different; it will start soon – the darkness will end, the day will dawn, terror will subside, and lost hopes will come to life and come true.

And we are not talking about a population of eccentrics and dreamers. There were 600,000 serious, tormented, frightened Jews who were struggling to cope. Children grew rapidly into youths ready for battle, and adults went into training and tightened their belts. It felt like Doomsday was coming, the eve of the end of the world. On the one hand, the terrible echoes of the immediate past could still be heard – the lengthy period of waiting, the fears, the general anticipation of better times and the sound of the ram's horn. And on the other, the magic word "state"; a "state," and everything would be different from now on. Fears would evaporate, hardships would ease up. A "state", and everything that had failed or had been missed out would come right in a minute. And the horrors suffered so recently by the European Jews, as well as everything that was too hard to endure in the tiny Jewish community here – poverty, helplessness, the endless Arab attacks, the never-ending British harassment, the begging, the failures wherever we turned, everything hanging from a thread for too long – now, a state would be founded and everything would become solid, terra firma, and the Jews would have a state.

People breathed it deeply, sensing its arrival like a farmer senses the coming rain. There was no need to prove anything or provide evidence or calculate or plan. It would all be self-evident. An entire nation would meet at one spot, in a single belief that the state would do that great, wished for, messianic and earthly thing for them. The Jews would have a state.

And a little man with a white mane walked before them, his sharp, commanding voice alarming them, driving them on, calling on them and exciting them, confirming that it would indeed be like that, that indeed a state was coming and everything was about to begin and would be different – as if the entire giant sun had shrunk into a single burning spot.

Of course, it is not hard to scoff at that faith now, to question the dream that a state can solve everything. It is not hard to prove how blind, naïve, or perhaps just too dejected they were; how gullible and even pathetic they were; and how they forgot about reality and the boundaries of imagination; how they ignored the hard facts just as they ignored the demands made by the Palestinians living next to them, as well as the reality of the Middle East and the ruthless economic laws that did not go weak at the sound of the word "state." They did not philosophize about a state being merely an instrument, and that it all depends on whose hands it is in and on where he is taking it and so on. But those were two or three years in which the entire world shrunk into a single demand, a single wish, a single faith dazzled by a big light; when man and nation were compressed into one spot – the State of the Jews. Such moments occur only once in the lifetime of a nation, only once in history. And regardless of whether this is the right answer or not, that moment, when the world shrunk into a single sizzling spot, with one little man running ahead, waving his arms in the air, urging them to follow, and they all ran after him – many of them never to run again – anyone who was there will never forget that one time in his life when everything, absolutely everything, became one thing.

14.5.**48**

"We Hereby Announce..."

At 4 p.m., the members of the National Committee gathered at the Tel Aviv Museum on Rothschild Street for the historic announcement of the establishment of the State of Israel. Prime Minister David Ben-Gurion, head of the caretaker government, excitedly read out the Declaration of Independence. Thousands were standing outside the hall, and tens of thousands listened to Kol Yisrael Radio, which broadcast the 40-minute ceremony.

"In Eretz Yisrael, the Jewish nation rose, and its spiritual, religious and political character was shaped," Ben-Gurion's voice thundered. "It is the natural right of the Jewish nation to live like any other nation, independent in its sovereign state... Therefore, we hereby declare the establishment of the Jewish state in Eretz Yisrael – the State of Israel... ". When he finished his speech, Ben-Gurion signed the Declaration of Independence, and the council members followed suit. Few noticed that Ben-Gurion had read his

14 May 1948 - The statutory Assembly gathers at the Tel Aviv Museum and announces the establishment of the State of Israel and the caretaker government. Photo: Hans Pin, GPO

announcement from a typed page, and not from the Declaration of Independence, which was not yet ready because of the hasty decision to announce the establishment of the State of Israel. When the ceremony ended, Ben-Gurion stepped out to meet the crowds waiting outside and was received with cheers. Throughout the country, people went out into the streets and danced and sang in honor of the newly born state. Rabbi Y.L. Fishman, the Jewish Agency's most veteran member, said *Sheheyanu* [the Jewish prayer, thanking God for "living to see this"].

However, even before the festivities ended, Arab armies invaded the State of Israel. The armies of Egypt, Syria, Jordan, Lebanon and Iraq invaded Israeli territory with the clear intention of preventing the establishment of the Jewish state at all costs. The War of Independence had begun.

**The Jordanian Legion –
cuts Jerusalem off**

**The Egyptian Army
– charges toward Tel Aviv**

**The Syrian Army –
approaches Haifa**

14 May

The Great Invasion of the Arab Armies

The war started on the first night of the state's existence. The Israel Defense Forces [IDF] was only just getting organized and seriously lacked guns and ammunition. It had to fight the Arab invaders with almost no means. According to the Arab plan, the Egyptian Army was supposed to conquer the Jewish settlements in the Negev, move on to Ashkelon, to Ashdod, and then reach Tel Aviv. The Syrian, Lebanese and Iraqi armies were supposed to move through the Yizre'el Valley and reach Haifa. But man proposes and God disposes.

The Egyptian Army was warded off by the Givati Brigade in the area of Negba, where fierce fighting took a heavy toll. Another Egyptian column was warded off west of Rehovot, again by the Givati Brigade. The Syrians, who were supposed to reach Haifa, started by taking Tsemach, Massada and Sha'ar Golan, and reached the gates of Degania. A Syrian tank even managed to enter the kibbutz, but was stopped short by a Molotov cocktail. The battle at Degania was a turning-point in the entire campaign in northern Israel because, from this point on, the Syrians did not try to launch an offensive to reach central Israel, and settled for attempts to seize territories north of Lake Kinneret.

A sheet iron model of the Syrian tank that penetrated the gates of Degania at the beginning of the War of Independence, as displayed on 1 May 1968 in Tel Aviv. Photo: Oded Stopnitski

The heaviest battles, however, were waged against the Jordanian Army, mainly in Jerusalem. The Jordanian Legion managed to cut the city off from central Israel, conquer the Old City, conduct battles inside the city, and even take Mt. Scopus. In fact, Jerusalem was under siege and the road connecting it to the coastal plain was cut off. Food and water supplies in the city were low and the city was being shelled by the Legion's guns. Heavy battles took place in the Latroun area, where the IDF made serious efforts to dislodge the Legion from its positions which cut Jerusalem off from Tel Aviv. All the attempts failed and the IDF suffered heavy losses. Contact with Jerusalem was eventually re-established when the "Burma Road" was built, running from Hulda to Jerusalem. Two weeks after the War of Independence started, it became clear that the Arab invasion had failed, due mainly to the heroic endurance, determination and fighting spirit of the IDF fighters and the Jewish settlements.

The first armistice came into effect on 11 June 1948. A month later, the IDF launched its first counter-offensive against the Arab armies.

Signalwoman with the Yiftah Brigade that fought for the opening of the Latroun- Jerusalem road. Photo: Boris Karmi

Arab warriors in Bab-el-Wad on the lookout out for Israeli troops during the battles of Sha'ar Hagai. Photo: AP

The War of Independence

1948

5-6 April

Operation Nachshon

The goal of Operation Nachshon, which started on the night of 5 April, was to reestablish contact with Jerusalem. A decision was made to change the tactics used by the convoy guards: they would man strongholds and ambush and raid enemy forces.

At the end of March, the Hagana staff met at Ben-Gurion's home in Tel Aviv and decided to carry out Operation Nachshon - the biggest operation of the War of Independence. "There is one burning issue at the moment," Ben-Gurion said, "and that is the battle for passage to Jerusalem. This is a crucial battle. The downfall of Jerusalem might deliver a death blow to the entire Jewish settlement of Israel." Upon his orders, the operation forces were beefed up and heavily armed.

Some 1,500 fighters took part in the operation that was led by Givati Brigade commander Shimon Avidan. The forces left the point of departure, Kibbutz Nachshon, at night, moving toward Jerusalem, blocking side-roads and even sabotaging some of them. Two previous operations had paved the way for this: The Kastel had been captured and the headquarters of Hassan Salama in Ramla (responsible for issuing the orders to attack convoys to Jerusalem) had been blown up. After the village of Colonia was captured, the operation commander announced: "The road to Jerusalem is open!" On 13 April, a convoy left Hulda for Jerusalem and returned safely.

Operation Nachshon - which symbolized the transition from guerrilla warfare to full-scale military operations aimed at inflicting casualties on the enemy or seizing territories - exacted a toll of 57 dead and 72 wounded. It laid the foundations for operations on a scale the Jewish settlement had not known before, and helped create the prototype of the brigade.

The "Burma Road" enabled vehicles to travel to Jerusalem. Photo: GPO

Jerusalem outside the walls was heavily bombarded by the Jordanian Legion.

28 May

The Jerusalem Jewish Quarter Surrenders

The battle over the Jewish Quarter ended two weeks after the establishment of the state with the surrender of the 1,700 Jews who remained there. The first battle, dubbed "the seven-hour fight", started in December 1947. In its wake, British soldiers entered the quarter to serve as a buffer. The British wanted the Jews to leave the quarter, so they made food supplies hard to come by.

The Hagana command faced a real dilemma: The Jewish Quarter had no strategic or military value. It only had historic and traditional significance. The question was whether large forces should be allocated to break the siege, or whether the *status quo* should simply be maintained. The dilemma was settled the day after the Declaration of Independence, when the Arabs began shelling the quarter. After three days of fighting, it became apparent that the quarter would not hold out without assistance. Palmach soldiers were ordered to break in: "Warriors! For the past 2,000 years, since the times of King David, no Jew has broken through the Old City walls. Be daring and succeed!"

The forces that were sent conquered Mt. Zion, intending to reach the Jewish Quarter, but the Arab shelling continued and escalated. The forces sent a cable back, stating: "We have no commanders, we have run out of ammunition and morale. If the attacks continue, we are lost!"

Arab pressure increased on 26 May, and the Jewish residents were gathered together in four synagogues. Repeated Palmach attempts to break through the gates failed. In view of this situation, two local rabbis were authorized to contact the commander of the Arab forces and negotiate a cease-fire to evacuate the wounded. He refused, saying he would only accept a total surrender. On Saturday, 28 May, the Jewish Quarter residents surrendered.

Jewish Quarter residents surrendered to and were taken captive by the Jordanians. Photo: John Phillips

Jerusalem was cut off from the coast for several months and its Jewish residents suffered a shortage of food, water and gasoline. Photo: Sygma

A Palmach unit was ordered to break into the Jewish Quarter in the Old City.

The War of Independence

1948

9 July

The "10-Day" Battles: The Conquest of Lod and Ramla

After an armistice of about one month, the IDF initiated battles that lasted 10 days, during which important areas were captured: Lod and Ramla, Nazareth, the entire Lower Galilee, and most of the Western Galilee. No one won the battles in Jerusalem and, in fact, the city was divided between Israel and the Jordanian Legion. On the Egyptian front, the IDF pushed the Egyptian forces south of Ashkelon, but the northern Negev settlements remained cut off. The Syrians still held the Hula Plateau region. On 18 July, both sides heeded the UN National Security call, and the second armistice began.

The Negev Brigade took Beersheba in a lightning operation. The city's Arab residents had fled a few days earlier.

15 October

Operation Yo'av – The Conquest of Beersheba

The operation was designed to open routes to the cut-off Northern Negev settlements and to establish Israel's control over the Negev. An Egyptian brigade was surrounded in the Faluja Enclave near Negba. The Egyptian Army, which was supposed to reach Tel Aviv, started retreating southward, unable to prevent the IDF conquest of Beersheba. Yig'al Alon, who commanded the southern front, was praised highly for his achievements. The Israeli offensive ended on 22 October, when a cease-fire was announced by the Security Council.

Photo: GPO

A couple of Negev Brigade Palmachniks in Beersheba. Operation Yo'av ended as a result of orders from the Security Council.

1948

29 October

Operation Hiram: Capturing the Upper Galilee

Operation Hiram was both the largest and the last operation of the War of Independence on the northern front. Its goal was to ward off the Arab forces that held the entire Upper Galilee and parts of the Lower Galilee, and to establish a new defense line along the northern border.

The operation was launched after Kaukji's Salvation Army attacked Kibbutz Manara. In a lightning 60-hour operation, the IDF stormed the Upper Galilee, launching a difficult operation, during which it liberated Meron, Gush-Halav, Tarshiha, and Sasa.

Yig'al Alon, commander of Operation Hiram, in which the Upper Galilee was conquered, and commander of the southern front in the War of Independence, 1948.

The siege on Manara was lifted and the Upper Galilee roads reopened for traffic. With the purging of the Galilee, Kaukji's army was, in fact, eliminated after suffering heavy losses. Kaukji himself fled the battlefield at the very last moment.

Yiftach Brigade soldiers, 1948.

22.6.48

The *Altalena* Arms Ship Goes Up in Flames

The Irgun brought guns, ammunition and volunteers from Europe on board the *Altalena*. When the ship anchored on the Kfar Vitkin shore, Irgun heads demanded that 20% of the equipment be handed directly to their men, despite the fact that it had previously announced that it was joining the IDF. Ben-Gurion greatly disapproved of the Irgun's conduct and rejected the demand, saying that it was a threat to the people's unity and constituted an attempted mutiny. He unequivocally demanded that all the weapons be handed over to the IDF.

The Irgun heads refused to obey government orders and decided to send the *Altalena* to Tel Aviv, where they hoped to rally a large number of supporters and sympathizers. But when the ship arrived at the shores of Tel Aviv, Ben-Gurion gave the order for it to be shelled, and it went up in flames. The shelling killed 16 people and wounded some 50. The commander of the force that sank the *Altalena* was none other than Lieutenant Colonel Yitzhak Rabin, who would later be Israel's prime minister.

The Altalena, *the Irgun arms ship, is shelled by the Palmach and burns opposite the Tel Aviv boardwalk.Photo: Hans Pin, GPO*

Dr. Haim Weizmann Arrives in Israel

30 October

State Council President Haim Weizmann and his wife arrived in Israel on board a special El Al flight. Weizmann, who was received in a full military ceremony, was very moved and had a lump in his throat when he met the cabinet members. Dr. Weizmann wrote in the plane log: "I had the great privilege of traveling for the first time on board such a fine Israeli airplane, in the company of such nice people."

First Immigrants Arrive at Tel Aviv and Haifa Ports

Immigrant ships started arriving at the Israeli ports of Haifa and Tel Aviv immediately after the Declaration of Independence, bringing thousands of immigrants from camps in Cyprus. Other ships carrying immigrants from all over Europe also arrived in Israel's seaports. Most of the immigrants were sent directly to the battlefields to fight for Israel's independence.

The first legal immigrants arrive in Tel Aviv one day after the declaration of the state. Photo: Hans Pin, GPO

Arab Residents Flee

During the War of Independence, about 250,000 Arab residents abandoned their homes – some having been encouraged to do so by the IDF – and fled to neighboring countries. They fled, believing that when the war ended and Israel was destroyed, they would return to their homes. Then reality dealt them a harsh blow. Israel did not let them return. This created the refugee problem that has not been solved to this day. For years, the Arab countries have nurtured the problem, using it as a weapon against Israel in every international forum.

Arab masses flee, initiating the refugee problem. Photo: GPO

48

2 February

The *Chizbatron* Starts Performing

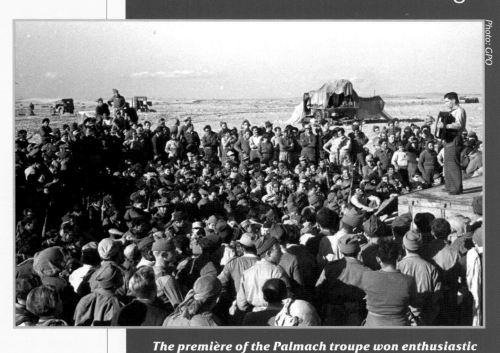

Photo: GPO

The première of the Palmach troupe won enthusiastic reviews and standing ovations. The Chizbatron, predecessor of the Army bands, included sketches of Palmach life, skits and songs in its performances.

10 March

Bread Prices Go Up – The Jewish Agency and the National Committee officially announced a rise in the price of standard bread: round bread – 47 mil; long bread - 52 mil.

22 April

The Battle over Barclays Bank - Fire was exchanged between Hagana and Irgun members when the latter tried to rob Barclays Bank in Tel Aviv.

20 September

An Armed Robbery in a Café - The first armed robbery took place in Tel Aviv. Three masked men stormed into a café, held the owner and waiters at gunpoint and stole IL35, a hefty sum in those days.

14 May

Nonstop Drafting throughout the Sabbath

The first public draft near the Meir Park in Tel Aviv during the War of Independence. Photo: Boris Karmi

29 September

Photo: Soskin

He Walked in the Fields

The Cameri Theater put on several plays: In Tel Aviv, Moshe Shamir's *He Walked in the Fields*, and in Jerusalem *The Inspector Is Coming*. Both plays were box-office hits and won rave reviews.

13 May

The four Etzion Bloc settlements fell after lengthy battles and a five-month siege. In the last battle, 157 Israeli soldiers were killed and 350 taken captive by the Jordanians.

14 May

David Ben-Gurion announced the establishment of the State of Israel.

22 June

The *Altalena* went up in flames after being shelled by IDF guns on the orders of David Ben-Gurion.

17 July

The Israeli lira (IL) was declared the official Israeli currency. Finance Minister Eliezer Kaplan announced that the new lira would have bills of up to IL50.

27 July

The IDF pledged allegiance to the State of Israel. Ya'akov Dori was appointed the first chief of staff.

28 July

The IDF's first military parade was held in Tel Aviv.

29 August

Golda Meyerson (Meir) was appointed Israel's envoy in Moscow.

14 September

The Supreme Court started operating in Jerusalem. Dr. Moshe Zmora was appointed president.

3 October

The Philharmonic Orchestra began a concert season with conductor Leonard Bernstein.

7 November

David Ben-Gurion ordered the dismantling of the Palmach headquarters.

8 November

The first population census was held in Israel: 716,000 Jews and about 70,000 others were counted.

19 December

Israel's request to become a UN member was denied.

A movie ad

1949

The Austerity: Aluminum "Wonder Pots" for those who could afford them. Photo: Fritz Cohen, GPO

The monthly food allocation per person. Photo: GPO

Days of Austerity
Cheating the Palate

Media person
Yaron London

I was nine. The radio, that big wooden box with Bakelite knobs, carried daily messages from the Ministry of Supplies and Rationing. Pregnant women, children and people with ulcers got extra food rations. Later, dietitian Tehia Bat-Oren told us all about cheating the palate by making a zucchini spread that tasted just like liver paté, or an eggplant stew that was just like goulash. Revstein, the grocer on the corner, cut out coupons from our food-stamp book with his blunt scissors, and stacked them up on a metal pick. Our religious butcher, Mendl Kribushei, who lived on our floor, once gave us a piece of prime meat that had miraculously fallen off his butcher block. And once we received "Script" coupons that Uncle Max had sent from America, and an authorized shop gave us a chocolate bar for them.

I don't remember longing for more or better food than what we were given in such small portions. We were not brought up with a taste for the finest. The decree, "Eat it with bread!" accompanied every mouthful.

Besides, I was an only child, and everyone in our house spared food from their plates for me: my parents, my unmarried uncle Moishe who lived with us, and even the tenants, the Benado couple, the new immigrants from Bulgaria who rented the big room in our three-room apartment.

The shortage was more acute for me at school because notebooks and pencils were scarce and given out sparingly. As I do now, I used to scribble on every piece of paper I laid my hands on, and I would cover my notebooks with drawings of Mickey Mouse and Donald Duck, filling them up long before my friends did. Our teacher, Efraim, was a Holocaust survivor, and I imagine he spent the war in starving Russia, hence his contempt for petty hardships. He introduced the custom of keeping little personal notebooks in class; we divided the pages into numbered squares that served as ration slips. A monitor was put in charge of the cabinet where the treasured notebooks and pencils were kept. Before he gave any of his peers a fresh notebook, he would carefully examine the old one to see that it was filled with writing on both sides of each page. Children had a lot of responsibility in my school, "The Educational Institute for Workers' Children".

The jargon of rationing included several fearsome and loathsome words. "Profiteers" were creatures of darkness who crawled up from the "black market", hiding plucked chickens under their coats and smuggling them into town to be sold for excessive amounts of money. The profiteers' clients were the "bourgeois" who voted for the General Zionists and, as always, cared only for themselves, forsaking the laborers. My mother, who dominated our house, believed that tormenting the flesh improved and purified man. Minister of Supplies and Rationing Dov Yosef was badmouthed in many houses; not in ours. Here, this British attorney, with his squeaky voice and funny little mustache, was considered a hero of the struggle for social justice.

However, my pioneering mother could not do away with the basic motherly instinct of feeding her young. Once, a profiteer appeared on our doorstep, speaking in a low voice and uncovering a bucketful of eggs. I stood behind my mother, certain that she would slam the door right in his face, maybe after giving him a good lecture on socialism. However, she bought ten eggs, and handed them over to me to put very carefully in the pantry. I took the eggs and threw them in the garbage can. My mother stood there for a while staring at the sticky mess running down the sides of the can, then drew her arm back like a tennis player and smacked me across the face. Then she covered her face with her hands and wept. She had a volatile temperament, and I had seen her screaming to high heavens or roaring with laughter, but I'd never seen her crying. After that, she came to her senses and threw her arms around me. I hugged her back. It was a moment of great joy.

13.1.49

Cease-Fire Agreements with Egypt, Lebanon, and Jordan

The negotiations on a cease-fire agreement with Egypt started on the Isle of Rhodes, under the auspices of UN envoy Dr. Ralph Bunch of the United States. The Israeli and Egyptian delegation resided in the Roses Hotel in Rhodes and, initially, only held indirect talks. Gradually, relations between the delegations grew warmer and personal ties were established. The talks started with both parties presenting far-reaching demands: Egypt demanded that Israel evacuate large segments of territory it had conquered, including the city of Beersheba. Israel demanded that Egypt withdraw to the British Mandate lines. During the negotiations, Israel made a gesture to the Egyptians, allowing them to evacuate an Egyptian brigade that was trapped in the Faluja pocket. One of the Egyptian soldiers was a young captain named Jamal Abd-al-Nasser, the future Egyptian president. After six weeks of negotiations, the parties reached an agreement according to which the Egyptians were to stay in the Gaza Strip, while the rest of the Negev would be Israeli territory. It was further agreed that the cease-fire lines would be armistice lines, and that the Nitzana area would become a demilitarized zone. The Israeli-Egyptian cease-fire agreement was signed on 24 February.

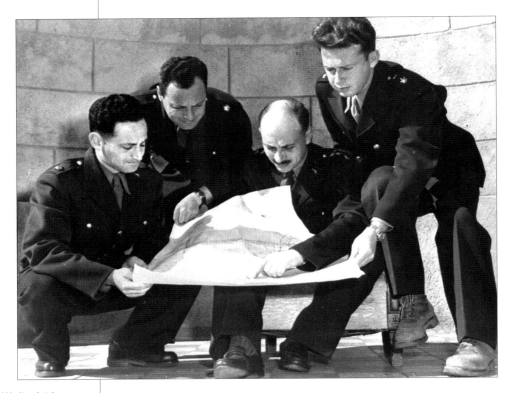

Yitzhak Rabin, Yiga'el Yadin, Arieh Simon and Yehoshafat Harkavi – the officers of the Israeli delegation for the cease-fire talks in Rhodes. Photo:GPO

Meeting in Latroun, under UN auspices, between the Israelis and the officers of the Jordanion Legion for the purpose of determining a cease-fire line. Photo: Sygma

After the talks with Egypt ended, Israel and Lebanon engaged in negotiations, held at Rosh Hanikra. Based on the agreement with Egypt, it was agreed that the international border line would serve as the cease-fire line. Israel agreed to pull out of 14 Lebanese villages and, following instructions from David Ben-Gurion, Israel gave up its demand that Syria withdraw from territories it held inside Israel. The agreement between Israel and Lebanon was signed on 23 March.

The third agreement was with Jordan. The negotiations were difficult, taking place while the armies engaged in combats during which Israeli troops reached Eilat, thus completing the occupation of the entire Negev. Negotiations with Jordan were held in Rhodes and in simultaneous meetings with Jordan's King Abdullah. The talks ended in an agreement according to which Israel was given control over the "small triangle" and the Wadi Ara road. It was also agreed that Israel would be responsible for the railroad tracks to Jerusalem. It should be noted that the Jordanian concessions were also the result of Israel's military pressure. The agreement between the two countries was signed on 4 April.

The Cease-Fire Accord With Syria

20 July

As expected, the negotiations with Syria were the toughest. The talks were held in the no-man's-land area of the Bnot Ya'akov Bridge and lasted four months. Five days before the negotiations started, there was a US-supported coup in Syria. The agreement between the two countries, like the ones Israel had signed with the other Arab countries, was also based on a withdrawal to the international border line. There was, however, one clear difference in the agreement with Syria: It was decided that the evacuated areas would remain demilitarized and that the Arab residents who had fled during the war would be allowed to return. The agreement with Syria was signed on 20 July. This officially ended the War of Independence.

First Elections in Israel

Dr. Haim Weizmann, President of the Provisional Council, addressing the Constituent Assembly.
Photo: David Eldan, GPO

Twenty-five lists (of candidates), or parties, ran in the elections for the Statutory Assembly (parliament); only 12 made it. Some 500,000 eligible voters took part in the elections, giving Mapai 46 seats, 19 to Mapam, 16 to the religious parties, 14 to Herut, 7 to the General Zionists, 5 to the Progressive List, and 4 to the Sephardim; three other lists shared a small number of seats. The results did not give any party a solid enough majority to form a cabinet without having to set up a coalition. The results also showed that, despite the fact that thousands of new immigrants took part in the elections, voting patterns did not change much when compared with elections for pre-state institutions.

Three weeks after the elections, on 14 February 1949, the Statutory Assembly gathered in Jerusalem. The gathering was attended by Dr. Haim Weizmann, president of the temporary State Council, the chief rabbis, judges, IDF generals, and many others. After singing the national anthem - *Hatikva* - the elected representatives pledged allegiance to the state, with the cabinet secretary reading the text and the members declaring "I do." Two days later, the assembly passed the transition law that named the parliament - Knesset - and the assembly was dubbed "the first Knesset." On the next day, February 17, Dr. Haim Weizmann was sworn in as Israel's first president. It was first decided that the president's term would equal the Knesset's - four years, but a later bill determined that the presidency would be a five-year term. One week after he was elected president, Dr. Weizmann commissioned David Ben-Gurion to form a cabinet and, on 8 March 1949, the first Israel cabinet was presented to the Knesset.

The twelve-member cabinet was established upon a narrow-based coalition of Mapai and parties to its right. The major portfolios were given to Mapai members: Ben-Gurion assumed the roles of Prime Minister and Defense Minister; Moshe Sharet was made Foreign Minister; Eliezer Kaplan - Finance Minister; Dov Yosef - Minister of Supplies and Rationing; and Zalman Shazar - Education Minister. Moshe Shapira, Rabbi Fishman and Rabbi Levine were Ministers for the Religious Parties. Progressive's Pinchas Rozen was made Justice Minister. The first Israeli cabinet started working, but not for long. Trouble and crises were right around the corner.

The first meeting of the government: Prime Minister David Ben-Gurion and his twelve ministers.
Photo: Hugo Mendelssohn, GPO

25 January
First elections for the 120-member Statutory Assembly in Israel.

16 February
The Knesset elects Dr. Haim Weizmann first president of the State of Israel.

24 February
A cease-fire agreement with Egypt was signed.

5 March
The beginning of Operation Uvda in which the IDF seized the southern Negev and the Bay of Eilat. The "Ink Flag" was hoisted on Eilat beach at the end of the operation.

11 March
The government decided that new immigrants should live in tents and barracks that would be built in immigrant camps until there was a budget for the construction of thousands of housing units.

23 March
A cease-fire agreement with Lebanon was signed.

26 April
In the Knesset, Prime Minister David Ben-Gurion announced an "austerity regime" - the rationing of basic food supplies. Dov Yosef was appointed Minister of Supplies and Rationing.

4 May
Israel celebrated its first Independence Day with festive parades in Jerusalem and Tel Aviv.

11 May
Israel was accepted as a UN member; 37 countries voted for, 12 against, and 9 abstained.

The National Austerity Menu

26 April

The cabinet declared a state of national austerity and rationing of basic food products. Minister Dov Yosef, who was Agriculture Minister in the first cabinet, was also nominated Minister of Supplies and Rationing. The citizens received their rations by means of local grocery stores. Minister Yosef provided a detailed program, according to which each citizen would receive a monthly supply of food worth IL6. The national austerity menu designed by the new minister was made up of the following daily rations: an unlimited amount of standard bread; 60 grams of corn; 58 grams of sugar; 60 grams of flour; 17 grams of rice; 20 grams of legumes; 20 grams of margarine; 8 grams of noodles; 200 grams of skim-milk cheese, 600 grams of onions, and 5 grams of biscuits. The meat ration was 75 grams a month per person.

7.11.49 The "Magic Carpet" Immigration

Jerusalem – Israel's Capital

5 December

Following deliberations at the UN Assembly which declared that Jerusalem should be subject to international rule, Prime Minister David Ben-Gurion declared that Jerusalem was the capital of Israel and an inseparable part of it. "Jerusalem is the very heart of the State of Israel," Ben-Gurion told the Knesset. On 9 December, the UN declared Jerusalem an international city. In response, the Israeli government decided to move all of its offices to the city. Four days later, the Knesset unanimously endorsed the Prime Minister's announcement.

The Magic Carpet was an operation in which some 50,000 Yemenite Jews, mostly children, were brought to Israel on some 380 flights. This was one of the most wonderful and complex immigration operations the state has ever known. British and American planes airlifted the Jews from Aden, the capital of Yemen, when they reached the city from all over Yemen after extremely dangerous and risky journeys. The operation was secret and was released to the media only several months after its completion.

Yemenite immigrants en route to Israel. Photo: Teddy Brauner, GPO

The year 1949 saw massive waves of immigration to Israel. Some 250,000 Jews who arrived that year alone were placed in military barracks and tent camps, and were later moved to *ma'abarot* [transit camps]. The state nearly collapsed under the burden. Calculations made that year showed that the state needed some $3,000 for the absorption of each immigrant, which meant that the state required about $700,000 for the whole campaign; the entire state budget was less than that. Yet, despite everything, the young state was more than willing to do all that was necessary to absorb the immigrants, believing that this was the reason for its establishment in the first place.

Herzl's Remains Buried in Jerusalem

17 August

Reproduction: GPO

The remains of Benjamin Ze'ev (Theodore) Herzl, the man who envisioned the State of Israel, were brought to Israel from Vienna, Austria. The reception ceremony at the airport was attended by the heads of the state, the army's general staff, and many dignitaries. The state funeral was held in Jerusalem and the guard of honor consisted was made up of the cabinet ministers. Herzl was buried on Mount Menuchot which was renamed "Mount Herzl" after the burial.

Israel Joins the UN

11 May

Israel was accepted as the 59th member of the United Nations one year after declaring independence. This followed a second request, after the first Israeli request was rejected. Thirty-seven states voted for, twelve voted against, and nine abstained. After the vote, Foreign Minister Moshe Sharet was received at the UN Assembly with warm applause and great love.

An Israeli flag is hoisted at the UN for the first time. Holding the flag, right to left: Moshe Sharet, Abba Eban and David Hacohen. Photo: Leo Rosenthal

49

30 August

The Austerity Budget – The first state budget was a modest IL40.1 million. The ministers settled for the slim budgets they were allocated without a protest or threat. Austerity prevailed.

2 November

The Cows are Coming to Israel – A first shipment of 3,000 US cows arrived in Israel as special emergency aid aimed at improving the quality of milk here.

22 November

A School for Juvenile Delinquents – At the end of the first year of Israel's existence, the social welfare authorities had to urgently establish a school for juvenile delinquents. They chose... Eilat – the tiny, hot and faraway town.

11 February

Photo: GPO

The State Council Approves the National Emblem – After nine months of deliberations and reviewing some 450 suggestions, the committee appointed to select the national emblem selected the work of the Shamir brothers. They designed a symbol composed of the *menorah* found on the Arch of Titus with an olive branch on each side. The artists maintained that "the *menorah* represents the glorious past of the Jewish nation and, unlike the Star of David, is a symbol no other nation or state in the world uses."

10 February

Habima's On the Negev Prairies Causes a Storm

Photo: Alexander

Yiga'el Mosinson's play **On the Negev Prairies** *opened the new season of the national theater, Habima. The play, starring Hana Rovina and Aharon Meskin, and directed by Shimon Finkel, brought a realistic drama from the Negev to the Tel Aviv hall. Mosinson wrote the play drawing on his experience as information officer in Kibbutz Negba during the War of Independence. The play caused a storm. Soldiers who took part in the defense of Negba demonstrated outside the theater, and the newspapers ran articles arguing over the need to be historically accurate when presenting a contemporary play.*

4 May

The Parade That Did Not March

It turns out that the IDF was not immune to chaos. The IDF parade on the first Independence Day never reached its destination. The route along which the soldiers were supposed to march was in complete disarray. Premier Ben-Gurion ordered the establishment of a commission of inquiry to find out the reasons why the parade didn't march.

Photo: Hans Pin, GPO

9 December

Passport Forgers Caught *– The police apprehended a group of passport forgers in a raid on a hotel on Hayarkon Street in Tel Aviv.*

17 May

The State Comptroller's Bill was endorsed after a brief discussion in the Knesset.

22 June

Education Minister Zalman Shazar introduced the Compulsory Education Bill according to which every child under the age of 14 must attend elementary school.

26 July

The first volume of the Hebrew Encyclopedia was published. A festive ceremony was held at the Habima theater and was attended by state and spiritual leaders who praised the first volume.

7 August

The train line to Jerusalem became operational again after a lengthy break. The first train from Tel Aviv was warmly received by the residents of Jerusalem, including David Ben-Gurion.

7 September

The Knesset ruled that all Israeli citizens must pay income tax.

1 November

A nationwide campaign of inoculation against tuberculosis began. All Israeli children were inoculated within several weeks.

9 November

Yiga'el Yadin was appointed the IDF's second chief of staff, replacing Ya'akov Dori.

1950

Tents and children at the Sha'ar Aliyah ma'abara, Haifa. Photo: Robert Capa

Tin huts in the Or Yehuda ma'abara. Photo: Teddy Brauner, GPO

The *Ma'abarot* Period
Soldier-Girl on the Roof

Writer Sami Michael

In the early 1950s, I served as a soldier in an Ordnance Corps base in the Tel Hashomer area, the very heart of old and familiar Israel. During my service years, the green fields and orchards around my base were overtaken by neighborhoods of ma'abarot [transit camps] that soon became infected wounds, covering the entire country – from Kiryat Shmona to Beersheba. They were crowded camps of tents, canvas huts and shanties. There was no electricity, but there were stinking cesspools and markets that offered rotten vegetables that even the black market would not have.

I and the other soldiers on base smelled those ma'abarot from afar. We heard the voices; we saw the figures emerging from the camps and walking in the roads like lost ants; we read about the unemployment and the fires that devoured fields and little children – but we stayed away. The lucky guys on base had families and apartments in solid buildings in Tel Aviv. The less fortunate, like myself and the Holocaust survivors, had no homes or family off base, but every one of us avoided the ma'abarot, trying not to smell, see or hear them. We were the generation that had lived through World War II, and we were sick and tired of the sight of refugees. And indeed, the people who lived in those ma'abarot were dispirited refugees. They were refugees who used whatever strength they had left attempting to escape the fate of refugees.

Even we soldiers who had no special place to go to on Sabbath or holidays were served meat daily. We showered in hot water summer and winter. We had clean uniforms and sparkling toilets. We had no sick and hungry children to take care of. We were the happy ones who resented the swamps of ugly misery. When our souls longed for light, we drove to Tel Aviv. When we wanted a breath of fresh air, we turned toward Tel Aviv. When we wanted to feast our eyes on pretty girls, we walked to Tel Aviv. Places with names such as Yehud, Sakia A and B, Heria, Pardess Katz and Kiryat Ono were not on our youthful agenda.

We could not, however, ignore disasters, and the ma'abarot encountered plenty of these, especially when the country was blessed with rains. Rivers overflowed, rainwater trapped in fields became stagnant, and floods swept through the huts and tents, wrecking them and forcing the inhabitants to fight the currents, hunger and the cold. We would leave our base and drive our jeeps, command-cars and half-tracked vehicles to bring them bread and milk or evacuate the people when the entire camp was flooded.

I remember once, when it had rained for days on end, a brook turned into a raging river and swept away an entire ma'abara. Thousands fled, but several thousand others were trapped. We drove out there in our heavy vehicles.

We got sopping wet while we pulled out stunned children and terrified old women. Some of the people there insisted they did not want to leave, hiding from us and the flood in their broken-down dwellings. Madness met with madness as the daylight slowly died away over the filthy water. When you are preoccupied with saving lives, you do not pay much attention to a cat trapped in a treetop. We fought our way through the muddy water, heading toward the moans of the old and sick, ignoring a strange wailing sound that came from somewhere in the background. Since there was no tree in the camp, we did not look for – nor did we even think of looking for – a cat.

When daylight was gone, everything became quiet. Only the whining, wailing voice would not stop. We looked around us, and saw a lonely hut at the edge of the camp, the water reaching its windowsills. On the roof, we saw a slim figure, a shadow or perhaps a chimney. I was sent there with a driver and a truck. Standing on the roof was a girl soldier who was serving as a teacher in the ma'abara. She was a Tel Aviv girl with a fresh face and fair hair. She was wet to the bone and her drenched uniform clung to her body. An impossible dream in an impossible situation. She had almost no strength left and, in fact, when we reached her, she could only mumble: "Mom, Mom, Mom... ."
Despite her misery, she was so beautiful against the gray sky and murky water. The driver and I climbed on to the hood, and she fell into our arms. "Thank you," she wept with pearly tears. "Thanks for saving me. I was so scared. I was afraid I'd have to spend the night here, in the dark, with them."

She did not mind the pouring rain. She was not scared of the rising tide. She was not terrified of the loneliness. But she was almost hysterical with fear of those creatures who lived in the canvas and tin huts. That night, I realized that two worlds had been created in Israel. I was not angry at her. I remember her as a beautiful girl to this day. My granddaughters will soon be her age, and as pretty as she. And, just like her, they are far removed from the development towns and the poor neighborhoods.

I am still caught in the middle, somewhere between my beautiful granddaughters and the inhabitants of that ma'abara who did not have a lucky break and remained trapped in the same despair.

24.5.50

The *Ma'abarot*: And the Earth Filled with Tents, Shanties and Huts

In the early 1950s, some 100,000 immigrants lived in *ma'abarot*. The first was set up in May in the Judean hills, and another 140 were later established throughout Israel. The *ma'abarot* consisted of tents, tin and canvas huts, and small barracks. Living conditions were unbearable and the supply network could not cope with the large number of residents. Residential conditions were disgraceful. Many families had to live together in large barracks, with no partition between them. Food was scarce, monotonous and tasteless. There was real hunger in many places, and the harsh winter of 1950 struck the new immigrants mercilessly. There were no heating devices and not enough blankets or warm clothes. The *ma'abarot* residents suffered greatly, with no solution in sight.

The idea of *ma'abarot* was first introduced by Levi Eshkol, Jewish Agency secretary general and future prime minister. Eshkol suggested that transit camps for immigrants be built all over Israel, and this is how *ma'abarot* were born. The immigrants were supposed to have temporary housing and do odd jobs until they were permanently absorbed.

Reality, however, was different. The immigrants had no work, and no one took the trouble to find work for them. They mainly did all sorts of busy work, but most of the time they were unemployed, despairing and bitter. The largest camp was Sha'ar Aliyah, near Haifa. Initially, it really served as a transit station to which the immigrants were taken from the Haifa Port for classification, registration, medical examinations, inoculations and fumigation with DDT – a traumatic and humiliating experience that many would remember for years to come.

Besides the daily struggles, the immigrants had to adjust to a new culture and language that were very different from their own. They were under heavy pressure to forsake the cultures they had brought with them from their countries of origin and to adopt a new cultural environment and a complicated and unknown language.

"In the *ma'abarot*," says writer Eli Amir, "the seeds were sown for social rifts, ethnic gaps, and the sense of deprivation and bitterness. These thing were later to cause a rift in Israeli society. And yet, despite everything, or perhaps as a result of nostalgia, it can be said that this was the finest hour of a young, poor and inexperienced country that was full of goodwill."

Moving to a new home in the Pardessia ma'abara. Photo: GPO

Floods in the Bet-Lid camp. Photo: GPO

The "Anti-Black Market Headquarters"

15 June

The economic situation kept on deteriorating and the austerity regime continued. The black market was a direct result of the grim economic reality. Basic food products were being sold at outrageous prices, and the government was doing everything it could to fight the phenomenon. The cabinet set up an Anti-Black Market Headquarters, and the Justice, Police and Supplies Ministries co-operated in the struggle. Special courts were set up in which profiteers were given speedy trials and heavy penalties: trade licenses were taken away, stiff fines were imposed and prison sentences were handed down. Cars were searched in surprise roadblocks, and large quantities of vegetables, chicken, liquor and other products were seized.

Police officers hunt down smuggled chicken. Photo: Fritz Cohen, GPO

Operation Ezra and Nechemia: The Aliyah of Iraqi Jews

Immigrants from Iraq at Lod airport.

Some 130,000 Jews arrived in Israel in Operation Ezra and Nechemia. Flying the Iraqi Jews to Israel lasted several months, and started after the Iraqi Government passed a special bill permitting their emigration. The Iraqi Jews were mostly wealthy and the local authorities gave them special privileges. When the Jews learned about the special permit they had been given, thousands arrived in Baghdad and gathered in registration centers where they registered for immigration to Israel.

According to Iraqi law, the Jews had to sell their property and liquidate their businesses before they could leave. Many sold large properties for ridiculous sums in order to win the right to immigrate.

Waiting in Baghdad was a tense and difficult period. Some 50,000 Jews signed up in one month, and two months later there were 90,000 on the list. This mass movement stunned the Iraqi Government, which had not expected the number of immigrants to exceed 8,000, and feared that administrative institutions run by Jews might collapse. At the same time, the Zionist movement issued a manifesto calling on the Jews to sign up for immigration. It started with the following: "O, Zion, flee, daughter of Babylon," and concluded thus: "Jews! Israel is calling you – come out of Babylon!"

The first planes flew to Israel via Cyprus in mid-May. Several months later, a giant airlift operated directly from Baghdad to Lod airport. Operation Ezra and Nechemia ended at the beginning of 1952, leaving only about 6,000 Jews in Iraq. Most of the 2,500-year-old Jewish community immigrated to Israel.

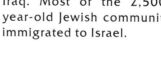
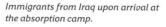
Immigrants from Iraq upon arrival at the absorption camp.

The Knesset Passes "The Law of Return"

4 July

The Law of Return, endorsed unanimously by the Knesset, determines that every Jew has a right to immigrate to Israel and receive Israeli citizenship. Prime Minister Ben-Gurion did not participate in the vote. The law was received with great joy because many believed it to be the legal embodiment of the goals of Zionism, and that it reflected the wish that the State of Israel serve as a home to all Jews wherever they may be. However, in later years, the Knesset has had more than once to address the question of how to decide who is a Jew, because while the law states that all Jews are entitled to immigrate to Israel, it does not elaborate on who is a Jew. This issue has been a bone of contention between religious and secular Israelis, has caused government crises, and has even been addressed by the Supreme Court.

---

30 January
The Knesset passed a bill according to which the minimum age of marriage is 17. People who wish to marry younger must obtain court approval.

3 February
Ramat Gan was declared a city. Avraham Krinitzi was its first mayor.

13 March
The conflict between the religious parties and Mapai regarding the education of immigrant children in the camps resumed. The religious parties threatened to dissolve the coalition if education in the camps was not the responsibility of religious teachers only.

23 April
An IDF parade was held in Jerusalem on Independence Day.

27 April
Britain fully recognized the State of Israel, two years after the British Mandate had ended.

1 May
The May Day parade was called off due to a serious disagreement between Mapai and Mapam regarding the text of the slogans that were to be displayed in it.

2 May
The IDF officially announced that half the girls who were supposed to enlist for military service had declared that they were religious and hence exempt from serving.

19 May
Operation Ezra and Nechemia began. It brought 130,000 Iraqi Jews to Israel.

29 June
The Knesset approved the state budget, to the tune of IL60.8 million.

4 July
The Knesset passed "The Law of Return", according to which all Jews are entitled to immigrate to Israel and receive Israeli citizenship.

16 July
The government decided to raise the salaries of judges by an average of 50% after they threatened to go on strike.

5.2.50

Rain and Snow All Over the Land

Polio in Israel

24 September

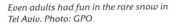

A polio epidemic broke out in Israel, mainly in the north. In Haifa, two children died after contracting the virus and another ten cases were discovered. Thousands of children throughout Israel were infected before the epidemic ended around the mid-1950s. Several isolated cases of polio were discovered in northern Israel at the end of the 1980s, but they were dealt with immediately.

The winter of 1950 was particularly harsh. Some say they remember nothing like it. Snow covered every village and town, including the central plains, Tel Aviv and even the northern Negev. Heavy snow fell in the mountains and temperatures dropped to minus 10 degrees Centigrade in the Galilee. The stormy weather caused floods that cut off many areas. Public transportation ceased to operate, and schools and government offices closed. The new immigrants who resided in the *ma'abarot* suffered the most. Many camps were flooded, and residents were evacuated for fear that the shanties and huts might collapse. Four Yemenite immigrants were killed in an avalanche that destroyed the hut they lived in at the Ein Shemer camp which was not evacuated in time.

Even adults had fun in the rare snow in Tel Aviv. Photo: GPO

24 May

IDF Radio on the Air

The army radio station, Galei Zahal, started broadcasting. The station first operated four hours a day, from 6 to 10 p.m. It mainly broadcast music and entertainment programs, information for the soldiers and lectures. The station workers were all regular soldiers. The station quickly gained popularity among soldiers.

Right: Staff Sergeant Rachel Levison, first IDF Radio announcer. Photo: GPO

Bottom: IDF Radio technicians taping at an officers' course. Photo: GPO

50

1 May

Breaking up the May Day Parade

Photo: GPO

The rising ideological tension between the left-wing parties caused the breaking up of the May Day parade. The reason for this was a heated and uncompromising argument between the two parties regarding the wording of the slogans on the placards to be carried in the parade. The debate erupted when Mrs. Golda Meyerson (second from the left) jeered at one of the banners against Ben-Gurion.

1 August

Merchants staged a general strike in protest against Minister Dov Yosef's policy of austerity.

3 September

In Jerusalem, the "Billion Conference" opened. It was attended by Jewish millionaires who were asked to help Israel by raising capital in the United States.

16 October

Prime Minister Ben-Gurion resigned as a result of the crisis with the religious parties over education in immigrant camps and *ma'abarot*.

1 November

After unsuccessful attempts to form a government, the task was again given to David Ben-Gurion.

14 November

The first municipal elections were held in Israel. The General Zionists won victories at the expense of Mapai. This led to the advancement of the 2nd Knesset elections.

14 May

A "Blue-and-White" Jaffa Brothel - The police raided a brothel operating in Jaffa and arrested two prostitutes and three men who were found on the premises. The brothel was discovered, the police said, as a result of surveillance, stakeouts and tip-offs.

28 October

The Israeli national soccer team won a surprising 5–1 victory against the Turkish team.

26 March

Hanna Senesh Returns Home

Hanna Senesh, the paratrooper who went to the rescue of the Hungarian Jews and never returned, was brought back to Israel in a coffin on board an Israeli warship. Many paid her last respects in a procession that started on the streets of Haifa and ended on Mount Herzl in Jerusalem. Behind the coffin marched her mother, Katherine Senesh, her brother, and Yoel Palgi, who represented Hanna's group in Caesarea.

The portrait of Hanna Seneshona JNF stamp.

Expose those who conceal the goods!
The black market frenzy has been stopped – let us eliminate it completely!

28 October

Knesset Speaker Yosef Shprinzak opened the first Maccabi Games in the State of Israel. This was the third time the games had been held, and this time they were at the Ramat Gan Stadium in the presence of 50,000 spectators. The games had been scheduled to take place in 1938, but they were called off due to rising Arab violence and the fear of the British administration that the games would increase the pace of the illegal immigration of Jews to Palestine. The slogan of the 3rd Maccabi Games – "Unity in Honor of the Jewish Nation and for the Glory of Sports" – symbolized a change in the concept of the games: From now then, the games were open to all Jewish athletes, not only to Maccabi members.

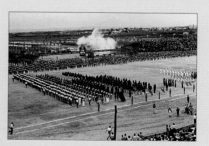

Delegations stand in readiness at the opening ceremony. Photo: GPO

An advertisement for Galai's radios.

(*1951*

The Israeli team at work drying the Hula. Photo: GPO

The 1990s. Work to re-flood the Hula Lake begins.

Drying the Hula
The Dying Lake

Writer Meir Shalev

"It seemed that it would be this way forever; could it ever be otherwise, without all of that?"

These are the words of photographer Peter Merom who wrote about his life on the shore of the Hula Lake in an album about its last days, entitled The Dying Lake.

Apparently, it could be otherwise, and everybody knows the dry (very dry) facts: The Hula Lake has been dried out, killed. It is gone but, like many other great victims, it refuses to be forgotten.

Ecologists, hydrologists and agronomists have discussed and will go on discussing the professional aspects of this drying. For us laymen, the Hula will forever be an allegory about brutality, blindness, arrogance and abuse of ideals. If this sounds familiar, let us not forget that we have acted the same way in other areas – hence the power of the allegory.

A review of the history of those days, just like a walk through the scarred Hula landscape, tells an irritating tale. Fifty years after the pioneers of the Second Immigration (1904-1914) dried the swamps, the State of Israel found itself a new swamp to fight, as if to relive its youth. Those who looked for signs of the old enemy in the Hula Lake – water, reeds, buffaloes and mosquitoes – found them all over the place. Those who wished to find land in it, found it at the bottom of the lake. And it was not just any land, either. It was virgin land that had never been possessed by man. Without Turkish footprints, Roman relics, Arab leftovers or Canaanite remains. It was land just like our ethos and pathos love it – pure, anticipating, waiting for redemption.

The newspapers of the time describe the drying of the Hula in the all-too-familiar and enthusiastic tone: "A great miracle," "a giant enterprise," "a pioneering act". It seems that in those days, everyone thought and acted according to the same formula. What's so surprising? We have been brought up that way. As soon as we are given some still waters, a few mosquitoes and some reeds, we take off on a tour of our conditioned and well-trodden thought patterns: You say drying, you mean swamp; by swamp, you mean malaria; malaria means pioneers; and they mean settlement, plowing the first furrow, dancing an energetic hora, values, vision, land, Zionism. And so, by the power of words which are too lofty and professionalism which is too low, the lake has been dried, killed and turned into an allegory.

Several years ago, I heard a very edifying little tale: Before the Hula was dried, a Dutch expert was brought here to study the issue and give some advice. He was not too enthusiastic about the entire affair and said, among other things, that our expectations regarding the quality of the turf supposedly waiting to be rescued at the bottom of the lake should not be too high. One of our experts stood up, banged on the table with his fist, and thundered: "Our turf is good turf; it is Zionist turf!"

Had this story been told about any other fool, we would laugh. Because he is our fool, we can only weep and mourn for him, for us, for the dying lake and, worst of all, for the kind of thought processes that dried it out. We find the very same approach today, everywhere. It is the attitude of "I know best," and "It will work out fine in the end," of arrogance and machismo.

It has been forty years since the lake was dried and, I am sorry to say, things did not work out so fine. It seems that the dying lake is fighting back with a vengeance. The water we had expected to collect is contaminated and contaminates Lake Kinneret. Wild animals and plants are disappearing, mice are multiplying, and the land – that virgin land that awaited us so – is not good Zionist turf, but simply barren wasteland. We could almost say that the Hula waters cry to us from the ground. However, because we have already attributed human qualities to the turf, let us leave the water alone.

The lake is dying. Part of it has been re-flooded, but not revived. The allegory, becoming clearer before our very eyes, teaches us the hard way (do we know of any other way?) that brute force is a double-edged saber – it swings right back and wounds those who rattled it. The Hula is dead, and this is its last will and testament.

We Came to Israel: Immigration and the Hardships of Absorption

1951 was characterized most of all by massive waves of immigrants to Israel which kept arriving from the East and the West. About 180,000 immigrants arrived that year. Israel, whose population had numbered approximately 600,000 people in 1948, had absorbed approximately 700,000 by the end of 1951 – an unprecedented phenomenon. In four years, a society that was still evolving absorbed a mass of immigrants that outnumbered it. This placed a very heavy economic burden on the young state. Yet, despite the difficulties and the need for giant budgets, the government and the veterans believed that absorbing this mass immigration was precisely the goal and purpose for which the State of Israel had been founded.

Israel, however, had neither the means nor the infrastructure for the enterprise. The first waves of immigrants were placed in deserted houses belonging to Arabs who had fled the cities and the villages. Later, the state set up camps and *ma'abarot* where the new immigrants were settled.

With the deteriorating economic situation that year, the problems of mass immigrant absorption started to increase. There was talk of slowing down the rate of immigration. In those days, it was said that the Israelis loved immigration, not immigrants. Veteran Israelis were forced to tighten their belts and change the way they lived, a way that was still evolving. The newborn society felt alienated from the immigrants, a cultural gap. The latter tried very hard to cast away their old cultures and adjust to the new one. The prevailing norm rejected the heritage and traditions of the oriental Jews, encouraging cultural unification along the lines dictated by the veterans – the absorbers. The idea was that a new Israeli culture must be formed, and the immigrants must adopt it as fast as possible.

Near the end of 1951, the rate of immigration slowed down. The people in charge of absorption in Israel began to worry that the Jewish communities abroad were sending mainly the sick, handicapped and elderly. They decided therefore on a new "selective" absorption policy according to which young and healthy immigrants received preferential treatment, while the number of old and invalid immigrants was cut down. The new policy was dubbed "immigrant regulation." And indeed, the number of immigrants again dropped significantly at the end of 1951.

New immigrants arrive at Haifa Port.
Photo: Robert Capa

Split in the United Kibbutz Movement

21 May

The United Kibbutz Movement (UKM) split on ideological grounds. After months of confrontations between Mapai and Mapam supporters in the Kibbutzim, the movement decided to split. The "divorce" came through after the UKM decided to expel all Mapai members. The confrontations escalated after the decision was made, turning violent and sometimes causing rifts in families over ideological issues. After the decision was made, 30 kibbutzim announced that they were leaving the UKM.

An immigrant family in a hut in Sha'ar Aliyah. Photo: GPO

14.2.51 Education Crisis in the *Ma'abarot* Causes the Cabinet to Resign

The Israeli cabinet resigned as a result of the stormy debate about education in the *ma'abarot*. The religious parties demanded that immigrant children receive religious education, claiming that most immigrants were religious and observant while the state, they claimed, forced secular education upon them. The Ministry of Education maintained the opposite, claiming that a network of unified national education schools should be set up, regardless of the existing streams. The framework was supposed to educate the pupils in the spirit of unity and the merging of the exiles, and to teach general studies, emphasizing modern life. A compromise was found eventually in establishing two education systems: secular and religious. The religious system was applied in full to the camps where most of the immigrants were Yemenites. This compromise lasted almost a year, but when the immigrants moved from camps into *ma'abarot*, the debate broke out again and the compromise did not work anymore. In early February, the Knesset rejected the education minister's suggestion that children in immigrant settlements be enrolled in the Workers' schools. Ben-Gurion, who viewed this as a vote of no confidence, resigned. He was very upset, and lashed out at the religious Knesset members from the podium: "No one will monopolize religion in this country... We will not let the religious parties have custody of religious education... ."

The Ben-Gurion government became a caretaker cabinet, and the Knesset decided to bring the elections forward to 30 July 1951. Having decided this, Ben-Gurion did not refrain from intensifying the crisis with the religious front. In March, in his capacity as defense minister, he presented the plenum with an amendment to the Security Service Bill, suggesting that religious girls be drafted for national service. Considering the move to be an act of vengeance, the religious parties turned to the Chief Rabbinate, which declared that "women must not be drafted." The crisis was put off to the next Knesset.

When it was cold outside, studies were held in a wooden hut. Photo: GPO

רשימת
מפלגת פועלי ארץ-ישראל
ובלתי מפלגתיים

"We Are Fed Up With Mapai's Rule"

30 July

The election campaign for the 2nd Knesset was very stormy. The General Zionists conducted a tough campaign against Mapai, under the slogan, "We Are Fed Up With Mapai's Rule." They attacked the policy of rations and austerity that Ben-Gurion's government had introduced. The General Zionists gained the most seats in these elections, going up from 7 to 20 Knesset seats, nearly tripling their power. Mapai kept its power – 45 seats; Mapam went down from 19 to 15 seats; and Herut lost 6 seats, going down from 14 to 8 Knesset members. The religious parties, which ran separately, maintained their power.

16 January
The Israeli Government sent an official letter to Western countries, demanding that the Germans pay reparations for the murder of six million Jews during the Holocaust.

20 January
The Hula drying project, designed to give settlements additional land, began. Later on, the operation created great tension with the Syrians.

30 January
An earthquake in central Israel, felt mainly in Tel Aviv, caused major panic.

14 February
The Ben-Gurion cabinet resigns over the *ma'abarot* education crisis.

27 February
A new town named Ashkelon was established in the south. It was populated mainly by immigrants from North Africa.

4 April
A grave incident with the Syrians occurred in the al-Hamma area. A Syrian unit entered a demilitarized zone and killed seven Israeli policemen.

9 April
An Air Force plane crashed into the sea during the Independence Day parade. The pilot was rescued, but died later of his injuries.

14 May
Member of an underground movement of young ultra-Orthodox Jews, dubbed "The Zealots' Pact," expecting to attain religious goals by force, were detained by the police.

17 July
The Knesset passed the bill of equal rights for women, stating: "One law applies to men and women."

25 July
The first Nahal Brigade settlement-camp was set up opposite Gaza.

4.4.51

Drying the Hula and the Confrontation With Syria

The dry Hula Lake. Photo: GPO

The Hula drying project, designed to provide the adjacent settlements with additional farming land, created a lot of tension with Syria, which disapproved of the project. The Syrian Army opened fire at the workers and the IDF soldiers guarding them, and shelled kibbutzim and settlements in the region. Tension reached its peak in early April when Syrian soldiers entered a demilitarized strip in al-Hamma, ambushed an Israeli Border Police patrol and killed seven policemen. The Israel Air Force retaliated by raiding Syrian outposts, but to no avail. A few days later, the Syrians shot two Israeli soldiers dead.

In May, another Syrian unit penetrated the area of Korazim, north of Lake Kinneret. An IDF force pushed them back after four days of fierce fighting, sustaining 40 fatalities and some 70 wounded.

Draining the Hula swamps. Photo: GPO

Photo: GPO

Schools for Teaching Hebrew

Hebrew Schools *(ulpanim)* opened throughout Israel. The most prominent and famous of them was *Ulpan Etzion* in Jerusalem. Olim from all over the world took Hebrew classes there, acquiring a basic knowledge of the Hebrew language.

51

1951

21 September

Refrigerator Production Increases

Photo: GPO

The Amcor Company was pleased to announce that it had succeeded in increasing the production of its electric refrigerators. That year, it produced 400 new refrigerators, barely meeting the rising demand. Most families in the young country had been using old iceboxes, refrigerating the food with ice blocks that were sold on the streets. A serious shortage in ice was created that year, when ice producers cut down on production, protesting the fact that the government would not permit them to raise prices.

1 November

A bread shortage was felt in central Israel - Although the prevailing atmosphere of austerity dictated settling for less, the bread shortage was seriously felt in central Israel, mainly in Tel Aviv. Long queues lined up in front of the bakeries in anticipation of the coveted standard bread.

Maccabi Tel Aviv won the national soccer championship. The national league resumed its activity this year, after a break of several years.

12 November

The Seamen's Strike

This was one of the first and most violent strikes Israel has known. The seamen went on strike after their demand to establish a non-Histadrut labor federation was rejected. The strike paralysed the Israeli fleet and forced the ports to shut down. It turned into a violent clash when members of the Histadrut's Hapoel guards tried to break the strike. Ten days into the strike, the police used force against the seamen, who barricaded themselves on board one of the ships, but to no avail. The strike lasted 43 days.

16 October

The First Mif'al Hapayis Lottery

Gambling became popular in three-year-old Israel. Mif'al Hapayis, the national lottery, which was established with the intention of collecting funds for educational institutions, was received with interest and curiosity. The first lucky winner was a resident of Ramat Gan.

Photo: GPO

30 July

Mapai maintained its power in the elections for the 2nd Knesset. The General Zionists went up from 7 to 20 Knesset seats, the religious parties kept their representation intact, and Herut went down from 14 to 8 seats.

5 August

All the movie theaters in Israel went on strike protesting the decision to raise the entertainment tax.

12 September

The Tel Aviv-Eilat bus line was inaugurated. The first trip took nine hours, and passengers included Knesset members and other notables.

11 November

The Egged bus cooperative was formed following a merger of several public transportation companies.

Photo: GPO

19 December

Dr. Haim Weizmann was elected president for the second time.

1952

Menahem Begin led the opposition to the German reparations. Photo: GPO

Riots outside the Knesset building during the vote on the reparations. Photo: David Rubinger

Reparations From Germany
"Paying for Sins With Blood Money?"

*Former Minister
Dr. Yosef Burg*

At the beginning of 1952 – the very first days of the second Knesset – we had to address an issue that was very upsetting for the entire nation: whether or not we should sign an agreement of reparations with the West German Government. The agreement was being promoted by German Chancellor Konrad Adenauer and Israel's Prime Minister David Ben-Gurion, who coined the phrase "a different Germany." Dr. Nachum Goldman, chairman of the board of the Zionist Federation, conducted the negotiations.

The introduction to the agreement explicitly stated that enormous crimes had been committed during the Nazi regime and that Germany was hereby expressing its desire to repair the damage it had done, if only in part. Germany pledged to pay the State of Israel and Jewish organizations some $800 million to cover partially the expenses of rehabilitating the Jews who had suffered Nazi persecution, compensate them, and help with their absorption in Israel. In addition, Jewish victims of Nazi atrocities were to be paid personal compensation.

The very idea that Israel should negotiate with and receive money from the Germans caused a storm in Israel, the question being whether money should be accepted from the Germans at all. The Knesset had already been faced with votes on issues of conscience, but the issue of German reparations was more than an issue of personal conscience. It was a tough deliberation. No one wanted to have anything to do with Germany, an outcast among the family of nations. Was the offer to pay reparations not an attempt on its part to pay for its sins with blood money? Also, there was the question of "Have you killed and also taken possession?" (I Kings, 21, 19)

On the other hand, there were practical considerations. We had to absorb over one million immigrants and we could not do this with Jewish donations alone. We had to bolster the IDF and procure equipment for it. That could not be done without the reparations money. Others, however, maintained that our economy and morals would be corrupted by the German money.

The night before the vote on whether to engage in negotiations with Germany, I did two things: I went to my bookshelf and selected a book by French philosopher René Descartes and read a little about the ways of meditation. I wanted to escape the emotional world, especially as I am a sentimental person. I believed that addressing an issue such as this required a clear mind. Whatever the decision may be, it must not be made in a state of emotional turmoil. Then I returned to my bookshelf and looked at the Mishna books that stood there. They had been printed in Germany, in 1947, with the help of the US Army. I had received them from the American Joint Distribution Committee.

I stood there wondering what my late father, who had died in 1937, would have done; what would my mother have said? And what would Rashi and the Tosafists have said if they had had to decide? I felt they would want us to stay alive – that this should be our consolation and revenge. No soul can live if the body is dead. Therefore, for the sake of consolation and for the sake of revenge – that we do exist despite the Holocaust – I decided to vote for the negotiations.

The Knesset building was on King George Street in Jerusalem. The Herut Movement, which headed the opposition to the reparations, staged a mass demonstration at nearby Zion Square. Herut leader Menachem Begin made the lead speech, and he did not mince any words. He called Ben-Gurion "a maniac" who had become the prime minister of Israel and was asking the German murderers for money for the blood of their victims. "This shall never happen," Begin declared. "We are willing to leave our families again, go to prison and face torture to prevent the disgrace." The demonstrators started rioting, overturning cars, and hurling rocks into the Knesset hall.

Yitzhak Refael, who supported the agreement, was halfway through his speech on the podium when a rock hit Hanan Rubin in the head. Most of the Knesset members left the hall. Ben-Gurion remained sitting, with me beside him. He told me: "If I leave, it will be the end of the Israeli parliament. I must not move." I would be lying if I were to say I was not afraid, but I did not want to get up while Ben-Gurion remained sitting. Deep in my heart, I knew he was right.

The vote was held on 9 January 1952; 61 voted for the reparations agreement and 50 voted against. Although each Knesset member should have been allowed to follow his conscience, we were subjected to factional discipline. Only Rabbi Norok was allowed to vote against. In September, the Knesset Foreign Affairs and Defense Committee decided, with a majority of 8 to 7, to authorize the government to sign the agreement.

The agreement was signed in Luxembourg on 10 September 1952, when the Knesset was in recess. It is hard to say that the event did not leave its mark. However, it was impossible to stop the momentum of life.

9.1.52 The German Reparations Affair

Menachem Begin: "This Will Be a Civil War Until Death!"

One of the stormiest affairs in Israel's history was that of the German reparations. The storm erupted after the German Government offered to compensate Jewish Holocaust survivors, and Prime Minister Ben-Gurion brought the issue before the Knesset, announcing that negotiations were being conducted. Public opposition was widespread and extensive. Among those opposing the reparations deal were many Holocaust survivors who claimed that this would seem like the Jews had forgiven the Nazi crimes and the German people. On the other hand, people who favored the deal maintained that the Germans were obliged to give back everything they had taken away from the Jews, and that the money would be used for the absorption of Holocaust survivors in Israel.

The debate was very passionate, crossing political boundaries. The Herut Movement, headed by Menachem Begin, led the struggle against the deal. It reacted sharply and organized stormy and violent demonstrations. On 9 January, the day the Knesset debated the issue, Herut organized a mass demonstration in Jerusalem in which Begin delivered a fiery speech saying, among other things: "When they fired their guns at us, I said – no! This time I will give the order – yes! This will be a civil war until death! We might be sent to the gallows again... ." The excited crowds stormed the Knesset with Begin in the lead. Thousands of demonstrators tried to break through the police barriers, while the police tried to ward them off with clubs and tear gas. The demonstrators did not give in, pelted rocks at the Knesset building and smashed several windows. In the evening, after a day of heavy clashes, the demonstrators dispersed. Some 200 demonstrators and 100 policemen were injured and several dozen were arrested.

Photo: Eliezer A. Sonderpen

Thousands demonstrate against the German reparations in Mugrabi Square in Tel Aviv. Photo: David Rubinger, GPO

Ben-Gurion Proposes: "Professor Einstein for President!"

9 November

When the seven days of mourning for Israel's first president, Dr. Haim Weizmann, ended, Prime Minister David Ben-Gurion made the surprising suggestion that Prof. Albert Einstein be elected Israel's president, calling him "the greatest man in generations". Einstein, however, declined. The Knesset chose to replace Dr. Weizmann with Yitzhak Ben-Tzvi, who won 48 votes. He ran against Peretz Bernstein of the General Zionists, who received only 18 votes.

Professor Albert Einstein visits Rishon Lezion, 1923. Photo: M. Amati

Yiga'el Yadin Resigns as Chief of Staff

Yiga'el Yadin resigned from his post as the second IDF chief of staff following disagreements over the army budget with David Ben-Gurion, prime minister and defense minister. At the end of 1952, due to Israel's grave economic situation, it was decided to cut the IDF budget significantly – from $150 million in 1951 to $64 million in 1953. Ben-Gurion demanded that the army perform an extensive downsizing program that included firing many career soldiers and significantly reducing procurement and training plans. Chief of Staff Yadin rejected Ben-Gurion's plan, offering an alternative downsizing plan. The prime minister insisted that the chief of staff execute his plan. Yadin refused and filed his resignation. He was replaced by Mordechai Maklef, and Moshe Dayan was appointed head of the Operations Branch. Maklef gradually implemented the changes imposed by Ben-Gurion and, during his 12-month tenure, managed to upgrade the combat level of the IDF soldiers and even to lower the average age of the senior offices.

Chief of Staff Yiga'el Yadin with Meir Amit (right) and Meir Zorea (left). Photo: Starphot

Ma'abarot Demonstrations: "We Want to Be Like the Ashkenazim"

Photo: Guttgold

26 October

Thousands of demonstrators in the three largest *ma'abarot* staged sit-in strikes and vast demonstrations protesting the decision to move tent dwellers to "permanent residences" in wooden and canvas huts built near the current camps. The immigrants charged that they were being discriminated against. They refused to move and demanded that, "like the Ashkenazim," they be evacuated to real permanent housing and not "be thrown to the dogs." Large police forces were deployed in case the embittered immigrants decided to assault government representatives.

1952

9 January
By a majority of 61 to 50, the Knesset ruled that the government should commence negotiations with the German Government on the reparations agreement. Before the decision was made, stormy demonstrations were staged outside the Knesset building.

16 January
The operation in which the Iranian Jews were brought to Israel began. Israeli planes flew the Jews from Teheran directly to Lod Airport.

1 February
The report that Mapam leader Mordechai Oren had been arrested in Prague shocked his friends in Israel. Oren was detained on suspicion of breaching state security because he had tried to locate his friend Shimon Orenstein.

26 March
The members of the ultra-Orthodox underground movement, "The Zealots' Pact", were sentenced to prison terms of up to 12 months.

13 May
The first class of medical doctors graduated from the Hebrew University in Jerusalem.

22 June
A bomb was thrown at the house of Transportation Minister David Pinkas as a protest against the decision to halt all private cars for two days a week.

25 June
Levi Eshkol was appointed finance minister, replacing Eliezer Kaplan who resigned for health reasons.

1 July
Teddy Kollek was appointed director-general of the Prime Minister's Office after completing a political tour of duty in the United States.

10 July
Finance Minister Levi Eshkol decided to raise the civil servants' salaries by IL12 a month.

19 July
For the first time, Israel took part in the Olympic Games in Helsinki.

4.4.**52**

Nutrition Experts:
"Food Rations are Wrong."

Nutrition experts sharply criticized the fact that the food rations allocated to the public were insufficient for healthy nutrition and were even basically wrong. The Nutrition Council members who examined the rations stated that Israel's residents were suffering from a shortage of calories, protein and calcium because they were not being given enough meat, fish, eggs and cheese. The experts suggested that portions of powdered milk and eggs be added to improve the situation. The experts further recommended that the sugar allocation be increased and, if that could not be done, they suggested adding jam that had a high sugar content. Referring to the food given to infants, the experts suggested that they be given rations of whole and fresh milk, which was absolutely essential for the proper growth of the young Israeli generation.

No Gasoline - No Cars

22 May

Due to a serious gasoline shortage, the government decided to impose two non-driving days per week on every car in the country. Each car had to display a sticker specifying the day on which it was not to be driven. Bus travel was reduced as well, with all busrides ending at 11 p.m. This resolution greatly angered the public.

Standing in line for dairy products. Photo: GPO

Locust Plague in Israel

27 April

Young Israel woke up one morning to an unfamiliar reality: Swarms of locusts covered the fields, vineyards and even roads.

The locusts landed in the Dan Region, Ramla, Lod, Rehovot and even the North. The headquarters for combating the locusts announced that the species that had appeared in Israel was the yellow desert locust. The locusts arrived in swarms, flying some 50 meters above the ground. Thousands of residents went out to the field to chase the locusts away before they caused real damage to crops. The locusts spent a few days here before moving northwards.

Kibbutz Sa'ad members fighting the swarms of locusts that covered their fields. Photo: GPO

52

1952

6 August

The First Choir Festival Opened in Jerusalem

Photo: GPO

Dozens of Israeli and foreign choirs arrived in Jerusalem to attend the first choir festival in Israel. The residents of Jerusalem did not only attend the events, but also the numerous rehearsals.

21 August

Yitzhak Sadeh, the first Palmach commander and an IDF general, died at the age of 62.

10 September

The reparations agreement was signed. Chancellor Adenauer signed for Germany and Minister Moshe Sharet signed for Israel.

19 September

A government crisis erupted over the issue of national service for girls.

5 October

Dov Shilansky and Ya'akov Heruti, former Irgun activists, were arrested outside the Foreign Ministry in Tel Aviv on suspicion of attempting to place a bomb there, protesting the reparations agreement with Germany.

9 November

Dr. Haim Weizmann, Israel's first president, died. He promoted the Balfour Declaration, and established the Weizmann Institute.

6 August

Films That Promote "Meals and Feasts" Disqualified – The Council for the Inspection of Films and Plays (the censorship) decided to disqualify movies that did not correspond with the concepts of austerity. The council announced that "films that promote hearty meals or grandiose feasts will be disqualified without hesitation." The council banned the screening of four American films that were "morally inappropriate" for the Israeli audiences.

28 February

Onions for Shoes – The Bulgarian Government commissioned some 30,000 pairs of the best quality shoes from Israeli factories. However, instead of paying cash, the Bulgarians sent a giant shipment of onions – a very scarce commodity in Israel. The Bulgarian Government announced that it would be willing to send more food products in return for shoes.

Lend Your Hand to the Rehabilitation of the Ma'abarot and Poor Suburbs. Signed: The Fund for Flood Victims.

3 January

General Strike of Grocery Shops

Grocery shops throughout the country went on strike because of Dr. Dov Yosef's treatment of grocery merchants. Citizens were requested to buy bread in good time. As a result of the strike, Dr. Yosef decided to give in to some of the merchants' demands to raise the prices of several products.

Photo: GPO

תן ידך לשיקום המעברה והפרבר
המגבית לנפגעי השטפונות

1953

Chief of Staff Moshe Dayan with officers of the 101 and paratroopers. Standing, right to left: Asaf Simhoni, Moshe Efron, Dani Mat, Ariel Sharon, and Meir Har-Zion. Sitting: Refael Eitan, Ya'akov Ya'akov and Aharon Davidi. Photo: GPO

Photo: Avraham Vered, Bamachaneh

48

A Shining Link in the Security Chain

*Former Chief of Staff
and MK
Amnon Lipkin Shahak*

The story of IDF Unit 101 is an important chapter in the history of Israel's security because the spirit of that unit is what makes the IDF strong even on the threshold of the year 2000. An invisible but strong thread connects those days and today, although our technological, demographic and geo-political reality has changed, thus causing some of our moral values to change.

This thread is the chain of names, places and events that constitute the IDF heritage, determining the army's and society's values. We must remember that our defensive identity has changed in the past, and is still under constant examination, but its foundations are solid and clear.

Unit 101 is a shining link in that ever-forming security chain. It is made of the same fundamental stuff as our security problems and solutions.

The fifth year of Israel's existence, 1953, found the Israeli defense establishment confused and indecisive in the face of threats and harassment. Those days were characterized by penetrable borders and by infiltrators who murdered and wounded civilians, committed theft and violence, and undermined our economy and morale. The Active Policy – that magic formula that was meant to end the harassment – worked only partially. The retaliation operations, carried out by large IDF units, did not yield satisfactory results, caused political resentment and sparked counter-violence.

Unit 101 was set up to solve these problems. It was a small and flexible unit that was based on originality of thought and operational determination. Its moral nature was not to everybody's liking but, after a series of successes, its shape was finally molded and remained intact until it merged with the Paratroopers' Brigade.

The nature of the 101 and the way it was born, the way it operated and the way it was acknowledged in Israel and world-wide are a microcosmic reflection of the complex existential security problems Israel had always had to deal with. An analysis of its nature and actions would, in fact, be an analysis of the nature of our problems and solutions at that time. By studying those, we may try to analyze differences between and similarities to those of today. Learning the history of that unit is tantamount to learning how the still-forming State of Israel exercised its power, how it dealt with challenges, what moral dilemmas it faced and what solutions were found. Some of the latter were perhaps not satisfactory, but they definitely set the ground rules for the rights and wrongs of the current system.

No nation, state or army can ever build its might and future without learning and understanding its past – in order to imitate it, to implement the lessons learned and to grow on the basis of past deeds and mistakes. In a short period of time, Unit 101, which originally numbered a few dozen soldiers under the command of Major Ariel Sharon, significantly changed the nature of IDF-initiated operations. In the things it did – the mistakes it made, its accomplishments – Unit 101 serves as a shining example of the unique way the IDF uses its power. It was unique because Israel's political and defense problems have always been extraordinary and complex. It was unique because the people were special and the methods they employed were unorthodox.

That uniqueness – of which Unit 101 was an early, original and major expression, both on the mythological and the practical levels – is the source of our power and might today. The IDF must preserve this uniqueness, while carefully and intelligently upholding its moral and operational code in a way that will further increase its strength.

12.2.**53**

The USSR Severs Its Ties With Israel

The USSR decision to sever its ties with Israel was made in Moscow after a bomb was thrown into the Soviet Embassy in Tel Aviv, wounding three embassy personnel, including the ambassador's wife. The USSR issued a statement accusing Israel of inciting hostile acts against it and even claiming that the Israel Police assisted the attackers.

The decision was preceded by a tense period in Jerusalem-Moscow relations. The reason for this tension was an anti-Israel campaign in the Eastern Bloc that started with the Prague Trials in which 11 Jewish members of the Communist Party were charged with treason and sabotage, and continued with the "Doctors' Trial", in which a group of Jewish physicians was charged with attempting to assassinate Soviet leaders, including Stalin. Most of the doctors were executed. Anti-Semitism was rising in the USSR. After the Doctors' Trial, the Israeli government filed a protest with the Soviet government against the blood-libel and anti-Semitism in the USSR. The Soviet Union changed its policy from enthusiastically supporting the young state to becoming a hostile adversary, eventually severing diplomatic ties with it.

This change of attitude toward Israel had an impact on the in-fighting within the Israeli Mapam Party. Mapam leaders Moshe Sneh and Ya'akov Riftin were dismissed for justifying the deeds of the Communist regime in the Prague Trials. Sneh quit Mapam and set up a one-man faction in the Knesset. Several months later, he established the Israeli Communist Party (ICP or Maki) that openly and consistently supported USSR policies.

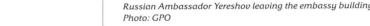

Russian Embassy staff members packing and leaving. Photo: GPO

Russian Ambassador Yereshov leaving the embassy building. Photo: GPO

Ben-Gurion Retires to Sde Boker

7 December

"The country does not depend on one man," David Ben-Gurion announced, and retired to Kibbutz Sde Boker in the south, surprising the public, the politicians and the cabinet ministers of his own party. The Mapai leaders tried to convince him to stay on in his position, but to no avail. Ben-Gurion's Sde Boker hut was built especially for him. Its photograph appeared on the front pages of every newspaper. Ben-Gurion suggested that Levi Eshkol take over as prime minister, but he declined. The Mapai leaders were certain that Moshe Sharet was the natural successor and, indeed, after Ben-Gurion resigned, the president assigned Sharet the task of forming a new government. Ben-Gurion spent a year in Sde Boker before returning to the cabinet.

Paula and David Ben-Gurion at the door to their Sde Boker hut.

Unit 101 Goes on Retaliation Missions

1953

Major General Moshe Dayan, Head of the IDF Operations Branch, initiated the establishment of a secret unit, number 101. It was to carry out retaliation missions behind enemy lines. Major Ariel Sharon was appointed commander of the unit. The unit was established against the backdrop of a deterioration in the security situation when murderous terrorist squads infiltrated from Jordan and attacked Israeli civilians. The IDF first retaliated with attacks against villages and military bases in Jordanian territory, but in most cases this did not stop the Jordanians. Secret Unit 101 was supposed to provide an effective answer to the attacks.

Its best-known operation took place on 14 October. Unit 101 attacked the village of Kibiah in Samaria, which was a known launching pad for terrorist operations. The unit overran the village and blew up the houses, not knowing that dozens of civilians were hiding inside. Some 70 people, mostly women and children, were killed in the blast. The operation caused a major storm in Israel and was followed by international condemnation.

Prime Minister Ben-Gurion announced that the operation had not been carried out by the IDF, but by Israeli border villagers who could no longer tolerate the sabotage and murderous attacks they had been subjected to. The operation, which resulted in a great tragedy, resparked the domestic debate about the retaliation operations. Ben-Gurion favored an iron fist policy and countermeasures to make the point that no terrorist attack would go unpunished.

Photo: Avraham Vered, Bamachaneh

Photo: Avraham Vered, Bamachaneh

The Israel Prizes Awarded for the First Time

20 April

On the fifth Independence Day of Israel, the Israel Prizes were awarded for the first time, in Jerusalem, for outstanding scientific research and original works of art and literature. Professor Ben-Zion Dinur, education and culture minister, said in his speech that "a nation reveals its independence in spiritual creativity." Ten scientists and philosophers received the prizes, consisting of IL 1,000 each. The oldest judge on the panel was Professor Martin Buber.

6.12.**53**

Moshe Dayan -
The Fourth Chief of Staff

Appointing Moshe Dayan chief of staff was the last thing David Ben-Gurion did before he resigned as prime minister and defense minister. When Chief of Staff Mordechai Maklef filed his resignation, Ben-Gurion quickly accepted it and appointed Dayan without consulting Maklef. The appointment was not unanimously approved by the cabinet. Some considered Dayan a "political" chief of staff and were concerned that he would become involved in political decisions. However, most ministers praised him for his skills and ability to lead the army at a time of rising security tensions and an increase in acts of sabotage and murderous attacks by infiltrators.

Upon his appointment, Dayan announced his resignation from the Mapam Central Committee. As the fourth IDF chief of staff, Dayan led the army in a series of retaliation operations, mainly carried out by Unit 101. The peak of his career at the time was leading the IDF to a decisive victory over the Egyptian Army during the Sinai Campaign (1956).

In his capacity as fourth chief of staff, Dayan led the IDF to its great victory in the Sinai Campaign. Photo: Yael Baron

The State Education Law Passes

12 August

The Knesset passed the State Education Law and canceled the "special streams" education system. The workers' schools that had existed for 30 years were abolished. The law stipulated that there would only be two streams in education in Israel: state schools and religious-state schools. Agudat Yisrael, the ultra-Orthodox party, decided that its schools would not fall under the auspices of the Ministry of Education and would operate as independent schools.

Photo: GPO

"Oh, The Red Rock of Petra!"

29 August

For many years, the red rock of Petra attracted young Israelis who believed that getting there was a great challenge. Many paid with their lives, without getting to see the rock. At the end of August, five young Israelis, including two girls, tried to get to Petra, but were caught and murdered by the Jordanian Legions.

1953

9 July

A Jewish Agency Official Sold Fabrics and Bought Apartment - A Jewish Agency official was suspected of selling fabrics, which the agency received as a gift from South America, without a tender. With the money he made, he bought a luxurious four-bedroom apartment in Tel Aviv, which he furnished beautifully; he even purchased handsome silverware. The agency board members demanded that he be dismissed from his post at once.

25 November

Jackals and Foxes Attacked Hens - Twenty-five hens belonging to Mr. Shalom Zubari of Moshav Bet Zayit were devoured by jackals and foxes that broke into the last house in the village. The villagers claimed that the predators came from across enemy lines.

2 December

Paper Production in Israel Began - The first paper factory was built in Israel. The first shipment of crepe paper was sent to the Israeli industry. The plant management announced that it would be able to produce all types and thicknesses of paper within two months.

6 December

Little Children Deserted in Tel Aviv - Three little children were found deserted in Tel Aviv after their father, a resident of Rehovot, abandoned them there. The father's friends said he had done so because of economic and personal hardships. The police took the children to a WIZO institution.

22 January

Shops Run Out of "Nelson" Cigarettes

The popular "Nelson" cigarettes suddenly disappeared from the shops. The reason - the factory received a shipment of the wrong tobacco and production stopped. Cigarette prices went up at the same time: a box of 20 cigarettes of Israeli-made Players would now cost half a lira.

17 April

Violinist Jascha Heifetz Attacked

The internationally acclaimed violinist was attacked by an unknown assailant, near the Edison Movie Theater, Jerusalem, after performing there. The assailant tried to break his left arm with a blunt instrument, but instead hit Heifetz in the chest. Incidentally, the violinist's hands were insured for IL300,000.

Photo: AP

13 October

Infiltrators from Jordan killed a mother and her two children in Yahud.

18 November

The Knesset passed the National Insurance Bill.

6 December

Moshe Dayan was appointed the fourth IDF chief of staff, replacing Mordechai Maklef.

7 December

David Ben-Gurion resigned as prime minister and defense minister.

24 December

Egypt confiscated 2,000 tons of clothes sent on board a Norwegian ship to Israel.

9 July

The première of the movie *Twenty-Four Hours of A Woman's Life* was held at the Chen Movie Theater in Tel Aviv.

1954

Moshe Sharet, Israel's second prime minister. Photo: GPO

Moshe Sharet meeting foreign diplomats. Photo: Hans Pin, GPO

The Alternative That Flickered
"My country has left me"

Ya'akov Sharet
Son of Moshe Sharet

The year 1954 was Moshe Sharet's only full year as prime minister. He served as Israel's second prime minister and foreign minister between January 1954 and August 1955.

This brief term can be explained by the fact that Sharet was given the post temporarily after Israel's first prime minister, David Ben-Gurion, suddenly resigned. Ben-Gurion went to Sde Boker at the end of 1953, but continued to exert his influence from there, since he remained party leader, and even declared that he would be back.

Some believe that Ben-Gurion's resignation at the end of 1953 was designed to distance Sharet from the cabinet because he opposed heating up the borders with retaliation operations and warned against launching a pre-emptive war, or even talking about it – because talk just might start it. Indeed, when Ben-Gurion retired, he recommended that his party appoint Levi Eshkol, not Sharet, next prime minister. This move failed, but before leaving, Ben-Gurion managed to plant two booby traps for Sharet: He chose the extremist Pinchas Lavon as defense minister, and appointed the belligerent Moshe Dayan chief of staff.

Sharet did not have the slightest chance of overpowering the defense establishment. The IDF top brass ignored his authority and conducted an independent retaliation policy behind his back. Chief of Staff Dayan, who sought a war with Egypt, openly incited the officers against Sharet. In an odd twist of fate, it so happened that in the days of Israel's most moderate prime minister, the IDF operated Intelligence Branch agents in Egypt in July 1954 – without Sharet's knowledge and while he was conducting secret negotiations with President Nasser – in what would later be known as "The Affair". When the whole affair exploded, it marked the end of Sharet's term. Ben-Gurion returned to the cabinet as defense minister (after Sharet fired Lavon) and, after the 1955 elections, was appointed prime minister again, replacing Sharet.

Being an intelligent man and a foreign minister who was sensitive to Israel's international status, Sharet realized that the very establishment of the State of Israel had put an end to the element of expansion in Zionism. He maintained that once the Jewish settlement had become a sovereign state and a member of the family of nations with equal rights and duties, new rules of existence applied to it. One of the most important of them was: no more conquering of territory.

Ben-Gurion did not agree. He did not consider the cease-fire lines of 1949 sacred. In his Independence Day speech in 1955, he declared: "Our future does not depend on what the gentiles say, but on what the Jews do."

Sharet rejected this ethnocentric and narrow-minded approach. Unlike Ben-Gurion, he maintained – right from the start, without having to learn the lessons of future wars – that Israel would not be able to live by its sword forever, nor could it surrender its resources to the military. Therefore, he demanded that Israel observe a policy of anti-escalation: Violent initiatives were doomed to breed counter-violence, in an endless vicious circle. Favoring restraint and compromise, Sharet drew on his personal experiences. He said in a lecture once: "I cannot expect all of you to spend two years in an Arab village, like I did, to realize that Arabs are humans; that they have a mind, reason, dignity and human emotions, and that they too can be shocked." (from Personal Diary, p. 1,507)

Ben-Gurion did not share these insights, hence the two were destined to collide. It was also obvious who would emerge victorious: Ben-Gurion was a charismatic leader of national and international stature. Sharet was a leader whose reasonable ideas and search for compromises could not excite the masses.

Faithful to his beliefs, Sharet managed to frustrate Ben-Gurion's initiatives to conquer the Gaza Strip and Sharm al-Sheikh, and prevented several retaliation operations. But it was he who authorized a large-scale retaliation operation (whose scope seems to have been expanded without his knowledge, and not for the first time) against the Egyptian Army in Gaza on 28 February 1955. Again, it was ironic that under this moderate prime minister, Israel conducted an operation that gave a push to the Egyptian-Czech arms deal which, one year later, led to Israel's first war of choice.

Sharet was the main stumbling block in Ben-Gurion and his allies' path to a pre-emptive war with Egypt. Ben-Gurion was thus convinced that Sharet must be removed from the cabinet. He was deposed four months before Israel went to war.

In his eight-volume diary, Sharet wrote that he should be counted among the casualties of the 1956 war, adding:

"My country has left ... It is not up to me to run this country, which seems to be an impossible thing to do without resorting to adventurism and deceit. I am incapable of either. I will forever weigh the risks and not rush into an adventure. I will be cautious and not gamble with our future. I am not being self-righteous nor am I pretending to be so. I am merely admitting to my limitations and accepting them. The two paths are entirely different; one cannot walk both at the same time. The country is going along a path that is not mine. Things have gone too far. Final facts have been established and basic concepts have been taught that can no longer be corrected in this generation. And the next generation is not mine anyway." (from Personal Diary, p. 1,834).

2.7.54 "The Affair": Who Gave the Order?

Two of the accused in "The Affair" – Marcelle Ninio and Robert Dassa. Photo: Eliahu Harati

Binyamin Jibli, the "senior officer" and operator of the Egyptian terror network.

"**T**he Affair" preoccupied Israel for many years. It caused serious political crises, the resignation of Defense Minister Pinchas Lavon, a rift in Mapai, and Ben-Gurion's retirement. What's worse, two young Jews paid the price and were executed in Cairo, and 10 others were given lengthy prison terms for their involvement. But, first things first...

"The Affair" started in July 1954, when post offices, movie theaters and libraries in Cairo and Alexandria were sabotaged by improvised fire-bombs. The bombs were planted by local Jews who had been recruited by the Israeli intelligence and trained in Israel for this purpose.

Thirteen young Egyptian Jews were caught after one of them was apprehended when the firebomb in his pocket ignited while he was on his way to carry out an attack on a movie theater. The cell members were put on trial and charged with terrorist activities in public locations in Cairo and Alexandria. The prosecution demanded that they be given death sentences. The court sentenced Dr. Moshe Marzouk and Shmuel Azar to death, and sent the others to prison for many years.

The dormant squad of Egyptian Jews belonging to the Intelligence Corps' Unit 131 was activated as a result of the progress that was being made in the Egyptian-British talks about the evacuation of the British Army from the Suez area. Israel was concerned about the British departure, and the IDF intelligence branch devised a mad and imaginary plan according to which terrorist acts would be perpetrated in Egypt in order to convince the British to postpone the evacuation, as Egypt was not responsible enough to protect the interests of the West. According to the plan, the attacks were supposed to spark unrest and riots proving that Egypt was not a stable country.

The details of "The Affair" were not published in Israel for a long time, under orders from the military censor. Only years later, it became apparent that the Egyptian network was operated by senior IDF officers without the knowledge of the political echelons. There is no doubt that Prime Minister Moshe Sharet was unaware of the operation. Chief of Staff Dayan was abroad at the time. "Senior officer" Binyamin Jibli resigned, claiming that Defense Minister Pinchas Lavon had given him the order to activate the Egyptian network. Lavon vehemently denied this, and the affair became more and more complicated. The question, "Who gave the order?" went on hovering in Israel's political sphere for many years.

The Bat Galim crew released from the Egyptian prison. Photo: GPO

29 September

"We Were Shackled... Egyptian Officers Slapped Us Across the Face..."

The ship, *Bat Galim*, and its crew were given an order to cross the Suez Canal, carrying a cargo of logs, meat and hides, as part of an Israeli effort to break through the blockade Egypt had imposed on the passage of Israeli vessels and goods through the canal. Despite signing the cease-fire agreement, Egypt insisted that Israeli vessels not be allowed to cross the canal. Chief of Staff Moshe Dayan suggested that the Egyptians be put to the test in front of the whole world. On 29 September, the *Bat Galim* reached the Suez Canal and was stopped by the Egyptian authorities, who claimed that its crew had killed two Egyptian fishermen. Ten crewmen were detained and the cargo confiscated. Captain Tzvi Shidlo said later, "The Egyptians searched the ship thoroughly, but found nothing, no guns or ammunition... Late at night, after completing the interrogation, they took us to a Cairo prison in shackles... Egyptian officers slapped us across the face there..."

After spending three months in the Egyptian prison, the ten *Bat Galim* crewmen were released. They received a heroes' welcome in Israel, and each was given IL5,000 as compensation for the time spent in the Egyptian prison. Egypt, however, remained adamant in its refusal to allow Israeli vessels through the canal for a long time.

Moshe Sharet – Israel's Second Prime Minister

Moshe Sharet presented his new cabinet to the Knesset at the beginning of January, with Pinchas Lavon as defense minister. There were 15 ministers in the cabinet, eight of whom were Mapai members. It was the first time in Israel that a government had been set up without Ben-Gurion as prime minister. Sharet's position was uneasy and often complicated. Ben-Gurion did not want him as his successor. The defense establishment was in the hands of three people: Lavon, Dayan, and Peres, who all disapproved of Sharet's moderate policies. In addition, Israel's international status was at an unprecedented low.

Sharet found it difficult to function with Ben-Gurion still serving as the oracle of the Israeli military and top political echelons and, in fact, continuing to run the state from his hut in Sde Boker. Even if major defense and foreign affairs decisions were made by the inner cabinet, Ben-Gurion's views were on everybody's mind and significantly affected decision-making.

Sharet served as prime minister for nearly two years, during which his relations with Ben-Gurion deteriorated drastically. After the elections for the 3rd Knesset in 1955, a new cabinet was formed with Ben-Gurion as prime minister once again and Sharet retaining his foreign ministry portfolio.

Moshe Sharet and David Ben-Gurion sign the Declaration of Independence. Photo: GPO

"Nathan, Nathan..."

18 February

Singer Joe Amar dedicated a song to Nathan Elbaz, a 20-year-old new immigrant from Morocco and an IDF soldier. After training, Elbaz was ordered by his commanding officer to disarm hand grenades. While doing this, Elbaz suddenly heard a click and realized that a pin had been released. He grabbed the hand grenade and yelled at the other soldiers to get away as far as they could. When he realized that he did not have enough time to throw the grenade far enough so that no one would get hurt, he threw himself on the grenade which exploded, blowing him to pieces. This story of self-sacrifice became a popular tale, and Chief of Staff Moshe Dayan gave Nathan's family a medal and a citation of honor for his heroic act.

1 January
The Tel Aviv Stock Exchange opened.

26 January
Israel's second prime minister, Moshe Sharet, presented his new cabinet to the Knesset. Sharet replaced Ben-Gurion who resigned.

1 February
The Law of Return was amended: Jews with criminal records who might be a danger to society will not be able to immigrate to Israel.

4 April
The Israeli National Insurance Institute started operating. The insurance money was to be paid via the Income Tax authorities.

6 May
The 6th Independence Day parade was held in Ramla

19 June
Jordanian terrorists entered Israeli territory and murdered a woman who lived in Mevo Betar, in the Jerusalem corridor.

24 June
The Municipality of Tel Aviv decided to build a university.

2 July
"The Affair" began: A Jewish spy network in Egypt carried out a series of terrorist attacks in Cairo and Alexandria, and was exposed.

1 August
Yitzhak Olshan was appointed Supreme Court president, replacing the late Moshe Zmora.

8 September
The big immigration of Moroccan Jews began.

Photo: Fritz Cohen, GPO

17.3. **54**

"I Saw Mom and Dad Die."

Eleven people, including children, were massacred in Ma'ale Akrabim when infiltrators from Jordan attacked a bus traveling from Tel Aviv to Eilat.

"I saw Mom and Dad die," said Mira Firsenberg, a five-year-old girl who survived the horror. The survivors said that the infiltrators hid behind the monument for the Engineering Corps and ambushed the bus. They opened fire as the bus was driving slowly uphill, taking the sharp curve. The driver was killed first and many passengers were wounded. The terrorists then boarded the bus and shot the passengers at close range.

"When the murderers came towards me," little Mira recalled, "I played dead... That's how they saw me... They thought I was dead and left me alone... Yes, yes, they killed Mom and Dad..."

The infiltrators' tracks led to the Jordanian border, 15 km east of the site of the attack. Jordan denied any involvement in the horrendous act. In protest, Israel quit the Israeli-Jordanian cease-fire committee.

After the attack on the bus at Ma'ale Akrabim. Photo: GPO

Going to the funeral of an attack victim. Photo: GPO

Knesset Member Shlomo Lorenz' Immunity

23 May

It seems that the battles conducted by Members of Knesset against the lifting of their parliamentary immunity are not unprecedented. The attorney-general recommended that Agudat Yisra'el's MK Lorenz' immunity be lifted because he was suspected of receiving money from an American Jew and not sending it to its original destination. MK Lorenz objected to the lifting of his immunity, the MKs believed him and they decided against it. How contemporary...

Terrible Disaster at Kibbutz Ma'agan

29 July

A Piper airplane crashed into a crowd of 2,500 people, killing 17 and injuring 30. The accident happened during a ceremony held to commemorate a fallen paratrooper from Kibbutz Ma'agan. The pilot had a letter from the president and was supposed to release it over the audience. The letter got stuck in the plane's wheels, causing it to plunge and crash into the crowd within seconds.

54

1954

Yad Vashem Inaugurated

Photo: Roni Na'aman

Yad Vashem, the national memorial set up to commemorate the victims of the Holocaust, was established. The picture shows a freight car that was sent from Poland to Yad Vashem as a monument to mark the destruction of the Auschwitz concentration camp.

15 September

An Achievement in International Chess - Israel tied 2:2 against USSR's strong chess team in the Amsterdam Olympics.

16 June

Israel Invited to Fur Fair in Leningrad - The Soviet envoy in Israel invited Israeli fur and animal hair companies to participate in an international fair in Leningrad.

10 December

"The Police Will Learn About 'Busi'" - This threat was made by a medium-sized, square-faced, starry-eyed young man sitting on the bench in the Rehovot courthouse. His name was Busi, and he had terrorized the entire neighborhood of Sha'arayim with his fists. According to the charge sheet, however, three of the policemen who tried to arrest him after he had overturned a market vendor's cart, needed medical treatment. When the police representative requested that the court extend Busi's detention, Busi threatened in a roaring voice: "Thefts and murders will multiply in the Rehovot area. You will all know who Busi is...!"

9 December

400 Tons of Sugar from Poland to Israel - 400 tons of sugar were imported from Poland in an emergency operation by the Ministry of Industry and Trade due to a grave sugar shortage in Israel.

29 September

The Kastner trial reached the stage of closing arguments. Prosecutor Haim Cohn, in a surprise move, said that if it were found that Kastner had collaborated with the Nazis, he should be sentenced to death. If, however, Grunwald had made false accusations - he too should die.

25 October

The country's national basketball team lost 49: 45 to the Chinese Republic team in a game in Rio de Janeiro.

1 December

The Bank of Israel, the country's central bank, opened. David Horowitz was its first governor.

7 December

Five IDF soldiers who crossed the Syrian border near Kibbutz Dan were taken captive.

20 December

Max Bennett, one of the prisoners in "The Affair", committed suicide in a Cairo prison. His body was found when he was about to be taken to court.

21 December

David Ben-Gurion, Mapai leader, met with Yitzhak Tabenkin, the leader of the *Ahdut Ha'avoda* Movement, to discuss cooperation between the two parties.

3 November

The North Station Opens

A new train station was inaugurated in north Tel Aviv. It was dubbed the North Station.

Photo: Starphot

Advertisement for a diaper dryer.

29 November

Boats Rescue Residents Of Flooded Houses

Heavy rains that fell on Tel Aviv last night caused serious flooding in several neighborhoods. The fire brigade, with its four trucks, was called 28 times during the night to pump water out of houses, mainly in the Nordia neighborhood. The Jaffa police used rubber boats to reach houses that had been cut off by the floods.

Photo: GPO

1955

Dr. Yisrael Kastner and his daughter Suzy.

Dr. Kastner with his wife during his term as Industry and Trade Ministry spokesman.

The Kastner Trial

Co-operation with the Nazis or the Rescue of Jews?

Acting Supreme Court President (Ret.) Haim Cohen

The horrors of the Holocaust and the misery of its survivors were not high on young Israel's agenda. In passing the bills "Trying Nazis and their helpers" (1951), "The Memorial for the Holocaust Martyrs and Heroes – Yad Vashem" (1953), and "Introducing the memory of the Holocaust and heroism as a state education goal" (1953), we felt we had done our share, and now it was time to address our more burning needs. Occasionally, the newspapers carried reports about corrupt public activists of the time, mainly members of the Judenrat, but we had already condemned them all, as if we would have done any better.

An eccentric old man from Jerusalem, Malkiel Grunwald, issued a pamphlet for his associates at the Mizrachi in 1953, accusing Dr. Yisrael Kastner, leader of the Zionists of Budapest during the Nazi occupation, of collaborating with the Nazis, laying the foundations for them to deport and murder Jews, collaborating with looters of Jewish property, and helping them escape trial after the war. At the time, Kastner was a senior civil servant. Although, in my capacity of state attorney, I was asked to look the other way on this, I demanded that a man who had been so accused take immediate legal steps to purge himself, or be removed from public office.

Kastner refused to file charges, and the minister under whom he worked (Dov Yosef) refused to remove him from office. I therefore filed a libel suit against Grunwald on behalf of the state, not before I had received the impression from Kastner that whatever he had done was with the purest and best intentions. The court had only to determine whether in his meetings with Eichmann and his associates, Kastner had intended to extort benefits and exemptions for the Jews, or whether he intended to serve as an instrument in the implementation of their evil scheme. Shmuel Tamir, attorney for the defense – a young, determined and witty lawyer, very much a politician – not only turned the trial into a fierce war against state institutions and the left-wing parties for allegedly backing Kastner, but also managed to convince Justice Binyamin Halevi that Kastner had indeed "sold his soul to the devil" and co-operated with the Nazis. Kastner's sentence was handed down in June 1955, after a gigantic show-case trial that was accompanied by hysterical and inciting ("criminal", the Supreme Court president would call them later) press reports.

In January 1956, after 17 days of closing arguments by the defense and the State, the Supreme Court overruled Halevi's verdict and determined that Grunwald's accusations were libellous, with the exception of Kastner's defense of Nazi war criminals during the Nuremberg Trials. But Kastner did not live long with his name cleared and his moral victory. He was murdered by extremists (in March 1957). They came from the extreme right wing, pronouncing themselves the executioners of the man who had been condemned by a judge from Jerusalem as a traitor to his own people. Justice Halevi's verdict also inspired no-confidence motions against the government: The left entered a motion because Kastner had not been charged according to the bill, "Trying Nazis and their helpers", and the right's motion was based on the very fact that Grunwald had been put on trial. Both motions were rejected by a vast Knesset majority, but because the General Zionists – a coalition member – abstained, Prime Minister Moshe Sharet handed in his resignation to the president on 29 June 1955. That same day, he was asked to form a new government, which he succeeded in doing.

31.1.**55**

"Wearing Red Robes, Frozen Expressions on Their Faces, They Marched to the Gallows."

Dr. Moshe Marzouk.

Shmuel Azar.

*The bodies of Marzouk and Azar were returned to Israel only 22 years later. Their state funeral on Mt. Herzl was attended by many leaders and notables.
Photo: GPO*

Rabbi Ovadia Matzliah entered the death-row cells in the Cairo Central Prison two hours before Moshe Marzouk and Shmuel Azar marched to the gallows. The two, who were sentenced to death on charges of spying for Israel, "wore red robes," Rabbi Matzliah later reported, "and the expressions on their faces were frozen. I prayed for them. They said the *Shema*. When they started walking toward the gallows, Dr. Marzouk turned to me and said: 'Honorable Rabbi, you must all go there... to Israel. There is no future for you here...' I walked behind him saying the prayer of confession. They were executed a few minutes later." The Egyptian authorities, who rejected international amnesty requests, kept a low profile on the event and prevented the media from reporting the executions. Dr. Marzouk and Shmuel Azar were buried secretly and the Jewish community was not allowed to place tombstones on their graves. The other members of the spy network (set up by the Israeli Intelligence Branch in Egypt) who had been arrested in July 1954 with Marzouk and Azar, were given lengthy prison terms. Among those arrested was Max Bennett, a major in the Intelligence Branch. The Egyptians claimed that he was the head of the spy ring. Bennett was badly tortured in prison and committed suicide several days after the trial started. Another person who was believed to be a key member in the spy network, Paul Frank, managed to flee Egypt. In Israel, the press dubbed him "the third man". He was later detained and charged with turning the members of the ring over to the Egyptian authorities. He was sentenced to 12 years in prison.

After the executions, relations between Egypt and Israel deteriorated. The spy affair started a serious public and political storm. The question, "Who gave the order?" echoed in Israeli political corridors for many years. The Defense Minister of the time, Pinchas Lavon, claimed that he did not know that the net had been activated, and David Ben-Gurion demanded that a commission of inquiry be set up to find the persons responsible for the fiasco in Egypt.

The Olshan-Drori commission appointed to investigate the affair could not solve the mystery. Its report stated: "We were not convinced beyond reasonable doubt that the head of the Intelligence Branch was not given an instruction by Defense Minister Lavon. At the same time, we are not certain that Lavon indeed gave the order attributed to him." Several similar commissions examined the affair in subsequent years, leaving no stone unturned, but did not come up with conclusive results.

---

28 February

Operation Black Arrow in the Gaza Area

31 August

Operation Elkayam against the Khan Yunis Police

2 November

Operation Volcano in the Nitzana Area

Retaliation Operations Against Egypt

In 1955, tension on the Egyptian border escalated and attacks by infiltrators against Israeli settlements in the south multiplied. Israel decided to retaliate with an operation dubbed "Black Arrow" on 28 February. The attack was carried out in the Gaza region by a paratrooper unit under the command of Ariel Sharon. The Egyptian Army sustained 42 casualties and the IDF lost eight men. An Egyptian spokesman said this was the most serious Israeli operation since the signing of the cease-fire agreements. However, terror attacks against Israel did not stop.

The second retaliation operation that year was on 31 August. It was known as "Operation Elkayam". In this operation, an IDF unit raided the Khan Yunis police station, home of the Palestinian battalion that carried out the terror attacks and planted mines inside Israeli territory. The Egyptians sustained 72 casualties. In reaction, President Nasser sent large forces into the Gaza Strip, and the two countries started exchanging artillery fire the next day. A large Egyptian-Czech arms deal was signed that month.

The third retaliation operation in 1955, dubbed "Volcano", took place a few hours before Ben-Gurion presented his new cabinet to the Knesset. IDF troops attacked in the area of Nitzana, after Egyptian forces entered an area that, according to the Rhodes agreements, was supposed to be a demilitarized zone. This was the largest operation since Operation Horev in 1948: 70 Egyptians were killed, 48 were taken captive and dozens were wounded. The IDF sustained seven casualties. After that, the area remained relatively quiet until the Sinai Campaign.

"Kastner Sold His Soul to the Devil"

In his verdict, Justice Binyamin Halevi determined that Yisrael Kastner, head of the Hungarian Jews' Rescue Committee during the Nazi occupation, had sold his soul to the devil, collaborated with the Nazis and abandoned the majority of the Hungarian Jews in order to save his friends and relatives. The judge added: "Kastner knew that his co-operation aided both the total deportation and the destruction of most Hungarian Jews... The Nazis could never have misled the Jews if false rumors had not been spread via Jewish channels...". Regarding Hanna Senesh, the judge said that Kastner had prevented her release, fearing that she might expose his collaboration with the Nazis. Upon hearing the verdict, Kastner said: "History and all those who know what really happened will speak for me and bring the truth to light."

The Kastner Trial was, in fact, a libel suit against one Malkiel Grunwald, who wrote in his pamphlet in 1953 that Kastner, an Industry and Trade Ministry official, had collaborated with the Nazis. This marginal libel trial soon turned into a political show-case trial that sparked a storm in Israel, causing a government crisis and the formation of a new government. Attorney Shmuel Tamir, Grunwald's lawyer, charged the Jewish Agency with deliberately concealing reports on the Holocaust.

Two years later, Kastner was shot near his house and died ten days later. One year before he died, Kastner filed an appeal against the verdict with the High Court of Justice, which overruled Binyamin Halevi's verdict, thereby acquitting Kastner of the charges of collaborating with the Nazis.

Thousands attended Yisrael Kastner's funeral. Photo: Hans Pin

Sharet Resigns, Ben-Gurion Returns

26 July

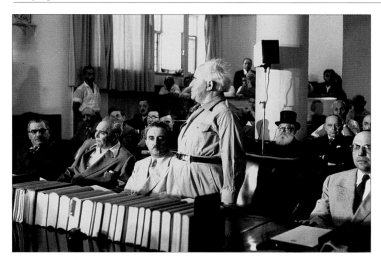

Prime Minister Moshe Sharet resigned and David Ben-Gurion returned to his post as Mapai head to lead his party to the 3rd Knesset elections. Mapai lost five of the 50 seats it had in the previous Knesset. The General Zionists lost 10 seats, and the Herut Movement went up from 8 to 15 Knesset seats. Forming a coalition was a complicated task this time, and it was not until November that Ben-Gurion managed to form a government.

Ben-Gurion returns as premier after Moshe Sharet's resignation. Photo: GPO

13 January

Uri Ilan, one of five soldiers held captive in Damascus, hanged himself. A note found in his clothes read: "I did not commit treason!"

31 January

Dr. Moshe Marzouk and Shmuel Azar were executed in Cairo after they were found guilty of spying for Israel.

9 February

Initial signs of oil were found in Zichron Ya'akov. "We have taken a significant step forward in our search for oil in Israel," official government sources announced.

Photo: GPO

21 February

Rabbi Yitzhak Nissim was elected first Sephardi chief rabbi, the "Rishon Letzion".

19 March

Herod's Palace was uncovered during archeological excavations on Massada.

27 April

The IDF unveiled a new submachine gun, the Uzi, at the Independence Day parade in Tel Aviv.

24 May

The first settlement, Otzem, was established in the Lachish region. Thousands of immigrants arrived in the region from North Africa later on and built many settlements there.

Photo: GPO

28 May

A bomb exploded in the print shop where the weekly *Ha'Olam Hazeh* was printed. This was an attempt to silence a newspaper which did not hesitate to publish stories about government scandals.

13.1. **55**

"I Did Not Commit Treason!"

El Al plane Downed Over Bulgaria

27 July

An El Al passenger plane was mistakenly downed by Bulgarian fighter planes, killing all 58 crew members and passengers. The Bulgarian government claimed that the plane had entered Bulgarian air space without permission. In order to cover up their responsibility for the affair, the Bulgarians cleared the wreckage from the disaster area.

Uri Ilan was one of five IDF soldiers who crossed the border into Syrian territory to work on a wiretapping device that was attached to the Syrian telephone system on the Golan Heights. The five were caught, imprisoned and tortured in a Damascus prison. Syria published a statement according to which the soldiers were armed with weapons, hand grenades, commando knives and communication equipment. The IDF spokesman, however, announced that the soldiers had been kidnapped from Israeli territory by Syrian troops. The General Staff decided to intercept a Syrian passenger plane to negotiate an exchange of prisoners. A plane was intercepted, but Prime Minister Moshe Sharet, who learned about this after the fact, ordered that it be released.

The Israeli soldiers were badly tortured in the Syrian jail. Uri Ilan of Kibbutz Gan Shmuel, hanged himself. When his body arrived in Israel, two notes were found in his clothes. One read: "I did not commit treason!" The other said: "They're killing us – revenge."

Memorial room for Uri Ilan. Photo: Edna Bar-Romi

Picking olives in Dimona. Photo: Erwin Farkash

"Dimona Is A Wonder of Wonders"

19 September

The development town of Dimona was built in the central Negev as one of a chain of settlements running along Israel's borders. Some 36 families from North Africa were brought on trucks from Haifa airport right to the middle of nowhere. A year later, a road to Eilat was constructed, and workers at the Dead Sea plants and additional immigrants started settling there. David Ben-Gurion, who visited Dimona, said: "I am drunk with joy and amazed at what I've seen. Israel is full of wonders, but Dimona is a wonder of wonders."

Kindergarten children walk the "streets" of Dimona. Photo: Moshe Pridan, GPO

55

8 March

A Purim Carnival in Tel Aviv

Photo: GPO

The first-ever Purim carnival was held in Tel Aviv with the participation of some 400,000 people. Schoolchildren, members of youth movements and regular folk marched in colorful costumes, playing musical instruments.

22 June

"Yisrael Kastner sold his soul to the devil," Justice Binyamin Halevi stated in his Jerusalem District Court verdict. The judge found Kastner guilty of collaborating with the Nazis.

26 June

Prime Minister Moshe Sharet resigned, causing the resignation of the entire cabinet.

26 July

In the elections for the 3rd Knesset, Mapai lost five seats, going down from 45 to 40; the General Zionists lost 10 seats; and the Herut Movement went up from 8 to 15.

27 July

An El Al plane was mistakenly downed over Bulgaria, killing 58 crewmen and passengers.

26 August

An emergency operation was launched to bring Moroccan Jews to Israel in the wake of riots which were part of Morocco's struggle for independence.

7 September

Mayors were elected in the three big cities: Gershon Agron in Jerusalem, Haim Levanon in Tel Aviv, and Abba Hushi in Haifa.

12 November

Wiretapping devices were found in the house of Dr. Moshe Sneh, a Member of Knesset for Maki [the Israel Communist Party].

11 December

Operation Olive Leaves: IDF forces raided Syrian posts on the Lake Kinneret shoreline in reaction to Syrian harassment of Israeli fishermen. Fifty Syrian soldiers were killed and 30 were taken captive. The IDF lost four men.

29 May

A Modern Version of the Original Sin - It seems that nothing has changed since the times of the Garden of Eden: Man still falls because of eating apples. Aharon Shabiki was brought to trial at the Tel Aviv District Court where the principal item of evidence was... a half-eaten apple. According to the police, Shabiki broke into a north Tel Aviv apartment and stole jewelry and cash worth thousands of lirot. While working, he could not resist the temptation to take a hearty bite of an apple he found there. The police made a cast of his tooth "prints" and thus discovered who the uninvited visitor was.

14 September

Revelations of the Income Tax "Book of Taxpayers" - The income tax book of taxpayers was officially published, listing 115,000 factories, companies and individuals who had filed their tax returns. The largest sum was paid by the construction company of Solel Boneh - IL1.4 million. Ata paid IL600,000; Etz Hazait paid IL120,000. The smallest returns by companies were paid by the Chen Movie Theater in Tel Aviv (IL28,000) and Angel Bakery in Jerusalem (IL13,000). A review of the book revealed, to the public's amazement, that some of Israel's richest are considered very poor...

Photo: Alexander Zoskind

31 May

Direct Inter-City Dial

For the first time in Israel, a direct phone link has been established between the three major cities - Tel Aviv, Haifa, and Jerusalem.

19 March

Hill 24 Is Not Answering

The première of the first Israeli film about the War of Independence was held in Tel Aviv. *Hill 24 Is Not Answering* won rave reviews.

(1956

The Sinai Campaign started with a battalion of paratroopers landing at the Mitleh Pass, some 30 km east of the Suez Canal in the Sinai.
Photo: Avraham Vered, Bamachaneh

Soldiers briefed before going into action.
Photo: GPO

Operation Kadesh, (the Sinai Campaign)
Delivering a Deterrent Blow to the Egyptians

Res. Colonel
Meir Pa'il

The Sinai Campaign (Operation Kadesh) was an offensive launched by the IDF against Egypt in the autumn of 1956. It started on 29 October and ended on 5 November, after the IDF seized the entire Sinai peninsula, except for a 16-km strip along the Suez Canal. The Operation was politically and militarily coordinated with Operation Musketeer launched against Egypt by Great Britain and France in an attempt to recapture the canal, which Egyptian President Nasser had nationalized earlier.

The Sinai Campaign had three goals: (a) Opening the Tiran Straits, which Egypt had closed in 1955, for the free passage of Israeli vessels. (b) Delivering a deterrent blow to Egypt to convince Egypt, Syria and Jordan to stop all terrorist infiltrations into Israeli territory immediately. (c) Curtailing the process of Egypt's military strengthening, after Egypt started receiving modern weapons from Czechoslovakia in 1955, sponsored by the USSR.

According to the coordinated plan, the IDF was to start by parachuting Battalion 890 into the Mitleh Pass on the evening of 29 October. This move would be presented by Israel as retaliation against the Fedayeen (infiltrators) operations. After that, Britain and France would issue an ultimatum, warning Israel and Egypt to stay 10 miles away from the canal. Israel would comply, but Egypt would naturally not, which would provide the French and British forces with justification to launch Operation Musketeer, while the IDF continued the Sinai Campaign and seized the Sinai desert. Indeed, this is how it happened: On 30 October, the IDF continued its assault, while on 31 October, the British started bombing the Egyptian airports. Three days later, they started moving forces to conquer the cities of Port Said and Port Fuad at the northern end of the Suez Canal. However, because their advance was awkward and slow, they were not able to reach the southern outskirts of either city before the campaign was halted by the UN Security Council on 5 November 1956.

The IDF, nevertheless, was most effective in three stages: The opening stage – After parachuting Battalion 890 in, the remaining units of the Paratrooper Brigade started moving to a rendezvous point, taking Kunatila, Thamed, and Nahel before meeting on 31 October. In a very difficult battle that same day, the paratroopers cleared the Mitleh Pass, while Israeli infantry and armored units conquered Kuseime and surrounded the fortified Egyptian stronghold in Abu-Agela and Umm-Ketef.

During the second, decisive stage, the IDF broke through the Egyptian Army bases in Rafah and seized them, opening the Mediterranean route to the Suez Canal. The Air Force attacked the retreating Egyptian forces and the reinforcements sent to assist them. The Navy captured the Egyptian destroyer *Ibrahim al-Awal* which tried to shell Haifa.

During the third stage, the IDF forces stopped 10 miles east of the canal. On 2 November, the IDF started conquering the Gaza Strip, which was fully surrounded, and captured it in two days. By 5 November, the IDF completed its conquest of the Sharm al-Sheikh region in southern Sinai, while the Navy took Tiran and Snapir – two islands in the southern Straits of Eilat.

The IDF lost 171 soldiers in the campaign, some of whom were killed in a bitter encounter between two Israeli tank companies in Abu-Agela. Some 6,000 Egyptian soldiers were taken captive, and the army seized spoils of tanks, guns, vehicles, ammunition and other equipment.

Pressured by the United States and the USSR, the British, French and Israeli forces evacuated the territories they had taken within five months. They were replaced by a special UN force. When the British and the French were in possession of the northern Suez Canal, three Israeli soldiers entered Port Said from the sea and convinced half the Jewish community there to go to Israel on board an Israeli Navy vessel.

Israel's three major achievements as a result of the victory were: (1) Israel had 11 quiet years on the Egyptian border, eight quiet years with Jordan and eight more years with Lebanon. The establishment of the Fatah organization, under Syrian auspices, heated up the Jordanian and Lebanese borders as of 1965; the Syrian border has remained hot ever since. (2) The Tiran Straits were reopened for Israeli ships, with US assurances. (3) The swift IDF operation attracted the attention of Third World countries, which started asking Israel for military aid and advice (Ethiopia, Singapore and the Kurds, to name a few).

We have to admit, however, that the chief victor of the Sinai Campaign and Operation Musketeer was Gamal Abdel Nasser's regime: He boasted of being able to repel two colonial superpowers, France and Britain, as well as the State of Israel, which he conveniently presented as an ally of the two superpowers – something which could not have been done during the War of Independence.

29.4.56

Moshe Dayan: "We Blame Ourselves for Roi's Death."

Roi Rothenberg, the Nahal Oz District commander, was murdered after he was shot and wounded in a clash with Egyptian soldiers near his kibbutz. After wounding him, the Egyptians dragged him to their territory, tortured and murdered him. His body was returned to Israel badly mutilated. Chief of Staff Moshe Dayan delivered a eulogy that deeply moved Israel:

"We do not blame the Gaza Arabs for Roi's death... we blame ourselves. Roi Rothenberg, the skinny blond kid who left Tel Aviv to build a home at the gates of Gaza and serve as our wall... whose eyes were blinded by the light in his heart, did not see the lightning that struck him. His longing for peace deafened his ears, so he could not hear the murderers lurking in the shadows. The gates of Gaza were too heavy for his shoulders..."

Before murdering Rothenberg, Egyptian soldiers and infiltrators carried out dozens of attacks against Israeli settlements in southern Israel. At the beginning of April, Egyptian guns shelled IDF outposts near Kibbutz Nirim, killing five soldiers. In another attack, infiltrators threw hand grenades into an Ashkelon house, killing a woman and wounding the other residents. A week later, an Egyptian squad arrived as far as Moshav Shafrir near Ramla, and opened fire at a group of schoolchildren in a synagogue. Three children and their guide were killed and five children were wounded. The IDF reacted with retaliation attacks against Egyptian outposts and other targets, but to no avail. The Egyptians were indifferent to these operations, which had gradually been losing their deterrent effect.

Roi Rothenberg's funeral at Kibbutz Nahal Oz. Photo: Moshe Eitan (Foxy)

Another Egg Per Person

10 January

A true relief in austerity and rationing: The officials in charge of food rationing decided that the residents of Israel would be allocated ten eggs a month per person, instead of the previous ration of nine. Another egg per person, and thank God for that...

The POWs Return From Syria

29 March

Four IDF soldiers returned to Israel after spending 15 months in Syrian captivity. The POW exchange took place at the Bnot Ya'akov Bridge, with Israel returning 41 Syrian POWs. The fifth IDF soldier, Uri Ilan, committed suicide in prison after being badly tortured.

Four POWs return from Syria. Photo: GPO

Photo: Avraham Vered, Bamachaneh

The Operation Against the Kalkilya Police

10 October

One of the biggest IDF operations since the War of Independence was carried out against the police station of Kalkilya in Jordan. Some 100 Jordanian legionaries were killed and dozens were wounded. The IDF toll was 17 dead and 60 wounded. The operation followed a series of infiltrations by terrorists and Jordanian soldiers who murdered Israeli civilians and soldiers: On 10 September, seven soldiers were killed by Jordanian fire in the Hebron Hills area; two weeks later, Jordanian troops opened fire at the participants of an archeological convention at Kibbutz Ramat Rachel near Jerusalem, killing four and wounding 19 people. The decision to launch the Kalkilya operation was a painful one. However, the IDF top brass realized that the retaliation operations were no longer effective as a deterrence and could not continue. That was another reason for the decision to initiate the Sinai Campaign.

18.6.**56** Ben-Gurion: "Sharet Must Leave the Foreign Ministry."

The relations between Ben-Gurion and Foreign Minister Moshe Sharet deteriorated that year. The prime minister decided that the time had come to replace Sharet with a more loyal minister who would not serve as a focal point for the opposition against him in the cabinet and the party. Ben-Gurion suggested that Sharet resign and serve as Mapai secretary general. "Sharet must leave the foreign ministry," he declared, but the foreign minister rejected the proposal. Ben-Gurion did not give up and threatened to disband the government. The Mapai leadership panicked and pressured Sharet to resign. On 18 June, Sharet filed his resignation. The man who led the moderate line in the cabinet was forced to quit.

Speaking at the Knesset, Ben-Gurion explained the move: "I have realized that, for the good of the state, there must be full compliance between the foreign and defense ministries and that the foreign ministry currently needs a different leadership."

Labor Minister Golda Meir was appointed foreign minister. She aligned herself with Ben-Gurion and supported him on defense matters. Her first mission came soon after assuming office: She was dispatched to France, together with Shimon Peres and Moshe Dayan, to coordinate the joint operation against Egypt, which had announced that it was nationalizing the Suez Canal - a move that astounded and enraged the West, and eventually led to the Sinai Campaign.

After resigning as foreign minister, Moshe Sharet served as Member of Knesset through to the fifth Knesset.

The Kafr Kasem Massacre: "God Have Mercy On Them."

29 October

A Border Police unit was ordered to impose a curfew on the Israeli Arab village of Kafr Kasem several hours before the Sinai Campaign started. The soldiers were ordered to shoot curfew violators. The unit commander asked the regional commander what to do about workers in the field who had not heard about the curfew. The commander said in Arabic: "May God have mercy on them." The unit commander understood that as an order to shoot to kill. Later that evening, when the villagers were returning from the fields, the Border Policemen fired at them and killed 43 villagers, including nine women and seven children. Eight Border Policemen, including the commander, were put on trial and convicted of murder.

Seven Border Police troopers and their commander were tried after the massacre.

The Sinai Campaign

19**56**

29 October

The Sinai Campaign: Israel Decides To Go to War Against Egypt

The IDF launched the Sinai Campaign in the wake of endless incidents with Egyptian and Jordanian troops who allowed infiltrators to cross into Israeli territory. The Fedayeen murdered civilians and sabotaged the border settlement, while Israeli retaliation operations failed to deter them or solve the problem. Chief of Staff Dayan called for an extensive military operation. Prime Minister Ben-Gurion made the operation conditional on the supply of French arms and the support of the superpowers, which followed without delay...

A paratrooper at the Mitleh – The battle was long and hard. The chief of staff commended eight soldiers of the paratrooper brigade for their performance. Photo: Avraham Vered, Bamachaneh

In July 1956, Egypt decided to nationalize the Suez Canal. Speaking in Alexandria, Nasser lashed out at the United States, Great Britain and France for refusing to finance the construction of the Aswan Dam, and announced a naval blockade on Israeli vessels in the canal. The Suez Canal Company, which owned the franchise for operating the canal, was owned by France and Britain. The decision shocked and enraged the West, which tried to consolidate a policy against the Egyptian president's decision. Britain and France sent thousands of troops to the Middle East and started discussing a joint operation against Egypt.

In Israel, the Egyptian move revived the idea of a pre-emptive war against Egypt. Ben-Gurion believed that such a war could only be conducted in an atmosphere that was more favorable to Israel, with the goal being the removal of Nasser. Weapon shipments that arrived from France in the meantime encouraged Dayan to keep pressing for a decision to go to war on Egypt. France felt that Israel should be included in a campaign for the capture of the Suez Canal. On 22 October, Ben-Gurion went to Paris to make the final arrangements and co-ordination of the joint British-French-Israeli operation. Six days later, Ben-Gurion notified the cabinet that he had decided to launch the operation, dubbed "Kadesh", and that 90,000 soldiers had already been deployed and were ready for battle against the Egyptian forces in the Sinai. The next day, in the afternoon of 29 October, the IDF was ordered to move into the Sinai. The war began...

The IDF Conquers The Sinai

The Sinai (Kadesh) Campaign lasted eight days during which the IDF conquered the Gaza Strip and the entire Sinai peninsula. The Egyptian Army was defeated and many soldiers were taken captive by Israel.

Following are the main moves of the campaign:

29 October

Paratroopers in the Mitleh

The Sinai Campaign started when a paratrooper battalion under Refael Eitan's command parachuted near the Parker memorial at the Mitleh Pass, some 30 km east of the Suez Canal. The paratroopers engaged in heavy fighting with Egyptian troops who were dug in there, and managed to seize strategic positions in preparation for the arrival of the paratrooper brigade's infantry, commanded by Ariel Sharon. Other IDF units started attacking Umm-Ketef, Abu-Agela and the Jabal Libni Junction.

30 October

A French-British Ultimatum

As agreed with Ben-Gurion, the British and the French issued an ultimatum against Israel and Egypt demanding that they each clear a 10-mile strip on both banks of the canal. As planned, Israel agreed; Nasser, however, rejected it angrily and announced a state of national emergency. The IDF continued its offensive in the Sinai.

29 October

The Navy Joins the War

The Navy attacked and defeated the Ibrahim al-Awal, an Egyptian destroyer that was shelling Haifa, taking 250 crewmen captive. That same evening, British and French bombers started bombarding Egypt, mainly the Suez region. The Abu-Agela and Jabal Libni Junctions were seized. The attack on Umm-Ketef continued.

The IDF conquered the entire Sinai peninsula within several days. Photo: GPO

The Sinai Campaign

19**56**

2 November

Gaza and El-Arish Conquered

The IDF conquered El-Arish, stopping 20 km away from the canal. Other IDF units captured the northern Gaza Strip and later the city. Heavy armored battles were waged in the area of Bir Gafgafa. At the end of the fourth day of the campaign, the Egyptian Army seemed to be falling apart. Many Egyptian soldiers started fleeing, and were taken captive by Israel.

The most important achievement of the campaign was the reopening of the Tiran Straits to Israeli vessels. Photo: GPO

3 November

Approaching the Canal

The IDF troops continued their conquest of Sinai, reaching some 20 km east of the canal. Egyptian soldiers fled, leaving tons of equipment behind. The IDF conquered Khan Yunis, completed the conquest of the Gaza Strip, seized the oil fields at A-Tur, and moved toward Sharm al-Sheikh. The UN passed a resolution calling for an immediate cease-fire.

4 November

The Cabinet Curbs the IDF

Ben-Gurion ordered Moshe Dayan to halt the IDF 15 km east of the Suez Canal. He decided that the IDF would not reach the canal. In southern Sinai, IDF units kept advancing toward Sharm al-Sheikh.

Chief of Staff Moshe Dayan with soldiers in Sharm al-Sheikh. Dayan was an ardent supporter of the campaign. Photo: GPO

5 November

The British and the French Land

In the morning, British forces landed in Port Said and French troops landed south of the city. The IDF conquered Sharm al-Sheikh. Israel announced that it was willing to heed the UN call for a cease-fire.

6 November

The Results of the Sinai Campaign

The IDF lost 170 soldiers and hundreds were wounded. Some 3,000 Egyptian soldiers were killed and 6,000 were taken prisoner by Israel. The campaign was a military success, but did not yield any significant changes in Israel's security situation. The region was quiet for a while, but tension along the borders prevailed. The most important achievement was the reopening of the Eilat Bay to Israeli vessels. The passage remained open for 10 years – until the Six Day War.

David Ben-Gurion decided to stop the IDF before it reached the Suez Canal. Photo: GPO

27 January

Hundreds of ultra-Orthodox Jews, mostly Neturei Karta, went to Tiberias to forcefully prevent archeological excavations at the grave of Maimonides.

2 March

President Nasser announced that "Egypt would be ready to recognize the State of Israel and discuss a peace arrangement with it, but only on the basis of the partition plan of 1947."

29 March

Four IDF POWs returned from Syria after 15 months. In exchange, Israel released 41 Syrian POWs.

11 April

Three children of 13-15 years old and their guide were murdered by infiltrators while praying at the synagogue of Moshav Shafrir near Ramla.

29 April

Roi Rothenberg, the Kibbutz Nahal Oz regional commander, was murdered by Egyptian soldiers. Moshe Dayan gave a moving eulogy at the funeral.

12 May

Czechoslovakia released Mordechai Oren, who spend five years in prison for espionage and undermining the state's security. "I am very happy to be free again," Oren said.

10 June

The National Religious Party (NRP) was formed when *Hamizrachi* and *Hapo'el Hamizrachi* merged.

18 June

Golda Meir was appointed foreign minister, replacing Moshe Sharet, who had resigned.

3 July

The Polish Government permitted the emigration of Jews. Israel expected some 20,000 Jews to arrive during the year ahead.

8.11.56

The Superpowers Urge a Withdrawal From the Sinai

The pressure started with a letter from USSR Prime Minister Nikolai Bulganin to the governments of France, Great Britain and Israel in which he threatened to take direct action if Israel did not withdraw from the Sinai. "The Government of Israel is criminally toying with the future of its nation," he wrote, and recalled his ambassador from Israel. To support the threats, the Soviets dispatched fighter jets to Syria and submarines from the Black Sea into the Mediterranean. It felt like a great war was about to break out at any moment. US President Dwight Eisenhower applied similar pressure on Israel in a harsh letter he sent to Ben-Gurion, saying, "It would be regrettable if Israeli activities should jeopardize the friendly co-operation between our countries."

Ben-Gurion did not have much choice. On 8 November, he announced that Israel was willing to withdraw from the Sinai. In a speech on *Kol Yisrael* Radio, he added that he would not allow a foreign force to enter Israeli territory or the territories it was holding in the Sinai. The only things that were negotiable were the pace and terms of the withdrawal.

Israel finally agreed to withdraw from the Sinai provided that no foreign force enter Israeli territory or the territories it was holding in the Sinai.
Photo: Efraim Arda

The Champion of Victory Dies

8 November

Major General Asaf Simhoni, commander of the Southern Command, was killed when the light plane he was flying in was downed by Jordanian Army anti-aircraft fire after it crossed the border. Three days before he died, 34-year-old Simhoni accepted the surrender of Gaza, completing his command over the IDF forces that had conquered the Sinai.

The IDF Seizes 2 Million Sheets and 1 Million Blankets

10 November

In addition to tanks, cannons, vehicles and weapons that the IDF collected in spoils, it also seized two million bed sheets and one million blankets. The bed-linen and what to do with it caused a serious headache in the Quartermaster's Department.

56

1956

15 March

Ofira (Erez) Navon - Sabra of the Year

Reproduction: Boaz Linor

Ofira Erez (20) was elected Sabra of the year by the weekly Ha'Olam Hazeh. "Her Sabra character shows in her external as well as in her inner qualities," the competition judges wrote. "Once she takes off her army uniform, she wears typically Israeli clothes, mainly Yemenite shirts... Her jewelry is also Israeli by nature... but above all, she is characteristically self-confident and honest." Ofira married Yitzhak Navon, who had later became Israel's fifth president.

15 April

The Menorah at the Knesset

Jewish sculptor Beno Alko's work of art arrived as a gift from British Jewry to the Knesset in Jerusalem.

Photo: GPO

The first settlers of Ashdod. Photo: GPO

25 November

The city of Ashdod was based on North African, immigrants. The city's infrastructure consisted of 22 immigrant families.

Ashdod was first called Ashdod-Yam. Photo: Fritz Cohen, GPO

31 July

Stelmach's Historical Header

In a soccer match between Israel and the USSR, Nachum Stelmach scored a goal with a header. The Soviets won the game 2:1. Stelmach's header was the most dramatic event of the time.

Photo: GPO

21 September

Ben-Gurion celebrated his 70th birthday at his Tel Aviv home. He would decide on the Sinai Campaign a month later.

23 September

A Jordanian soldier opened fire at an archeological convention at Kibbutz Ramat Rachel near Jerusalem, killing 4 and wounding many others.

10 October

Israel launched a big retaliation operation against the Kalkilya Police. Some 100 Jordanians were killed and dozens wounded. The IDF's toll was 17 dead and 60 wounded.

29 October

The Kafr Kasem massacre: A Border Police unit that imposed a curfew on Kafr Kasem, near Petah Tikva, opened fire at "curfew violators", killing 43 villagers, including women and children.

29 October

Israel launched the Sinai Campaign that lasted eight days during which it conquered the entire Sinai peninsula and defeated the Egyptian Army. Israel took numerous spoils and captured 5,000 Egyptian soldiers.

6 November

Israel seized Sharm al-Sheikh. The Sinai Campaign ended.

8 November

The USSR threatened to harm Israel if it did not withdraw from the territories it had conquered. U.S. President Eisenhower also demanded that Ben-Gurion withdraw from the Sinai.

8 November

Prime Minister Ben-Gurion announced on Kol Yisrael that the IDF would pull out of the Sinai after UN troops arrived.

(*1957*

Three Men in a Boat – 1957. Participants, left to right: Dan Ben-Amotz, Gavriel Zifroni, Amnon Ahi-Neomi, Shalom Rosenfeld, and moderator Yitzhak Shimoni.
Photo: David Rubinger

A remake of the radio show, Three Men in a Boat, 24 years later.
Photo: Shaul Golan

Three Men in a Boat – The First Satirical Radio Show
Lies Don't Need Legs

Satirist

Amnon Ahi-Nomi

It must be remembered and understood: This was the stone age. In 1957, everything was carved in stone. Every cliché a politician uttered was extremely important. Everything happened "for the first time since the state was founded." No one talked of sacred cows – there were no other cattle.

It had been only five years since the end of austerity, and people were still amazed at the fact that they could have a whole egg for breakfast even if they were not in the final stages of pregnancy. And we heard rumors, though unconfirmed officially, that there were pleasures in the world that surpassed even military service. It was no secret: We had no TV! The Kol Yisrael radio broadcast endless talks. The wildest form of entertainment was the annual Bible quiz. Suddenly, in the dry desert of profound Zionist seriousness, there appeared a ray of light: Three Men in a Boat. The eighth wonder of the world! A calf with three heads.

And this is how it was: As always with late bloomers, the beginning was modest. Yitzhak Shimoni and Yehuda Ha'ezrachi gathered together a bunch of wise-guys in a Jerusalem student club: Bet Hillel. They asked silly questions and received weird answers, some of which were even funny. Believe it or not, the audience roared with laughter and amazement. Poets like Aharon Amir and Dan Almagor wrote songs; our best composers - Meir Hernick, Mark Lavri, and Arieh Levanon - wrote the tunes; the songs were performed at the club, and we were overjoyed.

After several careful attempts, the professionals stepped in – Shalom Rosenfeld and Dan Ben-Amotz. No more accidental leftovers. No more pathetic spontaneous responses. From now on, the participants would be given the questions in advance, and the answers would be carefully worded. We "forgot" to tell the audience, and everybody was happy. We all drank Cognac out of coffee mugs, so no one could see our shame. Lies don't need legs; they can fly.

And then, to top it all, the *New York Times* published a favorable criticism. Imagine that: Humor in the eternal city of Jerusalem... It sounds strange even today. Soon enough, we realized that our small country extended beyond the city limits after all. The people were thirsty for a drop of moisture and insisted on enjoying whatever we had. Burdened by the demands of humor, the former boat-dwellers needed a transfusion, which we got when Ada Ben-Nahum and Shmuel Almog joined us.

The nation was in shock. The program was taped live and broadcast on the radio twice a month: A new program and a re-run. What a feast! We performed on stage in the strangest places (we even reached Haifa once!) and the halls were packed with people who watched us eagerly. Naturally, the radio only carried the answers that won enough applause (ratings, you know).

Before I wrote these lines, I glanced at the three books that were born out of our joint pregnancy. I was appalled to realize how, 40 years later, we are still dealing with the same problems...

Many who sailed on the boat are no longer with us. I myself feel like a survivor of the *Titanic*. What drowned us in the end was the tip of the iceberg of Israeli melancholy. Don't worry, be happy; things could get worse, and they are...

21.2.**57**

"You Must Order an Immediate Withdrawal"

IDF troops leaving the Sinai.
Photo: David Rubinger

This was the dramatic appeal US President Eisenhower made to David Ben-Gurion, demanding an immediate IDF withdrawal from the Sinai and the Gaza Strip. The Israeli premier was under heavy pressure from the Americans and the Soviets, who had recalled their ambassador to Moscow. He accepted the unequivocal demand for lack of a better choice. He could only negotiate the terms of withdrawal. Speaking at the cabinet session that discussed the withdrawal, Ben-Gurion said in tears: "I gave them the order to go to war, and now I have to explain our withdrawal to them." Ben-Gurion really did not have another option: Eisenhower threatened to impose stiff economic sanctions on Israel and, on 26 April, he officially asked France to stop its aid to Israel and freeze a $30 million credit. The US Administration insisted on an unconditional withdrawal, but Ben-Gurion managed to work out a formula by means of which Israel would reserve the right to self-defense according to the UN Charter, if it was not allowed to sail through the Straits of Eilat. The United States and several other countries agreed to note down this formula. On 6 March, the IDF unconditionally pulled out of the Gaza Strip.

Withdrawal from the Sinai was gradual, with the IDF destroying every military facility before moving out. UN troops took their place until, eventually, Egypt regained control of the Sinai. On 10 March, the USSR declared that the Tiran Straits were Egypt's territorial waters. However, the *Inga Topet*, a Danish ship leased by ZIM, crossed the Tiran Straits on 24 March unmolested. Although the withdrawal left Israel with no territorial gains from the war, the Sinai Campaign did provide Israel with freedom of passage through the Red Sea and a quiet Egyptian border for 10 years.

POWs Exchanged With Egypt

20 January

There was no doubt that Israel triumphed in the Sinai Campaign, but even victories cost. In addition to the casualties, both parties had soldiers held captive by the other side. Four Israeli soldiers were taken prisoner, including pilot Yochanan Atkes who said the Egyptians had tortured him and burned his lips and ears with matches. In the POW exchange deal, Israel handed over 5,850 Egyptian POWs in return for the four IDF soldiers. The exchange marked the end of the war and the restoration of quiet.

The four POWs returning from Egypt. Photo: GPO

1957

An Assassination Attempt at the Knesset

Ben-Gurion Saved Miraculously

The Knesset session was dealing with routine matters calmly when a hand grenade thrown by one Moshe Dowek exploded. When the dust settled, it appeared that Moshe Shapira, minister of religious affairs and social welfare, was badly injured. Prime Minister Ben-Gurion, Foreign Minister Golda Meir and Tourism Minister Moshe Carmel sustained light injuries. The country was enraged by the ease with which a deranged person could endanger Israel's most senior leaders. "I wanted the world to hear of the wrongs that were done to me," said Moshe Dowek in explanation. The public's attention, however, focused on the lax security at the Knesset. Defense officials wondered out loud how an armed man could enter the hall and come that close to the prime minister. It was clear that Ben-Gurion and the senior ministers had had a miraculous escape. Stiff security arrangements were introduced at the Knesset after the event, and a glass wall was built between the visitors' gallery and the plenum hall. Visitors to the Knesset had to undergo a body search.

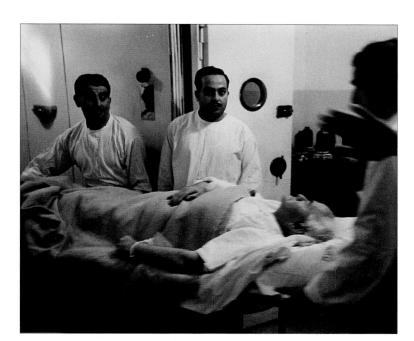

The prime minister receives medical care at a hospital. Photo: David Rubinger

The fifth Maccabi Games Begin

15 September

The Fifth Maccabia opened. The games were held under the shadow of the Sinai Campaign and troubled relations with the world, but the games continued in an orderly manner and without disturbances.

Kastner Murdered in Tel Aviv

3 March

Yisrael Kastner, who was charged of collaborating with the Nazis and providing them with trucks in return for which they allowed a group of Jews to leave Hungary for Switzerland during World War II, was shot and killed. This concluded an emotional and complicated affair that had preoccupied the Israeli public in 1954-55. The affair raised the issue that the Mapai leaders had done nothing during the Holocaust. Kastner, a government official, won an appeal against his conviction, but remained engraved in the public memory as a person who collaborated with the Nazis.

15 January

The IDF moved most of its units out of the Sinai, completing the second stage of withdrawal.

20 January

In a POW exchange deal, Israel returned 5,850 Egyptian soldiers in return for four Israeli soldiers, including pilot Yochanan Atkes. "The Egyptians tortured us," the returning soldiers stated.

9 February

A mass demonstration was staged in Tel Aviv against the withdrawal from the Sinai.

21 February

President Eisenhower made a dramatic demand on Israel to pull the IDF out of Sinai inmediately.

3 March

Dr. Kastner was murdered in Tel Aviv. The police questioned 300 people.

7 March

The last Israeli soldier left Sharm al-Sheikh by sea.

28 April

The satirical radio show *Three Men in a Boat* became one of the most popular Kol Yisrael programs.

6 May

The IDF staged the Independence Day parade in Tel Aviv, showing spoils collected from the Egyptian Army.

10 June

The workers of the Ata clothing factory started a strike that lasted three months.

12 June

Immigrants in Ashkelon and other places in the south rioted because of severe unemployment and dire economic straits. In some cases, the riots turned very violent.

17.7.57

"The Volunteers" Against Amos Ben-Gurion

School Uniforms in Tel Aviv

12 December

The Ministry of Education, the Tel Aviv City Council, and the PTA decided that schoolchildren should wear uniforms. They would be simple and affordable so that the lower economic groups could purchase them, too.

Deputy Police Chief Amos Ben-Gurion won a libel trial after he filed a suit against an organization called "The Line of Volunteers." The organization had charged that Amos Ben-Gurion comitted fraud and was involved in foreign currency violations. Ben-Gurion filed a libel suit and was exonerated, and the organization was fined IL5,000. The public opinion, however, was divided: Some believed the court was right in exonerating Amos Ben-Gurion. Others felt he had won the case because he was a member of the Mapai elite.

The Mann Auditorium Inaugurated

1 October

The Mann Auditorium in Tel Aviv was inaugurated with festivities and enthusiasm. The next day, a festive concert conducted by Leonard Bernstein was held in the elegant 3,000-seat hall. The orchestra played works by Beethoven and Noam Sheriff, a promising 22-year-old Israeli composer. The crowd that packed the hall cheered the orchestra and the conductor at the end of the splendid performance.

Leonard Bernstein, Arthur Rubinstein and the Israeli Philharmonic. Photo: GPO

They used to play soccer in front of the Mann Auditorium. Photo: GPO

57

1957

Ben-Gurion Stands on His Head

Reproduction: Paul Goldman, GPO

Ben-Gurion's "new" exercises included standing on his head. Everyone was amazed, except for his wife Paula, who scoffed at him.

6 October

USSR's Man-Made Moon Flies Over Haifa – The artificial Soviet moon crossed the skies of Haifa. It orbited Earth at an altitude of 90 km. Experts said that the satellite, picked up by the antennas of the Israel Postal Authority, would orbit Earth for a week, and then burn up upon re-entering the atmosphere.

12 September

El Al Bought A New Britannia – El Al was among the first companies to purchase the Britannia, a brand-new passenger plane. It took six hours to travel from London to Lod, which was considered a great achievement.

31 December

Merchants Sold Poison Believing It Was Citric Acid – Three businessmen were detained after selling large quantities of poison they believed was citric acid. Two police units were urgently dispatched to the shops to retrieve it. Thus far, the merchants had sold 110 boxes each containing 50 kg of poison.

1 August

A significant rise in the number of emigrants compared with the number of immigrants.

28 October

President Ben-Tzvi was elected for a second term.

29 October

A hand grenade was thrown inside the Knesset, lightly wounding Prime Minister David Ben-Gurion and two other ministers. Religious Affairs Minister Moshe Shapira was badly injured. Would-be assassin Moshe Dowek, had previously been hospitalized in mental institutions.

30 November

The drying of the Hula Lake. which began in 1951, was completed. As the lake emptied, fish started streaming into Lake Kinneret.

31 December

Prime Minister Ben-Gurion filed his resignation with the president as a result of a crisis with the *Ahdut Ha'avoda* ministers over Israel's military relations with Germany.

5 November

Baby Sinaia

This was the name given to a Bedouin baby found by soldiers in the Sinai, sitting next to her mother's body. The soldiers took care of her and named her Sinaia. Childless MK Fares Hamdan expressed a desire to adopt her. His wish was granted, and Sinaia joined the Hamdan family in Nazareth.

Little Sinaia loved and cared for. Photo: K. Weiss

14 July

The "Sparkling Burglar" Goes to Jail

Israel Benzioni, the "Sparkling Burglar" was sentenced to 10 years in prison after being convicted of theft, burglary, and offering bribes. He pleaded guilty to some 150 charges and stealing IL 108,000.

1958

Amos Hacham, International Bible Quiz laureate, worked as a clerk in the Jerusalem School for the Blind. Photo: AP

The award ceremony. Photo: GPO

The National and International Bible Quiz
A Cultural Connection With Our Roots

Former Minister
Shimon Shetreet

In 1958, marking Israel's first decade, a group of people with original ideas headed by Haim Gvariahu and encouraged by Prime Minister David Ben-Gurion, came up with the idea of bringing Israelis, especially the young generation, closer to the Bible by holding competitions and quizzes based on its verses, chapters and secrets. Studying the Bible as part of creating an Israeli culture served as an important instrument in strengthening our contacts with our roots in this land and added an original aspect to Israel's cultural and historical heritage.

The first national Bible was held on 4 August 1958 at the Mann Auditorium in Tel Aviv. Amos Hacham, a clerk at the Jerusalem School for the Blind (and son of Dr. Noah Hacham, a professor at the Jerusalem Teachers' Seminary), won the national competition and, several weeks later, the international one. Hacham became a media star and met the state leaders, including Ben-Gurion. To the public, Hacham symbolized the State of Israel's cultural connection with the Bible – which was so essential for the state that was only beginning to shape its culture.

Through the national and international quiz, 20th-century Israeli society returned to its ancestral saying:

"Do not let this Book of the Law depart from your mouth; meditate on it day and night." (Joshua, 1:8)

Ben-Gurion made an emotional declaration: "The Bible Quiz was the most important event of the decade. It showed that, upon becoming independent, the people of Israel returned to the Bible – the core and soul of the nation."

The young generation was enthusiastic as well. When the national and international quiz of 1959 was held, I was 13 years old, living in neighborhood A and attending the Erlich Elementary School in Tiberias. That year, I won the competition. My two runners-up were Matania Ben-Artzi of Tiv'on, currently a professor of mathematics at the Hebrew University, and Mr. Menachem Damari. Ben-Gurion shook my hand and hugged me warmly. He also said: "It is good that a new immigrant's son beat the Ashkenazim."

Ben-Gurion's decision to make Bible studies a national affair gave the quiz much prestige and encouraged the young generation and the public at large to study the Bible; in addition, it connected the secular population with its Jewish heritage. Bible studies not only connected the state and its children with the past, but also served as a basis for the renewal of signs of sovereignty dating back to the days of the First and Second Temple, and even before that.

Israelis everywhere felt they were following in the footsteps of their Biblical fore-fathers: Yoav Ben Zruyah and Avner Ben-Ner, the military leaders; Jeremiah and Isaiah, the spiritual leaders; Miriam, sister of Moses and Prophet Deborah, the nation's female leaders; Ezra and Nechemia the builders, and Uziahu, who built towers in Jerusalem. They and many others were brought back to life in a new form in the new state. Students of all kinds, religious and secular, drew on the Bible for values, principles and points of reference for their studies, research and writings.

Looking back, I can say that the Bible Quiz symbolically placed the Bible on bookshelves in Israel not only as a holy scripture, but as a work of art and culture that inspired human and Jewish values. The quiz brought the people closer to the Bible and the nation's ancient history – through healthy competition. Bible studies – the way Prime Minister Ben-Gurion encouraged them – were anchored in an approach that combined democracy and tradition in Israel. The message was that Torah and general education, tradition and democracy should be combined. We should not uphold only the secular and humanist world view. We can combine civil rights with close links to our ancient traditions.

It is hard to imagine Israeli culture as we know it today without the central dimension of the Bible's influence on literature, music and poetry.

1.7.**58**

The "Who Is A Jew" Crisis

Ben-Gurion: "We never resolved that the Jewish State should be a Halachic state."

Rabbi Y. L. Fishman-Maimon, Religious Affairs Minister.

The "Who is a Jew" crisis started when Interior Minister Yisrael Bar-Yehuda of *Ahdut Ha'avoda* found out that being registered as a Jew by the Interior Ministry required that the person who applied for citizenship present real proof that his mother was Jewish, and that making a statement to that affect was insufficient. This procedure was in effect during the term of the National Religious Party's Haim Shapira. Bar-Yehuda consulted Attorney-General Haim Cohen, who was known for his liberal views, and decided to instruct the registration clerks that anyone who honestly stated that he was a Jew should be recognized as such. The religious parties were very upset and Ministers Shapira and Burg resigned from the cabinet after their demand that the procedure not be altered was rejected. Moshe Toledano, a respected and religious Jew who was not identified with any party, was appointed interior minister. This, however, did not appease the religious parties which kept protesting against the ease with which anyone could be registered as a Jew. Trying to avoid a crisis, Ben-Gurion consulted a group of 50 rabbis, dubbed "Israel's sages". The rabbis supported the religious parties' stand, and Ben-Gurion had no choice but to announce that the old regulations were back in force. The religious parties returned to the coalition. Ben-Gurion had written to Rabbi Y.L. Fishman-Maimon, then Religious Affairs minister: "The Declaration of Independence never resolved that the Jewish state should be a halachic state ruled by rabbis... Just the contrary, we declared that it would not be a theocratic state and that men and women would have equal rights, which contradicts the Halachah..." However, it appeared that coalition considerations outweighed this aggressive declaration, and Ben-Gurion would rather have the religious parties in the cabinet than adhere to the principles of his letter to Rabbi Fishman-Maimon.

The "Crown" Arrived in Israel

23 January

The Aram-Zova Crown miraculously arrived in Israel and was presented to President Yitzhak Ben-Tzvi. The "Crown", the most important Hebrew manuscript, had been kept in Halab, Syria, in an ancient synagogue, from the time it had been brought there from Egypt by Maimonides' great-grandson. This is the first full handwritten version of the Bible, complete with reading annotations. In 1948, the Aram-Zova was damaged in a pogrom and vanished. Ten years later, it arrived in Israel. Halab-born writer Amnon Shamosh wrote a serious dissertation about this affair, entitled: *The Crown - the Aram-Zova Story*.

A page from the Aram-Zova Crown

The Shata Jailbreak

A prison riot of unprecedented magnitude broke out at the Shata Prison near Bet Hashita. After careful planning, the prisoners, mostly held on security-related charges, overpowered their jailers and tried to leave the prison while holding the jailers hostage. The large police forces that arrived on the scene were compelled to open fire, killing two wardens and eleven prisoners.

The swift and powerful police operation did not prevent 66 Arab prisoners from jail-breaking. Some of them were caught; others crossed the border into Jordan and disappeared. The incident sparked a storm in Israel. The ease with which so many security prisoners managed to escape cast doubt on the effectiveness of the prisons. Stricter security regulations in all prisons were introduced.

The Escaped Prisoners After They Were Caught. Photo: Hans Pin

Haim Laskov Appointed Fifth Chief of Staff

1 January

Major General Haim Laskov was appointed fifth IDF chief of staff. Laskov was the Armored Corps commander and member of the team that developed the corps' combat doctrine. In December 1957, he traveled to Germany with Defense Ministry Director- General Shimon Peres to purchase submarines for the Israel Navy. Laskov quit the post before the end of his term as a result of disagreements with Mossad head Isser Harel, who overrode his authority.

Change of chiefs of staff. Left to Right: President Yitzhak Ben-Tzvi, incoming Chief of Staff Haim Laskov, and Moshe Dayan. Photo: Warner Brown

1 January

Change of guard in the IDF high command: Haim Laskov replaced Moshe Dayan as chief of staff.

7 January

The three murderers of Yisrael Kastner were sentenced to life imprisonment.

9 February

The Finance Ministry considered lowering the high prices of gasoline set after the Sinai Campaign by up to 30%.

27 February

Violent riots and clashes with the police took place in Jerusalem because a swimming-pool was opened to both men and women.

28 March

Drainage works in the Hula Lake were resumed. The Syrian Army opened fire at the workers on the site. The IDF returned the fire, and skirmishes continued for a few days.

8 April

Thousands of former members of the Irgun and the "Stern Gang" staged a march in Tel Aviv.

24 April

An IDF parade and several other events took place to mark Israel's first decade.

27 April

The Hebrew University was inaugurated on Givat Ram in Jerusalem in a festive ceremony attended by MKs and many notables.

1 May

The May Day marches, organized by the Israeli Communist Party, headed by Dr. Moshe Sneh, turned violent. 100 demonstrators and some 30 police officers were wounded.

26 May

Four police officers were killed in a Jordanian attack on Mount Scopus. Colonel Flint of Canada, chairman of the Israeli-Jordanian cease-fire committee, was also killed in the attack.

24.4.58

Israel Marks A Decade

Special Plane Takes Reparations Claim to Germany

27 March

After a stormy public debate, a special plane left Israel for West Germany, carrying the reparations claim of the victims of Nazi persecution. The plane arrived in time to meet the deadline for the suits. On their part, the Germans doubled the number of people processing the flood of last-minute claims. The German Government estimated that it would have to pay some $1.8 billion in reparations. The argument about accepting German money continued for a long time in Israel, albeit in an undertone.

Top: *Decorated Tel Aviv streets packed with celebrating citizens.*
Photo: Fritz Cohen, GPO

Bottom: *The girls of the Nahal Brigade perform at the Ramat Gan Stadium.*
Photo: Moshe Pridan, GPO

With great pride, Israel celebrated the first decade of its existence. Considering the difficulties that the state had to contend with, its development was most impressive.

The festivities included an awe-inspiring IDF parade in Jerusalem, breathtaking performances by IDF soldiers at the Ramat Gan Stadium, and an exhibition in Jerusalem. The State of Israel, which had a population of 650,000 in 1948, tripled the number of Jewish citizens, reaching 1.8 million.

The young state anchored itself in the Middle East and established itself economically and militarily. Extremely impressive progress was made in the latter field. Having suffered economic depressions, sometimes bordering on bankruptcy, Israel managed to stabilize itself while facing an amazing challenge – absorbing one million immigrants, and giving them homes and jobs. The state was most successful in promoting agriculture. In only 10 years, Israel was able to provide most of the food consumed by its residents. The standard of living rose steadily, cultural and spiritual life progressed by leaps and bounds, and at the end of its first decade, it was clear that the State of Israel had overcome its birth pangs and was anticipating a better and more prosperous future.

Stormy Demonstrations Against A Mixed Pool

27 February

With the opening of a swimming-pool for mixed bathing in Jerusalem, ultra-Orthodox demonstrators staged protest rallies that soon deteriorated into violent clashes with the police. Many religious residents of Jerusalem felt that the pool was the last straw in the campaign against their way of life. Encouraged by their rabbis, dozens of Yeshiva students took to the streets and, driven by their faith, engaged in clashes and fist-fights with police officers. The uprising took quite some time to subside, and caused a large number of injuries on both sides.

58

16 January

Eilat Is Four Hours Closer

Photo: GPO

The highway to Eilat was inaugurated in a ceremony attended by Prime Minister Ben-Gurion and other officials. The 238-km road cut the driving distance from central Israel to Eilat by four hours, making a 2,000-year-old dream to spend a winter vacation in swimsuits come true.

25 November

"Immigration Loan" Imposed on Israeli Citizens - The rising need for funds for immigrant absorption compelled the government to impose an "immigrant loan" on the public to finance the absorption of the hundreds of thousands of immigrants. The goal was set at IL20 million, a hefty sum in 1958.

2 July

Treasury Officials Charged with Taking Bribes - Four Finance Ministry officials were charged with receiving IL12,000 in bribes from industrialists. Charge sheets were filed with the Tel Aviv District Court. Three industrialists involved in the affair were also charged.

11 November

An American Millionaire Marries an Israeli Scientist - Mr. Arthur Krim, president of United Artists, the big American film company, has become engaged to be married to Dr. Matilda Danon, a Weizmann Institute scientist. The two are getting married next month. Mr. Krim, who is also a wealthy Jewish New York attorney, has devoted much of his time to Israel and the Institute in particular, serving as a member of its board of trustees. For the past five years, Dr. Danon, his fiancée, has been working for the Institute's Genetics Department. She was a member of a team of scientists who came up with a method to determine the gender of a fetus five months before birth.

10 November

Prices of Cheap Cigarettes Go Up

The price of cheap cigarettes was raised by 60 mil a pack, with Degel, Adir, Washington, and Lux going up to 280 mil from 220 mil; Dafna, Negev, Semel and others going up from 200 mil a pack to 250; and Adam, Arye, Latif, etc. from 180 to 230 mil a pack. It appeared that cheap cigarette consumption had gone up by tens of percent. In August, these brands accounted for three million out of a total of ten million packs sold in Israel, constituting a 30% rise in consumption.

1 July

A government crisis over the "Who is a Jew" affair. The NRP ministers quit the coalition, creating a grave coalition crisis.

8 July

A young Israeli was sentenced to four years', imprisonment for revealing military secrets to Jordanian Army representatives.

24 July

Ezer Weizman was appointed Air Force commander and promoted to major general.

31 July

An unprecedented prisoners' mutiny broke out in the Shata Prison.

10 August

The first-ever meeting of religious Sephardim was held in Netanya protesting the fact that the Religious Affairs ministry did not appoint Sephardi rabbis even in places where the majority of inhabitants were Sephardim.

19 August

Amos Hacham won the first prize in the first international Bible quiz held in Jerusalem. Hacham, a polio victim, competed against 15 representatives from all over the world.

7 October

Habima Theater celebrated its 40th anniversary, and the Education and Culture Ministry pronounced it the national theater.

14 October

The cornerstone for the Knesset building was laid at the Government Compound in Jerusalem.

10 November

Defense Ministry Director-General Shimon Peres announced that he was resigning from his post in order to devote his time to political activities.

23 November

Ben-Gurion appointed Tel Aviv Rabbi Ya'akov Moshe Toledano Religious Affairs minister, replacing Minister Moshe Shapira who had resigned. The appointment of 76-year-old Toledano aroused fierce opposition among the religious.

1959

Stormy demonstrations at Wadi Salib. Photo: Oskar Tauber

The harsh living conditions of the locals. Photo: Oskar Tauber

The Wadi Salib Riots
Protesting the Big Misfortune

Prof. of Sociology
Sammy Samooha

The riots at Wadi Salib, a poor neighborhood in downtown Haifa, started on 8 July 1959 when a police officer shot and wounded a rowdy local drunkard called Ya'akov Elkarif. The neighborhood residents attacked the police station in response, and the next day staged a march to the station, protesting both the fact that an innocent man had been shot, as well as unemployment, harsh living conditions, poverty and ethnic discrimination. The Union of North African Immigrants that had been set up a few months earlier in Wadi Salib provided an independent and belligerent leadership, countering the National Organization of North African Immigrants that was ruled by Mapai. The demonstration quickly turned into racial riots, with the marchers storming Hadar, Haifa's uptown Ashkenazi residential and business center, attacking pedestrians and shops, causing extensive damage and injuring 13 policemen; 34 demonstrators were arrested. Within a few days, the riots spread to several development towns, mostly those populated by North African immigrants, but caused little damage. The government held an emergency session and appointed a commission of inquiry. A month later, the commission filed a "whitewashed" report documenting the hardships, the difficulties of ethnic merger and the feeling of being discriminated against, but not mentioning Mapai's iron-fist rule of Haifa and rejecting claims of ethnic discrimination. The press dealt with the issue extensively and the situation received some attention during the election campaign a few months later. David Ben-Harush, leader of the protest movements and chairman of the Union of North African Immigrants, ran on a separate list for Knesset, but failed to attain the minimum quota, as did other Sephardi-oriented lists.

The Wadi Salib riots were a traumatic event that emanated from protest over the great misfortune of the 1950s. Hundreds of thousands of immigrants from Asian and African countries were absorbed in disgraceful conditions. They came to Israel lacking education and capital, with large families, and without friends or relatives in the veterans' establishment. The establishment, on its part, took advantage of these weaknesses and sent the immigrants to border settlements and run-down moshavim and townships that were already plagued with poverty and unemployment. Most of the immigrants were given terribly overcrowded temporary housing and provided with the worst possible health, education and welfare services. Their lives were ruled by executives and party activists who followed orders from the establishment and foiled every attempt to create an independent leadership. The immigrants were termed "the generation of the wilderness" and "human dust" who must lose their Oriental backwardness in the Israeli melting-pot. Ben-Gurion's pseudo-democratic regime had all the power and used it to promote the veteran Ashkenazim (and through them the Ashkenazi immigrants) while discriminating against the Sephardim. The results of this policy were already evident in the 1950s. The "Orientals" were concentrated in the peripheries and small towns, forming the new proletariat – the poor and politically powerless. Their children failed in school and they felt increasingly humiliated, hurt and envious of the Ashkenazim who were doing well and improving their status steadily.

What were the results of the Wadi Salib riots? The leaders of the revolt were destroyed politically. To cover up the disgrace, the neighborhood was cleared of its residents and the government started rehabilitating other slums. Sephardi children were sent to low-level professional schools en masse to prove that the education gap was narrowing, and the quota of ethnic government appointments was increased. These steps, however, addressed the problem only partially. In March 1971, the Black Panthers Movement was formed to protest against the very same wrongs. When the Likud came to power in 1977, it initiated the Neighborhood Rehabilitation Project. The Sephardi protest was seen mainly in the alliance they struck with the Israeli right wing, with 80% of them voting for it in the crucial elections of 1996. However, the distress of Wadi Salib and other places like it, as well as their next generation, is seen in a large stratum – of which Israelis of North African origin are most prominent – that consists mainly of the working and poor classes, live in dire conditions, and whose children have little chance of escaping the same fate. They still feel socially underprivileged, hatred for the well-established Ashkenazim, and disappointment with the Right. The ultra-Orthodox Sephardi Shas Party is associated with this stratum and, in its own way, serves as the current representative of the distress in the Wadi Salibs of the 1990s.

1.4.59

The Night of the Ducks:
The Call-Up That Never Was

Major General Yehoshafat Harkavi, head of the IDF Intelligence Branch.

It was a routine and peaceful day, when the radio announced that a special bulletin would be broadcast at 9 p.m. The security situation was normal and there was no tension along the borders. At the designated hour, to the amazement and dismay of the civilians, the radio started broadcasting call-up slogans for IDF reserve units. One of the slogans was "water ducks", which is why the strange evening was dubbed "the night of the ducks". This started a major panic in Israel, the Jordanian Army was put on high alert, and Syria started calling up its reserve units. Calls started coming in from all over the world, inquiring about the sudden call-up. To everybody's embarrassment, the Foreign Ministry, the chief of staff and the IDF spokesman were all unable to explain what was happening. Eventually, it turned out that it had been a fictitious drill to test the reserve soldiers' alertness by calling up non-existent units. To add insult to injury, opposition leader Menachem Begin sent his blessing from the Knesset to the IDF soldiers on their way to a daring mission...

Ben-Gurion, who was not in the know either, established a commission of inquiry. He was doubly embarrassed because the queen of Belgium, who was in Israel on an official visit, thought she was caught up in a Middle East war. The commission's report was never published, but after it was filed, the chief of staff relieved Deputy Chief of Staff Meir (Zaro) Zorea and head of Intelligence Yehoshafat Harkavi of their duties. They were accused of being responsible for the fact that the chief of staff and the defense establishment had known nothing about the drill, and guilty of misunderstanding the ramifications of such an event. Ben-Gurion used the weird incident to make it clear that *he* was in control of the army and that he would not tolerate commanders who did not know what was going on. The event, that turned out to be a media farce, became synonymous with much ado about nothing.

Right: Major General Meir Zorea

Elections to the Fourth Knesset: "Say Yes to the Old Man!"
3 November

Before the elections and in view of frequent coalition and political crises, it seemed as if Mapai was losing ground and that Ben-Gurion would have difficulty staying in power. The results, however, were very surprising: Of the 900,000 voters in the elections, 370,000 voted Mapai, giving it 47 Knesset seats (an increase of 7). *Ahdut Ha'avoda* lost three seats and Mapam maintained its power. The religious parties made slight gains, and Herut won only two additional seats, despite the ethnic riots that had preceded the elections. Ben-Gurion's position was greatly strengthened after the elections, and the Mapai slogan. "Say Yes to the Old Man!", proved that he was still the party's main electoral asset. The Mapai list featured three new MKs: Moshe Dayan, Shimon Peres and Abba Eban. We will meet the three later in central events in this country.

Cabinet Crisis Over Weapon Sales to Germany

1959

A storm broke out in Israel when it was reported that Israel had signed a deal with West Germany regarding the sale of Uzi submachine guns and some 250,000 grenade launchers within 10 years. The German Defense Ministry spokesman said: "We decided to buy Israeli weapons because they are cheaper and better." Reactions in Israel, however, were very different. The approaching elections helped fan the flames and the coalition parties seized the opportunity to make political capital and create a serious coalition crisis, with Mapam and *Ahdut Ha'avoda* ministers adhering to an uncompromising line: "We cannot sell guns to the army that annihilated European Jewry."

Ben-Gurion insisted that the deal had been decided on long before by the cabinet and that all the coalition partners had agreed to it, but the coalition partners rejected the claim, seeking to weaken Mapai's power. They claimed that the resolution had not specified that the weapons were to be sold to Germany. A vote of no confidence was held in July and *Ahdut Ha'avoda* and Mapai did not support the government. Ben-Gurion had to hand in his resignation to the president, and the cabinet became a caretaker one. It turned out eventually that the issue of arms sales to Germany did not help the other parties nor did it harm Mapai in the election, as it was not central in the election propaganda, and the parties that harped on the issue lost power. The storm subsided on its own and Ben-Gurion emerged victorious from this crisis as well.

A Nuclear Reactor in Israel

8 May

The construction of an experimental US-made nuclear reactor began in the dunes of Nebi Rubin, near Rishon Letzion. Its output was one megawatt and its cost $800,000. Israel pledged to the United States that it would serve for research only. At the same time, Israel signed a deal with France for the construction of a 24-megawatt nuclear reactor. The construction of this plant had begun in 1958 near Dimona. Officially, Israel claimed it was building a textile factory, but the cautious security arrangements at the site attested to the fact that it was going to be a high-security facility. De Gaulle demanded that Israel declare that it did not intend to produce nuclear weapons, and Ben-Gurion had to agree. France continued assisting Israel in building and operating the reactor, despite protests from the world, especially the Arab countries.

The nuclear reactor at Nachal Sorek. Photo: GPO

29 January

Finance Minister Levi Eshkol announced that the government needed an additional IL175 million to cover drought damage and pay for the Jordan Plant. He decided to impose new taxes and cut subsidies to the tune of IL50 million.

1 February

The Austerity ended. Supervision and rationing of basic products was cancelled.

26 February

Colonel Issaschar Shedmi, commander of the brigade involved in the Kafr Kasem massacre, was acquitted of 25 charges of murder, found guilty of exceeding his authority, fined 10 mil and reprimanded. The commander of the battalion whose men fired at the villagers was sentenced to 17 years in prison.

3 March

The price of shoes rose by IL3-4 a pair. This was to be expected in view of the rise in the cost of unprocessed leather.

4 March

The Soviets offered Israel a book in Yiddish by Shalom Aleichem, printed in Moscow to mark the writer's 100th birthday.

1 April

The Night of the Ducks: A surprise call-up of reserve units that Kol Yisrael broadcast by mistake caused panic in Israel and put Jordan and Syria on the alert.

19 April

Yitzhak Rabin was appointed head of the General Staff's Operations Branch after Meir Zorea was removed from his post following the Night of the Ducks.

28 April

The Air Force received its first Voutour bombers from France. These were brand-new planes only recently introduced into the French Air Force.

8.7.59

The Wadi Salib Riots

The incident started after a brawl in a local café in the Wadi Salib neighborhood in downtown Haifa. It was a rundown neighborhood that had never been rebuilt after its Arab residents fled in 1948. The police were called in to stop the drunkards' fight, and shot and wounded one man. He was taken to hospital, but rumors spread in the neighborhood that he had died. The neighborhood residents staged a march to the local police station, where their rally turned into a major riot. Some 15,000 people, mostly of Moroccan origin, lived in the neighborhood. The feeling of being discriminated against and social deprivation burst out in full force. They broke into shops and looted them, torched cars and clashed with the police, injuring 13 officers. Two civilians were injured in the riots and 34 arrested. The riots quickly spread to southern and northern Israel and occurred wherever Sephardim resided. The incident served as a warning to the government that the "Orientals" were embittered and were willing to use force to improve their situation.

The Wadi Salib affair became the symbol of the struggle of the deprived strata against the establishment that had demeaned them during Israel's first decade.

Photo: Oskar Tauber

David Ben-Harush (right), leader of the Wadi Salib riots, outside the locked café where the riots started. Photo: Ronit Shani

Arrival of the Tanin Submarine

16 December

On a cold winter day with stormy seas, the Tanin – an upgraded British submarine – entered Haifa port. It was received by Navy commanders and the chief of staff. The destroyer *Eilat* fired 19 salvos in honor of its underwater sister, the Air Force performed an aerial salute, Navy vessels sounded their foghorns and the fire-fighters sprayed water.

Immigration From Rumania: The Problem of Parting

1 January

The joy over the mass immigration from Rumania was clouded by the parting from family members. The Rumanian authorities gave only some Jews exit permits, forcing them to leave their families behind. It is believed that about 10,000 families had to split, including 111 married couples. That year, most Rumanian Jews immigrated to Israel – some 150,000 of them. This was made possible when the Rumanian government allowed Jews to emigrate, despite Arab protests.

Photo: Fred Chasklin

59

16 January

The Nachal Brigade Band - A Hit

Photo: Mirlin-Yaron

The Nachal Brigade Band has become the most popular military band, performing nightly before soldiers and civilians with its hit songs.

8 May

Construction of a nuclear reactor began in the south. It was to be operative by the end of 1959.

5 July

Premier Ben-Gurion resigned over the Mapam and *Ahdut Ha'avoda* vote on the issue of arm sales to Germany.

8 July

There were riots in Wadi Salib as a result of ethnic tension and a feeling of deprivation on the part of the Sephardim. The riots originated from a drunkards' brawl and became really violent.

10 October

Fatah, the largest Palestinian organization, was established under the leadership of Yasser Arafat.

10 October

New lira bills in Israel:IL1/2, IL1, IL5 and IL10.

3 November

Mordechai Namir elected Tel Aviv mayor. For the first time since the establishment of the state, a Mapai member won the post. Up till then, all Tel Aviv mayors had been members of the General Zionist Party.

17 December

Ben-Gurion formed a new government with new ministers: Moshe Dayan, Abba Eban and Giora Yoseftal.

26 February

Actress Elizabeth Taylor Helps the Immigrants

Actress Elizabeth Taylor purchased $100,000 worth of Israeli immigrant absorption bonds at a Hollywood dinner. The total sum collected at the dinner was $1.3 million, earmarked for the construction of a village containing 400 housing units for immigrants to Israel.

17 July

Cardboard or Wood?

The Central Elections Committee became involved in a stormy debate over whether ballot boxes should still be the traditional wooden ones or new cardboard boxes manufactured by Cargal. A vote was held and the majority voted for wood, although cardboard could have been more economical...

Photo: Moshe Pridan, GPO

2 April

Secret Detective Unit Set Up by Tel Aviv Police - The purpose of the new unit was to monitor criminals. The number of highly skilled and trained detectives was kept secret. It was modeled on the King Unit of Britain's Scotland Yard.

6 November

The Carmelit Was Launched

The first Israeli underground train, the Carmelit, was inaugurated in Haifa in the presence of the mayor, MKs and other notables.

Photo: Moshe Pridan, GPO

(1960

Eichmann in a glass cell during his trial. Photo: GPO

Eichmann in the Israeli prison yard.

Capturing Adolf Eichmann
Our Historic Duty to the Deceased

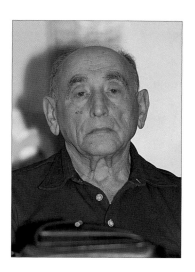

Former Mossad Head
Isser Harel

When I was appointed head of the Israeli Secret Services in 1952, I decided to deal with Nazi war criminals responsible for the murder of six million European Jews. At the top of the list was Adolf Eichmann. We started searching for him all over the world, but were consistently faced with failure.

The breakthrough occurred in 1957, when we received solid information from Dr. Fritz Bauer, attorney-general of Essen, Germany, according to which Eichmann was hiding with his wife and children in Argentina, under the name of Ricardo Clement. Our secret inquiries in Argentina verified the information.

When I received the information, I spent the night reading the Eichmann file. I received a picture of an arch-murderer who had committed crimes unprecedented in the history of mankind. He was the supreme authority on the Jewish issue, with every means of hunt-down and slaughter at his disposal. That night I decided: Adolf Eichmann would be caught.

Now we had to address the crucial question of how to do that. Naturally, we were obligated by law to notify the Argentine authorities of our suspicion that Clement was in fact war criminal Eichmann and wait for the lengthy extradition procedure to take effect. I knew for certain that once the official process started, Eichmann would be warned and would vanish - this time for good. I reached the conclusion, therefore, that we had no choice but to apprehend him ourselves, and this is how I presented the issue to Prime Minister David Ben-Gurion. We discussed the complicated issue of conducting a secret operation on the soil of another sovereign country from the moral and political points of view. Ben-Gurion stressed the historic value of holding a Holocaust trial in the Jewish state and the Israeli capital. He was mostly concerned about the youth. If they were made aware of the Holocaust, he maintained, they would understand that it was their historical duty to make sure that nothing like it ever recurred.

Eventually we reached the unhappy conclusion that we had no other choice but to capture Eichmann and bring him to trial in Israel. Despite our reservations, we knew that the State of Israel had the moral right to expose the horrors of the Holocaust and try the man in charge of the "final solution of the Jewish problem".

The operation, which was carried out in May 1960, was very complicated. From a distance of 15,000 kilometers, we had to make a positive identification, study the suspect's life patterns and establish the method and location of the capture. We also had to prepare a safe house in which to keep Eichmann after he was apprehended until a safe way was found to get him out of Argentina. Our people in the safe house initially believed that they would be dealing with an unusual person who might surprise them at any moment, a devious mind that could devise the most daring tricks. After several months of observation, they realized that they were observing a miserable criminal, a pathetic and scared man who groveled and humiliated himself with the sole purpose of making his new masters like him. It was hard to believe that this lowly creature was the same "superhuman" who had orchestrated the murder of millions of Jews.

Why should Israel – at the time burdened with problems of security, immigrant absorption and developing the land – undertake such a nationally, internationally and operationally complicated task? Israel had to do it because it was not just any state; it was the state of the Jews. It was called upon to perform an act of supreme historic justice: to punish the murderers of the Jewish nation and, mainly, to hold a public trial about the Holocaust. In that respect, capturing Eichmann was not an end, it was merely a means. The end was the trial; the trial of the Holocaust.

And what was so very important about a Holocaust trial?

"The final solution" was a terrible crime against humanity. Its aim was to eliminate the Jewish people totally. It was the duty of the State of Israel to expose this tragedy – its scope and its horrors. Historic justice and Jewish dignity made it imperative that the trial be held only by Jews in the Jewish capital – Jerusalem.

It was Israel's historic duty to the Jewish nation that had been massacred in the Holocaust. Had Israel avoided that duty, it would not be worthy of its historical calling.

23.5.60

"The Beast is in Chains!"

In a dramatic speech at the Knesset, Prime Minister David Ben-Gurion announced: "Eichmann is incarcerated in Israel and his trial will soon be held here." He told the ministers and MKs that the Israeli Security Services had apprehended Eichmann who, together with the heads of the Nazi regime, had planned the "final solution of the Jewish problem" which led to the murder of six million Jews. Ben-Gurion praised the services and said that this operation was their best ever.

The report stunned the Israelis. The details of the abduction were initially kept secret, but after a few days the story began to unfold. It appeared that Eichmann had escaped from Germany and was living in Argentina under the false identity of Ricardo Clement. He lived with his family in poor economic conditions in an old suburb of Buenos Aires. After several days of surveillance, he was apprehended on 11 May by a Mossad team. When he was caught, Mossad head Isser Harel cabled Ben-Gurion: "The beast is in chains!"

After his kidnapping, Eichmann was held in Buenos Aires and flown to Israel 10 days later, heavily sedated. He and his abductors were flown to Israel on board an El Al flight with an Israeli delegation that was returning from Argentina's 150th independence day festivities. When he arrived in Israel, Eichmann was taken to a secret facility in Jaffa; the team placed in charge of his interrogation was dubbed "Chamber 006". Eichmann was placed under heavy 24-hour guard and the police prevented the press from meeting or photographing him. Eichmann expressed his amazement at the Israeli abduction operation. "I could not believe Jews could do such a smooth job," he told his interrogators. Eichmann never denied his identity, but insisted that he was merely a regular soldier, following the orders of his superiors.

The Eichmann abduction caused a serious crisis in Israel's relations with Argentina, which demanded that Israel return Eichmann to Buenos Aires, and asked the UN to condemn Israel for the illegal abduction. Three months later, the differences were ironed out and the crisis ended.

Eichmann on his daily walk in prison.

Bar-Kochva Archives Found in the Judean Desert

8 April

Prof. Yiga'el Yadin announced that he had made a most important archeological discovery in the Judean Desert: The Bar-Kochva archives, which shed new light on the great Jewish revolt and the Roman siege. He found parchments, metal tools, clothing and scrolls with Bar-Kochva's brief and resolute orders which ended with warnings such as: "If this is not done, the rejectionists will be severely punished."

Yiga'el Yadin deciphering the Bar-Kochva scrolls.

An Historic Encounter:

Ben-Gurion and Adenauer

Israeli Prime Minister David Ben-Gurion and West German Prime Minister Konrad Adenauer met at the Waldorf-Astoria Hotel in New York in what was termed "an historic encounter". The meeting, widely covered by the world media, formally represented the reconciliation between the Jewish nation and the new Germany. Efforts to get the two together had continued for two years, with Ben-Gurion refusing to travel to Germany. When it was suggested that the meeting take place in New York, he agreed.

At the beginning of the meeting, Ben-Gurion stressed that Germany would not be able to erase its moral debt to the Jewish nation from its past, but he made a distinction between the crimes of Nazi Germany and the new Germany's efforts to pay for them. The meeting paved the road to the establishment of diplomatic relations between the two countries. The two leaders also extensively discussed economic aid, and the German prime minister announced that Germany would grant Israel a loan of $500 million for the development of industry and agriculture in the Negev, and promised a free supply of weapons.

David Ben-Gurion and Konrad Adenauer during their historic meeting at the Waldorf-Astoria Hotel in New York. Photo: UP

The "Where Is Yosale?" Affair

18 January

The affair, which in future years would reach dramatic heights, started with the Shuchmacher family and its economic plight. The family immigrated to Israel from Poland and, experiencing difficulties, asked the mother's parents - rich ultra-Orthodox Jews from Mea Shearim - to help raise the children. Their daughter Zina was sent to the Hassidic center at Kfar Habad, and the son, Yosale, was taken to his grandfather, Nachman Shtarkes. Having improved their economic situation, the parents asked for their children back. The grandfather agreed to return the daughter, and promised that the son would return toward the beginning of the school year. The family's attempts to regain custody of their son were foiled by the grandfather, who insisted that Yosale was liable to receive secular education that would place him among sinners. Then, Yosale vanished. Fearing that he might have been smuggled out of the country, the parents

The house on Moshav Komemiyut where Yosale was taken.

asked the court to intervene. However, the grandfather remained adamant, despite court orders he had received. The police stepped in, but could not find Yosale. They searched Jerusalem and Bnei Berak, but the child was already in New York. When the affair starting attracting public attention, making splash headlines in the press, Ben-Gurion decided to involve the Mossad in the search. Only three years later was Yosale found in Brooklyn.

18 January

The press reported that Yosale Shuchmacher had been kidnapped by his grandfather, an ultra-Orthodox Jew.

31 January

IDF forces raided the Syrian outpost of Hirbat Tawfik, built across the border from Kibbutz Tel Katzir, east of the Kinneret. This major retaliation operation followed Syrian attacks on the local settlers.

25 February

Deputy Defense Minister Shimon Peres went to France to purchase arms and discuss financial arrangements for the arms deal.

14 March

An historic meeting between the Israeli and German premiers was held in New York.

2 May

Israel's 12th Independence Day parade was held in Haifa. It started with a festive Air Force display and concluded with a demonstration by the Navy.

8 May

Attorney Gideon Hausner was appointed state attorney.

23 May

The prime minister informed the Knesset that Adolf Eichmann had been apprehended by a Mossad squad in Buenos Aires and brought to Israel.

27 May

An Egyptian plane was downed by Israeli planes in a dogfight.

16 June

The first Israeli nuclear reactor became operational in Nachal Sorek. The construction of a second reactor began in Dimona.

18 June

A Roman amphitheater was discovered in Bet She'an during archeological excavations.

21.12.60

"The Affair" Re-emerges:

The "Committee of Seven" Examines the Question: "Who Gave the Order?"

Pinchas Lavon, defense minister during "The Affair".

"The Affair" continued bleeding the political system this year as well. The tragic affair, that started with the apprehension of a Jewish spy network in Cairo, kept haunting the parties involved, with the central question: Who gave the order? Accusations were leveled at then Defense Minister Pinchas Lavon, who had been forced to resign in 1955. Lavon had been trying to clear himself for years, while in the background, rumors proliferated that the affair was fraught with lies and fraud. The issue resurfaced in the summer of 1960 when two officers were suspected of coercing witnesses to testify against Lavon. Once again, everybody asked: Who gave the order - Lavon or Chief of Intelligence Binyamin Jibli?

Ben-Gurion ordered a commission to be set up under Justice Haim Cohn to examine the issue. It found two senior officers suspected of perjury and falsifying documents. The prime minister then demanded that a legal commission of inquiry be set up, but the cabinet refused and decided to form a committee of seven ministers under Justice Minister Pinchas Rosen.

The "Committee of Seven" filed its conclusions at the end of December. It determined that Pinchas Lavon had not given the order and exonerated him. Ben-Gurion disapproved of the conclusions and took a long leave of absence. This, however, was not the end of the song and dance. In 1961, "The Affair" caused a split in Mapai and brought about early Knesset elections.

The IDF Raids Syria's Tawfik Outposts

31 January

Following unceasing Syrian harassment of Israeli settlements, including the shelling of kibbutzim and infiltrations into Israeli territory, the IDF raided the Syrian outpost of Hirbat Tawfik east of the Kinneret. The outpost, located in an abandoned Syrian village, overlooked the kibbutzim of Tel Katzir, Ha'on and Ma'agan. The IDF conquered the post after a heavy battle with artillery backup. Three IDF soldiers were killed. The Syrians sustained numerous casualties.

The Mother of Kibbutzim, Degania, Celebrates Jubilee

16 April

Degania marked its jubilee with a day's holiday. Early in the morning, the kibbutz members held a memorial ceremony for the fallen. Later, in another ceremony, kibbutz veterans were given honorary titles and three of them related the history of the kibbutz. In the afternoon, a plane flown by a kibbutz member flew over and dropped flowers and greetings from the kibbutz Air Force soldiers. A festive dinner and a play about the three generations of Degania concluded the festivities.

The first days of Degania.
Photo: Aroshkes

60

22 March

Paul Newman in Israel to Film *Exodus*

Photo: Carlyle-Alpina SA

Paul Newman landed in Israel with his wife, actress Joanne Woodward, and their little daughter. The Hollywood star came to shoot the monumental film Exodus, based on Leon Uris' best-seller. The film tells the heroic tale of the illegal immigration to Palestine and the founding of the State of Israel.

10 April

A Grand Victory – Israel's Soccer Team Defeats Yugoslavia: The Israeli national soccer team scored an unprecedented victory, beating the strong Yugoslav team 2:1 in Belgrade. Rafi Levy scored twice for Israel. Giula Mandi, Israel's Hungarian coach, said excitedly: "We achieved this major victory thanks to our fighting spirit... the players did their utmost... they are real heroes." The Yugoslav press praised the Israeli team: "We have never seen a goal-keeper like Hodorov... It is a great day for Israeli soccer and a bad day for ours..." A month after that victory, Israel defeated the Young England team with the surprising score of 4:0.

The four-day march of soldiers and civilians. Photo: Bamachaneh

Photo: Bar-David

15 July

The *Poalei Agudat Yisrael* Party (PAY) joined the coalition. The move caused a rift in the ultra-Orthodox camp. Binyamin Mintz was appointed Postal Minister.

31 July

Abba Eban was appointed education and culture minister, replacing Zalman Aran who resigned over disagreements with high-school teachers.

3 August

A new medical center, Hadassa, was inaugurated in Ein Karem, Jerusalem.

3 September

Drilling at the Negba-3 site revealed the highest quantity of oil ever found in Israel.

21 December

"The Committee of Seven", appointed to examine the Lavon affair, concluded that Pinchas Lavon had not given the order and found him not guilty.

6 July

The Air Force Gets Fugue Magisters

The Fugue Magister, the first training plane built by Israel Aircraft Industries (IAI), was presented to the Air Force in the presence of the prime minister, the defense minister, the Air Force commander and IAI heads.

Photo: GPO

9 November

Galia Golan – Miss World Runner-up

Miss Israel Runner-up Galia Golan was elected first runner-up to Miss World in a beauty contest in London. The Argentinian beauty queen won the title. Golan received a car, a trophy and £100.

1960

(*1961*

Pinchas Lavon at the height of "The Affair". Photo: Hans Pin

Gideon Hausner, prosecutor at the Eichmann trial. Photo: GPO

The Lavon Affair:

"Who Gave the Order?"

*Journalist
and Former MK
Uri Avneri*

The history of the State of Israel is full of "affairs", but even today when we say "The Affair", we mean the Lavon affair. The folklore of the 50s discussed the question, "Why was the Palmach dissolved?", while in the 60s we all asked, "Who gave the order?"

The "order" in question was given by an Intelligence Branch envoy to a network of Jewish spies in Egypt. They were instructed to place bombs in public places in Alexandria and Cairo, mainly in US and British cultural institutions. This was a triple scandal: placing bombs in public places risked the lives of innocent people; the very establishment of the network jeopardized the entire Jewish community in Egypt; and shifting it from espionage to terrorism was doomed to failure because the group was not professional. Its members were in fact caught red-handed, most of them receiving stiff prison sentences, and two being executed. Egyptian President Gamal Abdel Nasser could not have pardoned them even if he had wanted to because he had just executed the leaders of the Muslim Brotherhood and could not pardon Jews after he had hanged Muslims.

The man who delivered the order, a young man named Avri Zeidenwerk – an obviously deranged person – fled. The Israeli Intelligence Services suspected that he himself had betrayed the network.

"The Affair" cannot be understood without knowing the background: At the end of 1953, Ben-Gurion resigned as prime minister and defense minister and settled in Sde Boker – perhaps to serve as an example of pioneering for the young, perhaps to recharge his batteries, or perhaps because he was angry at his cabinet associates who blocked his extreme anti-Arab path. Perhaps he had hoped that they would not be able to do without him and would ask him to return on his own terms. He left the Defense Ministry to a sharp-tongued party activist, Pinchas Lavon, who at once turned from an extreme dove (by today's standards) into an extreme hawk. Some even suspected that Ben-Gurion had given the portfolio to an unsuitable man in order to prove that the cabinet could not do without him.

In those days, the British were about to evacuate their military bases along the Suez Canal, all that remained of their rule over Egypt. For some reason, all of Israel's leaders – from Ben-Gurion to Lavon – felt that this endangered Israel's existence. They saw the British as a buffer between Israel and Egypt and believed that handing the bases, with their equipment, over to the Egyptian Army would crucially reinforce it. In hindsight, it was utter nonsense, but the top echelons and the media were hysterical. The bombings of the Egyptian cities were supposed to give the impression that they had been perpetrated by an extreme nationalist underground, thus proving to the British that the Egyptian regime was weak and that they should not leave their posts. The bombings were also intended to convince the Americans that there was no point in approaching such a weak Egyptian regime.

In practice, the opposite happened. The network was exposed and its members subjected to public trials. Prime Minister Moshe Sharet, "a liar for the homeland", declared that this was an anti-Semitic blood-libel. However, secret inquiries were held behind the scenes; Pinchas Lavon was ousted and Ben-Gurion was recalled to the Defense Ministry, employing his "activist" line that led to the Sinai Campaign in 1956.

The affair could have ended at that, had Avri Zeidenwerk not been tempted to return to Israel. Because they could not prove that he had betrayed the network members, he was charged with other security offenses. In his secret trial, Zeidenwerk claimed that the charges against him were false and made to prevent him from revealing everything he knew about document forgery, pressuring witnesses and presenting false evidence during the investigation of the Egyptian affair. The judge who presided over the trial was shocked and sent the testimony to David Ben-Gurion, who was once again prime minister and defense minister, and who ordered a new investigation. Again, two main claims had to be resolved. Then Intelligence Branch Chief Binyamin Jibli claimed that he had been given a verbal order by Lavon. Lavon denied this. It was clear that one of them was lying through his teeth. Ben-Gurion sided with the officer, despite the fact that forgery of IDF documents had been proven.

The political establishment supported Lavon. When Ben-Gurion demanded that a "judicial commission of inquiry" be set up, though there was no law to approve this, the politicians set up committees that acquitted Lavon. Ben-Gurion kept insisting, and the issue became an obsession for him. He forced the Labor Party (then Mapai) to remove Lavon from his post as the Histadrut Labor Union secretary-general. The cabinet resigned, Ben-Gurion was re-elected (in 1961), but was dismissed or resigned (in 1963), quit Mapai, and established a new party that – relatively – failed in the elections (of 1965). Ben-Gurion – the man who had decided on and declared the establishment of the State of Israel and who had been idolized for many years, was eventually perceived as an old bore. His closest supporters (Moshe Dayan, Shimon Peres and others) rejected his authority and returned to Mapai, despite his objections.

"The Affair" hovered over Israel for 12 years. It played a central role in ending Ben-Gurion's rule, which brought one era to a close and started a new era in Israel's development.

11.4.61

The Eichmann Trial
"...Standing here with me today are six million prosecutors..."

The Eichmann trial opened in the Bet Ha'am Hall in Jerusalem with the defendant sitting in a bulletproof glass cell. The hall was packed with Holocaust survivors, reporters from all over the world, ordinary people and new immigrants. The eyes of the entire nation were focused on the trial. It opened with a speech by the prosecutor, Attorney-General Gideon Hausner, that sent shivers down everybody's spine: "Standing here now, Israeli judges, to prosecute Adolf Eichmann, I am not alone... Standing here with me are six million prosecutors... They cannot rise on their feet, point to this glass cell and shout at the person sitting there: 'I accuse you!'"

The trial was presided over by Supreme Court Judge Moshe Landau, while German Attorney Robert Cervacius spoke for the defense; the charge sheet was based on the bill entitled "Trying Nazis and their helpers", which entailed a death sentence. The trial lasted till August and some 100 Holocaust survivors testified, telling horrendous stories about the Holocaust. Writer K. Zetnik fainted on the stand, and writer Haim Gouri wrote: "Nobody will come out of here unchanged." During the trial, Eichmann was indifferent. Before the verdict, he only said: "I am guilty of being obedient to the obligation of serving during war time... I did not persecute Jews out of my own desire; the government did that... ." In their verdict, the judges wrote: "The defendant acted out of deep identification with the orders he was given and a strong desire to attain his criminal goal... ." Eichmann was sentenced to death.

Writer K. Zetnik faints on the witness stand. Photo: GPO

Poet Abba Kovner delivers a dramatic testimony. Photo: GPO

The Jerusalem courthouse was packed during the Eichmann trial. Photo: GPO

Spy Yisrael Ber Arrested: "I am not a Traitor!"

Yisrael Ber's arrest shocked the public – especially Prime Minister David Ben-Gurion. Ber, considered one of his associates, was a lieutenant colonel, military commentator, and the defense minister's adviser on military history. He had even served as the IDF military historian.

Under interrogation, he said he had had ideological motives and had never intended to undermine state security. "I am not a traitor. I did not side with the state's enemies. I tried to serve the country in everything I did. I never undermined state security."

Mossad head Isser Harel suspected him, saying he felt that Ber was a security risk because he lacked ideological backbone. Harel grew even more suspicious when Ber asked to meet with head of the West German intelligence, Glenn Weber, who was a primary target of the Soviet Bloc intelligence services. Although Harel would not allow a meeting, Ber met Weber in Europe. Harel then decided to put him under constant surveillance, which exposed his connections with an East German agent and the Soviet Embassy in Israel.

Ber was arrested on 30 March and charged with contacting a foreign agent and delivering classified information to a foreign country. He was given a 10-year sentence. An appeal to the Supreme Court resulted in his term being extended to 15 years. Ber died in prison. After his death, it became apparent that he had, in fact, been a Russian intelligence officer.

Kibbutz Tzor'a Abolishes Separate Children's House

26 September

Kibbutz Tzor'a members decided to close down the children's house and have the children sleep in their parents' homes. The decision was very costly as it was also decided that families with two children would be given two-room apartments.

Dr. Yisrael Ber (right) on his way to court.

Première of *Exodus*

21 June

Exodus, Otto Preminger's film about illegal immigrants who arrived in Israel from Cyprus, was shown in two premières in Tel Aviv's Tzafon movie theater. The public was not enthusiastic about the film, an adaptation of a book by Leon Uris, mainly because of the story's American slant. In general, however, the film was very impressive and became Israel's envoy to the world.

1961

1 January
Tzvi Tzur was appointed chief of staff, replacing Haim Laskov.

11 January
Forty-eight immigrants who left Morocco for Israel on board the *Egoz* drowned.

24 January
Yitzhak Rabin appointed deputy chief of staff.

31 January
Ben-Gurion filed his resignation because the "Committee of Seven" ruled that Pinchas Lavon had not given the order during "The Affair". Ben-Gurion disapproved of the committee's conclusions and said that it had assumed the role of a judge.

7 February
Prof. Kurt Sita of the Technion was convicted of espionage and sentenced to five years in prison.

15 March
The remains of Irgun commander David Raziel, who was killed in Iraq, were brought to Israel.

11 April
The Eichmann trial opened in Jerusalem. It was extensively covered by the world media, and attended by Holocaust survivors, ordinary people and new immigrants.

25 April
The Liberal Party was established when the General Zionists and the Progressive Party merged.

5 July
Israel launched the Shavit-2 – a 250-kg research missile – much to everyone's excitement.

12 September
The Haifa Theater opened. The first play it put on was *The Taming of the Shrew*.

15 August
Knesset elections held for the fifth time: Mapai lost five seats, Herut maintained its power, and the Liberals won three more Knesset seats.

5.7.61   The Shavit-2 Missile Launched

The first Israeli missile was launched. It was a 250-kg research missile, and the launch caused great excitement in Israel. The operation was kept top secret, and even the cabinet was notified only an hour before the launch.

Present at the launch site were Prime Minister David Ben-Gurion, Golda Meir, Shimon Peres, and senior scientists. After the launch, Ben-Gurion said: "This launch proves that Israeli scientists can build a fully made-in-Israel missile." However, some criticism was also voiced about the Shavit-2 launch being part of Mapai's elections propaganda.

The Israeli achievement was applauded by most of the world, but enraged the Arab countries, which demanded that the United States condemn the launch.

Elections Under the Shadow of the Lavon Affair

16 August

The elections for the fifth Knesset were held against the backdrop of the Lavon affair, which took a heavy political toll on everyone involved. Serious disagreements amongst the cabinet members regarding the findings of the Committee of Seven led to early elections. Naturally, the election campaign revolved around the affair and its ramifications, with commensurate results: Mapai lost five Knesset seats, going down to 42; Herut maintained its power with 17 seats; and the Liberal Party went up from 14 to 17 seats. Ben-Gurion assigned Levi Eshkol the complicated task of forming a coalition, which took two and a half months. At the beginning of November, Ben-Gurion presented his new 16-minister cabinet.

Stormy debates and demonstrations took place over "The Affair".
Photo: Yitzhak Berez

Soccer Champion Pele Arrives

11 June

Brazilian soccer superstar Pele came to Israel with his team, Santos, for a game against a team consisting of the stars of the Israeli league. The Brazilian team won 3:1 in the presence of 50,000 spectators who came to watch the Brazilian virtuoso in action.

1961

12 September

The Haifa Theater Opens

Photo: Photo Esther

The Haifa Theater opened to the public with Shakespeare's play The Taming of the Shrew. The theater later served as a model for the Beersheba Theater and the Khan Theater of Jerusalem. Yosef Milo fathered the idea and was the theater's first art director. Eight years later, when Bimat Hasachkanim actors joined the theater and Oded Kottler replaced Milo, the Haifa Theater took the revolutionary step of putting on plays that addressed the socio-political reality of Israel.

27 September

Ben-Gurion celebrated his 75th birthday.

4 October

Rabbi Yihya Alsheikh won the International Bible Quiz.

2 November

Ben-Gurion presented his new cabinet to the Knesset.

28 December

Operation Yachin began. During this operation, the Jews of Morocco were brought to Israel following an agreement with King Hassan II.

31 January

Two Women Rob A Beggar at Knife Point – Two women robbed an elderly Jerusalem beggar after they entered his room and demanded that he give them a loan so that they could get married. When the beggar refused, one of the women pulled out a knife and forced him to lie on his bed while the other searched the room. She found IL80 in bills and coins hidden in old socks under the bed.

The Israeli factory which produced the Susita. Photo: GPO

15 March

Bible Studies at Ben-Gurion's Home

Photo: GPO

The regular Bible class met at the home of Prime Minister David Ben-Gurion after a long recess. The prime minister delivered the opening speech about King Cyrus. He chose the issue on the occasion of the 2,500th anniversary of Cyrus' declaration about the return of Jews to Zion.

Photo: Oskar Tauber

9 January

Enzo Sereni's Wife Leaves Israel

The wife of Enzo Sereni, one of the Hagana commanders, decided to leave Israel, feeling that her work for immigrants was not appreciated. Ada Sereni, a member of Kibbutz Givat Brenner, had two daughters; her son was killed in a disaster on Kibbutz Ma'agan. Mrs. Sereni was very bitter because the state leaders did not acknowledge the great things she had done for the country, and decided to leave for Rome and join her family there.

31 May

The Ramla Prison Jailbreak

Nachman Farkash and Refael Blitz, two prisoners considered dangerous to the public, made a daring escape from Ramla Prison. A committee set up to investigate the affair found nine wardens guilty of negligence. It also determined that the Ramla Prison, where dozens of dangerous criminals were kept, was an unsuitable facility. Four years later, Farkash again escaped from the Ramla Prison, this time alone. He crossed the border into Egypt with the help of Israeli Arabs, and was returned to the Israeli border several days later, where he was found by two Kibbutz Nachal Oz members and handed over to the police.

(1962

Yosale's grandfather, Rabbi Nachman Shtarkes, waiting at the airport for his grandson who was returning from New York.
Photo: Micha Bar-Am

Yosale Shuchmacher came back home. Photo: Micha Bar-Am

The Kidnapping of Yosale Shuchmacher:
"Where Is Yosale?"

Writer Haim Be'er

For three years, the country asked, "Where is Yosale?" In addition to "Why was the Palmach dissolved?" and "Who gave the order?", this was clearly one of the most dramatic, militant and passionate issues to grip Israeli society over the past 50 years. The painful and emotional connotations of the question symbolized the great irreconcilable rift between the Jewish religion and the Jewish state.

The "Yosale Affair" started with a rather routine family dispute, typical of immigrant societies. Ida and Alter Shuchmacher, who had immigrated from Poland in 1957 and endured economic hardships, sent their son Yosale to Jerusalem to live with the wife's parents, Miriam and Nachman Shtarkes. One Saturday evening two years later, the parents came to the old couple's neglected apartment on the outskirts of Mea Shearim. They wanted to take their son back and enroll him in a religious-national school in Holon, where they lived. For various reasons, however, the grandfather refused to relinquish their son.

The grandfather was a Breslaver, a zealous Hassid whose spirit had been hardened by years in the Soviet hell of World War II and the Siberian camps. He claimed that his son-in-law wanted to leave Israel and convert the child abroad. Shtarkes obtained a decree from Jerusalem's Chief Rabbi Tzvi Pessah Frank, stating that "by the law of the Torah, Rabbi Nachman Shtarkes must prevent his grandson from leaving Israel and going where Jews are converted; after all, the same law applies to grandsons and sons... Anyone who can help in the matter must do so." It was this decree that served as moral grounds for the persistent and uncompromising stand of the grandfather and the ultra-Orthodox. It also transformed this story from one of many personal tragedies into one of the stormiest public affairs in Israel.

In February 1961, the High Court of Justice ordered the old man to return the child to his parents, but Shtarkes placed the child in the custody of ultra-Orthodox circles, and Yosale vanished. Yosale was smuggled out of the country and, traveling under several identities, moved from a Mea Shearim yeshiva to Moshav Komemiyut in the south, to Lucerne in Switzerland, to a small town outside of Paris, France, and to a Satmer milkman's home in Brooklyn, New York.

A key figure in the entire affair was, clearly, Ruth Ben-David – a Catholic Frenchwoman who had been a daring fighter in the French Resistance, and who had converted to Judaism, becoming the second wife of Rabbi Amram Balui, leader of the extremist Jerusalem Neturei Karta sect. Ben-David smuggled Yosale out of the country dressed as a girl with braids and traveled with him, telling him that his parents had betrayed him and his God. He lived like a criminal on the run, co-operating with his kidnappers.

In the middle of March 1962, Prime Minister David Ben-Gurion decided to send the Mossad in search of Yosale, having been convinced that law enforcement called for unorthodox methods. He summoned Isser Harel and ordered him to initiate the search. Operation "Gur" (cub), one of the biggest the Mossad had performed thus far, eventually tracked Yosale down and, on 1 July 1962, the country was astounded when the papers printed special editions reporting that the child had been found in New York and would be coming back to his parents very soon.

In 1996, 37 years after the kidnapping, Yedioth Aharonoth correspondent Amalia Argaman-Barnea interviewed Yosale – now married, a father of three daughters, and a manpower manager at a Hi-Tech company. She asked, "Why do you think the affair penetrated the biography of an entire nation so deeply and why has 'Where is Yosale?' been an Israeli idiom for so many years?" Yosale answered: "I believe that two things made this affair such a big story: my parents' insistence – the fact that they would not let up for a moment – turned it into a symbol of the struggle against religious coercion. The other thing was the extensive media coverage, which never lost sight of my personal tragedy."

1.7.62

"Mamele, Mamele!" Sobbed Yosale

For nearly two years, Mossad agents combed three continents to find Yosale Shuchmacher who had been kidnapped by his ultra-Orthodox grandfather; the grandfather would not return Yosale to his parents for fear that his beloved grandson might get into bad company. The search was extremely difficult because the ultra-Orthodox circles were almost impenetrable.

The first breakthrough was made in August 1961, when information was received indicating that Yosale was being hidden by the Kot family on Moshav Komemiyut in the Negev. The family members said Yosale had been brought there by his uncle, but had been sent abroad soon after that. The agents found out that Yosale had been smuggled out of the country, dressed as a girl, by Ruth Ben-David, wife of Neturei Karta sect leader Amram Balui.

Ten more months went by before the Mossad agents located Yosale in Brooklyn, New York, at the home of the Gartner family who belonged to the Satmer Hassidim. Two days later, the boy and his mother met at the New York immigration offices. The world's most famous boy entered the room cold and hostile. His mother cried, "My son!" in Yiddish, and burst into tears. Yosale was unmoved. The mother tried again, and they had the following conversation:

Mother: "Yosale, don't you remember me?" Yosale: "I don't remember who you are..." Mother: "I am your mama, don't you remember?" Yosale: "No, you are not my mom. My mother went away, but she will be coming back for me. Besides, I'm not Yosale. I'm Yankel Gartner."

Only when his mother showed him some photographs did Yosale start crying: "Mamele! Mamele!"

The family flew to Israel the next day and Yosale received a warm welcome here. The Yosale affair had a happy ending.

Yosale Shuchmacher with his father on their way home from the airport. Photo: Micha Bar-Am

Yosale and his mother meet in New York after a separation of 10 months. Photo: UP

Levi Eshkol: "There Is No Deluxe Devaluation."

In a special radio broadcast on Friday, just before the Sabbath, Finance Minister Levi Eshkol announced a "new economic policy" centered around a 70% devaluation of the Israeli lira. This was the first devaluation in 10 years. It caused a great public storm, mainly among businessmen and mortgagees whose debt suddenly rose by 70%.

Eshkol asked the public to be calm and patient until the government had stabilized the Israeli economy: "There is no deluxe or easy devaluation, but the move was called for," he said. However, the economy was strike-bound for a few days and thousands of laborers staged demonstrations against the policy.

In fact, the new policy was meant to accommodate the International Monetary Fund and reduce the import-export gap. Eshkol wanted Israel to join the European Common Market, and improving the state of the Israeli economy was a prerequisite. In reality, it turned out that the devaluation helped less in increasing trade with Europe than in causing unemployment and a recession that lasted until the end of 1967.

Hapo'el Tel Aviv Wins the State Cup

14 August

After Maccabi Tel Aviv won the State Cup for four consecutive years, Hapo'el Tel Aviv defeated Maccabi in the finals and won the cup. Erez Lustig scored the victory basket in the last seconds, placing the score at 50:48 for Hapo'el.

Photo: K. Weiss

Jewish Gangster Lanski Arrives in Israel

3 October

Meir Lanski, an international Jewish mobster whom the Italian Mafia wanted dead, arrived in Israel and applied for citizenship according to the Law of Return. Lanski, 62, arrived with his wife. He was notorious as the head of a drug-trading gang in New York and one of the leading assistants to the head of the Italian Mafia in the US. Interpol notified Israel of his deeds and asked the Israel Police to keep an eye on him. The police decided not to arrest him, but waited for his three-month tourist visa to expire, at which point he was deported.

5 January

Famous philosopher Martin Buber published a statement supporting the abolition of the military regime in Israel. He severely attacked Ben-Gurion's attitude toward the Arab minority in Israel.

Photo: Moshe Pridan, GPO

9 February

Finance Minister Levi Eshkol announced a new economic policy centered around a massive devaluation of the lira. Stormy demonstrations took place as a result.

12 March

Brother Daniel, a Carmelite monk, filed an appeal with the High Court of Justice demanding that the state recognize him as a Jew. He claimed that he was the son of a Jewish mother and had converted to Christianity during World War II, which is why he should be acknowledged as a new immigrant according to the Law of Return. The court granted his request.

16 March

IDF forces raided Syrian outposts in Nukeb after the Syrians attacked fishermen in the Kinneret. The IDF lost seven soldiers, the Syrians 30.

31 May

Eichmann was executed by hanging after the High Court of Justice ratified the sentence. Before his execution, Eichmann cried: "Long live Germany, long live Argentina, long live Austria – the countries I was associated with."

28 June

Dr. Robert Soblan who fled to Israel from the United States, where he had been sentenced to life imprisonment for spying for the USSR, was arrested and deported from Israel. He inflicted injuries on himself on the plane, and was hospitalized in London, where he died.

16.3.62

Golani Storms Syrian Outposts

At the beginning of 1962, the Syrians resumed their attacks on Israeli fishermen at Lake Kinneret and shelled Israeli settlements in the region. The Golani Brigade launched a major retaliation operation against Syrian posts in Nukeb, north of Kibbutz Ein Gev.

The Golani raided the outposts at night, but the lead force was spotted by the Syrians who opened heavy fire on it. A serious battle ensued, during which Air Force jets were sent to the region. The battle lasted over an hour. When it ended, the IDF suffered seven losses and the Syrians had 30 and many wounded. The operation was followed by a brief period of calm, after which the Syrians again fired at Israeli fishermen.

Photo: GPO

Hawk Missiles Arrive

27 September

American President John F. Kennedy decided to provide Israel with batterires of Hawk anti-aircraft missiles. This move made Israel the only non-NATO country in posession of such missiles, which were designed to intercept low-flying bombers.

Dr. Robert Soblan in London' after his deportation from Israel. Photo: UP

"Leave Me Alone, I'm a Sick Man."

28 June

Dr. Robert Soblan, a Jewish psychiatrist whom a US court sentenced to life imprisonment for spying for the USSR, escaped to Israel using his dead brother's name. Soblan was staying at a Tel Aviv hotel when he was found and detained, following a request from the US Government.

When he was taken from his hotel room to the police car, he yelled: "Leave me alone; I'm a sick man... I'm a Jew who wants to live in Israel."

Soblan was deported from Israel and tried to commit suicide on the plane. He was hospitalized in London, where he died two months later - of cancer. The deportation caused a storm in Israel because Soblan had not been allowed to go through all the legal proceedings before being deported.

62

5 June

The International Oriental Trade Fair

The International Oriental Trade Fair opened in Israel, for the first time since the 1930s, at the Tel Aviv Exhibition Grounds. Thirty-three countries were represented, and there were 800 commercial and industrial exhibits. Poland was the only Communist country to take part, and only in the book fair. For IL 1.5, the Israelis could enjoy attractions such as a cable car, an amusement park, an Israeli-made TV set, the Philharmonic Orchestra, or the London Festival Ballet.

1 July

Mossad agents found Yosale Shuchmacher hidden with a family of Satmer Hassidim in Brooklyn, New York. He returned to Israel after a emotional and dramatic reunion with his mother.

15 August

Air Force jets downed two Syrian MiGs during a dogfight east of Lake Kinneret.

27 September

US President John Kennedy announced his decision to sell Hawk missiles to Israel.

22 October

Haifa Port workers declared a general strike protesting the fact that the prices of hot meals had risen by 20 agorot.

30 October

Yitzhak Ben-Tzvi was elected for a third term as Israel's president.

21 November

A new city called Arad was established in Israel.

3 August

Cops Dress Strippers

The Tel Aviv Police vice squad arrested two strippers and two nightclub owners after the censorship board banned strip shows. The officers stopped a strip show half-way, and dressed the strippers in front of the audience.

12 October

"Ambulance Yoske" Does it Again

An Ashdod ambulance driver nicknamed "Ambulance Yoske" delivered yet another baby on his way to the hospital. Yoske had done this several times before. This time it was the first son of an immigrant couple. The delivery went smoothly, and mother and child were well.

Children of the Arad founders celebrating the new Negev settlement.

30 November

Attorney General Gideon Hausner, who won international fame as prosecutor at the Eichmann trial, decided to resign over differences with the justice minister.

22 October

General Strike at Haifa Port

A general strike broke out at Haifa Port after the management decided to raise the prices of hot meals from 50 to 70 agorot. The laborers opposed the decision, which was approved by the Histadrut Labor Federation. Housing Minister Yosef Almogi went to Haifa to try to get the laborers back to work until the matter could be settled, but the laborers rejected his offer. Prime Minister Ben-Gurion considered government intervention to prevent the total paralysis of the port after 18 ships had already anchored and another nine were waiting in the bay to enter the port.

(1963

Levi Eshkol, Israel's third prime minister (behind him, Shimon Peres). Photo: Y. Freidin

Eshkol observes the Old City. Photo: Moshe Milner, GPO

Prime Minister Levi Eshkol
The Number One Builder

*Former Minister
and Writer
Yossi Sarid*

I was 25 when I started working with Levi Eshkol. It was in 1965, right after the stormy elections that were marked by the struggle against Ben-Gurion and his boys. I was one of the Eshkol boys. I always had been, because I loved him, felt sorry for him and wanted to save him from Ben-Gurion who wanted to rip his successor's premiership apart. That was how I was dragged into the advisers' court.

Seven or eight months later, I could no longer take it and resigned. I loved my master and did not want to go free, but I felt like an adviser in a trap and wanted to break loose.

My soft spot for Eshkol stemmed from his weakness, which was advantageous to him. He was not a charismatic man, but he had a charm that enchanted and won over many people. Charisma frees its owner of the need to convince others and get them to agree because it speaks for itself and is independently convincing, even if it not clear why and how it does that. In contrast, a charm like Eshkol's is a soft drug that does not make people go out of their minds; they can still tell right from wrong. It is less addictive, hence it sells less.

However, Eshkol's advisers and associates wanted him to sell more, at least like Ben-Gurion, who could sell snow to the Eskimos. This is why, when the famous charisma could not sell a commission of inquiry on "The Affair" and "Who gave the order?", it quit the game. The advisers' court wanted Eshkol to be a Ben-Gurion – namely, to conceal all that was good and kind about him and become what he was not and should not have been. When they dressed Eshkol in the king's old outfit, I was no longer there.

Now, at the close of the first century of Zionism, when they reach out for the poison pen to rewrite history, Eshkol might be the main victim because he was the first among Zionists. Levi, son of Dvora and Yosef Shkolnik, was the Number One builder of the Zionist enterprise, with only Pinchas Sapir competing against him for the builder's crown. The years in which Eshkol worked the land, standing knee-deep in water, produced the best Zionist vintage with the best pioneering aroma.

Eshkol personified a sane Zionism that was productive and creative, normal and sober, open and tolerant, not yet contaminated with Messianism, adventurism, parasitism, prejudice and xenophobia. That is why, when the Six Day War broke out, after Eshkol had been dismissed from his post as defense minister as a result of enormous ingratitude, a new leaf was turned in the national book. Once again, he seemed like the right man at the right time. Only Eshkol, responsible and sensible Eshkol, could keep an eye on the good old wine and prevent the nationalistic demon from jumping out of the box. But the demon escaped because Eshkol was tired and beaten and could no longer hold out. The demons defeated the angels. Golda, Galili, Dayan and Alon defeated Eshkol. He stood there, the right man at the right time, with his eyes open, and saw how that bunch opened the door to the evil spirit, and the spirit came in and blinded their eyes.

Yes, the destruction started when the great builder was at the top. The man who had revived this country's soil lived to see the festivities of pagan worship all around him – and could do nothing about it.

25.3.63

Isser Harel Resigns Over the Mossad's Actions Against German Scientists

Mossad head Isser Harel decided to resign because of Prime Minister David Ben-Gurion's orders to stop the secret actions against German scientists and their families in Egypt. Harel had warned about the grave dangers of German scientists working in Egypt. He demanded that immediate and practical steps be taken against German scientists who helped the Egyptians produce missiles, planes and non-conventional weapons.

A confrontation between friends: Isser Harel and David Ben-Gurion
Photo: David Rubinger

Ben-Gurion rejected Harel's tough approach and did not accept his views regarding the gravity of the German scientists' actions. The prime minister feared that the Mossad's actions against the scientists - sending them letter-bombs, kidnapping them and making threats against their family members - might harm the developing relations with Germany. Ben-Gurion was very angry when two Mossad agents were detained in Switzerland while trying to foil an Egyptian attempt to recruit German scientists. Yosef Ben-Gal and Dr. Otto Yuklik were detained in Basel while trying to "convince" the family of one scientist not to help Egypt.

The arrest of the Israeli agents exposed the Mossad activities which were responsible for the disappearance of several senior German scientists who worked in Egypt. Following this affair, the German chancellor announced that his country had nothing to do with the scientists, who had been hired on a personal basis. The two Mossad agents were released a month later, after Israel exerted heavy diplomatic pressure on Switzerland. In the meantime, the disagreements between Ben-Gurion and Harel increased after the former ordered that all action against German scientists should cease. The Mossad head resigned, and his place was taken by Intelligence Branch Chief Meir Amir, who supported the prime minister's stand. No one imagined then that the prime minister was about to resign.

ZIM Builds Two Kitchens: One Kosher, the Other Not

27 August

The ZIM shipping company decided to build two kitchens on the ship *Shalom*: a kosher kitchen on the right side, and a non-kosher kitchen on the left. The decision was made after the ZIM management reached an agreement with an American "rabbinical institution" that gave it permission to build the two kitchens. Alas, 24 hours later, it became apparent that the "institution" was a commercial company that sold kosher stamps for a profit. This caused a major storm among religious Israelis, and the Chief Rabbinate announced that it would issue no kosher stamps for the company until it abolished the non-kosher kitchen. The storm subsided only after Prime Minister Eshkol intervened and the company decided against the opening of the non-kosher kitchen.

"Courage To Change Before Calamity"

11 January

Yitzhak Ben-Aharon [one of the founding fathers of the workers' movement in Israel], published one of his most important articles in *Lamerhav*: "Courage to Change Before Calamity Sets In". In it, he called on the workers' parties to unite forthwith. He wrote passionately and argued: "Let the three workers' parties establish an association of the Socialist Laborers of Israel - at once, and of their own accord. This unity will most definitely bring about the necessary change, and it can be done if the three join hands."

Ben-Aharon said later, when the article was first published: "I walked among them [the party members] like an outcast." Yet, at the end of 1963, Mapai and Ben-Aharon's *Ahdut Ha'avoda* began discussing a merger and, in February 1964, the two decided to form an alliance for the Knesset elections. Ben-Aharon's call was heeded.

David Ben-Gurion:
"I decided to resign for personal reasons."

Ben-Gurion's announcement of his resignation from the premiership and the Knesset surprised political circles - and the public even more so. He said that he "had decided to resign for personal reasons that had nothing to do with national problems." Ben-Gurion refused to elaborate on his real reasons until the day he died. One may only guess that his move followed a series of events and pressures that led him to believe he could not continue as prime minister and defense minister.

Ben-Gurion and the Mapai ministers decided that Levi Eshkol would be his successor. "Don't give in, as you always do; don't compromise; form a government at once and present it to the Knesset," Ben-Gurion told Eshkol. Ben-Gurion retired when Israel and Israeli society were stable and solid. His retirement symbolized the transition from the rule of an authoritative father figure to a more balanced and open regime under Levi Eshkol.

Ben-Gurion on a morning walk after his resignation. Photo: Micha Bar-Am

23 January
The Herut Movement decided to form a Histadrut faction. The decision was made by secret ballot – 324 for and 257 against.

3 February
Moshe Ben-Ze'ev, a district court judge, was appointed attorney-general.

20 February
The Knesset rejected a bill suggesting that the military government be abolished by a one-vote majority 57: 56.

6 March
Israeli public opinion was outraged by reports that German scientists had been working on the development of long-range missiles in Egypt.

25 March
Mossad head Isser Harel resigned over differences with the prime minister regarding the way Israel should handle the German scientists in Egypt.

21 April
The first International Book Fair opened in Jerusalem with the participation of hundreds of publishers from 30 countries.

23 April
Israel's second President Yitzhak Ben-Tzvi dies at 79.

29 April
Independence Day was marred by the death of President Ben-Tzvi. An IDF parade was held in Beersheba.

21 May
Zalman Shazar was elected Israel's third president.

26 June
Ten days after Ben-Gurion's resignation, Levi Eshkol presented his new cabinet to the Knesset. Eshkol assumed the role tailored by Ben-Gurion – prime minister and defense minister.

Zalman Shazar - Israel's Third President

21 May

Zalman Shneor Shazar, a Histadrut leader, editor of the daily *Davar* and the first minister of education and culture, was elected Israel's third president.

President Shazar on the streets of Jerusalem after he was sworn in. Photo: Y. Freidin

26.6.**63**

Levi Eshkol – A New Prime Minister

Ten days after Ben-Gurion's resignation, Levi Eshkol presented his new cabinet to the Knesset. Although he had never dealt with security issues, Eshkol assumed the role of prime minister and defense minister along the lines of Ben-Gurion. Moshe Dayan was uncertain about remaining in the cabinet as agriculture minister, but agreed to stay after Eshkol made him a member of the Ministerial Committee on Security Affairs. Pinchas Sapir replaced Eshkol in the Treasury while continuing to hold the portfolio of Industry and Trade. The education ministry was given to Zalman Aran, and outgoing Education Minister Abba Eban was made deputy prime minister.

Eshkol made great efforts not to anger Ben-Gurion, and even termed his cabinet "a sequel government". Ben-Gurion settled in Sde Boker, writing extensive articles about the events that had led to the establishment of the state, and studying the Bible and philosophy. He kept track of Eshkol's activities, but made sure he was not seen as interfering in his successor's work.

Prime Minister and Defense Minister Levi Eshkol reviews a guard of honor upon his arrival at the Defense Ministry in Tel Aviv. Photo: Fritz Cohen, GPO

IDF Compulsory Service Shortened

18 December

The government decided to reduce compulsory military service by four months. Accordingly, men would serve 26 months and women would serve 20. Prime Minister and Defense Minister Levi Eshkol explained the move saying that the IDF did not require the large number of men of draft age. The move would also save millions of Israeli lira, according to the Treasury figures.

POWs Exchanged With Syria

21 December

Israel received 11 POWs from Syria in exchange for 18 Syrian POWs. The Israelis said they had been badly tortured in the Syrian prison. The exchange was held under UN auspices at the Customs House near the Bnot Ya'akov Bridge. For years the Syrians had denied that they were holding Israeli POWs, and agreed to the exchange only after heavy international pressure had been exerted on them.

Hagashash Hahiver

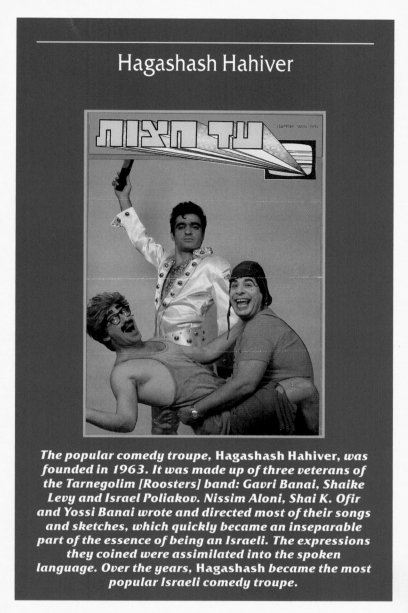

The popular comedy troupe, Hagashash Hahiver, was founded in 1963. It was made up of three veterans of the Tarnegolim [Roosters] band: Gavri Banai, Shaike Levy and Israel Poliakov. Nissim Aloni, Shai K. Ofir and Yossi Banai wrote and directed most of their songs and sketches, which quickly became an inseparable part of the essence of being an Israeli. The expressions they coined were assimilated into the spoken language. Over the years, Hagashash became the most popular Israeli comedy troupe.

26 July

Ultra-Orthodox Jews staged a stormy demonstration in Mea Shearim in Jerusalem protesting bus traffic on the Sabbath.

19 August

Syrian soldiers who entered Israel's territory shot and killed two Nachal Brigade soldiers in the settlement of Almagor, north of Lake Kinneret. The two were ambushed when they went to water the moshav fields.

19 August

The Israeli national basketball team won a surprise victory against the Yugoslav team, then No. 2 in Europe. The amazing score of 66:45 was both unprecedented and sensational.

21 October

In the Massada excavations, Prof. Yiga'el Yadin discovered the ruins of the synagogue where the zealots used to pray.

18 November

Shaver Thief Fined and Given Suspended Sentence

The Tel Aviv District Court found a man guilty of stealing a shaver and handed down a suspended sentence of six months in prison as well as a fine of IL400. The man stole the shaver from a delegate at the NRP conference at the Sheraton Hotel. The thief was also a delegate...

23 January

The Tel Giborim Affair - The bribery affair that rocked the country was associated with the building of a hospital at Tel Giborim. Yehuda Spiegel, deputy director of the Health Ministry, was suspected of receiving bribes for allocating hospital building contracts.

23 January

The American Princess

Nissim Aloni's play, *The American Princess*, was the first play put on by the Seasons Theater founded by Aloni and two young actors who quit Habima - Yossi Banai and Avner Hizkiyahu. This was Aloni's third play after *The Cruelest King* and *The King's Clothes* - "All three were about royalty; all three were failures, but they started an era." (from *The American Princess*) Aloni presented Israeli theater with enchanted, theatrical and colorful plays; magnificent scenes and heart-warming words that concealed an open wound; tales of deposed kings who could not find their place in the world; immigrants who carried the old country in their hearts; and gypsies in a world where "there are no more gypsies, only on records." (from Aloni's *The Gypsies of Yafo*)

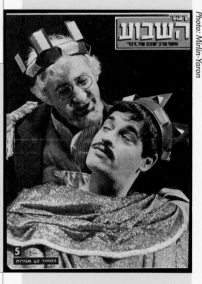

Photo: Mirlin-Yaron

21 April

The First International Book Fair Opened at Binyenei Ha'uma in Jerusalem - The fair was a meeting point for Israeli and international publishers and attracted thousands of booklovers. During the course of the fair, the Jerusalem Award was presented to a writer whose work expressed the freedom of man in society.

Photo: David Harris

1964

Scene from Salah Shabati, *a film by* **Ephraim Kishon.**

Haim Topol as Salah Shabati.

Salah Shabati

"Hey guys, does anyone know how to make movies?"

Writer
Ephraim Kishon

S*alah Shabati* was filmed 35 years ago and, in fact, was the second Israeli movie, after Eldorado by Menachem Golan, who also produced Salah. It is, therefore, small wonder that the conditions under which the film was shot were funnier than immigrant Salah's shenanigans.

In those pioneering days, there was only one usable movie camera in Israel – the Herzliya Studios' Ariflex. This prehistoric miniature camera could be used only five days a week because on Fridays it was used for filming the newsreel. The spotlights were as old as the camera, and when we had to shoot while in motion, we would sit the photographer and his camera inside a baby stroller and push.

Everything was outdated in this black-and-white movie, except for one very young actor, my dear friend Haim Topol, who made Salah Shabati very popular in Israel with his amazing talent which later turned him into an international star.

We must not forget that the film was shot in difficult times. Israel was busy absorbing one million immigrants, one of whom was Shabati's "spiritual father". I first met Salah in the 1950s, when my hut at the Sha'ar Aliya ma'abara was invaded by a family of North African immigrants blessed with lots of children. During the months I spent there, getting used to doing nothing, I tried to overcome the boredom by holding broken conversations with the head of the Moroccan family. The image of Salah started forming when I realized that my good neighbor did not know exactly how many children he had. When I asked him about his profession, he said that he was a steam-engine driver. I then inquired about the line he used to travel on in the old country, and he said with a mischievous smile: "I've never really tried it, but I hear it's a very nice profession."

My friends at Kibbutz Kfar Hahoresh rescued me from rotting away in the ma'abara, and my experiences in the lovely kibbutz influenced the script I wrote 12 years later.

In addition to these ancient turns of events, I must add that I arrived for the first day of shooting at the Kfar Hayarok without having the first idea about directing movies. My first question to the crew was: "Hey guys, does anyone know how to make movies?" No one answered. Still, I had the best cast of actors for the film, and they were all just as experienced as I was.

After I edited the movie with Dani Schick and added the wonderful score by Yochanan Zarai, it was time for the movie to hit the screens and prove its worth. Reactions to Salah Shabati varied: The critical message directed at the bureaucracy and party establishment provoked debates and condemnations. However, the audiences, especially the Sephardim, loved it. The critics expressed various opinions. After its première in Jerusalem, the most senior movie critic in Israel at the time wrote: "The standard of the film is as low as that of a commercial and the acting is bad because there is no script and no director." Shortly after that, Salah Shabati was sent to the San Francisco International Film Festival where it won the best script award and Topol received the award for best actor. Like I said, reactions varied.

It must also be understood that many in Israel disapproved of the fact that the movie had been sent abroad. This included not only the press, but also Prime Minister Golda Meir, who gave the order that the low-quality product, as the local critics described it, not be exported.

After Salah had been screened for nine consecutive months in New York and had won us two Golden Globe awards and an Oscar nomination for best picture, Mrs. Meir changed her mind. With a warm smile she said: "To err is human." I have often been asked about Salah's current occupation, and I always say that had he been real, he would most probably be serving as director general of the Ministry of Tourism; and if not him, then his son Shimon Shabati. In any event, for more information, please call his grandchildren. Or mine.

25.5.**64**

The Establishment of the PLO: "A Gun and an Olive Branch"

The PLO - Palestine Liberation Organization - was established at a conference of the Palestinian National Council, held at the Intercontinental Hotel on the Mount of Olives in Jerusalem. Initiator and moving force behind the event was Ahmad Shukeiri, who represented Palestine in the Arab League at the time. Shukeiri took advantage of a resolution passed during the first Arab summit in January 1964, calling for the establishment of a "Palestinian entity" and decided to form an organization that would be supported by all the Arab states. During the conference, Shukeiri was unanimously elected chairman, and the Palestinian National Covenant he drafted became the PLO foundation declaration.

The covenant states that Palestine is the homeland of the Palestinian Arab nation, that there is an affinity between the nation and the land, that it is a single and indivisible territorial unit of which the Palestinians are the legal owners. The covenant denies the State of Israel's right to exist and perceives the Zionist Movement as having aggressive goals and being racist by nature. According to the covenant, Judaism is a religion, not a nation; hence the Jews do not have a right to self-determination or a state of their own. Despite his views, the PLO under Shukeiri avoided adopting a policy of guerrilla activity against Israel, preferring logistic and political co-operation with the Arab countries. For this reason, Fatah and other left-wing Palestinian groups did not support Shukeiri's initiative and did not join the PLO.

After the Six Day War, Shukeiri and the old guard were deposed from the PLO leadership and, at the beginning of 1969, Yasser Arafat and the leaders of the Fatah and leftist movements seized control of the PLO. The change of guard in the PLO caused the organization to focus more on its national identity and led it to adopt a policy of armed struggle against Israel.

The Yom Kippur War and the political process that followed it made some PLO leaders rethink their goals and the means of attaining them, which caused disagreements among PLO leaders. The dilemma was expressed in Yasser Arafat's speech to the UN in 1974: "I come to you with a gun and an olive branch... ."

PLO Leader Yasser Arafat. Photo: GPO

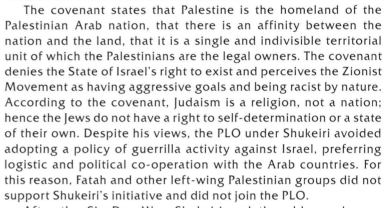

The Kinneret-Negev National Water Carrier

10 June

President Zalman Shazar pressed the button, the National Carrier pumps started working, and water started flowing from Lake Kinneret, through the Bet Nekofa Valley and Rosh Ha'ayin, to the Negev desert. The carrier, which took over 10 years to construct, was one of the largest development projects in Israel. Numerous pumping stations were built along its route, carrying 300 million cubic meters of water annually from Lake Kinneret to the south.

The activation of the National Carrier greatly angered the Arab world. Syria even demanded that the Arabs declare war on Israel. Egypt and Jordan preferred a more moderate approach, leaving the Syrians no choice but to initiate endless border skirmishes. The IDF was forced to retaliate severely against Syrian outposts. The PLO also earmarked the carrier as a primary target for attack. An attempt to sabotage it was thwarted and one of the terrorists was apprehended by the IDF.

Photo: GPO

The Pope in Israel:

An event "unprecedented in the history of mankind."

Pope Paul VI arrived on an historic visit to Israel. It was the first-ever visit to the Holy Land by the head of the Catholic Church. The Pope arrived from Jordan for only 11 hours and was received in a state ceremony at an archeological site near Megiddo by an Israeli delegation headed by President Zalman Shazar. The Pope, who never mentioned Israel in his speech, stressed that he was praying for the "nation of the covenant whose role in the history of religion [would] never be forgotten." This was a completely religious visit, and had no political significance, the Pope added.

President Shazar said that the Pope's visit was an event "unprecedented in the history of mankind." He added: "This land which Your Eminence has just entered is living proof that the prophets' vision of the ingathering of the exile and the revival of our sovereignty is actually being fulfilled." The president then gave the Pope a golden medal containing the map of Israel and an inscription in Hebrew and Latin: *He went on a pilgrimage to the Holy Land.*

After the ceremony, the Pope went to visit holy sites in Nazareth and the Galilee, and then traveled to Jerusalem. Mayor Mordechai Ish-Shalom received him with salt and bread at the entrance to the city, and the entourage continued to Mount Zion and the Dormition Abbey. The Pope returned to Jordan that same evening. The papal visit was extensively covered by the international media, which stressed that the visit represented a reconciliation between Judaism and Christianity. In Israel, criticism was voiced about the fact that the state reception had been held at Megiddo, not in Jerusalem. "It is a national humiliation," the critics said; but Prime Minister Levi Eshkol rejected the criticism, saying: "We shall walk tall to the Yizre'el Valley and meet him on Hebrew soil."

Pope Paul VI accompanied by President Shazar during his historic tour of Israel. Photo: David Eldan, GPO

Jabotinsky's Remains Brought to Israel

9 July

Some 24 years after the death of Revisionist leader Ze'ev Jabotinsky, the Israeli Government decided to grant his family's request to bring the remains of Jabotinsky and his wife Johanna for burial here. Jabotinsky, buried in the United States, wrote in his will: "If I am buried abroad, my remains are to be moved to Israel only upon the orders of a Jewish government, for I am certain one will be formed."

Herut leader Menachem Begin initiated the move, and Prime Minister Levi Eshkol granted the request, despite David Ben-Gurion's sharp opposition. Ben-Gurion considered Jabotinsky an ideological adversary who should not be forgiven even after his death. Jabotinsky was buried in a state ceremony on Mt. Herzl in Jerusalem.

Menachem Begin heading the guard of honor of Herut leaders accompanying the coffins of Johanna and Ze'ev Jabotinsky. Photo: Moshe Pridan, GPO

1.1.64

Yitzhak Rabin Appointed Chief of Staff

Yitzhak Rabin was appointed chief of staff at the age of 42 only after Ben-Gurion resigned as prime minister. Rabin was one of the most prominent commanders of the Palmach [the pre-state army], but Ben-Gurion had delayed his promotion because he had attended the rally protesting the dismantling of the Palmach, despite a specific order that banned officers on active duty from doing so. The fact that Rabin was associated with Yig'al Alon and the *Ahdut Ha'avoda* Party did not help his military career either.

Things changed when Levi Eshkol became prime minister and defense minister at the end of 1963. He decided not to extend the term of Tzvi Tzur, who was considered a Ben-Gurion and Peres man, and appointed Rabin – thus indicating that his main appointments would not be affected by Ben-Gurion's stands.

As soon as he assumed the post, Rabin called on former Palmach officers to join him on the General Staff, approaching commanders such as David Elazar, Yeshayahu Gavish, Uzi Narkis and others. One of the first public comments he made was the following: "Weapons are raw material. A gun is merely an instrument. If the man who holds it knows how to operate it well, it becomes effective and dangerous."

Yitzhak Rabin – the seventh IDF chief of staff. Photo: GPO

"Ben-Gurion, You Are Starting Fires!"

12 November

This was the accusation Prime Minister Levi Eshkol leveled at Ben-Gurion during a stormy session of the Mapai Central Committee. There was an unprecedented clash between the two, caused by another of Ben-Gurion's attacks on Pinchas Lavon, calling him a traitor, as well as the Mapai-*Ahdut Ha'avoda* merger. In reaction to the merger, Ben-Gurion announced that he was quitting the party. Levi Eshkol handed in his resignation to the president, again over the Lavon affair, but formed a new cabinet several days later. "The Affair" was pushed aside.

Moshe Dayan Resigns

3 November

Agriculture Minister Moshe Dayan resigned as a result of disagreements with Prime Minister Eshkol. In his letter of resignation, he wrote: "I could not continue serving as a cabinet member because I did not identify with the prime minister, which I should." Dayan's associates said that he was unhappy with the political line of Eshkol's cabinet.

1964

7 July

Actress Sophia Loren Arrives in Israel

Actress Sophia Loren arrived in Israel to act in the title role in the movie Judith. Her luggage – several trunks, a hairdresser's chair and personal effects – arrived at Haifa Port.
Above: Sophia Loren and Peter Finch in Judith.

10 June

The National Water Carrier was launched in a ceremony attended by President Shazar. The carrier conveyed water from the Kinneret – via canals, pipes and tunnels – to the Negev.

9 July

The Israeli Government decided to bring the remains of Ze'ev and Johanna Jabotinsky to Israel for burial. The move was initiated by Herut leader Menachem Begin.

5 August

Taxi drivers staged a general strike demanding a raise in rates.

10 September

The first families arrived in Carmiel – a new township in the north.

Photo: GPO

3 November

Moshe Dayan resigned as agriculture minister. He was replaced by Haim Gvati.

14 December

Levi Eshkol resigned as prime minister due to confrontations with Ben-Gurion over "The Affair". He formed a new government several days later.

National soccer team champions (left to right) Shlomo Levy, Mottele Spiegler and Motzi Leon holding the Asia Cup. Photo: GPO

3 March

Prime Minister Levi Eshkol Married the Knesset Librarian – Levi Eshkol married 34-year-old Miriam Zelkovich, the Knesset librarian. Ms Zelkovich, Eshkol's third wife, had been a friend of the family for years. His second wife, Elisheva, died in 1959. Miriam was described as a kind and modest lady of medium height, good looks, and simple but good taste. She held a Masters' degree in history, and specialized in the Middle Ages.

Levi Eshkol with Ms. Miriam Zelkovich, the Knesset librarian.

Mordechai Luke at Lod Airport after being turned over to Israel.
Photo: Aharon Yoselevich

16 November

Mordechai Luke, the Man in the Box, in Israel – Mordechai Luke was turned over to Israel after an abortive attempt by the Egyptian Embassy in Rome to smuggle him to Egypt in a box.
Three Egyptian diplomats were arrested a week earlier in Rome under suspicion of trying to kidnap a 30-year-old Israeli in a box. The Rome Airport police prevented the box from being loaded onto the plane when they heard moans and groans from inside it. Luke was found chained and drugged inside the box. Two days later, it became apparent that he was Mordechai Luke, a criminal from Petach Tikva who had escaped to Egypt in 1961 after involvement in a series of crimes. Interrogated in Israel, Luke said that he had been working for the Egyptian intelligence in Europe, engaging in economic espionage. According to him, however, he had provided no valuable information, but had only fed them false reports that confused them – which is why they had tried to kidnap him. Upon his request, he was returned to Israel on 25 November. Getting off the plane he said: "Don't hold on to me; I won't run away." He was sentenced to 13 years in prison for spying for Egypt.

3 June

Israel Wins the Asia Soccer Cup

Israel won the Asia Soccer Cup after beating South Korea 2:1 in the finals at the Ramat Gan Stadium in the presence of 35,000 spectators.

(*1965*

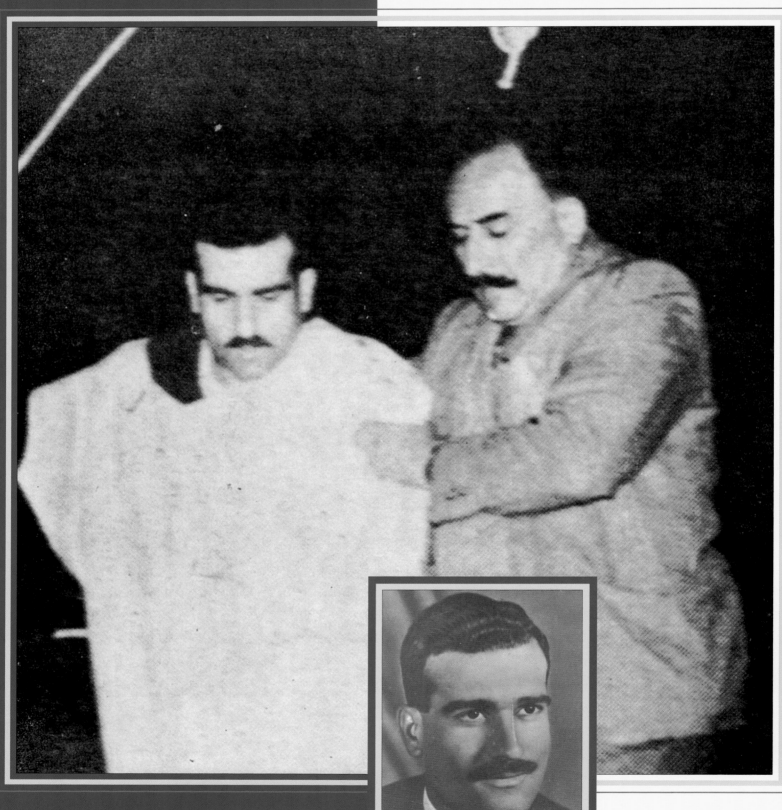

Eli Cohen taken to the gallows in Damascus. Photo: AP

Ever since Eli Cohen's execution, Israel has been trying to bring his body back to Israel for burial. Photo: GPO

Eli Cohen "May the Lord avenge his blood!"
The Undercover Warrior

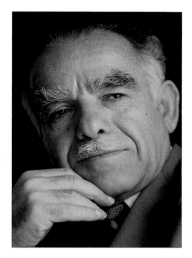

Former Prime Minister
Yitzhak Shamir

It was 1965, two years before the Six Day War, which led Israel to the highest military, political and economic achievements and earned it enormous prestige around the world and in Jewish communities.

As often happens during drastic changes, the period of dazzling success was preceded by gray and sad times. Israel was burdened with grave defense and economic difficulties. There was a sense of gloom, accompanied by apocalyptic jokes such as the last Israeli to leave should not forget to turn off the lights. One day in May, Israel was shocked by a report that an Israeli had been executed in Damascus in the middle of the night. His body was put on display, wrapped in a white sheet inscribed with a list of the amazing crimes of espionage he had committed for Israel. Syrian, Lebanese and other Arab newspapers were full of wondrous stories about the legendary achievements of the Israeli spy who had arrived in Damascus and for 4 years, provided the Israeli enemy with Syria's most classified security secrets.

According to the Arab press, Eli Cohen was born in Alexandria, Egypt, in 1924. His parents had immigrated there from Syria. He was an excellent student at the Jewish school and studied engineering at the Faruk University. He immigrated to Israel in 1957 and settled in Bat Yam. He worked as an accountant, married Nadia, an immigrant from Iraq, had children and lived a quiet family life until friends and associates learned about his character and talents. He joined the Israeli Intelligence in the early 1960s.

He was trained as an agent and, in 1961, his had commanders decided to build a cover story for him. He was to pose as an Arab who had been born in Lebanon, had immigrated to Argentina and had decided to return to the Middle East. He was sent to Argentina, where he received an ID card identifying him as Kamal Amin Tabat, a businessman. Quite easily, Cohen befriended several Arabs of Lebanese and Syrian origin and made a name for himself as a successful and serious man who cared about the Arab cause was an earnest supporter of the Syrian Ba'ath party, and wished to settle in Syria.

Cohen arrived in Damascus in 1962. He rented an apartment in a luxurious part of the Syrian capital and established a reputation as a successful businessman. He befriended mainly military men with whom he traveled all over the country. He had many friends, including some very prominent ones who spent time with him in his handsome apartment, in an atmosphere of carefree luxury. He gleaned extensive and valuable information from his conversations with his friends, which helped him answer queries from his Israeli commanders. The newspapers said that while he lived in Damascus, he sent hundreds of messages to Israel, thus enabling his operators to form a correct and balanced analysis of the situation in Syria. He used to travel on business to Europe every six months, where he met his contacts and received both money for expenses and instructions for future activities. During these trips, he also visited his growing family in Bat Yam.

The routine of short trips to Europe and brief visits home must have been difficult for him. His wife Nadia said that during his last visit, he was sad and nervous. Undoubtedly aware of the risks he had been taking, he nevertheless decided to continue his double life and returned to Damascus. It may be assumed that his operators had told him he was doing well, although, as the story goes, he had been warned not to make too many transmissions, as these might expose his activities. The Arab papers said that Cohen's lifestyle and multiple contacts with the military eventually made the Syrian security services suspect him, and they started following him.

There are various accounts of how he was caught. According to several sources, he was picked up by a radio detector and caught while transmitting to Israel. At first, he tried to deny his identity and mission but, after being subjected to severe torture, he revealed his modus operandi and even told his interrogators of the orders he had received on his last trip. It is said that the Syrians tried to force him to continue communicating with Israel but, following a prearranged stratagem, he managed to inform his operators that he had been caught.

His interrogation and trial lasted 3 months. He was hanged on 18 May 1965. Before he was executed, he was allowed to meet the Damascus rabbi and send a letter to his wife, asking her to remarry so that his children have someone to look after them. His Israeli operators went to great lengths to rescue him and the best French lawyers were hired, but they were not allowed to meet with him. Syria was offered large sums of money, and prominent international figures and organizations intervened on his behalf, but to no avail.

More than 30 years have passed since then. The Israeli public will forever remember Cohen as an honest and serious man who was devoted to his people and his country, and who operated with a deep conviction that he was serving his nation despite enormous but necessary risks. The image of his body dangling from a rope is etched in the hearts of many Israelis, and his name is spoken with reverence.

There are few like him in the Israeli Hall of Fame. Many heroes fought their peoples' enemies courageously, but few were spies, undercover warriors, who constantly risked their lives in solitude, conducting a war of minds. Eli Cohen is a member of the magnificent tribe along with Sarah and Aharon Aharonsohn, Avshalom Feinberg, Lishansky and Belkind – the members of Nili. And as the name "Nili" suggests ("The glory of Israel will not fail"), Eli Cohen's name will live forever in the memory of the people.

18.5.65

Eli Cohen Hanged in Damascus:
"I Went to Syria on a Mission for the Israeli Intelligence."

Eli Cohen: "The greatest Israeli spy ever to operate in an Arab capital." Photo: AP

Eli Cohen, our man in Damascus, was hanged at dawn in the Damascus Square of Saints with his hands tied behind his back and his body covered in a white sheet with an inscription reading: "Eli Cohen – sentenced to death by hanging." At midnight, Cohen was taken from the prison to the police headquarters in the heart of Damascus, and from there to the gallows in the square. He looked stunned, but calmed down a little after writing his last letter to his family. In the letter, he asked his wife Nadia to forgive him, to look after herself, and to give their children a good education. "Nadia darling, you are entitled to marry another man in order to provide our children with a better future... I ask you not to mourn what has happened, but to look to the future."

After writing the letter, Cohen walked to the gallows. The executioner held his arm as he walked up the steps, and then put the rope around his neck. Cohen was pronounced dead 90 seconds later, but his body was left hanging for another six hours. The Syrians described Eli Cohen as "one of the greatest Israeli spies ever to operate in an Arab capital." For nearly four years, he had sent coded messages to Israel on a small radio transmitter that he kept in his apartment, close to Syrian army headquarters. He was apprehended after the Syrian intelligence services began suspecting him, and a Syrian citizen identified him as a Jew who had been born in Egypt. His last message to Israel was composed by the Syrians. It read: "Kamal and his friends will be staying with us for a while... We will soon inform you of the fate of the others."

Cohen joined the Mossad and was sent to Syria after spending some time in Argentina where he associated with the local Syrian community and made a name as a successful businessman with family in Syria. He arrived in Damascus as a rich immigrant, under the name of Kamal Amin Tabat and quickly befriended members of the top Syrian echelons. He relayed information of supreme importance to Israel, mainly about Syrian Army movements and deployment along the Israeli border, and about critical decisions taken by Syrian leaders. For this reason, his exposure caused shock waves among the Syrian leadership. During the trial, Israel offered to exchange him for Syrian POWs, but Damascus rejected the offer, as it did the other pleas from various world leaders to pardon Cohen and not execute him.

Speaking in an interview with a Syrian reporter 24 hours before his execution, Eli Cohen said: "I went to Syria on a mission from the Israeli intelligence to secure a future for my wife, my children and my family... It was only for them that I was willing to undertake such a risky mission... I did not betray Israel."

Teddy Kollek – Mayor of Jerusalem
30 November

Teddy Kollek, the man whose name has been associated with Jerusalem more than any other, was elected mayor in November 1965, winning the seat from Mordechai Ish-Shalom, a Mapai member. Kollek, who was one of Ben-Gurion's boys and even served as director general of the Prime Minister's Office, ran in the municipal elections at the head of the Rafi list. After he was elected, he said: "If I had to draft a platform that would unite all the parties in the city, I would only say the following: 'Ask for Peace for Jerusalem.'"

The Six Day War, which broke out after Kollek had been in office for 17 months, united the two parts of Jerusalem. Kollek transformed Jerusalem from a small town into one of the world's most important cities. During his term of office, the city experienced unprecedented development and doubled its population. Kollek spent 28 years in the job he loved so dearly. On 2 November 1993, he lost the mayorship to Likud member Ehud Olmert.

Teddy Kollek: "Ask for Peace for Jerusalem." Photo: David Rubinger

The Mapai Split:

"This man does not deserve to stand at the helm!"

1965

At the Mapai conference of February 1965, Ben-Gurion and his men made two demands: (1) that the Lavon affair be examined by state institutions, and (2) that the electoral system be changed. Both demands were rejected by a majority of 60%, and Ben-Gurion lashed out angrily at Prime Minister Eshkol, saying: "This man does not deserve to stand at the helm!" He called on the party to name another candidate for prime minister in the next elections. The Mapai infighting grew stronger and Ben-Gurion's supporters quit the cabinet. There would definitely be a split.

At the end of June, Ben-Gurion summoned his people and announced that he was forming a new party: Rafi – Israel's Workers' list. The party split occurred. Shimon Peres joined Rafi at once, although he was not absolutely sure about the move. Moshe Dayan hesitated for a few days, and then also joined. Ben-Gurion explained in an interview, "We are not splitting Mapai; the only way to keep the real Mapai alive is by running separately in the elections."

Mapai decided to punish the dissidents. After a stormy debate at the Party Conference on 11 June, the party decided to expel them. Ben-Gurion was tried by the party court, which ruled to remove him from the party's ranks.

Rafi held an extremely energetic campaign, but its showing in the 2 November elections was very disappointing. Despite the fact that the party was led by Ben-Gurion, Peres, Dayan and others, it won only 10 Knesset seats. The Alignment, headed by Levi Eshkol, surprised everybody by winning 45 seats.

David Ben-Gurion addressing a Rafi election rally: "We are not splitting Mapai." Photo: Moshe Pridan

The *Naturei Karta* Leader and the French Convert

28 July

A dramatic turn occurred in the affair of Rabbi Amram Balui's marriage to the French convert when the rabbi appeared in person before the ultra-Orthodox community court and signed a pledge stating that he would not marry her if the court did not approve. *Naturei Karta* activists who opposed the marriage sent copies of the letter to various rabbis and public activists so that they could all see that the matter was not yet over.

Convert Ruth Ben-David Balui with a picture of her husband, Rabbi Amram Balui. Photo: Zoom 77

3 January
An attempt to sabotage the National Water Carrier was foiled. This was the first terrorist action by Fatah. One terrorist was wounded and apprehended.

24 January
The Mapai leadership decided to take disciplinary action against persons held responsible for ethnic-oriented grouping in the party.

17 February
At the Mapai conference, there was a serious clash between Ben-Gurion on the one hand and Levi Eshkol and Moshe Sharet on the other over the Lavon affair.

14 March
Israel and West Germany officially announced their decision to establish diplomatic relations. The Knesset approved the cabinet resolution on 16 March.

18 March
Shimon Agranat was appointed Supreme Court president, replacing Yitzhak Olshan.

26 April
A new political bloc was set up: Gahal. It comprised the Herut Movement and the Liberal Party. Following the merger, seven MKs quit the Liberal Party and formed the Independent Liberals.

18 May
Eli Cohen was hanged in Damascus after being convicted of spying for Israel.

19 May
Mapai and *Ahdut Ha'avoda* established "The Alignment" when the heads of both parties signed an agreement about running together in the elections for the Knesset, Histadrut and the municipalities.

3 June
Levi Eshkol was chosen as the Mapai candidate for prime minister.

127

Diplomatic Relations With Germany

16.3.65

PM Levi Eshkol: "Reason must prevail over sentiment."
MK Menachem Begin: "No absolution and no forgiveness."

The historic decision to establish diplomatic relations with the West German government was accompanied by heavy moral and emotional arguments and considerations. The decision was supported by 66 MKs and opposed by 29, while 10 abstained. Prime Minister Eshkol said, "...reason must prevail over sentiment... Our moral and historic account goes beyond any political act, but we must seize every opportunity we have to fortify the nation in its new homeland."

Herut leader, MK Menachem Begin, maintained that "...every German deserves to die... their hands are covered with Jewish blood... Therefore, there is neither absolution nor forgiveness, and no normal relations will ever be possible between us and them." After the resolution was passed, German Chancellor Ludwig Erhard said: "I feel a deep satisfaction that after years of tragedy and bad relations with Israel, we could find a basis for normal and fruitful relations." Bonn announced that it would provide Israel with economic aid to the tune of $50 million. This move enraged the Arab countries, and the Arab Foreign Ministers' Council decided to sever diplomatic relations with West Germany.

Spy Wolfang Lutz Caught in Egypt

7 March

Appearing on Egyptian TV, Wolfang Lutz told of his activities in the service of the Israeli intelligence, claiming that not all of the explosive packages he had received from Israel had been sent to the German scientists in Egypt. Lutz said that he and his wife had received $100,000, deposited to a Munich bank account, from Israel for his services. The "spy on the horse" added that the Israeli intelligence had ordered him to go to the Suez Canal region and file a report on the missile base there. Lutz showed TV viewers the wireless that he had kept hidden inside a kitchen scale. He said that he had instructions to destroy the wireless if he thought he might be exposed, but he was arrested before managing to do that.

"The Spy on the Horse," Wolfang Lutz. Photo: IPPA

10 May

The Israel Museum was Inaugurated

Photo: Ze'ev Hertz

The Israel Museum, the national home of art and culture, was inaugurated in Jerusalem in the presence of 1,600 dignitaries, including state leaders, foreign officials, museum directors from all over the world, and donors. Under the Management of Dr. Willem Sandberg and Israeli art curator Yona Fischer, the museum presented a new perception of art in Israel.

8 June

The Israel Broadcasting Authority was established after a bill by the same name was passed in the Knesset.

13 June

Prof. Martin Buber, one of the greatest Jewish philosophers, died at the age of 87.

29 June

Mapai split. Ben-Gurion announced that he was founding a new party, Rafi.

7 July

Moshe Sharet, former prime minister and foreign minister, died at the age of 70.

12 August

"The battle over water" continued on the northern front. IDF troops destroyed heavy Syrian equipment used to divert the Jordan River water sources, as well as three tanks.

2 November

Elections for the sixth Knesset were held: The Alignment under Eshkol won with 45 seats; Rafi under Ben-Gurion won only 10 seats.

21 January

The Shalom Tower

The tallest building in Israel, the Shalom Tower, was inaugurated in Tel Aviv by the Mayer family. The 36-floor building contained an area large enough for a department store, shops, restaurants and offices.

The Shalom Tower was erected where the Herzlia High School used to stand.
Photo: Efraim Kidron

23 August

The 7th Maccabia Opened in Ramat-Gan

The biggest Jewish Olympiad opened in the renovated Ramat Gan Stadium. The impressive opening ceremony was attended by 1,400 athletes from 30 countries. The ceremony included a magnificent display of exercises by 1,200 Young Maccabi members.

Photo: GPO

20 July

Young Tiberias Man Inherits IL22 Million

A young man from Tiberias, Meir Mizrachi, received IL22 million when a 70-year-old man died and left him the money as a reward for taking care of him when they shared an apartment and for handling the old man's money transfer to Israel.

(*1966*

**The termination of the
military government in
Bakka al-Gharbiya in
the Triangle.
Photo: Micha Bar-Am**

*A demonstration in Jerusalem in favor of terminating
the military government. Photo: Yig'al Mann*

The Termination of the Military Government
Discrimination on a National Background

Former MK
Azmi Bashara

The military regime was finally abolished in 1966. It had been imposed on the Israeli Arab residents of the Galilee and the Triangle and had served as the main channel through which relations between the state and that population had been organized since 1949, when the Arabs received Israeli citizenship – a precondition for the state's joining the UN. The military government was a daily reminder of the inherent conflict upon which the Israeli political entity was founded. On the one hand, the Declaration of Independence promised full equal rights to every Israeli citizen, regardless of religion, race or sex; on the other hand, some 18% of the Israeli population were living under the rule of a military government. The only difference between that and full military occupation was that the Arabs had been given the right to vote as citizens of the state.

No one can take citizenship seriously under a military regime. Even the most formal political rights lost their meaning in the face of the fear that marked the relations between the Arab citizens and the authorities. Fear was the law that governed those relations, a law under which all forms of political freedom of choice become paralyzed. The regional military governor had the authority to inflict direct punishment by imposing administrative detentions and issue restraining and restricting orders. He had the power to prevent the residents from earning a living by denying or canceling work permits or freedom of movement.

Through the military government, the state appeared to the Arab citizens as an occupying, hostile and ever-suspicious force. For the Arabs, there was no difference between the ruling party, the GSS, the army, the Arab department of the Histadrut, the Israel Land Administration or the JNF [Jewish National Fund]. They were all personified by the officer in charge or the GSS man. The military government did not only serve as an instrument of control over possible anti-Israel political activity, but also as a mechanism for recruiting votes for the ruling party and as a tool by means of which Arabs were deprived of their land – which then became nationalized or state-owned land from which the Arabs were excluded. Thus, the military government helped to turn the Arabs from farmers who worked their land into laborers in the Jewish market.

Another role played by the military government was preserving the traditional structure of the Arab village by placing mukhtars [village leaders] and heads of clans as middlemen between it and the population. When they applied for a work permit for a member of their village or asked for the appointment of a teacher, they pledged political loyalty. In addition, as terrorizing regimes always do, the military government operated a network of informers who dealt with even the finest details of everyday life, reporting on the papers the people read or the radio stations to which they listened, and even the names they gave their children.

The military government left a deep scar in the relations between the state and the Palestinian Arab minority in Israel. The Arab citizens were discriminated against even after that regime was abolished because as long as the state views itself as a Jewish state and the instrument for the realization of what it sees as the welfare of the Jews, relations between the Arabs and the state will remain unchanged. When the military government was abolished, the Arabs were allowed to benefit indirectly from the development of the Israeli economy and democracy, but this development was meant to serve the Jews. One may call this neglect or indifference; yet, when neglect and indifference are inherent in the way the state understands its role, we must call a spade a spade: discrimination on a national background.

One year after the termination of the military government, many more Palestinians fell under direct Israeli occupation. This time, those who stayed on their land were not granted citizenship.

10.12.66

Writer S.Y. Agnon Wins the Nobel Prize for Literature

For the first time in Israeli history, an Israeli writer won the Nobel Prize. Shmuel Yosef Agnon was born in Galicia. He lived in the Talpiot neighborhood of Jerusalem and wrote the novels *The Bridal Canopy, The Day Before Yesterday*, and many other simple and fascinating stories that made him the greatest modern writer of fiction in Hebrew. He shared the 1966 Nobel Prize for Literature with Nelly Sachs, a Jewish writer living in Sweden.

Swedish King Gustav V gave Agnon the award, saying: "May God give you many more creative years for your own people and for the whole world." Agnon replied in Hebrew: "Blessed is God for bestowing of his honor onto a flesh and blood king." In his speech, Agnon commented about the sources that influenced his work: "I will attempt to find out who gave me what. First, there are the Scriptures, the Bible, the Mishna, the Talmud and the Midrashim. After those, there are our holy arbiters and poets, and the wise men of the Middle Ages, first of whom is Maimonides... Moreover, I was influenced by every man, woman and child I met in my life... and so as not to deny anyone, I must mention beasts, animals and birds from which I learned and about which I wrote in my books... Finally, I wish to thank God for the privilege of living in the country He swore to give our forefathers and us... ."

Writer S.Y. Agnon. Photo: GPO

Before winning the Nobel Prize, Agnon won many other prizes, including the prestigious Bialik Award and twice the Israel Award "for his rich and unique stories and novels."

Samuel Josef Czaczkes was born in 1888, and his first poem was published in 1904 in Krakow in a Hebrew newspaper, *Hamitzpeh*. He immigrated to Israel in 1908 and published his story *Agunot* in a literary magazine under the name of S.Y. Agnon, which became his official *nom de plume*.

Left: S.Y. Agnon and his wife receiving the Nobel Prize in Stockholm. Photo: Reportagebild

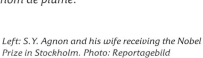
Photo: Avraham Vered

The IDF Raids the Jordanian Village of Samoa

13 November

IDF troops crossed the Jordanian border, reaching the southern Hebron Hills and demolishing dozens of houses in the village of Samoa and two other nearby villages. The operation came as a reaction to a series of terror attacks against Israeli targets, which had come to a head two days earlier when three IDF soldiers were killed and six wounded by a mine planted by infiltrators on the patrol road near the Jordanian border. The Samoa village operation was one of the largest since the Sinai Campaign. Some 18 Jordanian soldiers were killed, 44 wounded, and three taken prisoner. One Israeli soldier was killed: Lieutenant Colonel Yoav Shaham, the paratrooper battalion commander. In a dogfight that followed when the Jordanians started sending troops to the region, an Israeli Mirage downed a Jordanian Hunter. Prime Minister Eshkol said the operation was "a warning and retaliation designed to deter the Jordanian Government and the residents of the region from co-operating with terrorists operating against Israel."

The May Day Demonstrations:

"We Want Bread and Work!"

The year 1966 will be remembered as a time of recession. The Israeli Government launched a new and daring economic policy to curb the increasing prosperity. The government had several reasons for its decision to present a budget of recession: Large projects such as building the National Water Carrier, the Ashdod Port and the Dead Sea Works were ending; the slowdown in immigration caused a reduction in construction; and the Germans ended their payment of reparations. At the same time, security expenses increased, accounting for 50% of the GNP. The policy of recession was devised by the Eshkol boys, a group of young and talented economic experts who had joined the Treasury. Their policy consisted mainly of reducing the budget deficit by cutting down on government expenditures, eliminating subsidies on basic commodities, exposing Israeli industry to competing imports and a series of other steps which, all in all, increased unemployment.

In theory, the plan looked modern and promising, and even received positive reactions and comments. However, the euphoria came to an abrupt end when unemployed workers in Ashdod and Dimona clashed with marchers in the May Day parade, chanting: "We want bread and work!" The chants quickly turned into blows, stone-throwing and attacks on public buildings. The police were called in and soon there were injured and arrested workers as well as much bitterness about the authorities' attitude toward the unemployed.

The Knesset discussed the demonstrations, and Labor Minister Yig'al Alon said: "Violence, demonstrations and strikes will not solve the painful problem of the unemployed." But the problem kept growing. The policy of recession caused unemployment to reach 20% in the development towns. According to the National Insurance data, some 400,000 people lived under the poverty line that year. The feeling of resentment swept across the country. In 1966, the number of emigrants exceeded the number of immigrants. In the end, the policy of recession was a failure, stopped only by the Six Day War.

Unemployed workers demonstrating outside the Worker's Council in Petach Tikva. Photo: Fox

Instructional Television Goes on the Air

24 March

Instructional Television started its regular broadcasts for schools, making Israel the first country in the world to offer instructional television before it had a regular television channel. At first, the station, sponsored by the Rothschild family, broadcast nature, mathematics and English lessons with the teachers completing the material in school. In the 1970s, more programs were added and the station was placed under the authority of the Ministry of Education and Culture. During the Lebanon War, in 1982, the station started broadcasting a daily news magazine, *A New Evening*, and changed its name to Israel Educational Television.

1966

12 January

Levi Eshkol formed a new cabinet, noticeably appointing Aba Eban as foreign minister, Shapira as justice minister, and Galili as acting minister.

Photo: AGEP

10 February

A long strike began at the Ashdod Port over disagreements between the port management and the workers' union, headed by Yehoshua Peretz.

23 February

Post and telephone tariffs went up by 50%, which was expected to bring in IL60 million to the Israel Postal services.

1 March

Peace activist Abie Nathan was deported from Egypt after spending 24 hours in Port Said, during which he asked for an audience with President Nasser. The Egyptian daily *al-Ahram* wrote: "Abie is a pathetic clown."

24 March

Instructional Television starts regular broadcasts to schools.

16 April

The Coca Cola company opens a branch in Israel after many years of giving in to the Arab boycott. The move was expedited by the pressure of American Jewish businessmen.

25 April

In the Independence Day parade, the IDF displayed US-made Patton tanks and Super Perlon helicopters.

28.2.66

Abie Flies to Cairo

Abie Nathan took off in his plane, *Peace-1*, from the Herzlia airport at 08:15, heading for Cairo. He did not apply for an exit permit, nor did he co-ordinate his trip with the Egyptian authorities. "My only goal is peace, and my only hope is to contribute to peace between the two peoples," Abie told the al-Jamil Airport supervisor when he landed in Port Said. He later added: "I am here to meet with Egyptian President Nasser and hand him a petition for peace signed by 100,000 people."

Abie did not meet the president, but was allowed to return to Israel 24 hours after he had left. He was received with great sympathy by the crowds that gathered outside his Tel Aviv restaurant, *California*. However, the Cairo daily *al-Ahram* summed up Abie's peace flight thus: "It was a stupid comedy... Abie is a pathetic clown who deserves neither punishment or our attention."

Abie Nathan upon landing in Port Said, Egypt. Photo: AP

Abie Nathan went on his peace mission in a 40-year-old single-engine plane. Photo: AP

SS Man's Son Enrolls at the Hebrew University

4 September

A 21-year-old German, the son of a former SS officer, decided to enroll as a student at the Hebrew University in Jerusalem. Hans Manze decided to make the move to express his revulsion at his father's actions. The father was a Nazi war criminal who never stopped expressing his anti-Semitic views. The young man, who was already living in a youth hostel in Israel, announced that he was deeply impressed with the country and intended to study and even settle here.

An Iraqi Fighter Pilot Landed in Israel

15 August

Iraqi Pilot Munir Radfa landed in Israel with a USSR-made MiG-21, which is believed to be the most advanced jet used by the Egyptian, Syrian and Iraqi air forces. The landing was publicized worldwide and termed as "a great achievement for Israel and the West" because this was the first plane of its kind to arrive in the West. The pilot, who co-ordinated his move with the Israeli intelligence, explained his motives, saying: "I defected because I was not given a promotion to squadron commander."

Major General Motti Hod, Air Force commander, and the MiG-21. Photo: GPO

66

30 August

New Knesset Building Inaugurated in Jerusalem

Photo: Zoom 77

The new Knesset building on Givat Ram in Jerusalem was inaugurated in a state ceremony attended by the heads of the state, representatives of 50 parliaments and 47 Jewish communities, and 5,000 Israelis. The new edifice took five years to build and cost IL22 million.

26 April

Ezer Weizman retired as Air Force commander after eight years on the job. He was replaced by Motti Hod.

1 May

Stormy demonstrations were staged in Ashdod and Dimona against the government's policy of recession.

28 June

In a dramatic move, Herut Movement chairman Menachem Begin announced that he would not be running for the post again. The reason for the crisis was an attempted rebellion on the part of Shmuel Tamir and his associates.

30 August

The new Knesset building was inaugurated in Jerusalem. The state ceremony was attended by Israeli leaders, foreign parliamentarians, Diaspora representatives, and thousands of Jerusalem residents.

2 October

MK Ben-Gurion celebrated his 80th birthday in Sde Boker. Thousands of Israelis arrived to pay him their respects.

8 November

Prime Minister Levi Eshkol notified the Knesset that he was putting an end to the military regime imposed on the Arab villages in 1948.

10 December

In Stockholm, Sweden, S.Y. Agnon shared the Nobel Prize for Literature with Jewish poet Nelly Sachs, each receiving $30,000.

4 February

ZIM House Goes Up In Flames

ZIM House in Tel Aviv went up in flames. Dozens of workers and others who were in the building, unable to escape, gathered on the roof and were evacuated by Air Force helicopters. The pilots conducted amazing maneuvers, having very little room to move as well as near-zero visibility because of the smoke. People crowded the streets and avenues watching the scene and interfering with rescue operations. One man was killed and several dozen were injured in the fire.

Photo: GPO

20 November

Revolution in Milk Marketing in Israel

No more milk in bottles. The Tnuva company started marketing milk in plastic bags. But there is a catch: Milk will no longer be delivered to our homes – it will be sold in shops and supermarkets. A real revolution...

12 November

Tal Brody in Israel

Tal Brody arrived in Israel as a new immigrant. He fell in love with Israel when he was a member of the US basketball team at the 1965 Maccabia. He joined Maccabi Tel Aviv and then the national team. His arrival transformed Israeli basketball, moving it up a league. In 1967, during his first season with Maccabi Tel Aviv, the team reached the European cup-holders' finals for the first time. Brody's leadership, fighting spirit and belief that "no rival is invincible" changed conventional thinking, inspired everyone around him and made basketball very popular in Israel.

(19*67*

Defense Minister Moshe Dayan (center), Chief of Staff Yitzhak Rabin (right) and Major General Uzi Narkis entering the Old City through Lion Gate. Photo: GPO

Prime Minister Levi Eshkol hands over the Defense Portfolio to Dayan. Photo: IPPA

Moshe Dayan
A Myth That Should Not Be Shattered

Ariel Sharon

Moshe Dayan's magnitude as a natural leader who rose from the people, the fields and the battlefields constantly reminded his rivals of their natural size. Many could not forgive him for that.

I have no claim on Dayan, but I knew him better than many. Our paths crossed for nearly 30 years. We knew each other from the battlefields and became friends through occasional battles between wars.

I knew Moshe Dayan well. My memory of him consists of events, words and encounters. There was always the smell of soil, the memory of our country's landscapes, the caress of wheat; a "hot" mare running wild, and him bringing her under control in front of a group of amazed residents of a northern village; outside a Bedouin tent in the Lower Galilee at night; hissing embers, burning eyes, a fig plantation near Safed, loquat trees in Wadi Milek; him standing erect in front of the fire with a smirk on his face.

He could lean against a rock or lie on the ground and merge with them completely as easily as he sat in the parlors of the world's greatest. He could hold a conversation equally with an Arab farmer, a Bedouin shepherd and a foreign leader.

"As long as there are Arabs in this country, we will be able to live here," he told me once, ages ago, during a hike in the Galilee, "for only if we are constantly on guard will we handle this land." "If we become complacent, self-satisfied, or if our alertness falters for a moment, we will lose our willingness to pay the heavy price for living here."

He summed up his philosophical perception of living here in one sentence. When we returned to Kibbutz Kfar Aza from the raid on Gaza on the night of 28 February 1955, carrying our dead and wounded on our shoulders, he was there waiting for us. I approached him and told him that the mission was fully completed, but that the price had been high. He said wryly: "The dead are dead and the living live." In this brief sentence he delivered the harsh, albeit realistic message of Zionism in the last 100 years. There is a price to be paid for the establishment and bolstering of the Jewish state; and we should be willing to make a sacrifice, in many areas, any day or even any moment.

His perception of security was expressed in a statement in 1955: "We cannot ensure that no water pipe will be sabotaged and no tree uprooted; we cannot prevent the killing of workers in the field or families in their sleep; but we can make our blood very expensive."

In the 1950s, Dayan turned the IDF into an offensive army. No more Tel Hai heroism or Massada atmosphere. The war must be waged on enemy territory. Always, under all conditions, Dayan was the embodiment of this concept for the Jews and the whole world.

Our achievements in retaliation operations, the Sinai Campaign and – to top it all – the Six Day War would not have been possible if Dayan had not shaped the army in those stormy 1950s. He was the greatest revolutionary chief of staff the army has ever had. His imagination absorbed and encouraged operational plans. He invigorated the army. He set the fighting norms, the high standards. In his time, achievements were great because demands were high.

In his time, we started filing true battle reports. We also had basic principles to adhere to in our relations with the Arabs: reward and punishment, law and respect (punish when we should, never humiliate). He also set patterns for treating the enemy POWs which lasted for years.

I still remember his order to "take POWs on all fronts" so that we would be able to liberate our own POWs. The principle was: "We do not abandon comrades in the field and we do not leave soldiers in enemy hands." Indeed, we brought all our POWs back. These principles guided generations of soldiers.

He was politically daring. The small Israel of that time was involved in secret missions, international pacts and unknown fronts.

After the Yom Kippur War, many asked me – not too kindly – why I spoke in positive terms about Dayan and did not join those who condemned him. I replied: "Because he was the only one to come and visit us daily when we were in hell on earth. It was a hell of blood and fire, and few came to see it. He was there with us every day. Without him, the decision to cross the Suez Canal with my division, followed by additional forces, would not have been made. That move changed the fate of the war. It is important to remember that without it, there would not have been peace with Egypt".

What can we learn from Dayan, who left no clear-cut political legacies behind?

We can learn originality of thought, political daring and an insistence on the honor of Israel and the Jews as an essential factor in Israel's existence; ties with the homeland and its landscapes, and deep roots in the history of the people of Israel in its land – the land of the Bible; a correct defense policy to make the enemy aware of Israel's strength, thus removing the threat of war; the courage to stand outnumbered; getting to know the Arabs and learning how to live with them.

Dayan knew all of that.

May we learn from his deeds, which made him look bigger and go farther than most people of his generation.

19 67

What Sparked the War?

It started on 7 April, when the Syrians opened fire at Israeli tractors which had returned to work on the disputed land near Kibbutz Ha'on, east of the Kinneret. The IDF returned the fire. The Syrians increased their bombing and began shelling settlements in the region. Dozens of houses were demolished and an IDF officer was killed. IAF jets were sent to destroy the Syrian artillery batteries. Syrian MiGs were sent to intercept them, and the two air forces engaged in dogfights above Kibbutz Shamir. The IAF was given the go-ahead to pursue the Syrian jets into Syrian territory. Six Syrian planes were downed, two near Damascus. Syrian prestige was badly damaged. Based on a defense pact from 1966, Syria demanded that Egypt issue an immediate response to the Israeli provocation. Egyptian President Nasser faced a dilemma: If he reacted, the situation might escalate to war; if he did not, he would lose face in the Arab world. Egypt had not reacted to the massive IDF operation in the Jordanian village of Samoa and had been severely criticized by the Arab world.

While Nasser - as yet undecided - was examining the situation, Syria announced that Israel was amassing forces on the northern border, preparing an offensive. Israel denied this vehemently, but Soviet intelligence "confirmed" the reports to Egypt. Prime Minister Levi Eshkol invited the USSR ambassador to join him on a tour of the northern border and see for himself that there was no special army deployment. The ambassador refused. The Egyptian chief of staff was urgently summoned to Syria to "take a close look at the IDF concentrations near the Syrian border." Nasser was forced to protect his honor and status in the Arab world and ordered massive forces to be sent to the Sinai on 14 May. The snowball started rolling fast toward war.

Dozens of houses in the north were hit and demolished by extensive Syrian shelling. Photo: GPO

Egypt's President Nasser: "If Israel Wants War - *Ahlan Wasahlan*!"

Photo: London Express

22 May

After sending large forces to the Sinai, Egyptian President Nasser continued his provocation of Israel. He demanded that the UN evacuate its units from the Sinai and, when it did, he announced the closure of the Tiran Straits to Israeli vessels. Addressing his army officers in the Sinai, Nasser said: "The Tiran waters are ours; if the Israeli leaders and General Rabin want a war - *ahlan wasahlan* [welcome]... they will find our soldiers waiting for them." He then told the soldiers in the Sinai: "The people of Egypt and others are counting on you... each of us is willing to die for the most sacred cause... We are not intimidated by the imperialists... We shall march to victory..."

Nasser was fully backed by the USSR. The Soviet Prime Minister and the Communist Party's Central Committee sent a special message of support to Egypt "as it stands in the defense of its country and waters against the imperialists." The day after Nasser made his declaration, the army initiated the second stage of amassing forces in the Sinai, until it had some 80,000 troops there.

A National Unity Government: Calming Inner Pressures

1 June

The Israeli political scene was very stormy during the period of waiting. Many meetings were held and many ideas raised in an attempt to replace Levi Eshkol. Many doubted that he could lead Israel in trying times. Rafi members, headed by Shimon Peres, suggested that Ben-Gurion be recalled and made prime minister, but Mapai rejected the idea. Another suggestion, that Ben-Gurion join the cabinet as defense minister, was made, on condition that Eshkol leave the cabinet. That idea was rejected as well. Efforts were made to get Gahal and Rafi to join the cabinet, mainly to make Dayan defense minister. The national unity government was established on 1 June with three new ministers: Moshe Dayan as defense minister, and Menachem Begin and Yosef Sapir as ministers without portfolio.

The NRP tipped the scale eventually when it threatened to quit the coalition unless a unity government with Dayan as defense minister was formed at once. Dayan's appointment was very well received by the public, especially by the army, which perceived him as a leader who could lead it to victory.

The Waiting Period

Israel Prepares for War – Reserve Soldiers Called Up

Initial reports about Egyptian forces entering the Sinai reached Prime Minister and Defense Minister Levi Eshkol during the IDF parade in Jerusalem. The army decided to bolster its armored forces in the Negev, but not to call up reserve units as yet. The intelligence believed that Nasser's moves were a show of force designed to save face with the Arabs and demonstrate that his military move would prevent Israel from attacking Syria. However, on the following day, when Egypt demanded that the UN troops evacuate the Sinai, Israel started calling up its reserves. The call-up was gradual and ended on 19 May, after all UN troops had left the Sinai and Gaza.

Israel's city streets were empty and the economy was paralyzed. The top Israeli political and security echelons felt that Israel could not withstand this situation for a long time. Nevertheless, during the long waiting period, the supply of basic commodities did not cease, and the people on the home front behaved with great restraint. Many volunteered to help with transportation, food distribution and preparation of bomb shelters, as well as in factories and kibbutzim. There was an atmosphere of brotherhood and caring. The home front was doing well, but the situation at the front was much more complicated. Some 300,000 Israeli soldiers were deployed along the Egyptian border, anxiously awaiting the outbreak of war. Everyone was waiting for the cabinet to make a decision.

The frequent consultations that Eshkol and his ministers held were attended by Chief of Staff Yitzhak Rabin. He explained that the IDF was strong enough to repel any Arab attack and, if necessary it could also launch an offensive. Rabin stressed that he believed the army should attack as soon as possible, unless the government wanted time to try and solve the problem at the political level.

The political contacts started with messages from US President Lyndon Johnson calling on Israel to show restraint and let the tensions subside. Levi Eshkol responded that Israel would not be the first to attack. US Administration officials also asked Egypt not to escalate the situation further and not to prevent the freedom of passage through the Tiran Straits. In another attempt to calm the Egyptians, Prime Minister Eshkol announced in the Knesset that Israel did not seek war and was willing to promote peace and stability in the region, but the Egyptians did not heed the call. That same night, they announced the closure of the Tiran Straits, thus taking another step toward war.

Photo: Yitzhak Berez

On the home front, people volunteered and helped each other, while 300,000 soldiers waited on the front for the decision to go to war.

Photo: Yosef Lior

Chief of Staff Rabin Collapses

23 May

For Yitzhak Rabin, 23 May was a very busy day. He attended a meeting of the Ministerial Committee on Defense to discuss whether Israel should go to war or delay the decision by 48 hours. Ben-Gurion's words of the previous day still echoed in his ears: "You made a mistake... You should not have called up the reserves... You have placed the country in a very dangerous position, and you will be held responsible... You should not go to war... We are isolated..." Rabin agreed to wait 24 hours, as most ministers demanded. Then he had a meeting with the NRP Chairman Moshe Shapira, who also spoke harshly: "How dare you go to war when things are not in our favor? You will all be held responsible for jeopardizing Israel's safety..." This conversation had a bad effect on Rabin. That evening, he felt very tired and extremely gloomy; he had also smoked too much that day. He felt guilty of dragging Israel into a political and military morass. Eventually, he summoned Major General Ezer Weizman, then head of operations, told him how he felt and asked whether he should resign. Weizman calmed him down. A physician was called in and gave Rabin a tranquilizer that made him sleep through the next afternoon. Rumor of Rabin's collapse spread rapidly through the political ranks and eventually expedited the processes that led to the establishment of a national unity government and Dayan's appointment as defense minister.

Chief of Staff Yitzhak Rabin and Defense Minister Moshe Dayan. Photo: IPPA

The Six Day War

19**67**

IDF forces advancing toward Rafiah.
Photo: GPO

The IAF attacked airfields in the Sinai
and Egypt. Photo: GPO

The IAF destroyed the Egyptian,
Jordanian and Syrian Air Forces on the
first day of the war. Photo: GPO

5 June

The War Starts - The IAF Destroys Hundreds of Enemy Planes

In a few hours of massive and sophisticated attack, some 200 IAF jets managed to destroy the air forces of Egypt, Syria, and Jordan; 374 planes were destroyed on the ground and the rest were destroyed in dogfights. The IDF had complete aerial supremacy during the six days of battle.

In The South - The Divisions Charge

The IDF ground forces entered the Sinai in three columns. Yisrael Tal's division captured Chan Yunis, Rafiah and el-Arish, and surrounded Gaza; Ariel Sharon's division stormed the fortified zone of Abu-Agela; and Avraham Yaffe's division crossed the Egyptian border and advanced toward the rear of the Egyptian forces.

Jordan and Syria Attack Jerusalem and Haifa

The same morning, Jordan started shelling Jerusalem, firing its artillery day and night, inflicting casualties. Several shells were also fired from Kalkilya at the Dan District. At the same time, Syrian jets raided Haifa Bay and the northern settlements.

6 June

The Paratroopers Surround the Old City

The IDF troops moved forward throughout the whole of Samaria, conquering Latroun, Janin, Kalkilya and Ramallah in brief battles. Moshe Dayan ordered the Paratroopers' Brigade, under the command of Mordechai (Motta) Gur, to conquer the Old City of Jerusalem. The brigade conquered most of the Arab villages around the city and fought a very fierce battle in the bunkers on Ammunition Hill, where it sustained numerous losses and injuries.

The IDF Conquers Gaza

In the south, the IDF broke through the area of Umm-Ketef and Abu-Agela and took Gaza within a short time. That night, the Egyptian command ordered its troops to withdraw from the region and assume defensive positions at the Mitleh and Gidi Passes.

Water for a wounded soldier after the heavy battle on Ammunition Hill, Jerusalem. Photo: Starphot

IDF troops in Gaza.

Photo: GPO

The Egyptian military governor of Gaza signs the letter of surrender. Photo: GPO

141

The Six Day War

7 June

"Temple Mount Is in Our Hands... Temple Mount Is in Our Hands!"

At 10:00 a.m., the paratroopers broke through Lion Gate and liberated the Western Wall and Temple Mount. Motta Gur stood near the wall with his officers and announced on the radio: "Temple Mount is in our hands! I repeat, Temple Mount is in our hands!" After hours of fierce battles, the sweaty and weary paratroopers burst into tears. Major General Shlomo Goren, chief military rabbi, arrived at the site, blew the *shofar* and said a prayer: "This is the day we have been yearning for; let us rejoice in it."

The Navy Reaches Sharm al-Sheikh

The Israel Navy vessels that sailed out of Eilat reached Sharm al-Sheikh that afternoon and conquered the Tiran Straits without resistance. The paratroopers arrived later to complete the mission.

An Israeli battleship crossing the Tiran Straits after capturing them. Photo: GPO

Top: *Rabbi Goren blows the shofar at the Western Wall. Photo: GPO*

Bottom: *Paratroopers at the Western Wall. Photo: David Rubinger, GPO*

Right: *The Paratroopers' Brigade storms the Old City through Lion Gate. Photo: GPO*

Israeli vessels across from Sharm al-Sheikh.

1967

8 June

The IDF Reaches the Suez Canal

On the fourth day of the war, it became clear that the Egyptian Army had crumbled. The IDF advanced quickly to western Sinai, seizing Egyptian army bases and airfields. The IAF raided the withdrawing Egyptian convoys inflicting heavy damage. Thousands of Egyptian soldiers were left in the desert, separated from their units that were heading west, begging for food and water. At the end of the day, the IDF reached the Suez Canal, and the conquest of the Sinai peninsula was completed.

Thousands of Egyptians troops were left behind in the Sinai, separated from their units, without food or water.

On the fourth day of the war, IDF troops reached the Suez Canal, completing the capture of the Sinai. Photo: GPO

5 February

The government decided to pay unemployment benefits due to the significant rise in the number of unemployed as a result of the growing recession.

15 February

The Health Ministry decided to inoculate children against measles. The inoculation was administered mainly to under two-year-olds.

20 February

Rehav'am Ze'evi and Ariel Sharon promoted to major general.

14 March

Thousands of ultra-Orthodox Jews stage a demonstration in Jerusalem against performing autopsies. Dozens of demonstrators and policemen were injured during the riots.

31 March

A committee established to investigate the disappearance of Yemenite immigrants' children discovered documents according to which dozens had been adopted and approximately 100 had died of various diseases.

27 April

The Israeli national youth soccer team won the Asian championship for the fourth consecutive year.

15 May

During the IDF Independence Day parade, Chief of Staff Rabin was notified that Egyptian troops had started moving toward the Sinai.

16 May

The Atomic Energy Commission announced its opposition to bathing at Diplomats' Beach and Palmachim, near the Nachal Sorek nuclear reactor.

16 May

A partial reserve call-up began.

18 May

The UN abandoned its positions in the Gaza Strip, which were seized by Egyptian soldiers.

1967

The Six Day War

9 June

The IDF Charges the Golan Heights

Israeli tanks enter the city of Kuneitra in Syria. Photo: GPO

Major General David (Dado) Elazar, head of the Northern Command, was ordered by Defense Minister Moshe Dayan to launch an offensive against Syrian troops on the Golan early in the morning. During the battles at noon that day, most of the Syrian fortified posts, which had been terrorizing the Israeli settlements below, were captured by Israel. The battles were fierce. The IDF soldiers advancing on steep slopes were subjected to massive shelling that claimed casualties. The battles continued the next day, with the IDF storming Kuneitra. Damascus Radio announced that the city had fallen even before the IDF reached it, in order to pressure the UN Security Council to impose a cease-fire. The radio announcement, however, caused the Syrian residents to flee, and the entire Syrian deployment collapsed. By the time the cease-fire was enforced at 16:30, the IDF had completed the conquest of the Golan Heights. The Six Day War had ended.

Bottom: IDF troops conquer Tal al-Fahr on the Golan Heights.

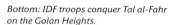
Photo: Ya'akov Sa'ar, GPO

67

15 June

Shavuot Celebrated at the Western Wall – Some 250,000 people came to celebrate Shavuot [Pentecost] in united and liberated Jerusalem. Although a temporary order banned this, hundreds climbed the new road to Mount Zion, walked down the stairs near the city walls, passed through Dung Gate and reached the Wall. The people wept, hugged and kissed the stones.

24 October

Rabbi Soloveichik: "The future of the territories is a matter for the government, not the rabbis."

Photo: Ya'akov Sa'ar GPO

Speaking before a religious gathering in the United States, Most Reverend Rabbi B.G. Soloveichik said: "I find the intervention of rabbis on the issue of which territories may or may not be returned to the Arabs completely unreasonable." The rabbi said further, "The entire matter of the territories is for political and security experts, not rabbinical meetings... The Israeli Government will act in accordance with security considerations, and its decision will be the rule." Speaking about holy sites, he explained: "I am fully aware of the sanctity of the Western Wall, Rachel's Tomb and the Cave of the Patriarchs; however, we must not go overboard. Judaism is not about holy places. Some places are sacred, but we do not sanctify graves... ."

15 May

Yerushalaim Shel Zahav [Jerusalem of Gold]

Naomi Shemer's song Yerushalaim Shel Zahav was commissioned by the organizers of the 1967 Israeli Song Festival and did not compete. Performed by Shuli Nathan, it became an instant hit. When the Six Day War ended, Jerusalem of Gold, originally a song of longing and nostalgia, became a victory anthem that was sung by the paratroopers who had conquered the Old City. On the same day, Naomi Shemer (in the picture) added two verses in honour of the new reality and performed them in front of IDF soldiers in al-Arish: "We're back to the water cisterns, to the market and the square. A shofar sounds on Temple Mount in the Old City."

14 May to 5 June

Israeli Artists Volunteer to Perform in front of the Troops – During the waiting period before the Six Day War, dozens of Israeli artists volunteered to perform in front of IDF troops. Singers, comedians and actors traveled all over and performed at any hour, some immediately on their return from abroad.

Arik Lavi, Shai K. Ofir and Uri Zohar performing in front of troops. Photo: Mula and Harmati

27 August

Lotteries in the Territories – The Mif'al Hapayis national lottery requested government permission to hold lotteries in the occupied territories as well because, among other things, the local residents who visited Israel showed a lot of interest. Those opposed to the idea expressed a fear of creating new points of friction by introducing an Israeli state-related institution into the territories

12 May

Oded Kottler wins the "Best Actor Award"

Oded Kottler, lead actor of the film Three Days and A Child won the "Best foreign actor award" at the Cannes Festival in France. The film was based on a novel by A.B. Yehoshua.

Oded Kottler in Three Days and a Child. Photo: Marian Vardi

12 June

POWs exchanged with Egypt: Israel returned 4,500 Egyptian POWs for 10 IDF soldiers.

28 June

East Jerusalem was annexed to Jerusalem, the Israeli capital.

28 June

Chief of Staff Yitzhak Rabin was awarded an honorary doctorate. He made his famous "Mount Scopus speech."

21 October

Israel Navy destroyer *Achi Eilat* was sunk across from Port Said when Egyptian boats attacked it with missiles. All 47 crewmen were killed.

23 October

In response, the IDF shelled the oil refineries in Suez, and the newspapers reported: "Suez is on fire – the city is in a sea of flames."

30 October

The Movement for Greater Israel was established, combining all the movements that opposed making territorial concessions in Judea, Samaria and Gaza.

(1968

The Israel Television newsroom, minutes before going on the air. Left to right: Mordechai (Motti) Kirschenbaum, Yoram Ronen, Haim Yavin and Dan Biron. Photo: Aharon Zuckerman

The Israel Television control room, Romema, Jerusalem. Photo: GPO

The First Israel Television Broadcast
All the achievements and all the mishaps

TV Anchorman
Haim Yavin

It was like a scene from a thriller – midnight, and we were standing in a dark and empty room, poring over maps and sketches. A table lamp lit our faces, casting huge shadows on the ceiling. We were trying to figure out just how many producers and directors Israel Television (ITV) would require once it got started, but paradoxically, we didn't really know how many hours we would broadcast – and what would go on the air. We worked in the dark. Then came frustration, impatience, anger. The first ITV workers wanted to broadcast, not push paper.

This drama took place in the offices of the ITV founding team – two humble rooms on 16 Shamai Street in Jerusalem. We used to come here every morning, dreaming of building the best TV station in the world.

One morning in February 1968, as I was making my way to the office as usual for another weary day of charts and sketches, the radio broadcast an item about preparations for the approaching IDF Independence Day parade, which was supposed to be the Six Day War victory parade. In the office, I ran into Elihu Katz, head of the founding team. "How about us broadcasting the IDF parade on TV?" I asked. Everyone in the room smiled gloomily. The idea sounded like a bad joke, at best.

Louis Lantin was standing right next to us. He was an Irish director who had come to help; an uncompromising man. "We can do it," he insisted. I went back to Katz. "Think of the prestige," I told him. "The first ITV broadcast will be the IDF victory parade!"

Katz was jalmost convinced when we suddenly remembered that we did not have a mobile broadcasting unit or even a studio; we had nothing. Uzi Peled, Katz's deputy, said that it so happened that he was going to London the next day. "If you find a mobile unit...," Elihu Katz said with a sheepish smile. Peled cabled us from London: He had found a mobile unit, made by Intel, used but in good shape, for £235,000. "Buy it!" Katz ordered. A week later, a gigantic deep blue studio on wheels rolled into Nachalat Shiv'a Alley. "She's old, but she's a beauty," said the technician who stepped out.

Lantin was made director, Yoram Ronen the announcer, and I the producer of the first ITV broadcast. We placed four cameras along the parade route, the Ramallah-Jerusalem road, and another on the roof of the Notre Dame Church. The Irish director could not speak a word of Hebrew, and the crew could not understand his orders. The army rehearsed at night and in the dark we could not tell whether the marchers were paratroopers or Armored Corps men, nor could we distinguish between an Israeli armored personnel carrier and a captured Egyptian tank. Ronen, the broadcaster, could only guess.

The 1968 Independence Day arrived and I went to the mobile unit at the bottom of French Hill. I was very excited. First time on the air, the IDF victory parade, and I was the producer! At 10:00 sharp, Lantin yelled: "Roll VTR!" The parade got under way and... it was nothing like the nocturnal rehearsals. We threw away our clipboards and started improvising. Ronen was speaking while I translated it for Lantin who, sitting in the tiny, blazing and crowded control room, kept yelling: "Tell me, tell me what comes next!"

And the marchers marched and marched and marched.... When it was all over, I went out to take a breath of fresh air and a happy man ran up to me. It was Elihu Katz, who hugged and kissed me and said in a faint voice: "We did it!"

The critics responded immediately. The next morning, *Ha'aretz* wrote: "ITV has just been born and it is already taking political orders from the government: Moshe Dayan was not shown even once!" But we knew the truth. Dayan had not been seen because it had all been one big mess...

Every ITV achievement and mishap was there in that first broadcast. We broadcast the parade – a complicated operation even for a veteran and organized station – without even a studio because everyone was impatient. Everyone – the TV workers and managers and the political establishment – wanted instant TV.

Sure there was a lot of personal ambition involved, but there was also devotion and integrity, daring and *chutzpah*. These were the qualities that made ITV what it is today. It was born out of the storm of the Six Day War with an idealistic and naïve vision of helping to promote peace. But television does not make peace. On the contrary: its close-ups only succeeded in bringing rival camps into confrontation. Our reports about the settlements angered the Palestinians and reports on terror attacks upset the Israelis. It helped pit *Gush Emunim* against *Peace Now*, religious against secular, Jews against Arabs.

Yet, at the end of the day, TV with its close-ups is the only medium that connects humans, regardless of race, religion or sex. It enables everyone to see the face of a rejoicing man or the image of a suffering victim – a victim of deprivation, discrimination, persecution, crime, terror or war.

25.1.68

The *Dakar* Submarine Is Missing: Questions, Grief and Shock

Photo: GPO

The last message from the *Dakar* submarine was received at the Haifa Naval Base on Thursday at 12:12. The transmission was bad and disjointed but bore no signs of distress. It had been a very hard winter, and that day was particularly stormy. The *Dakar* vanished without a trace, leaving questions and doubts, grief and shock. Navy vessels and IAF planes went out to search for it, aided by units from four other countries. At first, the Navy was optimistic, as there was great confidence in the abilities of the *Dakar*'s experienced commander, Ya'akov Ra'anan. As the hours went by, the optimism was gradually replaced by deep concern.

The *Dakar* had sailed from Portsmouth, England, after undergoing repairs and having a rescue cell for the sailors installed in it. It crossed the Straits of Gibraltar on its way to Israel, progressing on schedule. A more advanced and modern French submarine, the *Minerve*, disappeared mysteriously at the very same time.

Numerous speculations have since been made about the cause of the *Dakar*'s disappearance. The most plausible assumption was that the submarine had violated diving restrictions, but Navy experts, who knew the skills of the commander, could not accept it. Other possible reasons were a mechanical fault or an encounter with a Soviet submarine that sank it. The Egyptian government announced that it had not been involved. When all hopes of finding the *Dakar* faded, the foreign units returned to their bases. Israel continued its extensive searches, including Egyptian territorial waters, after obtaining permission from the Egyptians.

Eventually, Israel had to call off the search, and the *Dakar* and its 69 crewmen were pronounced missing. On 9 February 1969, a distress buoy was found on the shores of Chan Yunis. This led to more speculation that the submarine had released it in order to signal distress. The cause was never known

A memorial ceremony for the 69 Dakar submarine crewmen was held at sea on board the destroyer Yafo. Photo: GPO

The Dakar submarine and its crew before its last voyage

Heavy Battles at the Canal: The Suez Refineries Burn

26 October

The Egyptian artillery started shelling IDF bases along the Suez Canal heavily, killing 14 soldiers and wounding 31. Egypt had hoped that an escalation in the situation would compel the superpowers to intervene and force Israel to withdraw. The IDF retaliated with a series of raids on specific targets deep in the Egyptian rear. Most of the operations were successful because they were surprise attacks, performed swiftly by IDF elite units. The operations caused economic and military damage as well as heavy casualties. In response to attacks on IDF troops at the canal, the IDF shelled the Suez refineries on 26 October, setting them ablaze.

The Egyptian artillery action abated after these operations. As a result of the lessons learned from the artillery fire, it was decided that the IDF would bolster its fortifications which faced the Egyptians. Thus, the IDF adopted a defensive rather than an offensive doctrine - and this proved to be wrong during the Yom Kippur War.

Photo: Avraham Vered

The Karame Operation In Jordan

Paratroopers, Armored Forces and the IAF

In the wake of frequent infiltrations from Jordan and the inefficacy of IAF raids on terrorist bases, the IDF command decided to launch a daring and extraordinary ground operation. A large IDF force, accompanied by tanks and protected by aerial cover, crossed into Jordan and captured the village of Karame. The village was a known launching pad for terror activities and housed the Fatah headquarters. Leaflets distributed by the IDF to the villagers said: "Go to your houses immediately. Those who have weapons should place them in the street. Close your windows and doors and stay inside. Remember, we have nothing against you."

The aim of the operation was to make the terrorists feel insecure in their own territory. The operation was going well when the Jordanian Army, upset by the invasion, decided to intervene, and sent large forces to the village. A heavy and bloody battle ensued, and the IDF soldiers found themselves greatly outnumbered. They managed to pull out, killing some 60 Jordanian soldiers and some 150 terrorists. However, Israeli troops also sustained 28 fatalities, and some of the bodies were left behind. They were returned to Israel later. The IDF lost many vehicles and tanks, and even an IAF plane was hit and crashed in Israeli territory.

A stormy public debate arose about the necessity of the Karame operation, which seemed to have been a failure. The IDF had indeed proved that it could attack terrorists anywhere, but the terrorists had shown that they could fight back and cause serious damage. Although the terrorists continued to brag about their success in the Karame operation, the number of infiltrations was significantly reduced.

The Karame Operation – A bloody battle that started a public debate in Israel.
Photo: Shmuel Shaham.

Photo: Shmuel Shaham

21 January

The Labor Party was established when Mapai, *Ahdut Ha'avoda* and Rafi decided to merge.

25 January

The submarine *Dakar* disappeared en route from Britain to Israel.

20 February

Yitzhak Rabin assumed the post of Israeli ambassador to the United States. Haim Bar-Lev replaced him as chief of staff.

18 March

A bus carrying Tel Aviv high-school students went over a mine near Eilat. Three escorts, including a doctor, were killed and 16 students were badly wounded. Three days later, the IDF launched an extensive retaliation operation against the village of Karame in Jordan.

12 April

A group of religious Jews celebrated Passover in Hebron and announced that it had gone there to revive Jewish settlement in the city. The group stayed at the Park Hotel. Shortly afterwards, the government approved the establishment of Kiryat Arba.

1 July

Yig'al Alon was appointed deputy prime minister and minister of absorption.

23 July

An El Al plane en route from Rome to Israel was hijacked by Palestinian terrorists and landed in Algiers. The plane and passengers were released after 39 days of captivity.

Photo: GPO

"It's Moshe Dayan! A Mountain Fell On Him!"

20 March

"I swear on my mother's life! I'm not kidding. It's Moshe Dayan! A mountain fell on him!" This famous sentence was yelled by Gershon Birenboim at an archeological excavation site in the Holon industrial zone when a clay wall collapsed on Moshe Dayan, who was digging there. Birenboim and his son dug the shocked and injured Dayan out. He was rushed to the hospital where it turned out that his injuries were minor. He had suffered three broken ribs and a damaged vertebra. Israelis wondered how such a prominent and essential person could take such unnecessary risks.

28.12.68

"The Skies of Beirut Were Illuminated by Fire"

After a year of numerous and varied terror attacks, the terror organizations shifted to international activity against Israeli targets abroad, such as El Al planes and embassies. In retaliation, the IDF decided to attack Beirut Airport. A commando unit was flown in by helicopter and landed in the Lebanese capital in the middle of the night. The IDF soldiers blew up 13 civilian planes belonging to Arab companies, causing damage estimated at $100 million, but no casualties. *The New York Times* reported: "The skies of Beirut shone brightly, illuminated by the huge fires that burned for a long time."

The operation, which was a great military success, sparked a great deal of anger against Israel. The French government, which considered itself responsible for Lebanon, was particularly angry. France decided to cancel planned weapon deals with Israel. Other countries also wondered how Israel, which had been protesting against terror attacks for years, could employ the same methods. While the operation boosted the people's morale and strengthened the IDF's power of determent, it caused a political debate about its scope and necessity.

Hand Grenade Thrown in the Cave of the Patriarchs

9 October

Forty-seven people, mostly Jews, were injured when a hand grenade was thrown at a group of worshipers who were waiting to enter and pray at the Cave of the Patriarchs. The blast also damaged the site. The defense forces initiated a hunt for the culprit.
The incident caused great tension in Hebron and many shops were closed. The IDF had to beef up its forces in the city, and security measures around the site were intensified for the safety of the worshipers.

Photo: GPO

Beirut Airport after the IDF blew up 13 civilian planes.

The Labor Party Founded

21 January

Mapai, *Ahdut Ha'avoda* and Rafi decided to merge into a single party called Labor - despite Ben-Gurion's opposition. Golda Meir stayed on as secretary-general since Mapai constituted some 60% of the new party; the other two parties accounted for 20% each. This was followed by a cabinet reshuffle.

68

1968

1968

Military Bands Spring up

Photo: Nahum Guttman

With the IDF deployment covering vast territories, military bands began springing up after the Six Day War. Every branch wanted its own representative troupe, and thousands of bases, outposts and units were thirsty for entertainment. In two years, the number of performing military troupes rose from 4 to 17. The bands crisscrossed Israel in broken-down trucks and always constructed their own stages. The success of the bands was also due to the fact that the best Israeli writers provided them with material: Sasha Argov, Moshe Vilensky, Naomi Shemer, Haim Hefer, Yoram Tehar-Lev, Yair Rosenblum, Dan Almagor and others. In a short time, the military bands took the lead in Israeli show business and the IDF became the biggest producer in the country.

4 September

A terror attack at the Tel Aviv Central Bus Station – Terrorists planted explosive charges that killed one person and wounded about 50 others.

15 October

The Israeli national soccer team reached the quarter finals at the Mexico Olympics. This was a rare achievement in Israeli sports.

26 October

Fourteen soldiers were killed and 31 wounded when the Egyptians shelled posts along the Suez Canal. In retaliation, the IDF shelled the Suez refineries.

22 November

A car-bomb exploded in the Machaneh Yehuda market in Jerusalem, killing 12 and injuring 70.

Photo: GPO

16 April

"I Don't Deserve a Prize."

David Ben-Gurion refused to accept the Israel Prize or attend the Independence Day celebrations. He wrote to Education Minister Zalman Aran: "I don't deserve a prize for performing my duty to our country."

Photo: Zoom 77

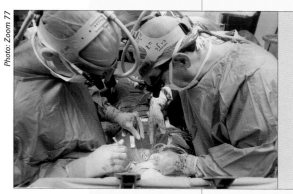

5 December

The First Heart Transplant in Israel

The first heart transplant was performed in Israel at Beilinson Hospital in Petach Tikva. The team of surgeons was headed by Prof. Maurice Levy, who was considered a pioneer in organ transplant in Israel. The patient, 41-year-old Yitzhak Sulam of Jaffa, died of complications two weeks later. The operation was performed a year and two days after the first-ever heart transplant was performed by Dr. Christiaan Barnard.

23 December

Israel Television started regular broadcasts. Initially, it broadcast three days a week.

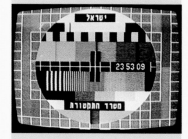

27 December

The United States officially announced its decision to sell 50 Phantom fighter jets to Israel.

Photo: GPO

21 March

Beware of Button Mines!

The Israel police warned the public against tiny plastic mines made in China. Police sappers said that they could cause severe bodily injury upon exploding. The security forces found dozens of these mines in the possession of Fatah terrorists.

(1969

Israel's fourth prime minister, Golda Meir. Photo: GPO

Prime Minister Golda Meir at a news conference with Yig'al Alon and Abba Eban. Photo: GPO

Golda Meir
Shrewdness That Did Not Prevent Serious Mistakes

*Former Minister
and MK
Yossi Beilin*

She was the Labor Party's choice by default. Labor was established in January 1968 when three political parties – Mapai, Rafi and *Ahdut Ha'avoda* – merged. It was feared then that a conflict between Prime Minister Levi Eshkol's two natural successors, Moshe Dayan and Yig'al Alon, would lead to either a rift or a takeover of the united party by a small faction. Finance Minister Pinchas Sapir went to 72-year-old Golda, who was recovering from an illness in a Swiss sanitarium, and brought her back to the center of the ring, just as she was about to retire from the Knesset and public life.

She was a clever and seasoned woman, blessed with political, diplomatic and social experience. The ultimate Jewish mother, emotional, a bit cynical, not charismatic, not popular; however, she quickly won broad public support once she settled in Eshkol's chair in March 1969.

Theoretically, this was a temporary appointment – until a successor was chosen in the elections of October 1969 – but, as in many other cases, a temporary solution became fact. Golda became prime minister, assisted by the wisdom of Yisrael Galili and the charisma of Moshe Dayan and Yig'al Alon. Together they ran a government that ruled Israel during the years of its great blindness – the years between the Six Day War and the Yom Kippur War.

Golda belonged to another generation. She was wise, humane and sensitive to social injustice. She is quoted as saying: "I will never forgive the Arabs for making us fight them." She loved the Jewish nation, but this did not help her deal with the central issues of her time: the Israeli-Palestinian conflict and the ethno-social crisis amongst the Jewish population. She felt she could solve these problems by minimizing them, making statements such as, "There is no Palestinian nation; I am a Palestinian," or "They are not very nice," in reference to the Black Panthers of Jerusalem.

She was a unique person, one of very few women to reach the upper echelons of Israeli politics, and she was greatly admired by American Jewry. On the one hand, she was a warm-hearted grandma; on the other, she was a symbol of Jewish determination, becoming aware of her extreme standpoints only in retrospect. In 1937, she had voted against the idea of partitioning Palestine, an idea of which Ben-Gurion approved. Decades later, she acknowledged her error, saying that we were historically fortunate that the Arabs had prevented the execution of the plan because otherwise she would have been held responsible for the fact that a Jewish state had not been set up before the Holocaust.

Her biggest mistake was rejecting the proposal that UN envoy Gunnar Jarring made to her in February 1971 – peace with Egypt in return for a withdrawal from the Sinai. To a large extent, the Yom Kippur War was a direct outcome of that decision. During the war, she endured the crisis well, encouraged the nation and even knew how to conceal the bitter truth from it in an elegant manner. Nevertheless, it was the Yom Kippur War that sent her home in May 1974 with the strong feeling that she had made a mistake.

In 1977, when Egyptian President Sadat arrived in Jerusalem, Golda could not understand why he had never come to see her, but had chosen Menachem Begin instead. When it became known that Begin and Sadat were to be awarded the Nobel Peace Prize, she maintained that the Oscar would have been more appropriate. Golda was even more perplexed when Begin acknowledged the rights of the Palestinian people, for she still believed that there was no Palestinian nation. By the time Sadat signed the peace accord with Israel, the "old lady", as he called her, was no longer alive. She died in December 1978 at the age of 80.

8.3.69

The War of Attrition at the Suez Canal Begins - "Endurance Alert"

The war of attrition started when Egyptian President Nasser announced that the cease-fire with Israel was null and void. Heavy battles started soon after that with massive Egyptian shelling of IDF posts along the Suez Canal and, in response, IAF jets bombing oil refineries west of the canal and the cities of Ismailia and Suez. The battles intensified the next day after Israeli gunners killed Egyptian Chief of Staff Abdul Munim Riadh in a direct hit. At the funeral, Nasser vowed to avenge Riadh's death, and over the next couple of weeks, Egyptian artillery shelled IDF posts along the canal daily.

Egypt launched the war of attrition after it had given up hope of forcing Israel to withdraw from the Sinai by means of international diplomatic pressure.

Knowing they could not beat Israel in a mobile war, they selected a doctrine of warfare dubbed "war of attrition" which exploited the fact that their army outnumbered the IDF. The war consisted of daily shelling of Israeli outposts and routes with the aim of harming soldiers, equipment and supplies. The IDF units, forced into a round-the-clock "endurance alert", were collapsing under the strain. The Israeli sensitivity to the loss of life undermined the soldiers at the canal outposts and encouraged the Egyptians to go on debilitating the Israeli troops.

Israel could not go to war utilizing its initiative and mobility because it was in a complicated political and military situation. The IDF, therefore, was left with the limited option of retaliation, employing mainly the IAF to inflict damages on the Egyptian enemy, targeting the canal cities and oil facilities. Commando units crossed the border regularly and attacked targets behind enemy lines; for example, the IDF destroyed the power grid that supplied electricity to Cairo, demolished Nile bridges and raided Egyptian Army outposts.

The prolonged war of attrition started a heated public debate about withdrawal from the Sinai. The people started feeling helpless and this increased as the war continued to take a heavy toll and the political echelons kept demonstrating helplessness.

An IDF soldier keeping an eye on the Suez towns from the banks of the canal. Photo: GPO

Photo: GPO

The Daring Raid on the Isle of Green

20 July

The Isle of Green, a fortified and armored Egyptian post at the southern end of the Suez canal, was conquered by the IDF on Saturday night. The island served as a basis for anti-aircraft guns. Six IDF soldiers were killed in the operation and nine were wounded. The Egyptians sustained dozens of casualties. The IDF unit conquered the fortress in a fierce battle and held the entire island for an hour, sabotaging equipment. The Egyptians shelled the island throughout the operation. The operation was a great success and remained etched in Israel's memory as one of the most impressive and daring IDF operations.

The Cherbourg Ships Slipped out of France

The French embargo on the export of arms to Israel forced Israel to resort to unconventional methods in order to take possession of five missile boats it had purchased in France. On Christmas Eve, Israeli Naval officers dressed as Norwegians boarded the boats and simply sailed from Cherbourg to Israel. The world was shocked by the Israeli *chutzpah*, while Israel feared that the French might give chase and attempt to sink the ships. In the event, the French did not react, creating an impression that they had given tacit approval to the operation so as not to be perceived as violating their own embargo.

The missile boats arrived in Israel after an uneventful voyage. Planes belonging to several foreign air forces escorted them, as did hoards of reporters. The boats were accompanied by an Israeli oil tanker and protected by Israeli submarines and planes. The main fear was that Arab armies might try to attack the ships, but no such attempt was made. France expressed "official anger", but imposed no significant sanctions on Israel.

Photo: GPO

Photo: K. Weiss

The al-Aksa Mosque Goes up in Flames

21 August

Early in the morning, a young Arab came running out of the al-Aksa mosque on the Temple Mount, screaming: "Fire, fire!" The Jerusalem fire-fighters could not do their job because hundreds of Arabs were crowded inside, insisting on performing the fire-fighting and rescue themselves. They were very angry and the security forces chose not to clash with them. The fire caused heavy damage to the mosque. There were very harsh reactions from the Muslim world against Israel, charging it of deliberate arson. Moshe Dayan was put in charge of the investigation, which revealed that the fire had been caused by an eccentric [non-Jewish] Australian called Michael Rohan.

1969

9 January

NBC TV reports: "Israel is about to produce nuclear weapons and missiles with nuclear warheads."

19 January

Labor and Mapam formed the Alignment, agreeing to run jointly in the Knesset, Histadrut and municipal elections.

27 January

Nine Jews were executed in Iraq on charges of spying for Israel and the United States.

18 February

Terrorists attacked an El Al plane in Zurich. One crew member was killed. An Israeli security guard charged at the five terrorists and killed one.

26 February

Levi Eshkol, Israel's third prime minister, died.

6 March

A bomb exploded in the cafeteria of the Hebrew University in Jerusalem, wounding 29 students.

8 March

Egyptian President Nasser announced the cease-fire agreement with Israel null and void. The war of attrition at the Suez Canal began.

17 March

Golda Meir presented her cabinet to the Knesset and won the confidence of the house.

8 April

Katyusha rockets fired from Jordan hit Eilat.

28 July

The Eighth Maccabi Games opened in Ramat Gan, attended by 1,500 athletes from 25 countries.

11 September

Eleven Egyptian planes were downed in dogfights after trying to attack IDF forces along the canal.

4.3.69

Golda Meir Appointed Prime Minister
"I would have been very happy had Dayan or Alon been given the post."

Prime Minister Levi Eshkol, who was suffering from cancer, died on 26 February. Golda Meir, herself ill with a serious blood disease, was in a Swiss sanitarium. The leading candidates for Eshkol's post were Moshe Dayan and Yig'al Alon, but the Mapai leadership ruled them both out due to "unsuitability", or - more precisely - for not belonging to the party. Golda was said to be a qualified candidate who would block Rafi member Dayan and *Ahdut Ha'avoda* member Alon, but she was not very enthusiastic. Furthermore, she was most unpopular at the time. After she was elected, she said: "I would have been very happy had Dayan or Alon competed for the post and won."

Nevertheless, when she assumed the post, it became apparent that she was tough and dominant, winning public support in a short time. She controlled Israeli foreign policy single-handedly and powerfully for five years, until after the Yom Kippur War.

Prime Minister Golda Meir at a consultation in her office. Photo: Micha Bar-Am

Prime Minister Golda Meir meeting security guard Mordechai Rachamim, who later became her bodyguard. Photo: GPO

An El Al Security Guard Rescues the Passengers

18 February

At 17:30, four men and a woman attacked an El Al plane with hand grenades and guns as it was preparing for takeoff from Zurich Airport in Switzerland. The pilot was shot six times. Mordechai Rachamim, an Israeli security guard, jumped out of the plane, fired at the assailants and killed one. The Swiss guards charged at the other terrorists, who preferred to surrender to the fire brigade, with the exception of the woman, who was apprehended by the local police while trying to escape.

The Popular Front for the Liberation of Palestine (PFLP) assumed responsibility for the attack which, thanks to the Israeli guard's fast action, did not end in disaster.

Knesset Elections: The Alignment Loses Seats

28 October

The Knesset elections were held against the backdrop of the ongoing war of attrition and Israel's political isolation. Although Prime Minister Golda Meir was quite popular, a movement was established supporting Moshe Dayan's candidacy for premier. The election results were disappointing for the Alignment, which went down from 63 to 56 Knesset seats. Forming a coalition was a very complicated task this time because of the numerous splits in the Israeli left wing. Nevertheless, Golda Meir managed to form a national unity government with Gahal.

69

2 December

"Let My People Go!" at the Malchei Yisrael Square

Photo: Micha Bar-Am

"Am Yisrael Chai [the people of Israel live] – anywhere and under any regime!" announced Prime Minister Golda Meir at a demonstration at the Malchei Yisrael square in Tel Aviv, demanding the release of Jews imprisoned in the USSR. The demonstration was attended by some 15,000 people, mostly youth movement members, high-school and university students and young party activists. They issued a unanimous call to the USSR Government: "Let My People Go!"

28 October

Elections for the 7th Knesset were held; Labor went down from 63 to 56 Knesset seats; Gahal won 26 seats.

14 December

Ezer Weizman retired from the IDF and was appointed minister of transportation for the Likud Party within the national unity government.

16 December

Yitzhak Ben-Aharon was elected Histadrut secretary general.

7 November

ITV to Broadcast on Friday Nights As Well

ITV started broadcasting on Friday nights, despite a government decision to the contrary which was made during the attempts to form a national unity government. The Friday night broadcasts were the result of a legal struggle by Attorney Yehuda Kessler and his brother-in-law Adi Kaplan. The two filed a petition with the High Court demanding that ITV broadcast on the eve of the Sabbath. "Because I pay Broadcasting Authority fees, I suffer from the fact that, due to various and irrelevant pressures, the Israel Broadcasting Authority has decided not to broadcast on Friday nights, which is against the law."

The Shin Duo - Giora Spiegel and Mottale Spiegler

26 December

Israel Makes it to the World Cup Finals

For the first time in history, the Israeli national soccer team was one of the 16 finalists in the World Cup Finals held in Mexico. Mordechai Spiegler scored the crucial goal in the match against Australia, thus earning the Israeli team a ticket to Mexico. The important goal was scored, despite pressure from the Australian team, in a combined attack by the two Shin's – Spiegel-Spiegler. Spiegel passed the ball accurately to Spiegler, who scored from 15 meters. Hundreds of Jewish spectators rushed into the field and hugged and kissed the rejoicing players. This return match took place in Sydney, Australia, after Israel had won the first game in Ramat Gan 1:0.

16 July

A Restraining Order Issued Against Singer Nechama Lifshitz

The Tel Aviv Rabbinical Court issued an order banning singer Nechama Lifshitz from leaving Israel. The singer, who had recently immigrated from the USSR, was about to go on a tour of Europe and the United States. The order was issued upon the request of her husband, who wanted to prevent her from leaving him. He explained: "Success has gone to her head and now, at the peak of her career, she wants to leave me. If she goes abroad, I will be left broke and all alone here." Nechama Lifshitz responded: "I married him fictitiously under circumstances upon which I will elaborate in court."

Singer Nechama Lifshitz and her husband. Photo: Y. Freidin

(1970

The Bathtub Queen by Hanoch Levin: a cornerstone in Israeli satire. Left to right: Germaine Unikovsky, Yisrael Gurion, Yossi Graber, Tikki Dayan. Photo: Mula and Harmati

On 19 May, the Cameri Theater decided to close down the show "due to heavy public pressure..." Photo: Mula and Harmati

Political Satire in Israel
From *The Bathtub Queen* to the *Harzufim*

Dr. David Alexander

The precise dictionary definition of the word *satire* links it to the dinner table in ancient Rome. *Satire* was a kind of stew or salad; hence, by allusion, it referred to a stage act that consisted of a variety of entertainment forms: songs, juggling, acrobatics and magic, as well as jesters who made fun of various people and issues by means of witty rhymes. Satire, however, never enjoyed the reputation of a good meal. It has always been closer to Saturn, the planet to which dark, malicious and even lethal qualities have been attributed.

The main thing that can be said about political satire in Israel is that it accompanied the realization of the Zionist dream and the construction of a new society from scratch with a critical eye and barbed words. The Israeli satirist has never been an onlooker; he has always been involved and provocative.

At its best, Israeli satire has always been an "event" – on stage, on TV or in the press. It deals directly with the very essence of Israeli politics and its ideological extremes. It is not plain "art"; it is a "war", dictated by emotionally charged issues, in which both sides – the satirist and the audience – use the most advanced techniques of calumny, insult and slander. In the 1970s, when the Cameri Theater put on Hanoch Levin's *The Bathtub Queen* (a masterpiece that proved to be a prophecy in the years to come), the playwright received a letter (one of many) which read: "Dear Mr. Self-righteous Hanoch! When I was in the concentration camp, I met a preacher like you... He too used to be a great humanist; but in the camp he was the worst collaborator with the Nazis. I wish you could have experienced being in that camp. You, however, would probably have become the same as him... Keep your dirty hands off the wounds of bereaved parents. You are not one to show anybody the way..."

This is an example of a controversial work whose content divided theater-goers into two ideological camps. It demonstrates how the horrors of the Holocaust and the agony of bereaved families are thrown back at the satirist who dares challenge belief, consensus and norms.

In 1973, the Haifa Theater put on a play called *Status Quo Vadis*, a satirical cabaret by Yehoshua Sobol. It attacked the religious establishment and caused heated debates in the Haifa city council as well as a motion to the Knesset agenda (MK Avraham Werdiger of *Poalei Agudat Yisrael* said it was "an unusual play; provocative, venomous, crude, inciting and dirty, its sole purpose being to kindle hatred of religion and faith... for all the Canaanites who infest the Bohemian crowds at cheap shows...").

When the Cameri put on *The Last of the Secular* ten years ago, playwright-director Shmuel Hasfari and the other artistic directors demanded that their names be removed from anything to do with the play after the theater "surrendered" to public demand that two extremely harsh scenes be taken out of the show. The play was about a state that had become ultra-Orthodox and was busy hunting the last secular person in order to make him repent. Before the play was even performed at the Tzavta Theater, the public was up in arms. The Israeli cabinet under Yitzhak Rabin (during his first term as prime minister) was twice forced to discuss controversial items which had been shown on the legendary satirical TV show, *Cleaning the Head*. The item that caused the biggest uproar showed the prime minister surrounded by "friends" who ripped an effigy of Rabin to pieces, limb by limb, all the while making harsh personal accusations.

Other TV shows – *The Cameri Quintet*, *Harzufim*, and even *Zehu Zeh* (which became famous because, while supposedly being a children's show, it made fun of the Gulf War terror when the missiles were falling here) – presented quite a few items that sparked controversy and turned into "events". Over the past several years, every weekend supplement runs a satirical page or insert. Clearly, *Zu Aretz* (printed in *Haolam Hazeh*), *HaDerech el HaOsher* (The Path to Joy, in *Ma'ariv*) and most of all *Davar Acher* (Something Else), which started in *Davar* and is now run by *Yedioth Ahronoth*, "contributed" headlines no less than the news pages did.

Ephraim Kishon, the spiritual father of many young Israeli satirists, often commented about the fact that the satirist is always frustrated because his work does not bring about changes in political thought or the ways of the government ("no protest, no opposition, no scandal, no change, absolute indifference").

Good satire often serves as a valve for letting off steam, taking stands and creating public controversies. A satirist's biggest achievement is, perhaps, when his work becomes part of a communicative and historical terminology which goes beyond the isolated piece and becomes a symbol. This is what happened with *The Bathtub Queen* and, to a certain extent, this is what happened to the political world of the *Harzufim* puppets.

When there is an immediate dialogue between the satirist and his "victim", when our eyes see, our ears hear, and our heart – always the heart, not the brain – is involved in the "event" with all the passion and emotion that are reserved for political debates – (for what isn't political in Israel!) – this is when the real hour of grace for Israeli satire occurs.

7.8.70

Bombing Deep Within Egypt Leads to a Cease-Fire at the Suez Canal

The constant state of war and the daily attrition experienced by the IDF compelled army commanders to adopt extreme and tough methods of operation. The aim was to inflict such enormous damage on the Egyptians that they would be forced to declare a cease-fire. This concept was devised when it was realized that the retaliation operations were not exerting enough pressure on Egypt, whose operations had become more complex and daring, thus increasing the number of Israeli casualties. At the same time, Israel's political isolation was growing and the United States was increasing its pressure.

The turning-point came when Israel received the first upgraded Phantoms. They could carry a heavier load for greater distances, allowing the IAF to strike deep within Egyptian territory and cause

Photo: GPO

serious damage. As of January 1970, the IAF shelled a series of military and civilian targets inside Egypt. The purpose of these bombings was to cause economic and military damage, thus engendering resentment against Nasser. The bombing did cause damage and hundreds, perhaps thousands of Egyptians, mostly civilians, were hurt, but most of the anger and hatred was directed toward Israel, while Nasser's popularity increased.

The most serious result of these in-depth bombings for Israel was that the USSR decided to give its full support to Egypt, providing it with ground-to-air missiles which restricted the Phantom's freedom of operation. The Soviets also provided Egypt with the most advanced MiG-21 jets, which posed a real threat to the Phantoms. They were flown by well-trained Russian pilots. The combination of the advanced planes and the ground-to-air missiles made the IAF operations dangerous and sometimes even impossible.

The increasing Soviet involvement in the war encouraged the Americans to find ways to resolve the serious situation. President Richard Nixon sent a letter to Israel vowing to maintain its military capabilities and support it economically. After prolonged and serious deliberations, Israel agreed to accept the Rogers Plan, after which a cease-fire was introduced. Gahal quit the government in the wake of this decision. The agreement, however, was violated by Egypt, which placed 21 anti-aircraft missile batteries along the Suez Canal, a move that would cost Israel dearly in the Yom Kippur War. Neither side emerged victorious from the war of attrition. Both sides suffered great damage and losses, although Egypt suffered more. This war openly involved the superpowers in Middle East affairs and exacerbated the arms race between Israel and the Arab countries.

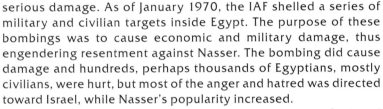

The Avivim School Bus Attacked

22 May

Terrorists who infiltrated from Lebanon attacked a bus on the northern road, killing nine schoolchildren, two teachers and the bus driver and wounding 24 others. The terrorists fired four bazooka rockets, three of which hit the bus. The murderous attack was accurate and lethal. The Israeli Government held a special session to discuss the issue and the Lebanese border was put on the alert. A mass exodus of Lebanese from the border area began in anticipation of Israeli retaliation. The IDF started escorting buses along the northern road, which provided a partial solution.

Motta Gur, head of the Northern Command, visiting the wounded children of Avivim.
Photo: GPO

Twelfth-Graders' Letter to Golda

Against the backdrop of the ongoing war of attrition, 70 representatives of twelfth-grade students sent a letter to Prime Minister Golda Meir saying: "Now that our government has turned down a chance for peace by rejecting Dr. Nachum Goldman's shuttle, we are no longer certain that we will be able to do our military service under the slogan, 'We have no choice.'" The letter was written after the Israeli Government refused to acknowledge Dr. Nachum Goldman, chairman of the Zionist Federation, as an official Israeli envoy when he was invited to Egypt to seek a solution to the war of attrition.

The students' explicit declaration that they might refuse to serve in the IDF created a great uproar in Israel. The signatories stated that they would be willing to establish a Nachal Brigade settlement and serve there, provided it was set up within the 4 June boundaries. They expressed their disapproval of conquering territories, of the war of attrition and of the impotence of the political echelons, as a result of which many young men were getting killed. Black humor started developing in Israel among the future recruits, who would arrange to meet in military cemeteries on memorial days.

The twelfth-graders' letter was one of the strongest expressions of rejection of government policies. The signatories were dubbed Leftists or Matzpenists [a leftist cell accused of spying for the enemy], but many others claimed the right to express their views in light of the great sacrifice that was being demanded of them.

Demonstrations for the release of Soviet Jews. Photo: Fritz Cohen, GPO

Soviet Refuseniks Who Hijacked a Plane:

"We did not betray our homeland because Israel is our homeland."

16 December

Demonstrations were held in Israel and abroad, protesting the verdicts issued at the Leningrad Trial in which Jews were convicted of hijacking a Russian plane and attempting to fly it to Israel with their families. Two of the hijackers, Mark Dimschitz and Edward Kuznichev, were sentenced to death, and nine others were sentenced to lengthy prison terms with hard labor. At the trial, the defendants rejected charges of treason, saying: "We never betrayed our homeland; Israel, not Russia, is our homeland." As a result of massive international protest, the Soviets decided to stay the sentence.

1 January

Shmuel Rosenwasser, a night-watchman from Metulla, was kidnapped by terrorists who reached the border fence. The terrorists handed Rosenwasser over to the Syrians.

15 January

Poet Leah Goldberg died at the age of 59.

22 January

A paratrooper force captured the Isle of Shadwan in the Suez Gulf, held it for 36 hours and inflicted many casualties on the Egyptians.

10 February

Terrorists attacked El Al passengers in Munich. Actress Hanna Marron was badly injured.

17 February

S.Y. Agnon, Nobel laureate and one of the greatest Hebrew writers, died at the age of 82.

22 February

A mother of seven from Moshav Elkosh near the Lebanese border was killed when an explosive charge planted outside her bedroom wall went off.

7 April

The Tel Aviv municipality decided to remove the parking meters and introduce parking cards that would be sold in kiosks throughout the city.

1 May

The Cameri Theater put on Hanoch Levin's *The Bathtub Queen*, which created an uproar due to its anti-war stand.

3 May

21 terrorists were killed in the biggest-ever IDF clash with a terrorist squad in the Jordan Rift Valley.

22 May

Terrorists attacked a bus carrying schoolchildren from Moshav Avivim. Nine pupils, two teachers and the bus driver were killed.

10.2. **70**

Actress Hanna Marron Wounded in A Terrorist Attack in Munich

Photo: GPO

Poet Nathan Alterman, "The People's Conscience", Dies

28 March

Nathan Alterman – poet, translator, columnist and playwright who won the Israel Prize for literature in 1968 – died of a heart attack during surgery on his stomach at the age of 60. Alterman began publishing his poems in the periodical *Turim* (Columns) and later in *Machbarot LeSifrut* (Literary Notebooks), which he had founded. He owed his fame to, among other things, *The Seventh Column*, a weekly poem dealing with current affairs published in *Davar* and *Ha'aretz*. Hundreds came to pay their respects to "The People's Conscience", as Ben-Gurion called him. His last request was to have a modest funeral, without eulogies, and to be buried "among simple Jews."

El Al flight 435 from Lod to London was attacked by terrorists during a stopover in Munich. The attack began at 12:50 when four terrorists, who had arrived on a flight from Baghdad, opened fire on the plane and threw hand grenades. Actress Hana Marron, a passenger on the flight, was badly wounded. She was rushed to a local hospital in critical condition and operated on. Her life was saved, but she lost a leg. When her condition stabilized, she returned to Israel.

Another passenger on the plane, Asi Dayan – son of Defense Minister Moshe Dayan – was not hurt. The pilot, Captain Uriel Cohen, shielded the passengers with his body and confronted a terrorist. Passenger Arie Katzenstein threw himself on a grenade and was killed instantly. Another terrorist was shot by German security personnel.

Realizing that the terrorists had managed to slip through the tight German security, the Germans improved security arrangements in their airports.

Hanna Marron returned to Israel after having been badly wounded in a terrorist attack in Munich. Photo: GPO

The Attack on the Isle of Shadwan

22 January

A paratroopers' force was flown by helicopter to the Isle of Shadwan (halfway between Ras Muhammad in the Sinai and Ghardaka in Egypt) and captured it after a heavy battle in the lighthouse area. The raid, dubbed Operation Rhodes, greatly embarrassed the Egyptian Army, whose units were unable to prevent the Israeli takeover. The Egyptians suffered heavy losses. The IDF unit evacuated the island after 36 hours.

Israeli helicopters during the raid of the Isle of Shadwan. Photo: Starphoto

70

1970

2 April

Habima Renovations Completed

Photo: Koko

The new Habima Theater was inaugurated after a long period of renovations. The building now included a cellar, Habimartef, for experimental plays.

30 May

Thirteen IDF soldiers were killed and two taken captive in a clash with Egyptian commando units.

1 June

Three were killed and 14 wounded in two Katyusha attacks on Bet She'an.

7 August

A cease-fire was signed between Israel and Egypt, ending the war of attrition, after the parties accepted the Rogers Plan.

12 August

Israel found out that Egypt had advanced 21 missile batteries and some 1,000 tanks to the Suez Canal area, in contravention of the cease-fire agreement.

30 December

Nineteen IDF soldiers were killed in an accident at a military base near Neot Hakikar when rains caused a giant rock to fall and crush the mess hall.

4 November

100,000 Students Out of School - The high-school teachers started a general strike after a heated debate that lasted eight hours and only ended at dawn. The strike, which lasted 40 days, was called because the teachers demanded that their salaries be adjusted to the level of the engineers' salaries.

11 November

Hebrew Lessons in Egyptian Army Bulletin - The Egyptian Army bulletin revealed that Egyptian soldiers were learning Hebrew. The paper read: "Egyptian warrior, learn your enemy's language... The battle against the Israeli enemy is drawing near, there is no doubt about that... Learn the words and phrases published in our paper so that we can use them in our next confrontation with the Zionist enemy... ." Among the Hebrew expressions the Egyptian soldiers were being taught: "Hands up." "Don't move." "Drop your weapon." "Where is your arms cache?" "Where is your command post?"

14 December

Israel in the Mexico Soccer World Cup Finals - The Israeli soccer team made it to the World Cup finals in Mexico for the first time ever [and the only time so far]. The team acquitted itself honorably, reaching a draw in two games and losing the third by a single goal. The players received high praise and returned triumphantly.

The Israeli soccer team in Mexico.

15 January

Poet Leah Goldberg Dies

Leah Goldberg - poet, writer, playwright and critic - died at the age of 59 after suffering from a terminal disease. Goldberg published several books of poetry, a novel (*And He Is the Light*), and the play, *The Palace Owner*, that was performed by the Cameri Theater. She also wrote children's books and was an excellent translator. In her last years, Goldberg, who was a professor, headed the Comparative Literature Department at the Hebrew University in Jerusalem.

Photo: GPO

12 December

Israeli Athletes Win Gold Medals in Bangkok

Israeli athletes won gold, silver and bronze medals at the Asian Games in Bangkok. Among the winners were track and field runners, Esther Roth-Shahamorov (right), Hanna Shezifi (left) and sharpshooter Shimon Friedman.

(1971

The Black Panthers demonstrated in Jerusalem, burning an effigy of Prime Minister Golda Meir. Photo: K. Weiss

Demonstrations in support of the Black Panthers' cause were staged all over Israel. (The placard on the left reads: "Golda, teach us Yiddish.")

"The Black Panthers":

An Unflattering Mirror in Front of Israeli Society

Labor MK
Haim Ramon

1971 seemed like a very good year. The kingdom of Israel stretched from the peaks of Mount Hermon, through Judea and Samaria, down to the shores of the Suez Canal. The war of attrition had ended in the summer of 1970 and, for the first time since the Six Day War, Israel's borders were quiet and there was no more war. Waves of immigrants were arriving from the USSR and the West. Many improved their economic status as a result of the state's enormous security expenditure and the state leaders of the time, primarily Golda Meir, used to say, "We have never had it better."

This political and social tranquillity and the quiet before the storm of the Yom Kippur War were disturbed at the beginning of 1971 by a group of young Jerusalemites who called themselves "The Black Panthers".

They emerged from the poor neighborhoods of Jerusalem, belonging mostly to large families with low incomes. They had arrived with their parents from Morocco or other Arab countries during the big waves of immigration of the 1950s. Most of them were school dropouts and many had tangled with the law and spent time in institutions for young delinquents. Most of them had never been called up for military service. They had no steady jobs and were labeled criminals. However, unlike their parents, they were determined to change their fate by every possible means – not always entirely legal ones. They wanted their children's fate to be different from their own in order to prevent the formation of a third underprivileged generation. Their enemy was the obtuse and satiated establishment which stubbornly ignored the difficult social problems of the "second" and "third" Israel.

In March 1971, the Black Panthers applied for a permit to stage a legal demonstration in the streets of Jerusalem. The police, unaware of the size of the organization, rejected the request and even made several preemptive arrests of activists. The police conduct, however, only gave the movement publicity and encouraged it.

The police move aroused a wave of sympathy and an unlicensed demonstration was held on 3 March. This was the day on which the first significant Israeli social movement was established. The demonstration received a lot of publicity and brought poverty and ethnic relations to the fore. The authorities were forced to react to the loud messages they were receiving. Even Golda Meir, who said that the Panthers were "not nice", had to establish a public committee to come up with a solution for the problem of the underprivileged youths. The Panthers met ministers, MKs, police commanders and Histadrut and Jewish Agency officials. However, it seems that the meeting that finally established the movement was the one with Golda Meir. She did not hide her rage and contempt for the young group, and refused to consider them as a social movement representing a problem that threatened to cause a rift in the Israeli society.

It was precisely Golda's approach that escalated the confrontation between the Panthers and the ruling elite. Sympathy for their struggle increased among large sectors of Israeli society. The movement was joined mainly by young men and women whose social background was similar to that of the founders. Many of the youngsters from poor neighborhoods placed themselves at the disposal of the movement, and even ethnic organizations that had gradually been waning were revived. While the movement was gaining strength, protest activities continued. Some were routine – demonstrations and posters, others were less routine – stealing bottles of milk and distributing them to poor children.

As the movement grew, a process of structural and ideological crystallization occurred. Its members were registered as a non-profit organization whose aims – primarily – were the eradication of the slums, free education from kindergarten to university, free housing for poor families and equal representation for the Sephardim in every state establishment. External activities and the institutionalization process were often affected by inner processes and infighting that harmed the Panthers' efficacy. Nevertheless, the movement reached the peak of its power in the Histadrut elections of September 1973.

As a movement and as individuals, the Black Panthers did not really leave a mark on Israeli society. Their image of having criminal records and being too young and inexperienced, coupled with organizational problems and internal conflicts, prevented the movement from becoming a significant force on the Israeli political scene. The Yom Kippur War in 1973 pushed social issues aside for a while and once again the issues of security and peace were given priority. In retrospect, however, it is evident that the Black Panthers did manage to change the shape of Israeli society. In the 1970s, the Knesset passed numerous social bills regarding unemployment, social welfare, housing and education, which significantly narrowed social gaps in Israel. Had it not been for the group of angry young men from the Jerusalem neighborhoods of Musrara and the Katamons, youngsters who would not put up with the establishment's obtuseness and indifference toward social problems, and had they not placed an unflattering mirror in front of Israeli society – there might have been a tremendous social explosion.

Ever since then, social issues have been an inseparable part of the Israeli political agenda and have influenced decisionmakers. Even the media, which had not bothered with social affairs before the Black Panthers arrived on the scene, give significant coverage and expression to social problems in the State of Israel. In this, therefore, lies the greatest victory of that group of young people from the poor neighborhoods of Jerusalem.

11.2. 71

"Israel Is Missing A Golden Opportunity To Make Peace With Egypt."

UN envoy Gunnar Jarring resumed his Middle East shuttle mission. Yet, due to both parties' intransigence, the negotiations reached a deadlock despite Jarring's unceasing efforts. In February, Egyptian President Anwar Sadat suggested that Israel and Egypt reach an "interim agreement" in which Israel would basically agree to a full withdrawal from the Sinai. According to the proposal, Israel was initially supposed to withdraw 40 km east of the Suez Canal. Golda Meir was prepared only for a 10-km withdrawal and refused to agree to anything further. In return, she demanded that Egypt allow Israel free naval passage through the canal as well as undertake not to resume hostilities. Egypt rejected this. In March, Israel received a new offer, according to which Israel was to withdraw to a distance of 40 km from the canal; the evacuated territory was to be demilitarized and Egyptian civilians were to be allowed to go as far as 10 km into the evacuated territory in order to prepare the canal for reopening. The Egyptians made the offer conditional on Israel's acknowledging that this would be an "interim agreement" and a pledge that it would withdraw further in the future.

UN envoy Gunnar Jarring at a meeting with Foreign Minister Abba Eban in Jerusalem. Photo: GPO

The proposal initiated a fierce debate in the cabinet. Moshe Dayan was willing to discuss it, but the majority, headed by Golda Meir, rejected it. The US Administration exerted heavy pressure on Israel, warning that it was missing "a golden opportunity to make peace with Egypt." Looking back, it does indeed seem that Israel missed a rare opportunity to make peace: In 1977, it accepted the very same terms that it had rejected in 1971. It is possible that the refusal resulted from excessive self-confidence, from faith in Israel's economic and military might, and from the belief that Sadat was a weak leader, which was the impression he gave in those days. Commentators tend to believe that, had Israel had the courage to accept the Egyptian offer in 1971, the Yom Kippur War could have been prevented.

"Two Atom Bombs Are Produced in Dimona Each Year"

18 July

In a special in-depth report, the French publication *Le Monde* revealed that Israel was producing nuclear bombs in the Dimona reactor. According to the report, Israel was capable of producing two 20-kiloton bombs annually. Under the headline, "Israel – The Land of Miracles", the French paper described Israel's ability to produce nuclear weapons, electronic devices for jamming ground-to-air missiles, and a laser system for tracking any moving target accurately. The report, which was very flattering to Israel, presenting it as a country in which science was "the very core of the national ideology", caused a reaction throughout the world and was extensively quoted by the Arab press. The Israeli Government chose not to comment.

The Black Panthers: "They Are Not Nice."

1971

The foundation of the Black Panthers movement added a new dimension to the social protest that had been escalating as a result of the widening gap between the rich and the poor. It started in the Musrara neighborhood of Jerusalem, inhabited by poor and mainly Eastern people. The protest expressed deep feelings of discrimination and deprivation which the immigration from the USSR exacerbated. The immigrants were given all kinds of benefits, popularly known as "Villa-Volvo", which caused great resentment and anger at the government and its policy.

The Black Panthers movement used various means to make the public aware of its struggle. Its members organized mass demonstrations, harnessing the media to the cause. Its charismatic leaders were frequently interviewed, portraying their cause as a national crisis. On 18 May, riots and clashes with the police reached their peak at a demonstration in Zion Square, Jerusalem, when the demonstrators threw three firebombs at the police. Some 20 police officers and demonstrators were wounded and 74 activists arrested. Golda Meir said that they were "not nice", but the cabinet was forced to address their plight and discuss ways of solving their problems. In the wake of the

The leaders of the Black Panthers, left to right: Eli Abichzer, Charlie Biton, Sa'adia Marziano, Roni Horowitz. Photo: NewsPhot

conclusions and proposals of a special committee, the ministries dealing with social issues received additional budgets, and extra funds were allocated to ease the distress of the weak strata.

Unfortunately, two years after the Black Panthers founded their movement, the Yom Kippur War broke out, as a result of which most funds were redirected to meet security needs. The movement failed in its attempt to become a political party, mainly due to infighting. Its leaders, however, joined other parties, through which they tried to continue promoting their social agenda. In the end, the movement's main achievement was increasing public awareness of the problem of the ethnic gap and social deprivation in Israel.

Photo: Yossi Roth

Citizen No. 3,000,000 – A Soviet Immigrant

11 January

Nathan Tsirolnikov, who immigrated from Russia on 11 January, brought the number of Israeli citizens to three million. The struggle for the Soviet refuseniks continued and even had positive results. Grisha Feigin, a USSR hero and a captain in the Red Army, who had been a refusenik for several years, received an emigration permit and arrived in Israel on 12 February. In 1971, 40,000 immigrants arrived in Israel, 13,000 from the USSR.

2 January
A tragedy in Gaza: Two toddlers, a boy and a girl, were killed when a terrorist threw a hand grenade into a car in which the Arroyo family was driving. Their mother was seriously injured.

16 February
A huge fire at the Shalom Tower caused IL1 million worth of damage.

5 April
Moshe Dayan told the Labor Party Conference: "We will not go back to the lines of 4 June 1967, even if this leads to war."

18 May
Stormy demonstrations were staged by the Black Panthers in Jerusalem. The demonstrators clashed violently with the police and dozens were arrested.

2 June
The first El Al Jumbo arrived in Israel.

9 June
Egyptian President Anwar Sadat threatened "a savage and ruthless war in which we are willing to sacrifice one million victims."

6 July
Yitzhak Tabenkin, leader of the United Kibbutz Movement and one of the founding fathers of the Labor Movement, died at the age of 84.

7 July
Katyusha rockets fired from Jordan fell on Petach Tikva, killing three women and a girl. This was the first time that Petach Tikva had ever been hit by Katyusha rockets.

9 August
Yitzhak Rabin agreed to extend his term as ambassador to the US by another year.

14.11. 71

The Netivei Neft Affair – Theft, Embezzlement and Corruption

Dr. Yitzhak Nevenzal, the state comptroller, exposed the corruption in the Netivei Neft Company which had drilled for oil in the Sinai and was financed by the state. The comptroller discovered financial irregularities, theft, embezzlement and peculiar personal relationships among the company workers. On 14 November, a commission of inquiry was set up, chaired by Justice Alfred Vitkon, and including Major General (Res.) Meir Zorea and businessman Avraham Kalir. The commission called many witnesses, mostly company workers, who described the directors' irresponsible conduct and mismanagement.

The commission's conclusions shocked the public because it did not demand the resignation of company director Michael Friedman "as no evidence was furnished against him regarding crimes he had supposedly committed, as some witnesses suggested" – this despite the fact that the testimonies supported the suspicions and accusations, of which the main one was wasting vast amounts of the tax-payers' money. The public demanded that someone be accountable, and the company manager resigned on 27 April 1972.

But the affair was not over. It later became apparent that the attorneys who had represented the various parties involved in the investigation had received particularly high fees – also from public funds. Justice Minister Ya'akov Shimshon Shapira assumed responsibility for this and resigned. Three months later, however, he returned to his post. This again sparked public protest, but this time to no avail.

State Comptroller Yitzhak Nevenzal exposed the Netivei Neft affair.
Photo: Yosi Rott

Two Arroyo Children Killed in Gaza

2 January

The Arroyo family tragedy shocked Israel. A 17-year-old Palestinian threw a hand grenade into the car of the Arroyo family near the Gaza Strip. The hand grenade entered the car and exploded. Daniel (5) and Abigail (7) were killed and their mother was seriously injured by the blast. Following this attack, Major General Ariel Sharon, head of the Southern Command, took harsh measures against terrorism in the Gaza Strip.

Israeli Oil Tanker Attacked in the Red Sea

11 June

The Coral Sea, an Israeli oil tanker on its way to Israel, was attacked in the Red Sea, in the Bab el Mandeb Straits near Aden. A speedboat carrying three terrorists intercepted the tanker and six bazooka rockets were fired at it. Several rockets hit the tanker and started a fire on deck. The terrorists' boat fled the scene quickly. The crew managed to extinguish the fire and the tanker continued on its way to Israel. Political sources said that the act required swift Israeli retaliation in order to prevent any risk to Israeli vessels en route to Eilat.

1971

18 April

First Mimuna Festivities in Jerusalem

Photo: GPO

Thousands celebrated the Mimuna with traditional North African songs, dances, costumes and food. The festivities were held in Jerusalem for the first time. Public officials, including the president, the prime minister, the mayor of Jerusalem, the Histadrut secretary-general and heads of the Zionist Federation came to wish the people well. Representatives of the Arab, Druze and Circassian minorities also arrived, bringing their traditional dishes as a goodwill gesture. During the festivities, there were performances of singing and folk-dancing as well as competitions for titles such as the prettiest dress, the nicest tea set and the proudest mother.

2 November

Corruption at the Top

The police began investigating irregularities in the "Autocar" car factory, including granting large discounts to public officials and institutions. Among the persons interrogated were senior government officials, former army generals and others. The people questioned said that the discounts they had received were reasonable and, in most cases, had been given as part of the campaign to promote the Triumph 1500.

At the same time, the cabinet decided to appoint a commission of inquiry on suspected corruption at the Netivei Neft national oil company.

Photo: GPO

17 October

Inauguration of the Jerusalem Theater
The Jerusalem Theater was inaugurated in a festive ceremony attended by President Zalman Shazar, Jerusalem Mayor Teddy Kollek and donor Miles Sherover whose contribution enabled the theater to be built. The opening night was directed by Gershon Plotkin, and the best Israeli actors performed together with American stars Eli Wallach and Ann Jackson.

19 April

The New Tel Aviv Museum Opens Its Doors

President Zalman Shazar inaugurated the new Tel Aviv Museum on Shaul Hamelekh Boulevard. The symphony orchestra of Tel Aviv University's Music Academy played a work by composer Paul Ben-Haim. A special concert to mark the occasion was held at the Mann Auditorium on the same day. It was conducted by Leonard Bernstein.
The museum opened with an exhibition of sculptures by Jacques Lifshitz and a display of works by the greatest 20th-century French artists.

Photo: Newspot

20 August

The government announced a devaluation of the Israeli lira, making $1 equivalent to IL4.20. The devaluation caused an increase in the prices of many basic products, including bread, milk, eggs, oil and sugar.

17 October

The Egged bus company launched its daily Tel Aviv - Sharm al-Sheikh line.

23 October

Israel's first quintuplets were born in Jerusalem to the Berman family.

26 October

The Agriculture Ministry and the Jewish Agency decided to expropriate land owned by a resident of Moshav Nitzanei Oz who had leased it to Arabs.

13 November

The media revealed for the first time that the people found guilty in "The Affair" were living in Israel after their release from prison in Egypt.

28 December

Defense Minister Moshe Dayan divorced his wife Ruth. Shortly after, he married Rachel, with whom he had been good friends for a long time.

1972

The Israeli athletes who were murdered in Munich are buried in Israel.
Photo: Micha Bar-Am

Memorial services for the 11 murdered athletes were held outside the Israeli Olympic dormitory in Munich. Photo: AP

The Munich Olympiad 1972
The Bloody Olympiad

Former Olympic Athlete
Esther Roth-Shahamorov

As soon as I took my first stride on the track in 1967, my coach, Amitzur Shapira, told me that he was preparing me for the Olympic Games. Here it was. In September 1972, we went to the Munich Olympiad. The Israeli delegation included 22 athletes, as well as coaches, referees and executives. The men were housed in one dormitory and swimmer Shlomit Nir and I in another, some 200 meters away.

When we arrived at the Olympic village, we were given final security instructions. We were especially told to beware of letter-bombs, which were "fashionable" at the time. Then we separated and mingled with athletes from all over the world. Observing the mixture of people there was a great experience. It was easy for us to guess the athletes' area of expertise by looking at their body structure: The tall ones were basketball players, the short guys were weight-lifters, and those with swollen ears were wrestlers. I was also enchanted by the colorful carnival of costumes. At the same time, I was full of anticipation for the competitions.

The festive Olympic atmosphere was suddenly shattered when we heard the terrible announcement that terrorists had entered the Israelis' dormitory and taken them hostage. Upon entering, they had killed Moni Weinberg, who had tried to block the door with his body. Then they killed Yosef Romano, who fought them although his leg was in a cast.

The night before the attack on the Olympic village, the Israeli delegation had been invited to see *Fiddler on the Roof*, starring Shmuel Rodensky, which was a great success in Germany at the time. I sat next to coach Amitzur who spoke German and translated the text for me. We were the guests of honor, and we were in a wonderful mood. Our group lifted Rodensky and me up, and we had our picture taken like that. The next day, I celebrated reaching the finals of the 100-meter hurdles, having set a new record. That evening, my coach and I arranged to meet at the cafeteria the next morning. Shlomit Nir woke me up in the morning, telling me that terrorists had got into our friends' rooms and that we must evacuate ours at once. We were terrified. We were taken somewhere else in the village where those who escaped had gathered, and together we listened to reports about the negotiations between the terrorists and our government, headed by Golda Meir. Every hour or so, we heard a shot that made us even more edgy and uncertain. I will never forget the moment I saw the nine athletes, their hands tied behind their backs, taken away by the armed terrorists.

They made their way in a line toward two waiting helicopters, climbed in and took off – illuminated by dozens of camera flashes – never to return. The helicopters landed in a military airport in Munich, where German snipers awaited them. The Germans, however, failed in their attempt to release the Israelis.

We returned to Israel with 11 coffins. Earlier, a ceremony had been held in the Olympic stadium to commemorate the slain athletes. Shmuel Lelkin, head of the Israeli delegation and speaking on its behalf, promised that Israel would continue to participate in future Olympiads. Indeed we did, but our dream had been shattered by the disaster. For me, the next Olympic Games were an attempt to realize my murdered coach's dream as well as a memorial to my athlete comrades. That was a mission that needed to be accomplished.

5.9.72

Athletes Slain in Munich

The Olympic flag was lowered to half-mast during the memorial ceremony at the Munich stadium. Photo: AP

Eight Arab terrorists entered the Olympic village at dawn and took over the Israeli athletes' rooms. Two Israeli athletes were murdered during the takeover and another nine were taken hostage. The abductors demanded that Israel release 200 terrorists in custody in Israel. The German security forces conducted nerve-wracking negotiations with the terrorists and eventually agreed to provide them with two helicopters that would take them and the hostages to the military airport in Munich, where a plane was waiting for them, supposedly to fly them to Tunis.

In the meantime, the Germans devised a rescue plan, but their performance was amateurish and clumsy, and the plan failed totally. The German snipers, whose rifles were equipped with infra-red sights, opened fire too soon, just as the terrorists were coming out of the helicopters to examine the plane that was waiting for them. The first volley did not eliminate all the terrorists, and those who remained managed to throw a hand grenade into one helicopter and spray the other with heavy automatic fire. All nine Israeli hostages, who were tied to one another in the two helicopters, were killed. The Germans killed five terrorists and captured three. A German police officer was also killed and the helicopter pilot was injured.

The world condemned the Munich massacre, but the games continued. A small number of delegations decided to leave in sympathy with the Israeli delegation. The Israelis returned home grieving, shocked and in pain. Although the world condemned the act, the Arab countries rejoiced. The terror organizations demanded that the Germans release the three captive terrorists, threatening that if their demand were not met, they would attack the Germans. The German government held lengthy discussions on the matter, but could not reach a decision. On 29 October, a German plane was hijacked and the hijackers demanded that the Germans release the three terrorists immediately. The Germans did not hesitate very much and gave in to the demand, releasing the three who had massacred the Israeli athletes.

Israel and the West were extremely critical of the move. In Israel, particularly harsh criticism was leveled at the Germans, relating also to the abortive attempt to rescue the Israeli athletes, which cost them their lives.

The Israeli delegation leaving the games. Photo: AP

Photo: GPO

David Elazar, the Ninth Chief of Staff

1 January

Major General David (Dado) Elazar was promoted to lieutenant general and appointed ninth IDF chief of staff, replacing Haim Bar-Lev. In the Six Day War, Dado served as head of the Northern Command and won the esteem of both the public and the politicians for his performance. Nevertheless, Dado will be remembered for his role in the Yom Kippur War fiasco. The Agranat Commission of Inquiry, set up after the war, determined that Dado was responsible for not preparing the army for war. Dado was forced to resign, but he remained popular among the public, who believed that he had been a scapegoat for the political echelons.

The Lod Airport Massacre

Bottom: *Knesset members commemorate the Lod Airport massacre victims. Photo: K. Weiss*

Japanese terrorist Kozo Okamoto being brought to the military court that sentenced him to life imprisonment. Photo: Yossi Roth

Three passengers on the Air France plane that landed at Lod Airport were Japanese terrorists who had been trained in Lebanon by the PFLP. The three were mercenaries, members of the Japanese terror organization, "The Red Star Army", who had agreed to carry out a terror attack in Israel in solidarity with the Palestinian organization that had trained them. When their bags arrived, they pulled out Kalachnikov submachine guns and started spraying lethal bullets in every direction. They also threw several hand grenades. Terrible chaos followed and the security guards in the terminal were unable to locate the terrorists among the hysterical crowd. One of the terrorists even managed to run back to the landing area and attack a planeload of passengers with his submachine gun and hand grenades. The results of the attack were horrendous: 25 people were killed and 71 wounded. Among the fatalities was Prof. Aharon Katzir, a brilliant and internationally renowned scientist who had won the Israel Prize for science. One year after his death, his brother, Efraim Katzir, was elected president of Israel.

Two of the terrorists were killed in the airport and the third, Kozo Okamoto, was captured, tried by a military court, and sentenced to life imprisonment. He was released from prison in a POW exchange deal after the of Lebanon War. After the terrible bloodbath, security arrangements at Lod Airport underwent drastic changes. Every passenger and his luggage were thoroughly checked and dozens of guards were hired to protect the terminal. Other airports in the world also tightened their security. The Japanese Government apologized to Israel officially for its citizens' involvement in the attack and even paid more than $1 million in damages.

Photo: IPPA

The Uprooted Residents of Ikrit and Bir'am Continue Their Struggle

23 July

The government decided not to honor a commitment which it had made to the uprooted residents of the Arab villages of Ikrit and Bir'am in the Galilee, and refused to let them return to their lands. After the War of Independence, the IDF moved most of the residents of these villages to the central Galilee, while others escaped to Lebanon. The government decision to renege on a past promise angered many Israeli circles.

9.5. *72*

Commando Unit Frees a Hijacked Sabena Plane

A passenger plane belonging to the Belgian Sabena company was hijacked by Fatah terrorists to Lod Airport. The terrorists demanded that Israel free hundreds of terrorists imprisoned here, threatening to blow up the plane with its passengers. Defense Minister Moshe Dayan conducted lengthy negotiations with the terrorists with the intention of wearing them down. At 16:00, a General Staff commando squad, under the command of Lieutenant Colonel Ehud Barak, approached the plane. The 16 commando soldiers were dressed in white El Al technicians' overalls. Among them was Benjamin Netanyahu. The squad attacked the terrorists and in a precisely orchestrated 10-minute battle eliminated two of them and captured two female terrorists. Three passengers were injured in the operation, one of whom later died of her injuries. The successful operation and the skill of the Israeli soldiers won worldwide acclaim. Chief of Staff Elazar commented later: "A brave and daring force conducted the operation. If other countries in the world were to do the same, there would not be a hijacking problem." A military court sentenced the two captured terrorists to life imprisonment, but they were released as part of the POW exchange deal after the Lebanon War.

The General Staff commando unit (in white overalls) breaks into the hijacked Sabena plane. Photo: David Rubinger

Spy Network Headed by Udi Adiv Exposed

7 December

A Jewish-Arab spy network was uncovered by the security services. The network was headed by Udi Adiv, a 26-year-old member of Kibbutz Gan Shmuel and a former paratrooper. The Jewish members had been trained in Syria and belonged to an extreme communist organization. They pleaded guilty to charges of relaying information to Syria regarding IDF camps and border security procedures, and admitted that they had been planning to perpetrate hostile acts against Israel. The fact that the Jews who were arrested were considered the "salt of the earth" caused profound shock in Israel. The public could not understand the members' motives for betraying their homeland. All the network members were given stiff prison sentences. The two leaders, Udi Adiv and Daud Turki, were given 17-year prison sentences.

Udi Adiv

Hanoch Langer and his bride. Photo: Yossi Roth

The Brother-Sister Affair is Over

19 November

Chief Rabbi Shlomo Goren cleared the names of the Langer brother and sister, who had been pronounced bastards. Goren ruled that they might marry whomever they wished. Prime Minister Golda Meir congratulated Goren and said: "I hope the new edict will guide people with a similar problem." Rabbi Goren's associates expressed the fear that ultra-Orthodox circles might take violent steps against him, and the police placed guards around his Tel Aviv home.

2 June

Azulai the Policeman Wins Awards and Compliments

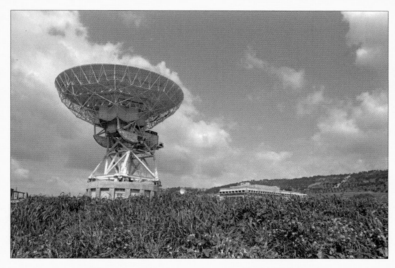

Ephraim Kishon's movie, Azulai the Policeman, starring Shai K. Ofir, won the Golden Globe, the award given by US movie critics. The film won rave reviews in other countries, too.

Photo: GPO

A ground station for satellite communications inaugurated near Bet Shemesh. Photo: GPO

5 September

The Munich massacre: 11 Israeli athletes were murdered during the Olympic Games by Black September terrorists.

15 October

Rabbis Ovadia Yosef and Shlomo Goren were elected Israel's chief rabbis, replacing Rabbis Yitzhak Nissim and Issar Unterman.

1 November

An ombudsman was appointed in the IDF.

21 November

Six Syrian MiGs were downed in the biggest battle between Israel and Syria since the Six Day War. In addition, the IDF destroyed 15 tanks and 20 artillery batteries, as well as causing heavy damage to Syrian Army camps.

Photo: GPO

8 November

"A New Life Is Only Just Beginning" - The arrival of David and Esther Markish to Israel caused great excitement at Ben-Gurion Airport. David Markish was the son of famous writer Peretz Markish, who was murdered together with other Jewish writers upon Stalin's orders in August 1952. "All last year we waited eagerly for this moment," David Markish said. "A new life for me in our holy homeland is only just beginning."
In 1972, the number of Soviet immigrants reached a new record of 30,000 Jews after international pressure had been applied to the USSR government to allow Jews to emigrate.

Photo: GPO

1 March

Moshe Sneh Died

Moshe Sneh, one of the prominent figures in the Israeli defense establishment, died at the age of 64. Before the establishment of the state, Sneh was head of the national command of the Hagana and a senior member of leading pre-state institutions. In 1947, he quit the General Zionists and joined Mapam, in which he formed a leftist cell that later merged with Maki – the Israeli Communist Party.

24 February

Elite Workers Strike

Thousands of workers at the Elite factory went on strike, demanding pay hikes and equal salaries for male and female workers. The strike lasted two months.

Photo: Arieh

1973

Chief of Staff David Elazar (center) on the Golan Heights during the fierce battles of the Yom Kippur War. Photo: GPO

The Yom Kippur War – a morning prayer before going to battle. Photo: GPO

Lieutenant General David Elazar
Commander of the Yom Kippur War

*Former Defense
Minister
Yitzhak Mordechai*

Lieutenant General David (Dado) Elazar, the ninth IDF chief of staff, will be remembered as the commander of the Yom Kippur War in October 1973. In those days which were so hard for the people of Israel, Dado stood out with his moral strength, his great wisdom and his superb heroism and commanded the most difficult war Israel has ever fought. The Agranat Commission, established after the Yom Kippur War, found him "personally responsible for what preceded the war, both in terms of situation evaluation and IDF preparedness" and recommended that his term as chief of staff be terminated. I, however, believe that he was done a great injustice because his decisions and the way he conducted the war were not investigated. Had this been done, he would most definitely have won much praise, and rightly so.

When I served as a paratrooper battalion commander – in the dreadful battles at the Chinese Farm, on the bridgehead on the banks of the Suez Canal, and elsewhere – Dado was etched in my heart as a commander and leader of the highest order. History did us a favor when it placed Lieutenant General David Elazar at the helm of the Israeli Army during this difficult war. Calm, rational and wise Dado demonstrated supreme qualities in those harsh, cruel days.

Chief of Staff Elazar and I, as battalion commander, established a unique relationship during the retaliation operations deep inside enemy territory. When we departed for the operation against the Palestinian naval commando base in Tripoli, Lebanon, Dado escorted me to the Navy vessel, and said one thing: "I'm counting on you; look after the boys."

During the battles of the Yom Kippur War, Major General (Res.) Rehav'am Ze'evi (Gandhi) got on to my battalion radio frequency and told me that Dado was personally interested in how my soldiers and I were doing. After the war, I saw Dado's agony when he met commanders; he carried the terrible pain, the loneliness and the deep sorrow for the loss of the best IDF soldiers, the boys who went to war and never returned. His heart could not take it. While in his prime, he collapsed under the burden of the horrors of the war and its results.

Dado belonged to a rare breed of IDF commanders, and was one of the most outstanding. He was the son of a warrior who had fought as a partisan and served as a captain in Tito's Yugoslavian Army. As a boy, he was raised in the spirit of the Zionist movement and kibbutz values. He was an intrepid soldier and one of the best IDF commanders ever.

He was a soldier in the Palmach, and took part in raids on government installations when we fought against the British mandate. During the War of Independence, he took part in Operation Nachshon, which opened the road to Jerusalem, and was wounded in the San Simon battles. He also commanded a platoon that attempted to break into the Old City. Later he was appointed battalion commander and fought with the Palmach-Harel brigade at the Radar Outposts, Latroun and in the Judean Hills. He participated in Operation Horev in the Sinai against the Egyptian Army. During the Sinai Campaign, he commanded an infantry brigade on the border of the Gaza Strip.

Dado was one of people who shaped IDF doctrine and prepared the forces for the ultimate test. He became commander of the Armored Corps in the 1960s; during his tenure, the corps expanded and reached the peak of its strength – a fact that was demonstrated during the Six Day War.

As head of the Northern Command, Dado was one of the heroes of the Six Day War. He initiated and pushed for the conquest of the Golan Heights in order to remove the Syrian threat from the Jordan Valley and Galilee settlements. He led the battles for the Golan and Northern Samaria. The Northern Command excelled under his command and he was greatly esteemed by both soldiers and civilians. During his term, the command relentlessly fought against rising terrorism. He was the hero of the northern settlements, establishing firm ties with the settlers and working hard for their security and well-being.

During his tenure as chief of staff, he initiated many daring operations against terrorist headquarters. The most outstanding of all was "Spring of Youth" against terrorist commanders in the heart of Beirut.

The people of Israel will forever remember Dado as a man who dedicated his life to Israel's security, and who made a significant contribution to the security of the northern settlements in particular as well as to the entire nation.

We will remember Dado for his calm and reassuring voice and for his calculated leadership; mostly, we will remember him as a superb military commander. The people of Israel won the Yom Kippur War, but paid very dearly for it. The war opened the road to peace with Egypt. Dado, whose life consisted mainly of wars and battles, died in his prime before seeing the advent of peace and before realizing his full potential and talents as a statesman.

His image, way of life, heritage and heroic deeds should be studied by Israel's youth. They are worthy of being emulated by Israel's soldiers and will remain in Israel's heart forever.

The Yom Kippur War

"Low Probability"

On the eve of the Yom Kippur War, the Israeli intelligence community assessed the probability of a Syrian-Egyptian attack on Israel as being "low". This assessment dictated Israeli political-security views, and ignored the fact that just a month earlier, in September, the Egyptian and Syrian armies had bolstered their forces in a most extraordinary manner. The Israeli intelligence assumed that this had been done for the purpose of maneuvers and the political echelons were quick to accept this assumption. Even reliable and confidential information from Jordan's King Hussein about when a war would break out did not affect the politicians, who chose to adhere to the "low probability" line.

For the sake of remaining calm or perhaps to salve the politicians' conscience, a decision was made to beef up the regular army forces on the Golan Heights and to put the IAF on alert. Prime Minister Golda Meir, however, did not cancel her official trip to Australia, scheduled for the day after Rosh Hashanah [New Year] - it was "business as usual." During the 10 days between Rosh Hashanah and Yom Kippur, Israel received more and more information that large Egyptian and Syrian forces, including armored columns, were moving to the border, but the heads of the intelligence branches would not change their earlier assessments, ruling out a possible imminent attack on Israel.

Photo: Yossi Roth

Three days before the outbreak of the war, Defense Minister Dayan toured the Golan Heights and warned that the IDF would retaliate harshly if Syria tried to attack Israel. The IDF Intelligence Branch now explained that the Syrian activity along the border with Israel was a reaction to the downing of 13 MiGs a month before. Discussing the situation, the government rejected a demand by Chief of Staff David Elazar to call up the reserves. Heading the opposition to the move was Moshe Dayan, who was backed by Prime Minister Golda Meir. Two days before Yom Kippur, Israel received a dramatic report from an extremely reliable source close to the Egyptian leadership which totally contradicted the previous assessment and undermined the confidence of the intelligence branch heads for the first time. The report said that Egypt and Syria were about to attack Israel. In order to verify the report, Prime Minister Golda Meir sent Mossad head, Tzvi Zamir, abroad to meet with a supremely important source. Meanwhile, the government decided on a partial call-up of the reserves. Zamir returned with unshakable, authorized, information: War was on the threshold. However, even in light of this information, the intelligence branch remained adamant: The probability of an all-out war was low; at most, the heads of intelligence claimed, there would be some border skirmishes.

Israel prepared for a calm, quiet day of fasting. Several hours into Yom Kippur, the "low probability" became a difficult, surprising and painful reality. The Yom Kippur War had begun...

6 October

Yom Kippur, Two in the Afternoon: The Egyptians Cross the Canal

It was a great surprise. Egyptian and Syrian forces launched a massive attack against Israel. Two hundred Egyptian warplanes attacked IDF forces in the Sinai, while their ground forces started crossing the canal with rubber boats and constructed bridges that would permit additional forces to cross over. The Egyptian troops, who had rehearsed the crossing well, were equipped with antitank rockets. Overnight, Egypt managed to move about 100,000 soldiers and dozens of tanks across the canal. Facing them were some 8,000 IDF soldiers, most of them from a veteran reserve brigade. The IDF had 300 tanks in the Suez Canal region, but when they tried to move toward the outposts, they ran into Egyptian infantry ambushes which operated massive quantities of antitank weapons, destroying most of the Israeli tanks. At the same time, the Egyptian armored forces and infantry that had crossed the canal over the two bridges they had constructed, captured most of the IDF outposts.

The attack on the Syrian front was another unwelcome surprise. Syrian planes attacked IDF units on the Golan Heights and their artillery shelled the civilian settlements. In parallel, hundreds of Syrian tanks rushed westwards and captured the Golan with almost no resistance. The IAF was given the task of warding off the attack. Waves upon waves of planes attacked the advancing Syrian Army, but they were struck at mercilessly by advanced missiles. The Syrian Army also sent three helicopters with dozens of commando soldiers who surprised the IDF soldiers in the intelligence base at the top of Mount Hermon and, in a swift battle, conquered the outpost that had always been called "the eyes of Israel". Dozens of Israeli intelligence soldiers were taken captive and the advanced electronic equipment that was in the post was sent to Damascus.

At dawn, the situation looked painful and grim: Egypt controlled most of the canal outposts, and its troops had conquered most of the Suez region and were quickly advancing eastward, into the Sinai. The situation was equally grave in the north. The advancing Syrian armored units were confronted by only one regular army division that had already lost many tanks and soldiers. There was nothing to do but wait for reinforcement from the reserves.

Egyptian President Anwar Sadat in conference with his senior officers. Photo: From the Egyptian book, The Ramadan War.

IDF columns headed for the northern front. Photo: GPO

Photo: AFP

Prime Minister Golda Meir's Announcement on 6 October:

"Citizens of Israel: Today, at around 14:00, the Egyptian and the Syrian armies launched an attack against Israel. They carried out a series of air force, armoured corps and artillery assaults in the Sinai and on the Golan Heights. "The IDF is fighting to ward off the attack, inflicting heavy losses on the enemy... Our enemies had hoped to surprise the citizens of Israel on Yom Kippur... but we were not surprised. Our intelligence services knew that the Egyptian and Syrian armies were preparing for a combined attack... We have no doubt that the IDF will win...".

The Yom Kippur War

7 October

The Counteroffensive: The Most Difficult Day of the War

On the second and most difficult day of the war, the IDF units on the southern front faced five Egyptian armored and infantry divisions of 400 tanks and 100,000 soldiers. The Israeli tanks failed in their attempt to link up with the canal outposts, suffering heavily from the effective use of the Egyptian antitank weapons. At the same time, because of the densely deployed Egyptian anti-aircraft batteries, the IAF was limited in its striking power. The Egyptian forces were establishing their new rear about five km east of the canal, while the IDF was withdrawing to the second line of defense. IDF reserves started arriving at the front, while the regular forces fought with whatever they had left to prevent the entire sector from falling.

The situation in the north was even worse: Two Syrian tank columns penetrated deep into the Golan Heights. In the central sector, one column reached as far as the Bnot-Ya'akov Bridge on the Jordan River. The distance from there to the Hula Valley is very short. In the southern sector, the Syrian forces came as close as seven km to Lake Kinneret, and in the northern sector, they surrounded the Golan division headquarters. In light of the situation, the IDF command decided to send the entire air force to ward off the Syrian assault. The two armored brigades that had been stationed on the Golan when the fighting started suffered heavy losses but kept on fighting. The reserve soldiers immediately engaged in the counteroffensive. It was another 24 hours before the divisions under the command of Dan Laner and Refael Eitan managed to curb the advancing Syrian forces.

Consultations at the Southern Command Headquarters during the counteroffensive battles. Photo: David Rubinger

Photo: Avraham Vered

8 October

Chief of Staff David Elazar:
"We will go on fighting until we break their bones."

While Dado was promising reporters in Tel Aviv that "we [would] break their bones", the IDF was engaged in its counteroffensive in the Sinai. A division under Major General Avraham (Bren) Adan was fighting in the northern sector, and Major General Ariel Sharon's division was sent to assist it from the south.

Initial reports from the field said that the counteroffensive was progressing well and the mood at the IDF High Command greatly improved. However, several hours later, it became apparent that the counteroffensive had failed terribly. Bren's division was repelled by the Egyptian troops, suffering heavy losses; 400 tanks were destroyed and dozens of soldiers killed or wounded. Sharon's division had been directed to attack the Third Egyptian Army instead of assisting Bren in his attack on the Second Army, thus "missing" the unsuccessful counteroffensive.

The IDF command was in a bad state. It decided to deploy the forces in the Sinai in defensive positions and forego additional attempts to push the Egyptians back across the canal. While the IDF was analyzing the situation, Egypt launched a counteroffensive in response, and only as a result of enormous efforts was the IDF able to ward it off.

Paratroopers on the Suez-Cairo Road. Photo: GPO

8 October

Moshe Dayan: "The Situation Might Lead to the Destruction of the Third Temple."

Defense Minister Moshe Dayan was surprised by the staying power of the Egyptian Army and the failure of the IDF counterattack. He was in a foul and pessimistic mood. The ministers were stunned when he said he felt that the IDF should withdraw deep into the Sinai and set up a new line of defense in the Gidi and Mitleh Pass area. Later that day, Dayan appeared before the Israeli newspaper editors' committee and informed them that the situation was very grave and might lead to the destruction of the third temple. The editors were astounded; some said it felt like an earthquake, others burst into tears. Dayan wanted to appear on TV and tell the public the bitter truth, but Golda Meir would not permit him to do so. In his memoirs, Dayan revealed that he had tendered his resignation, but Meir had rejected it.

11 October

IDF Units Approach Damascus

On the morning of the sixth day of the war, the IDF was ordered to launch the big assault on Syria. Until that day, the IDF had been involved in fighting the Syrians off and trying to shift the war on to Syrian territory. During the preceding 24 hours, the IAF had been bombing strategic targets around Damascus, including airports, military bases, oil refineries, government buildings and other targets. At the same time, the IDF managed to conquer the entire Golan Heights, and the Syrians retreated, leaving behind some 900 tanks, mostly damaged.

The attack on Syria was led by two armored divisions commanded by Refael Eitan and Moshe Peled. They broke through the fortified Syrian posts and, by the evening, were 40 km from Damascus.

Some people believed that the IDF could put a decisive and unequivocal end to the war by conquering Damascus, but political and strategic considerations tipped the scale in the other direction. The IDF decided that the best thing to do would be to hold on to the current easily defensible line, and to send as many units as possible to the southern front. On 12 October, all fighting on the Golan ceased. Israel regained all the territories it had held before the war as well as more land inside Syria.

Defense Minister Moshe Dayan at a news conference on the second day of the war. Photo: GPO

A photo taken on the road to Damascus as a souvenir.

The Yom Kippur War

19**73**

Israeli tanks crossing the Suez Canal.

Ariel Sharon consulting Defense Minister Moshe Dayan and southern front commander Haim Bar-Lev before crossing the canal. Photo: GPO

15 October

Sharon and the Paratroopers Cross the Canal

On the night of 15 October, paratroopers from Sharon's division crossed the Suez Canal in rubber boats and set up a bridgehead on the western bank. The place chosen for the crossing was the gap between the Second and Third Egyptian Armies. Sharon's division was supposed to seize a four-km-wide corridor through which forces could cross and set up a bridgehead on the western bank of the canal. Then Bren's division was to cross the Egyptian bridges, move south, capture airports, eliminate missile batteries and cut the Third Army off from the rear. Sharon's paratroopers started attacking vehicles and soldiers, and were later joined by the tanks that began to cross the canal on rafts.

The next day, after fierce battles, Bren's soldiers also crossed the canal, broadened the narrow corridor the paratroopers had created, moved south and eliminated the missile batteries that prevented the IAF from operating in the region. Sharon's brigade moved north toward Ismailia, trying to push the Second Army deeper into Egyptian territory. The Egyptians, at the same time, kept trying to attack the IDF bridgehead on the western bank, attempting to cut the Israeli forces off, but failed. On 19 October, when the Egyptian leaders realized just how far the IDF had penetrated Egyptian territory, President Sadat dismissed Chief of Staff Shazali. On 22 October, the UN Security Council declared a cease-fire, but the IDF kept fighting for another two days during which time it surrounded the entire Third Army. On 24 October, a unit of Bren's division attempted to break into and conquer the city of Suez, but it was repelled and suffered heavy losses: 80 soldiers were killed and dozens were wounded.

17 October

The "Chinese Farm" Battles

One of the most difficult battles was waged at a site known as the "Chinese Farm", when a paratrooper unit under the command of Lieutenant Colonel Yitzhak Mordechai entered a death trap. The paratroopers fell into a well-laid ambush of an Egyptian division that struck mercilessly at Israeli soldiers who could neither find shelter nor advance. Dozens of paratroopers were killed in this battle, and it took hours before rescue forces could evacuate the wounded and the dead.

Chief of Staff David (Dado) Elazar and General Arik Sharon. Photo: David Rubinger

1973

22 October

Conquering the Hermon – "The eyes of Israel"

After fierce and bloody battles, a Golani Brigade force managed to retake the Hermon outpost which had fallen into Syrian hands at the outbreak of the war. The battle, which was mainly fought face to face against a Syrian commando unit, took place during the night, with the Syrians preventing the Golani soldiers from reaching the peak. The fighting lasted 12 hours. When the post was taken, one of the soldiers told a TV crew: "These are the eyes of Israel."

An Israeli flag on the Hermon outpost. Photo: Yossi Roth

11 November

A Cease-Fire Agreement At Kilometer 101

The IDF sustained 170 casualties and hundreds were wounded. Some 3,000 Egyptian soldiers were killed and 6,000 were taken prisoner by Israel. The campaign was a military success, but did not yield any significant changes in Israel's security situation. The region was quiet for a while, but tension along the borders prevailed. The most important achievement was the reopening of the Eilat Bay to Israeli vessels. The passage remained open for 10 years – until the Six Day War.

Top: *UN troops guarding the tent where the cease-fire talks were taking place at Kilometer 101. Photo: Israel Sun*

Bottom: *The Israeli delegation headed by Major General Aharon Yariv and the Egyptian delegation headed by General Gamassi. Photo: IPPA*

Photo: Yossi Roth

21 February

IAF planes downed a Libyan Boeing passenger plane that entered the Sinai airspace, ignoring signals and warnings. 105 passengers were killed.

9 April

Operation Spring of Youth: IDF units raided the heart of Beirut, attacking the headquarters of terror organizations and eliminating three Fatah leaders in their homes. This was one of the most daring IDF raids: 43 terrorists were killed, including Arafat's deputy. The IDF sustained two fatalities.

Photo: Gamma

7 May

Israel celebrated its 25th birthday in a big IDF parade in Jerusalem viewed by 300,000 spectators.

24 May

Efraim Katzir was nominated fourth Israeli president, replacing Zalman Shazar. Katzir was a professor of biochemistry and one of Israel's most senior scientists.

11 July

Major General Ariel Sharon, head of the Southern Command, quit the army when he realized that there was no chance that he would be appointed chief of staff. He was replaced by Major General Shmuel Gonen (Gorodish).

1973

The Yom Kippur War

The Outcome of the War: Fatalities, Wounded and POWs

By the end of the war, Israel's casualties numbered about 2,600 dead and 7,000 wounded. The IAF had lost over 100 planes, and the Armored Corps had lost some 800 tanks, most of which had been destroyed by Egyptian antitank missiles operated by Egyptian soldiers. Egypt had 233 Israeli POWs while Israel had 8,300 Egyptian POWs. The POWs were exchanged on 15 November, with the Egyptians first releasing the wounded and two days later the remainder, including POWs held in Egypt for four years, since the war of attrition.

Memorial day on Mount Herzl. Photo: Micha Bar-Am.

The Israeli, Egyptian, Syrian and Jordanian delegations at the Geneva Peace Conference. Photo: AP

21 December

The Geneva Peace Conference

The conference opened with the participation of the foreign ministers of Israel, Egypt, Syria and Jordan under the auspices of the UN and the US and USSR foreign ministers. The conference was convened to discuss a just and lasting peace in the Middle East but, in fact, initially only addressed the issue of disengagement in the Sinai and on the Golan. The importance of the conference lay in the very fact that it had taken place, as well as in its ceremonial aspect. Indeed, several days after it started, the conference closed. The disengagement talks continued via US Secretary of State Henry, Kissinger.

1973

7 April

First Time in the "Eurovision"

Israel participated for the first time in the European "Eurovision" song contest, held in Luxembourg. Israel was represented by Ilanit who sang Ei Sham (Somewhere) by Nurit Hirsch and Ehud Manor. This was the first entertainment show relayed live to Israel via satellite.

21 December

The Geneva Peace Conference opened, attended by delegations from Israel, Egypt, Syria and Jordan. The world media described it as "a first historic meeting between Israelis and Arabs after four wars." The conference yielded disengagement agreements on the Syrian and Egyptian fronts.

31 December

Elections for the eighth Knesset were held. The Alignment went down from 56 to 51 seats; the other parties more or less maintained their number of seats. The influence of the Yom Kippur War fiasco was not yet reflected in the results.

18 May

"I Am Staying on the Boat Until Peace Comes."

Photo: Yossi Roth

Abie Nathan began broadcasting from the Voice of Peace radio station. His medium-wave transmission, almost at the end of the dial, was broadcast from the Peace Ship that was cruising along Israel's shoreline. On its first day, the radio broadcast mostly pop music. At 20:00, Abie came on the air and presented his credo in his own style and with much emotion.

11 March

"Quiet, We're Filming *Casablan*!"

The filming of the Israeli musical *Casablan* began. The movie was produced and directed by Menachem Golan and filmed by David Gurfinkel, with actor Yehoram Gaon, who had also starred in the stage version.

Casablan underwent several changes: It started as a novel by Yig'al Mosinson; in 1957, it was adapted for the stage and put on by the Cameri Theater, starring Yosef Yadin. American director Larry Frisch

used it for a film whose plot took place in Greece. In 1963, *Casablan* returned to the Israeli stage as a musical. Golan's new movie version did not focus on ethnic tension, but mainly on the gaps between the various social strata in Israeli society after the Six Day War. The film was a great success in Israel.

21 October

Danny Kaye "Joins the Reserves" - Actor-comedian Danny Kaye and French Singer Enrico Macias arrived in Israel on 20 October to perform in front of soldiers and the wounded in hospitals. At the airport, Kaye said: "I came to join the IDF reserves... I will do anything you ask me to, as long as I am helping soldiers." Several days earlier, Leonard Cohen had arrived in Israel and was immediately "drafted" to perform in front of soldiers on the front lines.

Photo: GPO

11 March

Israel's First Drive-In Movie Theater

Families equipped with food and drink packed the new drive-in movie theater in Tel Aviv. When the commercials took too long, the drivers blew their horns. The first movie shown on the giant 30-meter screen was Walt Disney's *Jungle Book*.

Photo: Dror Simchoni

(19 74

Gush Emunim *members march toward the settlement of Sebastia. Photo: David Rubinger*

Elon Moreh settlers evacuated from Mount Rojib. Photo: Zoom 77

The Establishment of *Gush Emunim*
The campaign for the redemption of the land began

*Former Minister
and MK
Zevulun Hammer*

The year 1974 was the starting point of two long and significant campaigns in which we are still engaged today and in which we will be engaged for years to come: The peace process and settlement of the land.

This was the year that followed the Yom Kippur War. The Egyptian and Israeli armies were still entangled. The war had ended, but not the attrition – there were attacks and counterattacks.

Henry Kissinger was working on the disengagement plan. In February, the IDF completed the evacuation of its forces from the western side of the Suez Canal. Today we know that this was when the seeds of peace were sown. Sadat would come to Jerusalem in 1977; the Camp David talks would be held in 1979 and end in a peace agreement. The peace campaign was beginning. At the very same time, in February 1974, *Gush Emunim* was founded. Settlement of Judea, Samaria, Gaza and the Golan had already begun, but religious Zionism – which believes that settling every part of the land is both the privilege and the duty of every pioneering Torah-learner – started operating as an official movement. The campaign for the redemption of the land began.

The two campaigns followed parallel trails in history, and it has gradually become clearer that the two are intertwined. Paradoxically – and this may not be understood by most observers – they are interdependent. Unless we seek every opportunity to make peace in this land, settlement does not have a moral national future; without settlement, peace has have no political or security basis. Deep under the surface of historic processes – which secretly mock the political groupings of the moment – lies the proof of the link between reconciliation with the Arab nations and the return of the people of Zion to their land. I am convinced that whatever the shape of peace between us and our neighbors will be, its geo-political essence will draw upon the reservoir of dedication, self-sacrifice and willingness to leave a familiar home and street in order to build a home on barren land, protect it and develop it.

The *Gush Emunim* Movement provided every Jew with a new perspective, and gave the State of Israel the strength to endure today's pressures for the sake of tomorrow's goals.

I am certain that the presence of *Gush Emunim* and its settlements will bring a peace which is far safer and more reliable than the one we would have made had we adopted the concept of keeping the territories empty of Jews, to be used as bargaining chips.

Gush Emunim was formed halfway to Israel's jubilee. I find this symbolic. The War of Independence ended on the cease-fire borders, which were incidental from the logical viewpoint and impossible from the political viewpoint. They cut through the heart of Jerusalem, dividing it in two and making it difficult for us emotionally. Fifty years later, we could have found ourselves not only giving back territories, but encouraging war. Between then and today, *Gush Emunim* laid the foundations for a different, permanent reality. The infrastructure of the bloc lay in the education of the knitted *yarmulke* generation – those who feel it is their duty to study the Torah, work, serve, defend and build the state.

That generation did not only build *Gush Emunim*. It also laid the foundation for the Hesder Yeshivas that combine military service with Torah studies, thus forging the link between knitted *yarmulkes* and state security. More and more religious officers feel that it is their duty to extend their IDF service since they consider security as part of their personal and national fulfillment.

In 1974, we did not know how important that was.

In the jubilee year, we know – our mission is not yet complete.

1.4. 74

The Agranat Commission:
The Military Echelon is Responsible for the Yom Kippur War Fiasco

The first session of the Agranat Commission. Left to right: Prof. Yiga'el Yadin, Supreme Court Justices Moshe Landau and Shimon Agranat, State Comptroller Yitzhak Nevenzal, Major General Haim Laskov. Photo: GPO

When the Agranat Commission published its interim report, the Israeli public was appalled: The state commission of inquiry determined that the main culprit was Chief of Staff Lieutenant General David (Dado) Elazar, and recommended that his tenure be terminated. According to the Commission's findings, Dado had delayed the call-up of the reserves before the outbreak of the war, did not formulate his own assessment as commander and did not prepare the army properly. Intelligence Branch head Eli Zeira and his deputy were also found personally responsible for failing to anticipate the war despite having plenty of intelligence material at their disposal. The Commission also ruled that the head of the Southern Command, Shmuel Gonen (Gorodish), was responsible for failing to have the forces on the Egyptian front in a suitable state of preparedness. The Commission recommended that those senior officers be dismissed.

The public was furious that the Commission had placed all the responsibility on the military while exonerating the political echelons, mainly Moshe Dayan and Golda Meir, for the terrible fiasco. The Commission indeed criticized Dayan, claiming that, with his military experience, he should have formed an opinion that contradicted that of the military, but the criticism was mild and inconclusive. The committee stated that Golda Meir's moves and decisions had been correct, and even commended her for deciding on the extent of the call-up of reserve soldiers on the eve of the Yom Kippur War. The fact that the committee laid the blame on the military while the political echelons washed their hands of any responsibility proved to the incensed public that the leadership was utterly insensitive and cynical.

Lieutenant General David Elazar resigned immediately, saying: "I am sorry to leave under such circumstances." The majority of the public sympathized with the chief of staff and would not let Meir and Dayan stay on as if nothing had happened. Vigils, demonstrations and petitions were organized, mainly by stunned, pained reserve officers who had returned from the war, calling on the two to resign. The public felt that the Agranat Commission had been more preoccupied with whitewashing than with revealing the truth.

Gun-Smuggling Archbishop Cappucci Arrested

8 August

Archbishop Hilarion Cappucci, a senior clergyman, was apprehended by the security services while smuggling weapons for the terror organizations. When his car, which enjoyed church immunity, was captured, it was found to be loaded with Kalachnikov rifles, pistols and some 200 kg of explosives. Cappucci was sentenced to 12 years in prison, but was released three years later as a gesture of goodwill to the Vatican. He was then deported.

Yitzhak Rabin Appointed Prime Minister

3.6.74

1974

Golda Meir led the Alignment in the Knesset elections held on 31 December 1973 and won despite the Yom Kippur War fiasco. The Alignment lost some power, going down from 56 to 51 Knesset seats, but Meir encountered no real difficulties forming a cabinet. However, this government existed on borrowed time. The Agranat Commission's report was published at the beginning of April and caused a major uproar. Meir was forced to resign and her cabinet became a caretaker government. A debate ensued in Labor as to whether Meir should be replaced or new elections called. In the end, the party decided to present a new candidate for premiership.

The leading candidates were Pinchas Sapir, Yig'al Alon, Shimon Peres and Yitzhak Rabin. Sapir, who was the natural candidate, refused to assume the post despite the pressure exerted on him. Alon was ill and would not take the job. Dayan was associated with the fiasco, and was therefore disqualified. The remaining candidates were Peres and Rabin. The latter had a security background which the Labor Central Committee members believed was essential for rebuilding the people's confidence in the party.

Prime Minister Yitzhak Rabin and Defense Minister Shimon Peres watching an Armored Corps exercise.
Photo: Shalom Bar-Tal

Peres was widely supported in the party because of his political skills. In a secret ballot by the Central Committee members, Rabin got 298 votes to Peres' 254. Rabin, who had the support of the veteran leadership, defeated Peres, a former Rafi member, by only a small margin. Peres' achievement showed that the former Rafi members had been reabsorbed into the party and that he was greatly esteemed. Upon his election, Rabin started forming a cabinet. He was in no hurry because Labor was still in power, thanks to the Meir caretaker government. He presented his new cabinet on 3 June – a cabinet which had an unstable coalition backing it. Peres was appointed defense minister.

Gush Emunim Settles Sebastia

25 July

Gush Emunim activists and supporters, accompanied by MKs, settled near Sebastia, receiving extensive media coverage. The settlers chained themselves so that they could not be evacuated easily. Four days later, refusing to evacuate the site themselves, a large IDF force was sent to evacuate them. The settlers employed passive resistance, and the soldiers had to carry them out one by one. The move sparked a public debate between those who were in favor of settling the territories and those who were against.

Photo: David Rubinger

18 January
The Israeli-Egyptian disengagement agreement was signed with the mediation of US Secretary of State, Henry Kissinger.

10 February
A protest movement led by Motti Ashkenazi called on Golda Meir and Moshe Dayan to resign following the Yom Kippur War fiasco.

25 February
Gush Emunim, a new Zionist-religious movement, was established with the aim of settling all parts of Eretz Yisrael.

1 April
The Agranat Commission published an interim report, laying the blame for the Yom Kippur War fiasco on Lieutenant General David Elazar, Intelligence Branch head Eli Zeira, and head of the Southern Command, Shmuel Gonen (Gorodish).

11 April
In a horrible terrorist attack in Kiryat Shmona, 18 were killed, including eight children and two soldiers.

14 April
Mordechai (Motta) Gur was appointed chief of staff following David Elazar's resignation.

15 May
Terrorists captured the Netiv Meir School in Ma'alot. Twenty-one pupils and three adults were killed in the rescue operation.

31 May
Israel and Syria signed a disengagement agreement in Geneva.

3 June
Yitzhak Rabin presented his new cabinet to the Knesset.

15.5. **74**

The Ma'alot Disaster: Terrorists Kill 21 Pupils

An IDF soldier involved in the rescue operation at the Ma'alot school carries his wounded sister.
Photo: Ya'acov Sa'ar, la'am

A band of terrorists from Naif Hawatme's organization crossed the Lebanese border and captured the Netiv Meir school in Ma'alot. The event was one of the most traumatic in Israel's history. On their way to the school, the terrorists burst into the house of the Cohen family and murdered the mother, the father and their four-year-old son. The terrorists took 105 pupils and 10 teachers hostage and conducted uncompromising negotiations, demanding that Israel release 20 of their comrades held in local prisons. The defense establishment believed that Israel should under no circumstances deviate from the policy of not surrendering to terrorists' demands.

Defense Minister Moshe Dayan ordered a rescue operation using force. An elite IDF unit was ordered to storm the school and free the hostages. The results were disastrous: 21 children and three adults were killed and 68 wounded. The IDF forces also suffered casualties, including one dead. Severe criticism was leveled later at the teachers who had fled, abandoning the children. The terror attack shocked Israel, mainly due to its serious results. The newspapers were full of photographs of the dead children and the stories of the survivors.

US Secretary of State Henry Kissinger arrives at Ben-Gurion Airport and is received by Foreign Minister Abba Eban.
Photo: Moshe Reicher

Kissinger Brings About a Disengagement Agreement in Sinai

18 January

As a result of his energetic activity and in spite of great difficulties, US Secretary of State Henry Kissinger managed to bring about a disengagement agreement between Israel and Egypt. This was the first time that the parties had accepted the participation of an American mediator, despite the Russians' disapproval. Kissinger put pressure mainly on Israel to make concessions, seeking to prove to the Arabs that the United States was the only power that could mediate between the parties and persuade Israel to adopt an attitude of compromise. Indeed, according to the agreement, Israel was to withdraw from all the territories it held west of the Suez Canal.

Photo: Neri Gavish

The POWs Return From Syria

1 June

Sixty-five IDF soldiers who had been taken captive by Syria were returned to Israel as part of an exchange agreement between the two countries. The POWs were received with warmth and affection by thousands of Israelis who came to greet them. In return, Israel handed over 408 Syrian POWs. Among the returning POWs were the soldiers who had been stationed at the Mount Hermon outpost and had been taken captive on the first day of the war. They said they had been tortured by the Syrians.

1974

6 June

Dancers Valery and Galina Panov Immigrate to Israel

"We feel like survivors returning home," said ballet dancers Valery and Galina Panov upon arrival at Ben-Gurion Airport. They were greeted by numerous fans who had came to applaud the successful outcome of their stubborn struggle for the right to immigrate to Israel. This was the big moment of the people who had supported the Panovs with demonstrations, petitions and pressure on the Soviet authorities. Galina came out of the plane first, and was showered with kisses and flowers. Valery emerged next and could not hide his joyful tears.

24 June

Terrorists murdered a mother and her two children after they broke into the family home in Naharia.

25 July

Hundreds of settlers settled in Sebastia, Samaria, and clashed with IDF soldiers. They were evacuated four days later.

19 November

Terrorists entered an apartment block in Bet She'an, killing four people and wounding 20. The IDF killed the terrorists.

11 December

A terrorist threw a hand grenade at the audience in the Chen Movie Theater in Tel Aviv, killing two and wounding five people.

8 November

Import of Private Cars Prohibited

The Israeli Lira was devalued by 43% and the prices of all imported goods went up by 22%. The government also canceled all subsidies of basic commodities and imposed a temporary ban on the import of private cars and other products. The public reacted sharply and staged protest demonstrations. At the same time, frenzied shopping continued until the very last moment, with people snatching sugar, rice, coffee and cigarettes off the shelves. Car importers sold their entire stock, long lines stretched outside gas stations, and policemen were placed on guard at the banks.

10 February

Motti Ashkenazi Leads the Protest Movements

Motti Ashkenazi, the commander of "Budapest", the only Suez Canal outpost that did not surrender, left hospital prematurely and started a vigil outside the Prime Minister's Office in Jerusalem, demanding that Defense Minister Moshe Dayan be fired. Ashkenazi launched a one-man campaign to change the Israeli leadership, accusing Dayan of being "the main, though not the only, culprit for the Yom Kippur War fiasco." His struggle prompted hundreds, including soldiers and reservists, to contact him and express willingness to join him in his struggle.

Photo: David Rubinger

19 November

War Widow Marries a Disabled Bedouin IDF Veteran

A nurse at Ichilov Hospital in Tel Aviv whose husband was killed in the war married Bedouin tracker Ibrahim Shibli, a disabled war veteran who had been cited for his bravery and exemplary conduct during the fighting at the Suez Canal. The civilian ceremony was held in the bridegroom's village, Arab al-Shibli, near Mount Tabor. The couple spent their honeymoon in the village. The Defense Ministry's Rehabilitation Department gave them IL4,000. After the honeymoon, the coupled moved to a flat in Ra'anana.

Photo: Michael Freidin

(1975

Yehoshua Peretz, chairman of the Ashdod Port workers' union, with Yerucham Meshel, Histadrut secretary-general, at the end of the port strike. Photo: Shalom Bar-Tal

Strike at the Ashdod Port. Photo: Yitzhak Nofech-Mozes

Yehoshua Peretz
The writing on the wall

Former Head of
Histadrut
Amir Peretz

Avraham Shushan, the Ashkelon District Court judge, decided to send Yehoshua Peretz, chairman of the Ashdod Port workers' union, to prison. This started a wave of protests and demonstrations that quickly spread around the city of Ashdod. The extent of the identification with the port workers as well as nation-wide reactions – that were critical but also very sympathetic – should have been the writing on the wall for the Labor Movement, preceding the elections of 1977 that brought about the most significant political upheaval in Israel's history.

Yehoshua Peretz was chairman of the union at the time when Labor ruled both the Histadrut Labor Union and the government. Co-operation between these two bodies was so tight that the workers had no room to protest or express any kind of displeasure. They were forced to accept as "God-given" whatever the ruling organizations agreed on and dictated, a fact which angered them greatly, and rightly so.

True, the way the struggle started was nothing to sympathize with. It started because Peretz ordered the Ashdod Port gates to be closed after a guard demanded that he identify himself. Clearly, this was just the spark that ignited the conflagration and, in the end, was rather marginal. Peretz, however, remains imprinted in our collective memory as a mythological, authentic, courageous and decisive workers' leader. It is also clear today that the protest did not start because of any particular event, but rather because thousands of workers were feeling frustrated and angry after years of having their rights ignored.

Peretz taught the workers just how important it was for them to get organized when fighting for a just cause. He led thousands who suffered from the social deprivation and the neglect which were the lot of manual laborers at the time. Clearly, he symbolized a shift both in working relations in Israel and in the manner in which the government, the Histadrut and the workers treated one another. His method of struggle expressed the independence of the heads of the workers' unions. This independence resulted from the fact that the workers really supported them, thus giving them room to operate without fear.

The Histadrut was in a real dilemma: On the one hand, it found it hard to accept the fact that local labor unions were not following its instructions and were breaking the law. On the other hand, it had to side with Peretz and even state that he had made his move as part of his job – in this way giving him its support.

The numerous articles the press published at the time also attest to the great distance between the laborers and the authorities who ignored their feelings and needs. One of the writers even dubbed Peretz "Idi Amin", hinting that he was unpatriotic and was sabotaging the essential interests of the State of Israel. Only a few really understood the workers' need for recognition.

The establishment treated the protest movement led by Peretz with the same indifference as it treated other outbreaks of social protest, but this time it was not a group of frustrated, hopeless, unemployed people. This was a group of working men who belonged to a very central and major production facility in Israel. This group united and spoke clearly and defiantly in support of a comprehensive ideological workers' struggle which emanated from a feeling of deprivation.

It is clear today, perhaps more than ever before, just how justified this outcry was; moreover, Yehoshua Peretz taught us how important it is for the workers to have an authentic, charismatic and relentless leader.

The Savoy Hotel – A Battle in the Heart of Tel Aviv

An eight-member Fatah terror squad reached the Tel Aviv shore in rubber boats and captured three floors of the Savoy Hotel on Geula Street. The terrorists took dozens of people who were in the hotel hostage and moved them to the top floor. They conducted negotiations with the security forces using Kochava Levy, a guest at the hotel, as mediator. The terrorists demanded that Israel free their comrades imprisoned in Israel and, as was customary in terror attacks for purposes of bargaining, the Israeli government conducted lengthy negotiations with them, attempting to wear them down. The entire country followed the negotiations closely, with the terrified and exhausted Kochava Levy going back and forth between the soldiers and the terrorists, trying to explain the situation to the former and to convince the latter not to kill hostages. By using Levy as a mediator, the terrorists made a big mistake, because she provided the security forces with a precise account of the number of terrorists, the type of weapons they had and their positions. At 05:00, nearly 24 hours after the terrorists had seized control of the hotel, the General Staff commando unit broke into the hotel, led by Colonel Uzi Yairi. The soldiers had to deal with the explosive charges the terrorists had planted in the hotel. The battle was difficult because the terrorists were well barricaded. Seven terrorists were killed and the eighth was apprehended. Colonel Yairi, who had commanded the paratroopers' brigade in the battle at the Chinese Farm in the Sinai during the Yom Kippur War, was killed. Two other IDF soldiers and three hostages were also killed and the hotel was very badly damaged.

The terror and shock caused by this incident were great. The Israelis felt that no place in Israel was safe from terror, not even Tel Aviv, which had been considered the safest place in Israel.

The Savoy Hotel after the battle with the Terrorists. Photo: GPO

The UN Rules: "Zionism Is Racism"

10 November

"When I stood on the UN podium, I remembered my father who in 1939 had ripped the British White Paper into shreds, and I decided to do the same." This is how Israel's UN Ambassador Haim Herzog described his dramatic speech at the UN General Assembly, during which he ripped to pieces the text of the UN resolution that determined that Zionism was racism. Herzog added: "I knew I had to make a dramatic gesture. I knew that this was an historic moment which was being written on a page of Jewish history, and that I had been chosen by Providence to be the messenger who represents all Jews." Israel found consolation in friendly gestures by its friends at the UN, primarily the United States, which announced that it would disregard the UN resolution. Other free-world countries leveled harsh criticism at the resolution.

Israel's UN Ambassador Haim Herzog ripping the UN resolution to pieces. Photo: AP

Israel and Egypt Sign Interim Agreement

Having brought about a disengagement agreement between Israel and Egypt, US Secretary of State Henry Kissinger decided to enter the local political arena in full force in an attempt to bring about an interim agreement between the two countries. He was not daunted by the Savoy Hotel attack, which had been intended to sabotage his efforts. The Americans were pleased with Egypt's compromising attitude, and decided to pressure Israel into showing flexibility regarding a withdrawal from the Suez Canal to the Gidi and Mitleh Passes. Israel agreed to the withdrawal, but made the move conditional on an Egyptian declaration of non-belligerency. Sadat, however, was unable to make such a declaration in return for only a partial withdrawal.

Realizing that the talks had reached a dead end, Kissinger used every means he had to pressure Israel. He threatened that the Geneva Conference would reconvene and that he would consider Israel's conduct as a personal affront. Eventually, he declared that the United States would "re-examine" its Middle East policy, hinting that the US might stop its support of Israel. Indeed, the administration acted very coldly toward Israel, freezing new arms contracts and sending out unofficial feelers in the direction of the PLO.

On its part, Israel used the influence of its friends in the US and even managed to get the support of the majority of the Senate members. The US maintained its cool treatment of Israel for about 18 months. In August, Kissinger returned to the region, this time managing to find a compromise. Israel agreed to return the Abu-Rodes oil fields to Egypt, withdraw to the area of the passes and set up two-way early-warning stations. The signing of the interim agreement started a "honeymoon" between Israel and the US, with the latter providing Israel with advanced F-15 planes and other sophisticated weapons. The interim agreement constituted another stage in the Israeli-Egyptian rapprochement.

Prime Minister Yitzhak Rabin signs the interim agreement with Egypt in the presence of US Secretary of State Henry Kissinger.

A demonstration in support of the interim Israeli-Egyptian agreement. Photo: GPO

Photo: Uzi Keren

Michael Tzur Sentenced to 15 Years

24 May

Michael Tzur, a prominent and well-known businessman, was sentenced to 15 years in prison after being convicted of fraud, theft, embezzlement and taking bribes. Tzur was director-general of HaHevra LeYisrael and was accused of taking advantage of his prominent public stand for personal gain. He pleaded guilty. His conviction and arrest reinforced the public feeling that corruption was rampant within Labor Party.

1975

15 January
A rising number of USSR Jews drop out on their way to Israel.

5 March
Eight terrorists attacked the Savoy Hotel in Tel Aviv and took dozens of hostages. During the takeover, the IDF unit killed seven terrorists and captured one. Three soldiers were killed, including Colonel Uzi Yairi of the paratroopers.

6 March
Gush Emunim activists and soldiers clashed during an abortive attempt to settle in Elon Moreh.

24 March
US President Ford announced a policy of "re-examining" the attitude of the US toward Israel because of the failure of Kissinger's shuttle mission. The US delayed weapon shipments to Israel as part of the sanctions.

24 May
Michael Tzur, former director general of HaHevra LeYisrael, was sentenced to 15 years in prison for taking IL 12 million in bribes.

29 May
Prime Minister Rabin offered Ariel Sharon the post of security adviser. Sharon accepted the offer.

26 June
The coffins of Eliahu Chakim and Eliahu Bet-Tzuri were brought to Israel for burial. The two were executed in Egypt in 1945 after having been charged with the murder of Lord Moyne.

4.7. 75

A Refrigerator-Bomb Explodes in Jerusalem: 13 Killed and 60 Wounded

A Hercules Crashes in the Sinai; 20 Soldiers Die

25 November

An IAF Hercules crashed in northern Sinai while attempting to fly over Mount Hilal. The Hercules was flying too low as a result of a navigational error. Its pilot, Captain Bustan, tried to fly over the top, but the plane crashed into the peak, failing to clear it by only five meters. Twenty crewmen and soldiers who were on the plane were killed. It took the rescue forces a long time to reach the crash site due to the rough terrain.

On Friday afternoon, Zion Square is one of the busiest spots in Jerusalem. This is why the Fatah terrorists chose it as the target of their attack. They hid the explosive charge inside a refrigerator that was brought to the square in a three-wheeled cart by a young Arab. Several citizens thought that the refrigerator looked suspicious, but when they opened the doors, they found it was empty. The lethal charge, consisting of two mortar bombs stolen from the IDF, was placed inside the refrigerator walls. The police were called in but arrived too late. The charge exploded, killing 13 people, including Arabs, and wounding another 60.

The police launched a manhunt after the terrorists, while several hot-tempered Jews tried to attack Arabs. Fist-fights started at the Machaneh Yehuda Market, where shop-owners had to defend their Arab workers. The police were harshly criticized for failing to arrive on time, which might have prevented the attack.

Yehoshua Peretz at a Histadrut demonstration in the 1990s.

Yehoshua Peretz Arrested

8 October

Yehoshua Peretz, leader of the Ashdod Port workers' union, was arrested after clashing with policemen who had arrived to disperse a demonstration he had organized. Tempers flared after his detention, and the police were forced to send more officers to the port. Peretz was tried, fined IL5,000 and given a two-month prison term. He appealed the sentence, claiming that this was a labor dispute that should not have been dealt with by legal proceedings. His image is that of a true workers' leader.

75

14 April

Kfir - the Israeli Fighter Plane

The Israeli fighter plane, Kfir, was unveiled to the public and the TV cameras in a ceremony preceding Israel's 27th Independence Day that was attended by cabinet members, MKs, the IDF General Staff generals, heads of the Defense Ministry, IAF commanders, reporters and, naturally, many of the Israel Aircraft Industries (IAI) workers, led by IAI Director General Al Schwimmer. Shimon Peres, one of the leading promoters of the IAI, said: "This is a great achievement for the State of Israel and the IAI. Of all the countries that produce planes, we are the smallest; and of all planes made in the world today – the Kfir is the best."

2 January

The Murder of Soldier Rachel Heller - The district court rejected an appeal against the extension of the custody of Yoram Bichonsky, 21, a disabled IDF veteran who was detained on suspicion of murdering his girl friend, 19-year-old soldier Rachel Heller. Her body was found in October 1974 by the side of the road leading to Caesarea beach. The police only had circumstantial evidence against Bichonsky and he was released after 45 days in custody.

21 October

Hadassah Hospital Returns to Mount Scopus

The Hadassah-Mount Scopus Hospital reopened in a festive ceremony attended by hundreds after being closed since 1948.

12 August

Pinchas Sapir, Mapai leader and finance, industry and trade minister, died of a heart attack at the age of 68.

1 September

Israel and Egypt signed an interim agreement mediated by Henry Kissinger.

26 September

MK Menachem Begin promised the Herut Movement Young Guard that if he were elected prime minister, he would never return the territories.

8 October

Yehoshua Peretz, leader of the Ashdod Port workers, was arrested after a clash with the police.

13 November

A bomb hidden in a cart on Jaffa Road in Jerusalem exploded, killing six people and wounding 46.

25 November

A disaster in the Sinai: An IAF Hercules crashed into Mount Hilal in the Sinai; 20 passengers and crew members were killed.

Photo: Rachamim Yisraeli

8 December

Gush Emunim activists agreed to a compromise by means of which they would move out of Sebastia into a nearby military camp. The compromise was presented to them by poet Haim Gouri on behalf of Minister Israel Galili.

3 August

Israel's Handicapped Team Wins the World Trophy

Fifteen disabled athletes, including some who had been wounded in the Yom Kippur War, participated in games in Britain, winning the world basketball championship and medals in other fields. The athletes then went to Belgium, where they took part in the basketball championship with 10 other countries. In the final game, the Israeli athletes played against the American team, beating them by 50:47 and winning the world trophy.

(*19* 76

The Entebbe Hostages Returning to Israel. Photo: Shabtai Tal

Yonatan (Yoni) Netanyahu, commander of the Entebbe Operation, who was killed during the rescue. Photo: IPPA

The Entebbe Operation
"Yoni and Entebbe Are One and the Same."

*Benjamin Netanyahu
and Ido Netanyahu*

Yoni was born far from Israel. He also died far from Israel. He was born on 13 March 1946 and died in the heart of Africa on 4 July 1976. When he was born, his parents were on a Zionist mission in the United States, and when he shed his blood on Ugandan soil, he was on a mission for the country his parents and grandparents had worked to establish, a country to which he had come when he was three years old.

Yoni did not believe that in modern times, the Jewish people could really exist anywhere but in its own country – Israel. He saw himself as "an inseparable part, a link in the chain of Israel's existence and independence," and this is how he operated. This is why he chose to dedicate his youth to the army instead of continuing his university studies or learning a profession. Yoni excelled in the army – as in everything else he had done – as a paratrooper, in the officers' courses and other courses, as commander of an armored battalion on the Golan Heights after the Yom Kippur War and, finally, as commander of the task force which he prepared for the operation that would be named after him.

No nation could ever win the struggle for its existence without individuals who were willing to sacrifice their lives for it. Yoni knew that well. Because he was at peace with his conscience, he was fully willing to sacrifice his life for his nation. "Death," he wrote at 17, "does not scare me; I am intrigued by it. It is a riddle that I, like many others, have tried unsuccessfully to solve. I am not afraid of dying because I do not think that living without a cause is worth much. If I had to sacrifice my life for a cause of my choice, I would do it gladly." Thirteen years after writing that, he died fighting for that cause.

In Entebbe, perhaps more than in any other incident in the history of Israel, Yoni and his men demonstrated the very essence of the Jewish state. The Jewish nation now has an army, power, the ability to operate – even on the Equator, 4,000 km from Israel. This operation is the best example of the revolution wrought by the Zionist movement on our very existence. When the people of Israel were forced into exile, they lost all powers of self-defense. Therefore, besides being a most daring operation, Entebbe will be remembered as a momentous symbol.

"Yoni and Entebbe are one and the same," Yitzhak Rabin said, eulogizing him. Indeed, the memory of Yoni will forever be associated with the Entebbe Operation and vice versa. However, Yoni will not only be remembered for this operation, for which he spent 48 hectic hours preparing his soldiers, and during which he ran in front of the glass wall of the terminal in full view of the terrorists, falling just seconds before they were eliminated. He was never to know that the operation was a success. He will be remembered for the things told about him by those who knew him. Yoni will perhaps be mainly remembered for his voice – of Yoni the thinker, the soldier, the son, the husband, the brother, the friend – which rings out from his letters, resounding in the hearts of thousands for a generation already. Yoni was famous in his lifetime, but when his letters were published, people who did not know him discovered who he was.

This is what Dr. Elisha Bar-Meir, Yoni's friend, wrote several days after Yoni died:

> *Yoni.*
> *Yoni means all that is different.*
> *Yoni means all that is beyond words.*
> *Yoni – challenges no one ever posed; missions no one ever accomplished; contests of endurance, using up the last drop of strength; deserts without water, huge mountains, dry rivers, faraway monasteries.*
> *Yoni means German Shepherds, little children in distant homes, rooms for an hour after a sleepless night. Chess games, a pipe, Edgar Allan Poe, Tchaikovsky's 1812, Alterman.*
> *Yoni means few friends. Friendships without words.*
> *Yoni means a constant battle against sleep, fatigue, overindulgence, forgetfulness, inefficiency, helpless-*
> *ness, falsehood.*
> *Yoni means making the impossible possible.*
> *Yoni – the beauty that we are lacking.*
> *Yoni – the infinity of Israel.*

Sometimes, people's deeds remain engraved in human history for generations. The collective memory of a nation makes it a nation. The Entebbe operation is one of those special events that add a layer to our national memory, becoming a component of our nation's ability to survive – fifty years after the establishment of the state, three thousand years after the foundation of the Kingdom of Israel.

4.7.76

Operation Yonatan – The Entebbe Raid

The Mercedes that served the commando unit in the Entebbe raid.

On 26 June, an Air France passenger plane on its way from Paris to Israel was hijacked by terrorists from a PFLP splinter faction. The hijackers landed the plane in Uganda, in co-operation with the local authorities and their leader, Idi Amin. After landing, they released all the passengers with the exception of the Israelis and several religious Jews. They presented an ultimatum, demanding the release of terrorists imprisoned in Israel and other countries within 48 hours. Israel announced that it was willing to negotiate.

The Israeli decisionmakers knew that a rescue operation would be very risky because not only was the destination 4,000 km away, but the Ugandan Army was co-operating with the hijackers. However, after extensive consultations and a comprehensive examination of the situation, the political echelons gave the rescue mission the go-ahead. The task force, comprising the General Staff commando unit under Colonel Yoni Netanyahu, paratroopers and Golani brigade soldiers, landed their Hercules planes at Entebbe Airport, immobilized the local forces and stormed the terminal where the hostages were being held. The operation was executed in the best possible manner. The surprised terrorists were eliminated in the first round of fire and all the hostages, some of whom were wounded, were taken to the planes that were waiting on the tarmac. Task force commander Yoni Netanyahu was the only IDF soldier killed. According to eye witnesses, he was shot by a terrorist when he led the charge. Soldier Surin Hershko was badly wounded. Hostage Dora Bloch, who had been taken to a local hospital earlier, was apparently murdered. On their way back to Israel, the Hercules planes made a refueling stop in Kenya. The great success was marred by Yoni's death. During the attack, the task force killed 20 Ugandan soldiers, and even took time to sabotage the MiGs standing on the tarmac in order to prevent them from pursuing the Hercules planes. The operation gave Israel a sense of intense national pride, and was praised by the world.

Confidence in the IDF ability to conduct daring and complicated operations was restored after it had been eroded in the Yom Kippur War. The feeling of helplessness in the face of terrorism was replaced by a feeling of self-confidence and control. Although the price was heavy, national pride reached its peak.

Photo: Yossi Roth

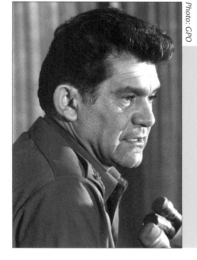

Photo: GPO

Former Chief of Staff David (Dado) Elazar Dies of a Heart Attack

15 April

David (Dado) Elazar died of a heart attack while swimming in the pool at his home in Tel Aviv. Dado, who began his military career with the Palmach, was the ninth IDF chief of staff. He was forced to resign following the findings of the Agranat Commission. He was convinced that there had been a miscarriage of justice and that he had been sacrificed to clear the names of Moshe Dayan and Golda Meir. Although the Agranat Commission found him guilty of the Yom Kippur War fiasco, the public supported him and believed that he had been made a scapegoat. Dado felt rage and frustration toward the commission, but never tried to contradict its conclusions. He died at the age of 51.

Land Day: Six Killed, Dozens Wounded

1976

March was a stormy month in the Galilee. Enraged by the government decision to confiscate over 100,000 dunams of their land, Arab villagers staged demonstrations and strikes. The police reinforced their forces in the region significantly, but could not gain control of the situation. By the end of the month, the Israeli Arabs were rioting. They formed an executive committee which decided that 30 March would be marked as Land Day – a day of struggle against the appropriation of lands – in a general strike.

The Arab youths, however, did not settle for a strike and clashed with the security forces, mostly in the villages of Sachnin, Arrabe and Dir-Hanna. Marchers in those villages clashed with the IDF soldiers who were brought there. The police used firearms against the Arabs. Six were killed, 69 wounded and over 250 detained; 16 policemen and soldiers were wounded as well. The unrest spread throughout Israel and even started being felt in the territories. The Land Day events also assumed a political nature. Elections for the local authorities were held around that time and the Israeli Arab public, affected by the events, delivered a painful blow to the old leadership, which was seen as moderate and pro-Jordanian. The main victors in the elections were the extremist candidates who were identified with the PLO. This sparked a storm of arguments and conflicts in the Israeli political establishment.

Border Police officers detain a stone-throwing rioter. Photo: Yossi Roth

Asher Yadlin Arrested and Sentenced to Five Years in Prison

18 October

Asher Yadlin, former chairman of the Histadrut Sick Fund and a leading Alignment activist, was Yitzhak Rabin's candidate for the post of Bank of Israel governor. Yadlin never got the job because the police arrested him on suspicion of theft and taking bribes. His detention brought to light one of the largest corruption affairs in Israel's history. Yadlin adamantly denied all charges, but an extensive investigation as well as secret testimonies received by the police combined to form a serious charge sheet against him. Yadlin was sentenced to five years in prison. His arrest constituted yet another blow for the Alignment, which was increasingly perceived as political corruption incarnate. It paid dearly for this when it lost the 1977 elections.

Asher Yadlin taken to prison. Photo: Yossi Roth

20.12.76

The F-15 Crisis and the "Brilliant Maneuver"

Three F-15 jets arrived in Israel, making a significant American contribution to Israel's security. The planes arrived on a Friday and performed an air show for cabinet ministers at the Hatzerim Air Force base. The show extended beyond schedule and the ministers had to drive home after the entry of the Sabbath. The religious parties decided to use this to test their power and bolster their position for the approaching Knesset elections. They did not plan to overthrow the government, only to protest the violation of the Sabbath, and chose to abstain in a no-confidence vote. The government, nonetheless, won by a majority of 55 to 48.

However, Yitzhak Rabin, who was worried by Shimon Peres' increasing power in the party, decided to take advantage of the situation. Immediately after the vote, he dismissed the NRP ministers and resigned. His cabinet thus became a caretaker government (which cannot be overthrown by the Knesset), giving Rabin room to act without the fear of no-confidence votes. Rabin forced the Alignment to bring the primaries forward, fearing that if he waited, Peres would gain more strength. Peres was in fact caught unprepared and Rabin won the Labor primaries by a narrow margin of 41 votes. This move was dubbed "the brilliant maneuver". Unfortunately for Rabin, soon after that the media revealed that his wife Leah had an illegal foreign currency bank account and he was forced to resign from the party leadership, leaving Peres to run against Menachem Begin in the 1977 elections.

The American F-15 planes served as a pretext for a vote of no confidence in the government.

Theft in the Jaffa Police Headquarters

12 January

Three not especially sophisticated criminals made a laughing-stock of the police when they broke into police headquarters in Jaffa and cracked a 400-kg safe containing IL 1.6 million. The police restored their lost honor by obstinately pursuing the three and capturing them. Years later, this event inspired a movie called *Under Their Noses* that was not very popular with the police.

"Dash" Formed: Yiga'el Yadin Goes into Politics

22 November

Yiga'el Yadin, a most esteemed and popular figure in Israeli politics, announced in a well-oiled publicity campaign that he was ready to assume a political role. The public believed him to be an honest and straight politician. Interviewed on the weekly TV program *Moked*, he made the dramatic announcement that he was forming the Dash Party - a new center movement whose platform was democracy and integrity. Yadin led the movement in the 1977 elections, scoring a major success: 15 Knesset seats.

Dash leaders - Yiga'el Yadin (center) and Amnon Rubinstein (right). Photo: N. Ben-Ami, Sunphot

76

11 July

Rina Mor Elected Miss Universe

Photo: La'Isha

Rina Mor, Israel's 20-year-old beauty queen, won the international title for 1976. When the outgoing Miss Universe crowned her, Mor burst into tears. She was a student at Tel Aviv University, an amateur glider and a youth club leader. When asked where she would like to travel after winning the title, she said: "I'd like to visit an Arab state, but I can't; so I'd like to go to Africa and see the jungles."

16 August

All grocery shops went on a three-day strike protesting the decision to force them to keep books.

18 October

Asher Yadlin, candidate for the post of Bank of Israel Governor, was arrested on suspicion of taking bribes.

22 November

Prof. Yiga'el Yadin announced that he was joining politics and established Dash – the Democratic Movement for Change.

21 December

Prime Minister Yitzhak Rabin resigned over a crisis with the NRP ministers concerning the arrival of the F-15s after the entry of the Sabbath. His resignation led to the elections being brought forward to 17 May 1977.

26 December

French businessman Shmuel Flatto-Sharon was arrested in Israel following an official extradition request from the French Government.

11 January

"I'm Innocent!"

Photo: Shaul Golan

"I'm innocent!" yelled Amos Baranes at the judge who found him guilty of murdering Rachel Heller and sentenced him to life imprisonment. This ended the second act of one of the stormiest murder trials ever held in Israel. The first act took place when Yoram Bichonsky, Heller's boyfriend, was detained as a suspect at the time. After spending 10 years in prison, Baranes was pardoned, but kept struggling to be totally exonerated.

28 July

Esther Roth-Shahamorov Makes History

Photo: A P

For the first time in the history of Israel's athletics, Esther Roth-Shahamorov reached the finals of the Olympic 100 meters' hurdles. She came in sixth with a time of 13.04 seconds.

10 February

Snow in Jerusalem, Hebron and Safed

About 10 cm of snow fell in the mountains of Judea, Galilee and the Golan. The main arteries of Jerusalem were cleared early in the morning. The snow that fell in the Galilee cut off roads from Acre to Rosh Pina and Safed, and brought traffic to a halt in the city. In the Hermon area, temperatures dropped to zero, and on Mount Meron, the temperatures reached minus three degrees Centigrade.

(1977

**Menachem Begin delivering his victory speech at Metzudat Ze'ev.
Photo: David Rubinger**

Prime Minister Menachem Begin and Egyptian President Anwar Sadat. Photo: Yaavoc Saar, GPO

Menachem Begin: The Man Who Caused the "Upheaval"
A rare breed of leaders

Former MK
Roni Milo

Some men go down in history for doing just one thing. Menachem Begin will be remembered for much more. The story of this unique leader - one of a rare breed of leaders - is linked to the recent history of the people of Israel.

The speech he delivered on the Irgun radio the day the state was established can teach us about his vision: "In our country, justice will be the supreme leader. Let no one among us go hungry, homeless, without clothing or basic education; remember, you were strangers in a strange land."

Begin was born in Poland in 1913, studied law in Warsaw, and became Betar leader in Poland in 1938. He followed faithfully in the footsteps of Ze'ev Jabotinsky, the founder and guide of the Betar Movement. Jabotinsky's teachings would accompany Begin throughout his life. When he caused a social upheaval with his "Neighborhood Rehabilitation Project" as soon as he was elected prime minister in 1977, he was not only paying a debt to the weak strata that had supported him and his movement for years, but also implementing Jabotinsky's teachings of the five basic needs (food, shelter, clothing, education, health).

When Warsaw was conquered by the Nazis, Begin fled to Vilna, where he was arrested by the Russians and sent to a labor camp. In 1942, he arrived in Israel, became the commander of the *Irgun Tzevai Leumi* [National Military Organization] and conducted an armed struggle against British rule. The Zionist leadership opposed the Irgun's belligerent methods, and relations between the two groups deteriorated to a near civil war. Only Begin's restraint and concern for the nation prevented them from crossing the red line. Even when the *Altalena*, the Irgun arms ship, was sunk while he was on board, he did not forsake his policy of restraint.

After the state was established, Begin formed and headed the Herut Movement, obstinately maintaining his unique views on foreign and security affairs, for better or for worse, even if they caused his movement to remain in opposition for many years.

In 1965, his movement joined forces with the National Liberal Party, which he initiated, and he continued expanding his political bloc after the Yom Kippur War. His political campaign culminated in his impressive victory in the Knesset elections of 1977, a victory that was dubbed "the political upheaval".

As mentioned earlier, as soon as he was appointed prime minister, he set in motion the "Neighborhood Rehabilitation Project", by means of which he hoped to bring about a real social revolution and advance the underprivileged strata. At the same time, he sought to put an end to the bloody dispute with our neighbors and decided to sign a peace agreement with Egypt, the strongest Arab country.

His bold move of signing the peace treaty is even more impressive when examined against the background of his previous stands: In the 1970s, Begin intended to bring down the national unity government over the Rogers Plan that linked an agreement with Egypt with a withdrawal from the Sinai. He claimed that, just like in a convoy, if the lead boat slows down, the last boat might get lost; if his movement showed weakness, other parties might weaken even more, and they might all lose their way.

In giving up the Sinai, Begin proved that he was willing to make sacrifices for peace, hence the great impression he made and the emotional reactions he inspired in Israel and abroad to his political moves as prime minister, when the burden of national responsibilities rested on his shoulders.

His political determination was always combined with his sensitivity to social injustice. In whatever he did – as a freedom fighter, opposition member and leader of the people – he championed equality and unity. He never let power go to his head and make him forget that he was working for the people.

His concern for the people was tragically tangible during the Lebanon War. I remember that one day, hearing on the radio that a father of four had fallen in battle, I went to his office and told him: "Mr. Begin, we must get out of Lebanon. The people can no longer tolerate this war." Begin turned to me and said: "Do you think I do not understand this, my son?" There was pain in his voice and he seemed broken. Seeing his face and hearing his answer, I knew he would not hold out under the burden. Indeed, a short while later, he retired.

Begin's legacy should guide every Israeli leader: sensitivity, understanding, adhering to principles while showing flexibility, honest consideration and true concern for the public's welfare and well-being.

This exemplary man will forever stand before our eyes as a real, living and breathing symbol. I am grateful to have had the opportunity of knowing him and working with him.

17.5. **77**

"Begin's in Power... Begin's in Power!"

At exactly 10 p.m., TV announcer Haim Yavin uttered the dramatic words: "A political upheaval!" which signalled the start of the Likud's celebrations. The activists watched the screens for a moment, not believing that they had actually won the elections, and then they burst out chanting, "Begin's in power! Begin's in power!" However, more than a Likud victory, it was the Alignment's defeat. The Likud went up from 39 to 43 Knesset seats, a nice but moderate gain. The Alignment, on the other hand, dropped from 51 to 32 seats in a clear vote of no confidence. The newly founded Dash party won 15 seats, but could not tip the scales. All the leftist parties lost power and, when the religious parties joined the Likud, it became clear that the era of Mapai as a ruling party had ended. When the NRP announced that it was willing to sever its historic alliance with Mapai and join a coalition with the Likud, nothing could stop Begin from becoming prime minister. He combined the Likud's 43 seats with the NRP's 12, the five seats of the ultra-Orthodox parties and Ariel Sharon's two, and formed a coalition of 62 MKs.

Begin did not settle for this tiny majority and, four days after the elections, he stunned Israel when he offered the Foreign Ministry to Moshe Dayan, who was an Alignment MK. Dayan accepted the offer, despite enormous adverse criticism, provided that the government did not annex the territories while peace negotiations

Menachem Begin with the Likud leaders at Metzudat Ze'ev on the night of the victory. Photo: Ronit Shani

were taking place. Begin agreed and, on 20 June, he presented a cabinet based on 63 MKs. From this powerful position, Begin contacted Dash, which considered his offer for some time and eventually joined the government. Yiga'el Yadin was appointed deputy prime minister, and the coalition now had a majority of 77 MKs. The fact that part of that majority belonged to the "peace camp" enabled Begin to keep his promises and work for the achievement of true peace for Israel and, some time later, to invite Egyptian President Sadat to Israel.

Photo: IPPA

The American Bank Account of the Rabin Family

7 April

"Very few would have acted as nobly as Yitzhak did," Leah Rabin said, summing up her husband's conduct when the affair of her foreign bank account was exposed. The media revealed the fact that Leah Rabin had a foreign currency bank account in the US, which was illegal in those days. Yitzhak Rabin said that the account had remained open inadvertently since the time he served as ambassador there, but maintained that he was as responsible for it as his wife. In a dramatic message - relayed on TV at the end of a basketball game in which Maccabi Tel Aviv won the European championship - Rabin announced his resignation as prime minister. He took a leave of absence and left Peres to take his place.

President Sadat in Israel: The Historic Visit

At nine p.m., Israel held its breath. So did the rest of the world. Egyptian President Anwar Sadat stood at the door of an official Egyptian plane that had just landed at Ben-Gurion Airport. An emotional scene, and a dream come true: The leader of the Arab world had arrived on an official visit to Israel. He was received by the entire political and military leadership: President Efraim Katzir, Prime Minister Menachem Begin, ministers, MKs, the chief of staff, IDF generals and many other dignitaries. Everyone was excited and gave Sadat a royal welcome. So did the Israeli public.

President Sadat inspects the guard of honor at Ben-Gurion Airport.
Photo: David Rubinger

Ten days before his visit, while addressing the People's Assembly, Sadat threw down the gauntlet, saying that he was willing to go to Jerusalem and visit the Knesset to make peace with Israel. Begin took up the gauntlet and sent an official invitation to Sadat. To the amazement of the entire world, Sadat accepted the invitation and landed in Israel. Some IDF officers, primarily chief of staff Gur, doubted Sadat's sincerity and warned that this was a trick. Defense Minister Ezer Weizman reprimanded Gur publicly for his scepticism.

Sadat spent three days in Israel during which he charmed the entire nation. He delivered a rather extreme speech at the Knesset, demanding a full Israeli withdrawal from the occupied territories and a solution to the Palestinian problem. Begin's reply was a courtesy speech; he made no significant political statement. On the last day of the visit, however, Begin agreed to declare that Israel would be willing to withdraw to the international border line with Egypt. Sadat then returned to Egypt well satisfied. The stakes had been high – and he had won.

Minister Avraham Ofer Commits Suicide

3 January

"Just tell me, what do you have against me?" Avraham Ofer begged. Ofer was housing minister in Rabin's government when public opinion convicted him of corruption – against the backdrop of stories of corruption involving the Alignment – even before the police had concluded their investigation. He was a suspect, but the police investigators would not tell him what the suspicions were based on. Ofer met Prime Minister Rabin and begged to be told the truth. His request was not granted. Upset and agitated, he drove to the Tel Baruch beach and shot himself in the head. The public was shocked. After his death, it was revealed that of the 33 charges brought against him, 30 were refuted and three were never investigated. Ofer chose to end the tragic affair himself.

---

17 February

In a dramatic game, the Maccabi Tel Aviv basketball team defeated CSKA Moscow 91:79 . Israel was jubilant.

20 March

Yassir Arafat was elected chairman of the PLO Executive Committee.

7 April

In a special speech on TV, Prime Minister Yitzhak Rabin announced his resignation because it had been discovered that his wife, Leah, had an illegal foreign currency account in the US.

7 April

Maccabi Tel Aviv won the European basketball championship after its 78: 77 victory in the final game against Italy's Varese.

17 May

A political upheaval in Israel: The Likud won the elections and Menachem Begin became prime minister.

26 May

Moshe Dayan announced that he was joining Begin's cabinet as foreign minister.

14 July

Thousands demonstrated in Bnei Brak, protesting car traffic on Hashomer Street on Saturdays.

Housing Minister Avraham Ofer.
Photo: Uzi Keren

29.10.77

Finance Minister Simcha Ehrlich Announces the "Economic Upheaval"

Finance Minister Simcha Ehrlich. Photo: Zoom 77

When the Likud won the elections, it was clear that things would change, mainly in the economy. The main change was the lifting of the government's strict supervision of the economy. In this framework, supervision of the foreign currency - buying, selling and owning - was eliminated, VAT was raised from 8 to 12 percent and subsidies were significantly cut. As a result, the prices of basic commodities rose, which did not please the public, to say the least. Many complained that the Likud, which had come to power as a result of the support of the weak strata, was raising prices drastically. Begin blamed the Alignment, "which had left it to the Likud to deal with the poor economy - the result of Mapai corruption."

The new monetary policy was followed by a major devaluation of the Israeli lira. Investors turned to the stock exchange, which rose steadily. Complaints about the price hikes subsided when people realized that they could make easy profits on the stock exchange. Thousands invested all their money there and nobody heeded the experts' warnings that Israel was headed for hyperinflation.

The memorial site for the helicopter crash victims. Photo: Zoom 77

An IAF Helicopter Crashes; 54 Soldiers Perish

10 May

An IAF Yas'ur helicopter carrying 44 paratroopers on a training mission crashed in the Judean Desert. All the paratroopers and the ten IAF crewmen were killed. An extensive debriefing determined that the cause of the accident was human error. The country was appalled, as this was the worst training disaster it had ever seen. As a result, the IAF introduced new flight regulations for Yas'ur helicopters.

Uri Zohar on his TV show, It's My Secret, when he had just begun to turn religious. Photo: Isaiah Karlinsky

Comedian Uri Zohar Becomes Religious

2 October

Actor, film director and comedian Uri Zohar, the symbol of Israeli secularism, announced publicly that he had decided to become religious. Zohar explained that he was tired of his superficial secular life; he added that he was quitting his weekly TV show, *It's My Secret*, and was about to dedicate his life to studying the Torah. Some of his friends could not believe this, saying this was yet another of Zohar's publicity stunts. However, when it transpired that he was attending a yeshiva regularly, they accepted the fact that the "most secular Israeli" had become religious.

77

1977

7 April

"Maccabi, Maccabi, Maccabi Tel Aviv!"

Photo: Yossi Roth

This was the year of Maccabi Tel Aviv. A historic year no Israeli sports fan would ever forget. It started with the sensational 91:79 victory over CSKA Moscow, the USSR champion, which shocked the Russians. Their Jewish coach, Alexander Gomelsky, told Tal Brody: "This was a political game, but Maccabi was undoubtedly the better team and deserved to win." Movie theaters were empty that night as everybody watched the game on TV. When it ended, thousands danced in the streets and drank champagne. Six weeks later, Maccabi defeated CSKA again, and subsequently won the final game against the Italian champion, Varese, by one point, 78:77, thus winning the European cup. Again the people danced in the streets and motorists blew their horns to express the nation's pride in the historic victory.

2 October

Uri Zohar appeared for the first time wearing a *yarmulke* at a meeting organized by the Esh Torah Yeshiva for newly religious Jews in Jerusalem.

29 October

Finance Minister Simcha Ehrlich caused an "economic upheaval" when he announced that the government had decided to lift its supervision of foreign currency.

19 November

Egyptian President Sadat landed in Israel for an historic visit during which the two countries initiated peace negotiations. Sadat was received very warmly.

18 December

Some 120,000 people attended a rally held in support of the peace process at Malchei Yisrael Square in Tel Aviv.

6 May

The First Tennis Center Inaugurated

The first tennis center in Israel was inaugurated in Ramat Hasharon. It consisted of 13 illuminated courts and a central 4,000-seat stadium. The president attended the inauguration. The center was constructed with the help of US and Canadian donors.

13 May

The Israeli-Made Merkava Tank

Israel produced a tank called the Merkava. It was developed by Major General (Res.) Yisrael Tal, and was considered one of the most advanced tanks of its kind in the world. Its uniqueness lay in the protection it provided to the crew. It was first exhibited on Independence Day. The design of the Merkava reflected lessons learned in the Yom Kippur War.

Photo: IDF spokesman

25 December

The El Al plane that took Prime Minister Menachem Begin to Egypt was flown by three pilots who had been held captive by the Egyptians during the war of attrition.

12 June

Vietnamese Refugees Rescued at Sea by Israeli Cargo Ships

In a dramatic speech, Prime Minister Menachem Begin announced that Israel was willing to grant 66 Vietnamese refugees asylum and citizenship. They arrived in Israel on board Israeli cargo ships that had pulled them out of the water after countries in the vicinity of Vietnam refused to accept them.

1978

Aharon Barak was appointed Supreme Court Justice in July 1978 and Supreme Court president in August 1995.
Photo: Ziv Koren, GPO

Supreme Court President Aharon Barak with his fellow justices (left to right) Eliezer Goldberg, Dov Levin, Meir Shamgar, Shlomo Levin and Gabriel Bach. Photo: Zoom 77

Aharon Barak
Flashing Like Lightning, Peace-Loving Like Aaron

*Former Minister
and MK
Shulamit Aloni*

Prof. Aharon Barak [lightning] appeared in the Israeli public arena like lightning, and the following thunder was heard all over the land. It was Justice Minister Haim Tzadok who appointed him attorney-general, correctly considering him - a wise, honest and broad-minded man - worthy of the position.

Clearly, when Barak addressed – in a most unorthodox manner – the affairs of Avraham Ofer and the Rabin dollar account (which led to the resignation of the prime minister), he had before him the unequivocal decree: "Do not pervert justice; do not show partiality to the poor or favoritism to the great, but judge your neighbor fairly." (Leviticus 19:15) Based on this principle, he later devised the famous "Buzaglo [everyman] test" – a simple test by means of which every citizen can ensure that he is being judged justly, without favoritism or surrender to political or other pressures.

There is no doubt in my mind that when he still was attorney-general and proposed the Foundation of Justice Bill, he based it on the Biblical edict: "Do not pervert justice or show partiality. Do not accept a bribe... Follow justice and justice alone, so that you may live and possess the land... ." (Deuteronomy 16:19-20) It appears, however, that at that time, Barak – the professor, legal expert and attorney-general – did not think that "Israel's Heritage" included, alongside universal human values, racism and ethnocentrism that discriminates between people. Or perhaps he knew, and believed that the courts and the spirit of democracy could deal with the xenophobia and ethnocentrism which, during our years of exile, had become introversion and defensiveness. However, when we became a nation of mighty conquerors after 1967, they manifested themselves, to our shame, in the oppression of and violence against anyone under our rule who was different.

In any event, when Aharon Barak assumed the Supreme Court post in 1978, he kept to the path he had set for himself during his tenure as attorney-general. He opened the court to perform justice for the people, even for representative groups, and extended the boundaries of the court authorities to cover the legislative and the executive branches. For him, everything was judgeable, since the court was the guardian of democratic rule, human rights and righteousness, as is written in the Bible: "Zion will be redeemed with justice, her penitent ones with righteousness." (Isaiah, 1: 27)

The Supreme Court president flashes like lightning, but is also peace-loving like Aaron, brother of Moses. I do not say that only because he played a part in reaching the peace accord with Egypt (when the government of Begin, Dayan and Ezer Weizman was in power), but because I believe that had he been put to the test as Aaron was, he too would have made a golden calf for the people. In saying that, I intend neither flattery nor criticism, but merely to shed light on another aspect of his public activities.

For years, Religious Affairs Minister Zerah Warhaftig and Prime Minister Golda Meir denied that the Chief Rabbinate possessed "black lists" of people disqualified for marriage based on information collected by informers as well as by the Interior and Health Ministries and the Jewish Agency. This was all done secretly, in the dark, with no objective test; the disqualified people would receive the unexpected notification and were unable to protest. In the end, reporter Yoella Har-Shefi and her colleagues at *Yedioth Ahronoth* got hold of the lists and gave them to us, typed and edited, just like they were distributed to the local Religious Councils and Rabbinical Courts. Their existence could no longer be denied. The public was enraged. The entire matter was handed over to the attorney-general who, to everyone's amazement, validated the lists. He ruled: "As long as all matrimonial affairs in Israel are under the sole jurisdiction of the Rabbinical Courts, the rabbinical judges have a right to seek out, investigate and locate bastards, or women who cannot marry *Cohanim* [descendants of the priests], or women who are forbidden to both their husbands and their lovers, or deserted wives, or women who must either marry or be excused by their deceased husband's brother – and all the others who are disqualified from marriage." The only thing he demanded of the compilers of those lists was that the victims who were to be prevented from establishing a family by the power of the religious establishment be notified of their status and given a hearing in order to find out that they had indeed been disqualified legally. This was not Barak the reformer! It was an example of the supremacy of the law, but not of the supreme right of adults and unmarried people to establish a family as they pleased.

This was Aharon the legal adviser. Today, I am more disturbed by Aharon the court president. After the murders committed by the members of the Jewish Underground and Ami Popper, after the massacre perpetrated by Baruch Goldstein at the Cave of the Patriarchs, after the Rabin assassination – when nothing was done to the families of the Jewish murderers, and their homes remained standing for them to receive consolation and support – Barak ruled that the house of the terrorist who had planted the bomb at the *Apropo* café in Tel Aviv be blown up and his wife and little children left homeless. I cannot understand this, just as I do not understand how he still supports those despicable emergency regulations that permit collective and regional punishment that is always – absolutely always – imposed on the weak, vanquished Palestinians, who are subjected to humiliation, appropriation and expropriation by us. This seems even more strange today when we are seeking peace and co-operation with the neighboring nation.

In my opinion, when Barak decided to continue imposing collective punishments on the Palestinians after the Hasmonean tunnel and the Har Homa crises, he was not Prof. Barak, fighter for justice, freedom and equality, but rather Aaron the priest, who heeded the people's clamor, asking that God be seen on every hill. Naturally, the decision is within the framework of the law - the iniquitous British emergency law of 1945. It is an undemocratic, non-Jewish law and it is not mandatory to implement it, especially since we are no longer the persecuted victim. We number nearly six million citizens, we have a strong and courageous army and the world is not entirely against us, except when we turn it against us as a result of our own deeds.

I must add that none of Prof. Aharon Barak's eight wise and enlightening books gives any justification or satisfactory explanation for discrimination against individuals and collective punishments. It appears that he is not very proud of these things, and he has every reason not to be.

11.3. 78

Terror Attack on Coastal Highway: 35 Killed and Dozens Wounded

Thirty-five Israelis were killed and dozens were wounded in a terrorist attack of unprecedented scope and brutality perpetrated by a Fatah squad. The squad was trained by Abu-Jihad, head of the Fatah military branch. While they were sailing to Israel in two Zodiacs, two terrorists fell into the water and were left behind. Minutes after the squad reached the shore near Ma'agan Michael, they encountered an American photographer and killed her on the spot.

The unusually large squad that had managed to elude the Navy defense ring kept to its original plan and divided up into two units: The first unit stopped a taxi on the Coastal Highway, murdered the driver and set off on a trip of murder and mayhem along the highway. The second unit stopped a bus that was traveling north from Tel Aviv, killing some of the passengers during the takeover of the bus and taking the rest hostage. The terrorists, who wanted to bargain for the release of their imprisoned comrades, ordered the driver to turn around and drive to Tel Aviv. During the course of the journey, they threw hand grenades and fired at passing cars.

The bus caught fire when the police anti-terror squad stormed it.
Photo: Shmuel Rachmani

By this stage, the security forces had already been informed of the terrorist infiltration and police cars started pursuing the bus. The security echelons were determined to prevent the bus from entering Tel Aviv, and they barricaded the Country Club Junction. When the bus reached the roadblock, the police shot at the wheels, forcing the bus off the highway. Some of the terrorists jumped out of the bus and opened fire on the policemen, using bazookas and shoulder-launched rockets. The police anti-terror squad, the first commando unit to arrive at the scene, stormed the bus and killed the terrorists who were still on it. Most of the passengers on the bus were injured in the heavy exchange of fire around them. Suddenly the bus caught fire and all the passengers on it were burned alive.

When the shooting subsided, the soldiers found only seven bodies belonging to the terrorists. Two terrorists were taken alive. As for the others, the security forces feared that they had managed to flee with the intention of reaching Tel Aviv and continuing the killing. Hundreds of soldiers, helicopters, light aircraft, dogs and trackers participated in the manhunt, and a closure was imposed on the Dan Region. The next day, however, it became apparent that all nine terrorists had been killed.

Photo: Shmuel Rachmani

Refael Eitan Appointed Chief of Staff

1 April

Refael (Raful) Eitan was appointed 11th IDF chief of staff, replacing Motta Gur. Raful, a veteran soldier with an extensive combat record, became known when he headed the paratrooper unit that parachuted over the Mitleh Pass in the Sinai in 1956. Defense Minister Ezer Weizman chose him rather than other IDF generals because of his operational experience, fighting spirit and modesty. During his term, his name was associated with the Sabra and Shatila massacre, but the commission of inquiry in the case did not recommend that he be dismissed. At the end of his military career, Raful turned to politics and established the Tzomet movement which did well in the [1996] elections.

Photo: Yossi Roth

The Litani Operation
The IDF Attacks Terrorists in Lebanon

1978

The terror attack on the Coastal Highway, aimed at sabotaging the peace process (see the next page), convinced the government that real action against the terrorists was called for. A large IDF force, including tanks, crossed the border and advanced north, after IAF planes bombarded targets in Lebanon, among which were villages that served as launching pads for terrorists. Because the operation was directed against terrorist bases south of the Litani River, the IDF did not enter the city of Tyre, which served as a major terrorist base. Fighting there would have resulted in numerous casualties, sparking international ire at Israel. Most of the terrorists fled north in the early hours of the operation, but several guerrilla units stayed behind, delaying the IDF advancement, although the IDF had already reached the Litani. Dozens of terrorists were killed in the exchanges of fire.

After the operation, it was reported that many Lebanese civilians had been shot by IDF soldiers. Other reports included accounts of abuse of civilians by soldiers, as well as theft and looting. Two officers were tried and sentenced to prison, but Chief of Staff Eitan commuted their sentences shortly afterward.

The IDF returned to the international border after it had cleared and broadened a strip of land controlled by Christian forces under Major Sa'ad Haddad. These forces, who had friendly relations with the IDF, constituted the foundation upon which the South Lebanese Army (SLA) was later established so as to secure Israel's northern border and make it difficult for terrorists to infiltrate. The Litani Operation provoked furious reactions, especially after the number of civilian casualties was made known. The Egyptians, who were conducting negotiations with Israel, were particularly angry and warned that the talks would cease if Israel did not pull out of Lebanon forthwith. Six days after it started, Defense Minister Ezer Weizman ordered a cease-fire and a start of the withdrawal process. In this way, the talks with Egypt, which would lead to the Camp David agreement, could resume.

An IDF unit enters the village of Marj Ayun in Lebanon.
Photo: Tzvi Roger

The residents of the village of Zabkiya in southern Lebanon watching the soldiers who had entered the area. Photo: Moshe Milner, GPO

Yitzhak Navon Elected President

19 April

Yitzhak Navon, Labor's candidate for president, was elected to the post despite the opposition of Prime Minister Menachem Begin. Navon was chosen to be Israel's fifth president. He ran against Prof. Yitzhak Shaveh, who had Begin's support and personal guarantee. Although the Likud had a Knesset majority, several coalition members chose to vote for Navon, whom they believed to be more stately and experienced than Shaveh. Begin was upset, but congratulated Navon, who served as president until 1983.

Photo: Yossi Roth

Israel and Egypt Sign the Camp David Accord

17.9.78

US President Jimmy Carter, Egyptian President Anwar Sadat and Israel's Prime Minister Menachem Begin signed the Camp David accord at the White House. This was the first-ever peace agreement that Israel had signed with an Arab country. The agreement stated that both countries would start negotiations for peace; that Israel would evacuate the entire Sinai, including civilian settlements; and that the Palestinians would be granted full autonomy in five years.

The Camp David talks lasted two weeks, during which there were many difficulties, crises and even threats to sabotage the talks and blame Israel. The main bone of contention between Israel and Egypt was the Palestinian issue. Sadat did not want to be perceived by the Arabs as been concerned with only his country, while Begin was unwilling to recognize the existence of a Palestinian nation. President Carter exerted heavy pressure on Israel in order to soften its stand. When it seemed like the meeting might really collapse, the prime minister conceded that the agreement would include clauses recognizing the legitimate rights of the Palestinians. Begin's concession, encouraged by Foreign Minister Dayan and Defense Minister Weizman, made the signing possible. The agreement was enthusiastically supported by both the Israelis and the Egyptians. The Knesset approved it by a majority of 84 MKs, with 19 voting against it and 17 abstaining.

US President Jimmy Carter, Egyptian President Anwar Sadat and Israel's Prime Minister Menachem Begin signing the Camp David accord at the White House. Photo: David Rubinger

Begin and Sadat Awarded the Nobel Peace Prize

10 December

The Nobel Peace Prize committee in Oslo could not ignore the Camp David agreement. Menachem Begin and Anwar Sadat were chosen to receive the award jointly. The committee also commended US President Carter for his efforts to achieve peace. Jewish American writer Isaac Bashevis Singer received the Nobel Prize for Literature the same year. Begin delivered an emotional speech, vowing to continue the struggle for peace. He also called for the speedy release of the Jews who were being held in Soviet jails because of their desire to emigrate to Israel. Sadat chose not to attend the ceremony himself, and sent his assistant Said Mar'i to receive the award in his place.

Prime Minister Begin and President Sadat's assistant, Said Mar'i, receiving the Nobel Peace Prize. Photo: AP

1978

22 April

Israel Won the Eurovision

Yizhar Cohen went down in history when he won first prize at the Eurovision song contest, singing A-ba-ni-bi by Nurit Hirsch and Ehud Manor. Having succeeded where all other Israeli competitors had failed, he said: "I still haven't grasped the magnitude of this event... It's been two hours of madness... they're almost killing us here with love... but it's great; everything's great!"

17 September

The Camp David Accords were signed in a ceremony in Washington by US President Jimmy Carter, Egyptian President Anwar Sadat and Israel's Prime Minister Menachem Begin.

7 November

Direct mayoral elections were held for the first time in Israel. Teddy Kollek (Jerusalem), Shlomo Lahat (Tel Aviv) and Arieh Gur-El (Haifa) were re-elected by a sweeping majority.

8 December

Former Prime Minister Golda Meir died of a malignant disease at the age of 80.

10 December

Prime Minister Menachem Begin and President Sadat were jointly awarded the Nobel Peace Prize.

21 December

A Katyusha salvo hit Kiryat Shmona; one person was killed and 10 wounded.

Local Newspapers Appear

This was the year of the local papers which started appearing mainly in the big cities. *Yedioth Ahronoth* and *Ma'ariv* started publishing local papers in Tel Aviv, Jerusalem and Haifa. The Schocken network published its first local paper in Jerusalem, and only in 1979 did it start a local paper in Tel Aviv as well. For the sake of historical accuracy, it should be noted that the first local paper was printed in Eilat in 1959.

Photo: Shalom Bar-Tal

11 February

Lemon Popsicle – An Israeli Box Office Hit

Boaz Davidson's film, *Lemon Popsicle*, premièred throughout Israel. This was the first Israeli movie in 14 years (after Uri Zohar's *Peeping Toms*) to participate in the Berlin film festival. The movie, which depicted Israeli youngsters in the 1960s, starred Anat Azmon, Yiftach Katzor and Yonatan Segal – all doing their military service.

12 February

Hirbat Hiz'a on Television

NRP's Education Minister Zevulun Hammer disqualified Ram Levy's film Hirbat Hiz'a for television, claiming that it might play into the hands of "the poisonous PLO propaganda". The Israel Broadcasting Authority, however, decided that the film would be broadcast that same night. The movie was based on a novel by S. Yizhar and describes the ambivalence of an Israeli soldier during the War of Independence when he and his comrades received an order to capture an Arab village and banish its residents.

Ram Levy (left) with actor Gidi Gov on the set. Photo: Michael Margolis

1979

US President Jimmy Carter, Egyptian President Anwar Sadat and Israeli Prime Minister Menachem Begin after signing the peace agreement between Israel and Egypt at the White House. Photo: David Rubinger

The Israelis enthusiastically supported the peace agreement with Egypt. Photo: IPPA [The blackboard reads: "Today the signing of the peace agreement with Egypt."]

The Peace Accord With Egypt:
The Greatness of Leaders

*The seventh
President of Israel
Ezer Weizman*

Some historians believe that there are several great currents in history and that their realization is just a matter of time. It requires fortuitous leaders – one or more – to ride those historic waves and make them happen. Otherwise, the moment of realization moves on to a later time.

The era of Israel's wars lasted approximately 30 years after the War of Independence. After the Yom Kippur War, especially once the disengagement agreement was signed with Egypt in 1975, a new era started: one that focused on attaining peace; the current era. While it is true that at the present time, terror is undermining us, I would like to recommend that Israel's leaders make every effort not to get involved in a fourth war (believing that it will bring security), but to base our security on dialogue that will lead to agreements. In 1978, three strong leaders stood out: Israeli Prime Minister Menachem Begin, Egyptian President Anwar Sadat and US President Jimmy Carter – each with his own reasons for reaching an agreement.

Judging from talks I held with Sadat, I understood that he wished to extricate himself from the Russian bear-hug and replace it with the American caress. There was not a lot of love lost between the Egyptian authorities and the Soviet advisers there. Egyptian President Mubarak, a former fighter pilot and Egyptian Air Force commander, once told me: "In 1972, when we heard that you had downed five jets flown by Russian pilots, our entire Air Force was happy." He did not elaborate, but I assume that they were glad because the Russians used to say that the Egyptian pilots were not up to standard, while the Egyptians claimed that the Israeli Phantoms and Mirages were better than their MiGs. Sadat did not like the Soviet presence either. He told me with pride: "In 1972, a year before the war, I ordered them to leave in two weeks. They left in 10 days. The war was waged exclusively under Egyptian command."

Sadat also wanted to break the political deadlock, which was one of the reasons he started the 1973 war. After the war, he remarked: "Now I can speak to my people with a clear conscience." I suppose that, in the wake of his military achievements, he thought to himself: Now I am ready to talk to the Israelis. Sadat was also seeking ways to change the socio-demographic situation of Egypt.

Facing him was Menachem Begin. In 1977, a member of the right wing, a representative of the historic Revisionism had been elected Israel's prime minister for the first time ever. I cannot read a man's thoughts, but I feel that besides sincerely wanting peace, Begin wanted to prove that he of all people, a right-winger, could bring peace.

The third leader, Jimmy Carter, had an obvious interest in a quiet Middle East because of the oil fields and, just as importantly, because of the Suez Canal which, when closed, caused the price of oil to double and triple. Another reason, and perhaps a deeper one, was that Carter was a religious man, a Baptist. His desire to bring peace to the region sprang from his sense of duty to bring peace to the "children of Abraham," as he put it.

During his first visit to Israel, Sadat delivered a speech that was hard for us to swallow. A month later, we – Begin, Moshe Dayan and I – traveled to Ismailia. It was winter and we were sitting in a closed room. The tension was rising. Begin was citing past peace accords, and I noticed that Sadat was wiping the sweat from his brow. I understood that he was under great stress. Begin kept on talking. "...According to an expert on international law, Prof. Oppenheim..." he was saying, when suddenly Sadat clapped his hands. One of the palace workers entered. "Open the window," Sadat ordered. "He is very tense," I whispered to Begin. "So am I," he replied.

The crises continued. The Israeli public, who had pinned so much hope on the negotiations, started feeling disappointed.

Then Carter made a move, perhaps a one-time move, and invited us to Camp David with an explicit request that we not leave until we had reached an agreement. After 12 difficult and tense days there, we signed an agreement according to which we were to return to the international boundaries, evacuate the settlers (no dismantling of settlements, only the evacuation of people) and, naturally, institute diplomatic relations and all the rest.

The agreement pointed the way for the Palestinian autonomy. Everyone understood that the autonomy should be an interim period of three to five years, after which the final status, including borders, was to be decided on. Autonomy was never mentioned as a permanent solution, only as an interim stage before the permanent agreement.

Begin was ambivalent about the issue of evacuating the settlers from the Sinai. I did not doubt his sincerity when he told the Knesset: "With pain in my heart, but with a quiet conscience, I will recommend [that the settlers be evacuated], because this is the path to peace." I could almost hear his heart breaking as he spoke. Some may say that we should have stood fast, not given in, not given up. I do not think so. The greatness of leaders is measured by their ability to free themselves of past slogans and outdated opinions, and understand the historic currents. This was the greatness of Sadat, Begin and Carter, as it manifested itself at Camp David.

26.3.79

Israel and Egypt Sign a Peace Accord in Washington

The signing ceremony on the White House lawn, six months after the Camp David accord was signed, was impressive. It started with the three national anthems, and then US President Jimmy Carter, Egyptian President Anwar Sadat and Israeli Prime Minister Menachem Begin signed the historic agreement. The signing was preceded by heavy pressure exerted by the Americans on Begin, who wanted to introduce some last-minute changes. President him, whose efforts had led to the agreement, had visited the Middle East in order to iron out differences and have the parties approve the final draft of the agreement. On Carter's arrival in Jerusalem, Begin told him that before the agreement could be signed, the cabinet and the Knesset had to hold an in-depth discussion about the nature of the autonomy. Carter was furious and American pressure was applied again.

Carter managed to persuade Sadat to drop his demands regarding autonomy for the Palestinians, which enabled Begin to bring the agreement before the Knesset. After a stormy debate that lasted 28 hours, the Knesset approved the agreement by a majority of 95 to 18 (the rest abstained or were absent). Carter commented: "This is an historic decision by the State of Israel."

The Knesset approval paved the prime minister's way to the signing ceremony at the White House. The peace agreement stated that Israel would withdraw from the entire Sinai within three years, that the two countries would enjoy full and peaceful relations, and that Israeli vessels could sail through the Suez Canal. It was also agreed that after the signing, negotiations for a Palestinian autonomy in the territories would begin.

The three leaders – Carter, Sadat and Begin – during the national anthems preceding the signing of the Israeli-Egyptian peace accord.
Photo: Ya'akov Sa'ar, GPO

Hassan Salame Killed "in an Israeli Commando Operation"

22 January

At 16:00, Hassan Salame, who planned the massacre of the Israeli athletes in Munich, left PLO headquarters in West Beirut. The No.1 security man of the organization walked to his car in the guarded parking lot which was reserved for him and his aides, surrounded by a dozen heavily armed guards.

He got into his Range Rover station-wagon with three of his associates. The other terrorists got into their cars, and as they all drove toward the highway, a tremendous explosion was heard. A remote-controlled car-bomb exploded, destroying two of the cars and killing Salame. The PLO hastened to announce that "the assassination was carried out by a special Israeli commando unit."

Terrorist Hassan Salame, planner of the massacre of the athletes in Munich.

After the Peace Accord: Revisiting Egypt

11 July – Robert Dassa Returns to Alexandria

Eleven years after he was released from the Egyptian prison where he spent 14 years as an "Affair" prisoner, Robert Dassa returned to his hometown of Alexandria. He met his sister with her husband and three children at the family beach-house. After the family visit, Prime Minister Begin joined Dassa for a visit to the Alexandria Great Synagogue. Seeing that the place was deserted, Dassa said: "This used to be the meeting-place of the Jewish community. This is where the choir used to stand." Looking at the balcony, he added: "I will never forget the celebration of my Bar-Mitzvah here."

After that, Dassa toured the places he had planned to attack when he was a young and enthusiastic member of the Jewish network – the Rex and Metro movie theaters – which led him to years in prison.

Robert Dassa, one of the accused in "The Affair", returned to Egypt 11 years after his release from an Egyptian prison. Photo: Shalom Bar-Tal

4 September – Shlomo Ardinest Returns to the Pier Outpost

Shlomo Ardinest, commander of the Pier Outpost, was the last Israeli to leave the post during the Yom Kippur War under the unhappy circumstances of his capture. Ardinest was also the first Israeli to return there after the peace accord was signed to look for bodies of soldiers killed in the war. "I was very moved," he said, "I couldn't talk. I walked through the post reliving everything that happened there: Here Avichai lost his hand... this is where Arieh was wounded... and many of our belongings were still lying there.... Suddenly I saw an IDF shirt. Then I saw a piece of paper with Hebrew writing on it... it was the guard-duty roster for that last night. It contained the names of people whose remains we had come to find. A Yom Kippur prayer book was lying there; a book we did not finish praying from six years ago..."

An Egyptian officer suddenly approached Ardinest: "I know you. You were the commander here. I knew you would come. Is it true you received a citation?"

"No," Ardinest replied. "I didn't... Others who deserved it did..."

Shlomo Ardinest, commander of the Pier Outpost, returned to look for his friends' bodies. Photo: Shalom Bar-Tal

Dangerous Prisoners Escape from Ramla Prison

8 January

Eight dangerous prisoners, including Solomon Abu, who had arrived from France and was considered one of the most dangerous prisoners, escaped from the Ramla Prison. Extensive searches were held when the jailbreak was discovered, including air- and seaports. The police warned the public that the prisoners were armed and dangerous. It turned out that they had escaped through the mess hall and the kitchen, climbed up on to the roof and down into the yard, and broken through a gate. Outside, they hijacked a taxi and fled. They were all captured during the following two months.

16 January
A miracle in Jerusalem: An old newspaper vendor discovered a car-bomb in the city center and called the police. The bomb squad arrived at the site and de-activated the charges.

8 February
The cabinet approved a new economic plan presented by Finance Minister Simcha Ehrlich; the plan consisted mainly of cuts in food subsidies.

10 March
US President Jimmy Carter arrived for a visit in Israel and Egypt to expedite the signing of the peace accord between them.

14 March
IDF soldier Amram Avraham returned to Israel after 12 months in terrorist captivity. Avraham was exchanged for 76 terrorists, including some who had been convicted of murder.

26 March
The peace accord between Israel and Egypt was signed in Washington.

10 April
A bomb exploded in the Carmel Market in Tel Aviv, killing three people and wounding 32.

29 April
Seven prisoners of Zion, including Mark Dimschitz and Edward Kuznechov who were convicted in the Leningrad Trials, arrived in Israel after their unexpected release by the Soviet authorities.

24 May
The IDF started evacuating settlers who had barricaded themselves inside buildings in the vegetable garden of Moshav Neot Sinai. The soldiers and the farmers exchanged harsh words and blows.

7.11. *79*

Yig'al ("I don't have") Horowitz Appointed Finance Minister

Inflation hits the roof, and the cake immortalizing it keeps growing.
Photo: Giora Shalmi

Israel's economy deteriorated fast in 1979. When the Likud came to power, it inherited an annual inflation of 20%. A year later, inflation reached 52%, and in 1979, it reached the unprecedented figure of 116%. The Israeli Lira was devalued 70% over the year, and price hikes became routine.

The cabinet, unable to make economic decisions, held stormy debates about the policy that should be adopted, mainly whether subsidies on basic commodities should be cut. One night, the cabinet met for a meeting that was deemed crucial. Everyone expected severe economic measures to be announced, but in the morning it became apparent that no decision had been made. That night was later known as "the night of the ducks."

However, the government kept surprising everyone. In an unprecedented move, it announced that the prices of basic commodities would rise by 50%. Strikes broke out all around Israel, demanding salary hikes - and inflation kept raging. It seemed that the government was losing control of the economy, and many demanded that Finance Minister Simcha Ehrlich be replaced. On 7 November, the cabinet appointed Yig'al ("I don't have") Horowitz to replace Ehrlich, leader of the Liberal Party.

A Father and His Two Daughters Are Killed in a Terror Attack in Naharia

22 April

Four terrorists who arrived in Naharia by sea entered a residential building and took Dani Haran and his daughter hostage. While they were trying to return to the shore - intending to sail back to Lebanon - the police gave chase, and one of the police officers was killed. When the terrorists arrived at the beach with their hostages, a gun battle broke out between them and an IDF unit. Haran, his daughter and two of the terrorists were killed. Two other terrorists were captured and triled, but that was not the end of the Haran tragedy. Dani's wife, Smadar, who had hidden in the attic when the terrorists broke into the house, had strangled her baby daughter to death in an attempt to prevent her from screaming.

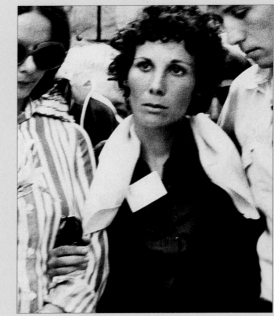

Smadar Haran at the funerals of her husband and daughters.
Photo: Haolam Hazeh

79

31 March

Second Israeli Win at the Eurovision: Gali Atari's *Hallelujah*

Photo: GPO

Singer Gali Atari and her song Hallelujah created one of the greatest sensations in the history of the Eurovision song contest. One year after winning the contest, Israel won again when the competition was held in Israel. The song, performed by Atari and the "Milk and Honey" band, was written by Shimrit Or and Kobi Oshrat and received a total of 125 points from the majority of the 19 countries that participated.

6 March

Death in a Refrigerator – two girls, 3 and 6, suffocated to death when they were trapped inside an old refrigerator that was standing in a yard in Petach Tikva. The police warned the public to beware of abandoned refrigerators, and a bill was passed prohibiting the dumping of old refrigerators in the public places.

26 March

The Postal Services sold some million first-day issue stamps and envelopes marking the signing of the peace accord with Egypt.

20 June

The National Team Wins a Silver Medal – The Israeli national basketball team won the silver medal in the European championship after losing the final game against the USSR. Mickey Berkovich was named MVP.

3 May

A Daring and Dangerous Bank Robbery

Four young men with masks on their faces pulled off one of the most daring and dangerous armed robberies ever in Israel. They walked away from a Bank Leumi branch in Ramat Aviv with more than IL2 million in Israeli and US currency. During the course of the rubbery, the robbers fired their pistols and Uzi submachine guns, and even threw two hand grenades in front of the bank. No one was killed, but the robbers brutally beat up several clerks and even threatened to murder the chief cashier. They fled with their loot after one of the robbers was wounded in the chest by a policeman who arrived on the scene by chance. The police pursued them and eventually captured them.

A police reconstruction of the capture of a suspect in a Ramat Aviv bank robbery. Photo: Oded Stopnitzky

27 May

President Sadat arrived in Beersheba for a meeting with Prime Minister Menachem Begin. The Israeli-Egyptian border was opened on the same day.

6 June

MK Geula Cohen quit the Likud because she opposed the peace accord with Egypt.

4 September

The price of frozen meat rose by 16% following a price rise on the international markets. This was the second price hike in six weeks.

24 September

IAF fighter planes downed four Syrian planes in dogfights over Lebanon. Three months earlier, the IAF downed five Syrian planes in the same place.

21 October

Foreign Minister Moshe Dayan resigned, stating that the main reason for his decision was his disagreement with Prime Minister Menachem Begin over the issue of Palestinian autonomy.

15 November

The Umm Hashiba installations that housed very advanced intelligence monitoring devices were blown up by the IDF bomb squad in preparation for the IDF withdrawal.

(1980

Deputy Prime Minister Yig'al Alon with Bedouin notables in the south. Photo: Moshe Milner, GPO

Yig'al Alon (right) with Yitzhak Sadeh (center) and Moshe Dayan (left) on the day they settled Hanita, 1938.

Yig'al Alon – The Warrior Rests
A son of the "plow and sword" culture

Writer Haim Gouri

One day, years ago, my eldest daughter asked me: "Who is this man you admire so much?" She was watching Yig'al Alon on TV. He was in his late fifties, struggling hard for sympathy in the political arena. She saw a wounded and scarred politician, fighting for his opinions and his place. Many believed that he had lost the chance ever to be Number One.

I told her to close her eyes and imagine a handsome young man from the Galilee who was admired and loved by a whole generation of young soldiers who looked up to him and followed him come hell or high water. This is how Yig'al was in my eyes. I see him as one of the chosen ones, one of the finest examples of the new Israeli generation. He went down in our history books as the man who built an independent Jewish military force and as the greatest military commander of the War of Independence. Later, he would be known as a politician who analyzed reality boldly and soberly.

I know that I am biased. I was one of the first soldiers of the Palmach "A" Company, of which Alon was the first commander. I remember the first time we met. One summer night in 1941, he came to a eucalyptus grove just outside the Kaduri school, where he too was in the first class. It was dark and he whispered to us, in his familiar hoarse voice, about the boat carrying 23 fighters which had been lost on the way to Lebanon, of what he and his friends had done in Syria. He urged us to join the special volunteer unit, the spearhead of the Hagana – the Palmach. I was one of those who were bewitched by the man and his words.

In his autobiography, *My Father's Home*, Alon writes: "I first saw the light of day in October 1918, in a small farming village, Kfar Tavor, at the foot of Mount Tabor, on its eastern and prettiest slope." He continues, "Kfar Tavor was blessed with an enchanting view, rich greenery, wild animals and magnificent birds." Like all great lovers, he describes the names of the plants and the smells, noting that "the smell of hay was always synonymous with the smell of love."

The Tabor and its surroundings are not just rolling expanses; they also represent time. Alon saw the Bible as a basic cultural experience. Among other things, he spoke of past events in the same region: "The images of Deborah and Barak, son of Avinoam... Sisera and Yael, the wife of Heber the Kenite, would appear before my eyes."

Yig'al was the son of a typical Israeli farming family, the son of the "plow and sword" culture. He was guided by the holy trinity of the time: Hebrew labor, Hebrew defense and Hebrew language. He belonged to the old settlements and was also a member of Maccabi. Later he joined the Labor movement, which was to win the political and cultural hegemony of Israel. He commanded the Hagana troops in the Lower Galilee during the events of 1936-9, and later joined the settlers of Hanita on the northern border. I remember that famous picture: Yig'al Alon and Moshe Dayan with Yitzhak Sadeh in the middle, embracing them as if to single them out for greatness. Yig'al and Moshe. The two who would later become bitter adversaries and whose rivalry would have a negative impact on Israeli politics.

Yig'al became a kibbutz member and very soon commanded the Palmach. He headed that force during the struggle against British rule and the beginning of the War of Independence. He fought on all fronts: in the north – as far as Lebanon; in the center – in Lod and Ramla; in Operation Dani; and in the massive campaigns in the south for liberating the Negev, fighting the Egyptian Army – Operations Yoav, Horev and Uvda which culminated in the hoisting of the "ink flag" in Eilat. No other commander shaped Israel's map like he did.

They say that this is where he started going down. Following an argument with Ben-Gurion, who esteemed and feared him, Alon resigned, or was forced to resign, from the IDF. As an opposition member with *Ahdut Ha'avoda* and Mapam, he was removed from the centers of power and influence. He studied at Oxford, but later returned to play a valuable role in Israeli politics. He united the Kibbutz Movement with the Labor Movement and served as a cabinet minister, but it always seemed as if he was late for something, as if he had missed the boat. He never became prime minister of Israel. Others did and he, who was a natural Number One, never got past being Number Two. Some say that as a politician he lacked the selfish and brutal ambition that characterized him as a military leader. Others "condemn" him, saying that he was too good a friend, too considerate, too committed.

To me and to many of his soldiers, he will forever be Yig'al who is at the top. The maxim according to which new things supercede the old applies only to the technological world. In the world of thought and spirit, art and literature and the historic acts that determine the fates of peoples and countries, things do not replace each other, but add up. This is where there is a place reserved for Yig'al Alon in Israel's history.

24.5.80

Menachem Begin: "The Government Is Malfunctioning."

The government under the leadership of Menachem Begin was fraught with problems. Ministers were in constant conflict, both in cabinet sessions and in the media. Begin was the target of the most severe criticism of all. It seemed as if he was losing control, and he admitted this openly, saying: "The government is malfunctioning."

The main source of conflict was Defense Minister Ezer Weizman, who adamantly opposed the defense budget cuts suggested by Finance Minister Yig'al Horowitz. He also attacked Begin's lack of willingness to promote the peace process. Weizman believed that the peace accord with Egypt had created a rare opportunity to attain peace agreements with all the Arab states, mainly the Palestinians; Begin, however, was not convinced.

Menachem Begin with his two deputies, Yiga'el Yadin and Simcha Ehrlich, during the Knesset debate on the state budget. Photo: Zoom 77

What angered Begin the most was Weizman's criticism of how he functioned on a personal level, about which he once said: "I will never forgive Weizman."

Weizman quit the cabinet at the end of May after his relations with Begin reached an unprecedented low. Weizman believed that Yiga'el Yadin would quit with him, causing the government to fall and leading to early elections. However, Yadin was concerned about the fact that his own party was falling apart. He knew that if the elections were moved forward, his party would crumble; he therefore chose to stay in the cabinet, and Weizman quit alone.

Ariel Sharon was very keen to be made defense minister, but Begin was reluctant to give him that important portfolio and decided to keep it for himself, the way Ben-Gurion had. Toward the end of the year, Begin suffered a mild heart attack which, his associates believed, was a result of overwork and stress.

The government kept moving in fits and starts, and everyone believed that it had run its course. Ministers quit one after another: Justice Minister Shmuel Tamir quit, Aharon Abu-Hatzira was put on trial and, worst of all, Finance Minister Yig'al Horowitz resigned at the beginning of 1981 because the economic situation of the state was deteriorating. Begin was powerless, and the Alignment looked as if it was going to win the coming elections.

Israeli Flag Hoisted in Cairo

18 February

The Israeli-Egyptian peace accord began to materialize with the opening of the Israeli Embassy in Cairo. The opening ceremony was held under heavy guard in spite of the objections of the Egyptian opposition. The Israeli flag was hoisted by Yosef Hadas, *chargé d'affaires* of the Cairo embassy, in front of several dozen astonished Egyptians. The opening of the embassy symbolized the beginning of the normalization process between the two nations. Several days later, the first Israeli ambassador, Eliahu Ben-Elissar, presented his credentials to President Anwar Sadat. In parallel, an Egyptian ambassador assumed his post in Israel and an Egyptian flag was hoisted over the embassy in Tel Aviv.

Photo: GPO

Bet Hadassah in Hebron Attacked; Six Settlers Killed

2 May

A group of settlers on their way to pray at Bet Hadassah in Hebron was attacked by terrorists with automatic weapons and hand grenades. Six settlers were killed and 16 wounded. The settlers' anger was directed mainly at Defense Minister Weizman; they claimed that the attack was the result of his lenient attitude toward the Palestinians. In reaction, the Hebron mayor, the city's religious leader and the Halhul mayor were deported to Jordan.

Photo: GPO

Yig'al Horowitz: "Look after the Lira"

Finance Minister Yig'al Horowitz and Histadrut Secretary General Yerucham Meshel at the Knesset. Photo: Zoom 77

While the cabinet was malfunctioning, the economy was deteriorating rapidly. Finance Minister Yig'al Horowitz made every effort to curb the rampant inflation and reduce budgets, but to no avail. His dramatic call: "Get off the roofs, madmen... look after the lira," did not succeed in making people aware of the situation. The public started abandoning the lira, and the US dollar became the going currency, with prices linked to it.

In October, the lira was replaced by the Israeli Shekel (IS), at a rate of IL10 to IS1, but this move did not help curb the price hikes either. Monthly consumer price indices reached double digits, and the government had to print more money to meet budgetary needs. By the end of the year, it became apparent that Israel's annual inflation had reached an all-time high of 131%.

The constant need to preserve the value of money due to the unprecedented inflation drove the public and the economy "crazy". The stock exchange was found to be a profitable alternative and many citizens invested there, some investing every last penny. The "madmen", as Horowitz described them, did not get off the rooftops. They suffered the consequences in the stock exchange crash of February 1981.

The Kidnapping of Oron Yarden Incenses the Country

8 June

The kidnapping of the child, Oron Yarden, and the drama that accompanied it whipped the country into a frenzy that lasted for many days. Oron was kidnapped by Tzvi Gur, who was mentally ill. Gur kidnapped Yarden in Savion after convincing him to get into his car on some pretext. Once in, Yarden was doomed. Gur drove him to an isolated place, gagged him and hid him in the trunk of his car. He then contacted the child's parents and demanded ransom money. After consulting with the police, the family agreed to pay, but instead of returning the boy, Gur murdered him and dumped his body near Netanya. The police found later that the child had been killed even before the negotiations had begun. Gur drove around with the body in the trunk of his car. He was captured and sentenced to life imprisonment plus 34 years.

2 January
Chief Superintendent Herzl Shafir was appointed chief of police.

7 January
Prices go up: a box of matches – IL1; a packet of margarine – IL11.5; a bottle of oil – IL57. Cigarettes – IL28, a 30% rise

2 February
Hanna Rovina died at the age of 90. She was one of the country's greatest actresses and a founder of Habima Theater.

18 February
In a festive ceremony, the Israeli flag was hoisted over the new embassy in Cairo.

29 February
Yig'al Alon died of a heart attack at 62. He was a commander in the Palmach, an MK, a minister and deputy prime minister. He was buried in Kibbutz Ginossar, where he had lived.

2 March
Snowstorms raged in the Galilee, Jerusalem and the Golan Heights. The Jerusalem highway was closed after snow in the city reached a depth of 30 cm.

10 March
Yitzhak Shamir was appointed foreign minister.

2 May
Terrorists attacked settlers on their way to pray at Bet Hadassah in Hebron killing six. Following the attack, local Arab notables were deported to Jordan.

24 May
Defense Minister Weizman resigned over differences with Prime Minister Begin regarding the autonomy in the territories.

2 June
Nablus Mayor Bassam Shak'a and Ramallah Mayor Karim Halaf were badly injured by bombs that were planted in their cars.

30 July
A big Knesset majority approved the "Jerusalem Bill", which invoked harsh reactions and condemnation worldwide.

7.4.80

"Mommy, Mommy!" Cried the Misgav-Am Children

The children's room in Kibbutz Misgav-Am after the battle with the terrorists. Photo: GPO

Five terrorists managed to enter Kibbutz Misgav-Am near the Lebanese border. The terrorists crossed the border fence undetected, carrying large quantities of weapons and explosives. They entered the kibbutz and succeeded in taking over the children's room, killing the kibbutz secretary who happened to be there with his wife. Seven children and a kibbutz member who was watching over them were then taken hostage. A large IDF force was deployed outside and negotiations with the terrorists began. As a result, the children were given food in the middle of the night.

The terrorists, already familiar with the IDF *modus operandi* in terror attacks for bargaining purposes, were ready when the IDF soldiers stormed the house. The first attack failed. The terrorists were well barricaded and trusted that the soldiers would be careful not to harm the children. The rescue forces retreated and a commando unit was sent in. It broke in at 10:00 and eliminated the terrorists. An IDF soldier and three-year-old Eyal Gluska were killed in the operation. The other children were rescued.

Actress Hanna Rovina, died

2 February

Actress Hanna Rovina, who was called "The First Lady of Hebrew Theatre", died at the age of 90. Rovina, a great actress with an impressive presence, acted in scores of plays during her lengthy career. In 1956, she was awarded the Israel Prize for her life's work and her contribution to cultural life and art in Israel. She was one of the founders of Habima Theater.

Hanna Rovina in Medea *by Euripides. Photo: Boris Karmi*

80

1980

7 January

While the Watchmaker from Safed was in Hospital, 34 of his Drawings were Stolen

Thirty-four drawings were stolen from the Zeichermacher (watchmaker) from Safed, Rabbi Shalom Moshkovich. They were worth millions because they were his last drawings. The thieves broke into his house while he was in hospital in the city, several days before he died. Moshkovich's naïve drawings were exhibited in museums worldwide. He started drawing because he could not earn a living as a watchmaker, and his achievements were impressive.

30 November

Tzvi Gur, the kidnapper and murderer of the child Oron Yarden, was sentenced to life plus 34 years in prison.

18 December

Shimon Peres defeated Yitzhak Rabin in the Labor Party vote for candidate for prime minister.

5 September

Tal Brody's Farewell Game

A farewell ceremony in honor of the greatest Israeli basketball player of all time, Tal Brody, was held at the Yad Eliahu Stadium. It was preceded by a farewell game in which Maccabi Tel Aviv defeated the European team. The moving ceremony was attended by Yitzhak Rabin, Moshe Dayan, ministers, MKs and many athletes. Brody thanked everyone, saying: "It was a wonderful evening. I am very touched. And the game was great."

8 August

Lovesick Soldier Runs Amok in an APC

A lovesick young soldier from Jerusalem chose a unique way to protest against his girlfriend's attitude toward him. He drove wildly through the streets of Jerusalem to her house in an armored personnel carrier (APC). Panicked pedestrians called the police and the soldier was caught after his fruitless pursuit of love...

1 November

The IDF Gives the US a Soviet Nerve Gas Antidote

A Soviet nerve gas antidote acquired by the IDF during the Yom Kippur War and later delivered to the US Army was recently banned for use. This was because soldiers who used it started hallucinating and developing loving feelings for... the enemy.

24 May

Cigarette Truck Stolen

A truck carrying IL10 million worth of cigarettes was stolen from inside the Dubek cigarette factory. Four robbers tied up the guard, took the keys from him and sped through Bnei Brak to a hide-out they had prepared.

21 January

"The Horowitz Era": Less Whisky, Salami and Nuts

The Israelis' consumption habits changed during the "Horowitz era". The public avoided purchasing expensive goods and sought cheap substitutes. It appeared that people were buying less whisky, salami and nuts, and more potatoes, cheese and fruit.

Photo: Hanania Herman, GPO

(*1981*

The Iraqi nuclear reactor after it was bombed by the IAF.

The Iraqi reactor in the final stages of construction.

The Bombing of the Iraqi Nuclear Reactor
Operation Opera – A different ball-game

Eitan Ben-Eliyahu

Ever since its establishment, the IAF has had several opportunities to demonstrate its remarkable might, skill and ability to use the tools at its disposal. The attack on the Iraqi nuclear reactor was definitely a fine example of this. It was a combination of initiative, imagination, planning and the ability to make decisions while performing a task that had never been attempted before. The target was apparently beyond the flight range and could only be reached through a series of improvisations. In addition, the bombing systems in the planes were not accurate enough, so the pilots had to be relied upon to perform their mission with greater precision than could be expected from the systems in the planes. The combination of all these elements led to an unprecedented historic achievement which had enormous political and military ramifications by any standards.

In 1963, Iraq built a Russian-model nuclear reactor in a research center south-east of Baghdad. The reactor became operational in 1969 and from then on it fulfilled all of Iraq's research needs. After that, France provided Iraq with a reactor dubbed "Osirak". There was a growing fear that Iraq would not stick to nuclear research, but would start producing nuclear weapons. The reason for that stemmed from a remark by Saddam Hussein, published in the Iraqi paper *al-Thawra*: "The Iranians need not fear our nuclear reactor; we have no plans to use it against Iran, only against the Israeli enemy...."

Planning the operation started in October 1979. Various methods were examined and even today it would not be wise to elaborate on them. The plans were constantly changed, updated and modified. The traditional IAF argument about who would do the job also took place. Every commander wanted the mission. Initially, we had planned that Phantoms should do the job, but after we received the F-16s and their pilots reached the required operational level, the Phantoms were ruled out. The F-15 squadron commanders argued with the F-16 pilots, each group insisting that the job should be theirs. In the end, we decided that the F-16s would carry out the attack and the F-15s would escort and protect them.

The plan was completed, launch bases were determined and the route and assault profile defined. We decided which bombs and which detonators to use to ensure accurate hits and penetration to the reactor core. The plan was highly classified and only a small number of officers knew everything about it. The pilots were given only some of the details – and even that was just before the operation took place.

The order was given on 5 June 1981, after several delays. Everyone was excited. The pilots whispered to each other; they expressed their pride at taking part in such an historic mission as well as some fear and tension. We had not carried out raids on Iraq since the Six Day War. Like others, I was excited and grateful for the privilege of taking part in the mission.

On Sunday afternoon, 7 June, the eve of Shavuot [Pentecost], Operation Opera got under way.

Our aim was to avoid inflicting casualties to the best of our ability, especially among the foreign advisers who worked on the site. This is why we chose a Sunday. The first foursome, heading the entire operation, was led by Lieutenant Colonel Ze'ev Raz, who was later commended by the chief of staff. The second formation was led by Lieutenant Colonel Amir. Lieutenant Colonel Moshe and I were at the head of the F-15s. Colonel Aviam, head of IAF operations and planner of this operation, was flying with the F-15s as the representative of the front command. Major General David Ivri, the IAF commander at the time, followed and guided the planning, made the decisions, made the recommendations to the government and commanded the operation from the IAF headquarters.

The planes flew silently at an altitude from which the pilots could almost see the faces of drivers on the highways below the flight path. The pilots were intent in their cockpits, performing what they had learned by heart, watching every point along the way, counting the minutes and seconds before they were to pull up and dive at the target.

The sun was setting in the distant and quiet west, and the twilight heralded the approaching holiday. At precisely 17:35, the eight F-16s, escorted by eight F-15s, dived toward the Iraqi reactor and, in a single volley, destroyed it to its foundation.

All our planes returned safely. The leaders reported "Alpha", meaning "Bull's-eye". The reactor had been destroyed and could not be reconstructed. The nuclear threat to Israel had been averted for many years to come.

7.6.**81**

The Bombing of the Iraqi Reactor: "A Perfectly Performed Operation"

Prime Minister Menachem Begin at a news conference after the bombing of the Iraqi reactor. Photo: Zoom 77

Eight F-16s and eight F-15s took off for Iraq. They flew 2,000 km, avoiding Jordanian, Saudi and Iraqi radar and, in two minutes, dropped 10 tons of bombs on the Osirak reactor near Baghdad. This operation effectively neutralized many years of Iraqi attempts to build a nuclear bomb. It was one of the most daring operations performed by Israel, with unprecedented success. Benny Peled, former IAF commander, said: "This was a perfectly performed operation worthy of the highest praise."

Iraqi President Saddam Hussein was furious and ordered that the commander of the anti-aircraft missile batteries stationed around the reactor be executed for not firing at the attacking planes. The Iraqi air force did not react either, possibly because it feared the F-15 escort. The reactor was totally destroyed but, because it was not active, there was no radioactive fallout. Prime Minister Menachem Begin used this very reasoning to explain the timing of the attack. He claimed that had Israel waited a few more weeks, the reactor would have became "hot" and bombing it would have released dangerous radioactive fallout and cost numerous lives.

The decision to bomb the Iraqi reactor was made after much hesitation and many delays. The timing was decided on after intelligence reports stated that Iraq was going to activate the reactor within a short time. Menachem Begin, Ariel Sharon and Yitzhak Shamir were the main supporters of the attack.

The Israelis were pleased with the operation, and the international media praised the IAF for its performance. However, the timing, three weeks before the elections, provoked public criticism of Begin. In a speech given after the operation, Begin claimed that the IAF operation had saved the State of Israel from a second Holocaust and that "a sword had been lifted off the Jewish nation's neck." Opposition leader Shimon Peres, however, maintained that the Iraqi nuclear option could have been averted by non-military means.

Photo: GPO

Zubin Mehta - The National Conductor

29 October

Conductor Zubin Mehta was appointed musical director of the Israeli Philharmonic Orchestra for life. On 18 July, Mehta stirred the emotions of 200,000 people who came to listen to the orchestra perform at the Yarkon Park in Tel Aviv. After leading the orchestra to great musical heights, Mehta was selected to be its director. His appointment was somewhat marred by his decision to include works by Richard Wagner, whose music was identified with the Nazis – and this sparked a public outcry.

A Stormy and Violent Election Campaign

The 1981 election campaign was very violent; some say it was the most violent ever. Two months before the elections, it looked like the Alignment was about to score a major victory. But then Menachem Begin pulled himself together and began to appear all over the country, where he was received with great enthusiasm. He mocked Peres and embarrassed him by displaying the letter Peres had written, opposing the bombing of the Iraqi reactor before the operation. Begin charged that Peres was willing to jeopardize Israel's security in order to win the elections. The inflammatory Likud campaign affected the opposition leader's rallies. Peres' appearances were constantly interrupted by Likud hecklers who booed and mocked him and threw a selection of the season's vegetables at him, mostly tomatoes. The police were compelled to appear at the Alignment rallies in large numbers to keep order and prevent brawls between the rival camps.

In the meantime, the gap between the two parties was closing, with Finance Minister Yoram Aridor distributing goodies to the people. The bombing of the Iraqi reactor tipped the scale in favor of the Likud for the first time that year. The Likud won the elections, with 48 Knesset seats to the Alignment's 47. Begin formed a new cabinet with the help of the right-wing and religious parties, and the second Begin cabinet was presented to the Knesset at the end of August, winning the support of only 61 MKs.

Likud supporters demonstrate at an Alignment election rally. Photo: Yossi Roth

Prime Minister Menachem Begin with his deputy David Levy at a Likud election rally in Malchei Yisrael Square in Tel Aviv. Photo: Nachum Guttman

Prime Minister Menachem Begin in Metzudat Ze'ev after hearing that the Likud had won the elections. Photo: GPO

11 January
Finance Minister Yig'al Horowitz resigned after the cabinet decided to accept the Etzioni Committee report regarding teachers' salaries, despite his opposition.

21 January
Yoram Aridor was appointed finance minister. Shortly after he assumed office, he implemented his "economics for the elections" which, some say, led the Likud to victory in the elections.

2 February
The Tel Aviv Stock Exchange collapsed with shares dropping 15% on average.

25 March

Yonatan Ratosh – poet, translator and linguist – died. Originally, he was a member of the Revisionist Movement, and later he headed the Canaanite Movement.

9 May

Photo: Y. Freidin

Poet Uri Tzvi Grünberg died at the age of 84. He was one of the greatest Hebrew poets, an MK and one of the leaders of the Revisionist Movement.

11 May
MK Flatto Sharon was sentenced to three years in prison, of which he would have to serve nine months, for offering his voters bribes during the 1977 election campaign.

24.5.81

Abu-Hatzira Acquitted:
"Not Guilty For All to See"

Aharon Abu-Hatzira after he was acquitted by the Jerusalem District Court. Photo: Zoom 77

Religious Affairs Minister Aharon Abu-Hatzira, who was charged with accepting bribes, was acquitted by the Jerusalem District Court. The charges against him were based on the testimony of state witness Yisrael Gottlieb, but the court cast doubt on his credibility, which destroyed the case against Abu-Hatzira. After his acquittal, his supporters held festivities in Ramla and Bnei Brak, during which Abu-Hatzira was carried on his supporters' shoulders as if he had been rescued from a vicious blood libel.

Abu-Hatzira announced that he would no longer run with Yosef Burg on the NRP list for the Knesset and that he was forming his own list - Tami, The Movement for Israel's Tradition. His party won three Knesset seats and joined the coalition. Abu-Hatzira wanted the Religious Affairs portfolio, but had to settle for the Absorption, Labor and Social Welfare Ministry. However, his joy was premature. He was charged with fraud and theft again, and his trial opened on the day the new cabinet was sworn in.

On 19 April 1982, Abu-Hatzira was found guilty. He was sentenced to three months of public service and was forced to resign. The conviction sparked his supporters' claim that it had been made on an ethnic basis.

Herzl Avitan Escapes

23 September

After visiting his sick father, Herzl Avitan gave his guards the slip and disappeared. Avitan, who was serving a 15-year prison sentence for robbing a bank, had been in prison for only two years. He did not waste his "free" time and managed to murder two more people during his escape - one of them the commander of the Ramla prison. A massive manhunt throughout the country got under way, as Avitan was considered an especially violent and dangerous criminal. In spite of everything, he succeeded in fleeing the country, and only two years later did the French police capture him and deport him to Israel.

A Black Day on the Tel Aviv Stock Exchange

2 February

Two weeks after Yoram Aridor was appointed finance minister, he was given a very stormy reception when the Tel Aviv Stock Exchange, which had flourished until then, crashed in one day. Shares dropped by an average of 15% and many people lost a lot of money. Some shares were wiped out completely. Aridor, who had implemented an election policy of giving out goodies to the people, was in shock. Although he called for the stabilization of the economy, his actions as finance minister caused just the opposite to happen. During his term in office, the Israeli economy deteriorated and Aridor's attempts to curb inflation failed miserably.

Top: Finance Minister Yoram Aridor. Photo: GPO
Bottom: The Tel Aviv Stock Exchange. Photo: Yaacov Saar, GPO

81

1981

26 March

Maccabi Tel Aviv Wins the European Cup Again

Photo: Moshe Shai

The final buzzer announced that Maccabi Tel Aviv had won the European basketball cup once again, after beating the Italian champion Sinodine Bologna 80:79 in the final game. This gave rise to festivities in Tel Aviv, during which excited youths jumped into the cold water of the fountain in Malchei Yisrael Square. Dozens of champagne bottles were uncorked and processions of cars drove through the city center, honking incessantly.

18 March

"I Was Left Alone in the Terrible Ocean." – Malka Stier, the only woman survivor of the *Massada* which sank near the Bermuda Triangle, told her shocking story: "There were 15 people in the lifeboat, tossed around for an hour in the stormy ocean, when suddenly a huge wave swept over us. The boat overturned and, although we were all wearing life-jackets, I was the only one who came back to the surface. I no longer saw my husband or anybody else. I was left alone in the terrible ocean." Four survivors were pulled out of the water near Gibraltar.

Photo: Yossi Roth

24 June

Begin and Peres Hold a TV Debate

A 30-minute TV debate between Menachem Begin and Shimon Peres was held. It was taped and the opponents received the questions beforehand.

3 August

Photo: Zoom 77

Ultra-Orthodox Demonstration in the City of David – Thousands of ultra-Orthodox Jews staged a demonstration demanding that the archeological excavations in the City of David near the Western Wall be halted. They claimed that the site was once a Jewish cemetery. To their chagrin, however, the High Court of Justice ruled that the diggings could continue.

24 May

Tami, a new Sephardi party, was founded by Aharon Abu-Hatzira after he was found not guilty in his first trial.

4 June

Finance Minister Yoram Aridor decided to allocate IS3 billion in subsidies for exporters. The Alignment claimed this was an election ploy.

7 June

IAF planes destroyed the Iraqi nuclear reactor.

15 June

The first international conference of Holocaust survivors from 30 countries was held in Jerusalem. Some 4,000 survivors attended.

30 June

At the end of a stormy and violent election campaign, the Likud, headed by Menachem Begin, won with 48 seats and the Alignment, headed by Shimon Peres, lost with 47.

6 October

Egyptian President Sadat was assassinated during a military parade in Cairo.

16 October

Moshe Dayan died. He had been the IDF chief of staff, an MK and a minister in several cabinets.

1 November

The Hebrew University school year opened at the Mount Scopus campus, which had been closed for many years.

14 December

The Knesset ratified the "Golan Bill", imposing Israeli sovereignty on the Golan Heights.

15 November

"Pladelet" Jumped Right Into the Policemen's Arms

A police stakeout outside a Ramat Gan house led to the capture of a Tel Aviv criminal dubbed "Pladelet" [steel door]. His capture put an end to a daring gang of robbers who, among other things, cleaned out the warehouse of the Shekem department store in Tel Aviv. A team of policemen knocked on the door of the man whose nickname reflected his enormous size. Realizing who was behind the door, "Pladelet" jumped out of the window, right into the arms of the police officers who were waiting for him downstairs. During his interrogation, he revealed that he was the head of a 13-member gang of robbers and fences that included two paratroopers and three women.

The Tel Aviv criminal, "Pladelet", is taken into custody. Photo: Shaul Golan

1982

Red Cross personnel clearing the bodies of Palestinians who were murdered by the Christian Phalangists in Sabra and Shatila. Photo: GPO

Bodies of Palestinian men, women and children on the streets of the Shatila refugee camp. Photo: DPI

The Lebanon War: The Sabra and Shatila Massacre
The Moral Awakening

Writer

A . B . Yehoshua

Sabra and Shatila are two refugee camps outside Beirut. On the night of 16 September 1982, the Christian Phalangists entered the camps and brutally murdered hundreds of Palestinian men, women and children. The IDF units stationed just outside the camp naturally did not take part in the massacre, and perhaps could not even guess at the scope of its cruelty. However, their very presence in the heart of Beirut provided backing and cover for the atrocities of their Christian allies, whose deeds were merely another link in the chain of atrocities perpetrated by all the parties in Lebanon: Christians, Sunis, Shiites and Palestinians.

The Israeli public seemed to have needed this vile incident in order to be thoroughly shocked and perhaps to undergo a moral awakening from this strange war we had initiated. It started, supposedly, as an extended military operation against the PLO bases in Lebanon, designed to push the Katyusha launchers northward, thus ensuring that the northern settlements were out of their range. It ended in a painful, deep and dangerous embroilment in the sick and torn Land of Cedars.

At first, most Israelis supported the war, believing in the illusion that, by simple means and with no particular problems, it would eliminate the Palestinian enemy, or at least completely remove it from Israel's borders. After the incident, the public began to understand not only how deeply Israel had sunk militarily and politically into the Lebanese quagmire, but also the moral corruption we were proliferating with our impossible demand that the Palestinian problem be solved by military force.

The Lebanon War took place exactly 15 years after the Six Day War. A simple comparison between the two wars would help us understand what had happened to Israel's policy when it deviated from its political and moral principles after the Six Day War. The 1967 war was clearly a defensive campaign imposed on us by the aggression of the Arab countries. I believe that because Israel acted in self-defense, it had moral supremacy which ensured a brilliant victory on the three fronts in an amazingly short time and with relatively few casualties. In the unjustified and irresponsible Lebanon War, the sophisticated Israeli war machine attempted to crush tiny Palestinian guerrilla units. And although the campaign lasted many days and the number of casualties equalled that of the Six Day War, there was no clear military achievement. Israel was forced to withdraw from most of the Lebanese territory without an agreement, and painful skirmishes continue to occur on the Lebanese border to this very day.

The Six Day War, which was a just war, provided a basis on which the conflict could be solved with the formula of "territories for peace". That formula brought Sadat to Jerusalem, served as an initial basis for the agreement between the Israeli and Palestinian nations and may lead to reconciliation between Israel and Syria. Miraculously, the injustice of the Lebanon War yielded two obvious results which to this day stand in absolute contradiction to the intentions of the Begin government that initiated the war.

That war indeed destroyed the small and imaginary Palestinian "state" in southern Lebanon, but not only was the Palestinian problem not eliminated – the war only made it clear just how essential a compromise between the two nations was. First, the *intifadah* broke out in the heart of the West Bank and the Gaza Strip several years later; then Israel and the Palestinians signed their first agreement in Oslo.

That war also established a bond of blood between the Golan Heights and southern Lebanon. Any solution for the security zone in Lebanon will, from now on, entail a peace agreement with Syria.

One clear lesson for the future was learned from that war: Israel will never again go to war unless it is absolutely and unquestionably necessary and unless there is a general consensus of public opinion. This may provide some consolation for the river of blood that has been shed in vain.

Operation Peace for the Galilee

19**82**

5 June

Operation Peace for the Galilee: This is How the Cabinet Decided...

Even before a new cabinet was formed after the 1981 elections, it was clear that Israel's northern border was heating up. The terrorists were carrying out numerous attacks and Operation Litani, aimed at pushing them north of the Litani River, had not succeeded. Defense Minister Ariel Sharon started pushing for an extensive military operation against the terrorist infrastructure in Lebanon already at the beginning of

1982. Sharon ordered the general staff to update contingency plans, of which there were two versions: "Small Pines" – a military takeover of south Lebanon; and "Big Pines", which was more ambitious and included a military breakthrough to Beirut. Sharon's pressures began to have results in April and May. The government decided to go to war, with only the question of timing and cause remaining open. The cabinet discussed launching a war on 17 May, but did not receive majority support. Begin and Sharon knew then that only a gross violation of the cease-fire by the terrorists would convince the ministers to assent to a military operation in Lebanon.

The excuse for the war came on 3 June when Israel's ambassador to Britain, Shlomo Argov, was badly wounded in a terrorist assassination attempt. The next day, the cabinet decided that IAF planes would raid terrorist camps in the Beirut area. Several hours later, the terrorists reacted with a massive shelling of Israel's northern settlements. The government felt that military action in Lebanon was inevitable, and approved an operation on 5 June, with only two abstentions. According to the government decision, the operation, dubbed "Operation Peace for the Galilee", was supposed

Galilee Panhandle residents in the shelters as hundreds of Katyusha rockets hit the region

to ensure that all Galilee settlements were out of the range of the terrorists' Katyushas. The ministers were given to understand that, as the range was 40 km, the IDF would not go beyond that. But war being what it is, the rolling snowball could not be stopped.

Photo: GPO

Photo: GPO

The Yamit Evacuation Battle

21 April

Thousands of IDF soldiers started evacuating the Yamit settlers. Hundreds of settlers barricaded themselves on rooftops and pelted the approaching soldiers with rocks and bottles, sprayed water on them and cursed them. Settlers and soldiers exchange blows in full view of international TV crews. All the while, an iron cage moved up and down the roofs to forcibly remove the struggling settlers. The sight of bleeding settlers and soldiers exchanging blows was a painful one.

A tough struggle ensued on the monument at the entrance to the city, where Tzachi Hanegbi and his student friends refused to get off the tower. Only after lengthy negotiations and extensive media coverage did Hanegbi agree to come down.

The evacuation of Yamit lasted four days, and when it was over, Defense Minister Ariel Sharon ordered that the city be bulldozed to the ground. When pictures of the destruction were screened on TV all over the world, harsh criticism was leveled at Sharon, who had not even bothered to receive cabinet approval for the move.

Photo: Micha Bar-Am

6 June

...And This Is How It Was in the Battlefield

On the morning of 6 June, the IDF communications networks sounded off the command: "All units, go! go! go! Roger and out." The IDF troops entered Lebanon, moving northwards in three columns and capturing their targets with minimal resistance. "Fatahland" was quickly taken, and the forces seized positions controlling the roads to Tyre and Sidon. The Lebanese coastal towns were surrounded, and Israel Navy missile boats shelled the routes running north from the towns in order to prevent terrorists from fleeing to Beirut. At the same time, the Navy dropped off large paratrooper units south of the city and they started capturing the hills overlooking the city. At the end of the first day of combat, it seemed like all the goals had been attained. The IDF high command now had to tackle the Beaufort Fortress, which served as a central terrorist base in south Lebanon and from which hundreds of Katyusha rockets had been fired at the northern settlements.

IDF armored personnel carriers entering south Lebanon.
Photo: IDF Spokesman

7 June

The Battle for the Beaufort

The Golani reconnaissance unit was given the task of conquering the most difficult target – the Beaufort Fortress. Situated 700 m above sea-level, it was a very strongly fortified target. The only access to it was up the steep mountainside. The IAF bombarded the site to soften it before the infantry moved in, but the terrorists did not withdraw. Late at night, under heavy Israeli artillery shelling, two Golani teams, commanded by Major Goni Hernick, started scaling the mountain's steep side. At daybreak, the Golani soldiers, in two flanks, broke into two wings of the fortress and fought a fierce battle with the terrorists who were hiding in the tunnels and firing at the soldiers from there. All the terrorists were eliminated, but not before Hernick and five of his men had been killed by terrorist fire.

Capturing the Beaufort opened the IDF routes northward, and the troops were able to advance without the threat of terrorists on the mountaintop. Several hours after the battle, Prime Minister Menachem Begin and Defense Minister Ariel Sharon arrived to congratulate the troops on a mission well accomplished. Begin believed that the mountain had been captured without any Israeli casualties because no one had briefed him. In debriefings after the war, the decision to attack the mountain was harshly criticized, and the operational importance of the move – mainly the decision to climb the steepest side – questioned. In spite of everything, the battle for the Beaufort still serves as an example of determination, courage and self-sacrifice.

Prime Minister Menachem Begin and Defense Minister Ariel Sharon visiting the Beaufort Fortress hours after the Golani Reconnaissance unit captured it. Photo: IDF Spokesman

Photo: GPO

Operation Peace for the Galilee

19**82**

9 June

The IAF Destroys Syrian Missile Batteries

In one of its most sophisticated and effective operations, the IAF destroyed dozens of Syrian missile batteries, using a variety of electronic means to jam the missiles. This time, the fighter jets defeated the missiles, having learned the lessons of the Yom Kippur War perfectly.

Realizing that it had suffered a harsh blow, the Syrian command was forced to send its fighter planes to protect the missiles. Dozens of Israeli and Syrian planes clashed in midair in what has been termed as "the biggest dogfight of all times". The results were indisputable: 100 Syrian planes were downed, while Israel did not lose a single plane. In one day, Syria lost one-third of its air power and half of its missiles.

Fighting on the ground continued in parallel with IAF operations. Photo: GPO

Major General Yekutiel (Kuti) Adam, deputy chief of staff. Photo: Zoom 77

10 June

Major General Yekutiel Adam, Deputy Chief of Staff, Killed

The highest-ranking IDF officer killed in Operation Peace for the Galilee was Major General Yekutiel (Kuti) Adam, deputy chief of staff. While driving with his assistant, Colonel Haim Sela, to the IDF command in Damur, they came under attack by artillery. Adam and those accompanying him sought refuge in a nearby building, not knowing that a terrorist squad was hiding there. The terrorists surprised the group of senior officers and killed them at close range. Another group of soldiers arrived there and eliminated the terrorists. Adam was considered one of the best IDF commanders and had an impressive military record. He had commanded armored brigades, as well as the Golani Brigade, and had headed the Southern Command. He had been mentioned as a potential successor to Refael Eitan, but he preferred the position of head of the Mossad. He quit his studies in the US in order to take part in the Lebanon War. The news of the death of this brave soldier shocked the country.

Photo: GPO

11 August

Surrounding Beirut and Evacuating the Terrorists

In the eastern sector, the IDF forces encountered tough opposition from well-equipped and dug-in Syrian units that tried to prevent the IDF from reaching the Beirut-Damascus highway. At the same time, other IDF units kept advancing toward Beirut's southern outskirts. The battle against the terrorists in Beirut started on the same day that US envoy Philip Habib attained a cease-fire agreement. The cease-fire collapsed two weeks later, and heavy fighting between Israeli and Syrian armored and infantry units broke out near the township of Bahamdoun on the Beirut-Damascus highway. Realizing that losing this battle might mean that Israeli tanks could reach Damascus, the Syrian Army sent large forces into battle. The IDF suffered 16 fatalities and 50 casualties in these battles.

In the meantime, the fight against the terrorists in Beirut resumed. The IAF shelled targets in west Beirut incessantly, and the IDF tightened its grip of the city. On 1 August, the IDF launched a massive offensive against the besieged terrorists, shelling the city heavily from planes, boats, tanks and artillery. The IDF forces seized key points in the city: the airport, the eastern neighborhoods and the Burj al-Barajne refugee camp which was a major terrorist stronghold. The fighting was fierce and inflicted heavy losses. Ten days after the battle for Beirut had started, an agreement was reached - mediated by US envoy Philip Habib - according to which the terrorists would be evacuated from Beirut by sea to Syria, Jordan and Iraq.

IDF soldiers on the southern outskirts of Beirut. Photo: GPO

22 July

Brigade Commander Eli Geva - A Conscientious Objector

Eli Geva, an armored brigade commander during the Lebanon War, wrote a letter to Chief of Staff Eitan asking to be relieved of his duties on conscientious grounds. He said he could not take part in the attack on Beirut and the killing of innocent people. The affair sent shock waves through the IDF command and exacerbated the dilemma regarding conscientious objectors. The chief of staff and the defense minister reacted very harshly and Geva's post as brigade commander was revoked shortly after that.

Colonel Eli Geva, an armored brigade commander who left his post halfway through the war on conscientious grounds.

21 February
Prof. Gershom Scholem, one of the greatest experts on Kabbalah, died at the age of 84.

11 April
IDF soldier Elliot Goodman opened fire at Arabs on the Temple Mount. Two were killed and 11 wounded. The Arab world was outraged.

3 June
Shlomo Argov, Israel's Ambassador in Britain, was shot and badly wounded by a terrorist.

5 June
The government decided to launch Operation Peace for the Galilee, the aim of which was to "get the Galilee settlements out of the range of terrorist fire". The operation was approved, with only two ministers abstaining.

6 June
The operation got under way with the IDF entering Lebanon in three columns, capturing all their targets with minimal resistance.

7 June
The Beaufort Fortress was captured. Golani soldiers climbed up the steep side of the mountain and fought a fierce battle inside the fortress. Six IDF soldiers were killed, including the force commander, Captain Goni Hernick.

9 June
The IAF destroyed the Syrian missile deployment using sophisticated means.

14 June
Finance Minister Yoram Aridor announced: "In the economy, we must act like the IDF does in Lebanon." He raised VAT from 12% to 15% and imposed a 2% sales tax on the stock exchange and a IS600 travel tax. The prices of basic commodities rose by 20%.

10 June
An IDF unit fell into a Syrian ambush near the township of Sultan Yakub. The unit suffered many casualties and three of its soldiers are still missing to this day.

Operation Peace for the Galilee

Families of Sabra and Shatila massacre victims. In Israel, a demand was made that a state committee examine the affair. Photo: Yossi Roth, GPO

16 September

The Sabra and Shatila Massacre

Two days before the massacre, Lebanese President-Elect Bashir Jemayel was killed by a bomb in his Beirut office. Jemayel was the commander of the Christian Phalangists. Seeking revenge, his men obtained the IDF's permission to enter refugee camps and capture terrorists who were hiding there. The Phalangists arrived in the camps on IDF vehicles and started murdering hundreds of Palestinian men, women and children.

Reports about the mass murder reached the IDF Intelligence Branch chief, but he did not bother to notify the political echelons. Prime Minister Menachem Begin heard about the massacre on BBC broadcasts from London. Shocking pictures were already being shown on TV screens worldwide. Israel's image was severely damaged, and it was blamed for looking the other way while the Phalangists were inside the camps. A great storm of public outrage erupted in Israel as well. The Alignment leaders demanded that the prime minister and the defense minister resign. They also demanded that a state commission of inquiry be set up to investigate the events at Sabra and Shatila. Two weeks after the massacre, the Kahan commission was set up and instructed to find out who was responsible for the bloody events in the refugee camps.

11 November

75 Killed in the First Tyre Disaster

A giant explosion demolished the military government building in Tyre, burying dozens of IDF soldiers. The seven-story building that housed the IDF command in the city turned into rubble within seconds. The building was full of IDF soldiers, General Security Service [GSS] and intelligence personnel, as well as Palestinian detainees who were being held in the basement. Special rescue forces with Engineering Corps equipment and large medical teams were rushed to the site, and trained dogs were used to locate signs of life. The operations continued for three days and three nights, in driving rain and extreme cold, but the results were shocking. Seventy-five bodies of IDF soldiers were dug out; 24 soldiers were injured. A special committee appointed by the chief of staff found no traces of a terror attack. It concluded that the cause of the explosion was a gas leak. The building could not have withstood the blast due to the low standard of construction in Lebanon.

Soldiers evacuating the bodies of their comrades from the military government building in Tyre. Photo: Michael Lovich, GPO

1982

3 April

The Great Whore Causes A Storm

Photo: Harmati

There was a commotion at the Cameri Theater during the première of Hanoch Levin's The Great Whore of Babylon. The theater was packed when, just before the play ended, veteran actor Yossi Yadin, who was in the audience, got up and yelled: "This is not what we established this theater for... You ought to be ashamed! Lower the curtain now!" There was a commotion, and many spectators left the hall with Yadin.

22 September

The First Test-Tube Baby Born in Israel - A 3.78-kg baby was born to a 32-year-old woman who had been married for 12 years but was unable to fall pregnant. Her treatment had started a year before at the special fertility clinic in the Shiba Medical Center at Tel Hashomer. Everyone eagerly awaited the historic birth, and the baby was delivered by Prof. Shlomo Mashiah, who performed a Caesarian section.

Photo: GPO

[The placards read: "Sharon, Go Home Now!" "No More Wars Like This!"]
Photo: GPO

3 July; 25 September

Peace Now Demonstrations - Two giant demonstrations were staged in Tel Aviv, representing the public debate in Israel *vis-à-vis* the Lebanon War. The longer the war went on, while deviating from its original goals, the more voices were heard in protest against Prime Minister Menachem Begin and mostly against Defense Minister Ariel Sharon. The first *Peace Now* demonstration (3 July) was attended by some 100,000 people who protested Israel's prolonged involvement in Lebanon. The second demonstration was held after the Sabra and Shatila massacre (25 September). According to the organizers, it was attended by some 400,000 people. The demonstrators at Malchei Yisrael Square demanded that a state commission of inquiry examine the Israeli Government's responsibility for the massacre. The pressure by *Peace Now* yielded results: The cabinet appointed the Kahan committee and decided to halt the war in Lebanon.

20 March

Nava Elimelech Murdered

The brutal murder of Nava Elimelech, a girl from Bat Yam, shocked the country. The girl was probably murdered on the day she was kidnapped. After the murderer abused her, he chopped up the body and put the limbs into plastic bags that he threw into the sea. Pieces of her body were swept ashore 10 days later north of Tel Aviv. A large police team held extensive searches for people suspected of sexual offenses as well as members of minorities in the region.

4 July
The IDF tightened the siege of South Beirut.

2 August
The IAF raided targets around Beirut, while the paratroopers captured the airport. The siege continued.

4 August
US President Ronald Reagan sent a harsh letter to Prime Minister Menachem Begin demanding that the shelling of Beirut cease.

11 August
IDF units reached the outskirts of Beirut. A cease-fire was attained by US envoy Philip Habib.

21 August
Some 15,000 terrorists left Beirut on ships.

29 August
Zionist Federation President Nachum Goldman died at the age of 87.

16 September
The Christian Phalangists perpetrated the Sabra and Shatila massacre.

1 October
The Kahan committee was set up to investigate the events in Sabra and Shatila. It was chaired by Supreme Court Justice Yitzhak Kahan, Justice Aharon Barak, and Major General (Res.) Yona Efrat.

14 November
Aliza Begin, wife of Prime Minister Menachem Begin, died. Begin, who was on a visit to the US, returned to Israel.

1 December
A new IS500 bill was introduced in Israel.

(1983

Emil Grunzweig (center in a light-colored sweatshirt) at a Peace Now demonstration in Jerusalem, shortly before he was murdered.
Photo: Vardi Kahana

A hand grenade thrown at the Peace Now demonstrators severely wounded Emil Grunzweig. Efforts to rescue him failed. Photo: Mike Taylor, GPO

Emil Grunzweig
The death of Israeli innocence

*Former Minister and MK
Avraham Burg*

When Emil Grunzweig was murdered, Israeli innocence died with him. There was not much left of it at the time, but the hand grenade ripped its remains into pieces that could not be put together again. We used to think that there was inner beauty in Israeli directness; that we could say anything, straight to the point; that these were the rules of the game. After all, we were in it together and we cherished the truth. Then we realized that absolute truth has a price. When one incites, another draws a gun; when one blames someone, another executes him. Since then, there has no longer been any truth in internal discussions in Israel.

When Emil Grunzweig was murdered, the last threads that connected religious Zionism with Israeli society were cut. Since his death, Israeli society has divided into settlers and their underground movement on the one hand and supporters of democracy at all costs on the other. This inner rift has pushed the parties in separate directions: the peace-seeking left toward Western culture and values and the religious right toward ultra-Orthodox fundamentalism. On the one bank stands modern and stately Israel with its political characteristics; on the other - the West Bank - stands the Kingdom of Judea, fortifying itself, actively and violently attempting to bring the Messiah against his will.

The myth that we are a different nation has died. We used to think that the gentiles were violent and we were merciful. Nonsense! Among us, there are violent killers just as there are in the worst of nations. Among us, there are racists in the worst sense of the word, who draw their inspiration from Jewish civilization. When Emil was murdered, all those demons emerged. We realized that the Judaism of murder has an underground, not God; it has murderers with no humaneness.

Facing Emil's untimely death, the Israeli left wing found itself staring cruelty in the eye and saw that it looked just like our enemies. We suddenly realized that the occupation had corrupted us and gangrene had spread in our bodies. Emil's death marked a shift in the views held by the Labor Party and its leaders. Peace ceased to be the wishy-washy word of the "bleeding-heart" liberals and became a bold and courageous policy that matured into a firm handshake 10 years after the unnecessary death of the true victim of peace. Emil's memorial site was the cornerstone for the building that Peres and Rabin inaugurated a decade later in Oslo and Washington. First Emil. We understood that we could not ignore the killing of innocent Arabs under the guise of "enlightened occupation", without that blood seeping across the Green Line and causing death among our own Israeli brethren.

Emil did not turn into a martyr. No one visits his grave. Teenagers do not spend nights there in honour of his memory. It has never become a tourist site. Only the right-wing madmen do that; see the memorial site for Baruch (the damned) Goldstein. Blood never spilled in both directions. The bullets were always fired from right to left, never the other way around. Our justice system also makes a distinction between acts of murder: If you murder a Jew for political reasons, you will rot in jail for many years. But if you kill an Arab on ideological grounds, you're a hero. You'll be released from prison in a short time, you'll receive preferential treatment, MKs will come to your rescue and your place will be kept for you. You're a saint, a precious guy. The Jewish underground members have long forgotten the stench of the prison latrines; they show no remorse and do not ask for forgiveness – not even outwardly, pretending. Repentance is not for them. Only Yona Avrushmi [who threw the hand grenade that killed Emil Grunzweig], who does not have an external protector, is deeply sorry and repentant – so he says; but then he is still being held in Ramla Prison. I believe that, had we asked Emil, he would have said: "Free Avrushmi, but don't you dare ever release the murderers of the Hebron and West Bank mayors." But that's how we are; we distinguish between blood and blood, between murderers and murderers – and we wash the blood off our hands.

The murder of Emil Grunzweig was a turning-point in the Israeli political struggle. It appears that there is a persistence in the left and in the peace camp that is unstoppable. This is not religious zeal. After all, Emil did not sacrifice his soul; it was taken from him by force. However, it turned out that the peace camp's regiments would not halt until the evil government, the one responsible for dividing the nation and breaking the national consensus, was removed. Still, it seems – at least from the present standpoint – that the peak of that struggle was also the end of the peace camp era. From then on, in fact, our camp has not really had an impact on major historical moves. Oslo was our heritage, thank God, so there was no need to protest then; but Oslo is dying before our very eyes, peace is slipping right through our fingers, and the Emil Grunzweigs of today are living well and don't lift a finger. The peace movement has deserted the streets, panicked, or just stopped. Many members of the inner circle say: "If Emil were here with us, we would have long been out in the streets." For Emil was not a leader of masses; he *was* the masses, that steady and reliable backbone every leader dreams of. We were 20 years old then. Where are the 20-year-olds of the 1990s?

No one will remember his name in a few years. This is the fate of the dead. His family and friends will remember and then we will also die. His epitaph and last will, however, are deeply etched in the hearts of many people, whether they knew him or not. His will calls on us to love peace and pursue it, to fight for our ideals, to know that wars cannot be won without victims and to be willing to sacrifice ourselves – for the people, the spirit, the future. Emil taught us that there are limits to democracy and that it too must learn to defend itself. But we also learned that there is no limit to the fidelity of those who are faithful to democracy; only democracy, fragile and compromising, is able to build a very narrow bridge joining all the opinions, communities and religions that surround us.

May he rest in peace.

7.2.83

The Kahan Committee: "Sharon Should Draw Personal Conclusions"

Defense Minister Ariel Sharon appearing before the Kahan Committee.
Photo: Zoom 77

The state commission of inquiry, headed by Supreme Court Justice Yitzhak Kahan, that was appointed to investigate the events which led to massacre at the Sabra and Shatila refugee camps, stated that Israel was indirectly responsible because the camps were under IDF control. The committee determined that the assertion that the massacre had been perpetrated without the army commanders' knowledge was not true, and that the Phalangists had entered the camps with the government's knowledge and the Army's permission.

The committee concluded that the persons responsible for the massacre were "those who were supposed to know of the intentions of the perpetrators of the massacre - the Christian Phalangists - and could have

taken measures to stop them." On the personal level, Defense Minister Ariel Sharon was severely criticized. The committee recommended that the defense minister draw personal conclusions from the flaws in his performance and, if appropriate, the prime minister should exercise his authority, based on "The Basic Law: The Government", enabling him to remove a minister from his post. But, although the committee made an unequivocal recommendation concerning Sharon, he refused to resign. Coalition MKs and ministers warned that if Sharon did not resign, they would overthrow the government. There were stormy arguments among the Israeli public, and demonstrations for and against Sharon were staged. One week after the Kahan committee published its report, the government endorsed it by a majority of 16 ministers against Sharon's single vote and decided to remove him from his post as defense minister. He stayed on in the cabinet as minister without portfolio and his place was taken by Moshe Arens, who was recalled from Washington where he was serving as Israel's ambassador.

The committee also leveled harsh criticism against Chief of Staff Refael Eitan for being indifferent to what had taken place in the camps but, because his term was nearly over, the committee did not recommend that he be dismissed. The committee also criticized Major General Yehoshua Sagi - head of the Intelligence Branch, Major General Amir Drori - head of the Northern Command, and Brigadier General Amos Yaron - commander of the Beirut sector.

The committee heard some 50 witnesses, including the prime minister, the defense minister, other cabinet ministers, the chief of staff, senior IDF officers, reporters and others. The political echelon was also severely criticized for its part in the affair.

The committee stated that Prime Minister Menachem Begin had failed to anticipate the consequences of allowing the Christian Phalangists to enter the refugee camps and that Foreign Minister Yitzhak Shamir had ignored a report that a massacre was occurring and had taken no steps to stop it.

Defense Minister Ariel Sharon and Chief of Staff Refael Eitan leaving a consultation at the prime minister's residence.
Photo: Zoom 77

Israel and the PLO Exchange POWs

23 November

Some 4,700 terrorists captured during the Lebanon War were exchanged for six Nachal Brigade soldiers who had been kidnapped by the PLO in Lebanon. During the 12 months of negotiations, the PLO demanded that Israel release terrorists who had carried out attacks inside Israel, but their demands were rejected. Most of the released terrorists asked to return to Lebanon, and only about 1,000 of them asked to be flown to Algiers.

Five of the six Nachal Brigade soldiers in terrorist captivity in Lebanon. Photo: Sygma

The Murder of Emil Grunzweig

"**N**ow!" The call came from a hill overlooking the Prime Minister's Office in Jerusalem, where a *Peace Now* demonstration was being held. The demonstrators, who were beginning to disperse, did not pay attention to the call. Seconds later, a blast was heard, sending terror through the area. The cabinet ministers heard the explosion of the grenade clearly. When the smoke cleared, Emil Grunzweig was found lying in a pool of blood.

Grunzweig, a 35-year-old *Peace Now* man and paratrooper officer in the reserves, was taken to the hospital where he was pronounced dead. Ten other demonstrators were injured, including Avraham Burg.

Emil Grunzweig, who came to demonstrate after completing a term of military reserve duty in Lebanon, wanted to protest against Israel's prolonged involvement in Lebanon. He walked with the other marchers from the center of Jerusalem to the Government Compound. Right-wing members harassed the demonstrators all along the way.

The police investigation lasted several months, at the end of which they detained Yona Avrushmi, a Jerusalem resident who pleaded guilty to the charge of throwing the hand grenade. He said that the police had prevented him from approaching the demonstrators, which was why he hid in a small grove of trees near the site of the demonstration and waited for them to begin dispersing. At that point, he threw the grenade. In his trial, Avrushmi claimed that he had been influenced by right-wing propaganda against left-wing demonstrators. He was sentenced to life imprisonment.

The murder of Emil Grunzweig is remembered as one of the darkest days in the history of the state. *Peace Now* people accused the right-wing leaders, including cabinet ministers, of incitement against the left.

The memorial site for Emil Grunzweig near the place where he was murdered. Photo: Zoom 77

Patients Died While the Doctors Were on Vacation at the Kinneret

22 May

The health system experienced a serious crisis in 1983. In an unprecedented move, the doctors left the hospitals and went on an organized vacation to Lake Kinneret in order to escape the confining orders that had been issued by the government. They left crowded hospitals, with departments and operating rooms manned by only a few doctors. Quite a few patients died because the doctors refused to operate or treat the serious cases.

The strike broke out after the government refused to let the doctors take money from every patient who came in for an examination. The doctors' struggle was fierce and unyielding. Even the prime minister's involvement could not resolve the crisis, which reached its peak when the doctors announced that they were starting an unlimited hunger strike on 14 June. Four months after the labor dispute began, a new agreement was signed between the doctors and the government in which the former received substantial salary hikes.

Doctors on strike in the hospitals. Photo: GPO

28.8.83

Menachem Begin: "Leave Me Alone; I Wish To Resign."

Prime Minister Menachem Begin made a dramatic and surprising announcement of his intention to resign and quit politics. "I no longer function like I used to," he said. "Leave me alone... I wish to resign."

He never revealed the reasons for his move to anyone except his closest family members. Commentators mentioned his deteriorating health, his wife's death, the unnecessary embroilment in Lebanon and the large number of casualties. Begin retired to the seclusion of his home and refused to explain his reasons or change his mind. "I weighed it all up before I decided," he said.

From the day he resigned until his death in March 1992, Begin maintained his silence. He had been Israel's prime minister for six years, and his greatest achievement was signing the peace accord with Egypt, which earned him the Nobel Peace Prize, together with the late Egyptian President Sadat.

Menachem Begin leaving the Prime Minister's Office in Jerusalem after announcing his resignation. Photo: Zoom 77

The Bank Share Crisis -Big Losses for Investors

11 October

On the day Yitzhak Shamir was sworn in as prime minister, the shekel was devalued by 23% and a rush on the dollar began. In its panic, the public sold its stocks and bought masses of consumer goods or dollars. The mass sales caused share prices to plummet and it was feared that the big banks, which up to that day had regulated the flow of their shares, might collapse if they went on with this practice. In order to prevent the collapse, the government intervened and set a minimum price it would pay people who were prepared to hold on to their bank shares for five years. The public, however, kept selling, despite the loss of a large percentage of the value of the shares.

The Second Tyre Disaster - 60 Dead and 30 Wounded

4 November

The Islamic Jihad succeeded in driving a booby-trapped car loaded with 500 kg of explosives into the courtyard of the IDF command in Tyre. The car sped into the compound at 06:00, and although the guards opened fire, the suicide bomber managed to reach the courtyard and detonate the charge. The blast destroyed the command offices of the GSS and the Border Police, killing 60 people - 28 Israelis and 32 local detainees - and wounding 30. The rescue teams that arrived at the scene implemented lessons learned from the first Tyre disaster and managed to rescue several people from the rubble.

The evacuation of one of the dead in the explosion at the IDF headquarters in Tyre. Photo: Nati Hernick, GPO

23 October

Tislam Disbanded

The "definitely final" farewell concert of rock group Tislam in Beersheba was accompanied by mass hysteria. The band – whose members were Yizhar Ashdot, Yair Nitzani, Yoshi Sadeh, Dani Bassan, and Tzuf Philosof – was established in 1979 and was an unprecedented musical success in Israel. It put out three albums, the first and most successful of which was Loud Radio, and represented a turning-point in the Israeli Rock scene.

27 November

Justice Meir Shamgar assumed the post of president of the Supreme Court, replacing Yitzhak Kahan.

2 December

A bomb exploded on a bus in Jerusalem, killing six and wounding 30.

Dani Katz' parents in the forest named after him.

11 December

Dani Katz Murdered

The child Dani Katz disappeared on his way home to the Denia neighborhood of Haifa. The police spent four days searching for him; his body was found in a cave near Sachnin in the Lower Galilee. Haifa was panic-stricken, and many parents would not allow their children to leave home unescorted. An extensive police investigation led to the detention of five suspects, all residents of the Arab village of Sachnin. They were found guilty and sent to prison for long periods. Later, however, they recanted, claiming that they had been forced to confess to killing the boy.

21 July

Rod Stewart in Israel

British rock star Rod Stewart's first performance in Israel was held at the Ramat Gan Stadium in front of an audience of thousands of fans, paving the way for other major international stars to appear in Israel.

24 September

Simon and Garfunkel in Israel

The famous duo, Simon and Garfunkel, performed in front of 50,000 people at the Ramat Gan Stadium, giving a two-hour concert in which they sang some 25 songs. "There's so much I want to say, but I cannot," Paul Simon told the audience. "I am so thrilled to be here." The audience could clearly see that the two had had a row during their European tour. In addition, they were not feeling well, and had eaten some hot chicken soup cooked by Nechemia Graf from Petach Tikva before going on stage.

25 January

"I Put All My Money in the Stock Exchange. Now I Can Jump off the Roof!"

The unprecedented stock exchange plunge brought many investors to the stock exchange on Allenby Street in Tel Aviv. People of all economic strata gathered there and stood in the rain to follow the the trading closely. "Our money is turning into garbage here," one of the investors yelled. "All the small investors have had it," said another. "Aridor tricked us," they said. "He promised prosperity, and there's a catastrophe instead...".

An elderly gentleman said with tears in his eyes: "I put all my money in the stock exchange. Now I can jump off the roof." Most of the shares lost half their value in a single day. The Finance Ministry announced it would not intervene, even after "Black Monday" on the Israeli stock exchange.

(*1984*

Prime Minister Shimon Peres answering a motion of no confidence at the Knesset. Photo: GPO

The national unity government under Shimon Peres on the eve of its swearing in. Photo: IPPA

Shimon Peres – The Greatest Politician
"Without him, Israel would have been less ready for war and less open to peace."

Journalist
Sever Plosker

MK Shimon Peres, born in 1923, currently holds no official office nor is he running for one. This for him is an unusual situation. Ever since he joined the pioneering youth movement, *Hanoar Haoved*, at age 15 until he quit the Labor Party leadership in the summer of 1997, Peres never laid down the tools of politics. He lived and breathed politics; it was in his blood, the love of his life, his reason for living. He never wore any uniform other than a politician's suit. He was never an officer, a businessman or a diplomat. He had wanted to be prime minister since his youth, but others in Mapai and later in Labor beat him to it by an inch and snatched the lead from him. Peres, forever Number Two, lost four elections. The public opinion polls treated him well, but time and again he fell into the trap of believing polls that fooled him into thinking that he was a sure winner. Nevertheless, Peres is no loser. He is a winner. His exciting and happy life is full of achievements. His family has been spared personal tragedies. Outside Israel, he has a political reputation second to none, and he has left a very deep mark on the State of Israel in many spheres. Israel without Peres would have been a different country, less important, less ready for war, less open to peace: less of a power.

Peres has amazing foresight, an ability to see decades ahead. In the 1950s, while Ben-Gurion was conducting the negotiations for reparations from Germany, Peres was already signing long-term contracts for the supply of advanced weapons for the IDF and beginning to establish the military industries. In the early 1960s, he understood the potential of nuclear weapons and connected Israel with France's nuclear potential. "I thought of a different concept," he wrote in his book, *The New Middle East*. "Israel should develop strategic deterrent strength. We built a nuclear reactor in the desert, in Dimona." Thus Peres created a non-conventional military option that protected the people of Israel in their country like an iron shelter, giving them an intimidating strength no other country in the region has.

Peres was responsible for settling the Galilee with Jews – Upper Nazareth and Carmiel were built upon his orders. In 1974, as defense minister in Rabin's cabinet, he lent his hand to the establishment of Jewish settlements in Judea and Samaria. The public considered him a hawk then, and he was. After that, Peres' ideas underwent numerous metamorphoses ("One must surprise, free oneself of past conventions," he would say after every shift he made), until he secretly signed, as Israel's foreign minister, a political agreement with the PLO in Oslo in August 1993. Peres believed Dimona and Oslo to be the peaks of his political career.

Peres was born in Lithuania to a wealthy Jewish family. He immigrated to Israel in 1931. His father was a hot-tempered, ambitious and adventurous Jew, and his mother was a teacher, an introvert librarian and a thinker. From his father he inherited his ambition, his skill at political wheeling and dealing and the passion for travel. His mother passed on to him an ability to philosophize, an openness to culture, the love of the written word and his legendary cool. Peres was only 26 when Ben-Gurion appointed him director-general of the Defense Ministry, which signalled the start of 50 years of public service. Peres was rarely seen crying in public, striking a table with his fist or using bad language. He endured in silence the extreme hostility shown him by part of the public. Peres was not one to avoid campaigning because he was afraid of being pelted with rotten tomatoes or of being spat on or cursed. Peres despised those who slandered him and they considered him condescending.

His manipulative skills blinded his judgement and, eventually, worked against him. His party members said he was "unreliable". And Yitzhak Rabin, in his 1979 book, *Service Book*, viciously dubbed him "an indefatigable underminer", giving him an image he could not shake off until the end of his political career. "Rabin legitimized the attacks against Peres," reporter Orly Azulai-Katz wrote in her biography of Peres, *The Man Who Didn't Know How to Win*. Peres did not forget, nor did he forgive Rabin, but he refrained from reacting, as usual.

Peres served as prime minister twice: as head of the national unity government from October 1984 and after Rabin's assassination. During his first term, he enjoyed levels of popular support known to no other prime minister since the first public polls were held, precisely because he was not trying to please anyone. During those two years in office, he made two especially difficult and courageous decisions: to effect an IDF withdrawal from Lebanon and to implement an economic stabilization plan. That plan immediately halted the Israeli economy's slide into hyper-inflation (meaning consumer price indices of 20% per month) and rescued it from the zero foreign currency crisis. The withdrawal from Lebanon helped to rebuild morale in the IDF and put an end to the bloody dispute within the nation. In October 1986, wrapped in the glory of a successful miracle man, he handed the premiership over to Yitzhak Shamir in accordance with their rotation agreement. He regained the post only after nine long years, when Rabin was assassinated. It was a brief term, only seven months long, and particularly bad – full of terror attacks, a war in the north, a deteriorating economy, a deep rift in the nation and Peres' own incomprehensible obtuseness.

Ever since he signed Oslo A and B, Peres has become the prophet of the "New Middle East" – a future vision of the countries in the region after they abandon the path of war and start co-operating in the economic, infrastructural, social and technological fields. The New Middle East was supposed to be liberal and democratic, with a global culture and American in its outlook. Israel stood in the center of this vision, which sent shivers down the spines of the ruling Arab elites and increased their fear of an Israeli economic and cultural domination. In Israel, Peres was called a "dreamer". Despite the fact that three Arab economic summit meetings were held in collaboration with Israel (in Casablanca, Amman and Cairo), the term "New Middle East" was mocked and despised, particularly after the terrorist attacks.

In 1996, Peres lost the first direct elections in Israel to the Likud's Benjamin Netanyahu by one percent – a painful but typical loss. Peres is Israel's greatest politician, but not its greatest statesman.

The 300 Bus Affair:

12.4.84

The GSS Accuses Yitzhak Mordechai of Killing the Terrorists

The 300 bus after the IDF soldiers attacked the terrorist squad that had hijacked it. The body of one of the terrorists is seen in the front of the bus. Photo: Havakuk Levison

An Egged bus, number 300 on the Tel Aviv-Ashkelon line, was hijacked by four terrorists. Holding the driver at gunpoint, they forced him to change direction and drive toward the Gaza Strip. Near Dir al-Balah, the security forces stopped the bus, on which there were 25 passengers. An elite IDF unit stormed the bus and killed two terrorists in the first round of fire. A female soldier, who was one of the passengers, was also killed during the operation. Two other terrorists who were at the back of the bus were captured alive and handed over to the GSS.

The next day, the reports said that all four terrorists had been killed during the rescue operation, but the press had pictures of two terrorists taken alive. Despite a censorship ban, the pictures were published, exposing the affair to the public. The exposure caused an outcry in Israel, and was followed by the setting up of commissions of inquiry in an attempt to discover the truth. The GSS and the IDF began an exchange of mutual accusations. A committee set up by Defense Minister Moshe Arens stated that Brigadier General Yitzhak Mordechai was guilty because he confessed to having beaten the terrorists during their interrogation. Mordechai was put on trial in the military court and acquitted. Eventually, it turned out that the story was a plot. Senior GSS members contacted State Attorney Yitzhak Zamir and informed him that the GSS men had co-ordinated their versions, twisted the facts and even destroyed evidence connecting GSS head Avraham Shalom with the killing of the terrorists.

Shalom, who was forced to resign later on, claimed that he was acting upon the prime minister's permission and authorization, but Shamir denied giving such orders and stressed that he had not even been aware of the killing. The affair sent shock waves through the GSS as well as the political and judicial echelons. Eventually, the heads of the GSS were pardoned even before facing trial.

Levinson Commits Suicide: "I Have No Strength to Fight."

23 February

Ya'akov Levinson, a major Israeli economic figure who had served as chairman of the Bank Hapoalim board of executives for several years, shot himself in his home after finding that he was no longer able to fight against the criminal charges that were being leveled against him. He left a note in which he wrote: "I must choose between fighting endlessly or killing myself; and I have no strength to fight anymore." Several days before his suicide, he was interviewed by Arieh Avneri of *Yedioth Ahronoth*, and said: "A gang of Bank Hapoalim and Histadrut leaders plotted against me using extortion and trumped-up evidence."

Levinson's suicide shocked the Labor Party and its members demanded that the Histadrut heads be questioned about their handling of the "Levinson affair". One of the major accusations leveled at him was that when he was director of the Ampal Company, he worked toward removing it from the control of Bank Hapoalim and transferring its assets to other concerns. A committee from the bank examined the affair and determined that there had been irregularities in Levinson's performance. The bank management and the Histadrut heads decided to hand their findings over to the police and, two days before the suicide, the police appointed Benjamin Siegel - commander of the fraud unit - to head the special team that was to investigate the affair. However, Siegel never got to interrogate Levinson, who wrote to his family: "I am ashamed of my weakness, but I have no strength left..."

Ya'akov Levinson in a rare appearance at the Labor Party's Central Committee.

The Unity Government and the Rotation

The national unity government was established because the two major political blocs had reached a tie. When the elections results were published, Likud and Labor started negotiating with the small parties in an attempt to establish a narrow-based coalition. They soon realized that the only acceptable alternative would be to form a national unity government based on a rotation agreement according to which during the first two years Shimon Peres would be prime minister and Yitzhak Shamir would be foreign minister and deputy prime minister, and the two would switch roles for the second half of the term. The two parties also agreed that the other ministers, including Defense Minister Yitzhak Rabin, would serve the full four-year term. The Likud and Labor held lengthy negotiations on the basis of that formula, at the end of which Peres presented a 26-member cabinet to the Knesset. There were several ministers without portfolio. It was also decided that an inner cabinet would be set up for major decisions; it would consist of 10 ministers, five from each party.

The unity government had two urgent tasks to address: Removing the IDF from Lebanon and curbing the inflation that threatened to destroy the Israeli economy. Although the two goals were attained during the national unity term, the government experienced quite a few serious crises and stormy debates.

Prime Minister Shimon Peres and his deputy, Foreign Minister Yitzhak Shamir, at the Knesset. Photo: GPO

A New Daily: *Hadashot* Takes Off

4 March

Hadashot, a paper competing with *Ma'ariv* and *Yedioth Ahronoth*, was published for the first time, full of hope of winning a slice of the market. It had a surprising and innovative look, with many color pictures and stories. During the years of its existence, the paper had a series of first-rate journalistic scoops, the most prominent of which was the 300 bus affair. The paper chose to ignore the censor's orders and published the photographs of the still-living terrorists as well as the fact that a commission had been established to investigate the affair. The paper was shut down for a few days because of this. In November 1993, newspaper publisher Amos Schocken decided to close it down. He called in the 400 workers and said: "I have reached the conclusion that there is no point in publishing *Hadashot* anymore, and only I am responsible for the failure."

The front page of the first edition of Hadashot.

20 January

Yona Avrushmi was arrested on suspicion of murdering *Peace Now* activist Emil Grunzweig.

23 February

Ya'akov Levinson, chairman of the Bank Hapoalim board of executives, committed suicide following an investigation against him on suspicion of a felony.

2 April

In a terrorist attack in central Jerusalem, one man was killed and 60 were wounded.

12 April

The 300 bus affair caused an outcry over the killing of two terrorists who had been captured alive during an IDF storming of a hijacked bus.

15 May

Yisrael Keisar was elected Histadrut secretary-general, replacing Yerucham Meshel.

19 June

The trial of 27 members of the Jewish underground opened. They were suspected of committing a series of crimes, from murder to planting bombs on Arab buses.

28 June

Six Israeli POWs were exchanged for 300 Syrians.

28 June

The High Court of Justice permitted the lists of Kahana and the Progressive List for Peace to run in the Knesset elections.

23 July

Elections for the eleventh Knesset were held. The results (in Knesset seats) were: Labor – 44, Likud – 41, Techiya – 5, the NRP and Shas – 4 each. The two major political blocs reached a tie.

27.4.84

The Jewish Underground Exposed

An extensive GSS investigation uncovered a Jewish underground operating in the territories against Arab targets. The members of the underground were young Jewish residents of settlements in the territories, some of whom were high-ranking IDF officers. They were well organized and equipped with weapons and explosives. They were captured after planting bombs on five Arab buses, and pleaded guilty to a series of grave offenses: attempts to assassinate West Bank mayors, murdering students at the Islamic College in Hebron, seriously injuring a police sapper who tried to detonate a bomb they had planted, and attempting terrorist attacks on the Temple Mount.

Twenty-seven members of the underground were put on trial and convicted of committing a series of serious crimes ranging from murder to planting bombs on Arab buses. Three of them were given life sentences and the rest long prison terms. The underground leaders were Menachem Livni and Yehuda Etzion. Livni, who

The members of the Jewish underground taken into custody. Photo: Zoom 77

was the prime suspect, had served as a commander of an Engineering Corps battalion and took advantage of his knowledge and the IDF means that were at his disposal. Most of the convicts spent relatively short periods in prison while others were pardoned by President Haim Herzog several years later. The lenient and forgiving treatment they were given drew harsh criticism from the public and the media.

Photo: AP

Benjamin Netanyahu – Our Man in the UN

16 September

Benjamin Netanyahu, who had served as a plenipotentiary at the Israeli Embassy in Washington, was appointed UN ambassador by Foreign Minister Yitzhak Shamir, with the agreement of Prime Minister Shimon Peres. Netanyahu attracted the American public's attention with his polished appearance and eloquence. He captured the hearts of his audiences, presenting Israel's stand in simple and familiar terms. He was the darling of the American media, where he appeared frequently, spicing his speech with baseball and football jargon.

"Throw the Nigger in the Ocean," the Israeli Captain Ordered

13 November

An incident in which an Israeli captain ordered a stowaway to be thrown into the ocean stunned the Israeli public. A black stowaway was found on board the *Moran* which was sailing from South Africa to Israel. The captain did not want to waste time by taking him back, so he ordered the stowaway to be taken off the ship and placed in a small rubber boat with food and provisions. As the ship was in mid-ocean, the captain was kind enough to show him the general direction of the shore. The incident actually took place in 1982, but was revealed only two years later by a retired Zim crewman. When asked why he had not disobeyed the order, he said: "For me, the captain was God." The fate of the stowaway was never known.

84

2 June

MK Porush Attacked by Gur Hassidim - Dozens of followers of the Rabbi of Gur attacked and beat up MK Menachem Porush in his hotel room. They broke his glasses, smashed lamps in the hotel synagogue and took off with his *streimel* [fur hat]. The attack came after his remarks had been interpreted as offensive to the Rabbi of Gur and his followers. He was hospitalized for one night.

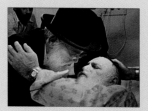

MK Menachem Porush in hospital, visited by Rabbi Schach, head of the Council of Torah Sages. Photo: Zoom 77

21 April

Dada Painter, Marcel Janco, Dies

Photo: Amit Levinson

Painter Marcel Janco died at the age of 89. He was one of the founders of the Dada movement, one of the most important currents in modern art. Playwright Eugene Ionesco wrote: "Surrealism cannot be understood without Dada; and Dada cannot be understood without Janco." Janco arrived in Israel in 1940, painted and taught art, and had a great influence on Israeli art. In 1953, he established the artists' village at Ein Hod near Haifa, hoping to combine individual creativity with community life.

10 September

Forgers' Gang Captured in Possession of 12 Million Forged Dollars - After a long investigation involving the CIA, the Israel police managed to capture seven Israelis from Jaffa who belonged to a network that had printed 12 million dollars of such high quality that they could fool any detection apparatus. The CIA kept the affair secret, fearing that the FBI might step in and take the credit.

Photo: Michael Kramer

13 January

"Kerosene Injector" Captured - Moshe Levy, a Holon resident who owned an electrical appliance store, was detained by the police on suspicion of having injected his girlfriend with kerosene, paralyzing the lower part of her body. During the investigation, it appeared that three years earlier he had killed his wife in the same way. He was sentenced to life imprisonment, and committed suicide in prison.

Photo: Shalom Bar-Tal

4 August

Charges were filed against the four major banks and their directors for manipulating share trade.

13 September

The national unity government was established. Shimon Peres was prime minister and Yitzhak Shamir was foreign minister and deputy prime minister during the first two years of its term; they switched roles for the second half.

16 September

Benjamin Netanyahu was appointed UN ambassador.

8 January

Rabbi Yisrael Abu-Hatzira died. He was the spiritual leader of the Moroccan Jews in Israel and was popularly called the "Baba Sali".

12 December

Soldier Hadass Kedmi Brutally Murdered

The initial findings at the site on Mount Carmel where the body of 20-year-old soldier Hadass Kedmi was discovered indicated that she had been cruelly murdered. There were signs of violence on her naked body. She had probably been strangled to death. Her clothing and handbag were scattered around the area. The police believed that the murder had been committed on nationalist grounds. When the report that her body had been discovered reached Kibbutz Kfar Masaryk, where she lived, the members were grief-stricken. "Our Hadass is gone," they wrote in a little note which they pinned up at the entrance to the dining-room.

(1985

Some 7,000 Ethiopian Jews were flown to Israel in Operation Moses. Above: Celebrating the 10th anniversary of Operation Moses at the President's Residence. Photo: Zoom 77

The Ethiopian immigrants – first moments in Israel. Photo: GPO

Operation Moses

From Addis Ababa to Israel

Meskie Shibro Sivan

Ever since I can remember, I wanted to immigrate to Israel. However, we had not always known that the State of Israel even existed. Just the opposite – we used to think that we were the only Jews in the world, and observed our tradition very closely. Our grandparents told us tales about the Land of Israel whenever they could, making us curious about that land and yearn for it. Driven by Zionism, my parents made preparations for the immigration long before Operation Moses happened. As children in Addis Ababa, we listened eagerly to stories about the Mossad, our man in Damascus [Eli Cohen], the Six Day War, the Entebbe operation – and we were proud.

Different, but so much alike, city and country people, we clung to each other and came to beautiful and difficult Israel.

Our ancient community has arrived home and started its last, but no less difficult journey – absorption. We are only at the beginning of this journey, but we are very excited to celebrate the 50th anniversary of our new-old homeland's independence.

This Child Is Our Hope

Dani Ababa

For hundreds of years, we, "The Homes of Israel" whom the gentiles dubbed Falashes (foreigners), lived in the mountains of north-west Ethiopia and adhered to unique customs of a Jewish nature. There are countless theories about the authenticity of our Jewishness and attempts to answer the questions of who we are and how we got there in the first place. Some of the speculations even go as far back as King Solomon and the Queen of Sheba.

For the time being, no one really knows to which of the twelve tribes of Israel that wander the globe we belong. A long and obscure exile accompanies our freedom in Israel since the 1970s.

There is no public controversy about our religious principles. There is, however, a stormy debate between the Ashkenazi Hassidim and the Sephardim about whether we are kosher Jews or not. In the late 1980s, the first Ethiopian immigrants started appearing in Israel, having been brought over in secret Mossad operations which were carried out in collaboration with the Israeli Navy in the heart of the enemy country, Sudan. The collective name of these operations was "Operation Moses". Over 15,000 Jews were taken out of Ethiopia on IAF planes or rubber boats belonging to the Navy in amazing secrecy. My family and I were among them, arriving from the heart of an enemy country.

Naturally, absorption in Israel was hard. We had to start life anew, learn a new language, understand a new culture and move from the 18th to the 21st century. The difficulties we encountered made us feel like our Zionist dream was falling apart abruptly. We met cold-hearted people in the community we had dreamed of for thousands of years and felt betrayed. Then they called us "Niggers" and afterwards they stuck disgraceful labels on us: "If your skin is black, you must have AIDS." Wishing to become part of the society, we joined the army, but then some officer proclaimed that blacks were not allowed in the military clinic. The country fumed for two days. A few months later, the state itself made the highly secret decision to throw out the blood we had donated, claiming that it posed a risk to society.

At present, there are some 65,000 Ethiopian Jews in Israel. Some of them have not yet been properly absorbed. The young are looking for a new identity, dancing to reggae and jazz music and remembering the old culture which the establishment had managed to bury. Many criminals sprang from among us, including big drug dealers. The Zionist dream we had had for generations was shattered in 13 years. Our spiritual leaders, the Keisim, spend their days in the Holy Land doing nothing. It is a grim reality. The authorities that deal with the problems of our community know this well, but they would rather speak of the nicer aspects, of our magnificent culture and of our contribution to society. At the same time, they are hiding the real facts about a large community. The Ethiopian youths of today hang around the Tel Aviv Central Bus Station, doing nothing. They just sit around and gaze at the stars. Yet it is not all bad in our country. There are successes. Many of us have managed to cross the terrible barrier and go far within a reasonable period of time. My heart bursts with joy when I see a loving mixed couple pushing a baby in a stroller. This child is our hope. I believe we can become part of Israeli society and feel that it is our turf as well. It could happen under one condition: if Israeli society makes us feel that this is our real home, without insulting us about the color of our skin. If it stops perceiving us as apes that fell out of a tree, we will be able to fit into the new land and build a multicolored Israel that upholds democracy and believes in equal rights for every human being.

The Journey Song

The desert road

Is winding

The day is long

The night is going on

Group after group of people

Some familiar, others strangers

Walk and talk, and suddenly cry

Some will not survive the remaining road,

Some will, but their thoughts wander:

Who did we bury, who did we keep?

Meskie Shibro Sivan

4.1.85

Operation Moses – Bringing the Ethiopian Jews to Israel

Some 7,000 Ethiopian Jews were brought to Israel in an air-lift from Sudan in a secret and dramatic rescue mission that has only now been revealed and which was dubbed "Operation Moses". The secret operation lasted several months, starting at the end of 1984, after reports had reached Israel that the Ethiopian Jews were being persecuted and were starving as a result of years of drought.

Once the national unity government under Shimon Peres made the decision to bring the Ethiopian Jews to Israel, the Mossad started the rescue operation. Most of the Jews lived in remote villages, and they had to walk hundreds of miles to neighboring Sudan, from where the Mossad agents flew them to Israel on board European planes. They arrived at Ben-Gurion Airport wearing their traditional garments, without money or property. Moving family reunions took place at the airport. "The scenes I saw," an immigration official said, "reminded me of the scenes of the days after the Holocaust when people went looking for their families. I saw youngsters with tears in their eyes looking for their parents and being badly disappointed. But there were also moments of joy when people discovered members of their families who they thought had died in Ethiopia or Sudan."

Operation Moses ground to a halt for a while because the media exposed it, causing embarrassment to the Sudanese and Ethiopian authorities, who hastily broke up the convoys of Jews and stopped the flights to Israel. The delicate situation was resolved when the American Administration intervened and pressured the Sudanese Government; the US Air Force sent cargo planes to rescue the rest of the Jews who were suffering from malnutrition and arrived in Israel very ill.

In May 1991, another 15,000 Jews were brought from Ethiopia in what has been called Operation Solomon. Currently, there are several hundred Jews and about 2,000 Falash Mura left in Ethiopia.

Ethiopian immigrants arriving in Israel. Photo: GPO

"An Economic Yom Kippur"

1 July

The newly established government set itself the goal of curbing inflation, in addition to the IDF withdrawal from Lebanon. Inflation had reached unprecedented proportions: about 400% in 1984 and 150% in the first half of 1985, which posed a real threat to the Israeli economy. A new economic stabilization program was introduced at the beginning of July. It included a 20% percent devaluation, a freeze on salaries and prices of products and services, cutbacks in the public sector and budget cuts. There were stormy discussions in the cabinet before the plan was approved; Prime Minister Shimon Peres said that Israel was facing an "economic Yom Kippur" and threatened to resign if the program were not approved. The effects of the program were already visible at the end of the year: After a 27.5% rise in the consumer price index (CPI) in June, the November CPI went up by only 1.3%. Inflation kept dropping during the following years. What seemed to be an impossible mission was proved to be possible, thanks to the resolute policy of the national unity government.

An economic consultation: (left to right) the prime minister, the finance, industry and trade minister, the labor minister and the social welfare minister. Photo: Zoom 77

Unity Government: "Pull Out of Lebanon"

One of the most difficult and daring decisions made by the national unity government was to withdraw from Lebanon. Prime Minister Shimon Peres, assisted by Defense Minister Yitzhak Rabin, managed to get the 16 cabinet ministers to vote for the decision; six were against it. The vote crossed party lines, so the Likud's David Levy voted for, while Foreign Minister Yitzhak Shamir voted against. The resolution stated: "The Israeli Government has decided that the IDF will redeploy in order to secure the northern border of Israel."

Photo: Yair Amikim. [The placard on the APC reads: "Farewell to the land that devours its conquerors."]

This somewhat obscure resolution was clarified in clause 2c: "The IDF will realign itself along the international border between Israel and Lebanon, while observing a security zone in south Lebanon which will be guarded by local forces (the SLA) with the backing of the IDF." After the cabinet session, the prime minister stated: "This is our last winter in Lebanon."

Soon after the resolution, the IDF started pulling out of Lebanon gradually, and the evacuation was completed in June. Some 2,000 soldiers stayed behind in the security zone, mainly to train the SLA. The general staff considered the security zone as a "protective layer" north of the Galilee settlements, where the IDF would maintain as few outposts as possible. Today, 12 years later, there are many more soldiers and units in Lebanon, contrary to the 1985 decision and plan.

After the decision was made, Defense Minister Rabin announced: "If the terrorists should return to southern Lebanon and attempt to attack our northern settlements, the IDF will not hesitate to enter Lebanon again in order to destroy the terrorist infrastructure."

The IDF withdrawal, executed in three stages, was accompanied by massive terror attacks on the withdrawing soldiers, inflicting heavy losses on the IDF.

Photo: UP

Pollard Arrested After Being Expelled from the Embassy

21 November

Jonathan Pollard, an American Jew, was arrested after the Israeli Embassy in Washington expelled him. He arrived at the embassy seeking political asylum. He had worked for the US Navy intelligence and was exposed after one of the workers there contacted the FBI, saying Pollard was showing an interest in matters that were not within his job description. After he was arrested, he admitted he had transferred classified material to Israel.

Pollard's arrest triggered off one of the worst crises ever in US-Israeli relations. In the wake of the affair, Israel had to recall several diplomats who were involved in it, including a senior IAF officer, Aviem Sela, who was Pollard's contact. Pollard was sentenced to life imprisonment, and, so far, every US president has rejected Israeli requests that he be pardoned.

4 January

Operation Moses, in which thousands of Ethiopian Jews were brought to Israel, was made public for the first time.

14 January

The government decided to pull out of Lebanon. The three-stage IDF withdrawal was completed in June.

10 March

12 IDF soldiers were killed in a terror attack in south Lebanon. A Shiite terrorist detonated a car containing 150 kg of explosives next to a truck packed with soldiers.

20 May

The Israeli Government decided to release 1,100 dangerous Palestinian terrorists in exchange for the release of three Israelis who were being held by the extremist organization of Ahmad Jibril.

3 August

Businessman Michael Albin jumped out of a window at the Jaffa police station where he was being interrogated, and was killed.

25 September

Three Israelis who were on a yacht anchored in Larnaka, Cyprus, were killed in what was dubbed "The Yom Kippur murder". Force 17, Arafat's elite unit, assumed responsibility for the murders.

29 September

The government approved the establishment of a second TV channel.

1 October

Operation Tunis: IAF planes raided the PLO headquarters in Tunis.

5 October

An Egyptian soldier opened fire on a group of Israeli hikers in Ras Burka in the Sinai, killing seven people and wounding four.

21.5.85

The Jibril Deal: "A Black Day for Israel"

Seven Israelis Murdered at Ras Burka

5 October

Seven Israeli hikers were killed and two wounded by an Egyptian soldier on the beach of Ras Burka, north of Nuweiba. Four of the fatalities were children, and three belonged to one family. The Israelis were on a hiking trip in the Sinai; they reached a sand dune when an Egyptian soldier opened fire on them at close range. The evacuation of the casualties took a long time, with the Egyptians refusing to allow an Israeli doctor who was at the scene to treat the wounded. The soldier, a devout Muslim, started shooting as soon as he had finished praying, yelling "Allahu Akbar!" [God is great]. President Mubarak sent a cable expressing his condolences to Prime Minister Peres and promising that the attacker would be severely punished. The soldier was sentenced to life imprisonment and committed suicide in prison.

The Israeli Government decided to release 1,100 Palestinian prisoners, including vicious killers who were serving life terms, in exchange for three Israelis who were being held by the extremist terror organization of Ahmad Jibril. The Israelis included Nissim Salem and Yosef Groff, who had been captured along with other six Nachal brigade soldiers who had been released earlier, and Hezi Shai, who had been captured at the Sultan Yakub battle during the Lebanon War.

Hezi Shai, one of the three Israelis released in the Jibril deal, is reunited with his mother.
Photo: Nati Hernick, GPO

The Jibril deal was severely criticized for the high price Israel paid for the three POWs. Bereaved families demonstrated outside the Defense Ministry, waving signs reading: "This is a black day for Israel." Demonstrations, mainly by settlers, were staged outside Prime Minister Peres' house as well.

Peres said, "This was one of the toughest decisions the government has had to make, and I can understand the reactions." Foreign Minister Shamir and other Likud ministers demanded that the Jewish underground members also be released from prison, but their request was rejected.

Photo: AP

The IAF Raided Terrorist Headquarters in Tunis

2 October

Eight IAF jets raided the PLO headquarters in Tunis. The planes flew a total of 5,000 km, refueling in mid-air, operating electronic radar-jamming devices and scoring accurate hits. Some 50 PLO members were killed and 115 wounded in a raid that was approved by the entire cabinet, except for Ezer Weizman. After the attack, Defense Minister Rabin said, "No PLO target is immune from attack anywhere in the world." The Tunis bombing came as a reaction to the murder of the Israelis in Larnaka.

29 September

Poet Yona Wolach Dies

Photo: Shalom Bar-Tal

Poet Yona Wolach died at the age of 41 after a three-year battle with cancer. She was a leading contemporary poet, along with Meir Wieseltier and Yair Horowitz. She defied rhythmic and linguistic norms and used daring sexual and violent images.

2 November

Jonathan Pollard was arrested in the United States on suspicion of spying for Israel. The arrest caused great turmoil in the US and a lot of embarrassment in Israel.

9 December

Eight IDF soldiers died in their sleep and seven were injured as a result of a fire on an IDF base in Samaria.

20 December

Tzvi Gur, the murderer of the child Oron Yarden, escaped from prison after he had been allowed to paint the outer walls of the prison. He was captured five days later.

16 August

The Rapist from the South

A female soldier who was given a lift in the vicinity of Beersheba was raped and shot in the head by the driver of the car. She was rescued by four young Bedouins who found her and called the police. The rapist was never caught.

Photo: Michael Kramer

2 July

Mall Madness

The Ayalon shopping mall in Ramat Gan opened and was inundated by crowds of people. Tens of thousands visited the mall and bought whatever they could lay their hands on. On the third Saturday following the opening of the mall, several shopowners closed their businesses, unable to cope with the crowds. Some 70,000 people visited the mall that Saturday and 27 children got lost. In the evening, the place looked like a battlefield.

Photo: Michael Kramer

Photo: Meir Azulai

11 June

The Habonim Disaster: A DeathTrip

In one of the most horrendous traffic accidents in Israel's history, three adults and 19 children were killed, and 16 injured. They were all in the same class at the Brenner School in Petach Tikva. A mother and her daughter and the class teacher were among the fatalities. The schoolchildren were on a Bar-Mitzvah trip to the north. At 08:50, their bus reached the railway crossing near Habonim Junction. Bus driver Ruth Davidov was attempting to cross the railway line when the Tel Aviv-Haifa express train approached at 100 kph. The train driver applied brakes, but was unable to stop in time and hit the rear end of the bus, hurling it 40 meters further on. The police and other rescue forces that arrived at the scene witnessed the horror. "In all my years on the force, I have never seen anything that horrific," a veteran policeman said.

1986

The families of POWs and MIAs demonstrate outside the Defense Ministry. Photo: Abigail Uzi

THESE EYES ARE COUNTING ON YOU.

Ron Arad with his daughter Yuval.

Ron Arad

"A Nation Can Never Feel What a Mother Feels."

Batia Arad
Mother of Ron Arad

Ron. I am writing to you now and I know you're there. You see, Ron, a mother knows when her son is alive... and I know you're there... alive... looking forward to this reunion just like Mom is...

My dear Ron, can you hear me now? Take care of yourself there. Mom is so worried about you. Mom loves you and is waiting for you.

You know, Ron, they call me "Ron's mother". Not "Batia". "Ron's mother..." And an entire nation misses you and thinks of you and would do anything to have you back. Whenever the smallest detail about you is mentioned, an entire nation forgets its daily worries, and clenches its fists... wishing...

And I can feel that nation inside me, although this great nation can never feel what one mother feels... Ron's mother...

I know you are out there, Ron... I can feel when you are cold... when you lose strength... when you hope with all your might...

I know you can endure a lot. I remember, when you were 10, we bought you new shoes. Two days later you started limping. When I asked you what was wrong, you said, "Nothing, Mom," and kept limping. Then I put your foot between my knees and saw this huge blister... and you said, "Nothing." Others would have fainted from the pain...

I know Ron – you are there, dreaming about Yuval, Tami, Mom... I feel it just like I felt it that night you parachuted into captivity... Inside me, I knew that something had happened to you. I felt what mothers feel through the umbilical cord whenever something happens to her child.

I can feel it when your captors are good to you or when they are cruel. You are inside me, Ron...

You have been inside me since the day you were born and I named you Ron – the joy of my life... and then at kindergarten and school and when you were a teenager and I took you to university to study because you were gifted... and I did not want you to skip a grade because you were always so shy and modest...

And when you completed the pilots' course and I sat in the audience, waiting for you to turn around and look at me and you didn't... at that moment I knew that my child was an adult – a pilot.

And when you came with Tami to tell me you were getting married, you went outside in embarrassment and, when I was left alone with Tami, she told me quietly: "Ron and I have decided to get married..."

And I knew that, Ron, because I am a mother, and mothers know... And it is so difficult for me, Ron, because I know how hard it is on you.

I remember when Yuval was four, I told her fairy tales and she stood there with a little stick she carried like a wand and asked: "Grandma, do you think I could turn the green leaves in our garden blue, like the good fairies?" And I asked: "Maybe you could cast a spell and make Daddy come back soon?"

She did not want to go on playing with her wand and I felt the burden little Yuval was carrying... and the burden on Tami... and your brothers, Chen and Dudu... and you, Ron? What about you?

My Ron. The country is turning 50 and you will be 40. I wish we could all sit here and tell your story. Or perhaps they will not need me in the Jubilee book... I wish... Ron is back and the tales would all have been told and retold...

But you are there, and I – Ron's mother – am hoping... and your name casts a shadow on every celebration in Israel... and the joy of the Jubilee is mingled with sadness and anger at what they have done to you in that long and unnecessary captivity... and my tears are all dried out. I don't cry any more. My sadness is tearless, and I hope, and I pray...

I only want to pray and plead that now, Ron, a moment before the jubilee...

Most of all, I would like to hug you. Give you a long, long kiss on the cheek... and cry... and you would wipe the tears with your sleeve and say, "Enough, Mom, it's all over..."

I open your door silently, while you, Ron, are asleep. I look at your closed eyes, listen to your silent and steady breath. And I cover you, so that you won't be cold... Ron... I don't want you to be cold... like it was there. And then I kiss you lightly on the cheek and whisper, "My Ron...," and you hear me... "This is Mother, your mother...," and you wake up suddenly and say, "What's wrong, Mom?" and I say, "Hush now, go back to sleep." I would ask for nothing more...

My God, what did I ask for? Can anyone make a simpler wish?

That Batia, Ron's mother, could hear her son say the word "Mother"?

26.10.86

Mordechai Vanunu Brought to Israel by Mossad Agents

The London weekly, *The Sunday* Times, reported that Mordechai Vanunu, "who revealed Israel's atomic secrets," was being held in detention in central Israel. The paper added that Vanunu had been brought to Israel by Mossad agents in a special operation on the orders of Prime Minister Shimon Peres. Later, it appeared that Vanunu had been captured in mid-ocean by a Mossad agent, Cindy, who lured him from London to Rome, supposedly for a romantic meeting. He arrived as arranged, and was kidnapped, taken to a hiding-place, drugged and brought to Israel.

According to *The Sunday Times*, Vanunu smuggled out 60 photographs he had taken secretly at the Dimona nuclear plant and relayed information about Israel's nuclear capability. Based on this information, the newspaper estimated that Israel possessed between 100 and 200 nuclear bombs - ten times as many as the world experts had assessed - which made Israel the sixth global nuclear superpower.

Israel would not comment about the newly published information. The prime minister only issued a statement, saying: "Israel's policy has not changed - it would not be the first to introduce nuclear weapons into the Middle East."

Vanunu was questioned by the GSS for days. When he was taken to court, he stuck his palm against the window for everyone to see the inscription in blue ink that read: "I was hijacked in Rome." He was tried and convicted of treason and serious espionage, and sentenced to 18 years in prison. He is serving his sentence at the Ashkelon prison in solitary confinement.

Mordechai Vanunu on his way to trial. Written on the palm of his hand: "I was hijacked in Rome 30.9.86."
Photo: Zoom 77

Ron Arad Taken Captive

16 October

An IAF Phantom that took part in a raid on terrorist targets in Lebanon was shot down. The two crewmen ejected and landed safely. The pilot was rescued in a swift helicopter operation while navigator Ron Arad went in search of a hiding-place and disappeared. It was impossible to rescue him. He was captured by members the Shiite Amal organization several hours later. Over the first two years, contacts were maintained with Arad through letters and intermediaries who tried to negotiate his release. But just the opposite happened. Arad was handed over to the Hizballah and Israel lost track of him. Ever since he was taken captive, every Israeli government has made enormous efforts to get him back, but they encountered a wall of indifference on the part of the Iranians and the Hizballah who refused to co-operate in solving the puzzle of Ron Arad's disappearance.

Israel left no stone unturned in its attempt to obtain information regarding Arad's whereabouts, including the abduction of senior Hizballah members, such as Sheikh Ubeyd, who was taken from his village Jibsheet in south Lebanon, or Mustafa Dirani, who had handed Arad over to the Hizballah for money - but to no avail. Israel holds Iran responsible for the fate of Ron Arad.

The first picture of Ron Arad in captivity.

The GSS Affair:
"A Black Day for the Rule of Law in Israel"

The picture that started the 300 bus affair - a captured terrorist is taken to an interrogation during which he died. Photo: Alex Libak

The GSS affair started when two terrorists who were captured alive during the rescue operation on the 300 bus were eliminated. It quickly became one of the most severe tests of the rule of law ever seen in Israel. Attorney-General Yitzhak Zamir decided to put GSS head Avraham Shalom on trial on a series of grave charges: Giving the order to kill the two terrorists, lying to the committees that examined the affair and soliciting perjury. Zamir claimed that the GSS leaders were responsible for tampering with the evidence and for laying the blame on Brigadier General Yitzhak Mordechai, chief paratrooper officer.

Prime Minister Shimon Peres strongly opposed Zamir's decision to take legal steps against Shalom, saying: "They want to throw the head of the GSS to the dogs." Peres, Shamir and Rabin even opposed the suspension of the GSS head by the special committee that was examining the affair until the end of the investigation.

Relations between the attorney-general and the cabinet deteriorated, mainly because the cabinet was trying to bypass Zamir by appointing private lawyers to advise on the affair. At the point where he could no longer investigate the affair, Zamir resigned. Justice Yosef Harish replaced him. He was expected to drop Zamir's charges against Shalom, but Harish said that he did not have the legal authority to do that.

After new lengthy discussions and power struggles behind the scenes, it was decided that Shalom should resign, and in turn, he and the other GSS agents involved would be pardoned. President Herzog agreed to go along with this deal, fearing that putting Shalom on trial might seriously undermine Israel's security. When the pardons were issued, the public was very critical. Former Justice Minister Haim Tzadok commented: "This is a black day for the rule of law in Israel."

A Terror Attack At a Givati Brigade Swearing-In Ceremony

15 October

The swearing-in ceremony of the new recruits of the Givati Brigade was held at the Western Wall, as usual. When it ended, terrorists threw hand grenades at them and their families, killing one and wounding 70 people. The terrorists managed to flee the scene. Three youths from the village of Silwan were apprehended several days later. They were members of the Islamic Jihad and they pleaded guilty, saying that they had chosen the spot because they wanted their act to have a religious meaning.

12 January

Hava Ya'ari and Aviva Granot were arrested on suspicion of murdering tourist Mela Malevsky at the Tel Baruch beach in Tel Aviv.

4 February

IAF jets intercepted a Libyan executive jet on its way to Damascus. Israel had received information that there would be senior terrorists on board the plane. This was found to be incorrect and the plane was released.

11 February

Prisoner of Zion Anatoli Sharansky was released from prison in the Soviet Union and arrived in Israel. He was given a royal reception at Ben-Gurion Airport.

17 February

The Hizballah abducted two IDF soldiers in south Lebanon, Rachamim Alshech and Yosef Fink, both Hesder Yeshiva soldiers. Their bodies were returned after lengthy negotiations.

27 February

John Demjanjuk, who was accused of murdering Jews during World War II, was extradited to Israel by the US authorities.

11 March

A divisive atmosphere at the Herut Movement conference. The discussions halted when fist-fights broke out. Shamir said: "The Herut Movement is committing suicide."

13 April

Finance Minister Yitzhak Moda'i was dismissed after calling Prime Minister Peres "a spaced-out prime minister." Moda'i was given the justice portfolio and Moshe Nissim took the Treasury.

5 May

Businessman David Blass was detained on suspicion of cheating the Kibbutz Movement out of large sums of money.

11.2.86 Anatoli Sharansky Arrives in Israel

Anatoli Sharansky, the symbol of the USSR Jews' struggle for the right to immigrate to Israel, arrived here after spending 12 years in solitary confinement in a Soviet prison. He was arrested in 1977 on charges of spying for the US, subversion, treason, incitement and anti-Soviet propaganda. He was released in an exchange deal for Soviet agents imprisoned in the US and Europe. The exchange took place in Berlin, where he was received by the US ambassador. Sharansky was taken to Israel in a special flight.

A warm welcome ceremony was held at Ben-Gurion Airport when he arrived. He was received by several thousand people, including Prime Minister Peres, Foreign Minister Shamir, ministers, MKs and other notables. At the ceremony, Peres announced: "We shall not rest until all the prisoners of Zion and people of Israel are released and allowed to return to their homeland."

On his arrival in Israel, Anatoli Sharansky was received by Prime Minister Shimon Peres and his deputy Yitzhak Shamir. Photo: GPO

In one of his letters to his wife Avital, Sharansky wrote: "I think that when I arrive in Israel, I will simply sit on the warm sand on a beach somewhere... until I calm down from this dreadful, long race. Only then will I be able to lead a normal life... One day, we will look back and wonder: Did this really happen to us?"

Natan Sharansky headed a new immigrant party, *Yisrael Ba'aliya*, in the 1996 elections. His party won seven Knesset seats and he was appointed minister of industry and trade.

---

21 October

The first liver transplant in Israel –The first liver transplant in Israel was performed at the Rambam Medical Center in Haifa by an extended team headed by Dr. Yig'al Kam. The first transplant patient was a 40-year-old Russian immigrant who had suffered from a chronic liver disease for years. The operation lasted 18 hours, at the end of which Dr. Kam said that it had been a very complex but successful operation. The patient died 19 days later.

An "Earthquake" in the Banking System

20 April

The Beiski committee, set up to investigate the collapse of the bank shares, concluded that the managers of the four big Israeli banks and the governor of the Bank of Israel were to resign within 30 days, or else they would be fired. The committee also criticized former Finance Minister Yoram Aridor. "Bank shares turned into uncontrollable monstrous pieces of paper," the committee stated. The bank managers were shocked by the seriousness of the committee's conclusions. Clali Bank Director-General, David Shoham, reacted by saying: "It is like in ancient Rome: They tortured 20 men for two years, and then fed them to the lions."

Leading bank managers at their Supreme Court appeal hearing. Photo: Zoom 77

17 June

The Last Picture Show

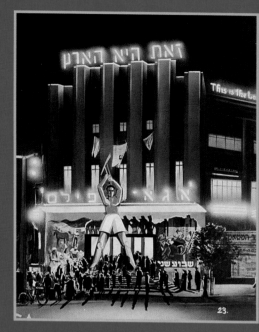

The Mugrabi movie theater burned down. The building, constructed in the 1950s in the Art Deco style, was one of the first movie theaters in Tel Aviv. It was a cultural center where not only films were shown, but plays were put on by the Cameri, the Ohel, the Matateh, and Li-La-Lo theaters. One of its major attractions was a removable rooftop that was opened to make viewing more pleasant on humid summer nights. After it burned down, it turned into a haven for junkies until it was demolished and turned into a parking lot.

5 August

Israeli Couples Adopt Romanian Babies – Dozens of childless Israeli couples "invaded" Romania to adopt children there, after Brazil – a former source of children for adoption - made the process complicated and expensive. The Israelis discovered that the Romanians did not cause any particular difficulties. A Haifa lawyer who specialized in adoption procedures denied rumors according to which most of the children offered for adoption were Gypsies.

Photo: Yitzhak Yismach

15 July

Agam - Fire and Water

Ya'akov Agam's sculpture, "Fire and Water", was inaugurated at Dizengoff Circle in Tel Aviv. The sculpture was a combination of a water fountain, a fire torch and music from Ravel's *Bolero*.

25 May

The GSS Affair: Attorney General Yitzhak Zamir demanded that GSS head Avraham Shalom be put on trial for his role in the 300 bus affair. A month later, President Haim Herzog pardoned all of the GSS personnel involved in the affair.

1 June

Yosef Harish replaced Yitzhak Zamir as attorney-general after the latter resigned over the GSS affair.

16 October

Navigator Ron Arad was taken captive by the Amal organization in Lebanon after his plane was downed.

20 October

Rotation: Yitzhak Shamir replaced Shimon Peres as prime minister, as per the agreement.

26 October

Mordechai Vanunu was kidnapped in Rome and brought to Israel by Mossad agents, according to foreign sources.

31 December

Interior Minister, Rabbi Yitzhak Peretz, resigned after the High Court of Justice ruled that convert Shoshana Miller should be registered as a Jew.

12 May

Man Shoots at Traffic Wardens' Car Because of Denver Boot

A drama in Tel Aviv: Avraham Tzadok, a 37-year-old grocer from Tel Aviv, whose car was immobilized by means of a Denver Boot, pulled out a gun and fired at the traffic wardens' car. He then demanded that they release his car. Instead, he was arrested and handcuffed by the police. One of the wardens commented: "It was like in the Wild West. It's really dangerous to work with Denver Boots."

(*1987*

***The** intifadah [uprising]
started in the Gaza Strip
and quickly spread to
the West Bank.
Photo: Sygma*

Children throwing stones at IDF soldiers in Nablus. Photo: GPO

The *Intifadah*
A Rare Opportunity to Get Out of the Duality Trap

Writer
David Grossman

On 8 December, an Israeli truck collided with two vans that were taking laborers home to the Gaza Strip. Four Gazans were killed and a rumor spread through Gaza that the accident was, in fact, a premeditated murder. The Gaza Strip ignited immediately. Huge demonstrations were staged, leaflets distributed and firebombs and, especially, thousands of stones – the symbol of the Palestinian uprising, the *intifadah* – thrown at the IDF soldiers.

After 20 years of oppressing the Palestinian nation in the territories conquered in the Six Day War, Israel found itself helpless, confused and surprised in the face of this uprising. Perhaps Israel was surprised because it had never admitted to itself clearly and directly that it was a conqueror; that there, in the "territories", lived a nation which Israel was oppressing and humiliating.

Twenty years after the Six Day War, the Palestinians turned into the menial laborers of the flourishing Israeli society. Overt and covert threads woven by the Israeli security forces trapped the Palestinians in a net of fear and submission.

Israelis and Palestinians would pass each other on the street and it seemed that the two had developed this special gaze – white and opaque – so as not to see nor understand what they were doing to each other and themselves by adjusting to the twisted reality.

A whole new language was devised in the Israeli press and public life – a devious, conflict-avoiding language designed to conceal the harsh reality, to whitewash it so that normal and routine life could continue in an illusion of a moral, enlightened and normal society.

Yet some forces cannot be undone by denial, and where people live, there is never an ongoing *status quo*. In December 1987, the Israelis realized that if you do not face up to the complexity of human reality, which is intolerable sometimes, it does not disappear. It only gains strength secretly, becomes impossibly compressed and one day explodes in your face, literally.

The riots that started in the Gaza Strip quickly spread to the West Bank. The Palestinians severed all of their ties with Israel and declared a popular uprising. "The children of the rocks" attracted the attention of the international media which took this new event and focused the world's attention on it. During the first couple of weeks, the IDF soldiers, who were not trained for such situations, killed dozens of Palestinians, including children. The Palestinians, armed with rocks and knives, killed settlers and soldiers, as well as many of their brethren whom they suspected of collaboration with Israel. In early 1988, the situation resembled a war between a giant and sophisticated army and an unarmed civilian community.

Naturally, that had a negative impact on Israeli society and on Israel's image – in the eyes of the world and its own citizens.

One month after the riots started, it was clear to all – except for the Israeli leaders – that there was no turning back. That a new Palestinian leadership was forming, not necessarily the one in exile in Tunis. More importantly, the Palestinians were forming a new and active concept of themselves, the aim of which was to realize the Palestinian nation's aspiration for its own state.

And yet, months or even years after the *intifadah* started, Israel's leaders of the time failed to understand that the Palestinians were offering us a rare opportunity to extricate ourselves from the duality trap and reshape the tragic relations that had worn down the two nations for 100 years.

To many Israelis, however, the *intifadah* was a great turning-point. Many realized that occupation and violence would only lead to ever-increasing destruction on both sides. This realization gradually translated itself into a change in political concepts.

This began to pave the way for the Oslo agreements and a tiny, fragile chance appeared for the two nations to recuperate. Time will tell whether that miracle will really happen.

9.12.*87*

The *Intifadah* Begins:
A dialogue via stones, sling-shots and firebombs

The *intifadah* began in December 1987, first in Gaza and then spreading throughout the West Bank. Ever since the Israeli occupation of the territories in 1967, there had been violent riots and demonstrations against the State of Israel, but such a widespread and intensive outburst had never been seen before. The *intifadah* expressed a new type of Palestinian extremism carried on young shoulders and conducting a dialogue with Israel via stones, sling-shots and firebombs. At first, the IDF did not attribute any importance to the uprising, expecting to quell the riots and demonstrations within a short time, just as before.

It became clear soon enough that the residents were willing to endure suffering and withstand the clashes with the soldiers. The IDF was compelled to send large units into the territories, but was still unable to subdue the riots, which were beginning to resemble civil disobedience. Gaza gave the signal and dictated the tone. On 9 December, the riots erupted at the Jabalia refugee camp after four of its residents had been killed and seven wounded in a traffic accident at the Erez crossing. This followed another incident in October in which the IDF had killed four local residents who were members of the Islamic Jihad. The conflagration started on 10 December and quickly spread to other refugee camps in the Gaza Strip and to the West Bank. Gaza has always been more violent than the West Bank, as it is overpopulated, economically stressed, packed with refugees and saturated with religious zeal. This prepared the ground for a violent outburst, but this time the West Bank was ripe for joining in. The *intifadah* activists in the villages and towns armed themselves with stones and firebombs and said what they had to say by means of songs and leaflets.

IDF soldiers in daily confrontation with Gaza residents. Photo: Micha Bar-Am

Photo: GPO

A Firebomb Thrown at the Mozes Family

11 April

Terrorists threw a firebomb at the car of the Mozes family while they were driving along the road from Kalkilya to Alfei Menashe. The mother, Ofra, and her daughter, Tal, were killed, and the father and two other children were badly wounded. In reaction to the incident, hundreds of settlers stormed Kalkilya, damaging cars, smashing windshields, burning fields and attempting to attack "suspects". Yitzhak Rabin, who went to meet settlement leaders, said: "Whoever chooses to live in the territories should know that they are taking a risk." That remark greatly angered the settlers.

The Demjanjuk Trial Opens in Jerusalem

John Demjanjuk during his trial in Jerusalem. Photo: Zoom 77

The trial was opened by prosecutor for the state, Yona Blatman, who described Demjanjuk's criminal activities: "The defendant smashed the heads of Jews who were on their way the gas chamber." The trial, which was held in front of a special panel of judges headed by Supreme Court Justice Dov Levin, was relayed live on TV and given extensive coverage by television networks worldwide. Hundreds of people, mostly Holocaust survivors, filled the hall every day.

Demjanjuk was accused of operating the engine that filled the gas chambers in the Treblinka death camp with lethal gas, causing the death of hundreds of thousands of Jews. The state also claimed that Demjanjuk was "Ivan the Terrible" who sadistically abused and killed Jews.

Demjanjuk's Israeli attorney, Yoram Sheftel, maintained that a terrible mistake had been made, and that his client was not "Ivan the Terrible", the man to whom the horrendous deeds had been attributed. He presented the court with documents proving the Demjanjuk was being held in a camp for Ukrainian POWs in Poland at the very time the state claimed he had committed the crimes in Treblinka.

Fourteen months later, "the second Eichmann trial", as it was called, ended. Demjanjuk was sentenced to death by hanging after he had been convicted of committing crimes against the Jewish nation. Demjanjuk appealed to the High Court of Justice, which acquitted him on grounds of reasonable doubt.

The Lavi Project Canceled: "A Blow to Zionism and the State"

30 August

The Lavi project began in 1982, when the government decided to develop an Israeli- made fighter plane. The project got under way, but soon encountered the opposition of the US Administration, which claimed that the Lavi would cost hundreds of percent more than had been planned, and that there was no economic logic for it. The opposition was led by Dov Zackheim of the American Defense Department. The cabinet held a long and stormy meeting, at the end of which it decided - by a majority of 12 to 11 - to halt the project. Following the resolution, Defense Minister Moshe Arens resigned, saying: "I consider this decision to be a blow to our security, to the Zionist enterprise and to the state."

16 February

The Demjanjuk trial opened in Jerusalem. The prosecutor, Yona Blatman, said in his opening statement : "Demjanjuk smashed the heads of Jews who were on their way to the gas chamber."

21 February

Meir Ya'ari, leader of Mapam and the National Kibbutz Movement, died at the age of 90.

4 March

Jonathan Pollard was sentenced to life imprisonment in the US for spying for Israel.

26 March

Former US President Carter visited Israel.

19 April

Dan Shomron replaced Moshe Levy as chief of staff.

24 May

Izat Nafso, who was sentenced to 18 years for treason and espionage, was acquitted by the High Court of Justice.

30 May

Betar Jerusalem won the national soccer championship.

30 August

The cabinet voted to halt the Lavi development project by a majority of 12 to 11 ministers.

7 October

Israel Broadcasting Authority reporters started a strike that paralyzed radio and television for two months, demanding that their salaries be raised to the level of the press reporters' salaries.

15 October

Ida Nudel arrived in Israel after a 16-year struggle to be allowed out of the USSR.

30 October

The state commission of inquiry on GSS interrogation methods and procedures, headed by Justice Moshe Landau, published its findings.

24.5.87

Izat Nafso, Acquitted

Photo: GPO

"I always believed that I would go free and that I was innocent. God answered my prayers. I would not have lasted in prison much longer... because it is hard to be in prison when you are innocent." This is what Izat Nafso told his mother in a telephone call to his Circassian village, Kafr Kama, after his release.

Lieutenant Nafso was convicted of treason and espionage in 1980 and sentenced to 18 years in prison after it had been proven that he had delivered information about the IDF to a senior Fatah commander and smuggled military equipment from Lebanon to hostile elements in Israel. Nafso filed an appeal with the Supreme Court, following an amendment according to which any military court ruling could be appealed. He claimed that he had confessed to the charges after his GSS interrogators abused and humiliated him. The Supreme Court acquitted him of most of the charges,

Izat Nafso arrives for his appeal hearing at the Supreme Court. Photo: Zoom 77

including those of treason and espionage. He struck a plea bargain by which he was convicted of exceeding his authority in a way that jeopardized state security. The judges severely criticized the GSS interrogators who "were out of line, adding insult to injury by lying to the military court."

Nafso's acquittal and the criticism of the GSS by the Supreme Court judges sparked a public outcry. Knesset members demanded that Prime Minister Yitzhak Shamir conduct a thorough overhaul of the GSS, which had not yet recovered from the 300 bus affair and was already involved in a new one.

The Night of the Hang-Glider

25 November

A terrorist who arrived on a hang-glider entered a Nachal Brigade base near Kiryat Shmona, killed six soldiers and wounded 10. He was eliminated after a shoot-out with one of the camp guards. Another terrorist, who had also tried to cross the border by hang-glider, was killed after landing in the security zone.

The fact that a terrorist had entered a military camp shocked the IDF commanders and the public. Chief of Staff Dan Shomron dismissed the Nachal Brigade commander and severely criticized the conduct of the soldiers and officers at the base. Military sources revealed later that the motorized hang-glider had eluded Israeli planes that had tried to intercept it, and had landed on a road outside the base.

Photo: Tzvi Tischler

1987

6 November

Zohar Argov Commits Suicide

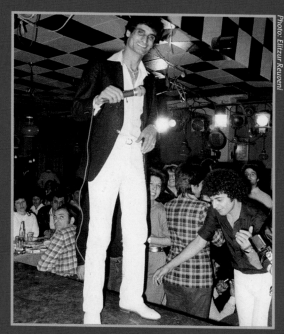

Photo: Elitzur Reuveni

Zohar Argov, the superstar of Oriental music, hanged himself in the detention cell of the Rishon Letzion police station. Argov, who had become a drug addict at the height of his career, tried to rehabilitate himself but failed. He stopped performing and got involved in crime. He committed suicide several hours after his detention.

8 December

The intifadah broke out following a traffic accident in which four Gazans were killed and seven wounded. Hamas, the Islamic Resistance Movement, was established five days later.

29 May

Major General (Res.) Shmuel Gonen (Gorodish): "I Planned to Murder Moshe Dayan" – "Right after I was dismissed as head of the Southern Command after the Yom Kippur War, I planned to murder Dayan. He was behind it all. He executed Chief of Staff Dado. We were pawns in his game." This was the opening remark Gorodish made in an interview with Adam Baruch of *Yedioth Ahronoth*, who visited him in the Central African Republic. Gonen went on: "I wanted to murder Dayan, and I would have done so had I not been politically aware. One thing stopped me: He was defense minister [a civilian] and I was a military man. I could not raise my hand to civilians. It was not a logical decision. It was pure emotion. I planned to walk into his office and shoot him at close range. No speeches, not even a word, I would just look him in the eye and shoot him right between the eyes. Don't you get it? Had I killed Dayan, I would have gone down in history much better than I have. The people would have realized what happened. They would have understood that in 1973, Dayan sacrificed us, me. He betrayed the soldiers in order to save his own neck in the Yom Kippur fiasco."

Photo: GPO

17 August

Shai K. Ofir, "The Father of Israeli Humor", died three days before a special gala performance in his honor at the Habima Theater. Ofir was an actor, pantomimist and director – a creator of Israeli entertainment and theater since the 1940s. He was one of the founders of the *Chizbatron*, and he performed in France with Marcel Marceau, directed the first shows by *Hagashash Hahiver*, and starred in many movies. His performance in Ephraim Kishon's movie, *Azulai the Policeman*, earned him international fame. Characters he had portrayed became items of classic Israeli humor. Haim Hefer dubbed him "the father of Israeli humor."

Major General (Res.) Shmuel Gonen (Gorodish). Photo: Efi Sharir.

15 January

Hava Ya'ari and Aviva Granot Sentenced to Life

The murder trial that electrified the entire nation for a year came to an end. Aviva Granot (left) and Hava Ya'ari (right) were charged with the premeditated murder of American tourist Mela Malevsky and sentenced to life imprisonment by the Tel Aviv District Court. At the beginning of 1985, a prostitute found the body of a dead woman on Tel Baruch beach. The woman was identified as Mela Malevsky, a 75-year-old Jewess and Holocaust survivor, mother of three and wife of a rich American Jew. Only at the end of 1985 did Superintendent Michel Hadad, head of the investigating team, come across material that helped him solve the case. The Malevsky family claimed that some $52,000 had been stolen from Mela's Jerusalem bank account. This led the investigators to Hava Ya'ari, a consultant on foreign shares at the bank. Ya'ari was arrested on January 10, 1986, after it was discovered that she had given Mela Malevsky financial advice. Four days later, the police arrested Ya'ari's good friend, Aviva Granot, a Tel Aviv pharmacist. The trial was very dramatic, with District Attorney Pnina Dvorin bringing 22 witnesses and presenting some 100 exhibits, while the two defendants exchanged mutual accusations. They maintained it was not murder, saying that Malevsky jumped out of the car they were driving after an argument. According to the defendants, she was killed when her head hit a rock. The state claimed that the murder was premeditated; that the defendants had picked up the victim in their car, hit her over the head with a rolling-pin, thrown her out of the car and run her over. The murder trial captured the media headlines for many months. Ya'ari's and Granot's appeal to the Supreme Court of Justice was denied.

1988

**State Comptroller
Miriam Ben-Porat
at the Knesset Audit
Committee.
Photo: Zoom 77**

*The state comptroller's annual report as submitted to the Knesset
speaker. Photo: Zoom 77*

State Comptroller Miriam Ben-Porat
An Effective Instrument in Fighting Moral Corruption

TV Host and Reporter
Ilana Dayan

In the summer of 1988, Israel's State Comptroller's Office was reborn. This low-key, sleepy institution that used to issue annual reports for the archives suddenly came back to life. A 70-year-old woman, who could have enjoyed a comfortable old age knitting for her grandchildren, brought about the change: Miriam Ben-Porat was the first state comptroller to show that she had teeth and even dared to bite.

Ben-Porat moved quickly: She forced the political parties to publish the names of their donors, enforced the implementation of the Party Financing Law, imposed fines, challenged political appointees, rebuked anyone who fixed balance sheets, exposed failures in immigrant absorption and established herself as the guardian of moral standards in Israel. She waged a battle of one against many: Miriam Ben-Porat vs. the corrupt. She appeared to be winning by points – and then the Gulf War broke out.

When the state comptroller heard that some of the gas-masks being issued to the public were good only for a masquerade and not against chemical attacks, she launched an offensive against the defense establishment. Ben-Porat really believed that the people were being misled by the defense industry because someone had not checked the situation out thoroughly. It is not clear, however, whether or not she appreciated the magnitude of the battle she had undertaken. The defense establishment rose on its hind legs: the army leaked information, the chief of staff briefed the press, the defense minister was interviewed - and the state comptroller was left to lick her wounds. This is what happens when a holy cow attempts to stick out its tongue at a holier and even fatter cow.

In my view, the gas-mask affair marked one of the comptroller's boundary lines. Here is a public figure – above reproach, the fearless iron lady, the Israel Prize laureate who is beyond all criticism – and she had cracked for the first time. Ben-Porat started making mistakes. For example, she got dragged into an insignificant squabble between Police Minister Moshe Shachal and Chief of Police Ya'akov Terner. She cleared one, tarnished the other, and received a reprimand from the High Court of Justice as a result. She also had to watch her former Supreme Court colleagues effectively overrule her decision.

At that stage, Ben-Porat experienced what any top model or new TV star knows: The media will help you acquire mythological dimensions only to get greater pleasure watching you fall. They will choke you with a warm embrace – first to be very close to you, later to hear your bones cracking. This is short-lived, fabricated love.

Toward the end of her first term in office, Ben-Porat became a controversial figure whose perception of her own job was problematic. The politicians were only too happy to make biting remarks about her and belittle her. They said she acted as if she were royalty, that she was cold, a populist and publicity-seeking. The political establishment argued over her status in the national hierarchy. (Where would she stand on the red carpet at airport receptions? Who would she sit next to at a dinner in honor of Hillary Clinton?) They collected receipts from a hotel she stayed in during a visit to Stockholm. They scoffed at her hair-do.

The attacks against Ben-Porat reeked of chauvinism and tabloid gossip. Some of the criticism against her was well justified. For example, why did she leave Ehud Barak wounded in the field when she failed to establish the facts of the Tze'elim affair? Why did she even take up this affair if she thought she did not have the tools to judge it correctly? To me, however, this is of lesser importance. Ben-Porat turned the State Comptroller's Office into something it had never been before: an effective instrument in fighting moral corruption amongst public figures. They were afraid of her, and she used this to her full advantage; or at least she did for most of her term.

The problem is, therefore, not in the way Ben-Porat perceives her job, but in the way we perceive her. This woman, who spent most of her professional life as a prosecutor and a judge, assumed the state comptroller's position when Israel's political system had hit rock-bottom.

Politicians defected, betrayed, embezzled, concealed, were tried and imprisoned, and generally disgraced themselves. The public felt nothing but contempt toward its leaders and waited for someone to put things in order. First it was Attorney-General Aharon Barak, then it was the High Court of Justice, followed by Ben-Porat. She was sucked into the vacuum and did not do too badly there, considering what can be done under such circumstances. But, at a certain point, she became too involved in fulfilling impossible expectations. She did not become the national baby-sitter because she wanted to, but because we forced her. It didn't do us any good, nor did it do her any good.

She will soon be 80. She will go home when she has had enough – tired but content. She will have done something with her life. The tough prosecutor who became a district court judge and then the first female judge on the Supreme Court bench has taught us an important lesson the hard way: When a government is bad, it should be sent home – not to the courtroom. Nor to the State Comptroller's Office.

The Election Results: The Likud and the Religious Defeat Labor

The ultra-Orthodox parties gained seats in elections of 1988. The picture shows an election poster in Mea Shearim. Photo: GPO

The elections were held at the end of 1988, after four years of a crisis-ridden national unity government. The campaign was relatively calm and the results showed a continuation in the rightward shift of the Israeli public. The Likud won 40 Knesset seats and Labor won 39. Both parties lost some power, with the main beneficiaries being the ultra-Orthodox parties: Shas went up from four to six seats, *Agudat Yisrael* went up from two to five seats, and *Degel Hatorah* (a new party consisting of the supporters of Rabbi Schach) won two. Together with the NRP, the religious bloc had 18 Knesset seats; the right-wing and religious bloc had 65 seats, against the left's 55.

Likud leader Yitzhak Shamir tried to form a narrow-based government with the religious, and so did Labor's Shimon Peres. However, because the religious parties made extensive demands regarding religious laws, the heads of the two major parties agreed that, despite its shortcomings, the national unity format would be preferable to surrendering to the religious parties' demands. The two parties decided to resume their co-operation on the basis of the same guidelines and proportion as in the previous cabinet, with the exception of the rotation. It was agreed that Yitzhak Shamir would be prime minister, Yitzhak Rabin – defense minister and Shimon Peres - finance minister for the entire term. Despite serious differences among its members, the national unity government survived until 15 March 1990.

"A Thousand Deaths Will Not Atone for His Deeds"

25 April

After 14 months of trial, Justice Tzvi Tal read out John Demjanjuk's sentence: "The defendant is no Eichmann, but he was the chief hangman who killed tens of thousands with his own hands, and willingly abused, tortured, humiliated and persecuted those wretched people... No law of limitations applies to such deeds, nor is there forgiveness... A thousand deaths will not atone for his deeds." After Justice Tal, himself a Holocaust survivor, finished reading Demjanjuk's death sentence, pandemonium broke out in the hall. Holocaust survivors burst into tears and sang songs of praise. Demjanjuk responded: "You tried an innocent man." Prime Minister Shamir commented: "The world's Jews are proud of their homeland today." Five years later, however, the Supreme Court decided to acquit Demjanjuk on grounds of reasonable doubt.

General Staff's Elite Unit Eliminates Abu-Jihad

1988

In a daring commando operation, 20 members of the General Staff's elite unit eliminated Arafat's deputy, Halil al-Wazir, alias Abu-Jihad. He was personally responsible for a large number of terror attacks that had been perpetrated in Israel. The squad arrived by sea in rubber boats and landed north of Tunisia. The members were driven from there by Mossad agents in rented cars to Abu-Jihad's luxurious villa.

After arriving at its destination, the squad assumed offensive positions around the house and waited for the signal. When the Mossad agents had made certain Abu-Jihad was in the house, the force moved in. First, a sleepy guard who was sitting in his car outside the house was killed. Then the force broke into the house using special engineering equipment and killed another guard before he even pulled out his gun. The soldiers, under the command of a young officer, went up to Abu-Jihad's study on the second floor. He realized what was happening and drew his gun, but one of the soldiers shot and killed him first. After the operation ended, the senior commander went into the house to make sure Abu-Jihad was dead. His wife and children, who were in the house, were unharmed.

Abu-Jihad, Arafat's deputy, was directly responsible for terror attacks carried out in Israel. Photo: Sygma

Before leaving, the soldiers collected secret documents from Abu-Jihad's study. They returned to the rented cars and vanished. Before the Tunisian authorities realized what had happened, the force was well on its way back to Israel. The world media covered the operation extensively , describing it as "a professional job, performed in less than five minutes." Israel denied having any knowledge about it.

Solomon's Judgment in Israel

22 April

Bruna, a Brazilian girl who was adopted by a childless couple from Ramla, found herself at the center of a modern "Solomon's Judgment" affair. The child was kidnapped from her mother in Brazil and given to an Israeli couple who adopted her and brought her to Israel. The biological mother followed her child to Israel and appealed to the courts to rule that she be returned to her. The long case concluded with the verdict that the child be returned to her biological mother. The adoptive parents and the girl were forced to part. It was learned later that the child and her mother live in a slum in very difficult conditions.

Bruna with her foster parents, Simone and Ya'akov Turgeman.

26.2.**88**

Defense Minister Rabin: "We'll Impose Order in the Territories"

The *intifadah* continued through 1988 as well. The riots in the territories intensified and became even more violent as the number of Palestinians killed by IDF fire reached scores every month. The world media broadcast extensive reports about the situation, and the Palestinians exploited the media, providing the foreign networks with "hot" items and terrible pictures of clashes between IDF soldiers and the residents of the territories.

The events reached a peak when, at the end of February, Israeli photographer Moshe Alpert published pictures showing IDF soldiers severely abusing a Palestinian West Bank resident. The screening of the pictures throughout the world sparked an uproar, and the world media sharply attacked Israel's policy in the territories.

The riots continued to spread and the IDF was forced to allocate large forces to deal with them. The Israeli leaders, primarily Defense Minister Rabin, repeatedly stated: "We will impose law and order in the territories, even if it hurts." But the declarations were ineffective. The population of the territories heeded calls by the Palestinian leadership to take part in violent acts against Israeli government branches through civil disobedience, consisting of throwing stones and firebombs, setting up roadblocks, burning tires, using knives and axes, clashing with the IDF, and taking measures against Palestinian collaborators.

Defense Minister Rabin during a visit to the territories. Photo: Defense Ministry Spokesman

---

A Woman and Her Three Children Burnt to Death in a Firebomb Attack on a Bus

30 October

A bus traveling from Tiberias to Jerusalem was attacked by firebombs when it passed through Jericho. The bombs started a fire on the bus. Attempts to rescue the passengers who could not escape failed. When the rescue forces put out the fire, they saw a ghastly sight: Passenger Rachel Weiss and three of her children had been burnt to death. The impact of this lethal attack on the Israeli public and on the elections that were held in the same week was very powerful and led to a rise in the power of the religious and ultra-Orthodox parties.

Shabtai Kalmanovich, A KGB "Mole" in Israel

10 January

Shabtai Kalmanovich, an international jewelry dealer, was arrested for spying for the USSR. Kalmanovich, who cultivated ties with top Israeli echelons, had access to classified information which he relayed to his Soviet operators. Before becoming a businessman, he was active in three political parties: Yig'al Horowitz's *La'am,* Labor and Flatto Sharon's list.

His trial lasted 10 months, at the end of which he was sentenced to nine years in prison. He was released after five years and returned to Russia, where he currently runs a large chain of businesses. Although he had been convicted, Kalmanovich declared that he had never relayed information that could jeopardize state security.

1988

1988

2 August

Royal Funeral in Jerusalem for Princess Alice – According to a request she made in her will, the body of Princess Alice, the mother-in-law of Britain's Queen Elizabeth, was exhumed from its temporary grave at Windsor Palace and flown to Israel for burial. Princess Alice, the mother of Prince Philip, the queen's husband, was buried in the Maria Magdalena cemetery in East Jerusalem 19 years after her death.

Photo: Zoom 77

19 September

The First Israeli Satellite, Ofek-1, Launched Into Space

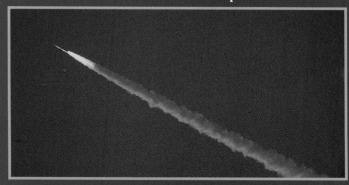

The first Israeli satellite, Ofek-1, was successfully launched into space and went into orbit around Earth, circling it every 98 minutes. Israel's technological skills were praised by many countries. Prime Minister Shamir said: "This achievement will earn Israel prestige and appreciation for its scientific skills; it will have great strategic importance." Western space experts noted that the satellite was designed to serve military needs, and that the launching missile could serve as a surface-to-surface missile. "The satellite launching proves that Israel can send missiles armed with nuclear warheads to every spot on the globe," NBC TV experts stated. Israeli experts asserted that the importance of the Ofek-1 launch into space lay in demonstrating Israel's capability to produce and operate very advanced satellites on its own, which would increase its power of deterrence and allow the implementation of military might that could be used in the future battlefield.

29 September

The arbitration between Israel and Egypt about the borderline in the Taba area concluded with Egypt winning the small piece of land.

19 October

A car-bomb exploded near the "Good Fence" in south Lebanon, killing eight soldiers and wounding seven.

1 November

The elections for the twelfth Knesset ended with the following results: the Likud won 40 Knesset seats, Labor won 39, and the religious parties improved their representation, reaching 18 seats.

9 December

Four IDF soldiers were mistakenly left behind after a raid on Ahmad Jibril's headquarters in the township of Nuweima in Lebanon. They were rescued several hours later. A debriefing held after the operation showed that there had been a discrepancy in the co-ordination between the operating forces.

22 December

Yitzhak Shamir presented the national unity government to the Knesset.

27 August

"If You Come Across Herzl Avitan – Shoot Him!"

The Israel Police launched an extensive manhunt for escaped convict Herzl Avitan who fled the Darom penitentiary in Beersheba. Hundreds of policemen and border policemen took part in the search. Senior police officers said that this was the largest manhunt ever conducted in Israel and that "Avitan is perhaps the most dangerous criminal ever to escape from jail in Israel."

Negev District Police Chief Haim Ben-On reported that he had told his officers to be ready to open fire the minute they see Avidan, who was known for his cruelty. Roadblocks were placed between Beersheba and northern Israel and the Border Police were asked to be extra careful. Before he escaped, Avitan told *Yedioth Ahronoth*: "If I ever escape from here, they will not catch me alive." He complained about his jail conditions, saying that the police and wardens had been abusing him. "I have been kept below the ground for nine years, living in complete solitary confinement, as if I were buried alive." Avitan was eventually captured in an apartment in Hod Hasharon in a "clean" operation by the police anti-terror unit.

Herzl Avitan in the Tel Aviv District Court. Photo: Michael Kramer

22 August

Gang Rape in Kibbutz Shomrat

A terrible incident in which a 14-year-old girl was raped by six youths for two weeks was exposed. The girl was badly abused and beaten, and raped repeatedly by the six. The affair sparked a bitter debate in the kibbutz, and in the end it was the girl's family which was eventually forced to leave the kibbutz. The affair made the headlines again several months later when the six defendants were found not guilty. They were convicted of rape only three years later, following an appeal by the state.

The women's lobby demonstrating against the verdict in the Shomrat rape case. Photo: Zoom 77

1989

Hamas activists at a show of force in Hebron. Photo: GPO

Hamas activists throwing rocks at IDF soldiers. Photo: Tzvi Tischler

The Hamas Year
Overcoming the barrier of fear

Professor of Sociology
Shaul Mishal

In 1989, the level of violence against Israel by the Hamas, the Islamic Resistance Movement, reached an unprecedented high since the beginning of the *intifadah*. The movement's presence in the local arena and its prominence on the Palestinian scene became an undisputed fact. Its involvement in the everyday life of the West Bank and Gaza communities increased twofold.

When the *intifadah* started in 1987, the Hamas was actively involved in organizing and initiating the everyday activities of hurling rocks and firebombs, erecting roadblocks, using the weapon of leaflets that turned into "orders of the day" – describing what should and what should not be done – and setting dates for strikes and opening hours for shops. The Hamas also addressed social issues, collected funds for the families of detainees and of people who had been killed, called for a selective boycott on Israeli products, urged laborers not to work in agricultural jobs in Israel that competed with local produce, encouraged civil servants to resign and called for attacks against the settlers.

The members of the Hamas military branch were the first to overcome the barrier of fear and the routine described above. In mid-February 1989, they abducted and murdered the paratrooper, Sergeant Avi Sasportas, and in early May, they abducted and murdered Corporal Ilan Sa'adon. The intrepidity of the Hamas would soon lead to a different kind of violence by knife-wielders and suicide bombers.

Israel reacted swiftly. In May, it arrested the Hamas founding father, Sheikh Ahmad Yassin. An extensive wave of detentions put the most senior Hamas leaders behind bars and went on to capture the mid-level field activists, heads of squads and regional commanders. The Hamas was outlawed; consequently, as it was illegal to be a member, its activists went underground. However, the assumption that these measures would deliver a painful blow to the movement later proved to be wrong. Pretty soon, Hamas activists from abroad, such as Dr. Mussa Abu-Marzuk, stepped in and, within a short period, hundreds of thousands of dollars started flowing in and hierarchic frameworks were established, side by side with informal and volunteer activity. The Hamas established a network of operatives in the Gaza Strip and the West Bank, constantly expanding its circle of supporters.

After Sheikh Yassin's arrest, the Hamas leadership became younger and more organized, with more progressive views, richer resources and better connections. It established ties with Syria and Iran, which provided it with financial support, weapons, military training bases and training in non-conventional military action. The Hamas opened an office in Amman, Jordan, which served as a channel for transferring money and sabotage materials to its squads in the territories. The movement also took root in Palestinian communities in exile, mainly in the United States, and formed an alignment of supportive organizations and bodies in Europe. Under Yassin, the Hamas resembled the institutionalized PLO under Ahmad al-Shukeiri, which assumed a Nasser-like pan-Arab image. Under Abu-Marzuk, the Hamas is closer in spirit to the radical PLO under Arafat after he took over its leadership in 1969.

The Hamas' organizational strengthening and improved status in Palestinian society was reflected, among other things, in its members' readiness to make independent decisions and undertake actions that were often in conflict with PLO positions. This could be seen, for example, in the elimination of Palestinians who were suspected of collaboration with Israel, or in setting general strike and memorial days that did not follow PLO dictates. These conflicts often deteriorated into violent clashes in the streets and in Israeli detention facilities.

Israel's image of deterrence was undermined by the fact that the Hamas had managed to establish a firm basis for itself among the Palestinian population despite extensive Israeli activity. At the same time, the success of the Hamas undermined the PLO's unquestionable status as the representative of the Palestinian nation and its national aspirations.

With the *intifadah* becoming a thing of the past and the Palestinian Authority (PA) establishing itself and becoming more deeply involved in everyday Palestinian activities, the Hamas has now started thinking and acting in a comprehensive way. It no longer seeks an all-out confrontation with either Israel or the PA. Although it will not officially recognize the PA's status and authority, it prefers co-existence to head-on clashes. Even though the Hamas consistently denies Israel's right to exist and champions violence as a solution, it does not rule out a possible dialogue with the aim of reaching a temporary arrangement. It has been proven on more than one occasion that in today's Middle East, so-called temporary arrangements frequently tend to become permanent.

6.7.89

"Death Ride" on the 405 Bus to Jerusalem

Evacuating the casualties from the bottom of the abyss. Photo: Zoom 77

A horrendous terrorist attack took place on an Egged bus, the 405 from Tel Aviv to Jerusalem. Yelling "Allahu Akbar", a terrorist pounced on the driver, grabbed the steering-wheel and forced the bus into an abyss opposite Abu-Ghosh. "I fought with him and pulled the wheel to the left, but he lay down and planted his feet firmly against the dashboard and pulled us into the abyss," the driver explained later. The bus, which was full of passengers, rolled down to the bottom of the abyss, came to a halt on its roof and caught fire. The stench of gasoline, burnt flesh and burning rubber filled the air. The screams of the injured could be heard on the highway 30 meters above the burning bus. People who arrived at the scene attempted to rescue the victims. Some of the rescuers carried them away from the fire without checking whether they were dead or alive.

Doron Levy, one of the rescuers, heard a woman scream: "Help me!" She was lying in the bushes, two meters from the burning bus. Levy tried repeatedly to reach her, but the flames and terrible heat prevented him from doing so. Helplessly he watched the flames moving toward her, consuming trees and bushes, finally surrounding her and drowning out her death cries. Rescue forces encountered difficulties in moving the casualties up the very steep slope. The IAF helicopters flying above the abyss could not find a place to land other than on the highway. The magnitude of the disaster was only seen when the fire was finally put out. The *Hevra Kadisha* [the organization that handles the dead] spent hours identifying bodies. "There were little children there," sobbed Eliezer Gelbstein, who headed the evacuation and identification operations. When the body count was completed, the toll of the attack was 16 dead and 27 injured.

Photo: Sygma

A Syrian MiG-23 Lands in Israel

11 October

The IAF control-room operators rushed to their radar screens. They had suddenly spotted a single enemy plane headed toward Israel. Before IAF planes had time to take off and intercept it, it disappeared from the screens. The plane landed in the small air-field of Megiddo and the pilot turned himself over to the IDF soldiers who arrived at the scene immediately. He said he had wanted to defect and free himself of the tyranny of the Syrian regime. His commanders had become aware of his dissatisfaction and he decided to defect before he came to any harm. Syria maintained, however, that the plane had been forced to land due to a mechanical malfunction and that the pilot had been taken prisoner by the Israelis. The "POW", however, was not keen to return home. He assumed a false identity and settled on a kibbutz in the north. The IAF took charge of the plane, examined it thoroughly, prepared it for flight and even flew it on IAF day.

Soldiers Avi Sasportas and Ilan Sa'adon Abducted and Murdered

16 February

Israel was stunned by the wave of abduction and murder of IDF soldiers. Paratrooper Avi Sasportas was abducted by Hamas terrorists from a junction near Ashkelon. Hundreds of soldiers and volunteers combed the area but could not find him. His body was found three months later, not far from where he had been abducted. On 3 May, soldier Ilan Sa'adon was also abducted by Hamas terrorists. He was apparently murdered shortly afterward. Following the murder, Israel arrested Sheikh Ahmad Yassin, spiritual leader of the Hamas. Sa'adon's body was found with the assistance of the PA only in 1996, buried in the dunes of Palmachim. His abductors, identified by the GSS, managed to escape to Libya.

IDF soldiers searching for missing soldier Ilan Sa'adon. Photo: Efraim Sharir

Sheikh Ubeyd Abducted

1989

Sheikh Abd-al-Karim Ubeyd, Hizballah commander in south Lebanon, was responsible for numerous attacks against IDF soldiers. The Israeli defense establishment decided to abduct him and trade him off for Israeli POWs, primarily Ron Arad. The General Staff's elite unit, which was given the mission, flew in by helicopter and landed near the village of Jibsheet, some eight km north of the security zone. Armed with guns with silencers, the soldiers surrounded Ubeyd's four-story house. One of the soldiers yelled in Arabic: "Open the door!" The sheikh and his family seemed less than thrilled about the unexpected guests. The soldiers did not wait for an invitation and they broke into the house after blowing away the front door. "The door suddenly burst open," the sheikh's son told reporters later, "and the Israelis came rushing in. They pointed their guns at the family, gagged Mother and tied her to a chair." The sheikh's five children were gathered in one room and locked in. The soldiers found three men in the house: Ubeyd, his uncle and a friend. According to the press, the three were forced to kneel while the soldiers searched the house. Some 30 minutes after the operation started, the

The house of Sheikh Ubeyd in the village of Jibsheet in south Lebanon, from which he was kidnapped by the General Staff elite unit. Photo: Reuters

soldiers and the three men were flown back to Israel by helicopter. The POW exchange plan (in which Israel expected to receive Yosef Fink, Rachamim Alsheikh and Ron Arad) never materialized because the Hizballah would not make the deal, issuing threats instead. Sheikh Ubeyd is still being held in an Israeli prison, waiting for a development that will allow him to return home.

Abie Nathan Imprisoned for Contacting the PLO

28 September

Abie Nathan, an energetic and stubborn fighter for peace between Israel and its neighbors and owner of the *Voice of Peace* radio station, was tried for violating the new law which banned contact with the PLO. Abie pleaded guilty and was sentenced to six months in the Eyal Prison. He refused to ask the president to pardon him, saying he was willing to sacrifice six months of his life for the sake of peace. Soon it became apparent that prominent politicians had also met with PLO members but had never been prosecuted. The law banning meetings with the PLO was only abolished three years later.

---

20 January

Defense Minister Yitzhak Rabin presented a plan to solve the Palestinian problem: tranquillity, elections in the territories and an autonomy or a federation with Israel or Jordan. The Jewish settlements would remain under Israeli jurisdiction.

28 February

In the municipal elections, Teddy Kollek won in Jerusalem and Shlomo Lahat in Tel Aviv. Likud candidates won the elections in five cities: Ramat Gan, Holon, Beersheba, Ashdod and Petach Tikva.

9 March

The Sikarii, an extremist Jewish group, torched the cars and front doors of journalists and writers, warning them not to write against the right wing.

27 March

Betzelem, an Israeli center for information about human rights in the territories, opened in Jerusalem.

3 May

A terrorist stabbed two Israelis to death and wounded three in Zion Square in Jerusalem.

23 May

US Secretary of State James Baker made a surprisingly harsh speech in which he called on Israel to abandon the "unrealistic vision of a 'Greater Israel' and halt the settlements."

5 June

President Haim Herzog commuted the prison sentences of the members of the Jewish underground from life to 10 years.

6 June

State Comptroller Miriam Ben-Porat sparked an outcry in the political establishment by publishing the names of people who had made donations to the election campaigns of the big parties.

22 June

Prof. Menachem Stern, a senior Israeli historian, was stabbed to death by a terrorist while he was walking through the Valley of the Cross in Jerusalem.

17.8.**89**

Record Unemployment: 150,000 Jobless in Israel

Unemployment in Israel reached a new high: 150,000 people, making up some 9.5% of the civilian workforce in Israel. The data were published by the Central Bureau of Statistics, which stated that this was a 60% rise in unemployment compared with the same period the year before. Contrary to expectations, unemployment increased not only in the development towns but also in the big cities. In July, 41 locations were registered as having a rate of unemployment of over 5%. Heading the list were Netivot (21.6%), Or Akiva (20.9%) and Kfar Yona (19.9%).

The dry statistics were painfully visible in reality. Shut-down factories with workers demonstrating outside the gates became a common sight. Laborers who had dedicated two or three decades of their life to a workplace were fired, and their lives shattered. The politicians' claims that this was reality and we had to live with it only fanned the flames. Worst of all, in several cases, it became apparent that the factories had not paid the pension funds on time, so the people who had been fired did not even get the severance pay to which they were entitled. Even those who were fortunate enough to be paid found no consolation due to their dismal prospects of finding employment.

Workers from all over Israel arrived at the Knesset to stage a demonstration to identify with the unemployed.
Photo: GPO

Yitzhak Shamir Fires Minister Ezer Weizman

31 December

When Prime Minister Yitzhak Shamir learned that Minister Ezer Weizman had been meeting PLO members, he did not hesitate to fire Weizman despite the shaky situation of the unity government.

Weizman's contacts with the PLO were uncovered when the GSS, which was wiretapping PLO activists' phone lines, found that Minister Weizman was one of the parties. Labor decided to support Weizman and pressured Shamir to recant. Eventually, Shamir agreed to have him back in the cabinet.

Photo: Zoom 77

21 February

Avia's Summer Wins a Prestigious Berlin Festival Award

Avia's Summer, a movie directed by Eli Cohen and starring Gila Almagor, won a prestigious award at the Berlin Film Festival. The movie, which tells the story of a 10-year-old girl's summer vacation at a farm in the early years of the state, was based on Gila Almagor's novel by the same name. Five years later, a sequel was made, also directed by Cohen and starring Almagor (right) and Kaifu Cohen (left).

16 June

The Last Temptation of Christ - Banned by the Censorship, Okayed by the High Court - After a public and legal struggle, Martin Scorsese's disputed movie *The Last Temptation of Christ* was released for screening in Israel. A year before, film and theater censorship ruled that it should not be screened in deference to religious sensitivities. The film distributor appealed to the High Court of Justice, and Court President Meir Shamgar overruled the censorship's decision, stating that "the court does not attempt to instill the judges' artistic taste in theater or movie audiences." The court also noted that the movie had been shown in Christian countries, which made banning it in Israel senseless. The picture shows actor Willem Dafoe as Jesus.

Photo: Sygma

14 September

Drugs and Orgies Videotaped by the Police - The gravest charge sheet ever submitted in Israel on drug-related offenses was filed with the Tel Aviv District Court. The police seized 50 kg of heroin and arrested some 80 people suspected of being involved in trading and distributing drugs. This was the culmination of a six-month operation during which police detectives filmed dozens of videotapes documenting drug parties and orgies conducted by the suspects at the Princess Hotel in Netanya.
The main suspects in the affair were a 35-year-old man whom the police dubbed "the biggest Israeli drug dealer" and a mother of three dubbed "the Madam". Another leading suspect was the owner of a private clinic. According to the charge sheet, the three purchased the large quantities of heroin in Lebanon and stored them in the house of the young doctor, where they also met to take drugs.
The "Madam" was the intimate friend of the prime suspect. The two used to meet, take drugs and indulge in wild sex, which was all taped by the police. People who saw the videotapes said some scenes there would put even the most daring pornographic movies to shame.

6 July

A terrorist seized the steering wheel of the 405 bus from Tel Aviv to Jerusalem and drove it over the cliff. Fourteen people were killed and 27 wounded.

19 September

A huge fire destroyed large tracts of the Carmel Mount forest. The authorities suspected arson by hostile elements.

Photo: Emanuel Ilan

16 November

Rami Dotan, head of the IAF procurement department, was questioned on suspicion of accepting bribes from American firms that sold equipment to Israel.

26 November

Scoop: The family of an Egyptian spy immigrated to Israel. The father of the family, Ibrahim Shahin, had worked for Israel for seven years, providing precise information about Egyptian Army movements. "My husband warned Israel about the Yom Kippur War. He was hanged in Cairo," his widow said.

15 March

Rafi Nelson's Village Closed - Rafi Nelson's holiday village was closed by the Egyptians after Taba was returned to Egypt. They claimed that the atmosphere of the place clashed with the values of Islam.

Photo: Joe Kot

8 April

"With You Gone, Who'll Play the Piano in This Whorehouse?"

Writer Dan Ben-Amotz, who had been suffering from cancer for months, threw a special "Farewell to Life" party at the Hamam Club in Jaffa, to which he invited 150 of his friends - writers, movie and TV people, actors, journalists and businessmen. Ben-Amotz received his friends dressed in a white *galabieh* [Arab caftan], and they kissed and hugged him. Leading Israeli singers sang for him and the crowd joined in. Among the people present were also members of the hospital staff who were treating him, including Prof. Feldman of the Weizmann Institute, who spoke about cancer and ways of fighting it. During the party, writer Amos Oz recounted an anecdote from President Truman's biography and concluded with a question to Ben-Amotz: "With you gone, who'll play the piano in this whorehouse?"
Ben-Amotz died six months after the party. He was of the most important Israeli writers and founders of an authentic Israeli culture in the press, literature, radio, cinema and satire. He became famous when he participated in the *Three In A Boat* show in the 1950s. Among his famous works are *The Book of Lies* that he wrote with Haim Hefer and Shaul Biber, *Don't Give a Damn, Screwing Isn't Everything* and *The Comprehensive Dictionary of Spoken Hebrew* which he wrote with Netiva Ben-Yehuda.

Dan Ben-Amotz at his farewell party with singers Yehudit Ravitz and Nurit Galron. Photo: Alex Libak

(1990

Rabbi Ovadia Yosef and MK Arieh Deri at a conference of Shas supporters in Jerusalem. Photo: Zoom 77

Rabbi Ovadia Yosef and MK Arieh Deri in consultation. Photo: GPO

Rabbi Ovadia Yosef
"Restoring Past Splendor"

Professor
Aviezer Ravitzky

Ever since Rabbi Ovadia Yosef – a great scholar and daring religious ruler, chief rabbi of Israel (1972-1983), spiritual mentor and political leader for hundreds of thousands – became an important figure, he has never stopped surprising the Israeli public. In the rabbinical world, his ascent was mind-boggling: he was elected Chief Rabbi (the *Rishon Letzion*) despite his entry into the race only two weeks before the elections and running against the incumbent chief rabbi. His political moves were even more astonishing. His supporters, gaining strength against all odds, currently hold 10 Knesset seats. He effected a surprising social change when he gradually removed himself and his followers from Ashkenazi patronage and became fully independent in the sphere of religious education. He surprised everyone when, making an ideological-halachic stand, he stated that territories of Eretz Yisrael might be given to the Arabs (for the purpose of saving lives), thus destroying the conventional Israeli dual stereotype concerning the opinions of a man who was both religious and eastern. He repeatedly crossed the lines of routine and customary divisions when, for example, he ruled that his followers should recite the Song of Praise [from Psalms] on Independence Day, the way the religious Zionists do, but supported his political ruling with the age-old oath sworn by the people of Israel: not to rebel against the sovereign of the place where they live – the way the anti-Zionist ultra-Orthodox do.

These achievements and daring moves made Rabbi Yosef a primary rabbinical authority in Israeli society and gave him enormous social and halachic power. He is worshipped by masses of an unprecedented size and variety – ultra-Orthodox, religious and traditional. No other extra-political Israeli figure wields so much political clout; and, despite all this, most of his time is devoted to studying, reading, writing and teaching.

What is his secret? As always, it is a combination of personal qualities and historic circumstances. He was born in Baghdad in 1921, immigrated to Israel at the age of four, lived in poverty and was educated at the Porat Yosef Yeshiva in Jerusalem, "the Oxford of the Oriental Jews." He was a very diligent student blessed with a phenomenal memory and an active mind. His career was meteoric: He was ordained at the age of 19; at 23 he was made a rabbinical court judge; he served as a rabbi in Egypt and Israel; he became a municipal rabbi and then a chief rabbi; and he wrote dozens of books. He is gifted in expressive powers and creativity, and is capable of retrieving the contents of hundreds of books from his memory and implementing them in practice. It seems that quite early on, he sensed his intellectual advantage over those around him, including the Ashkenazim, which is why he never felt inferior to them or a need to emulate them. On the contrary: As soon as he was elected Sephardi rabbi of Tel Aviv, he announced that, unlike his predecessors, he would not bow to Ashkenazi rulings, but would reinstate the Sephardic ones. This allowed for an interesting meeting-point between his personal qualities and his focus on Sephardi and Oriental traditions, namely: extensive knowledge, prodigious memory, the practical study of Halacha and daring and lenient rulings combined with disregard for conceptual and deductive thinking ("Argumentation leads to confusion") and the absence of any association between Halacha and philosophical thought.

Thus, unlike other extinct socio-ethnic movements, Rabbi Yosef is a positive symbol of a cultural renaissance for his followers, not a negative protest against economic deprivation. He did not try to heal past wounds but rather to revive an identity. He came into power at a time when the Sephardi Rabbinate was at a low ebb; he filled the void and called on his numerous students to go back to their traditions, which were not only legitimate and different, but also more authentic and direct. His people are indeed causing a revolution today in setting up establishments to replace the former religious systems: student associations, *yeshivas*, women's organizations, a court for financial matters, an authority for issuing kosher stamps, and so on. In his eyes, there is one deep meaning for the existence of the State of Israel: "The State of Israel today is the center of the world's knowledge; and there is no knowledge like Israel's Torah." According to him, Israel's Torah of today flows from the springs of the Sephardi and Eastern Jews.

The truth, however, must be told. A large part of this Sephardi "tradition" has been newly created. The oriental Jews never had *Kolels* in which hundreds of young men studied the Torah, having no other profession; do the young Sephardi rabbis who studied in Lithuanian *yeshivas* still follow the same teaching methods they were brought up with? Are they unique in their clothing, songs and even prayer melodies? Furthermore: Is looking up to the "greatest man of our generation", whom everyone should follow, not paradoxically imitating the myths and traditions of European ultra-Orthodox Jews? In any event, that myth proves effective in the Sephardi community, not less than it is in the Ashkenazi communities – and perhaps even more so.

Rabbi Yosef is a charismatic leader whose personality combines majestic splendor with being an ordinary person, aloofness and intimacy. He is able to move easily from highly sophisticated and learned language to common and juicy expressions, to crack a joke, and sometimes even to lash out at ministers and judges. His Halachic leadership is not less daring. He does not hesitate to issue edicts on sensitive matters that other rabbis have avoided: accepting bastards into the community, conversions, allowing deserted woman to remarry, accepting Karaite and Ethiopian Jews into the nation (without *tevila*), and so on. He assumed the posture of a leader who is willing to take religious risks and responsibilities, wishing to lead the community and perhaps even history. He took similar risks in the political arena *per se*. It is hard to conceive of another religious leader who would allow a single religious party to join a left-wing coalition of Labor and Meretz, unequivocally support the Oslo accords and send a positive signal to Syria. Indeed, when he was chief rabbi, he already ruled that territories may be returned for the sake of saving lives, but this stand only made a substantial difference when he managed to establish solid political power around him.

15.3.90

"The Stinking Maneuver" Overthrows the Unity Government

The idea to overthrow the national unity government and form a narrow-based government under Shimon Peres was conceived in January 1990. Peres and Shas Party leader Arieh Deri forged a plan according to which they would overthrow the Shamir-led unity government by voting against it in a vote of no confidence. The main obstacle in their path was Defense Minister Yitzhak Rabin, who believed that Labor should refrain from opportunistic parliamentary tricks for that purpose. On Peres' request, Deri met Rabin and told him that Shas and *Agudat Yisrael* would help overthrow the government and establish a narrow-based coalition under Peres – a government that would promote peace. Rabin was convinced and the plan got under way.

Shimon Peres and Arieh Deri co-operated in the plot to overthrow the national unity government. Photo: Zoom 77

Labor's excuse for a vote against the government came when the Likud chose to reject the political initiative of US Secretary of State James Baker. When Shamir learned that Labor was initiating a vote of no confidence, he immediately fired Peres, saying: "A man who wishes to overthrow the government cannot be a cabinet member."

Once Peres was fired, all the Labor ministers resigned. On 15 March, the government fell in a vote of no confidence in which *Agudat Yisrael* voted with Labor, while Shas and *Degel Hatorah* abstained. This was the first time in Israel that a government had been brought down by a no-confidence motion. President Herzog assigned the task of forming a government to Shimon Peres, but he failed because the Lubavicher Rabbi and Rabbi Schach ordered the *Agudat Yisrael* Knesset members, Avraham Verdiger and Eliezer Mizrachi, not to support a Peres-led government. Verdiger and Mizrachi went into hiding and would not answer Peres' calls. The country followed the political drama with bated breath, asking the crucial question: Where are Verdiger and Mizrachi? It eventually turned out that the two were hiding at the homes of relatives, waiting for the time Peres had to form a government to expire. "The stinking maneuver", as Rabin called it, had failed. Peres could not form a coalition. President Herzog ordered Yitzhak Shamir to do so, and he formed a narrow-based coalition within two weeks.

The "Tent Movement" Settles in the City Squares

A new protest movement was organized in Israel in 1990. Homeless young couples from deprived neighborhoods who felt that they had been discriminated against compared to the benefits received by new immigrants, put up tents and settled in city squares and public parks. They were protesting against their plight and bringing it to the attention of the public and the government. They were known as the "Tent Movement" and received extensive media coverage. The authorities refrained from using force to remove them from public areas and, eventually, the homeless were provided with appropriate solutions.

Tents of homeless in south Tel Aviv. Photo: Tzvi Tischler

Temple Mount Riots:
17 Arabs Killed and 200 Wounded

The whole thing started during the *Succot* festival [Tabernacles]. Some 20,000 Jews came to pray at the Western Wall, performing the traditional pilgrimage to Jerusalem. At 10:30 a.m., a group of Temple Mount Faithful met near the Pool of Silwan for the cornerstone-laying ceremony for the Third Temple. This gathering sparked tremendous unrest among the East Jerusalem Arabs. The Silwan village muezzin started chanting "*Allahu Akbar*", and masses of Arabs immediately rushed to the Temple Mount and started pelting the Jewish worshippers below with rocks, bottles and metal bars, injuring 20 of them. The Arab masses then burst into the police station on Temple Mount and set it on fire. The local police force, consisting of 45 policemen, could not stop the rioters. The policemen were surrounded by thousands of angry Arabs and were forced to open fire, which left 17 Arabs dead and some 200 wounded. The next day, heavy riots broke out in the territories and Jerusalem. A Jewish motorist was murdered near Abu-Ghosh and three Jews were stabbed to death in Jerusalem's Bak'a quarter by an Arab youth.

Mass detentions followed the big riots on the Temple Mount. Photo: Sygma

Following the Temple Mount incident, the police were severely criticized for their deployment and *modus operandi*, mainly in view of the fact that the GSS had provided them with intelligence information about expected riots in Jerusalem. Police Minister Roni Milo, whose orders to beef up the Jerusalem police force had not been carried out, set up a commission headed by former GSS chief Tzvi Zamir to examine the performance of the police. The commission leveled harsh criticism at police chief Ya'akov Terner, who had not been on the scene during the incident, and at the district commander, Deputy Commander Arieh Bibi. Israel was harshly condemned by the UN Security Council, which decided to send a special delegation to investigate the bloodshed on the Temple Mount.

Photo: GPO

Mass Immigration From the USSR

31 December

Some 200,000 immigrants, most of them from the USSR, arrived in Israel during 1990. The state had to deal with a wave of immigration the size of which it had not faced since 1951. The most serious problem was housing. The immigrants were placed temporarily in IDF camps, hotels, recreation facilities and mobile-home neighborhoods. The other problem was employment. Most of the immigrants were professionals – physicians, engineers, scientists and economists – but had to settle for odd jobs such as cleaning streets or working on production lines in factories. While the people were willing to absorb the new immigrants, many expressed resentment at the fact that some of the immigrants were non-Jews who used false documents to receive state benefits.

20.5.90

Ami Popper Murders Seven Arab Workers

At 6:15 a.m., 21-year-old Ami Popper arrived at the Gan Havradim Junction, south of Rishon Letzion, armed with a Galil rifle he had stolen from his brother, an IDF soldier who was at home on leave. Dozens of Arab laborers were waiting at the junction to be picked up by their Israeli employers. Popper held the workers at gunpoint, demanding that they stand in line and show him their ID cards. He then stopped a passing car with Gaza license plates and ordered its occupants to get out. When they did, he opened automatic fire at them and the group of laborers and then fled. Seven Arabs were killed and more than 20 were wounded by the shooting.

A three-day mourning strike was declared in the territories following the murder, and the Palestinians clashed violently with IDF troops. Eleven Palestinians were killed and dozens wounded in the riots. The police and the GSS launched a massive manhunt for Popper, but were unable to track him down. Eventually, Popper turned himself in. He told his interrogators that he was in a state of depression because his girlfriend had left him. He was sent for psychiatric observation and declared sane. At that stage, he changed his version and claimed that he had been sexually abused by an Arab eight years before and had wanted to take revenge ever since. The Tel Aviv District Court sentenced him to seven consecutive life imprisonment sentences

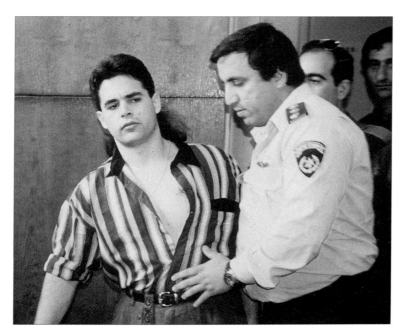

Ami Popper being brought into court to hear his sentence. Photo: Michael Kramer

and another 20 years for attempting to murder the 20 Palestinians whom he had wounded. In the meantime, Popper has become religious, and he and his family have been making great efforts to get the president to pardon him.

Victor Ostrovsky Exposes the Mossad: "Your Life Will Be in Danger if You Publish the Book."

5 September

Victor Ostrovsky revealed Mossad secrets in his book *By Way of Deception* that was published in Canada. Israel tried unsuccessfully to prevent the book from being published. The book gives a precise account of the organizational structure of the Mossad, its methods of operation and how it became one of the best espionage organizations in the world. When the Israeli authorities realized that they could not prevent the book from being published, they decided to ignore it and discredit Ostrovsky, who told the press that two Mossad agents had threatened him, saying, "If you publish this book, your life will be in danger."

Photo: Shaul Golan

Rami Dotan Admits to Accepting Bribes - "He Betrayed Us All"

28 October

Brigadier-General Rami Dotan was arrested by the police on suspicion of accepting bribes while serving as IAF chief of procurement. The affair was revealed toward the end of 1989 and reached its peak by the end of 1990. Ofer Pa'il, a member of the Israeli Defense Ministry procurement delegation to the United States, filed the complaint against Dotan, and the Einan committee, appointed by Defense Ministry Director-General David Ivri, determined that there had been irregularities in the way the Israeli delegation had made contracts with US plants and that the police should look into the matter.

Ivri decided to let the Israel Police and the Military Police examine the committee's findings. Dotan denied the charges against him and claimed that several elements had conspired against him because he would not buy equipment from them. He broke down when the suspicion arose that he had played a part in the attempted murder of Ofer Pa'il. Eventually, Dotan confessed to the charges and agreed to a plea bargain according to which he would return the bribe money he had received, would be stripped of his rank and discharged from the army and would serve up to 10 years in prison. Major General Avihu Bin-Nun, then IAF commander, said: "Dotan betrayed us all - the Air Force and me personally." Dotan pleaded guilty to charges of theft, taking bribes and fraud and was sentenced to 13 years in prison and a demotion to the rank of private.

In March 1997, the parole committee decided to release him after six and a half years in prison due to his "dangerous" state of health. The decision sparked a storm in Israel; the defense minister and the chief of staff criticized it and the High Court eventually ordered the parole committee to reconsider Dotan's early release.

1990

13 March

The Music Revolution Reaches Israel

MUSIC TELEVISION®

MTV, the world leader in pop music, began broadcasting in Israel after the station managers made a deal with the Israeli cable company. The station broadcasts were initially picked up by 5,000 households in Beersheba which had already been connected to the cable TV network.

18 October

Roni Leibovich, the "motorcycle bandit", was captured after 22 bank robberies.

21 October

Some 500 Ethiopian immigrants staged a demonstration outside the Prime Minister's Office demanding that their families be brought to Israel urgently because they were in mortal danger in Ethiopia.

14 December

Hamas activists from Gaza murdered two men and a woman in an aluminum factory in Jaffa.

24 December

Saddam Hussein warned he would attack Israel if the United States attacked Iraq.

26 December

Israel and the USSR re-established diplomatic relations after 23 years.

Photo: Shalom Bar-Tal

8 July

"New Driver" Signs Compulsory for Two Years – Following a series of traffic accidents involving young drivers, Transportation Minister Moshe Katzav issued a new regulation according to which new drivers would have to put a "New Driver" sign in their car's rear window for two years.

Photo: Chock

16 May

Ohana, Rosenthal and Tikva Watch Israel Beat the USSR from the Stands

A scandal at the Ramat Gan Stadium: Soccer stars Eli Ohana, Roni Rosenthal and Shalom Tikva refused to play against the USSR team after their demands for insurance arrangements were rejected. Rosenthal, for example, demanded that if he were injured in the game, he would be paid 1.5 million in compensation, as this might lead to the cancellation of his contract with the British team, Liverpool. Negotiations with the three players continued in the stadium. Eventually, however, they decided not to play. They saw the Israeli 3:2 victory from the stands.

4 April

"We Won't Let Them Steal Our Country!"

A demonstration held at the Malchei Yisrael Square demanding that the system of government be changed was one of the largest ever in Israel. A group of disabled IDF veterans joined a hunger strike that had been started by Avi Kadish, Eliad Shraga and David Meital. The speakers at the demonstration spoke against the ministers' "love of their seats", and Kadish cried: "We won't let them steal our country!"

Photo: Efi Sharir

(1991

Prime Minister Yitzhak Shamir addressing the Madrid Conference. Photo: GPO

The wreckage of a house in Savion which suffered a direct hit by an Iraqi Scud missile. Photo: GPO

The Gulf War
Yitzhak Shamir – The Power of Restraint

Minister and Former MK
Dan Meridor

At noon on 2 August 1990, we were surprised when a telegram arrived from Washington. Our representatives in the United States had asked the US Intelligence people whether they believed that a war with Iraq would break out. Their answer was a categorical no. That same night, the Iraqi Army wiped Kuwait off the map. The war clock started ticking. US President George Bush started getting the coalition countries together and preparing a military force of some half million soldiers. Israel began to receive threats from Saddam Hussein according to which, if Iraq were attacked, he would attack Israel.

Prime Minister Yitzhak Shamir convened a small group of ministers and military and intelligence people to analyze the situation and prepare for the possibility of an Iraqi missile attack on Israel. Later, the inner cabinet convened to discuss the current events. The US attacked Iraq on 17 January 1991, and several hours later, Israel was attacked by Scuds. Prime Minister Yitzhak Shamir immediately understood the major difference between this war and previous wars. This time, the "game" was different – Israel was not one of the main players. Shamir realized that the situation called for a different type of policy. Israel had to curb its natural instinct to retaliate when attacked. It was obliged to show restraint and allow the Americans and the coalition countries to attack Iraq and destroy the Iraqi army.

This situation revealed Shamir's iron logic, his ability to withstand pressure and his characteristic restraint. Even after the missile attacks caused a great deal of damage and the ministers demanded immediate military action, Shamir made a cold calculation and would not permit resolutions that would drag Israel into a war that might complicate the situation for the Americans and dissolve the coalition President Bush had formed. Yitzhak Shamir set an example of how to deal with a war crisis intelligently and with restraint – contrary to his image of belligerence. I stood by him during that difficult and tense time, day and night, reading the intelligence reports and watching his quiet leadership and his power of restraint.

If the Gulf War led Shamir to a policy of restraint, the reality that followed led him to the conclusion that progress could be made in the peace process. He surprised many when he went to the peace conference in Madrid, becoming the first Israeli prime minister to speak with the Syrians and the Palestinians face to face. The "do-nothing" policy that was appropriate for the Gulf War was replaced by political initiative. Shamir saw the great changes that were occurring in the world: The USSR had come apart; the Arab front had cracked open as a result of the Gulf War; the Palestinians, who had supported Saddam and had danced on the rooftops when the missiles hit Israel, had begun to despair; the *intifadah* was waning; and Israeli-US relations were becoming closer. In view of the new reality, Shamir decided to intensify the political initiative. I left for Washington on a mission for the prime minister and held a secret meeting with Secretary of State James Baker, in which we agreed on the principles that would form the basis of the Madrid conference.

Historically, it will be shown that the Madrid conference was a turning-point in the history of the Middle East conflict. Things did not develop as fast as we would have liked them to, for quite a few obstacles surfaced along the way, but the conference practically opened the channel for direct negotiations with the Arab countries and the Palestinians. Yitzhak Shamir was the man who led the Israeli government to this point. In the span of a year, Yitzhak Shamir was revealed in all his strength: restraint during the Gulf war and political initiative in Madrid.

17.1.*91*

The Gulf War: *Nachash Tzefa!* - Scud Warning

At 01:30 on Thursday morning, the US Air Force started bombing Baghdad. Hundreds of planes dropped tons of bombs on the city and dozens of Tomahawk cruise missiles hit strategic locations in Iraq. A state of emergency was declared in Israel. The citizens were ordered to seal rooms, prepare themselves for a lengthy stay in them and open their protective gas-mask kits. Some 24 hours after Operation Desert Storm began, the first round of missiles hit the Dan Region, causing serious damage to property. Many people from Tel Aviv and its surroundings left their homes and moved to safer locations. Tel Aviv Mayor Shlomo Lahat called them "deserters", received an angry response - and apologized.

While the "coalition countries" continued attacking Iraq, the Israelis sat and waited for the radio and TV to broadcast the unwelcome password, *Nachash Tzefa* [viper], warning that Iraqi Scuds were about to fall on Israeli

US Patriot missiles launched to intercept an oncoming Iraqi Scud over Tel Aviv.
Photo: Nathan Alpert, GPO

territory. This was the signal for the sirens which sent the Israelis into their sealed rooms. Over a period of six weeks, Israel was hit by 39 missiles altogether. The experts' pre-war predictions that Saddam was only making empty threats were proven to be totally wrong. At the same time, Saddam, who promised that this would be the "mother of all wars", used "only" conventional missiles against Israel, although it became known after the war that he did in fact possess chemical weapons.

The missiles caused damage mainly to property: some 7,000 houses were hit, and serious damage was caused to businesses and private property. Luckily, loss of life was minimal, with only one person killed and some 300 injured. Prime Minister Yitzhak Shamir agreed to the US request that Israel act with restraint and not attack the Iraqi missile launchers. US President George Bush feared that if Israel attacked Iraq, the anti-Iraqi coalition he had worked so hard to form might crumble.

Operation Desert Storm ended on 28 February after Kuwait was liberated from the Iraqi occupation. The Iraqi Army suffered a painful defeat, many army installations were demolished and thousands of soldiers were captured by the Allied forces. Only then did life return to normal in Israel. This was the first time in Israeli history that the home front became the battle front.

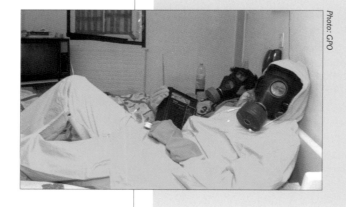

Photo: GPO

Who Was Responsible for the Gas-Mask Fiasco?

18 March

In a very harsh report, State Comptroller Miriam Ben-Porat stated: "One third of the gas-masks used during the Gulf War provided no protection... The political echelons are responsible for the blunder..." Defense Minister Moshe Arens said in reaction: "We did not forsake the public." Senior IDF officers claimed that the comptroller's investigation had been conducted by unprofessional people, but the public believed her, not the government or the IDF.

Operation Solomon: Ethiopian Jews Arrive

Photo: Nathan Alpert, GPO

The airlift in which Ethiopian Jews were brought to Israel started on a Friday evening. Operation Solomon lasted over 24 hours, during which 36 planes landed in Addis Ababa airport one by one and brought 14,400 Jews to Israel. The operation, commanded by Amnon Lipkin-Shahak, was the culmination of Operation Moses which had started in 1984, when some 8,000 Jews were brought to Israel. The operation was halted at that point because of a press leak, and many families had to wait long years for their reunion.

The civil war in Ethiopia worsened in 1990, as did the situation of the Jews who were left behind. They fled from the battle zones to transit camps in Addis Ababa, where they lived in difficult conditions. The Jewish Agency supported them there and helped them organize and prepare for the immigration to Israel.

In May 1991, when the rebels started closing in on Addis Ababa, the Israeli government decided to launch the airlift rescue operation. The US Administration exerted a great deal of pressure on the Ethiopian authorities to permit the Jews to emigrate, and diplomatic contacts were made with the rebel leaders. Eventually, all the parties gave their long-awaited permission and the operation got under way. Special units were sent to organize the transfer of the Jews to the airport where, in their best clothes and in an orderly way, they boarded the planes in groups. Several hours later, they arrived in Israel, the land of their dreams. In that operation, El Al broke a record when over 500 people were packed into one Jumbo.

Secret Unit Revealed

23 June

Everyone criticized the fact that Israel TV's first channel broadcast an item on its Friday news program about the IDF's undercover *Duvdevan* and *Shimshon* units. Senior officers claimed that the report exposed the units' *modi operandi*. Chief of Staff Ehud Barak said in reaction that the exposure was a means of deterrence. Meretz MK Ran Cohen said: "A country that wants to remain democratic cannot let such units exist."

Undercover soldiers arrest Hebron stone-throwers. Photo: Zoom 77

30.10.91

The Madrid Peace Conference - "Historic Opportunity for True Peace"

The international peace conference in Madrid was an historic event that received extensive coverage. The conference opened with an impressive ceremony in the royal palace. It was attended by an Israeli delegation headed by Prime Minister Yitzhak Shamir, and four Arab delegations from Syria, Lebanon and Egypt as well as a joint Jordanian-Palestinian delegation. Shamir, who had persistently opposed an international conference, only agreed to attend after pressure had been exerted on him by President Bush's administration and after the frameworks and goals of the conference had been limited. Foreign Minister David Levy, offended by the fact that Shamir, and not he, would head the Israeli delegation, decided not to attend. The main achievement of the conference was that Israelis held direct meetings with Arab delegations, especially the Jordanian-Palestinian

President George Bush addressing the Madrid Peace Conference. Photo: GPO

one which included people from the territories under the guidance of Yasser Arafat from his residence in Tunis. Furthermore, the conference created a framework for additional meetings between the parties involved in the Middle East conflict.

The sponsors of the conference, besides the Spanish king, were the United States and the USSR. The invitation to the conference stated: "There is an historic opportunity to promote the chances of true peace in the Middle East through direct negotiations between the parties." The conference was impressive, but had no practical results. The political stalemate continued for many more days.

British Billionaire Robert Maxwell Drowns at Sea

5 November

British billionaire Robert Maxwell, who had numerous investments in Israel, drowned while on a cruise on his private yacht. Maxwell gained control of *Ma'ariv* and invested money in many Israeli firms. After his death, it turned out that he had incurred enormous debts and had emptied his employees' pension funds. His death remains a mystery. It is still not clear whether it was suicide, murder or simply an accident.

Photo: Michael Kramer

"Motorcycle Bandit" Gets 20 Years

26 February

Roni Leibovich, dubbed the "motorcycle bandit", was sentenced to 20 years in prison after pleading guilty on 22 counts of armed robbery of banks all over Israel. He was caught in October 1990 when he parked his dark-gray motorcycle in the parking lot of a Bank Leumi branch in Givataim on his way to commit his 23rd robbery. The license plate of the bike was covered with adhesive tape, which alerted the suspicions of a neighbor who then called the police. When a patrol car arrived, Leibovich jumped on his bike and fled with the car after him. Many other patrol cars joined the chase, but Leibovich managed to give them all the slip. He was eventually caught because of a police helicopter which kept track of him from above until he arrived at his parents' home, which was near the bank he had planned to rob. "What do you want? I live here," he told the policemen who came to arrest him. Superintendent Haim Pinchas, head of the investigating team, was not convinced and, after briefly questioning Leibovich, decided: "This is our man. This is the 'motorcycle bandit'. We've got him!"

91

21 February

Fashion at War

Photo: Amir Weinberg

Creativity and a sense of humor did not disappear, even under the threat of Scuds. Several young fashion designers put on a special show in Tel Aviv, inspired by the war. The most striking outfits were a wedding dress presented by a model who donned a gas mask (above) and a transparent dress with a picture of a skeleton on it and the inscription: "War is dangerous for your health."

30 October

The Madrid conference opened with the participation of Israel, Egypt, Syria, Lebanon, Jordan and the Palestinians.

17 November

Twelve Iranians who fled their country crossed the border from Jordan and requested political asylum here.

22 January

Birth Under Fire

A dramatic birth took place at the Carmel Hospital in Haifa. The delivery took place during a Scud missile attack, with the mother and medical staff wearing gas-masks. The birth was quick and the baby was named Or [light].

20 January

Tel Aviv Residents Flee the City – After the first salvo of Scuds hit the Dan Region, many residents left the area and headed north or south. Some 100,000 frightened people inundated the hotels in Eilat, Arad, Jerusalem and Tiberias. The demand for outgoing flights increased as well.

Long lines at the ticket counters of the Ben-Gurion Airport. Photo: Amir Weinberg

January

"End of the World" Parties

The UN ultimatum to Saddam, in which he was asked to "be reasonable" and withdraw from Kuwait, expired on the morning of 16 January. Several days before the zero hour, Jerusalem and Tel Aviv residents attended "end of the world" or "the moment before" parties. The clubs were packed and some of the venues even handed out appropriate accessories, such as sachets of mustard. Theaters and cinemas were deserted. Everyone was either riveted to their TV screens or preparing a sealed room. The prices of adhesive tape, drinking soda and plastic sheeting skyrocketed.
At the Israel Museum, the expensive paintings in the Sam Spiegel collection – including drawings by Matisse, Monet, Picasso and Degas – were removed from the wall upon the request of the managers of Spiegel's estate, for fear that they might be damaged in the anticipated bombing.

The owners of the Habima Café in Tel Aviv hung a 27x15 meter Israeli flag across the front of the theater "to boost the morale and urge those who left town to return."

Photo: GPO

20 May

Lech Walesa in Israel – Polish President Lech Walesa visited Israel for the first time. The former leader of the workers' movement, Solidarity, which ignited the struggle against communism, met the president, the prime minister and other notables. In an historic speech at the Knesset, he asked the Jewish nation's forgiveness for what had been done to it during the Holocaust.

אין סאדאם העומד בפני הרצון

Two popular bumper stickers from the Gulf War.

נשארתי ב & רבתי!

(1992

Yitzhak Rabin delivering his victory speech. Photo: Meir

Yitzhak Rabin shown much affection during his visit to the Katamon neighborhood of Jerusalem. Photo: Zoom 77

The 1992 Elections –Yitzhak Rabin's Political Upheaval
Determined to change, correct and mainly to try and bring peace

Leah Rabin

The elections for the 13th Knesset were held on 23 June 1992. We gathered in the study of our house – Yitzhak, myself, our children and our grandchildren – sitting in front of the television set, waiting for the results of the exit polls at 10 p.m. Many of our friends wanted to be with us for the moment of the long-awaited victory, but Yitzhak was determined that only family members be with him before the results were made known. Conversation did not stop, but we spoke much more quietly. Occasional brief telephone calls from various aides gave us the updated forecasts.

Nine fifty-eight, nine fifty-nine, and then silent tension. We were glued to the TV set, waiting for the results of the exit polls. Anchorman Haim Yavin appeared on the screen and said one word: "Upheaval." This was all we needed to hear to indulge in a joyous round of hugs and kisses. An upheaval – the enchanted lever that released a river of happy tears.

The word *upheaval* was first heard in a political context in May 1977,when the Likud won the ninth Knesset elections. Until that stuffy night of June 1992, that word had only negative connotations for us. Not any more. Now it spelled victory.

People started pouring into our apartment, but the joy we felt inside the house was dwarfed by the cheers of joy we could hear from all over the neighborhood, a huge chorus from the multi-story buildings whose windows resembled wide-open, concrete mouths, congratulating us. It made me think of the cheers with which Yitzhak was received when he arrived at Bloomfield Stadium in 1977, several days after he had announced his resignation. This time, however, it was a thousand times stronger and without limits.

Only one person in the room kept his cool. Only one person did not cheer or weep with joy – and barely smiled. When he heard the word *upheaval*, Yitzhak didn't even react. He only warned us that the final results might be different. He quietly thanked the first few people who called to congratulate him, but I could see he was very happy inside. We hugged and kissed him, but he did not rise from his chair. "Let's wait and see," he said.

The phone never stopped ringing. We have a photo album showing the incredible number of floral arrangements we received. What a sight! Not an inch, table – shelf, carpet or corner – was free of glowing and intoxicating colors.

The Labor Party's victory celebration at the Dan Hotel in Tel Aviv was in full swing when we arrived there at 1:00 a.m. Music, dancing, endless chanting: "Israel is waiting for Rabin." Making his victory speech there, Yitzhak thanked and praised the people who had toiled so hard to put him back at the helm. Then he made the statement that would be quoted repeatedly: "I will navigate; I will decide."

At 4:00 a.m. he finally went to sleep, happy and self-assured, already planning the next day. He said good night in his personal manner: "My wife, please wake me up at a quarter to seven." After three hours of sleep, he got up and went to work. That was his way. The brief sleep was enough for him, and he went off to work like everyone else; he had much work ahead of him.

I remembered that night several years later, when I read Doris Kearns Goodwin's charming book *No Ordinary Time*. The paragraph describing Winston Churchill assuming the post of British prime minister in May 1940 says: "When he went to sleep that night, after that extraordinary day, he clearly felt very relieved. 'Finally, I may issue orders regarding the entire picture. I feel as if I am following the path of destiny, that my life so far has been just a preparation for this hour and this task.' " Indeed, Yitzhak had had years of preparation for this most important task.

Yitzhak held two portfolios in the new cabinet: prime minister and defense minister. He knew he had to control the two offices directly if he were to promote the peace process. This time, it was going to be his show, his agenda. Above all, he really felt he was the best candidate for both jobs. He was not blind to the irony of the situation and would often tell the cabinet: "I speak to you now as the defense minister, and I want you to know that in that capacity, I've got problems with the prime minister."

On 13 July, Yitzhak presented his cabinet to the Knesset. When we drove to Jerusalem for that occasion, I wrote in my diary:

"Yitzhak is sleeping next to me in the car, and I am sitting and reading the speech he will make in a few hours. I like the speech very much, and all in all I'm very excited. Could it be? Is it really happening that here we are on our way to Jerusalem – with everything that means – 15 years after we left it under such sad circumstances? Is there some invisible hand or power that has been trying for years to rectify a wrong which was done then, and now it is happening and the wrong is being rectified? It is happening; Yitzhak is coming back in full force, with the warm greetings of very many Israelis, representatives of the world's nations and the Jewish Diaspora. The eyes of so many are turned to him this day with so much hope and expectation. And he is aware of the burden these hopes and expectations place upon him, and he is determined to change, correct and especially, especially – to do whatever is possible to try and bring about peace... ."

All our children were in the Knesset – Dalia and Avi, Yuval and Eilat, and our three grown grandchildren who came to see their grandfather on his festive day – their festive day. Our closest friends were there with us as well. They had been at the Knesset when Yitzhak presented his cabinet in 1974; they had stayed with us for a week when he resigned under those extraordinary circumstances; clearly they belonged there on July 13.

Yitzhak called his speech "A Determined Government". I feel it was one of his finest speeches.

23.6.92

Yitzhak Rabin's Victory Speech:
"I Will Navigate, I Will Determine, I Will Decide!"

In the elections of 1992, Israel placed its confidence in Yitzhak Rabin. Under his leadership, Labor won 44 Knesset seats against the Likud's 32. There were many reasons for his victory: His image as "Mr. Security", his public credibility, the unity he had succeeded in forming in his party's leadership, the public's weariness of personal terror on the city streets, as well as the desire to thaw the political freeze that constituted the cornerstone of Yitzhak Shamir's policy. The Likud, on the other hand, was fraught with internal squabbles, breaking down into camps. The state comptroller's report that had been published just before the elections did not improve the image of the Likud, which had to deal with Labor's slogan, "We are tired of your corruption!"

In the last stages of the campaign, the Likud attacked Rabin personally, recalling his collapse on the eve of the Six Day War and even dubbing him "a drunk", but nothing could stop Rabin's forward charge. His victory was clear and unequivocal. When the election results were publicized, Rabin addressed Labor activists in a victory speech that went down in political history under the heading: "I Will Navigate, I Will Determine, I Will Decide!"

Rabin managed to form a bloc of 61 MKs - Labor, Meretz and the Arab parties [who were not in the coalition, but would not join the Likud], and Shas joined later. The slogan, "Israel is waiting for Rabin", materialized when the new cabinet won the confidence of the Knesset on 23 July. While Labor celebrated its victory, the Likud was in a major crisis. Outgoing Prime Minister Yitzhak Shamir announced that he was thinking of quitting the Likud leadership, a position he had held since Begin's retirement in 1983. MK Benjamin Netanyahu seized the opportunity and announced that he considered himself a suitable candidate for the leadership of the Likud, stating that he had the power to reinstate a Likud government. Thus, while Rabin was starting his term as prime minister, the race for the Likud leadership started as well.

Yitzhak Rabin watching television on the night of his election victory.
Photo: Zoom 77

[The banner reads: "Israel Is Waiting For Rabin"] Photo: Israel Hadari

500,000 People Below the Poverty Line

6 January

A National Insurance Institute report on poverty in Israel stated that about half a million Israelis, including many children, lived below the poverty line. This serious piece of information not only caused a public outcry, but was discussed at the Knesset and was extensively analyzed in the media. It disappeared as quickly as it had appeared. This figure kept featuring in National Insurance reports in the years that followed, but no solutions were found.

Tze'elim B Disaster: 5 Killed, 6 Wounded

1992

Chief of Staff Ehud Barak coming out of a cabinet session. Photo: Zoom 77

During an exercise that took place at the Tze'elim training base in November 1992, five General Staff elite unit soldiers were killed and six wounded when they were hit by a rocket that was launched by mistake. London's *Sunday Times* reported in January 1994 that the soldiers were rehearsing the assassination of Iraqi President Saddam Hussein. Chief of Staff Ehud Barak, his deputy Amnon Lipkin-Shahak, intelligence branch chief Uri Sagi, drill commander Amiram Levin and unit commander Lieutenant Colonel R., who was not in charge of the exercise, were present at the scene. The chief of staff appointed a committee headed by Major General (Res.) Menachem Einan to investigate the disaster. The committee found the junior officers responsible, while Amiram Levin was held only indirectly responsible. Several months later, the Military Police began an investigation into the affair, also laying the blame on two officers of the elite unit and minimizing the responsibility of Major General Levin. The Military Police report was presented to Brigadier General Ilan Schiff, military attorney-general, who rejected the report's conclusions and decided to put Levin on trial. Eventually, Levin had a hearing after which he was reprimanded by his commander, but not put on trial. The two junior officers, however, were convicted of negligent manslaughter, given three-month suspended sentences and demoted.

The affair reached its peak in July 1995. When Ehud Barak was about to be appointed minister in Rabin's cabinet, after he had quit the army, *Yedioth Ahronoth* published a report under the headline: "The Big Cover-Up". The report claimed that Barak "did not help the wounded and took off in his helicopter without evacuating any of them." The paper added that Barak gave conflicting versions in the two investigations.

The report created an uproar regarding Barak's conduct, and he chose to answer the accusations on the TV show, *Conference Call*. He rejected all the accusations and claimed that "the report [was] basically mendacious, biased and twisted... I never abandoned wounded soldiers, nor did I flee the scene... I told the truth to the two committees, as I always do... ."

The Knesset Audit Committee asked the state comptroller to investigate the affair. On 9 July 1997, the comptroller notified the committee that she had decided not to examine Barak's conduct during the evacuation of the wounded "because [she lacked] the legal tools with which to examine the conflicting testimonies." Barak reacted: "This is an unequivocal acquittal; the comptroller cleared me fully... ." The Likud claimed, however, that "the state comptroller had not clarified the affair."

The Direct Election of a Prime Minister

18 March

After a stormy and tense debate in the Knesset, the bill for the direct election of a prime minister [personally, not as head of a party] passed by a majority of one (57:56). The only coalition MK who voted with the opposition was Benjamin Netanyahu, who was not afraid of supporting the bill despite the fact that it was bitterly criticized by the heads of the Likud. The new election system was implemented in 1996 and, as a result, Netanyahu was elected prime minister.

Representatives of the bereaved families from the Tze'elim B disaster at a news conference. Photo: Oren Agmon

5 January

Eleven thousand Ethiopian immigrants were lodged in hotels because there was a delay in the connection of the caravan sites to the water pipes and electricity grid.

3 February

Ezer Weizman announced his retirement from politics and the Knesset.

14 February

Israeli Arabs attacked an IDF encampment near Kibbutz Gil'ad and axed three soldiers to death.

19 February

Yitzhak Rabin was elected Labor's candidate for prime minister after winning the party chairmanship, beating Shimon Peres by a slim majority.

9 March

Menachem Begin, former prime minister and Likud leader, died at the age of 79.

17 March

In Argentina, a car bomb blast destroyed the Israeli Embassy building in Buenos Aires, killing 22 and wounding 250.

2 May

A terrorist from Gaza stabbed 15-year-old Helena Rapp from Bat Yam to death. The murder sparked a riot in the city and stormy anti-government demonstrations were held.

23 June

A change of guard in the Knesset elections, with Labor under Yitzhak Rabin beating Likud under Yitzhak Shamir.

21 July

IAF soldier Amir Melet was killed and soldier Lilach Bar-Natan was badly wounded in a game of "net roulette" in an IAF base in the south.

8 September

Four social workers were murdered by a mentally disturbed young man who was in their care. He came to the premises to protest against the treatment he was receiving. After the murders, he barricaded himself on the roof of the building and was shot to death by the police.

17.12.92

The Deportation of Hamas Leaders to Lebanon

Non-Stop Rain

2 January

1992 was the year of rains and floods. Israel suffered stormy weather and the rainfall was far above average. The heavy rains caused floods, even forcing the Ayalon Highway, a major route in central Israel, to close down several times during January. The ones who were most affected by the floods were the residents of the caravan sites, who were evacuated due to repeated flooding.

After a stormy debate, the cabinet decided to make a dramatic move and deport 429 Hamas and Islamic Jihad activists from the territories to Lebanon for two years. The decision was made after a series of terror attacks, the last of which was the abduction and murder of Border Policeman Nissim Toledano by a Hamas squad. The decision was leaked that same night, and representatives of the deportees rushed to file a petition with the Supreme Court. Justice Aharon Barak issued an interim injunction ordering that the deportation be stopped. The next day, a seven-judge panel in the High Court of Justice approved the deportation by a majority of five to two, stating that the government had to give its reasons for choosing to carry out the deportation in that manner within 30 days. All that time, the deportees were waiting on buses near the Metulla border crossing, blindfolded and handcuffed.

The deportees were taken to the Zumariya crossing in the coastal region, between the Israeli-controlled security zone and the area controlled by the Lebanese. The deportation sparked a wave of international criticism, especially from the United States. The deportees were given very sympathetic media coverage that focused on the hard physical conditions with which they had to cope.

The deportation seriously harmed Israel's image. Following massive intervention by the US Administration, it was decided that 100 deportees would return at once, and the remaining ones – numbering over 300 – the next year.

The Hamas deportees' temporary camp at Marj al-Z'hur in Lebanon. Photo: Sygma

Menachem Begin Dies

9 March

Former Prime Minister Menachem Begin died at Ichilov Hospital in Tel Aviv at the age of 79. He was the Irgun commander before the founding of the state, and served as a Knesset member for the Herut Movement since 1948. In the early 1950s, he headed a campaign against the reparations agreement with the German Government. On the eve of the Six Day War, he joined a national unity government with Yosef Sapir and Moshe Dayan, but resigned when the government accepted the Rogers initiative. In May 1977, he headed the Likud in a political upheaval that made him prime minister. His biggest and most important achievement as prime minister was signing the peace accord with Egypt. In 1983, a year after Lebanon War (Operation "Peace for the Galilee"), Begin resigned as prime minister and lived in seclusion in his home until the day he died. Begin was one of the greatest and most admired Israeli leaders.

28 February

Aviv Geffen: "We Are a F*****-up Generation"

Photo: Razi

"I am not Yehonatan Geffen's son – he is Aviv's father."
Thus spake eighteen-and-a- half-year-old singer Aviv
Geffen, who was about to put out his first album,
in an interview. He was not serving in the IDF. "I
decided," he said, "that if I joined the army, I would
not see different things." His lyrics, often extremely
provocative, enraged the public. His song, We Are a
Fucked-up Generation, sparked sharp protests.

10 February

Kibbutzniks May Purchase Private Cars with Their Own Money - For the first time in the history of the Israeli Kibbutz Movement, kibbutz members were permitted to purchase private cars with their own money. This decision was made by Kibbutz Genigar. The kibbutz plenum ruled by an overwhelming majority that members could use money allocated to them by the kibbutz as personal budget, as well as funds from other sources such as gifts or inheritance, to buy themselves private cars. Four members of Genigar bought cars within two weeks after the decision was made.

1 August

First-Ever Israeli Medals at the Barcelona Olympics

For the first time ever, Israelis won Olympic medals: 24 hours after Yael Arad won a silver medal in the Women's Judo competition, Judoka Oren Smadja won a bronze medal. Smadja inflicted an Ipon (the Judo knockout) upon five rivals and then lost the semi-finals. Arad lost the finals to Frenchwoman Catherine Fleurie.

Yael Arad after winning the semi-finals. Photo: Yossi Roth

Photo: Ziv Koren

6 November

McDonald's in Israel, Too

McDonald's fast food chain arrived in Israel. The American company gave the franchise to run the company's branches in Israel to Omri Padan, who for several years previously was chairman of the Kitan textile company. A year later, the first McDonald's restaurant opened at the Ayalon mall in Ramat Gan.

4 October

An El Al 747 cargo jet crashed into a residential neighborhood in Amsterdam, Holland. Three Israeli crewmen and one passenger died in the disaster, as well as some 250 neighborhood residents.

15 October

Shas' battle against Education Minister Shulamit Aloni, demanding that she be removed from her post in view of her anti-religious remarks, reached its peak. Shas threatened to initiate a coalition crisis.

5 November

The Tze'elim B disaster: Five soldiers were killed and six wounded by a rocket that was fired at them by mistake during an exercise of the General Staff's elite commando unit at the Tze'elim training camp.

3 December

The remains of the 42 passengers of the *Egoz* were brought to Israel for burial. The *Egoz* sank in 1961 while smuggling Moroccan Jews to Israel.

17 December

In the wake of a massive wave of terrorism, the Israeli government decided to deport 429 Hamas and Islamic Jihad activists to Lebanon.

28 August

Knesset Member Yair Levy's Trial Begins
The trial of Shas MK Yair Levy opened at the Tel Aviv District Court. Together with his wife, he was charged with stealing half a million shekels from the *El Hama'ayan* fund. Levy claimed that the rabbis knew where the money was going, but refused to elaborate. Justice Arieh Segalson convicted Levy and issued a stiff sentence despite the plea bargain that had been worked out. Levi was sentenced to five years in prison.

1993

Signing the agreement between Israel and the PLO at the White House in Washington. Photo: Sygma

Prime Minister Yitzhak Rabin speaking at the ceremony. Photo: Sygma

The Oslo Agreement
The first, not the last step

Shimon Peres

Many people believe that in signing the Oslo agreement, Israel went the extra mile toward the Palestinians. The truth is, however, that Israel went an extra mile toward itself. The Labor Movement declared that it did not wish to rule over another nation – the Palestinian nation – against its will. To Yitzhak Rabin and to me, the Oslo agreement was a moral decision: We felt that Israel was strong enough to stop ruling over others.

The Oslo agreement was not only about making a moral decision; it was also about telling the truth. Our presence in Gaza was pointless. Our soldiers only served as targets for rocks and bullets, while we did not have a solution for the Gaza Strip and its inhabitants. The Gaza Strip had a negative strategic value because its 360 square km (of which the settlers occupied 50) were no compensation for the need to forcibly control one million people, very poor for the most part.

On the other hand, Arafat came to Oslo not because he believed that he could destroy Israel, but because he realized that the only way he could fulfill the Palestinian desires was through compromise.

It is easy to make moral decisions and tell the truth in theory. In practice, such decisions change old thinking patterns, expose our mistakes and cause resentment. In times of confrontation, when the nation negotiates with itself, we convince ourselves and settle our differences. However, when negotiations start with the opposite side, it appears that what we are looking for is a middle ground, namely, a compromise. Then it transpires that many people who support peace are not prepared to pay the price for it. It seems that it is easier to live with the price of war because it has been forced upon us. They forget that war costs incomparably more than peace.

To make an agreement, one needs a partner, a plan and a majority to support it. We realized that, of all the Palestinian partners, the PLO under Arafat was the most serious. We saw that the stories about the "Village Associations", the "local leadership" or the Hamas were incorrect. The PLO has always been the most important organization and Arafat its most authoritative leader. And it was not easy for us to come to terms with either the PLO or Arafat. I remember how hard it was for the late Yitzhak Rabin to shake Arafat's hand on the White House lawn. After he had done so, he whispered in my ear: "Now it's your turn," as if we were going through hell.

Yet, if it were not for Arafat, there would have been no agreement – not because he was the most extreme, but because he was the most realistic and flexible. He never became a Zionist, but he came to several difficult decisions: to leave terror behind; to advance in stages; to learn to live with the existing settlements; to leave Jerusalem out of the autonomy; and to understand that he would have to make compromises in the final stage as well. I am certain that deep down in his heart, he knows that the Palestinians will have to undergo a serious process of compromise regarding their future aspirations.

The Norwegians helped us with their modesty, discretion and enthusiasm which enabled our delegations and their heads – Uri Savir for Israel and Abu-Ala for the Palestinians – to create a suitable atmosphere for dialogue. We were assisted by Egypt. I believe that after I convinced President Mubarak of the importance of the first step (Gaza first), he was the one who convinced the Palestinians, after Rabin and I had agreed to add Jericho to the start of the process in order to counteract the impression that it would only be Gaza. We were greatly helped by the Americans. Warren Christopher and his team as well as Dennis Ross and the peace team were open to any idea and willing to provide any assistance. Clearly, however, most of the burden lay on Rabin as prime minister and, to a large extent, on me as foreign minister. It was our luck that after years of conflict between us, we found common ground: We decided that at our age, with our experience and prestige, we had to make difficult, inevitable and upsetting decisions so that the young generation would be able to enter a new era without yesterday's burdens and today's obstacles. This was not the custom, as politicians are thirsty for popularity and often postpone tough decisions for the next generation for the sake of popularity in their day and age.

The Oslo accord is a good agreement. There are problems because the government elected in 1996 is not a good government. It is neither faithful to Oslo nor does it have an alternative. After all, what is the point of talking about a permanent agreement where there is permanent disagreement on every point it requires?

I believe that the present government will fall and the Oslo agreement will last. I cannot see a force or majority that will take us back to Gaza, Nablus or other Palestinian villages and cities. I cannot see a force or majority that will be able to revoke the Palestinians' right to run their own affairs or their right to the territories or our recognition of them. "Repentance" will only lead to war; I cannot see a majority in Israel that would opt for another war of choice.

The Oslo agreement was a revolution in a land where the majority are conservative. This is why it is a controversial revolution. As we make progress toward the future, however, we will come to realize that it is the only true option because only a true understanding between us and the Palestinians, between us and the Jordanians, will secure a true peace. Israelis, Palestinians and Jordanians will have to live together, despite the fact that they may resemble Norwegian fjords, where sometimes the land invades the ocean and at other times the situation is reversed. There is no alternative to co-existence under such circumstances. I believe that we can already establish a sort of Benelux – economic co-operation between the three entities. I believe that none of the parties can prevent the Middle East from entering a new economic era of open borders, industry, agriculture and technologically and scientifically advanced services.

Israel is still divided into left and right, an old-fashioned division. Today's true division is between the forces of the past and the forces of the future. Oslo was the first step, not the last, that Israel made, daringly and intelligently, toward the future that belongs to our children and to the global future that already belongs to most of the world.

13.9.93

The Israel-PLO agreement: "No More Victims on Either Side"

The dramatic climax of the signing of the "document of principles" at the White House was the historic handshake between Yitzhak Rabin and Yasser Arafat. Although Rabin was clearly uncomfortable with the situation, the gesture signaled to the world, especially to the Israelis and the Palestinians, that the period of the bloody dispute between them was over. "Enough tears and blood," Rabin said in his speech. "No more victims on either side... ."

*The historic handshake between Yitzhak Rabin and Yasser Arafat.
Photo: Avi Ochayon, GPO*

According to the agreement signed by Shimon Peres and Abu-Mazen, Israel would recognize the PLO, withdraw from Gaza and Jericho, allow the establishment of Palestinian self-rule while the IDF withdrew from the West Bank towns, and start negotiations on a permanent arrangement that would be completed five years after the implementation of the Gaza and Jericho agreement. At the same time, the PLO would pledge to make peace with Israel, stop terror activity and expunge the clauses in the Palestinian Covenant that called for the destruction of Israel.

The agreement with the PLO was attained after a series of secret meetings that began in London, and continued in Oslo, the capital of Norway. They were conducted by two historians, Dr. Yair Hirschfeld and Ron Pundak. Deputy Foreign Minister Yossi Beilin was responsible for the initiative and, when the time was ripe, he let Foreign Minister Peres in on the issue. Prime Minister Yitzhak Rabin, who was informed about the talks at more advanced stages, gave the go-ahead.

The agreement was violently rejected by the Israeli right, which called for a civilian revolt and held stormy demonstrations all over Israel. There were also Palestinians that opposed the agreement. The rejectionist organizations – the Hamas, the Islamic Jihad and the PFLP – announced that they would sabotage the agreement by increasing terrorist activity against Israel.

Benjamin Netanyahu: "They Are Trying to Blackmail Me Over a Love Affair That I Had"

14 January

The "hot tape" affair started with a dramatic appearance by MK Benjamin Netanyahu on the Mabat tekevision newscast in which he told the astonished viewers: "Senior Likud members have been trying to blackmail me over a love affair I had. I was briefly involved with a woman, but it's over now." Those same people, Netanyahu added, warned that if he did not quit the race for Likud leadership, they would publicize a tape documenting his intimate relations with that woman. "I know who is behind this... He is a senior Likud member who is surrounded by criminals... A person who spies on others, taps phones and breaks into private property does not belong among the leaders; he belongs in jail," Netanyahu charged. Although he obstinately refused to reveal the name of the would-be blackmailer, it was obvious to all that he was referring to David Levy, who reacted immediately and sharply, accusing Netanyahu of "recklessness". The police became involved in the affair, but soon reached a dead-end. In the meantime, the identity of the other woman was revealed: a marketing consultant named Ruth Bar.
Ultimately, the "hot tape" affair did not harm Netanyahu's image. He defeated Levy roundly in the Likud primaries for party leadership, with 52% to Levy's 27%.

Benjamin Netanyahu and his wife Sarah. [The newspaper's headlines read: "Bibigate: He is no womanizer; women chase him"; "This is hard on us."]

Knife-Terrorism: 47 Murdered

A wave of knife-terrorism swept Israel during the year. March was the worst month, with 14 Israelis stabbed to death by Hamas and Islamic Jihad terrorists all over the country. The atmosphere was terrible, and the police commissioner urged citizens to carry weapons at all times. The public pressured the government to fight terrorism in every possible way. Numerous protest vigils were staged, demanding that Yitzhak Rabin step down as defense minister. Rabin, who vowed that he would fight terrorism relentlessly, imposed a closure on the territories and beefed up IDF units there.

Terrorism continued nonetheless. There was a brief lull until Israel and the PLO signed the agreement in September, but between mid-September and mid-November, seven more Israelis were murdered by rejectionist front terrorists.

At the end of December, Lieutenant Colonel Meir Mintz, the Gaza Brigade operations officer, was murdered by a Hamas squad. He was the highest-ranking officer to be killed since the *intifadah* first started. The Hamas issued a leaflet stating that Mintz had been murdered in order to avenge the death of Imad Akil, head of the Izz al-Din al-Kassam squad. In 1993, 47 Israelis were murdered and 86 wounded by Palestinian terrorists.

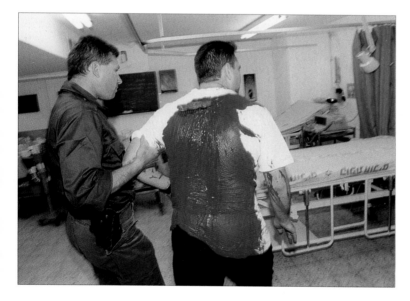

Eli Glicker who was stabbed in the back in Jerusalem is taken to hospital. Photo: Zoom 77

Ezer Weizman Elected Israel's Seventh President

Photo: Daniel Morzansky

24 March

The Knesset elected Labor candidate Ezer Weizman president: 66 MKs voted for him, while 53 voted for Likud candidate Dov Shilansky. He replaced Haim Herzog. After his election, Weizman said: "I know quite well what I may not do in my new capacity, but I do not know what I may do. But don't worry. I will not do anything unless I have the government's permission. I have plans for a new concept of the presidency."

Israel's Soccer Team Beats France

Photo: Avi Ochayon, GPO

13 October

The Israeli soccer team achieved international success when it beat the strong French team in Paris, 3:2. The lead went back and forth several times, and the victory goal was scored by Reuven Atar during the very last seconds. The Israeli team, however, did not make it to the World Cup finals.

11 January

The state comptroller harshly criticized Labor's conduct on the issue of party financing, stating that the party "purchased control with money".

9 February

Bank of Israel Governor, Ya'akov Frenkel, said that the stock exchange was a "financial bubble" and caused sharp drops in share prices.

21 February

New chief rabbis were elected: Rabbi Eliahu Bakshi-Doron as Sephardi Chief Rabbi and Yisrael Lau as Ashkenazi Chief Rabbi.

24 March

Ezer Weizman was elected Israel's seventh president.

31 March

Rafi Peled was appointed the new commissioner of the Israel Police.

30 May

The crisis between Shas and Meretz Minister Shulamit Aloni ended. Aloni was replaced by Amnon Rubinstein as education and culture minister and received the communications and science portfolio instead.

20 June

A bill of indictment was filed against Shas Minister Arieh Deri. He resigned after the Supreme Court had intervened.

7 July

A magnificent mosaic floor dating from the first centuries and showing a zodiac was excavated at Tzipori.

25.7.93

Operation Accountability: Reaction to Katyusha Shelling

Following the extensive shelling of Kiryat Shmona and the Galilee, the IDF reacted with a massive shelling of 60 terrorist targets in south Lebanon. The Hizballah retaliated with additional Katyusha salvos that killed two Israeli civilians and wounded 13. The deterioration of the security situation lead to Operation Accountability. The IDF shelled terrorist targets from land and air, and then shelled Shiite villages, intending to make the residents flee northward toward Beirut. The government and the IDF believed that the residents' plight would pressure the Lebanese Government and the Syrians into forcing the Hizballah back to the old rules according to which civilian settlements were not to be attacked.

Not only did 400,000 Shiite civilians flee the region following the IDF shelling, but many of the Kiryat Shmona residents fled the city and moved south as well.

The international community and Israeli public opinion fiercely opposed Operation Accountability, which ended six days later in a cease-fire attained through US mediation. The parties reached understandings according to which the Hizballah would not fire at the northern settlements and the IDF would avoid firing at south Lebanese villages.

IDF troops going on Operation Accountability. Photo: Avi Ochayon, GPO

New Mayors: Milo, Olmert, and Mitzna

2 November

Three young men won the municipal elections in Tel Aviv, Haifa and Jerusalem. Olmert defeated Teddy Kollek, who had been mayor of Jerusalem for 27 years, after reaching an agreement with the ultra-Orthodox community, thus tilting the electoral balance in his favor. Roni Milo, who ran on an independent ticket, defeated Labor candidate Avigdor Kahalani, replacing Shlomo Lahat. Amram Mitzna won a relatively easy victory in Haifa, where he replaced Arieh Gur'el.

Left to right: Jerusalem Mayor Ehud Olmert, Tel Aviv Mayor Roni Milo and Haifa Mayor Amram Mitzna. Photo: Tzvi Tischler

93

1993

17 June

In Spite of Everything... Elton John Returned to Israel

Photo: Abigail Uzi

Elton John's single concert in Israel took place at Tel Aviv's Yarkon Park 48 hours after the scheduled date. The day before, John left Israel before the concert "because of incidents at the airport and the hotel that jeopardized his safety." He was finally convinced to return. At the beginning of his concert, the rock idol apologized to tens of thousands of his fans, who welcomed him with unqualified enthusiasm.

25 February

Yehezkiel Aslan, Crime Leader, Murdered - The authorities feared that a war might break out in the criminal underworld following the murder of Yehezkiel Aslan, who was considered one of the heads of Israeli crime. He was shot five times in the back at close range while he was leaving a restaurant at dawn. His bodyguards were not with him. Thousands of residents of the Hatikva neighborhood came to the funeral. Another leading criminal, Ze'ev Rosenstein, was later arrested as a suspect, but was released.

Photo: Michael Kramer

18 August

The New Tel Aviv Central Bus Station Opens - Twenty-six years after a decision was made to construct it, the new Tel Aviv central bus station was opened. The construction of the station was finally completed after the building had stood empty for many years, becoming an environmental hazard. The opening was fraught with legal battles and stormy demonstrations by the residents who lived nearby. They claimed that, contrary to what they had been promised, they had not been compensated for damage to their property and the deterioration in their quality of life.

19 May

Maccabi Tel Aviv Loses the Championship

The Maccabi Tel Aviv basketball team lost the title for the first time in 23 years. It lost the fifth play-off semi-finals game against Hapo'el Galil Elyon 88:80, losing the series 3:2. Pini Gershon, the winning coach, roared to the TV cameras: "We've taken a giant step... I am like a bear that loves cream, but really wants the cherry on the top... ." The team from the Galilee later won the finals against Hapo'el Tel Aviv and, for the first time ever, even won the state championship.

Doron Sheffer, captain of Hapo'el Galil Elyon, holding the championship trophy.
Photo: Ariel B'sor

25 July

Operation Accountability got under way in south Lebanon after Kiryat Shmona and the Galilee were hit by Katyusha rockets. The IDF first shelled 60 terrorist targets and then villages north of the security zone, attempting to force the residents to flee north. After six days, a cease-fire and new understandings were reached between the two sides.

13 September

Israel and the PLO signed the "agreement of principles", and Rabin and Arafat shook hands in Washington.

2 November

Municipal elections were won by Ehud Olmert in Jerusalem, by Roni Milo in Tel Aviv and by Amram Mitzna in Haifa.

4 November

Television's commercial Second Channel began broadcasting.

2 December

MIA Zecharia Baumel's dog-tag was given to his parents by PLO representatives. He has been missing since the Sultan Yakub battle during the Lebanon War.

30 December

Israel and the Vatican signed an agreement for the establishment of diplomatic relations.

25 January

Prof. Yeshayahu Leibovich Renounces the Israel Prize

The dispute surrounding the nomination of Prof. Yeshayahu Leibovich as Israel Prize laureate ended when the professor announced that he was renouncing the award. "I did not expect the uproar that followed the announcement that I would be awarded the Israel Prize. Now I do not want it. I have been paid tributes, and I have all the honor I need." This is how the professor explained his decision. He added that one of the reasons that led him to his decision was Prime Minister Yitzhak Rabin's reaction that he would not attend the ceremony. The right wing was pleased to hear Leibovich's announcement.

Photo: Zoom 77

(1994

The massacre in the Cave of the Patriarchs: The widow of one of the dead with her ten children.
Photo: Zoom 77

Evacuating the wounded after the massacre. Photo: Zoom 77

The Massacre in the Cave of the Patriarchs
Terror Wearing a *Yarmulke*

Rabbi Yehuda Amital

It was early in the morning of Purim 1994 that Dr. Baruch Goldstein, a resident of Kiryat Arba and physician by profession, entered the Isaac Hall at the Cave of the Patriarchs and suddenly opened fire on Muslim worshippers. He killed 29 people and wounded scores. The shooting came as a reaction to a series of murderous attacks by Palestinian terror groups in which some of Goldstein's friends had been killed. However, the act should not be seen as merely one of vengeance. Goldstein was attempting to ignite the territories in a heroic and dramatic move, in the hopes that this would halt the talks between Israel and the Palestinian Authority, thus preventing the implementation of the Oslo agreements.

He failed in this mission, but he did manage to stain the Jewish people and the Torah with the blood of the innocent. In addition to the moral and religious baseness of killing innocent people while they were praying to the Creator, the dreadful murder profaned the name of God in the eyes of the whole world.

The Israeli public was appalled to discover that the phenomenon of ideological violence against innocent Arabs could exist within it – violence which might be directed against political rivals, Jews, and which could lead to bloodshed. Indeed, there had already been several frightening warnings: Ami Popper killing Arabs in a city street, or Yona Avrushmi killing *Peace Now* activist Emil Grunzweig in Jerusalem.

That Purim was different, however. Dr. Goldstein was admired by his community; he was a devoted physician, a public activist, an idealist and a God-fearing man. The worst thing of all is that his behavior was apparently motivated by his religion.

He probably chose the holiday of Purim for the murder so that he could obey the biblical injunction to "eliminate the Amalekites", thus de-humanizing all Arabs. Our ancestors realized that, when placed in the wrong hands, the Torah might turn into deadly poison. But it was still impossible to imagine that anyone might perpetrate a massacre in the name of the Torah, about which Maimonides said: "The only revenge the Torah takes is through mercy, compassion and peace in this world."

The sin against the children of Ishmael, son of Abraham, is just one aspect of the problem. Another aspect is the terrible sin against God and the Torah, whose path is peaceful. How could this man dare to clothe the Torah in such cruelty and hideousness? It became apparent that not only Islam, but orthodox Judaism too might have a harmful weed growing at the periphery of its garden; that terror might be wearing a *yarmulke*; that not enough had been done to eradicate such twisted and distorted concepts and ideas from those who teach and study the Torah.

Fundamental principles were undermined when a nationalist-religious ideology was created here, flaunting its extremist political standpoint against the backdrop of the bloody 100-year-old Israeli-Arab conflict. Central ideas such as personal and national morality and the sanctity of human life were shoved aside by belligerence, hatred, nationalism and racism. Meir Kahana's followers symbolized most of all that dangerous and malignant tumor of distorted nationalism in Israel. The Kahanist hoodlums were supposedly going by Kahana's "Jewish idea" when they casually damaged Arab property, smashing windows and water tanks and slashing the tires of cars, not to mention threatening, badmouthing and cursing political rivals whose ideas did not fully correspond with Kahana's. Baruch Goldstein was an avowed Kahanist.

The massacre in the Cave of the Patriarchs shocked every decent human being. Not less shocking, however, was the extent of support and sympathy for Goldstein's act. For the first time, the public was exposed to the unexpected magnitude of the understanding, agreement and even admiration for the murderer and his deed. Before the massacre, Israeli society knew about the narrow marginal Kahana group, but it appeared that the mass murder in Hebron was supported by a much wider margin. Indeed, political and educational establishments publicly condemned the murders, but in the ordinary ranks of various Jewish circles, there was a completely different picture.

Kiryat Arba rejoiced. Residents of many settlements in Judea and Samaria burst into songs of praise, and youngsters all over Israel, both religious and secular, spoke of Goldstein as a hero or a saint.

A handful of Kiryat Arba educators who wished to condemn the murder publicly were too afraid to do so. Important rabbis refused to condemn the murder unequivocally, nor did they attempt to explain or justify its motives. Hundreds of religious Jews in traditional ultra-Orthodox clothes participated in Goldstein's funeral. The head of the largest yeshiva in Kiryat Arba eulogized him, calling him a saint. His grave has turned into a shrine and a memorial has been erected there. Jerusalem bookstores sell books praising the deeds of the heroic doctor. And we are amazed: How could such a simplistic and dangerous idea – that everything can be settled by force – take root here?

Apparently, quite a large number of circles in Israel believe in the naïve concept that the use of force is the only solution to everything: to the Israeli-Arab conflict, to terror, wars and violence; the reason for our problems and our national plight is that we do not wield this force.

It seems that Goldstein's horrendous act led to an escalation of Arab terrorism. More innocent people died – this time Jews. Revenge attacks were waged in Afula and Hadera shortly after that, and the overwhelming waves of hatred, hostility, violence and bloodshed gained strength yet again.

One of the people who attended Baruch Goldstein's mass funeral was an unknown young man from Herzlia. He was stirred by the "devotion" of Goldstein and his followers. That man was Yig'al Amir who, in less than two years, would perpetuate the terrible madness by spilling the blood of Israel's prime minister.

25.2.94

The Massacre in the Cave of the Patriarchs: "A Loathsome Man"

Early on Friday morning, the festival of Purim, Baruch Goldstein, a Kiryat Arba resident and physician by profession, arrived at the Cave of the Patriarchs. He was wearing a military uniform with the insignia of a captain and carrying an M-16 automatic rifle. The IDF soldiers guarding the site recognized him and, thinking he had come to pray, did not detain him. At the entrance to the cave, a Muslim Wakf guard stopped him, telling him that he could not enter the Isaac Hall. Goldstein replied that he was an IDF officer, went around him, entered the hall and started shooting in every direction like a madman. As he was trying to replace the fourth clip, one of the worshippers managed to overpower him, snatch his gun and smash his head with an iron bar. Before he was eliminated, Baruch Goldstein killed 29 Arab worshippers and wounded 125.

The news of the massacre spread rapidly throughout the territories. The sight of bodies being evacuated from the Cave of the Patriarchs, the screams of the wounded and the pools of blood sparked an unprecedented outburst of fury in the territories. Massive riots and disturbances broke out all over the West Bank. The Arab world issued grave threats against Israel, and Jordan, Syria and the Palestinian Authority suspended political negotiations with Israel. The cabinet held a special session after the massacre, and decided to establish a state commission of inquiry, headed by Supreme Court President Meir Shamgar. Addressing the Knesset session, Prime Minister Yitzhak Rabin called Baruch Goldstein "a Jewish Hamas member, a loathsome man from Hebron who disgraced us all... I tell him and the likes of him: You do not belong to the nation of Israel... You are an alien strain, an evil weed. You shame Zionism and disgrace Judaism...."

The Shamgar commission summoned numerous IDF officers in order to determine whether or not the security arrangements at the cave were sufficient. Most convincing was Chief of Staff Ehud Barak who said in his testimony: "This incident fell upon us like a bolt from the blue." The committee determined that Goldstein had operated alone and had not been assisted or covered by others. It recommended that the security arrangements at the Cave of the Patriarchs undergo drastic changes.

The Cave of the Patriarchs after the massacre. Photo: The Muslim Wakf

Photo: GPO

Rabin, Peres and Arafat Receive the Nobel Peace Prize

10 December

Israeli Prime Minister Yitzhak Rabin, Foreign Minister Shimon Peres and PA Chairman Yasser Arafat received the Nobel Peace Prize for their efforts to promote peace in the Middle East and solving the Israeli-Palestinian conflict. Rabin and Peres tried to play down the historic event, and their demeanor was in fact reserved and low-key.

Peace Agreement With Jordan Signed

Photo: Sygma

Israel and Jordan signed a peace agreement in a moving ceremony at the new border crossing of Evrona, north of Eilat.

The heat and strong desert wind notwithstanding, the ceremony was attended by King Hussein, President Ezer Weizman, Prime Minister Yitzhak Rabin and the guest of honor, US President Bill Clinton. A grain of sand got into Clinton's eye, causing his eyes to tear and making the ceremony look particularly human and emotional. King Hussein made a moving speech, saying: "This is the day in which hopes, promises and determination shall prevail... We, all the children of Abraham, shall cherish and remember this day, which is the dawn of a new era of peace." Prime Minister Rabin said: "I have but one dream – to give the next generation a better and more peaceful world."

The signing of the Israeli-Jordanian peace accord at a ceremony in the Arava, attended by US President Clinton, Jordan's King Hussein, President Weizman, Prime Minister Rabin and many guests. Photo: GPO

The ceremony in the Arava symbolized the culmination of 30 years of secret talks between Israel and Jordan. King Hussein always feared holding overt talks with Israel, mainly because of the Syrians. He accepted Rabin and Peres' invitation to initiate overt negotiations for an official peace contract between the two countries only after the agreement with the PLO had been signed. The US Administration played an important part in expediting the negotiations, promising King Hussein that Jordan's debts would be canceled, while economic and military aid would be granted.

On 25 July, three months before the ceremony in Evrona, a meeting took place in Washington in which Hussein and Rabin signed the "Washington Declaration", according to which "the two countries recognize their right and obligation to live in peace with each other as well as with all states within secure and recognized boundaries. The two states affirm their respect for and acknowledgment of the sovereignty, territorial integrity and political independence of every state in the area."

Before the agreement was signed, the parties had to deal with problems and disagreements, mainly about water rights and border demarcation. But, thanks to the warm personal bonds forged between Hussein and Rabin, the disagreements were settled in direct talks between the two. The peace accord with Jordan won the enthusiastic support of the Israeli public; 105 MKs voted for it, while only three Moledet MKs voted against it. The agreement with Jordan was given national consensus and accompanied by a hope for true peace with our neighbor in the east.

Nachshon Wachsman Abducted and Murdered

9 October

The Hamas squad that abducted Soldier Nachshon Wachsman involved the entire country in its deed by means of a videotape in which the abducted soldier was seen appealing to the government, asking that it release Hamas leader Sheikh Ahmad Yassin. After an investigation by the intelligence branch, the house where the soldier was being held was located – a fortified house in the township of Bir Naballah. A General Staff elite force that stormed the building could not break through the barricaded iron doors and, by the time the soldiers got in, the terrorists had murdered Wachsman. Captain Nir Poraz, commander of the raiding force, was also killed during the operation.

A masked Hamas member with soldier Nachshon Wachsman on the abduction tape.

1994

25 February
Baruch Goldstein murdered 29 Muslim worshippers and wounded 125 in the Cave of the Patriarchs, causing rage in the Arab world, massive riots in the territories and angry reactions in Israel.

23 March
Demanding that the state investigate the affair of the missing Yemenite children, Rabbi Uzi Meshulam and a group of his followers barricaded themselves in a house in Yahud and fired at anyone who approached them. The police captured him only two months later. His followers turned themselves in.

10 April
The Jerusalem District Court sentenced the defendants in the banker's trial, fining some and sentencing others to prison.

13 April
A suicide terrorist blew himself up on a bus in Hadera, killing five and wounding 30.

17 April
There were initial reports in the press that the dailies, *Yedioth Ahronoth* and *Ma'ariv,* had been wiretapping each other.

10 May
Haim Ramon and his list *Haim Hadashim* [New Life] won a landslide victory in the Histadrut Labor Federation elections, defeating the Labor list under Haim Haberfeld. Ramon was later made Histadrut secretary-general.

16 May
The IDF completed the evacuation of the Gaza Strip, ending 27 years of Israeli rule there.

12 June
The Lubavicher Rabbi died at the age of 92. After declaring him the Messiah, the Hassidic sect of Habad were in total shock.

1 July
Yasser Arafat arrived on his first visit to Gaza after the IDF evacuation.

18 August
Prof. Yeshayahu Leibovich, the "prophet of doom" who was considered the greatest Israeli philosopher, died at the age of 91.

16.5.**94**

The Evacuation of the Gaza Strip

Netanyahu: "The beginning of the second War of Independence."

IDF soldiers leaving Gaza City.
Photo: Eyal Fisher

In a quick march, IDF soldiers completed their evacuation of the Gaza Strip. The muezzins broadcast chants of joy and the residents raided the building of the IDF command in the strip, trying to break into the symbol of the 27-year Israeli occupation. The majority of the Israeli public also sighed with relief because the Gaza Strip had become a burden for the IDF soldiers who had to deal with violent demonstrations, stone-throwing, firebombs and occasional attacks with firearms that left many soldiers dead or wounded.

The evacuation was preceded by lengthy negotiations that reached their peak at the signing ceremony in Cairo, attended by heads of state and foreign ministers. In a dramatic, last-minute move, Arafat refused to sign the maps. Prime Minister Rabin announced that there would be no agreement made unless Arafat signed. The negotiations resumed in front of international TV cameras, with everyone exerting heavy pressure on Arafat. Eventually, President Mubarak, nervous and angry, managed to convince Arafat to sign the all the maps and documents together with Yitzhak Rabin.

The agreement was severely criticized by the opposition. MK Benjamin Netanyahu, the Likud leader, declared: "Today, Rabin signed the beginning of the second War of Independence."

The Government Decides to Impose a Capital Gains Tax

16 August

Prime Minister Yitzhak Rabin deliberated for a long time before approving the Finance Ministry proposal to impose a capital gains tax. Finance Minister Avraham (Baiga) Shohat convinced him that it would benefit the economy and, in the long run, would turn the stock exchange into a better and more stable investment instrument. Rabin finally agreed.

The storm started the next day. Some $2 billion worth of shares were put out for sale and indices plunged. The stock exchange panicked and investors were enraged. The media also criticized the decision and senior economic experts attacked the tax. When Rabin realized the magnitude of the criticism, he decided to recant – and his associates leaked his decision. Baiga Shohat reacted angrily: "Leaders must have strength of character and determination, and not act according to popularity charts and wheeling and dealing." Rabin, however, was determined to cancel the tax. "It is permissible to admit to a mistake," he said. At end of January 1995, the finance minister announced officially that the tax had been abolished, and the stock exchange celebrated by massive share purchasing.

Haim Ramon after his election as Histadrut secretary-general. Photo: Zoom 77

"New Life" In the Histadrut

10 May

Ever since the Histadrut labor union was founded in 1920, Labor ruled it unchallenged. On 10 May 1994, this rule ended after the *Haim Hadashim* [New Life] faction, led by Haim Ramon, won a landslide victory over the Labor list headed by Haim Haberfeld. Ramon, a former health minister, won some 50% of the votes, surprising the entire political establishment. Ramon quit Labor after his health bill initiative was never put to the vote due to the pressure of his opponents in the Knesset and the Histadrut. He served as Histadrut secretary-general for 18 months and made several organizational changes that significantly weakened the labor union. He returned to the cabinet after Rabin's assassination and was replaced by Amir Peretz.

94

12 June

"Long Live Our Messiah King!"

Kfar Habad, the center of the Habad Hassidic sect, was shocked and embarrassed when the Lubavicher Rabbi died. Although many sang, "Long live our Messiah king!", other more worried voices could be heard as well. One of the Hassidim said: "I do not know what I will do tomorrow. A whole set of goals must be re-examined. We believed that the rabbi was the Messiah. Now that we realize he is not, we do not know what to do."

Photo: AP

11 August

Mickey Berkovich Goes to Play for Hapo'el Tel Aviv – "When I go to their court for the first training session, I will be making history," Mickey Berkovich said at a news conference. Berkovich, the superstar of Maccabi Tel Aviv, is considered the best Israeli basketball player ever. His last club was Hapo'el Tel Aviv. At the end of 1995, a special farewell game was held in his honor: the European team against Maccabi Tel Aviv. In the second half, the local team consisted of the mythological players who won the European cup for the first time: Aulcie Perry, Jim Boatwright, Lou Silver, Motti Aroesti and Tal Brody.

Photo: Moshe Shai

16 October

Amos Mansdorf Retires Tearfully – The superb tennis player, Amos Mansdorf, quit the game after losing the final game of the Ramat Hasharon tournament to South African Wayne Ferreira. Thousands of his fans came to watch him play his farewell game. He thanked them and burst into tears. Mansdorf, who was considered the best Israeli tennis player ever, was also very successful worldwide.

7 March

An IDF Soldier Facing A Gaza Child

An AP photographer immortalized a drama that occurred at the Jabalyah refugee camp in Gaza. A soldier aimed his gun at a child who was throwing rocks at him but, seeing that the child was not deterred, retreated. The picture created a public uproar. The left justified the soldier's action, but NRP Rabbi Haim Druckman said: "The soldier has twisted moral values; he should have shot the child."

26 August

Yehoshafat Harkavi, an Israel Prize laureate and one of the founders of the Israeli intelligence branch, died. He was a professor at the Hebrew University and a world expert on the Israeli-Arab conflict.

9 October

Soldier Nachshon Wachsman was kidnapped by Hamas terrorists and held in a village near Ramallah. An attempt to rescue him failed. The terrorists shot him as soon as the battle started.

19 October

A suicide bomber blew himself up on a number 5 bus near Dizengoff Square in Tel Aviv, killing 22 people and wounding dozens.

26 October

Israel and Jordan signed a peace accord in the Arava, in the presence of President Clinton.

10 December

The Nobel Peace Prize was awarded jointly to Arafat, Rabin and Peres in Oslo.

6 November

The Tank That Ran Amok on the Highway – A tank mechanic, Sergeant Amit Nechemia from Yahud, stole a tank from the Julis base and sped down major highways in southern Israel. He was chased for over 20 km. Near Moshav Ben Zacai, the tank hit a bus, lightly wounding eight passengers. He surrendered at 01:30 a.m. after lengthy negotiations during which he fired at the policemen. "He was very distressed because his relations with people on his base were bad," Superintendent Yifrach Duchovny said after convincing Nechemia to give himself up.

Photo: Appelbaum

10 May

The Uzi Meshulam Affair: The Drama Ends – Uzi Meshulam and 100 of his followers managed to drive the country crazy after he barricaded himself in his house in Yahud and threatened to shoot anyone who tried to break in. Meshulam demanded that the state establish a commission of inquiry to investigate the fate of the missing children of Yemenite immigrants in the 1950s. All the attempts to get the group to surrender of their free own will failed, and the people inside the house fired at the policemen and passing cars.
Police Commissioner Assaf Hefetz put an end to the affair when he managed to convince Meshulam to meet him late at night at the nearby Avia Hotel. When Meshulam and his cohorts arrived, they were apprehended by the police and taken into custody. The police then broke into the house in Yahud, but Meshulam's people would not surrender and fired at the police officers and even at a police helicopter. A police sapper shot at one of the men, Shlomo Assoulin, and killed him.
Meshulam was sentenced to eight years in prison. He appealed the sentence and the High Court of Justice reduced his term to six and a half years.

Photo: Tzvi Tischler

(*1995*

Thousands of candles in front of the coffin of late Prime Minister Yitzhak Rabin at the Knesset plaza in Jerusalem

The world's greatest leaders came to pay last respects to Yitzhak Rabin. Photo: Zoom 77

In Memory of Yitzhak Rabin
Only a Warrior Would Have Been Able to Meet Us Halfway

King Hussein of Jordan

With an outstanding record of a man such as Yitzhak Rabin, there is indeed very little to add. As a soldier, he defended his country for many years. As a premier, his record stands for strengthening his country's economy, and as peacemaker, he was a joint recipient of the Nobel Prize for Peace in December 1994. That was his greatest legacy, for it took a warrior to cross the divide, take courage and meet us half way. He laid the foundation necessary to heal the wounds, he brought the Middle East closer to peace, and he was Israel's courageous champion of peace.

Rabin fell as he took a stand against violence, as he sang the song for peace. My friend fought for as long as there was no chance for peace. These were his words at the Tel Aviv Rally the night he fell. When the right moment came, my friend and partner rose up to the challenge. The majority of the Israeli people supported him, as did a majority of the Middle East. With my friend, we stood against the forces of darkness, violence and the enemies of life and true faith. With my friend, we stood for those who wished a better and brighter tomorrow for the Children of Abraham, the followers of the three monotheistic religions. They all deserve a better life.

He was determined to work hard for peace. He fell for the cause. Israel and the entire world mourned him. We mourned him. We know the meaning of losing a leader, for we in Jordan have lost leaders in the cause for peace. My grandfather fell in Jerusalem for peace. Both were martyrs of peace. The people of the Middle East should learn and take lessons from their honourable and worthy legacy.

Before Jordan's peace treaty with Israel was signed in October 1994, both Rabin and I signed the Washington Declaration and addressed a special joint session of the United States Congress. When he addressed the Amman Economic Summit in October 1995, he spoke of his "desire to weave a fabric of co-existence and co-operation, a fabric resistant to the pressures, scepticism and outright sabotage to disrupt and derail the peace process". We worked together exactly to avoid such a situation. During that time, he showed enough humility and displayed so much courage to understand our point of view and our position. Eventually it took two sides to make peace. I shall always be grateful for his understanding.

We all hope that our coming generations will not suffer as we did, and will enjoy the fruits of peace that we could not. There is still a great chance for peace. Our achievements thus far must not be allowed to wither. Existing agreements must be given the opportunity to prove not only that peaceful co-existence can prevail, but normality, humanity and co-operation become the mark of the day. Yitzhak Rabin provided the lead to his people and left a legacy unsurpassed in the Middle East. My hope and aspiration is to build further, to replace despair and hopelessness by honour and dignity among all peoples of the region. This is what my fellow shepherd of peace, Yitzhak Rabin, wished for his people. It is my hope and wish too. Both Arab and Jew must not lose that spirit. Both Arab and Jew, who yearn for peace surely, miss him.

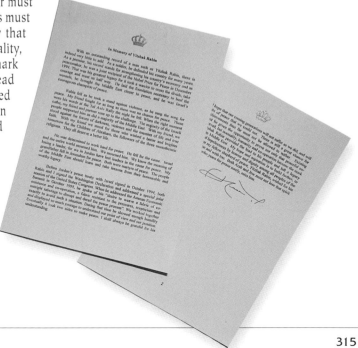

Shocked citizens outside Ichilov Hospital
upon hearing the announcement of
Prime Minister Yitzhak Rabin's death.
Photo: Ziv Koren.

Yitzhak Rabin – Commander of Commanders
His heart stopped beating, but his soul sparked renewed hope

Ehud Barak

When Yitzhak Rabin's coffin was lowered into the grave, when tears flowed unceasingly, when earth filled the pit and the *El Maleh Rachamim* prayer rent our hearts, I looked at the prime minister's grieving family and weeping friends all around me. Then I looked a little further, several meters behind the guard of honor and the crowd that was gathered there, down the mountain. In the shadow of the lush trees, the ground was crowded with marble tombstones and inscriptions in the color of clay: Soldiers' serial numbers, ranks, first names, last names, dates of birth and dates of death. Mount Herzl is covered with graves. It was only symbolic that the commander of commanders, the IDF guide, was laid to rest on the peak of Mount Herzl, surrounded by thousands of his warriors, IDF soldiers who went to their death, some while following his orders. And they belonged to all eras: fighters from the convoys to Jerusalem; those who broke the siege and died before their prime; those who were lost in retaliation operations; victims of routine security operations; those who died in the Sinai Campaign; those who liberated Jerusalem in the Six Day War; paratroopers; soldiers of the "Harel" and the Jerusalem Brigades; pilots; infantry men; pretty young girls; and boys who had not even started shaving.

I believe that the Six Day War was the highest peak of Yitzhak Rabin's life. He knew many good hours, perhaps more than any other Israeli leader, but also many moments of grief. Yitzhak, who was born in Jerusalem and commanded weaponless boys there during the War of Independence, presented the people of Israel with the city as a painful gift in June 1967. The commander of the "Harel" Brigade during the War of Independence and the chief of staff during the Six Day War led his soldiers back to his own cradle and that of the nation. We were very young boys when Yitzhak Rabin, himself a boy, led the "Harel" Brigade in the cruel battles of 1948. We were young boys when we were first given guns. Since then, for decades, when we looked up at the top of the Israeli defense establishment, he was almost always there: A commander and a guide, a tutor and an educator, a man and a friend.

Now he is up there, and we are here, alone.

In the 1960s, Yitzhak Rabin sent us across the border for our first retaliation operations. Time after time, he sent us deep into enemy territory, letting us be chief of staff in the field; but he stayed up all night, waiting for us in the front command post, worrying, chain-smoking, almost biting his nails, in order to provide us with the safety net of his backing and experience. We could hear his heart beating miles away from our home and the border.

Years later, when he was defense minister, I sat with him in an IAF command post, listening silently and tensely to the voices of our pilots over the radio, watching them on the monitors as they raided targets. We looked straight into his eyes when the moment of truth arrived and he had to make a decision to send our troops off on a mission from which some might not return. We saw some of the greatest moments of victory, satisfaction and pride together; but Yitzhak was also always first on the black or red phone to receive the bad news of casualties like heavy hammer blows. We always went to meet the soldiers in the field, to look into the faces of the 18- or 20-year-olds after battles in which they had lost their commanders and friends. And Yitzhak questioned them about every detail, never letting up or cutting corners, demanding, urging the commanders on, supporting and backing up the young soldiers.

Together we went to meet the families, choked with tears. To see the wide-open eyes of the bereaved parents, widows and children who had lost their loved ones. And Yitzhak would grit his teeth, gird his loins and talk straight to their broken hearts.

With Yitzhak we knew, as all IDF soldiers have always known, that making our existence safe was the only thing that guided his decisions. Nothing was dearer to him than human life, and we knew he would not put lives at risk if it were not to that end. IDF soldiers and members of other security branches always knew that, beyond his close family, they were his first love. That is why they followed him and always believed in him.

Rabin's leadership was established upon five central pillars. First: The shy naïvety of a gifted boy from the Kaduri School, and the simplicity and truthfulness which radiated from all his deeds. Second: The ruthless and realistic sobriety of his judgment and assessments. Third: His sharp and decisive appraisal that enabled him to distinguish between the wheat and the chaff. Fourth: Knowing how to get the people around him involved in creative co-operation. And last, and perhaps most important: Always being a captain with a compass, not a weather-vane; always knowing the right direction to follow, not the direction of the wind.

He carried these five elements with him during his military service as well as during his political life. Hand in hand with Shimon Peres, he made the historic decision to lead the peace process and the separation from the Palestinians – from a position of choice based on power and self-confidence combined with political wisdom, strategic daring and security considerations – and led us to where we are today.

This combination of political determination and responsibility to security will not be stopped either by the bullets of a Jewish gun or by the explosion of an Islamic Jihad bomb. A sovereign state and an elected government are not supposed to surrender to terrorism, regardless of its source. Yitzhak's heart stopped beating, but his soul sparked renewed hope in this pain-filled country. The youngsters who wept for Yitzhak Rabin in the city squares and lit candles for him will not forget his magic – the magic of a brave soldier and a courageous leader who showed us the path and the hope, and paid with his life for doing so.

I loved Yitzhak when he was alive. We all did. The bloodstain on the sheet containing the lyrics of the *Song of Peace* that was in his pocket sanctified this love of ours. After all, it was he who loved to hear the words of *Hare'ut* [The Song of Friendship] so much: "Love sanctified with blood / will keep on blooming among us."

Farewell, our beloved Yitzhak.

Yitzhak Rabin Assassinated:
"Shalom, Haver!"

Yitzhak Rabin singing the "Song of Peace" minutes before he was assassinated. Photo: Michael Kramer

Chief of Staff Amnon Shahak laying a wreath on Yitzhak Rabin's grave. Photo: Zoom 77

"**V**iolence is eroding the foundations of Israeli democracy. It must be condemned, denounced and isolated. It is not the way of the State of Israel." Prime Minister Yitzhak Rabin made these remarks in his last speech during the peace rally on 4 November 1995 at Malchei Yisrael Square in Tel Aviv.

The mass demonstration, organized as a show of support for the peace policy of Rabin and his government, ended with the *Song of Peace*. Rabin's voice could be heard clearly as he tried to overcome his shyness of singing. He left the platform to the chants of "Rabin, Rabin!" and reached the area that was supposed to be "sterile", that is, free of anyone who was not a bodyguard, on his way to his car. Murderer Yig'al Amir was waiting for him there. Before Rabin managed to get into his car, Amir fired three bullets into his back at point-blank range. The stunned bodyguards pushed Rabin into the car, which sped off to Ichilov Hospital. He was brought into the operating room unconscious and died on the operating table. At 23:14, Eitan Haber, the prime minister's bureau chief, announced: "The Israeli Government announces with shock, great sorrow and profound grief the death of Yitzhak Rabin, who was assassinated in Tel Aviv this evening. May he rest in peace."

The people who had gathered at the entrance to the hospital burst into tears and clutched their heads in disbelief. The entire country was appalled and enraged. No one could believe that a heinous murderer would dare to kill an Israeli prime minister, despite the fact that during the six months prior to the assassination, attacks against the prime minister had become increasingly violent and outspoken. They reached their peak at a right-wing demonstration in Zion Square in Jerusalem, where the demonstrators flaunted a picture of Rabin in Nazi uniform with his eyes ripped out, and chanted, "Rabin is a Nazi! Rabin is a traitor!"

The prime minister's funeral was held two days later and was attended by 80 heads of state, including US President Clinton, who eulogized Rabin emotionally, saying: "The world has lost one of its great men; a fighter for the freedom of his people and for peace." He concluded his speech in Hebrew, saying: *"Shalom Haver!"* [Farewell, friend.] A few hours after the funeral, the name of Malchei Yisrael Square was changed to Rabin Square. Thousands of youngsters filled the square, lit candles, sang and wept. The walls of the municipality building were covered with graffiti expressing people's enormous rage and pain.

Four days after the murder, hundreds of rabbis and leaders of the religious-Zionist movement – to which assassin Yig'al Amir belonged – held a soul-searching conference. The central speech was given by Rabbi Yehuda Amital, head of the *Meimad* movement. He said: "We are deeply ashamed... because, had words like 'government of destruction', or 'government of treason' not been uttered from among us, this murder would not have been committed... We cannot say that our hands are not stained with this blood..."

Murderer Yig'al Amir was sentenced to life imprisonment and an additional six years for wounding Rabin's bodyguard, Yoram Rubin.

The Oslo B Agreement:
"We Make Concessions for Peace"

Fixing their ties before signing the Oslo B Agreement, (left to right) Israeli Premier Yitzhak Rabin, Egyptian President Husni Mubarak, Jordanian King Hussein, US President Bill Clinton, and Yasser Arafat. Photo: White House Spokesman, GPO

Two years after Israel and the PLO signed the Agreement of Principles, the parties signed the Oslo B agreement which was designed to increase Palestinian control over Judea and Samaria and regulate the relations between the parties for the next five years, until the permanent arrangement was agreed on. The signing was preceded by many crises and obstacles, but it was eventually decided that the IDF would evacuate all of the West Bank cities except Hebron, most of which would be under Palestinian control. The arrangement determined that the Jewish settlers would not be evacuated before the permanent agreement was reached, and that the elections for the Palestinian Council would be held before the IDF withdrawal.

The signing ceremony was held in Washington. Prime Minister Yitzhak Rabin said in his speech: "We are not withdrawing and we are not leaving; we are making concessions for peace." Yasser Arafat said: "This agreement proves that the peace process is irreversible." The Israeli opposition reacted harshly, staging stormy demonstrations in which the crowd chanted: "Rabin is a traitor", "Rabin is a murderer", and "We'll get rid of Rabin with blood and fire." Addressing one of the demonstrations, Likud Chairman Benjamin Netanyahu said: "Today the Knesset was presented with the document of surrender and withdrawal, dubbed Oslo B, which will be approved by a slim majority based on an anti-Zionist pro-PLO party." The agreement was approved by a majority of 61 MKs; 59 MKs voted against it. This slim majority was indicative of the public debate that split the nation in two. The prime minister, however, was not deterred and adhered to the path of peace. Five weeks after the agreement was signed, Rabin paid with his life for aspiring to make peace between Israel and the Palestinians.

David Levy Forms the *Gesher* Movement

18 June

Addressing hundreds of enthusiastic supporters in Givataim, David Levy announced he was quitting the Likud and running for premiership in the 1996 elections. Levy reached this decision as a result of his bad relationship with Likud Chairman Benjamin Netanyahu following the "hot tape affair" in which Netanyahu accused Levy and his cohorts of threats and attempts to blackmail him. The accusations were later proven false, but the main reason for Levy's resignation was Netanyahu's decision to change the Likud primaries system in a way that would prevent minority groups from being represented properly.
Five months after quitting the Likud, Levy announced that he was establishing *Gesher* – a social-national movement that would run for the Knesset. Levy was joined by David Magen, Ya'akov Bardugo, Maxim Levy, Michael Kleiner, Yehuda Lankri and others.

The ceremony during which the establishment of the Gesher movement was announced. Photo: Meir Partosh

Aharon Barak Appointed President of the Supreme Court

19 July

Justice Aharon Barak, who became well known as a result of his activist approach to Israeli law and his aspiration to apply it to the entire spectrum of political life, was elected president of the Supreme Court, replacing Meir Shamgar. Barak applied his legal interpretations to areas never covered before, basing his approach mainly on the "constitutional revolution" – the new basic laws that the Knesset had approved in 1992 regarding human dignity and liberty and the freedom of occupation. These bills served as the legal foundations upon which Barak established his liberal and activist approach to the law, and this often angered ultra-Orthodox circles.

Photo: Yaakov Sa'ar, GPO

1 January
Amnon Shahak replaced Ehud Barak as chief of staff.

22 January
In two consecutive suicide terror bombings at the Bet Lid Junction, 21 people, mostly IDF soldiers, were killed. A full closure was imposed on the territories after the attack.

9 April
A double terror attack in the area of Kfar Darom killed six soldiers.

18 April
Foreign Minister Shimon Peres declared for the first time that Israel would be willing to withdraw from the Golan Heights to the international border in return for a full peace agreement with Syria. The declaration sparked a public outcry in Israel.

14 June
Natan Sharansky decided to form a new immigrants' party – *Yisrael Ba'aliya*.

12 July
The national-religious rabbis issued a decree according to which orders to evacuate IDF bases or settlements in Judea and Samaria should not be obeyed. The decision created dissent among the public, including those belonging to the National Religious Party.

24 July
A suicide terror bomber detonated a bomb on a bus in Ramat Gan, killing seven and wounding scores. The prime minister and the chief of staff who arrived at the scene were booed by the crowd.

21 August
A suicide terror bomber detonated a bomb on a bus in Jerusalem, killing five and wounding some 100 people. Stormy anti-government demonstrations were held all over Israel.

4 September
The celebrations of Jerusalem's 3,000th year began. Numerous guests from abroad attended.

22.1.95

Suicide Terror Bombers Kill 21 and Wound 34 at Bet Lid

The hitch-hiking station at Bet Lid after the murderous attack.
Photo: Avi Ochayon, GPO

A lethal operation carried out by the Islamic Jihad terrorists at the Bet Lid Junction took a heavy toll: 21 killed and 34 wounded, mostly IDF soldiers. The attack was carefully planned and precisely executed. The terrorists chose Sunday morning for their attack because the hitch-hiking stations are crowded with soldiers headed for their bases. One of the terrorists arrived at the Bet Lid junction wearing an IDF uniform and carrying a large bag. He approached a kiosk where scores of soldiers were standing and activated the charge. Several soldiers were hurt by the blast. Dozens of soldiers and civilians rushed to their aid. Among them was a second terrorist, also in disguise. He took advantage of the crush and panic, activated a second bomb and caused many more casualties.

It was later learnt that a third terrorist had arrived at the junction to blow himself up and increase the number of casualties, but had panicked and fled the scene, leaving his bomb in a nearby orchard. That terrorist was captured a year later and took his interrogators to the orchard where he had hidden the bomb. This attack was one in a series of serious terror attacks that sparked angry protests against the policy of Yitzhak Rabin.

A Hijacked Iranian Plane Lands in Israel

19 September

The IAF warning systems picked up an approaching plane that was identified as Iranian. Shortly afterwards, the pilot asked for permission to land, and the request was immediately brought to the attention of the prime minister. Rabin, who feared that this was a trap and that the Iranians were planning to detonate the plane over Tel Aviv, finally decided to allow it to land at the Uvda airfield in the Negev. After the landing, it transpired that the plane had been hijacked by a steward who requested political asylum in Israel. The plane was refueled the next day and departed for Iran.

Photo: GPO

Amnon Lipkin-Shahak Appointed Chief of Staff

1 January

Amnon Lipkin-Shahak of the paratroopers replaced Ehud Barak as IDF chief of staff. Shahak was one of the most talented IDF officers, held in high esteem by both the army and the political echelons headed by Yitzhak Rabin. Shahak commanded the IDF during the period of serious terror attacks by the Hamas and the Islamic Jihad, of constant clashes with the Hizballah, and of handing over the West Bank towns to the Palestinians. He also had to deal with the fact that the motivation of youngsters to serve in the IDF had decreased.

95

27 April

Sasha Argov, "King of the Hebrew song", Dies

Photo: Efi Sharir

Composer Alexander (Sasha) Argov died at the age of 81. Argov, known as the "king of the Hebrew song", composed over 1,000 songs, many of which have become classics. Argov wrote for the best bands: the Chizbatron, the Nachal troupe, the Tarnegolim, Hagashash Hahiver, and many others. He also wrote music for over 30 plays, including several musicals such as King Solomon and Shoemaker Shalmai, that became huge hits. In 1987, together with Shoshana Damari, he received an award for his contribution to the Hebrew song.
The picture shows Argov with singers Achinoam (Noa) Nini and Netanela at a gala tribute to him which was held at the Mann Auditorium in Tel Aviv.

1 November

The Site of "Rabin's Lights" – Four days before he was assassinated, Prime Minister Yitzhak Rabin attended a ceremony to mark the completion of the Israel Electric Company's new coal power station in Hadera. His father, Nechemia Rabin, had been one of the company's most veteran employees. Two months later, the company decided to name the new station – which is Israel's primary power source – "Rabin's Lights", after the late Yitzhak Rabin.

20 September

Reconciliation: Yehuda Wachsman Meets Sheikh Badr - Yehuda Wachsman (left), father of the late Nachshon, met Sheikh Yassin Badr (right), the father of the terrorist who abducted and later killed Nachshon, and was himself killed by IDF soldiers. In their reconciliation meeting, the two called for a fight against terrorism and violence and for the death sentence for murderers. They decided to establish an Israeli-Palestinian center for tolerance and education.

22 June

Alice Miller: The Battle for the Pilots' Course - The Supreme Court discussed a petition by 23-year-old Alice Miller who applied for admission to a pilots' training course. Miller claimed that, in dealing with her request, the army's policy was discriminatory and dealt a blow to sexual equality. She further claimed that biological differences between men and women were immaterial as far as the pilots' course was concerned. The IDF representative claimed, on the other hand, that the army was not an instrument for the attainment of social goals and that the fact that, by law, women can only do reserve duty up to age of 38 was crucial because it might undermine the strength of the IAF. Eventually, the court accepted Miller's claims. She was invited to take the admission tests for the course, but failed the psychological tests. As a result of her campaign, the prestigious course was opened to women. In 1996, seven female soldiers were accepted to the course, thus fulfilling Miller's dream. None of them graduated, however.

Photo: Zoom 77

8 February

Female Soldier Abducted - Keren Gertler, a 19-year-old soldier, was abducted at gunpoint upon leaving her home for her army base and taken to Magdiel, where she was sedated. Her father, diamond dealer Asher Gertler, was kidnapped shortly after that. The abductor, Avi Sapan, asked for a five-million-dollar ransom, threatening to kill the Gertlers. According to Asher Gertler, "the abductor sat next to me with a gun and said: 'I've got nothing to lose. If I don't get the five million dollars, you'll be the first to die.' I told him: 'Are you crazy? I am not as rich as you think.'"
Three hours later, Gertler escaped from his abductor. Sapan was shot to death in a clash with the police. Keren, who was being held by the daughter of Sapan's girlfriend, was released.

Asher Gertler and his daughter Keren. Photo: Haim Ziv

28 September

Israel and the Palestinians signed the Oslo B agreement, according to which the IDF was to pull out of all West Bank cities. The right reacted with stormy demonstrations, calling Rabin "a traitor".

4 November

Prime Minister Yitzhak Rabin was assassinated when he left a peace rally at Malchei Yisrael Square. The assassin was Yig'al Amir, who belonged to the extreme right wing. Israel and the world were stunned and enraged.

4 December

Edna Arbel was appointed state attorney, replacing Dorit Beinisch who was appointed Supreme Court judge.

19 December

The trial of assassin Yig'al Amir opened at the Tel Aviv District Court.

18 July

The Arad Festival Disaster

Three youngsters were killed and hundreds injured in the Arad Festival disaster. Some 25,000 fans pushed and crowded together to watch *Mashina* perform, causing many to be crushed. Ido Cohen, 17, said: "Suddenly, probably because of the pressure, the gates [of the stadium] burst open and we were all pushed in. I saw this guy with his face in the dirt, right under me. This went on for some 20 minutes." The rescue teams that arrived at the scene found total chaos. They evacuated the wounded to hospitals in the region. Three youngsters, who had come to hear music at the Arad festival, lost their lives.

(1996

*Prime Minister Elect
Benjamin Netanyahu
and his wife Sarah
after his election
victory. Photo: Sygma*

*Yitzhak Mordechai with enthusiastic supporters at the Likud
headquarters upon hearing the election results. Photo: Avi Ochayon,
GPO*

Benjamin Netanyahu – Prime Minister
He does not know

Journalist and Former Minister and MK Joseph Lapid

Bibi Netanyahu was not elected prime minister in 1996 because Yitzhak Rabin was assassinated, because Shimon Peres is a loser, or because Bibi Netanyahu is a media wizard. Bibi Netanyahu was elected because the majority of the Jewish public could not accept a deal in which we give up territories while the Palestinians blow up our buses. Such a formula was too lethal and did not leave much room for pure logical considerations.

Bibi Netanyahu's primal sin was that he dared get elected despite the holy trinity: the media, academia and the white (as in non-Sephardi and non-ultra-Orthodox) establishment. The liberal left which earnestly champions free, universal and democratic elections finds it difficult to accept the fact that the majority might vote "wrongly". Hence the persistent and arrogant attempts to delegitimize Bibi Netanyahu as prime minister. It was no accident that MK Ra'anan Cohen, Labor Knesset faction whip, rushed to the Supreme Court to file a petition against the election results. Judging from the sensation in the clogged arteries of the left, Bibi's election was in conflict with the law – if not the laws of the land, then the laws of nature.

Out of consideration for American pressure, Bibi Netanyahu did not destroy the Oslo document, did not set it on fire and did not dance wildly around its ashes. But he gave the right their money's worth: He stopped the peace process. The left is suffering from an optical illusion when it says that the fact that the peace process has stopped proves that Netanyahu has failed. On the contrary – this is exactly what he was elected for.

At the same time, Netanyahu is fulfilling the expectations of the left by showing amazing incompetence in running the affairs of the state. Like a skier who believes that the aim of the slalom is to bump into every little flag in his path, Netanyahu never misses a chance to get bogged down in a domestic or public scandal. At times, he demonstrates frightening obtuseness with regard to the basic concepts of proper government.

However, future generations will not judge him for his family scandals or the outrageous appointments he made. Netanyahu will be tried by history for failing to present a plan that could serve as an alternative to the Oslo agreement. Ever since he came to power, no one has been able to fathom where he is headed. No one knows what his political, geographic or strategic goals are. Whenever he is asked questions on the issue, he spews out a string of worn-out slogans, prepackaged for media consumption. Even his followers do not know his secret.

Every morning when Bibi Netanyahu wakes up, he is happy to find that he really is prime minister, that the state has not yet fallen to pieces and that his agenda is full of crucial missions, important conversations and meetings fraught with significance. But his eyes are watching a virtual reality that is not substantial. This is the nagging worry felt by everyone who follows Bibi Netanyahu's deeds and misdeeds: that the Israeli prime minister does not know where he wants to lead the state. And, even if he does, he is unable to reach the desired goal.

29.5.96

Netanyahu Elected Prime Minister; Peres Narrowly Defeated

After Rabin's assassination, Shimon Peres was appointed acting prime minister. He was very popular and faced a great temptation: he could exploit the situation to his advantage and bring the elections forward, thus gaining four more years in power. Peres, however, was worried that this might be perceived as a cynical exploitation of Rabin's murder for political gains. In the end, signals from Damascus indicating that there was some willingness to discuss a peace accord tipped the scale against bringing the elections forward. Peres chose to use the brief time at his disposal to see the Syrian process through. However, in early February, when the polls showed he was leading by 20% and Syrian President Assad rejected an offer to meet him, Peres decided that it was time to bring the elections forward.

Benjamin Netanyahu, David Levy and Yitzhak Mordechai at the Likud headquarters after the victory. Photo: Avi Ochayon, GPO

Peres and his men were certain that they would defeat the inexperienced Netanyahu easily, but reality dealt them a cruel blow. A wave of Hamas suicide terror attacks in reaction to the killing of "engineer" Yihya Ayyash caused the deaths of 59 Israelis in 10 days. A new reality was created in Israel. "A Terrorized State," proclaimed the *Yedioth Ahronoth* banner headline. The sense of a personal lack of safety was at an unprecedented peak. Netanyahu seized the opportunity and came up with a new election slogans: "Safe Peace" and "Fighting Terror to the Bitter End". The gap between Netanyahu and Peres gradually decreased as election day approached. In addition, Netanyahu managed to unite the Likud with the *Gesher* and *Tzomet* movements, which made him the only right-wing candidate for the premiership. The Likud campaign focused on the slogan, "Peres will divide Jerusalem", ignoring Peres' denials. Netanyahu's messages were internalized and totally believed by the public. At the same time, the Labor election headquarters decided to soft-pedal the campaign and disregard Netanyahu. Ehud Barak, head of Peres' campaign headquarters, claimed after the elections that he had recommended a more aggressive line against Netanyahu, but his proposal had been rejected. In April, a month before the elections, the government initiated Operation Grapes of Wrath against the Hizballah. After the Kafr Kana disaster, the Israeli Arab leadership called on its public not to vote for Peres in the elections. Peres was still leading in the polls, but it was clear that the race was undecided. Three days before the elections, the two candidates participated in a televised debate which had a crucial effect on the outcome. Peres appeared tired, hard-pressed and gloomy, while Netanyahu impressed the public with his vigorous, youthful and self-assured appearance.

At 22:00, at the end of election day, TV anchorman Haim Yavin announced that the two candidates had reached a tie. The Labor members started celebrating, but the true results came in early in the morning: Netanyahu had won the elections by a margin of 29,500 votes, winning the support of 50.49% of the voters, as opposed to Peres' 49.51%. Netanyahu was the first Israeli prime minister to be elected according to the new law of direct elections.

Photo: Zoom 77

"They Are Spilling Our Blood," Yelled Thousands of Outraged Ethiopians

28 January

Thousands of outraged Ethiopian Jews went to Jerusalem to stage a demonstration outside the Prime Minister's Office after *Ma'ariv* published a report according to which the Magen David Adom blood bank had been destroying Ethiopian blood donations for fear they were contaminated with AIDS. The rally quickly turned into one of the stormiest and most violent demonstrations Israel has ever seen. The deeply offended immigrants vented their fury on everything in their path and attacked policemen with rocks, bottles and sticks. The policemen, who had not expected such a degree of violence, tried to ward them off with tear gas, rubber bullets and water cannons. Some 40 policemen and 20 demonstrators were wounded. The managing director of Magen David Adom was fired because of the affair. The cabinet established a special committee headed by former president Yitzhak Navon to examine the affair.

Operation Grapes of Wrath

Hizballah activities against the IDF in southern Lebanon escalated at the beginning of 1996. The actions of the organization became more daring every day. In a massive Katyusha attack on Kiryat Shmona in April, 36 civilians were injured. The inhabitants of the northern settlement exerted heavy pressure on the government to react firmly. Pressured by the approaching elections and attempting to rid himself of the image of a yielding leader, Peres was forced to abandon his policy of restraint and accept the demand of his party ministers, headed by Ehud Barak, to unleash massive military force against the Hizballah.

Prime Minister Shimon Peres touring an IDF base in the north during Operation "Grapes of Wrath". Photo: Avi Ochayon, GPO

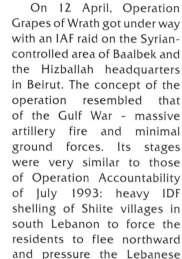

On 12 April, Operation Grapes of Wrath got under way with an IAF raid on the Syrian-controlled area of Baalbek and the Hizballah headquarters in Beirut. The concept of the operation resembled that of the Gulf War - massive artillery fire and minimal ground forces. Its stages were very similar to those of Operation Accountability of July 1993: heavy IDF shelling of Shiite villages in south Lebanon to force the residents to flee northward and pressure the Lebanese and Syrian governments to curb the Hizballah. The bases and command posts of the organization were indeed shelled incessantly and tens of thousands of villagers fled toward Beirut, but the Hizballah was not deterred and continued firing Katyushas on the Galilee.

On the seventh day of the operation, an IDF artillery battery shelled a UN post near the village of Kafr Kana. A large number of local residents were hiding there. Some 100 people were killed and scores were wounded. In the wake of the furious international reactions, Peres decided to call off the operation. However, heeding his advisers who were anxious about his security image, he was forced to change his mind. The operation ended with the intervention of the Americans. Secretary of State Warren Christopher drafted a plan based on "improved understandings" of Operation Accountability: Refraint from firing at civilians, a ban on firing into Israeli territory and the establishment of a committee to monitor the implementation of the understandings. In fact, Israel and the Hizballah agreed to restrict their confrontations to the security zone. On 28 April, after 16 days of fighting, a cease-fire went into effect.

The Ultra-Orthodox Riot on Bar-Ilan Road

6 June

Protesting the fact that Bar-Ilan Road, which runs through their neighborhoods, was not closed on Saturdays, thousands of ultra-Orthodox Jews spent their Sabbaths staging demonstrations that led to severe clashes with the policemen who were present. They pelted the police with rocks, cursed them and spat at them. Following the Supreme Court's orders, Transportation Minister Yitzhak Levy established a committee, headed by Tzvi Tzameret, that was supposed to suggest "solutions in the spirit of religious tolerance". The recommendations it made upset both the religious and the secular, and were rejected. Levy notified the court that he would use his authority to close the road during prayers on Sabbath and holidays. He added that "suitable arrangements" had been made. The court eventually went along with Levy's decision and, after finding alternative solutions for the secular residents of the area, Bar-Ilan Road was closed on Sabbath and holidays.

5 January

Yihya Ayyash, "the engineer", was killed. He was responsible for a series of terror attacks which cost the lives of many israelis.

8 January

GSS chief Carmi Gillon resigned following the investigation into the Rabin assassination. He was replaced by Ami Ayalon.

25 February

Twenty-six people were killed in two simultaneous suicide terror attacks, one on the number 18 bus in Jerusalem and the other at a soldiers' hitch-hiking station in Ashkelon.

3 March

Nineteen people were killed in a suicide terror attack on a bus in Jerusalem.

4 March

Thirteen people were killed in a terror attack at Dizengoff Center in Tel Aviv. This attack was followed by violent anti-government demonstrations.

13 March

The Likud, *Gesher* and *Tzomet* signed an agreement to run together in the elections.

28 March

Yig'al Amir was sentenced to life and another six years for assassinating Prime Minister Yitzhak Rabin.

11 April

Operation Grapes of Wrath against the terrorist infrastructure in Lebanon got under way. On the seventh day of the operation, 100 Lebanese citizens were killed in the IDF artillery shelling of Kafr Kana.

29 May

Benjamin Netanyahu won the elections for prime minister by a margin of nearly 30,000 votes, 50.49% to Peres' 49.51%.

24.9.96

The Western Wall Tunnel:
"We Are Touching the Very Foundations of Our Existence"

Visitors at the Western Wall tunnel.
Photo: Zoom 77

The Western Wall tunnel was already fully excavated in the summer of 1995 but, following recommendations from the defense establishment, then Prime Minister Yitzhak Rabin postponed opening it to the public, fearing that the Palestinians might view it as a provocation. When Netanyahu came to power, the tunnel issue was discussed again in various forums of ministers and security experts. After consultations and deliberations, the prime minister decided to open it after Yom Kippur. No member of the defense establishment knew about this, and the prime minister notified Defense Minister Yitzhak Mordechai only hours before the decision was implemented. The minister immediately notified the chief of staff, and large police and IDF forces were sent to the capital. The tunnel opened, causing an outburst of rage from the Palestinians, the Arab world and the international community. Arafat said the next day: "God has bought the believers' souls and possessions because they will go to heaven fighting for their people... kill and be killed... ." This was all the Palestinians needed to hear. Riots broke out on the same day in Hebron and Jerusalem. Prime Minister Benjamin Netanyahu reacted by saying: "A visit to the tunnel is a very moving experience. We are touching the very foundations of our existence."

The next day, 25 September, the territories ignited. For the first time since the PA entered the Gaza Strip and the West Bank, Palestinian policemen fired at IDF soldiers. The most serious incidents took place in Kfar Darom and Joseph's Tomb in Nablus, where a small IDF force was attacked by thousands of Arabs. The IDF announced a state of emergency in the territories, tanks were placed on the outskirts of the cities and large numbers of troops were sent to the conflict areas. During the three days of battle, 14 IDF soldiers and 69 Palestinians were killed, and 1,290 Palestinians were wounded. The United States applied pressure and a summit meeting was held in Washington the following week between Prime Minister Netanyahu, PA Chairman Arafat and Jordan's King Hussein. This restored calm to the territories. The Israelis could now start arguing about who was responsible for the decision to open the tunnel.

Photo: GPO

Identity of the New Head of the Mossad Revealed

2 June

For the first time in Israel's history, the identity of the head of the Mossad was revealed upon assuming his post. Dani Yatom, a former military secretary of Prime Minister Yitzhak Rabin, replaced Shabtai Shavit, who retired after 32 years of service.
The exposure of Yatom's identity heralded a new era in the history of the Israeli secret services - they became less secret and more open to the media.

"Engineer" Yihya Ayyash Killed by a Cellphone

5 January

Terrorist Yihya Ayyash, dubbed "the engineer", who was responsible for the death of dozens of Israelis and the wounding of hundreds more, was killed when he answered his cellphone. The booby-trapped phone was delivered to Ayyash by a collaborator. When Ayyash's father called him, he put the phone to his ear and said "hello". This was his last word. A digital signal sent to his phone detonated a tiny but powerful charge that immediately blew his head off. After his death, Ayyash became a *shahid* - martyr - in the eyes of the Palestinians. The GSS logged in an impressive achievement in the fight against extreme Islamic terror.

"Engineer" Yihya Ayyash

13 June

Signed Birth and Death Certificates of Yemenite Children Found

Photo: Zoom 77

The state commission of inquiry appointed to investigate the fate of the missing children of Yemenite immigrants from the 1950s discovered a box full of pre-signed birth and death certificates in an archive. Yehudit Hivner, who had directed the Population Registry for many years, claimed: "I never came across lists like these."

22 October

The French President in Israel: "I Am Going Back to Paris" – The entourage of French President Jacques Chirac were of the opinion that there was no need for extensive security measures during his tour of East Jerusalem. His Israeli hosts thought differently, and they filled the alleys with bodyguards. The visiting president was outraged; he pushed the guards and charged them with "initiating provocation." He even warned he would cut his visit short and return to Paris, but his visit ended the next day, as planned.

5 September

Prime Minister Netanyahu met with PA Chairman Arafat for the first time at the Erez crossing.

24 September

The Hashmonean Tunnel opened upon Benjamin Netanyahu's orders. Bloody riots started the next day in East Jerusalem and the territories, resulting in the death of 14 IDF soldiers and 69 Palestinians.

12 November

Azzam Azzam, an Israeli Druze citizen, was arrested in Egypt on suspicion of spying for Israel.

11 August

Murder Suspect Arrested – The mystery of the disappearance of scientist Amiram Hochberg and his 12-year-old son was solved. Hochberg, who was suspected of murdering his wife and her mother, was found in a rented apartment in Basel, Switzerland. He was arrested and his son, who the police believed to have been kidnapped by his father, was handed over to the Israeli Consulate. The two had disappeared three months earlier. At around the same time, the body of the child's grandmother, Ida Bleichman, was found. The mother is still missing. Hochberg escaped to Switzerland via Taba, Egypt and Italy. When the Swiss police arrived at the apartment, the child had a long braid that made him look like a girl. Hochberg told his landlord that he and his daughter had come to study German.

13 September

Ruth Nachmani Won Her Frozen Ova

By a majority of seven to four, the Supreme Court judges ruled that Ruth Nachmani was entitled to gain possession of her ova that had been fertilized by her ex-husband's sperm. This concluded a long legal battle between Ruth and Dani Nachmani over the fate of the frozen fertilized ova that were being kept at Assuta Hospital. Ruth Nachmani said: "The court told me that I was a living being, and permitted the same cycle that connects me to my life to connect me with my child. This cycle must not be broken. I will start looking for a surrogate mother immediately. I expect some calls today." Dani Nachmani did not show up in court. His attorney said: "This was the first time in history that a child was created in court by a pen... ."

Ruth Nachmani and her attorney Ziv Gruber. Photo: Zoom 77.

Photo: Zoom 77

23 December

Copaxon: An Original Israeli Drug – The US Food and Drug Administration officially authorized the Teva Company to produce and distribute its new medicine for the treatment of multiple sclerosis in the US. This was the first original Israeli drug approved by the US authorities. It had been in the process of development for 15 years since a discovery by Weizmann Institute scientists. Until that time, Teva only produced "imitation" medicine after the rights of the original companies had expired. With the FDA approval of Copaxon, Teva joined the circle of path-breaking pharmaceutical companies.

3 January

Carmela Bouchbout, Who Murdered Her Husband, Released from Prison –Carmela Bouchbout, who murdered her husband Yehuda after he had abused her for years, was released from custody after 456 days. After her discharge, she said: "I know it is hard to understand how a loving wife can shoot her husband. I asked my children to forgive me for taking their father away from them. I wanted us to be a warm and close family, which is why I kept silent for so many years. Had I dared to talk about what Yehuda really did to me, I would have been dead a long time ago. He would have killed me. I say to all battered wives: 'Do not hide your pain. Ask for help. Don't take my case as an example.' Remorse is so bitter. I would give everything just to turn the clock back."

Carmela Bouchbout with her two sons after her release from prison. Photo: Hai Ziv

Amiram Hochberg (left) with his attorney Sassi Gez. Photo: Dani Solomon

1997

Prime Minister Benjamin
Netanyahu at the site the
of the helicopter crash in
She'ar Yashuv.
Photo: Avi Ochayon, GPO

The bridge that collapsed during the opening of the Maccabi Games.
Photo: AP

Israel Turns 50: The Age of Transition
A country that improvizes its disasters

Journalist
Nachum Barnea

The authorities forgot to supervise, the engineer cut corners in the planning, the contractors skimped on materials, and the bridge that was supposed to enable the delegations to cross over into the opening ceremony of the Maccabi Games collapsed, causing the Australian team to fall into the poisonous sludge of the Yarkon River. This happened on 14 July 1997. The collapse of the bridge took the lives of four Jewish athletes from Australia and caused irreversible physical harm to several others. Numerically, it was not the country's worst disaster in 1997, but it was perhaps the most insulting. It symbolized several worrying cracks in the health of Israeli society on the eve of its 50th birthday.

The first insulting discovery was that Israel is still stricken with the "don't worry, trust me" disease. Yes, there are clear construction regulations, Israeli standards, accountability, municipal and district committees, police authorizations and so on. Gigantic organizations. In practice, this is a country which improvizes its disasters one by one. There are many good intentions, but there is a lack of seriousness. This year it became apparent that even a high-class establishment such as the IAF – which allegedly cultivates its own set of standards – is actually sheltered by the big "trust me". The collision of the helicopters in the skies of She'ar Yashuv was a result of cumulative sloppy working procedures and human errors. The punishment for the errors was dreadful: 73 soldiers killed. Quite a few fatal "human errors" were made this year.

The second insulting discovery that emerged from the Maccabi Games was that when a disaster occurs, no one takes responsibility. All the resourcefulness and sophistication that were conspicuous by their absence when the wretched bridge was being built, came to the fore when it collapsed. The Maccabia organizers blamed the project operators, who blamed the engineer, who blamed the contractors, who blamed the tractor that drove over the bridge several hours before it collapsed. Only the tractor had nothing to say.

The third insulting discovery was the most painful of all: while people were fighting for their lives in the waters of the Yarkon River, the festivities continued inside the stadium nearby; this is what the organizers had decided. Most Israelis watched the event on split-screen TV: one half showed the disaster area; the other half showed mass gymnastic routines, dancing and, finally, fireworks. Ironically, the show that had to go on to the bitter end was a celebration of 100 years of Zionism.

Domestic solidarity used to be one of the secrets of Israel's success; and suddenly something cracked. Veteran Israeli society has been undergoing major changes recently. The tight, involved frameworks that used to sanctify the collective will are falling apart. Instead, an open and pluralistic society is emerging, which is tailored to the individual's will. Caring about others, once the outstanding feature of Israel, is dying out. It can still be found with the ultra-Orthodox and settlers – two politically rising groups – but, regrettably, they care mainly for themselves.

Something has gone rusty in the old Israeli sense of involvement. Somebody else's disaster is frequently just that – somebody else's. It may be wrong to draw such conclusions from individual cases, but the cases are hard to forget. For example, the story of Grisha Pessachovich, the boy who immigrated from Russia. He was Jewish enough to get killed in the terror attack in the Machaneh Yehuda market in Jerusalem, but not Jewish enough to be buried in a Jewish cemetery. His first funeral, a Christian one, was not attended by any of his classmates from his prestigious Jerusalem high school. His mother refused to have him buried as a Christian, so eventually he was buried in splendid isolation in the section reserved for those of "uncertain religion".

Or on another level: the Rambam Hospital staff who did not send an ambulance to meet a helicopter which was carrying two wounded IDF soldiers from Lebanon. When the ambulance finally arrived, one of the soldiers, who was critically injured, was given unbelievably poor treatment. Human error, the hospital said, and laid the blame on one of the nurses.

Fifty is an age of transition. Human beings sometimes reach their peak then; sometimes they begin to wilt. In the history of countries, age is even more complex. Israel enjoys the image of a young country, although it is one of the world's most veteran (and stable) democracies. The prime minister who was in power in 1997 was the same age as the state, the first prime minister to be born into the existing state. This is all very well. But that prime minister's biggest achievement in 1997 was the very fact of his survival, in spite of mistakes and crises. Survival is the achievement of the aged.

Israel has been blessed with the vitality of a fresh society: It is full of energy and ambition; it is open to new technologies, amenable to new ideas. At the same time, it has been cursed with a bunch of childhood diseases for which, at 50, it is too old, as well as some geriatric illnesses that have afflicted it much too soon. At 50, however, it is still one of the most fascinating countries in the world.

Perhaps we should not expect too much. Like that Australian woman who was asked for her opinion of Israel the day after the bridge collapsed. She said: "I've thought many things about Israelis. But it never occurred to me that they couldn't build a bridge."

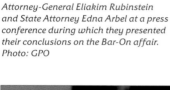

10.1.97

The Bar-On Affair – "A Threat to the Rule of Law in Israel"

In its 10 January session, the cabinet approved the appointment of Attorney Ronny Bar-On as attorney-general, with Minister Benny Begin objecting and five ministers abstaining. When the appointment was made public, Bar-On was severely criticized by the media and resigned 60 hours after assuming the post.

Ten days after his resignation, ITV correspondent Ayala Hasson exposed the deal that had led to the appointment under the headline, "Bar-On for Hebron". According to the report, Bar-On promised Arieh Deri a plea bargain in his trial if he were appointed attorney-general. Shas' support of the Hebron agreement was also conditional on Bar-On's appointment. The public was outraged, but Netanyahu dismissed the report out of hand. All the other people involved also denied that such a deal had ever existed.

Addressing the cabinet after the report had been made public, Netanyahu announced that as a result of fierce criticism, he had decided to let the police investigate the affair. State Attorney Edna Arbel ordered that an investigation be opened, and Commander Sando Mazor, head of investigations, was assigned the case.

Attorney-General Eliakim Rubinstein and State Attorney Edna Arbel at a press conference during which they presented their conclusions on the Bar-On affair. Photo: GPO

Dozens of politicians were questioned, including the prime minister, who was questioned under caution. Also, in an extraordinary move, Supreme Court President Aharon Barak was called to testify and claimed that he had opposed the Bar-On appointment.

At the height of the investigation, Attorney Dan Avi-Yitzhak resigned as Arieh Deri's attorney. In his resignation letter, he confirmed the television report that Deri had wanted Bar-On to be nominated, saying: "I have been informed that you went behind my back and slandered me and my wife... all because I committed the big sin of daring to oppose your plan to appoint Bar-On attorney-general."

On 15 April, the police recommended that Justice Minister Tzachi Hanegbi, MK Arieh Deri and the director general of the Prime Minister's office, Avigdor Lieberman, be indicted. Some 24 hours later, another shocking report was leaked to the media, according to which the police recommended that Prime Minister Benjamin Netanyahu be indicted on suspicion of fraud and breach of confidence.

On 20 April, after reviewing the police recommendations, the state attorney and the attorney-general announced that they had decided to file charges only against Arieh Deri on suspicion of fraud, breach of confidence and obstructing justice. Moreover, they decided to close the cases against the prime minister and the justice minister for lack of sufficient evidence. However, the investigation into the matter of Lieberman and senior businessman David Appel would continue. "There was a threat to the rule of the law in Israel... criminal elements interfered with the appointment of the attorney-general," the attorney-general and the state attorney stated in their conclusions.

Photo: Sygma

Disaster at the Maccabi Games: The Bridge Collapses

14 July

During the opening ceremony of the 15th Maccabi Games, a bridge collapsed, causing the deaths of four members of the Australian delegation and injuring 64. The bridge, which was built over the Yarkon River to enable the delegations to cross over into the stadium, collapsed while the 370 members of the Australian delegation were on it. While the rescue forces were busy pulling the people out of the river, the president officially opened the Games in a ceremony which took place a few meters away from the disaster area. The Dotan Committee, appointed to investigate the circumstances of the disaster, stated that it had occurred as a result of the incompetence of almost everyone involved in its construction.

The Government Decides to Evacuate Hebron

Hebron residents celebrate the IDF pullout. Photo: Zoom 77

After a stormy nocturnal session, the cabinet decided to pull the IDF out of the Arab sections of Hebron, in accordance with the Oslo B agreement. Eleven ministers supported the move and seven opposed it. At the end of the tense session, Minister Benny Begin announced his resignation from the cabinet. The evacuation decision was preceded by lengthy negotiations with the Palestinians, culminating the night before the cabinet session in a meeting between Benjamin Netanyahu and Yasser Arafat.

The IDF completed the evacuation the next day, quietly and in perfect order.

The Hebron agreement was the first document the Netanyahu government signed with the PA. The settlers and the right wing reacted sharply, but made do with restrained acts of protest.

A Jordanian Soldier Murders Seven Schoolgirls in Naharaim

13 March

Ahmed Mussa, a Jordanian soldier, opened fire at a group of eighth-grade schoolgirls from the Forest School in Bet Shemesh. They had arrived for a tour of the Naharaim enclave, which is in Jordanian territory. Seven pupils were killed and a teacher and five more pupils were wounded and taken to a nearby Jordanian hospital. The event shocked the Israeli public and Jordan's royal court, which immediately condemned the attack. King Hussein, however, did not settle for just the condemnation and, in an unprecedented move, came to express his condolences in person to the bereaved families. "I feel like I lost my own children," the king said. The murderer was given a life sentence with hard labor, but earned the admiration of many Jordanians.

Jordan's King Hussein visits the families of the girls killed in Naharaim. Photo: Avi Ochayon, GPO

Construction at Har Homa – A Crisis With the Palestinians

14 March

The government decided to construct a Jewish neighborhood in the area of Har Homa, south of Jerusalem, and a neighborhood for young Arab couples next to it. The land was expropriated in 1991 but, because the issue was politically sensitive, interior ministers in previous governments had never issued final construction permits.
Pressured by the MKs from the Greater Israel Front, Prime Minister Benjamin Netanyahu decided to start building on Har Homa. Two weeks later, bulldozers began working at the site, sparking harsh reactions from the Arab world and the international community. The Palestinians halted the talks with Israel, but ensured that their reaction was restrained.

Work on Har Homa begins. Photo: Avi Ochayon, GPO

1997

1 January
IDF soldier Noam Friedman opened fire at local residents in the Hebron market, wounding nine people. He told the police that he had intended to follow in the footsteps of Baruch Goldstein. He was examined by three psychiatrists, who declared him insane.

10 January
The cabinet approved the appointment of Ronny Bar-On as attorney-general, but he resigned 60 hours later, following sharp public criticism.

14 January
The cabinet approved the evacuation of Hebron: 11 ministers voted for the evacuation, and seven ministers against.

4 February
In a midair collision between two IAF helicopters, 73 soldiers were killed.

13 March
At Naharaim, in Jordan, a Jordanian soldier shot at schoolgirls from Bet Shemesh, killing seven and wounding five others plus a teacher. The soldier was given a life sentence.

14 March
The cabinet approved construction works on Har Homa in Jerusalem. The decision angered the world in general and the Arab world and the Palestinians in particular.

21 March
Three women were killed and six people injured in a terror attack on Café Apropo in Tel Aviv. A bomb planted by a terrorist exploded on Friday, the eve of Purim, when the place was packed.

27 March
Businessman Shaul Eisenberg died of a heart attack at the age of 76 while on a tour of China.

9 April
The body of soldier Sharon Edri, who had been missing since September 1996, was discovered.

17 April
Haim Herzog, Israel's sixth president, died at the age of 79.

4.2.97

73 Soldiers Killed In
A Helicopter Disaster

Two IAF Yas'ur helicopters collided in midair over She'ar Yashuv on the northern border, killing 73 soldiers who were on their way to outposts in Lebanon. The helicopters took off from the Machanaim camp near Rosh Pina, flying in formation. They were supposed to split up near the border and fly to their destination separately. Before they were cleared to cross the border, they cut their lights and - possibly - lost eye contact and collided.

The wreckage of the helicopters at She'ar Yashuv. Photo: GPO

Candles and poems in memory of the fallen at She'ar Yashuv. Photo: Meir Azulai

This was the worst disaster in IAF history. A national day of mourning was announced on the day of the funerals. Defense Minister Yitzhak Mordechai appointed a committee headed by former IAF commander David Ivri to investigate the accident. The committee findings were published on 17 April: "What happened there during the last seconds will remain a mystery. We still do not know why the two helicopters came so close to each other." The committee recommended that structural changes be introduced in the IAF command; that clear instructions be drafted regarding formation flying and changes in flight routes; that the squadron commander and his deputy be dismissed; and that the commander of the Tel Nof air base be reprimanded.

Ehud Barak Elected Labor Chairman

3 June

When Ehud Barak was elected Labor Party Chairman, it signaled the end of an era in party history. After the party had been led by Yitzhak Rabin and Shimon Peres for 23 years, Barak won 50.3% of the votes, bringing about a change of guard in the party. Other candidates in the race were Yossi Beilin, who won 28.5%, Shlomo Ben-Ami (14.7%), and Efraim Sneh (6.6%). The next day, Barak said: "The Labor Party is starting on a new path this morning, a path of hope for the State of Israel... I will unite the party, instill it with hope and bring about change...".

A Nightmare in Machaneh Yehuda

30 July

Two suicide terrorists blew themselves up at the two ends of a narrow alley in Jerusalem's Machaneh Yehuda market. The terrorists, dressed in suits and ties, were carrying explosives in their attaché cases. They had Jordanian currency in their pockets. Fourteen people were killed in the blast and some 160 wounded, 13 of them seriously. Eye-witness reports said: "We saw burnt people, screaming in pain... The stalls were on fire and the ground was drenched with blood and watermelon juice... People whose limbs had been blown off screamed for help... ." US President Bill Clinton held a special news conference in which he said that this was a "barbaric act", and called on the PA to put security measures into practice. He implored both parties to increase their co-operation in security matters. The Israeli security cabinet convened after the attack and decided to stop the negotiations with the Palestinians until terror had been totally eradicated; moreover, it demanded that the PA arrest hundreds of Hamas and Islamic Jihad terrorists, and that funds to the PA be halted; it requested that the US and Europe stop granting assistance to the Palestinians; and it imposed restrictions on the passage of Palestinian VIPs from the West Bank to Gaza.

1997

Eshkolot Payis – A Science and Art Project

אתה זוכה המדינה זוכה

The Mif'al Hapayis national lottery decided that, over the coming three years, it would invest some 800 million shekels in the Eshkolot Payis project. In the framework of the project, 81 centers for art and science would be constructed throughout Israel. Mif'al Hapayis has recently invested 200 million shekels in computers for Israeli schools. It is expected to have an income of 2.5 billion shekels in 1997, of which 60% percent will be paid out in prize money and some 30% invested in local authorities.

2 April

Only 3 weeks after a Jordanian soldier shot and killed seven Israeli girls on the Isle of Peace in Naharayim, tensions lifted a little when the Jordanians decided to let the Israel Electricity Company board and executives visit the ruins of the hydroelectric power plant, which has been defunct for nearly 50 years. This tour materialized after Mr. Arafa, Jordanian Electricity Company director general, visited Israel and toured the Orot Rabin power station.

Ruins of the Naharayim power station. Photo from 1977

20 April

The attorney-general and the state attorney published their report on the Bar-On affair, deciding to indict only MK Arieh Deri. They also criticized the prime minister and the justice minister for the way Attorney Bar-On had been appointed attorney-general.

26 May

Hapo'el Beersheba soccer team won the state cup for the first time in history, after winning the finals against Maccabi Tel Aviv 1:0.

3 June

Ehud Barak was elected Labor Party chairman.

5 July

In a terrible traffic accident on the Jordan Valley Road, Uri Pell, his parents and two of his friends were killed. They were on their way to Uri's wedding that was to be held at Moshav Hazor'im near Tiberias.

14 July

At the opening of the 15th Maccabi Games, a bridge collapsed, killing four members of the Australian delegation and injuring 64.

30 July

Fourteen people were killed and about 160 wounded in a suicide terror attack in Jerusalem's Machaneh Yehuda market.

3 January

Israeli Composer Moshe Wilensky Dies

One of the greatest Israeli composers, Moshe Wilensky, died at the age of 87. Wilensky, an Israel Prize laureate, composed hundreds of songs, many of which were performed by Shoshana Damari, the Yemenite queen of Israeli song. On hearing of his death, she said: "One cannot begin to describe our lengthy relationship... About six months ago, I asked him to write a tune for me. Even though he did not believe he could, he tried to write a perfect Wilensky song... ." Ehud Manor, Israel's leading lyricist, said: "He knew how to write music that connected with the big world, while we still believed we should be dealing with more important things. To me, Wilensky is the musical equivalent of [poet] Natan Alterman... ."

Moshe Wilensky and Shoshana Damari. Photo: Yossi Roth

5 January

Photo: Meir Partosh

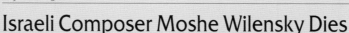

The Night of the Aliens – Thousands of Israelis armed with cameras, telescopes and binoculars awaited the arrival of aliens after TV host Dudu Topaz promised they would be coming. "It's amazing; they're early!" yelled people in the "UFO command" in Ramat Chen at 18:00. Their joy soon changed to disappointment when they realized that the "UFO" was a passenger plane headed for Ben-Gurion Airport. The dream of aliens ended at dawn and life in Israel returned to normal.

16 April

Hebron Tea Pourer Gets Three Years

The Jerusalem District Court sentenced Yisrael Lederman to three years in prison after convicting him of pouring boiling tea on MK Yael Dayan. Lederman, a tour guide from Jerusalem, threw the tea in Dayan's face in October 1996 during a tour of Hebron. During the course of the tour, Lederman offered Dayan a cup of tea. When she said that she would love one, he threw the tea in her face, causing burns on her neck. "I offered her tea, but I was pushed," he said in his defense. The judges rejected his claim and sent him to prison.

Yisrael Lederman taken into custody. Photo: Zoom 77

(1998

**Linor Abargil, Miss Israel and Miss World 1998.
Photo: Tzvika Tischler**

*Linor Abargil testifying against Nur Shlomo, who was convicted of raping and attempting to murder her.
Photo: Hadar Cohen*

The Courage to Expose a Brutal Rape

*Journalist
and Anchorwoman
Mickey Haimovich*

In November 1988, a young, curly-haired Israeli woman stood on a Seychelles stage looking stunned. Miss Israel Linor Abargil was just crowned Miss World, but her victorious smiles soon turned into tears.

Twenty years after Rina Mor won the title, another Israeli proudly and gladly received the international beauty queen title. Yet, very few in Israel were aware of her appalling tragedy, which she had kept secret for months. The Netanya girl was brutally raped by Nur Shlomo, a former Israeli travel agent, while on a fashion shoot in Italy.

With the tiara, pride, and joy, Linor Abargil could have put this dark affair behind her and keep smiling for the cameras, but she made a different choice. Two months later, she filed a complaint and Shlomo was detained in Israel. Abargil's royal year of sweet global tours turned into a courageous journey of a young woman who decided not to rest until the man who victimized her is brought to justice.

Starting in Israel, the trial naturally drew international attention. Miss World was called to the stand in the Tel Aviv District Court, where she elaborated on her rape in Italy in great detail.

Testifying in court is an almost intolerable experience for abuse and rape victims. They are not only called upon to relive the horrible moments, but often feel shame and self-blame. For their own protection, their identity is often kept secret, but this was not the case. Abargil appeared in open court, extensively covered by the media. She was not a dark silhouette. Everyone knew her. Everybody talked about it.

With a trembling voice and heart-breaking sobs, she related how she contacted the travel agent, who came recommended by her modeling agency. Shlomo, who was born in Egypt and had been married to an Israeli, was reputed for quickly finding cheap flights to Israel, and Abargil was eager to get home. On the next day, Shlomo called her and said he had a ticket. He offered to meet her at the Milan train station, but arrived too late for Abargil to catch her train. He then offered to drive her to Rome, so she does not miss her flight too. On the way there, he suggested that Abargil take a nap in the back seat, which she did. Soon after that, he stopped the car in a forest, put a knife to her throat, and brutally raped her. He gagged her with an adhesive tape, raped her again, and tried to strangle her. Abargil testified that through this, she felt detached from reality, as if in another world. "When he realized he could not kill me, he changed again and started begging me to forgive him. I swore I would tell no one," she related. When she returned to Israel, she first told some relatives about this, but then she took the stand, and told the world.

After facing vicious rumors that she won the international title because of her tragedy, she had her moment of truth in court, looking solid as a rock. She withstood even the cross-examination by Shlomo's lawyers, who tried to convince the court that she fabricated the rape story and that she and Nur had consensual sex, but they failed. The judges believed her. They unanimously convicted the rapist, fully and unquestionably trusting Abargil's story. Nur Shlomo was found guilty and handed down a 16-year sentence.

When the trial ended and Abargil spoke to the media for the first time, she wished to make her difficult personal story an example of determination for all rape victims who struggle to punish the men who violated them. "The most important thing that happened here today," she said, "is that now I can cry out loud and tell all the women who hear me: speak up, file complaints, don't be afraid. This is the most important thing. Each and every one of you, no matter who she is, has the power."

This article is written in 2007, in the shadow of the President Katzav affair, which makes Abargil's words even louder and clearer, but followed by a question mark. In 1988, at least, it was clear as day: Linor Abargil was the most beautiful woman on Earth, and the bravest.

23.10.98

A Netanyahu-Arafat Accord in the White House: "No More Violence"

The Second Beat Accord, better known as the Wye Plantation Agreement, was signed in the White House. US President Bill Clinton, Israeli Prime Minister Binyamin Netanyahu, Jordanian King Hussein, and Palestinian Authority Chairman Yasser Arafat entered the East Room of the White House at 16:00. King Hussein arrived from a nearby hospital where he was treated for cancer.

President Clinton said the agreement is good for Israel's security and the Palestinians' economy, promising both parties some generous aid. He called Netanyahu "a peace warrior." When the ceremony started, Netanyahu approached Arafat and they shook hands warmly. "Today we pledge there would be no more violence or conflict between the parties," Arafat vowed.

Right to Left: Binyamin Netanyahu, Bill Clinton, King Hussein, and Yasser Arafat signing the Wye Plantation agreement. Photo: Jacob Saar, GPO

King Hussein and Queen Nur with Sara and Binyamin Netanyahu. Photo: Avi Ohaion, GPO.

The main points of the agreement: Israel pledged to pull out of 13.1% of area C, under its full control; of 14% of area B, under its security control; and that area A, under a full Palestinian command, would expand from 3% to 17.5% of the West Bank. Israel also promised to release prisoners and open the Gaza airport. The Palestinians pledged to revoke the Palestinian Covenant clauses that call for the annihilation of Israel, to detain fugitives, and collect illegally held weapons. The Wye agreement enraged the Israeli right and opposition, whose members launched an initiative to advance the elections. The settlers called Netanyahu "traitor," and Likud MK Beni Begin said, "The agreement is horrendous and must be rejected."

In the wake of the agreement, Israel and the United States signed a defense memorandum where Washington pledged to increase Israel's defensive and deterrence capabilities and help it against the missile threat.

President Clinton visited Israel and Gaza in mid-December to encourage the parties to implement the Second Beat agreement, and attended a special meeting of the Palestinian leaders where the relevant Palestinian Covenant clauses were nullified. After the Clinton visit, Foreign Minister Ariel Sharon said, "the permanent agreement with the Palestinians will be completed in 20 years."

Sharon District Youth Hacks Pentagon Computers

9 March

Ehud Tenenbaum, 18, managed to hack into Pentagon computers using the network of a well-known Negev school. He left a message reading: "Your Pentagon system can be breached. Please, close it."

Top FBI agents tried to track the hacker for a very long time and when they did, they were amazed to hear Tenenbaum say, "I did not do it for political or financial reasons. I only wanted to test my limits." Pentagon's John Hammer, however, was not convinced. "This was the most organized and systematic attack the Pentagon has ever encountered," he said.

Tenenbaum was found guilty and handed down an 18-month prison sentence, of which he served 6 months doing community service.

After serving his time, he said he regrets what he did and that he is already working on an original product that would make him a fortune. Tenenbaum became a computer whiz while still in high school. He was a gifted child, but did not excel at school because he was dyslexic. He spent his nights working on his computer and gained great expertise.

מדור אזרחי
מדור פלילי

Photo: Michael Kramer

Tenenbaum in court, awaiting trial.

Manbar "Harmed the State's Security for Lucre"

Nahum Manbar, who was born on Kibbutz Givat Haim in 1948 and was a paratrooper's officer, became involved in criminal and unlawful financing activities. When his creditors started breathing down his neck, he decided to make money through arms deals. He bought weapons from the Polish Army and subsequently sold them to Third World countries, but he really crossed the line when he made deals with Iran. The prosecution proved that he sold large quantities of weapons, as well as chemical substances that are used in the production of weapons, to the Iranians. When rumors of this reached the Defense Ministry, some of its staffers warned him and even cut off their ties with him. Alas, Manbar persisted.

Nahum Manbar (Left) in court.
Photo: Oren Agmon

He was detained in 1977, after the Mosad obtained unequivocal evidence that he provided Iran with guns, information, and substances associated with chemical warfare. Manbar denied the charges against him, claiming he had been framed for no reason, but the court found him guilty of serious breach of the state's security, such as assisting the enemy in its war against Israel and providing an enemy state with security-related information while intending to harm the state's safety.

Manbar appealed his sentence, but the High Court of Justice rejected it and Justice Theodore Or wrote in his verdict: "This is one of the gravest cases of security breach ever tried in Israel. Manbar committed crimes that can harm the state's security for lucre."

To this day, Manbar keeps claiming he is an innocent man and an Israeli Dreyfus, insisting that he had been wronged and unjustly framed.

1 January
Yehuda Wilk assumes duty as Israel Police chief, replacing Asaf Hefetz.

3 January
Defense Minister Yitzhak Mordechay suggests IDF pull out of Lebanon without signing a peace treaty.

6 January
Data on Israeli education: In percent points, the number of high school graduates is one of the lowest among developing countries.

12 January
Threats against Rabbi Ovadya Yosef in leaflets distributed all over Israel: "The angel of death will take you soon and throw you in hell." This, because the rabbi agreed to give territories to the Palestinians.

13 January
Many Israeli cities are paralyzed due to a snowstorm. Zafed sages: "We have not seen so much snow in 50 years."

18 January
Community Police chief: "Juvenile violence will soon be Israel's main problem."

20 January
The first batch of F-15i fighter jets land in Israel. This $2-billion deal was the largest the Israeli Air Force ever made.

Photo: Efi Sharir

Veteran Paratrooper Commanders Reunion

16 June

A reunion of veteran paratrooper commanders was held at the Kfar Maccabiah Center in Ramat Gan. Two of the most prominent guests were Unit 101 commander Ariel Sharon and warrior Meir Har-Zion.

Ariel Sharon and Meir Har-Zion at the reunion.

20.2.98

A First: Surrogate Mother Gives Birth to Twins After Parents Wait 10 Years

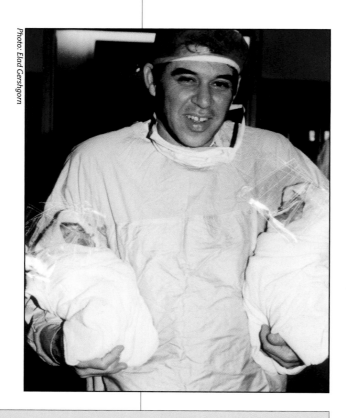

Photo: Elad Gershgorn

A 30-year-old surrogate mother gave birth to twins at the Rambam Hospital in Haifa. She did this for economic reasons, serving a religious couple that had been trying to conceive for more than 10 years. During the Caesarean section, the couple stood waiting outside the operating room and nearly fainted with excitement when they saw the twins. The mother burst into tears and thanked the Lord for "the gift I have been given." Hearing the babies cry, the surrogate mother whispered, "I don't want to see them... Take them away from me."

Another 15 couples have so far been given permission to have children under the Surrogate Parenting Act.

Mestings End IDF Service

11 January

After 50 years of IDF service, the "mesting" - the distorted Hebrew name of the tin mess kits that soldiers eat from in the field - is released from duty and replaced by disposable utensils.

Israel Is 50; the Jubilee Songs

3 May

These are the top 10 Israel songs of all times, as chosen by the Reshet Gimel radio Listeners:

1. *Yerushalayim Shel Zahav* (Jerusalem of Gold) - Shuli Natan

2. *Hare'ut* (Comradeship) - Shoshana Damari

3. *Shir Hashalom* (Song of Peace) - the Nahal Band

4. *Uf Gozal* (Fly Away, Baby Bird) - Arik Einstein

5. The Children of Winter '73 - Education Corps Band

6. *Tapuhim U Tmarim* (Apples and Dates) - Rami Kleinstein

7. *Hallelujah* - Halav U Dvash

8. *Haperah Begani* (Flower in My Garden) - Zohar Argov

9. *Livkot Leha* (Crying for You) - Arik Einstein

10. *Atur Mitzhech* (Your Forehead Adorned) - Arik Einstein

Photo: Michael Kramer

The Largest Ever Purim Parade Staged in Tel Aviv

13 March

The largest ever *Adloyada* (Purim parade) was staged in Tel Aviv in front of some quarter of a million spectators. The attractions included floaters, clowns, Muppets, celebrities, and entertaining shows.

98

Photo: Tzvika Tischler

22 April

50 Years of Israeli Fashion

One thousand fashion designs of the first 5 decades of Israel were shown in a Park Hayarkon pageant by 380 models.

10 May

Dana International Wins the Eurovision

Photo: Ziv Koren

Dana International's "Diva" won the first prize in the Eurovision Song Contest. At the end of a close and tense vote, the Israeli representative collected 174 points, while the song of Malta came in second with 166 points. Thousands celebrated the victory at the Rabin Square, and Dana declared, "I won because God loves me!" This was the third Israeli song to win the Eurovision Contest: Abanibi by Yizhar Cohen won in 1978, and Hallelujah won in 1979 in Jerusalem.

20 January
Prime Minister Netanyahu meets President Clinton and agrees to cede territories as part of the Second Beat.

20 January
Zvulun Hammer, education minister and vice premier, dies.

11 February
Yafa Yarkoni and Ehud Manor win the Israel Award.

26 February
Two Mosad agents are detained in Switzerland. They were captured attempting to bug Hizballah offices in Geneva. A suspecting neighbor called the police after surprising the two in the building basement.

5 March
Ezer Weizmann elected Israel President for a second term after defeating Shaul Amor.

6 March
Dalia Rabikovich and Amos Oz win the Israel Award for poetry and literature.

10 May
The government appoints Shaul Mofaz IDF chief of staff.

Photo: Haim Ziv

25 February

Yosi Banai - Israel Award Laureate

Yosi Banai won the Israel Award for theater. "An artist to the core, Banai is a stage animal who through his talents, personality, and creative world presents a unique combination of actor, director, and writer," the prize panel wrote. Banai, a man full of laughter and a great lover of Hebrew, passed away in May 2006 after struggling hard with cancer. He spent his last days working on a play named The King Is Dying.

14 May
Statesman and former Minister Yitzhak Mudai dies.

10 December
A Supreme Court historic precedent: The ultra-Orthodox' army exempt rendered illegal.

30 April

Bathsheva Performance Cancelled

The Bathsheva Dance Company performance at the Jubilee Bells show marking Israel's 50th anniversary was cancelled after the religious Knesset factions demanded that the *Ehad Mi Yode'a* number from *Anaphaza* be taken off or altered. This was followed by protests against "religious coercion."

The band performing Ehad Mi Yode'a

Photo: Gadi Dagan/PR

1999

Victorious Ehud Barak on Israeli prime minister election night.
Photo: Moshe Milner, GPO

Barak campaigning on Tel Aviv's Carmel Market.
Photo: Dani Solomon

Ehud Barak – Prime Minister
The man who tried to change the rules of the game

Writer Eli Amir

When Ehud Barak was elected prime minister in 1999, it felt like a new day dawned on Rabin Square, like a sweeping outburst of a hope. Barak promised peace and security (his election slogan), one nation (as he renamed Labor) one draft (national service for everyone), a blooming economy, minimized social gaps, and naturally - a solution for the "old lady in the corridor" (which he promised when he toured a crowded hospital). Having suffered Bibi Netanyahu's let down, and wishing for some correction and change, center and left voters chose Barak. The nation yearned for a leader to promote some compromise with the Palestinians, take the IDF out of Lebanon, and follow on Rabin's set of priorities. Barak was viewed as Rabin's successor, speaking of Ben-Gurion-like decisions, and the nation chose him and watched with anticipation.

Barak pulled the IDF out of Lebanon in a bold and controversial move. He scored quite a few achievements during his short term that ended prematurely. His coalition fell apart. The peace accord with Syria fell through over a 60-meters strip of land near Lake Kinneret. The Camp David conference, where Barak and Arafat met in July 2000, ended with an insulting picture of Barak shoving Arafat, with positive intentions, and incomprehensibly refusing to speak to the Palestinian leader alone during the 4-day conference. The hospital for the "old lady in the corridor" was eventually built as Barak promised (only to be inaugurated by Ariel Sharon), but it somehow left the feeling that the old lady is still out in her corridor bed.

The great euphoria ended in disenchantment. The commander and leader who knew victories and admiration was defeated by Sharon. The crown was taken from him and he withdrew, going back to his home piano where he tried to stomach the unfamiliar taste of failure. He took time off to regain his self-confidence, leaving his supporters bewildered.

I remember a moment in Barak's home when he set dates for the Lebanon pullout, for ending the conflict with the Palestinians, and for signing a peace accord with Syria, even defining their order of priorities. He did that as if there were no second and third parties, as if he could do it all one-sidedly, on his own, as if it was all up to him. Our hearts yielded to his wishes because we badly wanted to end the conflict and live in peace. Yet, a nagging thought persisted: how can he set dates for peace accords with old foxes such as Asad and Arafat. How can he be so sure?

"I mean to change the rules of the game in the Middle East. No more Oriental bazaar of hagglers, cheaters, and conmen, but a bold and courageous leaderships that puts it all on the table," Barak repeatedly declared, as if he were alone out there in the ring. Alas, the Middle East is a bazaar, whether we like it or not. Negotiating with the Arabs is an art form where you may never show your every card. At war, you may choose the location and timing of a clash, deliver a surprise. Ceremonies, however, require that both parties want them and set the time for their attainment. Barak was a loner, a man who lived by himself even when he was surrounded by advisers. He talked more than he listened. He adhered to his goals even if a mountain appeared on his way there. He dismantles watches and reassembles them alone. Regrettably, diplomacy, politics, and leaders do not work that way. It takes two to tango and, in our case, we even need an orchestra to play along and support the dancers. We need the USA, Russia, the Arab states, and Europe. At the same time, the "circumstances must be ripe," the other parties must be willing, leaders on both sides must be determined, the timing must be right, and then and only then, perhaps, agreements can be attained. Barak may have understood that in his mind, but not in his heart. "There is no partner on the other side," he declared - and then came the second intifadah.

Barak raised enormous hopes, and the media played a part in that. The media create superhuman, supreme, flawless heroes, pump them up, admire and empower them and we, redemption-hungry as we are, are tempted to believe. There was a moment that chemistry worked between voters and elected leader because of a promised salvation, but then reality slapped us in the face, and we left him alone. Members of his cabinet and party, who had been hurt by him, now abandoned him, stood on the sidelines, and gloated at his downfall.

How did that happen? Just like Rabin in his first term as prime minister, Barak made it to the top too fast. He did not have the time to acquire political and diplomatic experience, patience, and tolerance. He was not forged by the fires of disappointments and failures. He had no deep knowledge of party politicking, knew little of honorable and honest cooperation with party members, and was not familiar with concepts such as modesty and teamwork. He did not realize that reality runs its own course, it is complex, and you cannot dictate terms and schedules to it. Furthermore, expectations that a leader creates are dangerous for him and his nation because they must be fulfilled.

After quitting, Barak disappointed many who resented his choice to "look after his home" - starting a detrimental fashion that spread among us. After succeeding as a businessman he came back, almost hysterical, to erase the failure and seek the crown.

Israeli politics include the option of revival and return, which is why we need to ask: Is Barak worthy? The answer is - Yes, definitely. He is worthy, skilled, razor-sharp, bold, creative, and the best in the neighborhood.

Barak came back a changed man who has been through an exhausting campaign of conversing with every party member who so desired. It is the same Barak, plus some newly acquired caution, attentiveness, and understanding of the limits of power and complexity of the issues at hand. Barak knew he would not be given another chance. It may be assumed that with his historic vision, intellectual skills, and wise diplomatic views - he knows he must not miss the opportunity he is given in 2008. He knows he cannot miss again and repeat his past mistakes.

17.3.**99**

Convicted Arye Deri: "I Was Terribly Wronged"

In an unprecedentedly grave verdict, the court found Arye Deri guilty of pocketing $155,000 in bribes. The 917-page verdict contains harsh remarks by the justices concerning the conduct of Deri and the other three defendants. "They attempted to obstruct justice, coordinate testimonies, forge documents, file false affidavits, and exerted political pressures," the judges stated.

Nine years after the investigation started and after 4 years of trial, Deri sat in the courtroom and heard a piercing verdict that recounted his crimes: He collected bribes from the public coffers, and deposited extensive sums in his and his wife's bank accounts, financed trips abroad for him and his family, and paid for his Jerusalem apartment.

Reacting to the verdict, Deri said, "I committed no crime and stole nothing. I was terribly wronged. I am innocent before God and Men." Outside the court, SHAS supporters staged vigils and carried signs charging, "Sephardim Deported by Ashkenazim!" and claiming that "He is Innocent!" and "Deri, Born Free!"

Constant demonstrations of support for Deri were encouraged by Rabbi Ovadya Yosef, who determined: "He is not guilty by law! Rabbi Arye Deri is innocent!" The justices, however, made no secret of their criticism of Deri, handing down a 4-year prison term and fining him 250,000 shekels. The court also ruled that he comitted a flagrant offence, which is why he is may not hold a public role or office for 10 years after serving his time.

On 12 July, the court mitigated his sentence, cutting a year. The Deri trial pushed ethnic tensions in Israel back to surface, and made many feel that the establishment persecuted Deri due to his ethnic background and his political clout as SHAS leader.

Arye Deri celebrating the mitigation of his sentence. Photo: Tzvika Tischler

Sympathizers escort Deri outside the Jerusalem Court. Photo: Ziv Koren

Photo: IDF Spokesman

Submarine Dakar Found Drowned and Broken

30 May

Some 31 years after it mysteriously vanished near the Isle of Crete, Israeli Navy Submarine Dakar was found on the 2,900-meter deep bottom of the Mediterranean. Experts stated that no bodies would be found and salvaging it was impossible.

Over the years, 25 attempts were made to find it, but failed. This time, an American search team discovered a metal object and more debris later in the deep. Eventually, the vessel was found split in two. The Navy lost 69 crewmen in the Dakar disaster.

Barak Wins Elections: "Dawn of a New Day"

Ehud Barak secured a landslide victory and was elected Israeli prime minister by 56% of the voters. When the ballots closed, tens of thousands gathered at Rabin Square to celebrate and heard Barak promise: "A dawn of a new day has broken." He vowed he "will be prime minister for everyone... We will do everything we can to end wars and bring peace and prosperity."

Political observers were unanimous that more than a massive show support for Barak, the election result was a show of protest against the conduct of outgoing Prime Minister Benjamin Netanyahu. Many Likud voters turned their backs on Netanyahu, upset by his acts and behavior more than by the Oslo arrangements and his policy regarding Arafat and the exploding busses. They set ideology aside and punished Netanyahu for his term.

When he realized how badly he was beaten, Netanyahu announced he was stepping down as Likud Party leader as well. "I am taking a time-out," he told his bewildered supporters. "This is our Yom Kippur," one of them whispered. Ariel Sharon replaced Netanyahu as Likud chairman.

Barak started his term with a very supportive public and great hopes of diplomatic breakthrough, mainly with hope for "the old lady from the hospital corridor."

Ehud Barak at the Labor headquarters after his victory was announced.
Photo: Moshe Milner, GPO

Pilots Returned from Lebanon Hanging in Midair

11 June

Two Cobra helicopters were sent to rescue wounded soldiers from Lebanon when one of the helicopters malfunctioned and its pilots were forced to crash-land it in a pitch-dark ravine.

The other Cobra immediately landed next to it. The two pilots strapped themselves to the chopper glides and were flown back to Israel hanging in midair. "The pilots showed great resourcefulness and courage," their squadron chief said.

1999

4 January
By a vote of 85 against 27, the Knesset advances the elections to 17 May 1999.

24 January
Appearing live on the radio, Prime Minister Netanyahu fires Defense Minister Yitzhak Mordechay who decided to quit Likud and head Center Party.

28 February
Brigadier General Erez Gerstein, commander of the Lebanon Liaison Unit, killed in a Hizballah attack in the security zone.

Photo: Efi Sharir

14 March
The right-wing parties decide to merge and run in the Knesset elections on a single ticket, National Union. Their candidate list is headed by Beni Begin and Rehavam Zeevi.

16 March
In a report on the Zeelim disaster, the state comptroller states: "Barak did not run away" as charged.

4 May
Prime Minister Bibi Netanyahu: "The elites hate Sephardim and immigrants."

10 May
Rabbi Ovadya Yosef special offer: "Vote SHAS and go to Heaven."

17 May
Knesset and prime ministerial elections held, with Netanyahu running against Barak.

The "First Lady" of the Air Force

1.1.99

Lt. Sheri, the first woman air combat navigator. Photo: Giora Neuman, IAF Journal

When Lieutenant Sheri completed her march on the Israel Air Force (IAF) base parade ground and IAF commander pinned pilot's wings on her blouse, the crowd stood and cheered. After all, Sheri was the first woman to graduate an IAF pilot's course in 48 years. She was assigned as combat navigator with an F-16 squadron.

IAF chief Eytan Ben-Eliahu lavished praises on the new navigator, saying, "I hope that many women will follow you." Indeed, between then and now, 10 women have served as fighter pilots with the IAF.

The IAF first changed its stand on women pilots after, in 1995, the High Court of Justice ruled against the defense minister and in favor of Alice Miller, stating that women may volunteer to serve as IAF pilots. In the wake of this basic ruling, the IDF assigned numerous women to various combat positions. In 2007, the Knesset passed an act, according to which women may serve in any IDF position, and even volunteer for elite units.

Mosad Agent Fabricated Information on Syria

13 March

Mosad agent Yehuda Gil was found guilty of fabricating information with the intention of harming the state's security and sent to prison for 5 years. The state charged him of producing false documents, allegedly warning that the Syrians are planning a snatch operation on Mt. Hermon and reporting on suspicious Syrian Army movement along the border. The information made the defense establishment consider calling the reserves. In his trial, Gil denied charges that he had been misleading his superiors for years.

According to foreign media reports, Gil used to have a "source" in the Syrian government, but he had to quit his senior post and was no longer able to feed Gil with updated data. Gil, however, kept pretending the "source" was still giving him information. He even traveled abroad to supposedly meet his source, and brought back "information" he made up.

Photo: Hadar Cohen

Serial Rapist Beni Sela Captured

16 December

In a dramatic news conference, Tel Aviv District Police chief Shlomo Aharonishky announced excitedly, "The nightmare is over. We captured the serial rapist." An 18-month manhunt ended when Beni Sela was caught after trying to molest two young women in Tel Aviv. The police held him suspect on 34 counts of rape, attempted rape, and sexual assault. The detectives found two cameras and dozens of films depicting him in the act. His last victim was a 12-year-old girl from Ramat Hasharon. The detectives related that Sela used to make his victims shower after the attack and destroyed the sheets to eliminate the evidence.

Sela was found guilty and sent to 35 years in prison. In December 2006, he escaped while on his way to a hearing in a Tel Aviv court, but was captured a few days later near Nahariya and returned to the Rimonim Penitentiary, where he is held in total isolation.

Playwright Hanoch Levin Dies

19 August

Hanoch Levin, viewed by many as the greatest playwright and theater director in Israel, died after a long and bad illness. Levin produced 34 provocative, fascinating, and controversial plays before he succumbed to cancer at the age of 56. He directed his last play, *Ashkava* (Requiem), to his last day, suffering great pain.

Photo: Gadi Dagon, Cameri Theater PR

Scene from a Levin play

99

6 July

The Carmiel Festival

Photo: Elad Gershgorn

The 12th Folk Dance Festival opens in Carmiel featuring local and foreign dance groups.

6 June

Israel's national soccer team beats Austria 5:0 in the European Championship qualifiers, marking one of the greatest victories of Israeli soccer.

6 July

Ehud Barak's cabinet, the 23rd Government of Israel, is sworn in at the Knesset.

13 July

The longest trial in Israel's history, a civil suit, ends after 19 years in the Tel Aviv Magistrates Court.

4 September

Ehud Barak and Yasser Arafat sign the Sharm (amended Wye) Agreement.

1 October

Ted Arison, the richest Israeli in the world, dies at 75.

15 October

Dr. Yosef Burg, former minister and National Religious Party leader, dies.

15 December

Israel-Syria peace talks begin in Washington with Clinton, Barak, and Al-Shara.

20 December

National Insurance Institute report: 1 million Israelis, including 440,000 children, live under the poverty line.

Photo: Hadar Cohen

8 April

Guinness Kissing Record Breakers Hospitalized

A young Petah Tikva couple had themselves a 30:45' hours non-stop kiss on Rabin Square in Tel Aviv and broke a Guinness record. They competed against several dozen couples and won a flight around the world. "Our bodies ache, our muscles are sore, and our mouths feel on fire," the winning couple said.

Photo: Meir Azulay

7 October

A Bedouin-Russian Love Story

Love at first sight between a Jewish soldier who emigrated from Russia and a young Bedouin from the village of Arab al-Shibli led to a traditional village wedding. The Bedouin bride's parents were against the match, while the Russian soldier's parents begged him to "find a nice Jewish girl," but - as always - love triumphed. They married against all odds in an Israeli Bedouin-Russian love story.

10 March

Rana Raslan -

The First Arab Miss Israel

Haifa born, 21-years-old Rana Raslan won the title of Israel's 1999 beauty queen. "It does not matter if I am an Arab or a Jewish woman. We are all humans," Miss Israel said.

Photo: Tzvika Tischler

2000

The last IDF tank leaves Lebanon.
Photo: Efi Sharir

IDF soldiers rejoice upon leaving Lebanon.
Photo: Alfi Ben-Yaacov, GPO

We Are the Lebanon Generation

*Chief of Staff
Gabi Ashkenazi*

For nearly a generation, Lebanon was the landscape that shaped me. First and foremost, there was the Beaufort - that ominous fortress that became a symbol. You may leave Lebanon, but the Beaufort will never leave you. It rises high and mighty, dominating borders and houses, stating its presence. Around it - the same old ravines, crevices, villages, bridges, good and bad Lebanese, boulders, and shrubs where we spend many a nerve-wrecking nights. For 18 years, Lebanon has been a very central location on my and my generation's agenda: planning missions, assigning units and tasks, going in and out in convoys. There were moments of fear and worry, hope and glory, of partnership with the SLA, and of rage and pain at funerals of fallen friends and with their families. Lebanon robbed an entire generation of a part of our lives and very many comrades and commanders, friends and warriors.

Yet, when I sat down to write of 2000 - the year in which we pulled out of Lebanon, when I was Northern Command chief - it was faces I remembered, not the landscape. I remembered the outstanding people that Lebanon tore away from their families, the entire State of Israel, and my soul. I remembered the late Major General Yekutiel Adam, my former commander in Golani and a role model, who was the highest-ranking soldier the IDF lost in Lebanon when he served as deputy chief of staff. I remembered Major Goni Hernick, commander of the Golani reconnaissance unit, a brother in arms, who fell on the Beaufort, leaving a legacy that still lives in his unit. I remembered Lt. Col. Amir Meital, who fell fighting against terrorists of Ahmad Jibril's organization in the village of Nueima, deep inside Lebanon. Amir was a promising commander and warrior. If he were alive today, he would have been at the top of the IDF. I remembered Brig. Gen. Erez Gerstein, my brother, who fell while leading a convoy, as a true commander in the IDF. He was head of the Lebanon Liaison Unit and his death shocked us all. There are many fine commanders in the IDF, but men like Erez - courageous and honest leaders, warriors, and dreamers - are rare. Each year, there were fewer of us, commanders, as we stood on the hill overlooking Lebanon, that beautiful and cursed land, whose soil is drenched with the blood of my friends, my generation, hundreds of names, faces, families.

I clearly remember that Wednesday morning, 24 May 2000, when the forces under my command left the Land of Cedars. Many Israelis sighed with relief on that day. The front pages and TV screens were filled with pictures of dust-covered soldiers riding tanks and APCs through Israel's international border crossing back to Israel. For them, Lebanon was a divided and cursed land. Our presence there was much debated in Israel, but for us - the soldiers whose boots were covered with its gore, blood, mud, and dust - Lebanon was more than that. It was our life's essence and mission. There, we tested values such as self-sacrifice, selflessness, comradeship, and professionalism. Many of us were transformed there from young recruits to seasoned commanders and warriors. We grieved for our fallen brothers. We fought, dreaming of a better future. We learned first-hand how to keep our independence. In Lebanon, we sobered up! Against our will, we became the Lebanon Generation. I was wounded there during Operation Litani and I carry its memory on my body.

Leaving Lebanon that day, I remembered the years, the fallen friends, their smiles and visages. I still think about our valiant allies, the soldiers and commanders of the South Lebanese Army - brave souls whom I learned to love and respect, who were suddenly cheated and turned homeless. I meet some of them in Israel, now and then. Their feet are here, but their hearts are in the Land of Cedars. I remembered the long nights we spent inside Lebanon, when rank and role made no difference, as we watched the glimmering lights of Kiryat Shemona, Dovev, and Kfar Yuval, remembering the grave terror attacks they had suffered, knowing why we were there.

Leaving Lebanon that day, I did not look back, but knew: A sovereign Israeli Government under Menahem Begin decided in 1982 to send the IDF into Lebanon, and a sovereign Israeli Government under Ehud Barak decided in 2000 to realign its troops along the international border. The incursion and the pullout were both decisions made by a strong cabinet, one that trusted the IDF might and courage of its warriors.

Recently, after the Second War of Lebanon, I was recalled to the army and assumed post as chief of staff. Surveying the honorary guard, I looked for the faces of Erez Gerstein, Goni Hernick, Amir Meital, and Avraham Hido. If they were alive, they would have been there. They and many other good men are missing from our ranks. I am here for them!

24.5.00

"Mom, We're Out of Lebanon!"

Leaving Lebanon: IDF soldiers hoisting an Israeli flag. Photo: Ziv Koren

The IDF soldiers quickly cleared its outposts in Lebanon after spending 18 years there. All through that final night in Lebanon, the sound of exploding Hizballah bombs could be heard, Air Force helicopters hovered above, and many tanks secured the roads to ensure a smooth, victim-free pullout.

Reyhan, Ayshiya, Dla'at, Karkom, and of course the Beaufort, outposts that became symbols for IDF soldiers in Lebanon ,were blown up at dawn. At 04:00, Brigadier General Beni Gantz, commander of the Lebanon Liaison Unit, was the last soldier who crossed the border into Israel and the big gate north of Metula was locked behind him. Then, the telephones began to ring. Soldiers and officers called home, and happy voices could be heard yelling: "Mom, we're out of Lebanon!" "The nightmare is over!"

Soon after the IDF pulled out, Hizballah warriors seized took control of southern Lebanon, and thousands of South Lebanon Army soldiers and their families gathered at Fatma Gate, hoping they would be allowed into Israel.

Deciding to pull the IDF out of Lebanon, Prime Minister Ehud Barak put an end to a tragic and bloody chapter in Israel's history during which 1,547 soldiers and civilians were killed. The majority of Israelis supported the move that ended a sharp debate in Israel, and marked the great victory of the Four Mothers Movement, that has been urging the pullout for years.

IDF soldiers taking down a Lebanon outpost gate.
Photo: Yael Engelhart, GPO

Photo: Yaacov Saar, GPO

Israel-Syria Peace Talks Begin

3 January

Peace talks between Israel and Syria resumed in Shepherdstown, West Virginia. US officials said that the gap between the parties is merely 60 meters. The Syrian foreign minister said, "The Israeli withdrawal is a done deal," and Israel's Prime Minister Barak stated, "We can reach an agreement with the Syrians."

Above: Prime Minister Baraq, with US President Bill Clinton to his right and Syrian Foreign Minister Faruk al-Shara to his left.

Photo: AFP

IDF Soldiers Lynched in Ramallah

13 October

One of the worst incidents of the intifadah took place in Ramallah when reservists Yosi Avrahami (38) and Vadim Norzech (35) took a wrong turn on their way to base. Palestinian police officers detained them and took them to a local police station, which was attacked by a bloodthirsty Palestinian mob. They raided the station, tortured the soldiers, and eventually threw a mutilated body to the street. The crowd went on to abuse the body, tied it to a car, and dragged it to the city square, where they torched it. The other body was badly abused as well. A few days later, the lynch perpetrators were captured in a combined operation of the Shin Bet and an elite IDF unit and brought to trial in Israel.

A Palestinian youth proudly showing the incited crowd his palms covered with the blood of the Jewish soldiers.

The Al-Aksa Intifada: 1,110 Israeli Fatalities

Al-Aksa Intifadah was the name given to the war between Israel and the Palestinians that broke out in September 2000 and continued intermittently until the Palestinian civil war of June 2007. During that period, 1,110 Israelis were killed in terror acts. The immediate cause of the intifada (popular uprising) was Ariel Sharon's visit to Temple Mount on 28 September, which sparked riots in East Jerusalem on the same day.

A few days later, the Palestinians were joined by Israeli Arabs who rioted for 3 days, blocking roads and hurling rocks. Trying to disperse them, the police used live ammunition, killing 13 of them. In the wake of the October Riots, a national commission of inquiry was formed, headed by Justice Theodore Or. The intifada continued with terror attacks by suicide bombers, carbombs, and guns.

Veiled Palestinian youths hurling rocks outside Lion's Gate of the Old City of Jerusalem at the end of the Ramadan Friday prayers. Photos: Ziv Koren

3 January
Israel-Syria Peace talks resume in Shepherdstown, West Virginia, between Prime Minister Baraq, US President Bill Clinton, and Syrian Foreign Minister Faruk al-Shara

26 January
The High Court of Justice precedent ruling: Parents may not hit their children; not even a slap on the wrist.

6 March
Israel's Government makes a historic decision to pull the IDF out of Lebanon after 18 years of presence.

21 March
Pope Paul II makes a historic visit of Israel.

10 July
President Ezer Weizmann resigns after a 5-months criminal investigation against him on suspicion of wrongfully collecting funds from businessmen. The attorney general decided not to press charges, but criticized the president's conduct.

10 July
SHAS and the NRP quit the Barak cabinet, leaving it with only eight members. Nevertheless, the prime minister decided to go to Washington for a summit meeting with Arafat. "The people gave me a mandate, which I use to decide on the state's fate.

"Tell Me How to Stop the Tears"

24 February

"Tell me how to stop the tears / Tell me where there is another world to live / Along the shore, not waves, but the world / Smashed to droplets on the pier."
Ofra Haza (1958-2000) struggled for two weeks until her heart stopped beating after a mysterious hospitalization. Rumors abound about her medical condition.
Throughout the fortnight she spent at the Shiva Hospital, admirers, fans, friends, and relatives packed the place and prayed for her recovery. Dr. Zeev Rothstein, hospital director, announced her death, but refused to elaborate on its causes. It took a few days before the truth came to light: Haza died of a virus contracted because she had AIDS. Her family accused her husband, Doron Ashkenazi, as did Bezalel Aloni who was her personal manager for years. "Ask her husband how she got that way," he said.
Haza, a Cinderella with a golden voice from the Hatikva neighborhood of Yemenite Jews in Tel Aviv made it to the top of international charts and the hearts of Israelis, and went on to make an international career with songs such as *Im Ninalu* (If Heaven Gates are Locked).

Ofra Haza

Photo: Tzvika Tischler

30 July
Unprecedented medical achievement: Permanent artificial heart planted in a patient's chest.

7.10.OO Soldiers Abducted on Mt. Dov

Photo: Yario Katz

A New View of the Dimona Reactor

18 August

New pictures of the nuclear reactor in Dimona were taken by an American satellite and published in Israel as well. The site's last available pictures were taken 30 years ago.

Photo: US satellite

The Jeep from which Beni Avraham, Adi Avitan, and Omar Suwad were abducted. Reproduction photo: Tomeriko

Hayim Avraham, father of abducted soldier Beni (center) with an IRC representative (left). Photo: Shaul Golan

On a Sabbath afternoon, a Hizballah squad attacked an unshielded IDF patrol traveling along the Lebanese border on Mt. Dov, on the northern slopes of Mt. Hermon. The patrol was manned by Corps of Engineers soldiers Beni Avraham, Adi Avitan, and Omar Suwad. The terrorists detonated a powerful bomb, and then broke through the border gate, dragged the three soldiers, who were wounded or dead, across the border, and took them into Lebanon.

The IDF tried to slow the abductors down with mortar and tank shells and Air Force raids of Hizballah outposts, but failed. The army confirmed that the three soldiers were injured during the abduction. Barak said that "Hizballah, Syria, and Lebanon are responsible for the soldiers' wellbeing." Hizballah announced, "The soldiers are in a safe place that Israel cannot reach." A week later, on 15 October, Hizballah Secretary General Nasrallah announced that they abducted reserves Brigadier General Elhanan Tannenbaum in Dubai, where he went to make a drug deal. He was sedated, and flown to Beirut.

Mosad Successfully Smuggles Torah Scrolls Out of Iraq

7 May

Dozens of Torah scrolls that Saddam Hussein ordered destroyed were smuggled to Israel in a Mosad operation. Some 50 scrolls were hidden in a Baghdad warehouse by Jews who immigrated to Israel in the 1950's. The scrolls' rescue was part of a larger operation where Mosad agents salvaged valuables belonging to the Jewish community of Iraq.

"Captive" Torah Returns from Egypt

7 July

A Torah scroll that was taken captive 27 years ago, when the Suez Canal outposts were overrun by the Egyptian army in the Yom Kippur War, was given back to Israel. It was seized from the Mezah Outpost, which was the last one conquered, and whose 37-men crew was taken captive. Outpost commander Shlomo Ardinest said, "We decided to take the book into captivity with us believing it would keep us from harm."

OO

28 February

The Gashash Hahiver Win Israel Award

Photo: Michael Kramer

The comic trio received the Israel Award laureate for its life's work. The panel explained: "The Gashash created a unique language that assimilated with contemporary Hebrew."

Photo: Zio Koren

31 March

The Pope in Israel

Pope Paul II arrived on a historic tour of Israel. Visiting Yad Vashem, he said: "I deeply sympathize with the Jewish nation."

---

7 January

"Internet Burns Souls"

Use of the Internet and computers was banned in the ultra-Orthodox community because it introduces pornography. The community court issued an edict that was published on billboards and Haredi newspapers in Jerusalem and Bene Berak. The ads read: "It is strictly forbidden to get on the Internet, which poses a great threat to the sanctity of the Land of Israel and the future generations." Surveys conducted in the community, however, found that some half of the ultra-Orthodox households have computers.

---

22 February

"Landscape With Dog" Donated to the Israel Museum

A Paul Gauguin painting, worth some $15 million, was donated to the Israel Museum after several years of negotiations. The renowned French artist painted "Landscape With Dog" in 1903, a month before he died.

---

1 March

The Largest Diamond Robbery in Israel

Three armed robbers broke into a Ramat Gan diamond-polishing workshop, bypassing the guards and a sophisticated alarm system. They tied the 25 workers there and left the place a few minutes later with some 10 million shekels worth of diamonds. The police said they had inside information and were pros.

---

31 July

Contrary to political forecasts, Moshe Katzav was elected state president after defeating Shimon Peres.

22 September

Poet Yehuda Amihai dies.

28 September

The Al-Aksa intifada starts with riots in East Jerusalem.

1 October

13 Israeli Arabs are killed in the October Riots as policemen and Border Police officers fire at crowds of intifadah sympathizers.

7 October

Three IDF soldiers abducted in the Mt. Dov region.

16 October

Elhanan Tannenbaum, a reserves officer, kidnapped in Dubai and brought to Beirut by Hizballah.

20 October

Some 52 Naval Commando soldiers who trained in the Kishon River contract cancer. After 20 of them died, the IDF acknowledged their injuries were sustained in the line of duty.

10 October

Ehud Barak resigns as prime minister and calls elections for 6 February 2001.

2001

Prime Minister Ariel Sharon with his dog on Sycamore Ranch. Photo: Michael Kramer

The full Sharon cabinet; on Sharon's right, President Katzav. Photo: Amos Ben Gershom, GPO

Ariel Sharon,
The Hawk Who Knew How To Be a Dove

Ehud Olmert

Every nation and state has a fundamental ethos. In ours, Ariel Sharon is not only a central figure. He actually authored it as a military commander, political leader, and statesman. On 6 February 2001, Sharon ran against Barak in "special elections" for prime minister and scored a stunning landslide victory with more than 60% of the votes. Soon after that, he established a national unity government, as he promised on the eve of the elections. Some 30 years after launching his political career, he was at the top and the heart of the Israeli consensus.

As he started his term, Sharon managed to muster broad national support for his leadership and policies. He had a deep, perhaps intuitive understanding of the complex and fascinating mixture of the Israelis. This did not surprise me. The Mapai (Labor) member who established the Likud, the hawk who knew how to be a dove, the farmer who believed in advanced industry, the warrior with a season ticket for the Philharmonic Orchestra assumed post as prime minister with national unity already built into his personality. He started his term in one of the worst years Israel ever experienced. In 2001, the wave of terror reached unprecedented dimensions, leaving 208 dead and more than 1,500 wounded. In hindsight, this was the year of great disillusionment of the traditional political theses of the left and the right. Facing all this, Sharon stood up and navigated the State of Israel soberly and skillfully as politician and statesman. He never promised magic solutions. He was responsible, seasoned, and wise enough to realize that no single political or military act could end the deep and complicated conflict between the Palestinians and us.

The Israelis admired him for that. I remember those sad and bad days when Palestinian terror struck at us daily. As Jerusalem mayor, I visited attack sites. It was not easy. I will never forget the horror. I saw the depth of pain and heard the people's cries of rage. In those days, Sharon's leadership acquired special meaning. He was perceived as one who can deal with the problems of terror and its consequences for the Israeli society and economy. Indeed, as always, Sharon was not stagnant. He followed various tracks to handle the bulk of Israel's problems, primarily the terror problem. In those years, as I worked by his side as Jerusalem mayor and later as a member of his cabinet and his deputy, I studied him up close. I was deeply impressed with his original thoughts on political issues, admired his determination, and was amazed with his courage. I also grew fond of his personal style, his sense of humor, dispassionate mind, and the huge power emanating from him.

Much has been written about Ariel Sharon the commander, leader, and statesman, but people who knew him first hand knew he was first and foremost a family man. I still remember the look on his face when he was elected prime minister in February 2001. There was joy, but there was great sadness too. Delivering his victory speech in the Tel Aviv Fairgrounds, he spoke candidly. "So far," he told the excited crowd, "whenever I assumed new duties, in every moment of my life, joyous or harsh, my wife Lili was there, beside me. Now that the nation showed it trusts me to lead the state in the coming years, Lili is not here with me and I miss her."

Five years later, at the peak of his glory, Ariel Sharon's body failed him. For the first time ever, something stopped Sharon. In my mind still echo the words of Cabinet Secretary Israel Maimon, who called me that night of 4 January 2006 and said, "The prime minister lost consciousness and is incapacitated. You are to assume the duties and powers of prime minister." It was almost inconceivable. Suddenly, his incessant activity stopped. I still miss the long hours we worked together, his voice, body language, and special sense of humor. I yearn for the day when he opens his eyes and come back to us, mainly to his sons Omri and Gilad, and grandchildren Rotem, Yoav, Uri, Dania, Aya, Avigail, and other members of his family that he loved so much.

6.2.01

Israel's Prime Minister Ariel Sharon: "Peace Means Painful Concessions"

Photo: Ziv Koren

Ariel Sharon was elected prime minister by a majority of 61%, while runner up Ehud Barak collected 38.1%. For many years, Sharon was one of the most disputed figures in Israeli politics and the left's most hated politician in the 1980's. He started his race for prime minister only 60 days before the elections. It was the race of his lifetime, an end all be all stance in the ruthless Israeli political scene. His aides prepared a campaign that presented him as the loving grandfather, with children and sheep on his farm, who will bring peace, security, and unity to Israel. It worked perfectly.

As soon as the results were made known, he appeared before his followers and, calling for the establishment of a national unity government, he stated: "Peace means painful concessions by both sides." He started his victory speech commemorating his late wife: "Now that the nation showed it trusts me to lead the state in the coming years, Lili is not here with me, and I miss her."

On the following day, he sent emissaries to Europe and the United States with calming messages, after the world media expressed concern over "the election of this frightening person." A similar message was dispatched to Syrian President Asad, saying that Israel would be willing to resume negotiations without preconditions. He even talked to Yasser Arafat on the phone and told him, "I took part in every war here, so I understand the importance of peace..."

The national unity government was sworn in at the Knesset on 7 March; it had 26 ministers, including Binyamin Ben-Eliezer as Defense Minister, Shimon Peres as foreign minister, and Silvan Shalom in the Treasury.

The Versailles Disaster: "The Dance Floor Vanished"

24 May

Some 700 people partied at a wedding in Versailles Halls in Jerusalem when the floor suddenly vanished. Hundreds of guests fell through the breach in the floor all the way to the basement, and dozens were trapped under the debris. More than 100 ambulances evacuated 23 fatalities and another 377 injured guests to hospitals. The survivors said, "It was horrible... the dance floor just disappeared beneath our feet."

Police investigation led to indictments on charges of manslaughter, criminal negligence, and illegal profiteering. The courts sentenced the hall owners to 2.5 years in prison, and Engineer Eli Ron, inventor of the PalKal construction method, was handed down a 4-year sentence after being found guilty of causing death through negligence.

Ruins of the Versailles Halls in Jerusalem.
Photos: Ziv Koren

Dolphinarium Horror: 21 Youths Killed

Some 300 partying youths jammed the Dolphinarium complex, waiting for a dance party. There were many CIS immigrants, students who attended the Shevah School of Science.

Suddenly there was a huge explosion. A suicide bomber walked unnoticed right into the crowd and detonated a bomb he carried on his person. The club entrance looked like a war zone, with hundreds crying for help and dozens ambulances carrying away the victims. The horror was revealed when the dust settled: 21 youths were killed and 103 were wounded. This was one of the worst terror attacks in Israel's history.

The attack caused great rage all around the world and was sharply condemned. The Shin Bet started hunting the perpetrators, eliminating most of them by early November.

Photo: Jeremy Feldman

Police combing the terror attack site.

Minister Gad Zeevi Assassinated in Jerusalem

17 October

At around 07:00, a Palestinian assassin shot and killed Tourism Minister Zeevi in the Hyatt Hotel in Jerusalem. The minister took the elevator from the dining hall to his eighth floor room, where the assassin awaited him. He shot the minister three times, using a gun with a silencer, hitting him in the head. The minister collapsed, and his wife later found him lying in a pool of blood. He was taken to hospital, where he was pronounced dead.

Nicknamed Gandhi, Zeevi was a Palmah warrior, an IDF general, Greater Israel advocate, and a disputed politician. He refused a bodyguard after he became minister, saying, "I have a gun and I'm not afraid." He paid with his life for his insistence.

Zeevi's killers were detained a week later and pleaded guilty.

Photo: Yoav Galai

6 February

Ariel Sharon elected Israel's prime minister.

14 February

Seven soldiers and a woman are killed as a bus driven by a Palestinian rams a bus stop in Zerifin.

1 March

A research finds 250,000 Israelis, including 65,000 children, use drugs. Some 7 tons of heroin and 50 tons of marijuana and hashish are smuggled into Israel annually.

4 March

Suicide bomber kills 3 in central Netanya.

21 March

Yitzhak Mordechay is found guilty of sexual abuse and not guilty of harassment; given an 18 months suspended sentence.

18 May

Terror attack in Hasharon Mall: 5 killed.

1 June

Terror in the Dolphinarium: 21 youths killed and 103 wounded.

20 June

First Ethiopian immigrant to become an army doctor: Dr Avi Yitzhak, who immigrated 10 years earlier, is assigned to a paratroopers' battalion, where he is cited.

16 July

2 soldiers killed in terror attack outside the Binyamina train station.

9 August

Terror attack at Sbarro Restaurant in Jerusalem: 15 killed, including 6 children and 5 members of the same family.

9 September

Terror attack at the Nahariya train station: 3 killed. The perpetrator was an Israeli citizen.

1 October

The state attorney orders a criminal investigation against Prime Minister Sharon and his son Omri for allegedly collecting 6 million shekels from foreign donors in violation of the Elections Act.

Rabbi Elazar Shach, Ponibezh Yeshiva Head, Passed Away

Crowds of followers attend Rabbi Shach's funeral. Photo: Tzvika Tischler

Rabbi Elazar Shach dies at the age of 107. He was a Lithuanian and a strong opponent of Hassidim and Jewish mysticism, a brainy rationalist who deeply hated secularism. He believed Zionism is a bitter enemy that must be fought, viewing the yeshiva students as soldiers in God's army. He held moderate political views, believing that life is more sacred than land. His call for the establishment of a Sephardic ultra-Orthodox party led to the creation of SHAS.

Photo: Tzvika Tischler

Olim Arrive Despite Terror

23 August

Some 45,000 *Olim*, new immigrants, arrived in Israel since January despite the grave terror attacks. Only last week, some 1,225 students from the former Soviet republics landed in the Ben Gurion Airport, planning to settle in Israel.

On the left: Students arrive from Ukraine and Russia.

Rabbi Ovadya: "Women Must Be Beautiful"

1 August

In a sermon he delivered to mark Love Day, SHAS mentor Rabbi Ovadya said: "He who marries a woman with a nose like a watermelon will have a son looking like a cucumber..." The rabbi therefore recommended that men marry only beautiful women "so that they could help them bring handsome sons into the world..."

Photo: Israel Aerospace Industries

The Arrow Hits Bull's Eye

28 August

The Arrow-2 missile made a significant operational leap. This anti-missile missile, designed to defend Israel from Scuds and other missiles like it, hit its designated target and destroyed it.

01

13 May

"Everybody Knows - Europe's Color is Yellow"

Photo: Oren Agmon

The Maccabi Tel Aviv Basketball Club wins the European championship after beating Panathinaikos 81:67 in the final, 20 years after Maccabi last won the European title. Some 8,000 fans packed the Paris hall and did not stop cheering. At the end of the game, Prime Minister Sharon called Coach Pini Gershon, congratulated him and said, "The nation is proud of you." While the few hundred lucky fans celebrated in Paris, thousands took to the streets in Tel Aviv, dancing and chanting - "Everybody knows - Europe's color is yellow."

22 February

Hot Summer

The Castro Fashion House presented its new sensual and tight summer collection.

Photo: Alex Kolomoisky

Leading the campaign that year, Sandy Bar, House Model

17 October

Minister Rehavam Zeevi murdered by a Palestinian assassin in Jerusalem's Hyatt Hotel.

25 November

Scientific breakthrough in Israel: An internationally unique research at the Weizmann Institute produced a vaccine that totally stops juvenile diabetes.

29 November

Terror in Hadera: 4 women killed by 2 terrorists in a drive-by shooting.

23 November

The number of Israeli unemployed reaches an all-time high: 532,000; also, 1.5 million under the poverty line.

29 November

Terror in Pardes Hana: 3 killed as suicide bomber attacks a bus traveling from Nazareth to Tel Aviv.

1 December

Double suicide terror attack on Ben Yehuda Street in Jerusalem kills 11.

2 December

Terror in Haifa: 15 killed as suicide bomber explodes on a bus.

16 July

The 16th Maccabiah Opens in Jerusalem

Despite warnings of terror attacks and last year's trauma with the Ramat Gan disaster, the 16th Maccabiah games opened in festive ceremony in Jerusalem. Some 3,000 athletes from 43 countries came to take part in the games.

Photo: Avi Ohalon, GPO

Photo: Meir Partosh

3 January

Magic Violin

Yitzhak Perelman, the world's greatest violinist, conducted an exciting concert in Tel Aviv's Mann Auditorium where 600 violinists aged 6 to 16 played "Spring" from Vivaldi's "Four Seasons" while Perelman played the solo parts.

(2002

Terror attack on an Egged Company bus near Mahane Yehuda Market, Jerusalem.
Photo: Alex Kolomoisky

Netanya's Park Hotel dining room demolished on Seder night after suicide terrorist blows himself up.
Photo: Tal Cohen

Wave of Terror Followed by Operation Defensive Shield
"Fighting for Home"

Former Minister
of Defence
Shaul Mofaz

I clearly remember the worst day of 2002. It was Passover eve. As chief of staff, I celebrated the Seder, with my wife and four children, together with 1,000 soldiers who had no family in Israel. As we feasted and rejoiced, Lieutenant Colonel Hagai Mordechay, my bureau chief, handed me a note: "There has been a terror attack at Park Hotel in Netanya."

The pagers of officers around me started beeping, as if screaming the magnitude of the horror. I ordered Hagai to summon the General Staff for midnight and told Chief IDF Rabbi Israel Weiss to go on with the Seder ceremony as usual.

At midnight, I talked to Prime Minister Ariel Sharon, briefly, as always. "We have no choice," I said. "This time, we have to raid all the Palestinian towns and refugee camps." "Well," he said, "we think alike." It was clear to both of us that this night was like no other night indeed. I distinctly remember the General Staff meeting, with all of us sitting with stern faces, still wearing our white holiday shirts, knowing that this was a special night. We decided to go to war.

I served in the defense establishment for 40 years, going from simple soldier to army commander. I had been trained to deal with tough challenges, but we had no doctrine for dealing with suicide terrorists. There was nothing harder than heading the strongest and best military system in the Middle East, while dealing daily with this loathsome and ruthless form of terror attacks whose perpetrators do not wish to go back home.

We deliberated long and hard trying to choose a strategy, and I must say we did not always know if we were making the right move. One thing was clear, however - if we are determined to leave no stone unturned, we will defeat the terrorists. I was often told there are no magic solutions, that terror cannot be beaten, but we insisted that if we keep scratching the barrel walls, we'd get to the bottom.

Clearly, this wave of terror cannot be stopped on the beach. We have to get into the ocean and curb it there. This meant that we had to carry out a massive invasion of the Palestinian towns and refugee camps - which has never been done. Operation Defensive Shield was underway.

Through 2001, we prepared all the army echelons for an extensive antiterror operation, including procuring equipment and making detailed plans for the standing and reserves units. Now came the time to implement that.

Having made the decision to launch Defensive Shield, we prepared a force of unprecedented proportions. We called up hundreds of thousands reservists, and it warmed our hearts to see them all reporting for duty. The Israeli nation realized this was a trial time. "We are fighting for our home," was the message I delivered to the thousands of soldiers and officers during the long days and nights that I commanded the operation, looking in the eyes of the warriors, believing in their determination to eliminate the threat that was looming over Israel's children and houses.

In a large-scale logistical operation, the IDF entered every town, village and refugee camp in Judea and Samaria - almost all at the same time - smashing the infrastructure of terror it found there. This was one of the most complicated, elaborate, and extensive IDF operations ever. In it, we combined aerial, armored, infantry, and elite units, operating all at once in a densely populated urban region. The doctrine that the IDF devised and used in Operation Defensive Shield is currently studied worldwide. The terror organizations sustained a very tough blow, from which they were unable to recover, regardless of extensive aid they received from the outside. In the wake of the operation, the IDF was now able to operate freely all over Judea and Samaria, creating a situation that still exists.

The value of victory, of winning every clash with the enemy, which I had stressed since I became chief of staff, led the IDF troops and was realized at an unbearable price: The operation ended after 43 days during which 29 soldiers were killed and hundreds were wounded.

There is nothing worse for a commander who sends soldiers to battle than hearing that they fell. Still, clearly it was the IDF job - to defeat the terror that was imposed on us, to change the security situation and feeling of safety for every Israeli citizen.

Today, six years later, I still ache with the families that lost their loved ones in ruthless Palestinian terror attacks, and in IDF operations where soldiers fought for our right to live in this land.

Today, six years later, as I see the Israelis living their lives normally, I know we did the right thing: We gave Israel's citizens and visitors a sense of safety and security.

27.3.02 Seder Night Massacre at Park Hotel in Netanya: 30 Killed, 144 Wounded

The Palestinian Al-Aksa intifadah continued in full swing this year too. Some 60 suicide bomber attacks collected a heavy toll in 2002 - 453 were killed and 2,309 wounded - nearly twice as many as the year before. Nevertheless, until the terror attack on Park Hotel, the IDF reaction was rather mild.

A suicide bomber arrived in Netanya from Tulkarm. He entered the hotel dining hall, where some 200 guests were sitting at the holiday tables, about to have the Passover dinner. The terrorist wore a wig and carried an explosive belt on his person. He stopped in the center of the large hall as the waiters started hading out the dishes, and detonated the bomb. Exploding in a closed-in space, the

Photo: Tal Cohen

detonation blast and flying debris left almost everyone who were present hurt: Thirty people were killed and 144 wounded, nineteen of them sustained serious injuries.

The massacre caused great rage all over Israel and the public started calling for retaliation.

The cabinet members were summoned for an emergency session, after which Prime Minister Ariel Sharon ordered the IDF to launch Operation Defensive Shield in the West Bank.

The Big Recession Year

3 January

The recession expanded this year, among other things, because of the intifada. The number of unemployed reached 300,000, a negative growth record was logged (-7.2%), quality of life level reached an all time low (-2.8%), and the exchange rate peaked at some 5 shekel per US$. By the end of the year, Israel had a recorded number of poor: over 1 million, half of them children.

Photo: Shaul Golan

Photo: Joe Cott

"Karine A" Weapon Ship Captured

6 January

Precision intelligence on the Karine A, a ship sailing from Iran and smuggling weapons for the Palestinians, started the operation. After training extensively, a most complicated commando operation was ready to roll. The Navy commandoes went on the mission as the chief of staff accompanied it from an escort plane. The warriors surprised the vessel crew at dawn, in the Red Sea, jumping from helicopters and climbing on board from rubber boats.

Some 8 minutes after the operation started, the crewmembers were lying gagged on deck and an Israeli flag was hoisted on the mast. The IDF captured 50 tons of weapons and ammunition, including Katyusha, Lao, and Sager rockets, mortars, mines, and more. An investigation traced the ship back to Iran and found that Arafat personally approved the smuggling operation.

Operation Defensive Shield in the West Bank

2002

17 January

Terror in Hadera: 6 killed in an attack on a wedding party.

2 March

Suicide terror attack on the Bet Israel Yeshiva in Jerusalem leaves 11 dead.

9 March

Suicide terror attack in Café Moment in Jerusalem leaves 11 dead.

20 March

Terror attack on Bus No. 825 outside Megiddo Prison leaves 7 dead.

27 March

Terror attack on Park Hotel in Netanya on Seder night: 30 killed.

Photo: Ata Auisat

IDF operation in the Janin refugee camp

Photo: Ata Auisat

Realizing that Israel's residents lost all sense of personal security and that the state's security concept crumbled, Sharon decided to take drastic steps to rectify this. Operation Defensive Shield sent soldiers into West Bank towns, where they were to capture wanted terrorists, seize weapons, and destroy terror centers and labs.

The first move was a raid on Ramallah where a siege was clamped on the Mukata, Arafat's office complex. The soldiers were instructed to isolate Arafat. "No one should dare see him," Sharon ordered. Later (on 2 April), the IDF entered Nabulus, meeting minimal resistance.

The harshest battle took place in the Janin refugee camp. The Palestinians booby-trapped it with tons of explosives and ambushed soldiers in the alleyways. On the 7th day of the operation (9 April), a group of reserve soldiers came upon such an ambush and lost 13 of its men. That same night, bulldozers were sent into the camp and razed houses where numerous terrorists took refuge. The Janin operation collected a heavy toll: 23 soldiers were killed and 75 wounded.

The Palestinians charged that Israel committed a massacre there, but a UN committee investigated the incident and found no proof of that.

In the wake of the operation, the number of suicide terror attacks dropped significantly, Arafat was kept under siege, numerous fugitives were captured, and large quantities of explosives and ammunition were captured.

Photo: Ata Auisat

The Mukata Compound blasted

20.7.O2

Biggest Bank Burglary: 451 Safes Robbed

A real-life movie: A gang of professional burglars broke into the central Discount Bank branch in Tel Aviv, cut through the thick wall of the safes' room, crawled in, and spent peaceful hours emptying 451 safes. They took jewelry, gold coins, foreign currency, and other savings worth dozens of millions of dollars.

Many clients arrived at the bank upon hearing of the break-in. One of them yelled at the bank officials: "They promised it was the best protected safe-room in Israel! I had jewelry there that my grandmother brought from Morocco and money I saved to buy my son an apartment."

Photo: Tzvika Tischler

Meir Dagan Named Mosad Head

18 September

Prime Minister Sharon announced that Meir Dagan will replace Efraim Halevi as Mosad head. Dagan, a Gallantry Medal laureate, served with the paratroopers, commanded an Armored Corps brigade, headed the Antiterror Staff, was chief of IDF Operations, and served as special adviser to the chief of staff.

Record Embezzlement

25 November

Eti Alon, Israel Trade Bank clerk, was found guilty of stealing 250 million shekels, handed down a 17-year prison term, and was fined 5 million shekels. The judge sharply criticized Alon saying, "She did it cleverly and systematically, showing her clients no mercy."
Eti Alon said: "I gave the money to my brother, Ofer, who begged and pleaded me, fearing he would be killed..."

Photo: Yuval Erel, Israel Police

"Hodaya Smiled at Me, Then I Drowned Her"

8 December

This murder shocked Israel. "How can a father do that?" everyone asked. It started on Saturday morning, when 20-months old Hodaya was with her father. He called his divorcee and told her their daughter was missing. "I went to the bathroom, and she must have got out and disappeared."
Thousands of police officers and volunteers combed the region. The father, the girl's killer, cynically joined the searchers and told the media he believed the child was alive. The police, however, were suspicious right from the start and eventually received a tip on the place where the father buried his daughter. He was arrested and after denying for a while, he broke down. "Hodaya smiled at me, then I drowned her!" he confessed. "I wanted to hurt her mother." The diabolic father, Eli Pimstein, was sentenced to life.

The 'missing' ad for Hodaya Pimstein.
Photo: Sebastian Shiner

O2

9 September

Israeli Scientist Wins Nobel Prize

Photo: AP

Professor Daniel Kahneman (68) won the Nobel Prize in economy. The Israeli scientist, who also holds an American citizenship, received the prize for work combining psychology and economy in which he collaborated with an American counterpart. Kahneman teaches at Princeton and is a staff member in the Hebrew University. He won the prize for "laying the foundations for a decision-making process under stressful and uncertain terms."

Photo: Michael Kramer

28 January

Channel 10 Launched

The new commercial TV channel started broadcasting. It intends to challenge Channel 2 and made programs to reflect that. Its newscast anchor is Yaacov Eilon.

Photo: Yariv Katz

4 August

The 'Valley Train' Is Back on Track

The mythological Valley Train - which was built by the Turks some 100 years ago, ran from Haifa to Damascus, and stopped working after the War of Independence - was put back on track and driven over an old Turkish bridge with a reconstructed car.

Photo: Efi Sharir

First Cherries

The first cherries of the season picked ahead of the First-Fruit Festival.

29 March
Operation Defensive Shield starts.

31 March
Suicide terrorist kills 15 in Haifa's Matza Restaurant.

10 April
Suicide terrorist kills 10 on bus No. 960 near Kibbutz Yagur.

7 May
Suicide terrorist kills 16 in a Rishon Lezion club.

5 June
Carbomb explodes near bus No. 830 at Megiddo Junction, killing 17.

18 June
Suicide terrorist kills 19 on bus No. 32a in Jerusalem.

16 July
Suicide terrorist kills 9 on a bus from Bene Berak to Imanuel.

31 July
A terrorist kills 9 in the Hebrew University in Jerusalem.

4 August
Suicide terrorist kills 9 on a bus at Meron Junction.

19 September
Suicide terrorist kills 6 on bus No. 4 in Tel Aviv.

21 October
Explosion on bus No. 841 at the Karkur Junction: 14 killed.

10 November
Terrorist breaks into Kibbutz Metzer and kills 5, including a woman and her two small children.

15 November
Col. Dror Weinberg, commander of the Hebron Brigade, killed with 11 of his soldiers in ambush in Hebron.

21 November
Suicide terrorist kills 11 on bus No. 20 in Jerusalem.

2003

Shuttle Columbia liftoff.
Photos: AP

Late Ilan Ramon, the first Israeli astronaut.

Ilan Ramon - "Will You Hear My Voice?"
Late Ilan Ramon, the first Israeli astronaut.

Rona Ramon

"**S**ee you after I land," were the last words my love wrote me. On the way to Florida, Asaf asked if the landing would be as exciting as the takeoff. Will we be moved and cry? "We'll wait and see," I said. We stood there, on the benches, having our picture taken, smiling and excited. The world already knew. We did not.

The countdown ahead of the landing of the Shuttle Columbia started on Saturday, 1 February 2003, as she returned from 16 days in space. We sat there proud, excited, happy, waiting to receive our Ilan, the first Israeli astronaut, with his six crewmen. Minutes went by, one by one, until the sky fell on our heads: The shuttle disintegrated while reentering the atmosphere.

Ilan and I first met in 1986 and we got married very much in love six months later. Ilan "informed" me that he wanted a large family, believing it is our duty as humans to create the next generation. So we had four children, all conceived with great love: Asaf (19) who loves the skies like his father; Tal (17) who has his dad's musical talent; Yiftah (14) who inherited his Ilan's looks, nature, and charming smile, whom Ilan used to call "mini me"; and Noa (10), Ilan's princess.

Ilan was a loving and loved family man. He enjoyed stirring my pots and pans, tasting boiling dishes (he believed I am the world's greatest cook!!). He always took photos of family occasions. When he was home, he dedicated himself fully to the children and to me, not letting the job in the house after long hours of work.

As a professional, Ilan believed that a good commander always takes care of his subordinates. He did not speak much, but when he did, he spoke wisely. His comrades said that in discussions, they always waited for his input.

On 7 June 1981, Ilan and seven other Air Force pilots took part in the fateful mission whose consequences still affect Israel: the raid of the Iraqi nuclear reactor.

The decision to train an Israeli astronaut and send him into space was made in 1996, when then Prime Minister Shimon Peres met US President Bill Clinton. Three years later, Air Force commander Eitan Ben-Eliahu decided to act on this decision. "You will never believe the phone call I received," Ilan said. "Nisim from the Air Force called and asked if I want to be an astronaut. I told him to leave me alone because I only wanted to get home, but he said, 'seriously, we're looking for IAF candidates for NASA.' So I told him I'd ask you and get back to him in the morning." So it started, like some prank. When Ilan told me about it, it sounded unreal, but I felt it could be a special and fascinating adventure. Ilan presented his candidacy and was chosen from of a list of 20 to be the first Israeli astronaut.

Ilan felt this mission of going to space as an Israeli astronaut was of special significance for the Jewish nation and the State of Israel. He wanted everyone to feel that the Jewish state is independent and evolving, that the Jewish nation has a unique tradition that saved it over the ages, and that after surviving the Holocaust, it is expanding its horizons and starting a new age.

He wrote in his diary: "Is it not a miracle? I, the son of a Holocaust survivor, an Israeli aviator, am about to open new frontiers for the State of Israel." Feeling on a national mission, Ilan took with him meaningful and symbolic items: the Scroll of Independence, a Torah from Auschwitz, a special mezuzah symbolizing the Holocaust, a Kiddush cup, the IAF flag, the emblem of his university, the flag of his city of Ramat Gan, a flag of the Blich High School he attended to symbolize the education of the future generation, and the flag of the IAF museum, symbolizing its history.

On 16 January 2003, the Columbia space shuttle took off (on Mission No. STS-107), with Ilan sweeping us all with excitement. Our family and the entire State of Israel were elated. We had something to be proud of. This handsome Israeli, a fighter pilot, representing our small country, sending a message of hope and peace from space. I felt great love for my man and was very optimistic. There he was, making his dream come true, having the time of his life, making us all proud. The days he spent in space were very exciting for me. I felt I was falling in love with him again. After all the delays and crises, there he was, happily floating in space.

Ilan Ramon was buried on 11 February 2003 on Kibbutz Nahalal. On his tomb, next to the Columbia and IDF insignia, I wrote: "The first Israeli astronaut" followed by the words of Rachel: "Will you hear my voice, wherever you are..." and signed, Rona.
I will forever believe he does hear me wherever he is...

16.1.03

Ilan Ramon: "I Was Very Excited Seeing Israel From Above"

Photo: NASA

At 17:39, the Columbia chariot, carrying the first Israeli astronaut Ilan Ramon, stormed skyward with fire and smoke, and went on a 16-day journey in space. The takeoff was perfect. Everything ran smoothly. NASA Director Sean O'Keefe praised Ramon: "He's a real professional."

On the day before he took off, Rona Ramon gave her husband a CD with four songs, and gave each crewmember a *hamsa* - good-luck charm. "I was very excited seeing Israel from above," Ramon reported from space. That morning, the crew woke up to the sounds of Rachel's "Will you hear my voice."

Everything went according to plan as the crew members performed their assigned tasks and started preparing to land. Near the landing strip, everyone was waiting for the Columbia that was about to arrive in 3 minutes. "Something is wrong," a NASA official whispered. "We were supposed to hear the sonic booms already." The scheduled landing time came and went, but the shuttle did not show. A few minutes later, the worst nightmare materialized. The Huston center announced it lost contact with the shuttle, and soon the bitter news came: the Columbia broke apart upon reentry, above Dallas, Texas.

The disaster caused a great shock that was felt in Israel as well. NASA officials estimated that a part of the space ship disconnected from the shuttle, hit its wing, and caused the disaster. Eulogizing her husband, Rona Ramon said: "Ilan was killed in a place he loved, around people he loved, and his last days were happy. This is how we will all remember him."

Soldier Yuval Arad receiving a citation from Chief of Staff Yaalon.
Photo: Haim Tzah

Yuval Arad: "Why Did You Abandon My Father?"

27 August

In a rare monologue, Tami Arad said: "Ron is no longer relevant for them... Israel accepted a situation where Ron Arad is forever missing."

Tami, wife of missing IAF navigator Ron Arad, made the remark while Israel was engaged in negotiations with Hizballah for the release of Elhanan Tannenbaum and the bodies of the three abducted soldiers, in return for Mustafa Dirani and Shaykh Ubeid.

Tami spoke up after a long period of silence, sharply attacking the negotiations. "That scoundrel Dirani was the one who captured Ron, stuck him in his trunk, and drove him all over Lebanon like a sack of potatoes. When the State of Israel releases him, it would mean the state has given up on Ron."

Yuval Arad, who has not seen her father for 17 years, met Prime Minister Sharon and charged: "Have you no shame? Why did you abandon my father? He will never come back because you, as prime minister, do not believe he is alive." Listening to the excited girl, Sharon's eyes filled with tears, but he remained supportive of the exchange deal.

Sharon: Netanyahu, My Finance Minister

Photo: Alex Kolomoisky

Prime Minister Ariel Sharon, Industry and Trade Minister Ehud Olmert, Education Minister Limor Livnat, Public Security Minister Tzahi Hanegbi, and Transportation Minister Avigdor Lieberman

The establishment of the second Sharon cabinet was followed by schemes, twists, turns, and dramas. The election results created a complicated political map with the right-wing bloc winning 96 Knesset seats, the left had 25, and Shinuy in the center won 15 seats.

Sharon feared that if he formed a narrow-based right-wing government, he would not be able to make progress on the diplomatic track. At the same time, he did not have enough seats to form a national unity government with Labor (19 seats). For lack of a better choice, he formed a coalition with Shinuy (15), Meretz (6), the National Religious Party (6), and the National Union (7), leaving SHAS and the Orthodox parties out.

The most surprising move Sharon made was appointing his nemesis, Binyamin Netanyahu, finance minister. It would later appear that this was a fortunate move as Netanyahu, with Sharon's backing, took Israel from recession to growth, sliced the state budget and allocations, privatized sectors, and made the Israeli economy attractive to foreign investors.

On the diplomatic level, Sharon initiated the disengagement plan, after he announced at the Herzliya Convention on December 2003: "There will be no Jewish settlement in Gaza." The program he promoted conflicted with Sharon's ideology so far (having said in the past that Netzarim and Tel Aviv are one and the same).

His second term in office was conducted under a cloud of suspicious of crimes he committed involving the Greek island and Cyril Kern. He was questioned by the police on suspicions of taking bribes. In June 2004, the state prosecutor determined that there is no evidence to support suspicions against Sharon on the Greek island affair.

In his second term as prime minister, Sharon upheld his tough and belligerent approach toward terrorism, ordering the assassination of HAMAS leaders such as Ahmad Yasin, Aziz Rantisi, and others.

The Missing Holy Grail

26 May

Some 116 rare and precious objects of the famous Gross collection were stolen from the Diaspora Museum. Among the Judaica treasures taken, which are worth several millions, were unique scrolls, menorahs, Torah ornaments, lamps, wine cups, and holy grails.

The holy grail. Items from the collection

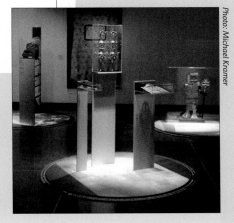

Photo: Michael Kramer

---

1 January
A 30% drop in marriage rates in Israel, according to the Central Bureau of Statistics. The number of couples who had a civilian wedding declined as well. At the same time, the number of divorces in Israel also dropped by 26%.

5 January
A double suicide bombing in Tel Aviv's old Central Station: 23 are killed, including six foreign laborers.

16 January
Ilan Ramon, the first Israeli astronaut, was sent into space in the Voyager shuttle, which disintegrated upon reentering the atmosphere 16 days later.

28 January
Knesset election day ends: the Likud wins, 38 Knesset seats; Labor, 19; Shinuy, 15.

16 February
First ultra-Orthodox Jerusalem mayor, Uri Lupoliansky, replaces Ehud Olmert.

18 February
Isar Harel, the man who established the Mosad and the Shin Bet, dies at 91.

5 March
Suicide bombing on bus No. 37 in Haifa leaves 17 dead.

20 March
Israel is second to Spain in unemployment rates in the West with some 300,000 jobless individuals.

1.7.03

Zeev Rosenstein, "Wolf with 7 Souls," Injured in an Assassination Attempt

This was yet another attempt to assassinate the Israel Police's No. 1 fugitive. As he does every day, Zeev Rosenstein came to see his moneychanger on Yehuda Halevi Street in Tel Aviv. When he returned to his car, there was a huge explosion. Rosenstein was injured in the arm and his bodyguards rushed him to hospital, but 3 innocent bystanders were killed and 42 were wounded.

This was the first incident in Israel's criminal history that an assassination attempt hurt so many innocent people. The police believe the war between crime families was expanding.

The Remedia Affair

7 November

This affair was exposed after the Health Ministry announced that the "Super Vegetarian Formula" baby food lacked vitamin B_1, the absence of which causes diseases and is essential for baby's growth. It turned out that 3 babies died having consumed the product, which led to a criminal investigation against the Remedia Company. In September 2006, the state decided to press charges on suspicion of causing death through negligence against several Remedia executives.

Photo: Tzvika Tischler

Photo: Hen Mika

"The Baby Proved: Life Wins"

18 March

Ronit Ilan (34), who lost two children in a Jerusalem terror attack where a suicide terrorist walked into a Bar-Mitzvah party in the Bet Israel neighborhood, gave birth to a bay boy.

After labor, she said: "I missed the voice of a baby in the house, and now I hear the baby. I got pregnant soon after the disaster to prove that life always wins."

The Ilan family: daughter Noy, father Shimon, mother Ronit, and the newborn baby.

Photo: Yariv Katz

A Real European Winter

23 February

Winter struck hard today, with snowstorms, strong winds, heavy rains, and floods. The authorities decided to open the two dams in Naharayim to prevent the Yarmuk River from overflowing.

On the left - the Yarmuk flooded.

03

28 August

Ninett - A Star is Born

Photo: Dani Salomon

Ninett Tayeb won the final of the first "A Star is Born" show, running against Shiri Maimon and Shay Gabso, and singing Zohar Argov's "Sea of Tears." She was chosen by 49% of the viewers, collecting more than 720,000 votes. She was born and raised in Kiryat Gat, where she also started her singing career.

7 April

Israelis - The West's Most Fertile Women

Fertility rate in Israel was found 75% higher than the average in the West, according to UN data. It turned out that Israeli women have twice as many children as women from Japan and 40% more than the Americans.

30 April

Yemenite Jews Live Longer

A 20-year research established that Yemenite Jews enjoy the largest longevity period. The Ashkenazim's life is shortest. One of the reasons is that traditional Yemenite food is healthier, and that Yemenite Jews smoke less and engage in physical activities.

8 October

Workaholic Israelis

Who said Israelis do not like to work?! A recent study by the Haifa University placed the Israelis as third on the world's workaholic chart, after the United States and Japan. Some 91% of the workaholics are males.

7 March

The Internet is Why Children Sleep Less

Israeli children sleep less that their European peers. This emerged from a study conducted at the Tel Aviv University. As a result, the children lose some of their ability to pay attention, concentrate, and remember things, which leads to declining learning abilities. Prof. Avi Sade called on parents: "Be kind to your children: Disconnect them from the Internet and the TV and send them to sleep."

20 March

Israel declared full alert as soon as the US attack on Iraq started (the 2nd Gulf War). The Israelis were asked to carry their gas masks at all times and prepare sealed rooms. While half a million children did not go to schools, Prime Minister Sharon said: "Chances that Israel would be attacked are slim."

30 April

Terror attack at "Mike's Place" on the Tel Aviv waterfront, perpetrated by British nationals, kills 3.

18 May

Suicide terror attack on No. 6 bus in Jerusalem leaves 7 dead.

19 May

Terrorist stopped from entering Afula mall; kills 3.

5 June

Shinuy Party's Yona Yahav elected Haifa mayor.

11 June

Suicide terror attack on bus No. 14a in Jerusalem leaves 17 dead.

19 August

Suicide terror attack on bus No. 2 in Jerusalem ("children attack") leaves 23 dead.

1 September

The Or Committee, which studied the Israeli Arab riots of 2000, where 13 Arabs were killed, publishes its report, recommending steps against Minister Ben-Ami and Police chiefs Wilk and Ron, criticizing Prime Minister Barak.

9 September

Two suicide terror attacks: 8 killed in a bus stop near Zerifin; 7 killed in Café Hillel in Jerusalem.

4 October

Suicide terror attack at Maxim's in Haifa leaves 21 dead.

28 October

Mayors elected: Tel Aviv, Ron Huldai; Ramat Gan, Tzvi Bar; Beersheba, Yaacov Turner; Ashdod, Tzvi Zilker; Herzliya, Yael German.

(2004

The hall in Stockholm, Sweden, where Nobel Prizes are handed out. Photo: AP

Four Nobel laureates: right to left: Professors Avraham Hershko, Israel Auman, Daniel Kahneman, and Aharon Ciechanover (opposite page).
Photos: Amit Shabi, Alex Kolomoisky, and Roni Shitzer

The Nobel Decade
Four Israelis Win the Nobel Prize in a Decade

Nobel Prize Laureat in
Chemistry, 2004
Prof. Aharon Ciechanover

During the sixth decade of Israel's existence, four Israeli scientists received the most important recognition that the international community accords researchers and explorers - the Nobel Prize. In 2002, Prof Daniel Kahneman (Princeton and the Hebrew University) received the "Sveriges Riksbank Prize in Economic Sciences in Memory of Alfred Nobel" for using a combination of psychological research and economic science to understand the process of human judgment and decisionmaking under conditions of uncertainty. In 2005, his colleague, Prof. Israel Auman (Hebrew University) received the same award for the way he used Game Theory to understand international processes such as interstate collaborations or conflicts. In 2004, Prof. Hershko and I (Technion) won the Nobel Prize in chemistry for discovering the process that living cells use to replace their damaged and unusable proteins with new ones. This discovery was significant in the study of the mechanisms of various diseases, including malignant ones, and brain degeneration. The discovery is used by pharmaceutical companies in the development of drugs that heal those diseases.

It would seem that we have every reason to be pleased with an achievement that states older, bigger, and richer than the State of Israel would be proud of. The fact that the Nobel Prize is given for achievements whose importance and significance to humanity only becomes apparent after decades of hard work gives hope that this might be a new beginning. If this were the early autumn rain, we may have been looking at a very wet winter and achievements of Israeli science may receive growing international recognition. Is this so? I am afraid not. Due to an accumulation of reasons, we are in for a rather dry winter. It should be stressed that the prize is not an end in itself, nor does it necessarily serve as the best reflector of nations' achievements. Hence we must not seek it, but rather seek achievements in education, science, and technology while preserving and instilling spiritual values - culture, history, and religion - thanks to which we are an independent nation, living on its land. The Nobel comes second, and is a mere recognition of an investment made.

It is a fascinating question whether the fact that the Jewish nation returned to its land and reestablished its sovereignty after 2000 years of exile diminished the Jewish genius. Some 25% of all Nobel laureates are Jews - an amazing achievement for this small, dispersed, and persecuted nation. Nevertheless, considering that half the Jewish nation currently resides in Israel, the share of Israeli Nobel winners is smaller than may have been expected. Simple mathematics shows that Israel should have had some 40 laureates. We cannot avoid the frightening question concerning the role of the Diaspora in creating the Jewish genius. Is it possible that constant persecution - being unable to settle on solid ground for so long for fear of church and king - forced the Jews to seek professions based on knowledge you can store in your head and take with you? Is this why Jews specialize in medicine, science, law, commerce, and religious studies? Did the Diaspora turn learning and getting an education into a uniquely Jewish art of a level unattainable by others? It now seems that the establishment of the State of Israel, making a 2,000-years-old dream come true, reversed the process: We are now a nation like any other.

Over the years, this important question was burdened with numerous changes in the Israeli society - political, cultural, national, religious changes, accompanied by parallel changes in the nature of its leadership, order of priorities, election method, and manner of conduct. On top of this, Western culture influenced us, pushing aside age-old and important values such as deep education, creativity, and culture, and replaced them with a culture of seeking economic success, entertainment, and sports. Today's idols are not found in the ivory towers or yeshivas, but in investment rooms and on the pitch.

The Nobel Prize and mainly the road leading to it, the investment it requires, the deep culture that backs it up - the culture of generations of Jews - will probably not produce a flood similar to the past 5 years. Even if we have more laureates, if the media ask them what they are going to do with the money and not what they discovered and why it is important, they will remain marginal on the Israeli scene. To me, staying on the margins has been a blessing. Studying the wonders of Creation undisturbed, being a curious tourist in God's world is the greatest gift I ever received. The way I see it, the change in the Israeli state and society's leading values that drives people to marginal issues poses an existential threat.

29.1.04

Elhanan Tannenbaum and 3 Soldiers in Coffins Return to Israel

When the coffins of abducted IDF soldiers Beni Avraham, Adi Avitan, and Omar Suwad landed in Israel, hope faded from the families' hearts. Along with the bodies, Hizballah also released Elhanan Tannenbaum.

The POW exchange deal was completed after 1,200 days of captivity, ending one of Israel's most painful episodes. Israel released 400 Palestinian terrorists and Lebanese nationals Mustafa Dirani and Shaykh Ubeid, who had been abducted in an attempt to obtain information on Ron Arad.

IDF soldiers carry the coffins of the three abducted servicemen, wrapped in Israeli flags, at the reception ceremony in Ben Gurion Airport.
Photo: Michael Kramer

Observers stated Israel had no other choice because, being a democracy, it could not just forsake citizen Tannenbaum in Hizballah hands, nor can it remain indifferent to the pain of the abductees' families. Collecting the body of Beni, his father said, "We closed a cycle, but the pain is only starting."

Tannenbaum was taken for medical checkup and was later interrogated. Prime Minister Sharon asked the interrogators to "show him some mercy, as he went through hell in the hands of savages."

Elhanan Tannenbaum and his family upon landing at Ben Gurion Airport.
Photo: Avi Ohaion, GPO

Shaykh Ahmad Yasin, "Palestinian Bin-Laden," Assassinated

22 March

The decision to eliminate Yasin was made by a small ministerial forum after a terror attack in Ashdod left 10 Israelis dead. Surveillance of Shaykh Ahmad Yasin was no easy task, though advanced means were used, since he was very cautious and did not sleep at home. He did, however, keep praying in a nearby mosque. An initial plan to take him out as soon as leaves the mosque was rejected because the crowd around him was too large. The Air Force waited patiently for an opportunity, which came 24 hours later. Yasin left the mosque at 05:00, with only four men pushing his wheelchair. They were some 100 meters away from the mosque when they took a direct hit by three missiles and were killed on the spot.

Prime Minister Sharon soon reacted: "Israel eliminated the leading Palestinian murderer." Defense Minister Mofaz added that, "Yasin was Palestinian Bin-Laden."

Ahmad Yasin believed that destroying Israel was his prime target and orchestrated several hundred lethal terror attacks against Israel.

Yasser Arafat Dies in Paris, Buried in the Mukata

Palestinians by the thousands surround Arafat's coffin as it is taken off an Egyptian chopper. Photo: Amit Shabi

Yasser Arafat died after 10 days in a Paris hospital. There was no definite cause of death. He was buried in the Mukata in Ramallah. Thousands of Palestinians who attended the funeral were unable to contain their grief or hold back their tears. For the Palestinians, Arafat was a national symbol, the "father of the nation" who fought for their independence and dignity.

For the most part of his life, Arafat believed in terror and is responsible for the deaths of thousands of innocent people in Israel and worldwide. First, he was a students' leader, then an international terrorist, and finally a statesman who signed a peace accord with Israel, which broke into pieces with the outbreak of the intifada.

28 January
Meni Mazuz replaces Eliakim Rubinstein as state attorney.

29 January
Terror attack on bus No. 19 in Jerusalem: 11 killed.

2 February
Prime Minister Sharon makes dramatic and surprising statement: "There will be no Jewish settlement in Gaza. I gave the order to start planning the evacuation of settlements there."

22 February
Terror attack on bus No. 14 in Jerusalem: 14 killed.

14 March
Terror in Ashdod: Two terrorists break into the Port, blow themselves up, and kill 10.

8 May
Terror attack in Kfar Darom: Tali Hatuel and her four daughters are shot point-blank and killed.

18 May
Sporting history: Sons of Sakhnin is the first Israeli Arab soccer team to win the national cup.

6 June
Palestinian leader Marwan Barghutti convicted of involvement in 4 terror attacks and sentenced to 5 life terms.

The APCs Disaster: 11 Soldiers Killed in Gaza

11–12 May

Fate struck twice at IDF soldiers in the Gaza Strip. Two APCs that were loaded with ammunition, as part of ongoing activity, exploded killing 11 soldiers. Their bodies spread over an area of some 500 meters. The first APC was hit in the Zaitun neighborhood, killing 6, and another 5 soldiers were killed on the Philadelphi Road near Rafah.

Photo: Barkai Wolfson

Soldiers sifting through sand searching for body parts on Philadelphi Road.

19.7.**04**

Justice Adi Azar Murdered; "A Shot at the Heart of Democracy"

"I'm Ashamed I'm Hungry"

1 February

An 8-years-old child did not go to school for a week because he had no food for his lunch break. "I'm ashamed in class because when the other kids have their lunch, I've nothing in my bag," he said. His mother supports 6 children on a 2,600-shekel allowance. The child was convinced to return to school after his teacher promised to bring him a chocolate sandwich. He is one of 700,000 children under the poverty line.

For the first time in Israel's history, a judge was murdered. Justice Adi Azar arrived home that evening and parked his car in the garage when an assailant emerged from the shadows and shot him dead. The smashed windshield, pierced car door, and bloodstains on the car seats attested that the judge was shot point-blank by a cold-blooded killer. Israeli crime has thus crossed the last red line.

The murder stunned Israel. Cabinet ministers said it was "just as grave as the Rabin assassination," and Supreme Court President Aharon Barak said "murdering a person only because he is a judge is a shot at the heart of democracy."

An intensive police investigation revealed that lifer Yitzhak Zuziashvili sent another convict, Rafi Nahmani, decided to murder the judge, intending to shorten his term and take their revenge of the justice system. Azar had no previous connections with the killers and was chosen because there was an easy escape route from his house. The two killers were given a life term each.

Police officers and civilians around Justice Azar's car after the murder. Photo: Tal Cohen

A First Israeli Gold Medalist

19-25 August

Wind-surfer Gal Friedman became Israel's first Olympic gold medalist ever after winning the Mistral sailing competition in Athens 2004. "I'm dreaming and I don't want to wake up," said Friedman.

Judoka Arik Zeevi won the bronze medal in the same Olympic Games. After the medals were handed out, the Israelis in the crowd started singing the national anthem, Hatikva, and Zeevi could not hold back his tears, He wept and said: "I'll never forget this moment."

Right, Gal Friedman; left, Arik Zeevi. Photos: Reuven Schwartz

04

6 June

Gila and Yehoram - Israel Award Laureates

Photo: Meir Partosh

Gila Almagor, the first lady of the Israeli cinema, received the Israel Award for Cinematic Achievement after some 50 films and 44 years on camera. Yehoram Gaon, the national singer, won the award for Hebrew Songs, "having sang the history of this land for the past 47 years," the panel stated.

1 May

Jerusalem Is No. 1

Hapoel Jerusalem's basketball team won the ULEB Cup (European Championship) defeating Real Madrid in the final.

Photo: Reuven Schwartz

2 August

First Cinema in Dimona

A new 300-seat cinema hall was inaugurated in Dimona, serving 40,000 residents who had to travel to Beersheba to catch a movie.

Photo: Meir Partosh

29 June
Arik Lavie, esteemed singer and actor, dies at 77.

1 August
Moshe Karadi assumes post as 15th Israel Police chief.

31 August
Simultaneous suicide terror attacks on two busses in Beersheba leave 16 dead.

26 October
A vast Knesset majority votes in favor of the disengagement from Gaza and northern Samaria.

2 November
Ben Gurion Airport's Terminal 3, better known as Natbag-2000, opens.

23 November
Refael Eitan (75), former chief of staff and cabinet member, drowns in the stormy waters of the Ashdod Port.

5 December
Azzam Azzam released from Egyptian prison after 8 years.

17 March
The first-ever artificial heart planted in the chest of Edmund Peretz.

26 June

Naomi Shemer, Songs Forever

Poet and songwriter Naomi Shemer ("Jerusalem of Gold") passed away at the age of 74. She wrote more than 1,000 moving songs that became part of the Israeli heritage. "Her songs will live forever," she was eulogized.

8 February

Famous Cashier 'Luba' on US Media

Luba - a tough, but kind-hearted Russian-born cashier who is one of the characters on the "Wonderful Country" satirical TV show, portrayed by comedian Tal Friedman - was shown on US media that extensively covered the phenomenon.

29 September
Two children killed by a Kassam rocket in Sederot. Locals stage a demonstration outside Ariel Sharon's nearby farm.

2005

Bulldozer razes houses in Peat Sade, implementing Ariel Sharon's disengagement plan. Photo: Avigail Uzi

David Hatuel, who lost his wife and four daughters in a terror attack outside Gaza, marries Limor Shem-Tov. Photo: Ofir Avitan Eshed, Ashkelon Photos

Evacuating the Gaza Strip Settlements
"We will return tomorrow... We will yet walk like lovers in the fields."

Former Settler
of Katif Bloc
David Hatuel

I was born in Ashdod in 1969. When I was 1 year old, Kfar Darom was resettled by Nahal Brigade soldiers. The state was thus paying a debt of honor to the 1948 heroes who tried to establish a religious kibbutz there, but were driven away by the storms of war. In the 1970's, when I was a child, the governments of Golda Meir and Yitzhak Rabin, may they rest in peace, built a new and beautiful settlement strip on the Negev's western shores. In 1987, I arrived in the Yamit hesder yeshiva, where I studied and served as a paratrooper. In 1992, I married Tali of Ashkelon, may God avenge her blood.

It was only natural for us to build our new and young home in the Katif Bloc dunes. We joined Katif, a religious and young moshav where we found friends - young couples of farmers and professionals - a developed community life, and comradeship. We felt we were the followers of the old Jewish settlers of Gaza, dating back to the days of Abram. Here, we combined work with Torah, religion with a simple and friendly life.

The Katif Bloc spread before us: an enchanting land of golden dunes running to a blue sea, spotted with the bright green of palms and acacias, with a unique human mosaic of young children and older people, religious and secular, and all lovers of the Land of Israel. A living fabric of settlers with a pulsating pioneering spirit. With time, I graduated from university and started teaching, first in Ofakim and later became the principal of the Maimon School in Ashkelon. Tali was a social worker in Azata and then in Katif. We were living our dream as a young and loving couple, with a nice house and beautiful children, living a simple life. In those dunes, we had four daughters - Hila, Hadar, Roni, and Merav - may God avenge their blood. They used to swim in the sea, under a shining and gay sun, trotting the dunes peacefully, softly, with a grace and joy that even long years of intifada, Kassams and mortar fire could not extinguish. Despite the enemy's threats and domestic talk of withdrawal, we built a home of faith and love for humanity, for the Torah, for this Land. We flourished and grew with our beautiful moshav and the entire Bloc community.

Our future looked bright, despite the hardships, until in 2003, the Israeli Government under Ariel Sharon decided, for reasons that are not clear to this day, to turn its back on the Jewish settlement enterprise and the majority of Jews in this land. In a surreal move, it decided to withdraw unilaterally and raised the sword of deportation to the settlements of the Katif Bloc and northern Samaria. We then launched a massive PR campaign, trying to convince the public of the importance of settlements and stupidity of withdrawals. We believed and hoped that common sense and honesty would prevail, that Jewish solidarity would surface. Many Jews in Israel and abroad, thinkers and warriors, supported our struggle. As a result, Prime Minister Sharon decided to ask his party members to vote on his plan.

On 2 May 2004, the day of the Likud referendum, my wife Tali, who was then nine-months pregnant, and our four daughters - Hila (11), Hadar (9), Roni (7), and Merav (2) - put on orange shirts, symbolizing our struggle, and drove to a Likud ballot to convince the voters to side with us. Two terrorists from Khan-Yunus lay in ambush by the side of the road. When our car passed them, they came out and started firing their AK-47's. After Tali lost control of the car, which stopped on the road, the terrorists ran to them and shot them all dead point-blank.

A sticker on the front of the car that was shot full of holes, said: "Jewish Hearts Vote Against."

I was left alone, broken, deprived of my beloved wife and daughters that filled by life with everything God can bestow upon a man.

Our campaign was largely supported, but the prime minister went on with his plan and in the month of Ab the year later, he chopped down the Katif settlement. All the bloc residents were deported and turned refugees, homeless, exiles, with no place to work and no income, scattered all over Israel. Their houses were turned into rubble.

On my 36th birthday, I too was deported from my home. This ended 35 years of blooming settlement. Yet, the pain, disappointment, prayers, togetherness, and powers of faith that emerged on the eve of the deportation were not all in vain. The Nation of Israel proved that even if we are uprooted time and again, we will always find our way back home. I chose faith in my personal life as well, and while dealing daily with grief and intolerable pain, I decided to rise from the ashes and not despair.

On 9 December 2004, I married Limor and made a new Jewish home.

On 25 March 2006, our first daughter, Tehiya, was born.

In 2008, as these lines are written, the Katif communities have not yet been revived, despite government promises.

When she was 10, the late Tali wrote to her classmates: "A person's deeds outlive him: the home he built, the book he wrote, the tree he planted. Do your deeds attentively."

The home we built is gone, the tree we planted was uprooted, but the book we wrote, the heritage and spirit of our struggle still live on.

Farewell, my beloved family, farewell my dream home. I will remember you always.

"We will return tomorrow... We will yet walk like lovers in the fields."

This song cannot be stopped!

The Disengagement

20O5

Right-wing demonstration outside the Knesset against the disengagement plan.
Photo: Alex Kolomoisky

Public Debate: Demonstrations, Roadblocks, Protest Marches

This was one of the most dramatic, traumatic, and difficult events the State of Israel ever endured. Very few such historic decisions were made throughout the state's history. For nearly 40 years, no government made any changes in the state's permanent borders. It is no wonder, therefore, that a loud and heated debate broke out when the disengagement decision was made, bringing ideological differences to a head.

The settlers and their supporters, who exacerbated their struggle with demonstrations, roadblocks, and protest marches, demanded a plebiscite to approve the plan. They claimed the cabinet decision contradicted the Likud platform and Sharon's own statements before the elections. Sharon and his cabinet, that supported the move, were aided by the  Israeli left. Together they claimed there was no reason to let Jews reside in the Gaza Strip while surrounded by over a million Palestinians, which made offering them security very difficult. The ultra-Orthodox joined the debate. Rabbi Ovadya Yosef even cursed Sharon: "How cruel is this evil man. May God strike him down, and he'll die and not get up."

Photo: Gilad Kavalerchick

15 August

The Disengagement Starts

At midnight, all roads leading to the Gaza Strip were closed. On the next morning, the Katif Bloc settlers were handed eviction orders. Addressing the nation, Sharon said: "This move is hard for me personally... (but) we cannot hold Gaza forever..."

16 August

Many settlers left willingly, holding emotional farewell ceremonies, but in some locations (Neve Dekalim, for example), the security forces encountered verbal abuse and even physical violence.

17 August

The "forceful evacuation" starts. Security forces begin evacuating Neve Dekalim, home of some 700 families. By evening, the local yeshiva that turned into a stronghold with hundreds of locals and supporters fenced in, was evacuated too.

17 August

Some 1,500 fenced themselves inside the Neve Dekalim synagogue, but the security forces pulled out the men, who showed passive but stubborn resistance, and the women who cried and prayed.

Soldiers evacuating a Nisanit resident.
Photo: Amit Shabi

Photo: Amit Shabi

18 August

The Kfar Darom Synagogue

Hundreds disengagement opponents fenced themselves on the synagogue rooftop, vowing not to let the village "fall again." The settlers attacked the soldiers and policemen with rocks and sticks, and even sprayed them with liquids. After a 3-hour struggle, in which 14 settlers and 60 officers were injured, the last bastion of the disengagement opposition fell. Around midnight, the settlements of Kfar Darom, Neve Dekalim, Netzer Hazani, and Gan Or were cleared.

Photo: Amit Magal

Eley Sinai residents walking out of the village, carrying the entrance sign

Settlers fenced in on the Kfar Darom synagogue rooftop throwing things at the evacuating forces

19 August

The evacuation of Gadid, Shirat Hayam, and Kfar Yam is completed.

21 August

The Katif Bloc evacuation ends with Eley Sinai, Katif, Shalev, and Atzmona. The Eley Sinai settlers build a shantytown near Kibbutz Yad Mordechay.

22 August

The residents of Netzarim, considered the hardcore of Gaza settlers, evacuate their settlement without any violence, as promised.

23 August

In northern Samaria, Homesh and Sa-Nur are evacuated. Some 60 settlers that resisted evacuation and sat on the fortress roof were taken down in containers.

Photo: Avigail Uzi

Netzarim settlers leave the settlement.

The Disengagement

20**05**

24 August

All Locations Clear: 25 Settlements Demolished

Some 15,000 residents of 25 settlements are evacuated. For them, it was a tragedy inflicted upon them after 38 years of believing they were on a national mission and building flourishing settlements. Now they had to leave their homes and even watch them razed. The settlers showed maturity and great restraint, and horror predictions of violent clashes did not materialize. Eventually, democracy was the big winner of the struggle over the disengagement.

Photo: Avigail Uzi

Rehabilitation of the Evacuees: "A Big Blunder"

The cabinet pledged to find housing and employment solutions for the evacuees, but in most cases, it did not deliver. A report by the state comptroller, published on 8 March 2006, termed the evacuated settlers' treatment as "a big blunder." The evacuees felt they were cheated by the state, and mainly by Sharon, who used to be "the father of settlements."

Photo: Shaul Golan

Boy trying to stop evacuating soldiers. Photo: Gilad Kavalerchick

Ganey Tal resident pleads not to be evacuated. Photo: Gadi Caballo

Photo: Oded Balilti, AP

Children from Bdolah in the Katif Bloc bid their home farewell. Above: Netzarim residents move out.

Menahem Begin: The Most Important Leader

In an extensive public opinion poll, the Israelis named Menahem Begin the most important Israeli leader of all times. Begin received 32.8% of the votes, followed by David Ben-Gurion (30%), Yitzhak Rabin (14.1%), and Arik Sharon (7.4%)

Photo: David Rubinger

Photo: Amit Shabi

Ezer "Cute Scoundrel" Weizmann Dies

24 April

Ezer Weizmann, Israel's 7th president, died today at age of 81. He was the ultimate Sabra, the most flamboyant figure on the Israeli political and security scene. Most of his charm followed from his being a man of contradictions, as his friend Eitan Haber said: He was an ardent believer in Greater Israel, but the first to realize that this dream was dead. He was a killer hawk in war and a white dove in peace times. For him, Sadat was Israel's bitter enemy one day, and a dear friend on the next.

Weizmann was the man who built the Israeli Air Force ahead of the 6-Days War, but received no glory when it was won. He orchestrated the 1977 political upheaval, helping the Likud win the elections for the first time, played a central role in making the peace accord with Egypt, established the Yahad Party, but then joined Labor's Alignment. He quit the Knesset in 1992 and was elected president of the State of Israel on 13 May 1993.

Menahem Begin used to call him, "the cure scoundrel," but many others just referred to him as "bigmouth." His second term in office ended with a police investigation and early retirement.

13 January
Terror attack at the Karni crossing: 3 terrorists blow themselves up, killing 6.

18 January
Stanley Fischer elected Israel Bank Governor.

29 January
Israel's leading satirist Efrayim Kishon dies at the age of 80.

25 February
Suicide terror attack at the entrance to The Stage Club in Tel Aviv leaves 5 dead.

8 May
Maccabi Tel Aviv wins the European basketball championship back to back.

15 May
Yuval Diskin assumes post as 12th Shin Bet head, replacing Avi Dichter.

1 June
Dan Halutz assumes post as IDF chief of staff, replacing Moshe (Bugi) Yaalon, whose term was not extended.

25 July
Teva purchases American medication giant Ivax for the incredible sum of $7.4 billion.

4 August
Jewish soldier Natan Eden opens fire at Arab residents on bus in Shefaram, killing 4. He was later lynched by a mob.

The Sharm Summit Ends the Intifada

8 February

The Sharm al-Shaykh summit was attended by Prime Minister Ariel Sharon, Egyptian President Husni Mubarak, Jordanian King Abdallah, and PA Chairman Mahmud Abbas. After extensive talks, the Israeli and the Palestinian representatives declared that the intifada ended, vowing: "After 4 bloody years, we are letting peace speak instead of guns."

Photo: Avi Ohaion, GPO

Right to Left: Abdallah, Mubarak, Sharon, and Abu-Mazen (Abbas)

1.10.05

Israel's Economy Soars - Foreign Investors Infuse it with Billions

Photo: Zvika Tischler

This year, Israel's economic situation is the best ever. Foreign investors infuse its economy with billions of dollars - $10 billion were invested in shares of Israeli companies and another $7 billion in Israel's industry. When compared with the two preceding years, the standard of living in Israel rose by 10.5%, gross national product expanded by 11%, the number of unemployed dropped by 18%, and some 180,000 new jobs were created.

Here is some more amazing data: Israel's exports leaped up 25%, its balance of payments turned positive, and government deficit dropped to almost zero. The Tel Aviv Stock Exchange reflected this improvement with share indexes rising some 90% over the past two years, while public-owned financial assets expanded by 370 billion shekels, or 30%. We failed in only one area - minimizing poverty. In 2005, 1.5 million of Israel's residents, of which half a million were children, were considered poor.

Excavations at the City of David site near the Western Wall.
Photo: Hayim Zah

King David's Palace Uncovered in Jerusalem

5 August

Secret archaeological excavations in the City of David exposed the remains of a splendid building that researchers believe was "the 3,000-years-old palace of King David."

A Beautiful Mind

10 December

Professor Israel Uman (75) won the Nobel Prize in economy. Uman is considered one of the world's greatest researchers of Game Theory, and is the first who managed to create a model that most precisely forecasts economic and political processes.

Moved the Fence to Save the Cave

11 March

Work on the security fence does not only breed political debate. During construction work of the fence, a magnificent and millennia-old stalactite and stalagmite cave was discovered about a kilometer from the settlement of Har Adar. The Defense Ministry agreed to shift the fence route to save the cave.

Inside the saved stalactite and stalagmite cave.
Photo: Amnon Nachmias, Nature and Parks Authority

12 April

Poet Ehud Manor Passed Away

Photo: Gilad Colorchik

Poet and songwriter Ehud Manor died of heart attack at the age of 64. Manor was an inseparable part of the Israeli entity and is considered one of Israel's greatest lyricists, writing hundreds of immortal lyrics to songs such as "I Have No Other Country," "My Young Brother Yehuda," "Eternal Union," and many more.

9 March

IDF-Approved Dreadlocks

The IDF gave new recruit Shmuel Waladi a special permit not to shave his full head of dreadlocks upon recruitment. "I told my commanders that I have been growing this hair since I was a small child in Ethiopia, and it is part of my faith," he explained.

Photo: Meir Azulay

15 June

Pretty Bukhara

Photo: Zvika Tischler

Bukharan Community Day was marked for the first time this year, after Pentecost (Shavuot). Thousands attended the Pretty Bukhara Festival, initiated by the Bukhara Jewry Congress and its President Lev Levayev.

15 August

The disengagement gets underway: the Kissufim checkpoint closes after 38 years of Gaza Strip occupation.

23 September

Sederot and its vicinity are hit by a volley of 38 Kassam rockets merely two weeks after the Israeli pullout of Gaza Strip.

26 September

Suicide bomber kills five in the Hadera city market.

9 November

Amir Peretz elected Labor Party leader.

21 November

Ari'el Sharon quits the Likud Party and establishes Kadima.

5 December

Terror attack at Netanya's Hasharon shopping mall kills five Israelis.

18 December

Prime Minister Ari'el Sharon suffers a stroke. He is hospitalized, but released and sent home 40 hours later.

24 June

The Israelis' Favorite Poets

Natan Alterman

Yehuda Amichay

Yona Wolach

Natan Alterman is the most popular Israeli poet. This emerged from an extensive public opinion poll conducted by Yedioth Aharonoth that produced a list of Israel's 10 most popular poets. Three poets came a close second - Leah Goldberg, Rachel, and Yehuda Amichay - scoring almost the same. National poet Hayim Nachman Bialik came in fifth, followed by Natan Yonatan, Yona Wolach, Dalya Rabikovich, and Alexander Penn

2006

**Evacuation of wounded
IDF soldiers from the
battle on Bint J'bail, south
Lebanon.
Photo: Alex Kolomoisky**

*Tomer Bohadana, commander of paratrooper's company,
makes the V sign after being wounded in a clash with terrorists.
Photo: Elad Gershgorn*

"Combs with Iron Teeth"

Ro'i Klein, of blessed memory, who was awarded the Medal for Bravery

Rabbi Haim Sabato

"The precious sons of Zion, worth their weight in fine gold, how are they reckoned as earthen pots, the work of a potter's hand?" That is the lament in Eichah (Lamentations). Our rabbis taught that their lustre put fine gold to shame. What was this radiance of the sons of Zion that stirred up the envy of the great men of Rome? What made them brighter than fine gold? Not external beauty, but internal brilliance.

We are told that on the first day of Creation, God created a great light, one beyond anything a human being ever experienced. God saw that the world was not worthy of so great a light, and thus He hid it for the Righteous in the World to Come. On occasion, sparks of that concealed light break forth and light up our world. Where does this light come from? From the depths of the pure souls of all generations. From Rabbi Akiva, who expired as he breathed the word "One." From Rabbi Chanina ben Teradyon, who was burned alive, wrapped in the parchment of a Torah scroll. He saw the parchment burn but the letters rose upwards above the flames, and he said: "He who saves His Torah, to Him I render my soul." From the mighty generations of the spirit who offered up their lives - it is from these Jews that that light emanated.

Adino the Etznite that was the name of King David's general who went out to battle. Our Sages interpreted his name: that he would make himself as lowly *(me'aden atzmo)* as a worm in the study hall, but when he went out to war, would make himself as firm as a tree *(eitz)*.

Ro'i Klein, of blessed memory, was a gentle soul to everyone who knew him. His was a poetic, sensitive soul. He was able to see the letters rising upwards, and he studied Torah lovingly in the *beit midrash*. But when he donned his uniform, he was cloaked in a spirit of heroism. His was a courageous heart when he commanded his soldiers in the battle.

When Rabbi Akiva was taken out to be executed, it was the time for reciting the Shema, and the Romans flayed his skin with combs with iron teeth. Each time they flayed his skin, he would recite the verse: "The Rock, His work is perfect; all His ways are justice; a God of faithfulness and without iniquity, just and right is He." A Heavenly Voice proclaimed: "Blessed are you, Rabbi Akiva, for all your ways were perfect and just, and you gave up your soul in perfection and justice." When Rabbi Chanina ben Teradyon and Rabbi Yehudah ben Baba heard about this, they rent their clothes and said: "Our brothers, know that Rabbi Akiva's execution was a sign for us."

When they flayed his skin, his thoughts focused on accepting the Yoke of the Kingdom of Heaven in love. His disciples said to him: "Our master, even now?" He said to them: "My entire life I was baffled by the verse, 'and with all your soul,' which means that 'even if He takes your soul' (you must love Him). 'When will I have the opportunity to fulfil this?' Now that I have the opportunity, shall I not fulfil it?" He dwelled on (the last word of the Shema verse) "One," until his soul departed. A Heavenly Voice proclaimed: "Blessed are you, Rabbi Akiva, that your soul expired with the word 'One.'" Sometimes God is merciful to a person who is undeserving, and sometimes ... sometimes He goes down into His garden, to the bed of spices, to gather lilies.

One who owns a fig tree knows when to gather figs. Who, though, can understand the thoughts of the Creator of man?

In whose hand is the soul of every living thing, and the breath of all mankind?

The soul is Yours, and the body is Your handiwork.

Take pity on Your creation!

Master of all souls, the soul is Yours, but the body, too, is Your handwork. And You created him to sanctify Your name in Your world. Lord of the Universe, take pity on Your creation!

And when Ro'i Klein, one of the precious sons of Zion, worth more than fine gold, may his name be a blessing, fell on the hand grenade and sacrificed his life to save his soldiers, he called out in a loud voice, "Hear O Israel, the Lord our God, the Lord is One," and he died with "One" on his lips.

What does the Heavenly Voice proclaim now?

Major Ro'i Klein, RIP

from the settlement of Eli, was deputy commander of Battalion 51 of the Golani Brigade. While fighting in the Bint J'bail sector in Lebanon, a hand grenade was hurled at Klein and his men. He threw himself at the grenade and was killed by the blast and shrapnel while protecting all the other soldiers from injury. His men later related that he yelled "Shma Israel" as he jumped. This act accorded him with a Citation of Bravery for "adhering to the task, taking responsibility, setting a personal example, and comradeship in battle."

Second War of Lebanon

2o06

12 July

Ehud Goldwasser and Eldad Regev Kidnapped and Taken to Lebanon

The Second War of Lebanon started on 12 July, after Hizballah shelled IDF units and northern settlements with mortars and rockets. Using the shelling as diversion, an ambush attacked two IDF Hammers that were patrolling the border fence. In this attack, 3 soldiers were killed, 2 were injured, and another two - Ehud Goldwasser and Eldad Regev - were kidnapped and taken into Lebanon. Soon after that, the IDF launched a massive attack on Hizballah targets. An Armored Corps unit was sent into Lebanon, but one of the tanks hit a roadside bomb and its 4-men crew was killed. A rescue unit was sent in, but it only lost another man.

The Israeli Government held an emergency session in which it decided to launch an attack against Hizballah, vowing to fight "until the threat on our northern border is eliminated and the abductees return." When this is written, the two soldiers are still missing.

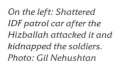

On the left: Shattered IDF patrol car after the Hizballah attacked it and kidnapped the soldiers. Photo: Gil Nehushtan

Eldad Regev

Ehud Goldwasser

Beirut buildings turned to rubble after an IAF raid. Photo: AP

13 July

Air Raids: Thousands Lebanese Targets Shelled

Following the recommendation of Chief of Staff Dan Halutz, the security cabinet ordered the IDF to start the attack of Hizballah targets with a massive air raid, without sending troops in. A few thousand Hizballah targets, outposts, ammunition depots, south Lebanon command posts, rocket bases, and the Beirut Airport - were raided in an attempt to prevent the Hizballah from reacting. One of the major IAF achievements on that day was the near-destruction of the Hizballah mid- and long-rage rocket setup.

The IAF expanded the scope of its attacks every day: On 14 July, it bombed the Beirut-Damascus highway, bridges, and oil depots, seriously damaging the Balabak region and Hizballah strongholds in the Dahiya neighborhood of Beirut. On 15 July, it raided roads leading to Beirut and cut south Lebanon from its northern part. On 16 July, residents of south Lebanon started fleeing north. On the 18th, the IAF attacked a convoy of ammunition trucks coming from Syria. On 20 July, 23 tons of bombs were dropped on a south Lebanon bunker where, according to intelligence, Hizballah leaders and Secretary Nasrallah were present. The IAF pounded Lebanon, but this did not yield the desired shift. The theory that the Air Force could win the war alone failed the test of reality.

13 July

Hizballah Reacts: Thousands Rockets Hit Israeli Towns

Reacting to the massive air raids, Hizballah started shelling northern Israel with thousands of rockets. In the first 6 days of the war, 625 rockets killed 13 civilians. Hizballah fired more than 100 rockets daily, striking at Haifa, Ako, Nahariya, Zafed, and other locations, forcing the Israelis to remain in bomb-shelters. On 14 July, Hizballah fired a Chinese-made C802 missile at an Israeli missile boat, the Hanit, killing 4 soldiers. On 16 July, several rockets hit the Israel Railways main workshop in Haifa, killing 8 workers. The IAF responded with a massive raid on the Dahiya quarter in southern Beirut.

In reaction, Hizballah warned it would attack the petrochemical plants in the Haifa Bay. On 17 July, rockets fell in the Golan Heights and Migdal Ha'emek for the first time.

Katyushas hit Haifa.
Photo: Shaul Golan

Katyusha strikes at the Israel Railways workshop in Haifa. On the left, Nahariya house hit by Katyusha rockets.

Photo: Alex Kolomoisky

Photo: Tal Shahar

Second War of Lebanon

20O6

19 July

Ground Incursion: Hizballah Outposts Attacked

The incessant volleys of rockets fired at Israel made the government decide on a land operation in Lebanon, which was meant to destroy the frontal Hizballah posts. The IDF units first moved 2km deep, to damage the rocket launchers. On 23 July, the incursion expanded with infantry and tanks raiding Hizballah outposts and Lebanese villages, in an attempt to create a security zone and push the launchers further north.

IDF soldiers entering Lebanon.
Photo: Ziv Koren

The IDF soldiers encountered strong resistance. Hard skirmishes took place in and around Bint J'bail. After the IDF first took Marun al-Ras (23 July), a township overlooking Bint J'bail, the battle there started (25 July). After Golani and Paratrooper Brigades' soldiers captured the town with the help of tanks and fighter jets, Brig. Gen. Gal Hirsh told reporters on site: "We have full control."

On the next morning (26 July), however, dozens of Hizballah warriors surprised a Golani unit there, killing 8 of its soldiers and wounding 22. The Israeli soldiers later said they "felt like sitting ducks."

In the end of July, the government decided to call up the reserves, and on 1 August, three reserve divisions joined the forces in Lebanon. While fighting along the border, the IDF carried out some operations deep inside Lebanese territory. On 1 August, a Sayeret Matkal commando unit raided a Hizballah command post in a Balabak hospital. After rockets were fired at Hadera, the Naval Commando went after several Hizballah commanders in Tyre on 6 August. On the next day, a rocket hit a group of reserve soldiers near Kfar Giladi, killing 12. In response, the IDF was given permission to conquer southern Lebanon. On 9 August, the chief of staff announced that his deputy Moshe Kaplinsky will serve as his representative at the Northern Command. This was viewed as a de-facto deposition of the regional commander, General Udi Adam. On the same day, 15 IDF soldiers were killed in fighting in south Lebanon; 9 of them were hit by an antitank rocket while hiding inside a building in the village of Dibl.

Photo: Efi Sharir

13 July – 14 August

The Rear: 45 Civilians Killed, 4,304 Wounded

A Nahariya living room hit by Katyusha. Photo: Yariv Katz

The Israeli home front was totally unprepared for the Hizballah attack. During the war, the rear was hit by 3,970 rockets and missiles; 520 of them struck at Kiryat Shemona, which sustained most of the hits; 45 civilians were killed in these attacks, while 4,304 suffered various degrees of injury; and 12,000 houses were damaged. The incessant firing made many residents of northern Israel seek refuge in the center and south.

The war pushed social and economic gaps clearly to the surface, and exposed the malfunctioning government support and assistance apparatuses. Practically, hundreds of thousands of citizens were forsaken, left without shelters, water, and often food, and did not know who to call for help. Thus, they received help from private entrepreneurs. Billionaire Arkadi Gaidamak built a tent town on Nitzanim Beach, which sheltered some 6,000 residents of northern Israel.

The balcony of the Nahariya house that was hit by Katyusha. Photo: Yariv Katz

Lev Hatzafon shopping mall in Kiryat Shemona was hit by a Katyusha Photo: Michael Kramer

12–14 August

The War Ends; 119 Soldiers Killed and 750 Wounded

While the UN Security Council was in session, approving the final draft of the cease-fire agreement, the Israeli Cabinet ordered the IDF to launch an extensive ground operation that was meant to seize the territory south of the Litani River. The operation, in which soldiers were taken deep into Lebanon on helicopters, extended past the approval of the cease-fire and ended with 35 IDF fatalities.

The decision to expand surface activity was severely criticized after the war, as many asked why it was necessary to launch it and what considerations were factored in.

The cease-fire agreement went into effect on 14 August, ending a 34-day war in which 119 IDF soldiers were killed and 750 were wounded; more than 1,000 Lebanese civilians were killed, including 28 in Kafr Kana; and the number of Hizballah fatalities is estimated at 700. The war cost Israel some 52 billion shekels.

Soldiers leaving south Lebanon. Photo: Michael Kramer

Second War of Lebanon

20O6

4 November

Critics and Protesters Call on Cabinet to Quit

The results of the war were followed by serious public criticism and calls for the establishment of a national commission of inquiry. Mostly criticized were the performance of the prime minister, the defense minister, and the chief of staff. Criticism was also leveled at the fact that the rear and the army were not prepared for this war, and at the decision to launch an extensive operation in the final hours of the war.

In early September 2006, the cabinet ordered the establishment of a governmental commission of inquiry headed by Justice Eliahu Winograd (see in 2007 for its conclusions).

The Second War of Lebanon ended with no clear victory: the abducted soldiers were not freed, the missile threat on northern Israel remained, and Israel's power of deterrence was eroded. It did manage to drive the Hizballah away from the border, destroyed terror infrastructures, and led to the deployment of a multinational force in southern Lebanon.

Photo: Tomeriko

Elections 2006: Kadima Wins, the Likud Crushed

28 March

The big winner of the Knesset elections was Kadima, which became the largest party in the house with 29 seats. The big losers were the Likud, which dropped from 40 to 12 seats, and Shinuy that was eliminated completely after previously holding 15 seats. The elections surprise was the Pensioners Party, which won 7 seats. Other ideological parties retained their relative power: rightist Israel Betenu (11) the National Union (9), and leftist Meretz (5). Practically, the results showed the center-left bloc, which supports the "painful concessions" policy, won the elections.

Prime Minister Ehud Olmert, Vice Premier Shimon Peres (2nd on the Kadima list), and Defense Minister Shaul Mofaz. Photo: Ata Awisat

---

4 November

Author David Grossman: "Our Leadership Is An Empty Shell"

A memorial rally marking the 11th anniversary of the assassination of Prime Minister Yitzhak Rabin was attended by some 100,000 people. The speakers called for a commission of inquiry of the war of Lebanon. Author David Grossman, who lost his son in the war, sharply attacked the Israeli leaders: "Our political and military leadership is an empty shell, filled with swords and intimidation, the delusion of power, and the wink of the charlatans. They are trading everything we hold dear. Given our complicated and misguided situation, this is not the leadership we need today."

Photo: Efi Sharir

Left: David Grossman speaking. Above: Some 100,000 attended the rally.

2006

4.5.06

Gilad Shalit: "I Need Lengthy Hospitalization"

At dawn, eight terrorists entered Israel through a tunnel, attacked an IDF outpost near Kerem Shalom, killed two soldiers, and blew up a Merkava tank. The terrorists also kidnapped Gilad Shalit, whose shoulder was wounded, and dragged him with them to Gaza. Following the attack, the IDF sent special forces to the Gaza Strip and its jets raided Gaza targets. The army also launched an investigation into the mishaps that made possible the worst terror attack after the disengagement.

On the next day, a spokesman for Izz a-Din al-Kassam Battalions announced they are holding Shalit. While the IDF launched Operation Summer Rains, diplomatic activity started in an attempt to free Shalit.

Responding to Egyptian efforts, HAMAS demanded that Israel free 1,000 Palestinian prisoners for Shalit, but Israel rejected the idea and instead detained one-third of the Palestinian Government ministers as bargaining chips.

A year after he was kidnapped, his abductors released a tape on which Shalit called on the government to accept their demands. "I, soldier Gilad son of Noam Shalit... am sending regards from prison... I miss you all... My health is deteriorating... I need lengthy hospitalization... I regret the fact that the Israeli Government is not interested in my fate."

Kidnapped Corporal Gilad Shalit (19) of Mitzpe Hila.

2 January
Elected Histadrut Chairman Ofer Eini: "Strikes must not be an end in itself."

4 January
Prime Minister Sharon has a severe stroke and goes into a coma.

28 January
Rabbi Yitzhak Kaduri, the oldest Cabalist, dies at the age of 106. State leaders used to pay their respects to him.

1 February
In violent clash between settlers and evacuating security forces in Amona, 219 were wounded, including 45 officers. The evacuation sparked a storm.

14 February
Shoshana Damari, queen of Hebrew songs, dies at the age of 83.

3 March
Zeev Rosenstein, Israel Police's most wanted man, charged with smuggling 1.5 million ecstasy tablets to the USA, turned over and given 12 years in a plea-bargain there.

Arik Sharon's Last Battle

4 January

Prime Minister Ariel Sharon had a severe stroke and was rushed to an emergency operation. This incident came two weeks after Sharon overcame a lighter stroke. Before he went into hospital, Sharon complained of fatigue, disorientation, and chest pains. Despite the doctors' efforts, Sharon went into a coma. His powers were relegated to his deputy Ehud Olmert.

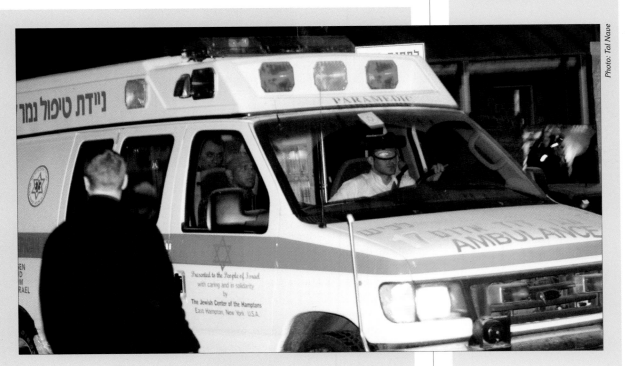

Photo: Tal Nave

391

4.5.06

Ehud Olmert Elected Prime Minister

Prime Minister-elect Ehud Olmert making
a victory speech. Photo: Ziv Koren

Three months after replacing Sharon as acting prime minister, Ehud Olmert presented the Knesset with his 25-member cabinet and held a swearing-in ceremony. As expected, Olmert demonstrated fine political skills and established a broad-based coalition, making good deals with Labor, SHAS, and the Pensioners Party.

Nevertheless, in a land where no one is given even 100 days of grace, Olmert soon found himself engaged in a new war in Lebanon, which turned the political tables around. When the war started, Olmert appeared as a man of stature, leading his nation with responsibility and determination. He was very popular and politically supported across the board.

As the war got entangled, however, his public standing was eroded. When the war ended, even though he attained a reasonable cease-fire agreement, Olmert was severely criticized and called upon to resign. Widespread criticism and demonstrations led to the establishment of a government commission of inquiry under Justice Eliahu Winograd. In its interim report, the committee stated that Olmert, Peretz, and Halutz were responsible for the mishaps and malfunctions it discovered.

Olmert's term as prime minister was further clouded by suspicions and investigations into his involvement in alleged criminal acts in the Bank Leumi affair, the house on Cremieux Street in Jerusalem, and favoritism in Industry and Trade Ministry appointments. While observers forecasted Olmert's political doom, he remains as Israel's prime minister.

Aharon Barak and Dorit Beinisch at the swearing-in ceremony. Photo: Amit Shabi

Beinisch, Supreme Court President

15 September

Dorit Beinisch was sworn in as 9th Supreme Court President, replacing Aharon Barak who said that Beinisch "is the right person, in the right time, and is worthy of the position." Beinisch said, "I do not feel glad assuming this post, but I worry for the burden of my new responsibilities."

Warren Buffet Purchases ISCAR for $4b.

7 May

The world's greatest investor, Warren Buffet, purchased the ISCAR Company from the Wertheimer family for $4billion, announcing: "I believe in Israel's economy." Prime Minister Ehud Olmert said, "This is a historic breakthrough for giant investments in Israel." Steph Wertheimer: "The deal was made to ensure the future of the Galilee industry."

06

6 May

Sami Ofer Buys a Van Gogh

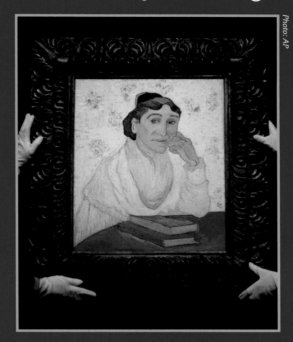

Photo: AP

Israeli shipping magnate Sami Ofer bought a Van Gogh for $40.3m. It is an 1890 portrait of Mme Gino, owner of an Arlet café that he and many artists frequented. Ofer is considered one of the world's two greatest art collectors.

11 June

1,400 Letters by A. Einstein Discovered in Jerusalem

A collection of letters by Nobel Prize laureate and author of the Theory of Relativity was discovered in the Hebrew University in Jerusalem. The letters reveal that the genius loved the ladies as much as physics. He emerged as an emphatic and warm person, who was married twice and had at least seven affairs.

17 April

Iraqi Musician Underground

The secret story of Salah al-Kuweiti, one of the greatest Iraqi composers, was revealed these days. Saddam ordered that his works be destroyed and his Jewish origin kept secret because he was admired all over the Arab world. After Saddam was overthrown, Iraqi TV revealed his origin and broadcasted his works. Salah and his brother, Daud, immigrated to Israel in 1951, but their musical talent was not acknowledged here.

Reproduction by Tomeriko

1 February

Israel's Greatest Athletes

Legendary soccer goalie Yaacov Hodorov and basketball coach Ralph Klein won the Israel Award in sports. Hodorov, named Israel's greatest goalkeeper ever, "became a symbol for every sports fan in Israel," the panel said. Klein was awarded thanks to his unique contribution to Israeli basketball as a player and as coach of Maccabi Tel Aviv and the national team.

Ralph Klein

Photo: Yosi Rott

Yaacov Hodorov

14 March
The assassins of Minister Zeevi are brought to justice in Israel after IDF troops surround the Jericho Prison and capture them there.

28 March
Elections for the 17th Knesset held. Kadima emerges the largest party with 29 seats.

17 April
Suicide bomber kills 9 in a Tel Aviv restaurant.

4 May
Israel's 31st cabinet under Ehud Olmert sworn in at the Knesset. Dalia Itzik becomes the first woman to serve as Knesset speaker.

11 May
Yosi Banai, one of Israel's culture giants, dies at 74.

20 May
Yitzhak Ben-Aharon, mythological Histadrut chairman, dies at 99.

21 August
Author S. Yizhar dies at 90. His monumental work, "Days of Ziklag," was published in the 1950's. He served as MK for Mapai and Rafi.

31 December
Yaacov Hodorov, Israel's greatest goalie, dies.

2007

Babian family house in Sederot hit by a Kassam rocket.
Photo: Gadi Caballo

Wounded woman evacuated from missile hit location.
Photo: Gadi Caballo

Kassams Upon You, Sederot

"Sederot is a mirror of our proven guilt."

Singer and Song Writer
Shlomo Artzi

Morality, sanctity, the land, and its people make the thread that runs through this year's history. And even if looking for morality in a land of overflowing government corruption is a bit old-fashioned, I would not stop searching. The three abducted soldiers are still trying to find their way home, and a trail of blood in the sands of the northern Negev marks the way to the Kassam-stricken town of Sederot. So I muse as I drive to see Dani, a friend who lives in the Besor, a strip of land near the Rafah border. Dani cut himself off central Israel and for $20,000 bought himself a small piece of land where he grows cherry tomatoes that he exports to Europe. Soccer player Yosi Ben-Ayoun is not the only prize tomato we export.

My friend Dani does not fear the Kassams, watching them as they fly over his house like some spaceships. Emerging from the murder labs of Rafah, they make their way to Sederot, that is given a 30-second "red alert" warning. On my way to Dani, I must cross the Sederot Junction and I pray that no Rafah-made rocket strikes me now, as the guys there fire indiscriminately at this beautiful road, that fading summer painted yellow on both sides. I notice there are fewer cars as I head south because what fool would willingly drive in that Kassam-stricken land, and on a holiday no less?

Now, that we have grown sour like the juice at the bottom of an old can in my fridge, Sederot has become our mirror. If we look closely, we will see our wrinkles, the wrongs we did, the madness we let creep in and did nothing against. Are we still a moral society? I ask myself and nod at the flock of birds overhead.

I want nothing from Sederot and it wants nothing from me, but we bug each other with our very absurd existence. I did want to help. I dropped by one Friday to do some shopping for the Sabbath in its empty mall, as a human gesture for the shop-owners who keep losing clients. It was, however, very little to do and in this age of publicity, it was only remembered for its PR value, because it did not really save their business.

What more could I do? I even volunteered to sing in the city square, named after murdered Rabin, but only a small crowd even bothered to show up. Perhaps this is because many felt sorry for this southern town, but chose not to think about it too much and went to dance in Tel Aviv clubs or had some sushi, instead of dealing with this Kassam mess.

To be sure, it is scary and it ruins your appetite, but Sederot cannot be suppressed. It is here to stay, with its passive existence, unemployment, and calls for help by its proud residents who chose to build their splendid homes here. Sederot is a scar on our beating heart. In this town, that produced an unprecedented number of musicians and composers (more than "A Star is Born"), live proud people whose sorrow made them follow the trail of money laid out for them in the Bereshit Forest on the Yarkon River bank by one Arkadi Gaidamak, the expressionless billionaire.

A guy from Sederot who lost both his legs to a Kassam came to see one of my concerts and said: "This is nonsense. I will live with it." And he smiled and drove away in the wheelchair that replaced his legs. Sederot will never be Israel's most beloved town. It is a pain in the state's ass. It is so naïve, honest and true. It makes one's heart yearn for more towns like it. Yet, we will not throw ourselves at its feet and ask it to forgive us for abandoning it. In 2007, it served as more proof that we exist, that we get up in the morning and go chasing our job hunting, or the tired lady in our bed, as we beg to slide in for a moment of love and passion.

The fields are so pretty here in the end of this silently fading summer, I think as I drive to Dani's, that it distorts the complicated truth we live in. Dani shows me around his tomato hothouse, where the plants grow tall and strong. "You did it all by yourself?" I ask. "Yes," he says, not hiding his pride, "me and my 14 Thai farmhands, my wild horses." And he laughs hard as we hop and skip barefoot in his hothouse, like the children we once were.

There are no stains of blood on Sederot's streets, no monuments for the victims. The wheelchair boy I met must have had his prostheses fixed by now. The birds around here won't be bought for a buck nor scared away by rockets. They bite into leftover peppers thrown outside the hothouses. For them, this is the sushi of life.

"There is wonderful friendship, where people don't forget each other. There must be love in this world, and safe places where people are not shot by rockets each morning," I tell Dani, "but where are these places? Definitely not here." "You are wrong," he says, fixing a slumping tomato bush. "Listen how quiet it is here. Hear the wind blowing through the fields. Look at the open skies and the passing clouds. The fact that I chose to build a home here proves this place has a future, despite the sorrows of war."

Though his optimist is catchy, I fire a demanding question at him. "Tell me, Dani, where is God? We've been looking for him all year."

"God?" Dani says and laughs. "God is inside the cherry tomatoes. Just look and listen carefully."

13.6.**07**

Shimon Peres: Milkman-Gone-President

At the age of 84, Shimon Peres managed to attain his most coveted goal: President of the State of Israel. This enterprising statesman, who did for this state more than any other living politician, the most popular Israeli in the world, won over 86 MKs who opened the President's Residence for him. Having lost elections so many times during his age-long career, Peres could now look at his rivals' and sympathizers' eyes and declare: "I am no longer a loser!"

Soon after winning the vote, he called his wife Sonia and told her: "You married a milkman, but you got the president." Peres thus because the first and only person in Israel's history who served as both prime minister and president of Israel. "I never dreamt of becoming a president... As a young man, I dreamt of being a shepherd or star-gazing poet," he said when he was sworn in. He was supported across political sectors and camps.

His biographer Michael Bar-Zohar said that though popular, Peres remains an enigma: He is artist of Hebrew, but speaks with a foreign accent; an ultimate security man who never wore a uniform; a mediocre politician, but a great visionary statesman; a kibbutznik with no official education, but a man of culture; romantic, but shy. A complex man.

History will remember him as the architect of Israel's ties with France; the man who helped building the Dimona nuclear reactor; who played a part in the Entebbe Operation; who as prime minister (1984) quelled the inflation and pulled the IDF out of Lebanon; the leader of the Oslo process, who replaced Rabin as prime minister after he was assassinated (1995), but lost the 1996 elections to Netanyahu. Together with Yasser Arafat and Yitzhak Rabin, Peres won the Nobel Peace Prize in 1994.

Israel's 9th President Shimon Peres sworn in at the Knesset.
Photo: Alex Kolomoisky

The Air Force Raids Nuclear Facility in Syria

6 September

IAF fighter jets attacked and destroyed a nuclear facility dubbed "farming factory" in the town of Dir Azur in northeastern Syria - according to international media. The Washington Post reported that the Israeli and US intelligence found out that this seemingly innocent plant produced uranium from phosphates, and that it was raided three days after a mysterious shipment arrived from North Korea in the Port of Tartus in northern Syria.

The Observer of London further related that eight F-16 and F-15i fighter jets took part in the raid, bombing the location with precision Maverick missiles and 250km bombs. Reportedly, the target was kept secret and the aviators who raided it were only briefed in midair. According to the Sunday Times, an IAF commando unit, named Shaldag, waited at the rendezvous point, marking the target for the approaching jets with laser beams.

Official Israel declined reacting to the reports, but IDF Intelligence chief Amos Yadlin said, "Israel rebuilt its power of deterrence." The Syrians threatened that "Israel will pay for the operation."

Winograd : "Grave Failures in War Management"

Established on 18 September 2006, the committee under Justice Winograd was a government commission of inquiry into the events of the Second War of Lebanon. It published an interim report seven and a half months later, leveling serious accusations at Prime Minister Ehud Olmert, Defense Minister Amir Peretz, and IDF Chief of Staff Dan Halutz. The committee determined that the three failed in planning the war, their decisionmaking process, and managing it. Olmert "seriously failed in using his judgment, responsibility, and caution." It said that Amir Peretz, "did not understand the issues, but consulted no one," and that Halutz "was unprofessional, imposing his views on the defense minister, taking advantage of his lack of experience, and silenced alternative views in the General Staff."

The committee members, right to left:
Prof. Yehezkel Dror, Prof. Ruth Gabizon,
former Justice and committee chairman
Eliahu Winograd, and former Generals
Menahem Eynan and Haim Nadel.
Photo: Amit Shabi

Chief of Staff Halutz resigned before this report was published saying, "I did not shake off responsibility; I quit." Amir Peretz quit his post on 15 June, after Ehud Barak replaced him as Labor chairman. Olmert rejected the calls on him to resign: "I will not quit because only I can get things right."

After the report was issued, the political establishment urged Olmert to resign, and 100,000 people attended a Tel Aviv rally calling on him to quit. Eventually, when the committee issued its final report, it did not make personal recommendations.

2 January

Teddy Kollek, legendary Jerusalem mayor, dies at 96.

17 January

Chief of Staff Dan Halutz files resignation in the wake of the Lebanon War.

28 January

Historic event: Ghaleb Majadla becomes the first Israeli Arab cabinet member.

Zeiler Committee Report

18 February

The Zeiler Committee was appointed to examine the performance of the police and the State Attorney's Office in the Farinian brothers affair (the murder of criminal Pinhas Buhbut and other felonies). In its conclusive report, the committee leveled harsh criticism at police chief Moshe Karadi saying, "he did not speak the truth, and thus may not serve as police commissioner." Referring to the police top brass, Justice Zeiler said, "there is a norm of lies, negligence, and corruption there." Commissioner Karadi resigned after the report was published.

8th President Moshe Katzav: "Spilling My Blood"

2006-2007

Most of Katzav's term as president (2000-2007) was moderate and stately. He cruised through national consensus, steering clear of controversial issues. During the disengagement, he tried to create a dialogue between the settlers and Prime Minister Sharon. Like his predecessor, Weizmann, he made a point of visiting bereaved families and wounded soldiers, extensively touring Israel, mainly its trouble spots.

On 8 July, the media reported that the president complained with the attorney general that a former employee was trying to blackmail him. Attorney Mazuz decided to launch an investigation. On 23 August, Katzav was questioned at the Residence. On 23 January, Mazuz filed a charge sheet against President Katzav, accusing him of suspected of rape, sexual harassment, indecent act, dishonesty, and badgering a witness. The president denied all charges.

On the next day (24 January), Katzav appeared live on TV, sharply attacking the police and the attorney general ("who did everything they could to find me guilty"), the media ("they are spilling my blood without checking the facts"), and the plaintiffs ("they have no real evidence against me"). At the end of his very stormy speech, Katzav yelled: "They want to execute a man without a trial. I am innocent!"

After a hearing with the attorney general, where the president's attorneys presented new evidence, the charge sheet was amended and a plea bargain deal sought. On 28 June 2007, the deal was signed. In it, the president pleaded guilty of indecent acts and sexual harassment. Assuming the blame, he decided to quit and was given a suspended prison sentence. The deal sparked a storm, protest vigils, and a petition with the Supreme Court.

Photo: Amit Shabi

President Katzav addressing the media

14.2.07

Gabi (Bulldozer) Ashkenazi - Chief of Staff

Photo: Guy Asiag

Half of New Officers are Religious

26 August

The number of religious officers in the IDF rose sharply recently. Some 45% of the graduates of the recent combat officers' courses come from the religious-Zionist current, turning into the army's backbone. This figure if far greater than their relative part in the population. "

Incoming Chief of Staff Gabi Ashkenazi, dubbed Bulldozer, is the first Golani Brigade graduate to reach that position. His father is a Holocaust survivor and his mother emigrated from Syria. He had served as Northern Command chief, deputy chief of staff, and Defense Ministry director general. Ever since he assumed duty, he has been dealing with the lessons learned from the Second War of Lebanon. His wife, Ronit, said he will be "a soldiers' chief of staff." Ashkenazi led the complicated task of the IDF evacuation of southern Lebanon in 2000 two years after assuming command over northern Israel, and in 2002 became deputy to Moshe Yaalon. Having lost the race for the army chief to Dan Halutz in 2004, Ashkenazi quit and became Defense Ministry director general in 2006.

Photo: Oded Balilti, AP

The winning picture: A girl opposing the disengagement wards off the evacuating police.

Israeli Photographer Wins Pulitzer

17 April

Israeli photographer Oded Balilti won the prestigious American prize for a picture he took of the Amona evacuation in February 2006. This picture won another 10 awards in other international competitions.

Photo: Yoav Galai

Butterflies Have Names

9 January

Schoolchildren from all over Israel are taking part in a project of painting half a million butterflies, one for each child that perished in the Holocaust. They are joining an international campaign where hundreds of thousands children paint paper butterflies to commemorate the children murdered during World War 2.